Charles Seale-Hayne Library
University of Plymouth
(01752) 588 588
LibraryandITenquiries@plymouth.ac.uk

Basins on the Atlantic Seaboard
Petroleum Geology, Sedimentology and Basin Evolution

Geological Society Special Publications
Series Editor J. BROOKS

GEOLOGICAL SOCIETY SPECIAL PUBLICATION NO 62

Basins on the Atlantic Seaboard
Petroleum Geology, Sedimentology and Basin Evolution

EDITED BY

J. PARNELL
Department of Geology
Queen's University of Belfast
UK

1992

Published by

The Geological Society

London

THE GEOLOGICAL SOCIETY

The Society was founded in 1807 as the Geological Society of London and is the oldest geological society in the world. It received its Royal Charter in 1825 for the purpose of 'investigating the mineral structure of the Earth'. The Society is Britain's national learned society for geology with a Fellowship in the region of 7000. It has countrywide coverage and approximately 1000 members reside overseas. The Society is responsible for all aspects of the geological sciences including professional matters. The Society's publishing house is the European distributor for publications of the American Association of Petroleum Geologists.

Fellowship is open to those holding a recognized honours degree in geology or cognate subject and who have at least two years relevant postgraduate experience, or have not less than six years relevant experience in geology or a cognate subject. A Fellow who has not less than five years relevant postgraduate experience in the practice of geology may apply for validation and subject to approval will be able to use the designatory letters C. Geol. (Chartered Geologist). Further information about the Society is available from the Membership Manager, Geological Society, Burlington House, London W1V 0JU, UK.

Published by The Geological Society from:
The Geological Society Publishing House
Unit 7
Brassmill Enterprise Centre
Brassmill Lane
Bath
Avon BA1 3JN
UK
(*Orders*: Tel. 0225 445046)

Printed in Great Britain by Galliard (Printers) Ltd, Great Yarmouth

Distributors
USA
 AAPG Bookstore
 PO Box 979
 Tulsa
 Oklahoma 74101−0979
 USA
(*Orders*: Tel: (918)584−2555)

Australia
 Australian Mineral Foundation
 63 Conyngham St
 Glenside
 South Australia 5065
 Australia
(*Orders*: Tel: (08)379−0444)

British Library Cataloguing in Publication Data
A catalogue record for this book is available from the British Library

ISBN 0−903317−76−1

Contents

Basins on the Atlantic Seaboard: introduction

JOHN PARNELL

School of Geosciences, Queen's University of Belfast, Belfast BT7 INN, UK

Much basic information on the basins on the western seaboard of the British Isles is available in an excellent compendium by Naylor & Shannon (1982). More recently, several volumes have been published containing much data pertinent to the basins of the North Atlantic region, including works by Manspeizer (1988) and Tankard & Balkwill (1989) for the North American margin, and Brooks & Glennie (1987) for the European margin.

This volume reviews research into the development of basins of Carboniferous to Tertiary age on the north west seaboard. There is currently much interest in the extensive series of basins stretching from west of Shetland through the Hebrides to Northern Ireland and the west coast of Ireland. Each of these regions has seen drilling activity as part of hydrocarbon exploration programmes. The volume brings together a diverse range of expertise, from fundamental studies of basin extension to environmental palaeoecology, and includes several contributions directly related to the hydrocarbon potential of the region. Information and discussion on the basins west of Britain and Ireland have been supplemented by papers on the North American margin and the region north of Britain to give a full coverage of the northern Atlantic region (Fig. 1).

Many plays on both sides of the North Atlantic depend upon Carboniferous source rocks, and several contributions assess the maturation level and source potential of these rocks in Scotland/Northern Ireland (*Parnell, Stein, Dean*) and on the Canadian margin (*Mossman*). The Jurassic also contains potential source rocks, but in many places they are immature, including the Hebridean region (*Thrasher*).

Most of the research undertaken on the Atlantic seaboard concerns the Mesozoic basins (Fig. 1), whose late Triassic-mid Jurassic stratigraphy and palaeogeography is reviewed by *Morton*.

In the post-Carboniferous succession offshore west of Scotland, Jurassic sandstones represent the most likely reservoir target. However, thick Permo-Triassic sandstones occur in some basins, and their diagenesis has been studied by *McKeever*. The subsequent Triassic–Jurassic evolution of the Hebridean region, in a half graben with faulted western margin, is described

by *Morton*. The reservoir potential of the thick mid-Jurassic deltaic sandbodies of the region is assessed by *Harris* in terms of facies distribution patterns. Concretionary cementation reduced the porosity in these Jurassic sandstones, although the timing of the cementation is equivocal (*Wilkinson*). Isotopic studies of the clay mineralogy in the Jurassic sequence suggest a predominantly Dalradian provenance, with admixed penecontemporaneous ash and subsequent alteration by meteoric waters, possibly during Tertiary times (*Hamilton et al.*). The outcrop of Cretaceous rocks in the Hebrides is very limited, but *Lowden et al.* show that the Upper Cretaceous could include good reservoir sandstones based upon a study of the Lochaline Sandstone. *England* discusses the role of Tertiary igneous activity in the evolution of the region, and concludes that magmatism had a negligible effect on the maturation of Jurassic source rocks. Fission track analysis records localised thermal effects around the Skye Tertiary igneous complex, but beyond the complex the region has not experienced a regional annealling event since the late Carboniferous (*Lewis et al.*).

Mitchell discusses the evolution of Carboniferous sedimentary basins in Northern Ireland and draws parallels with similar basin evolution in the Canadian Maritime Provinces. *Philcox et al.* use stratigraphic data to describe the evolution of the Carboniferous Lough Allen Basin in North West Ireland, where a number of gas shows have been recorded. The potential reservoir sandstones onshore in the north of Ireland are Carboniferous and Permo-Triassic. *Buckman* assesses the palaeoenvironment of a Carboniferous sandstone succession using ichnological and sedimentological evidence, and *Wang* shows that secondary porosity in Carboniferous sandstones was produced during Permian deep weathering. The history of Permian and Mesozoic sedimentation onshore in Ireland is summarized by *Naylor*, and *McCaffrey & McCann* focus on the post-Permian basin history in Northern Ireland, deduced from borehole and outcrop data. Offshore from the north of Ireland, *Dobson & Whittington* describe a graben complex which includes the Inner Hebrides Trough, the Malin Basin and the South Donegal Basin.

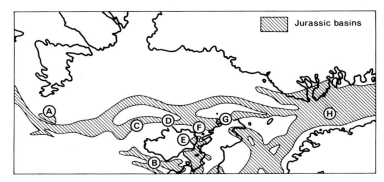

Fig. 1. Regions of basinal sedimentation in the northern North Atlantic during the Jurassic. Contributions in this volume: A, Canadian margin (Srivastava & Verhoef, Mossman); B, Celtic Seas (Ruffell & Coward); C, Porcupine (White et al., Moore, Shannon, Tate); D, offshore north west Ireland (Trueblood); E, onshore north Ireland (Mitchell, Philcox et al., Buckman, Wang, Naylor, McCaffrey & McCann); F, offshore north Ireland, south west Scotland (Dobson & Whittington, McKeever, Dean); G, Hebrides (Stein, Thrasher, Morton, Harris, Wilkinson, Hamilton et al., Louden et al., England, Lewis et al.); H, north east Atlantic seaway (Doré); also regional studies of north west seaboard (Parnell, Morton).

The hydrocarbon potential of the Slyne Trough to the west of Ireland has been evaluated by *Trueblood*, who reports source, reservoir and sealing rocks all within the Jurassic succession. *White et al.* show that there have been two main phases of stretching during the history of the Porcupine Basin, during the late Jurassic and Palaeocene. *Moore* particularly emphasises the transition from the syn-rift (extensive tectonism) to post-rift (thermal subsidence) phases of the Porcupine Basin, during which fault-bounded sub-basins developed. Early Tertiary submarine fan deposits in the basin may be potential hydrocarbon reservoirs, although they lie in deep water (*Shannon*). *Tate* discusses the structure which separates the main Porcupine Basin from the Seabight Basin, which appears to be an extension of the Clare Lineament, interpreted as a relic transform fault. To the south of Ireland, *Ruffell & Coward* suggest that reactivation of the 'Variscan Front' and associated thrusts in the late Jurassic controlled uplift and subsidence patterns reflected in the Mesozoic successions of the Celtic Sea basins and the Bristol Channel area.

Beyond the British Isles, *Doré* has documented the evolution of the seaway between the Laurentian Shield and Baltic Shield from late Permian to Cretaceous, using a series of palaeogeographic maps. The evolution of Mesozoic basins around the central North Atlantic has been reconstructed using techniques for the restoration of present plate margins to their pre-stretched configurations (*Srivistava & Verhoef*).

References

BROOKS, J. & GLENNIE, K. 1987. *Petroleum Geology of North West Europe* (2 vols). Graham & Trotman, London.

MANSPEIZER, W. 1988. *Triassic-Jurassic Rifting*. Elsevier, Amsterdam.

NAYLOR, D. & SHANNON, P. M. 1982. *The Geology of Offshore Ireland and West Britain*. Graham & Trotman, London.

TANKARD, A. J. & BALKWILL, H. R. 1989. *Extensional Tectonics and Stratigraphy of the North Atlantic Margin*. American Association of Petroleum Geologists Memoir **46**.

Basin histories and hydrocarbon source rocks

Burial histories and hydrocarbon source rocks on the North West Seaboard

J. PARNELL

School of Geosciences, Queen's University of Belfast, Belfast BT7 1NN, UK

Abstract: The basins on the North West Seaboard of the British Isles had widely differing burial histories and consequently contain different successions. Basins active in the Permo-Triassic saw early maturation of Carboniferous source rocks, but Jurassic sections remain immature. Basins active in the Cretaceous–Tertiary saw later maturation of the Carboniferous, followed by maturation of the Jurassic. Potential source rocks range from Ordovician to Tertiary age, but Carboniferous source rocks are probably the most widely distributed. Samples from onshore Carboniferous outcrops in Northern Ireland and western Scotland give good pyrolysis yields, with a potential for gas and limited quantities of oil. The Jurassic rocks of the Hebrides include bitumen-impregnated sandstones where Jurassic shales have achieved maturation in the vicinity of Tertiary intrusions. The North West Irish Basin shows evidence for oil migration in Carboniferous rocks and the burial history suggests that gas may have been generated from the Carboniferous in eastern Ulster where the succession is analogous to that in the Morecambe Gas Field.

A system of sedimentary basins extends the length of the North West Seaboard of the British Isles, from offshore west of Ireland, north through the Hebrides to the region west of Shetland and extending northwest to the Faroes. The system impinges onshore in the Hebrides and Northern Ireland, where it connects with the basins of the Irish Sea region (Fig. 1). The basin system is itself part of a larger system of basins extending down the eastern Atlantic seaboard from the Arctic to the Iberian region. Basin subsidence along the continental margin commenced during the Carboniferous at a time when oceanic lithosphere was possibly forming in the Rockall Trough region (Fig. 2; Haszeldine & Russell 1987).

Hydrocarbon exploration is being undertaken along the length of the North West Seaboard. This paper reviews some aspects of the post-Devonian burial histories and source rock potential of the basins.

Burial histories

The basins have a complex history from the Carboniferous onwards: different basins had widely differing histories. Basin subsidence occurred particularly during the Permo-Triassic, the Cretaceous and the Tertiary, but the locus of sedimentation changed through time and it could be argued that there are several successive basin systems which are superimposed upon each other. The successions are superimposed upon each other in different ways and are separated by variable degrees of uplift. The variations are illustrated by summary successions

for four basins at intervals along the North West Seaboard (Fig. 2). A succession for the Porcupine Basin is based upon well 26/28–1 (Croker & Shannon 1987, MacDonald et al. 1987), the succession for the Rathlin Basin is combined from the Port More borehole onshore (Wilson & Manning 1978) and an offshore gravity profile (Evans et al. 1980), the Hebridean succession is modified from that of Kilenyi & Standley (1985) and the Faroe–Shetland sequence is based upon well 206/5–1 (Bailey et al. 1987; Meadows et al. 1987). The Porcupine and Faroe–Shetland successions are from near the basin margins: thicknesses are considerably greater towards the basin centres.

There are a number of fundamental distinctions between the successions. The two more oceanward basins have a substantial Cretaceous sequence, but lack Permo-Triassic. (N.B. Other Faroe–Shetland wells do include some Permo-Triassic.) The more inshore basins were established in the Permo-Triassic and only have a thin Cretaceous cover. Jurassic sedimentation was not so constrained by basins, and was deposited more uniformly although early Cretaceous erosion stripped most of it off in the Rathlin Basin and there are local thickness variations due to intra-Jurassic uplift/erosion. All of the sequences have a thick Tertiary cover; predominantly volcanic in Rathlin and the Hebrides, mixed volcanic and sedimentary in the Faroe–Shetland Basin and predominantly sedimentary in the Porcupine Basin.

Distinctions between the successions gave rise to concomitant distinctions in their burial histories. In terms of hydrocarbon prospectivity,

From PARNELL, J. (ed.), 1992, *Basins on the Atlantic Seaboard: Petroleum Geology, Sedimentology and Basin Evolution.* Geological Society Special Publication No 62, pp 3–16.

3

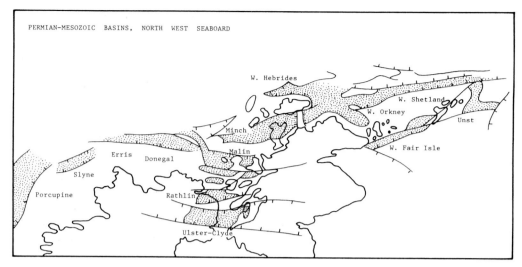

Fig. 1. Permian–Mesozoic basins on the North West Seaboard.

source rock units within the successions would have reached maturity at different times. To highlight these variations, time–burial plots have been reconstructed, based upon the successions in Fig. 3, and assumptions about erosion made from the regional geology. Erosion is documented particularly within the Jurassic and Cretaceous, but this may partly reflect the good stratigraphic resolution possible in these rocks.

The time-burial plots (Fig. 4) have the oil-window superimposed, bounded by time-temperature indices (TTI) of 15 and 160. The indices were calculated using the Lopatin reconstruction method of Waples (1980) with in-house modifications. For simplicity, the reconstructions assume a constant geothermal gradient of 30°C/km and a surface temperature of 10°C. It is very likely that there were temporal and spatial variations in the geothermal gradient. In particular, episodes of magmatic activity represent heat pulses.

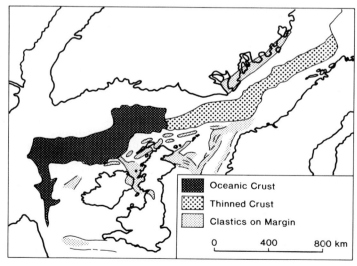

Fig. 2. Palaeogeography of the northern North Atlantic region at end of Carboniferous, showing distribution of clastic basins along continental margin (after Haszeldine & Russell 1987).

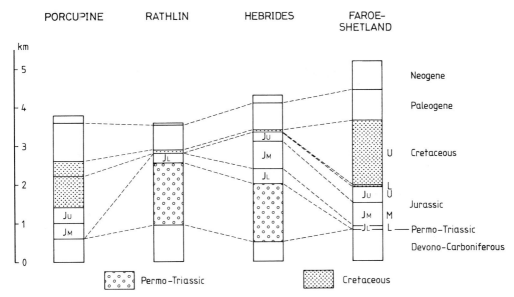

Fig. 3. Typical successions for Rathlin and Hebrides Basins, and marginal parts of Porcupine and Faroe–Shetland Basins (see text for sources).

Onshore in northeast Ireland, three phases of extrusive vulcanism (Carboniferous, Permian, Palaeocene) are recognized, which must have increased the heat flow at those times. However, the observed maturity of Carboniferous rocks in the region are consistent with the predictions of the simple time−temperature reconstruction. The reconstructions suffice to emphasise the variations in burial history between the basins. The basins which contain thick Permo-Triassic sequences saw relatively rapid maturation of the Carboniferous, early in the Mesozoic. Potential source rocks in the Jurassic are not deeply buried in these basins and are predicted to be immature. Although the Jurassic rocks in both the Rathlin and Hebrides Basins have experienced substantial Palaeocene magmatism, oil has only been generated in the very immediate vicinity of intrusions in the Hebrides (see below) and most Jurassic shale samples are immature

In the sequences with negligible Permo-Triassic sediments, maturity of the Carboniferous was delayed until later in the Mesozoic, but burial beneath thick Cretaceous and Tertiary successions brought the Jurassic rocks to maturity relatively quickly. It should be emphasized that the Porcupine and Faroe−Shetland basins are much thicker at their centres, and as a result the timing of source rock maturation would be progressively earlier towards the

centre. Much of the Faroe−Shetland basin contains a Permo-Triassic sequence which would have hastened the maturation of Carboniferous rocks. The reconstructions do not show Carboniferous rocks emerging beyond the oil window, but the deeper Carboniferous rocks are predicted to be overmature with respect to oil generation in the central parts of the Porcupine and Faroe−Shetland basins.

Source rocks

The predominant source rocks, as highlighted in the burial reconstructions (Fig. 4), are of Carboniferous and Jurassic age. However, potential source rocks are present through most of the Phanerozoic, from Ordovician to Tertiary (Fig. 5). The westward extension of the Midland Valley of Scotland into Northern Ireland includes Ordovician and Silurian inliers which have undergone only low-grade metamorphism, with graptolite reflectances of less 2% (Illing & Griffith 1986; Parnell 1989). These rocks may be gas-prone. On the north coast of Scotland, high oil yields are obtainable from Devonian lacustrine laminites in the Orcadian Basin (Parnell 1985). Similar rocks may occur in the West Orkney Basin and adjacent areas (Enfield & Coward 1987). The Devono-Carboniferous sediments of the Clair Field west of Shetland may represent a transition between the lacus-

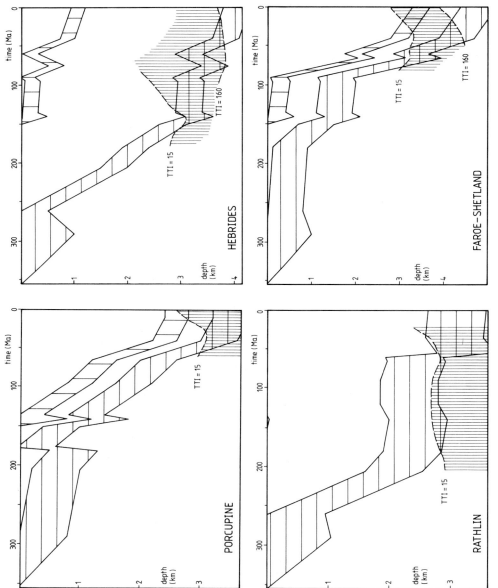

Fig. 4. Time-burial reconstructions for Carboniferous and Jurassic rocks in successions in Fig. 3. Assumptions about erosion based on regional geology.

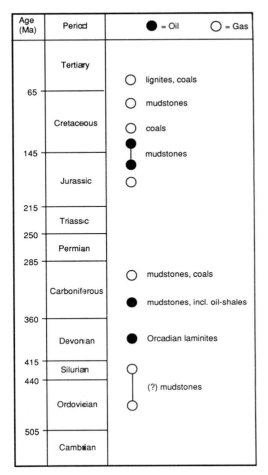

Age (Ma)	Period	● = Oil ○ = Gas

Fig. 5. Stratigraphic distribution of hydrocarbon source rocks on the North West Seaboard.

trine sediments of the Orcadian Basin and an upland environment to the west (Hitchen & Ritchie 1987). Carboniferous source rocks are either known or suspected in many basins, and are generally assumed to be gas-prone as in the Porcupine Basin (Croker & Shannon 1987). They are necessary to hydrocarbon potential in the Hebridean region (Kilenyi & Standley 1985) where Carboniferous rocks are tentatively identified in seismic profiles (Fig. 6) and have been collected from the seabed west of Skye (Eden et al. 1973). Onshore data confirm that the Carboniferous does have source rock potential (see below). The main oil source rocks in the Porcupine Basin are thick upper Jurassic shales (Croker & Shannon 1987). Similarly, the richest source rocks in the Faroe−Shetland Basin are upper Jurassic − lowermost Cre-

taceous, with a potential for both oil and gas (Bailey et al. 1987). Rocks with a limited potential for gas also occur in the Mid-Jurassic. Thick Liassic rocks occur in the Hebridean region, but they are immature. In the West Shetland Basin, well 205/25−1 penetrated eleven coal seams in the Lower Cretaceous (Hitchen & Ritchie 1987). Analyses of upper Cretaceous mudstones have generally revealed only a limited potential for gas (Bailey et al. 1987). Lignitic beds occur in the Tertiary of the Porcupine Basin and west of Shetland. High potential yields have been obtained from Porcupine samples (Croker & Shannon 1987) and the onshore Lough Neagh Group in Northern Ireland (authors' unpublished data). They are predominantly immature, except possibly in the central part of the Porcupine Basin.

Data for Carboniferous source rocks

Hydrocarbon prospects in western Scotland and Northern Ireland rely on the existence of Carboniferous source rocks. Exploration programmes in the Hebrides Basin (Kilenyi & Standley 1985) and the Ulster Basin in Antrim (Illing & Griffith 1986) assume that the Mesozoic successions are underlain by Carboniferous rocks. The Carboniferous outcrops quite widely in Northern Ireland, and also in Kintyre (McCallien & Anderson 1930) and at Inninmore Bay in Morvern on the Sound of Mull (MacGregor & Manson 1934; Love & Neves 1964) (Fig. 7). Pyrolysis data are available for three distinct sequences in Northern Ireland; the thick North West Basin of Lower Carboniferous spanning the border with the Republic of Ireland in the west, a sequence of Westphalian coals at Coalisland in East Tyrone, and shales and coals from North Antrim (details in Parnell 1991). The North Antrim sequence can be correlated with the Carboniferous of the Midland Valley of Scotland, but not with sequences elsewhere in Ulster. New pyrolysis data are reported here for the Kintyre and Morvern outcrops.

Hydrogen indices have been calculated from the pyrolysis yields and plotted against the temperature of maximum yield during pyrolysis (T_{max}), which allows reference to standard curves for kerogen maturation and vitrinite isoreflectance (Fig. 8). The samples generally have good yields with hydrogen indices over 100 mg/g, and plot between the curves for kerogen types II and III. Some samples from North Antrim, including samples of oil-shale, give higher yields up to 650 mg/g and plot between the curves for kerogen types I and II.

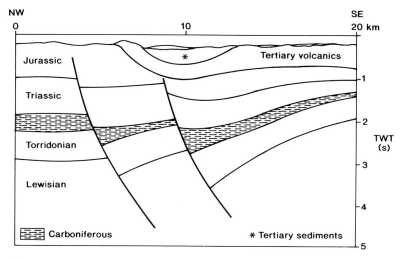

Fig. 6. Carboniferous strata in interpreted seismic profile south of Skye. Reactivation of basement faults controlled location of Oligocene sedimentation in Canna Basin (after Stein 1988).

This is consistent with petrographic observations that the oil-shales contain *Botryococcus*-type algal bodies similar to the lacustrine Oil Shale Group, their time-equivalents 170 km to the east in the Midland Valley. Less oxygen index data is available, but a cross-plot of the data against hydrogen indices on a modified van Krevelen diagram (Fig. 9) similarly suggests a substantial component of type-III (terrestrial) kerogen. The samples are relatively immature, just entering the oil-window at vitrinite reflectance levels of about 0.6%. However, the

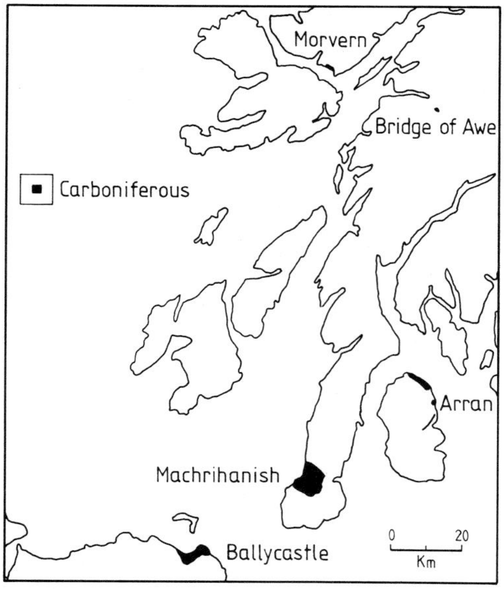

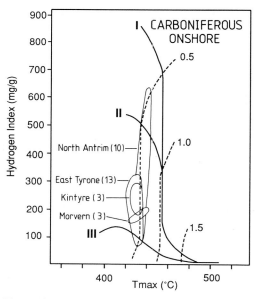

Fig. 8. Cross-plot of hydrogen index against temperature of maximum yield during pyrolysis for Carboniferous rocks in Northern Ireland/ western Scotland (sample numbers in brackets). Curves for kerogen maturation and vitrinite isoreflectance are superimposed.

Fig. 7. Outcrop of Carboniferous rocks in North Antrim and western Scotland.

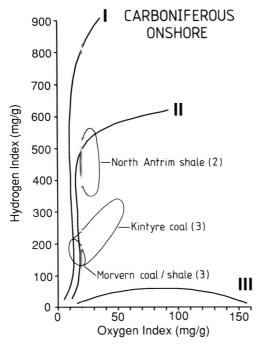

Fig. 9. Modified van Krevelen diagram, plotting hydrogen index against oxygen index, for Carboniferous rocks in North Antrim and western Scotland (sample numbers in brackets). Kerogen maturation curves superimposed.

samples are from surface outcrops which are not buried beneath Mesozoic basins, where they would be more mature and are likely to have generated hydrocarbons.

Most samples which have been submitted to pyrolysis-gas chromatography do not yield hydrocarbon distributions beyond C_{10} and appear predominantly gas-prone. However some samples from near the top of the Lower Carboniferous yield alkane−alkene doublets to about C_{25} and have a mixed potential for oil and gas (Fig. 10). These samples include the oil-shales from North Antrim. Trial distillation of the oil-shales produced oil yields of up to 17.4 gallons/ton (Wilson & Robbie 1966). It is notable that across the North Channel, cannel coals and oil-shales in the Carboniferous of Kintyre were considered to be sufficiently abundant and to have a high enough oil yield to warrant proposals for a distillation plant (McCallien & Anderson 1930). Samples from Kintyre and Morvern also yield pyrolysis chromatograms which indicate a mixed potential for oil and gas (Fig. 11). The vitrinite reflectance of Westphalian coal from the Inninmore outcrop

(Love & Neves 1964) is variable, due to weathering, but modal values in the range 1.2 to 1.5% suggest that the coal is at the mature limit of the oil window (Fig. 12).

Hydrocarbon shows

Hydrocarbons have been encountered in several of the offshore basins, particularly in those with thicker Permo-Triassic sequences. For example, there are significant, but non-commercial, volumes of oil in the Porcupine Basin (MacDonald *et al.* 1987) and west of Shetland (Bailey *et al.* 1987). The reasons for a lack of commercial discoveries are probably multiple. In the ocean-ward basins, the timing of hydrocarbon generation relative to trap formation may have been unsuitable. There is also a serious problem in the Tertiary reactivation of fractures (as in Fig. 6) which may have allowed the leakage of reservoired hydrocarbons. This report documents the onshore shows on the North West Seaboard.

Onshore, hydrocarbon shows are found in two particular regions: Skye and Eigg in the Hebrides, and North West Ireland. In Skye, Jurassic sandstones at several levels are coloured black because they are impregnated with bitumen. Notable black sandstones include occurrences in the Cullaidh Shale Formation at Inver Tote, the Elgol Sandstone Formation at Elgol and the Valtos Sandstone Formation at Rigg (locality details in Lee 1920; Anderson & Dunham 1966; stratigraphy after Harris & Hudson 1980). The occurrences at Inver Tote and Elgol appear to be related to the nearby intrusion of Tertiary sills into Jurassic black shales. North of Elgol, bitumen also occurs in calcite-filled fractures in sandstone which are similarly a product of Tertiary hydrothermal activity associated with an intrusion. The intrusions have yielded bitumen from vugs. Minor bitumen shows have been recorded in Eigg in the Valtos Sandstone Formation. The Triassic sandstones of the Hebrides are generally tightly cemented, but I have recorded bitumen nodules in Mull nucleated around zircon grains; a phenomenon documented in other basins which have seen hydrocarbon migration (Parnell *et al.* 1990). Below the Mesozoic sequence, hydrocarbons appear to have migrated through fractures in the basement; traces of bitumen occur in fractured Torridonian sandstones on Skye. In all these cases the likely source rocks are Jurassic. In addition, very minor hydrocarbon shows in the Tertiary rocks of the Hebrides could have been generated from interbasaltic lignites cut by intrusions.

In the Carboniferous of North West Ireland,

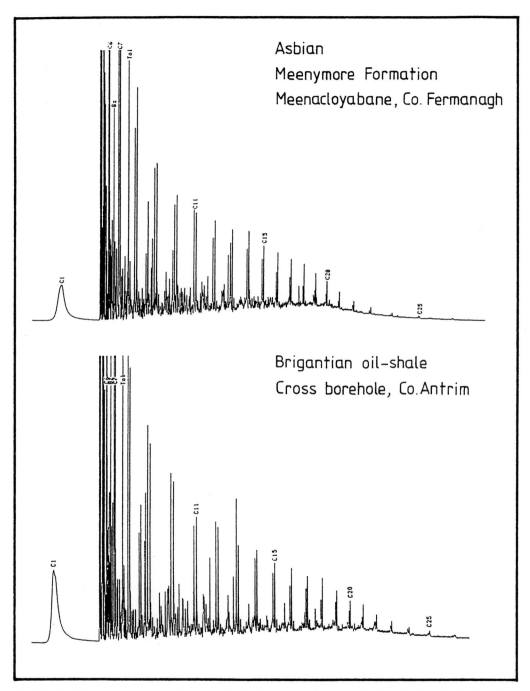

Fig. 10. Pyrolysis gas chromatograms for two Carboniferous samples from Northern Ireland, indicating mixed oil and gas potential.

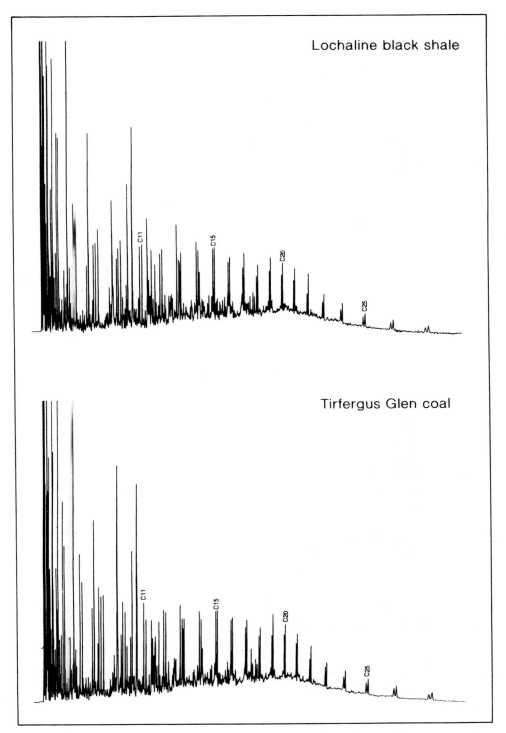

Fig. 11. Pyrolysis gas chromatograms for two Carboniferous samples from western Scotland, indicating mixed oil and gas potential.

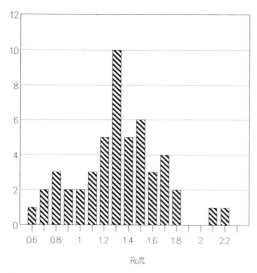

Fig. 12. Histogram of vitrinite reflectance for coal from Inninmore bay, Morvern.

hydrocarbons occur in several settings, including impregnations in sandstones, fracture-fillings in limestones and some widely distributed accretionary nodules. The only available sources for these hydrocarbons are within the Lower Carboniferous. The occurrences include a 2 cm wide pure bitumen vein in Co. Fermanagh along a NW−SE fracture, possibly of Tertiary age. This instance is interesting because it may be evidence for leakage along Tertiary fractures as discussed above.

In addition, hydrocarbon shows are also widespread in the Devonian rocks of the Orcadian Basin. Numerous sandstones contain bituminous residues at outcrop (Parnell 1985), particularly in Caithness and Orkney where Devonian source rock thicknesses are greatest. Bitumens also occur as fracture-fillings and deposits in hydrothermal mineral veins.

The bitumen shows in sandstones predominantly infill secondary porosity after the dissolution of carbonate cements (Fig. 13). In the case of the Jurassic sandstones on Skye, leaching of cement was probably by fluids generated during Tertiary intrusive activity. However, in the Jurassic sandstones of Eigg bitumen also occupies some residual primary porosity remaining after concretionary carbonate cementation (see Wilkinson, this volume). In the North West Irish Basin, the sandstones are arkosic, and bitumens occur in secondary porosity formed by the dissolution of both carbonate/sulphate cement and feldspar grains. Sandstones in the Orcadian Basin show bitumen post-dating a kaolinite cement which was

A

B

C

Fig. 13. Bitumen infilling secondary porosity in sandstones on the North West Seaboard. A, bitumen (black) infilling foraminiferal test (centre) and also as blebs between sand grains, Jurassic Elgol Sandstone Formation, Elgol, Skye. B, Bitumen (black) infilling intragranular dissolution porosity in feldspar grain, Carboniferous Mullaghmore Sandstone, Mullaghmore Head, Co. Sligo. C, bitumen (black) infilling secondary porosity after dissolution of calcite cement. Note irregular pores due to grain replacement by calcite before dissolution, Devonian Eday Group, Grimsetter, Orkney. All field widths are 2 mm.

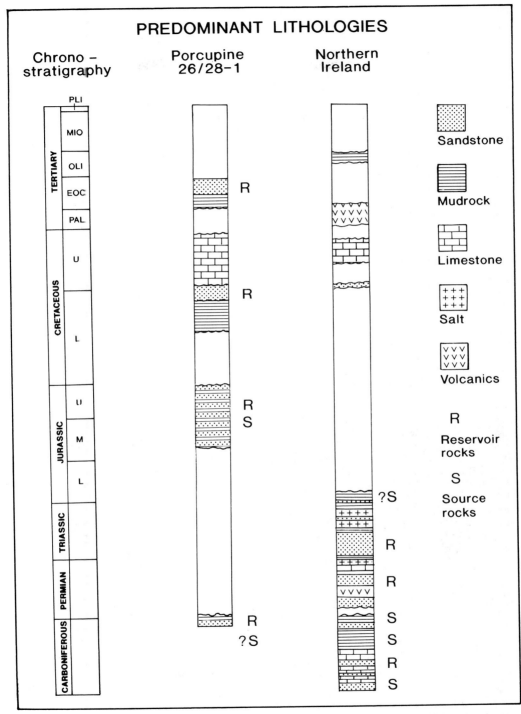

Fig. 14. Chronostratigraphic logs for Porcupine well 26/28−1 (from Croker & Shannon 1987) and a Northern Ireland composite section, indicating potential source and reservoir rocks.

14 J. PARNELL

deposited after calcite dissolution, probably during Carboniferous–Permian uplift.

The stratigraphic distribution of potential reservoir rocks varies between basins according to their burial histories. Figure 14 shows successions from the Mesozoic-dominated Porcupine Basin (data from Croker & Shannon 1987; MacDonald *et al.* 1987) and a composite section for onshore Northern Ireland which is dominated by pre-Jurassic sediments (data from Illing & Griffith 1986). The reservoir targets in the Porcupine Basin include sandstones of late Carboniferous, middle and late Jurassic, early Cretaceous and Eocene age. Some sections in the basin also include Triassic reservoir sandstones (Croker & Shannon 1987). The Northern Ireland basins include deltaic Carboniferous and continental Permo-Triassic sandstones.

Onshore exploration

In the past decade, exploration programmes have been conducted to investigate most conceivable onshore plays in the UK. The North West Seaboard is no exception, and onshore licenses were awarded for exploration in the North West Irish Basin (with contiguous license in the Republic of Ireland), the Ulster Basin, the Rathlin Basin in Rathlin Sound, the Stranraer Basin, the Clyde Basin, and in several parts of the Hebrides–Minch system (Fig. 15). Onshore licenses were also awarded for the Devonian rocks in the Orcadian Basin in Caithness and Easter Ross. Excepting the Orcadian Basin, and the North West Basin which is exclusively Carboniferous, all the plays are in Mesozoic basins. As discussed above, the plays depend on the presence and maturation of Carboniferous source rocks. In the larger basins (Hebrides–Minch) the burial depth is adequate for hydrocarbon generation from the Carboniferous, but there must be some doubt about the maturation level in the smaller basins like the Ulster Basin and Stranraer Basin (and see Dean, this volume).

In the eastern part of the Ulster Basin, maximum burial histories are similar to that reconstructed for the Rathlin Trough (Fig. 4), dominated by thick Triassic sedimentation and a substantial pile of Palaeocene basalts with the additional thickness of Tertiary sills within the Mesozoic rocks. Such a burial history should be adequate for at least some hydrocarbon generation from the Carboniferous. Carboniferous rocks are thought to be present beneath eastern Antrim, based upon seismic evidence (Illing & Griffith 1986). The hydrocarbon prospectivity of this region is highlighted by a close compari-

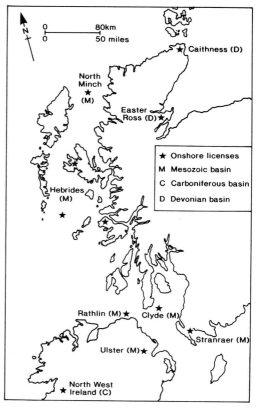

Fig. 15. Regions of onshore licence allocation on the North West Seaboard up to 1988 (onshore allocations include some inshore waters).

son with the succession in the Morecambe Gas Field on the opposite side of the Irish Sea (Fig. 16). They share probable Carboniferous source rocks, Permian and Triassic sandstone reservoirs, and Permian and Triassic evaporative mudstone seals. The first drilling activity in Antrim yielded only minor gas shows (Illing & Griffith 1986). However the setting is attractive for exploration and at the time of writing (November 1990) a further drilling programme is in progress. It is likely that the Ulster Basin will remain an exploration target for the forseeable future.

I am most grateful to B. Monson for use of his Lopatin reconstruction program, to Humble Instruments & Services for some of the pyrolyses, to the Geological Survey of Northern Ireland for access to core samples, and to G. Alexander, E. Mulqueeny and M. Pringle for technical assistance. The manuscript benefitted from reviews by A. Hurst and S. Trueblood.

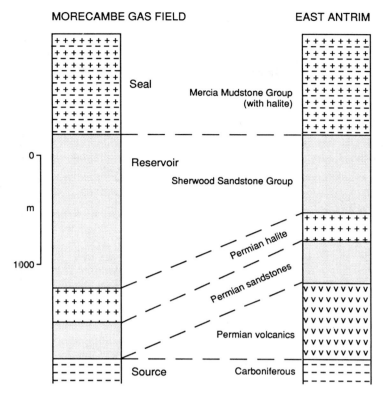

Fig. 16. Comparison between successions in Morecambe Gas Field and East Antrim (partly after Ebbern 1981; Penn *et al.* 1983).

References

ANDERSON, F. W. & DUNHAM, K. C. 1966. *The Geology of Northern Skye*. Memoir of the Geological Survey of Great Britain. HMSO, Edinburgh.

BAILEY, N. J. L., WALKO, P. & SAUER, M. J. 1987. Geochemistry and source rock potential of the west of Shetlands. *In*: BROOKS, J. & GLENNIE, K. W. (eds) *Petroleum Geology of North West Europe*. Graham & Trotman, London, 711–721.

CROKER, P. F. & SHANNON, P. M. 1987. The evolution and hydrocarbon prospectivity of the Porcupine Basin, offshore Ireland. *In*: BROOKS, J. & GLENNIE, K. (eds) *Petroleum Geology of North West Europe*. Graham & Trotman, London, 633–642.

EBBERN, J. 1981. The geology of the Morecambe Gas Field. *In*: ILLING, L. V. & HOBSON, G. D. (eds) *Petroleum Geology of the Continental Shelf of North-West Europe*. Heyden, London, 485–493.

EDEN, R., DEEGEN, C., RHYS, G., WRIGHT, J. & DOBSON, M. 1973. *Geological Investigations with a Manned Submersible in the Irish Sea and off Western Scotland*. Report of the Institute of Geological Sciences, 73/2.

ENFIELD, M. A. & COWARD, M. P. 1987. The structure of the West Orkney Basin, northern Scotland. *Journal of the Geological Society, London*, **144**, 871–884.

EVANS, D., KENOLTY, N., DOBSON, M. R. & WHITTINGTON, R. J. 1980. The geology of the Malin Sea. *Report of the Institute of Geological Sciences*, **79/15**.

HARRIS, J. P. & HUDSON, J. D. 1980. Lithostratigraphy of the Great Estuarine Group (Middle Jurassic), Inner Hebrides. *Scottish Journal of Geology*, **16**, 231–250.

HASZELDINE, R. S. & RUSSELL, M. J. 1987. The Late Carboniferous northern North Atlantic Ocean: implications for hydrocarbon exploration from Britain to the Arctic. *In*: BROOKS, J. & GLENNIE, K. W. (eds) *Petroleum Geology of North West Europe*. Graham & Trotman, London, 1163–1175.

HITCHEN, K. & RITCHIE, J. D. 1987. Geological review of the West Shetland area. *In*: BROOKS, J. & GLENNIE, K. W. (eds) *Petroleum Geology of North West Europe*. Graham & Trotman, London, 737–749.

ILLING, L. V. & GRIFFITH, A. E. 1986. Gas prospects in the 'Midland Valley' of Northern Ireland. *In*:

BROOKS, J., GOFF, J. C. & VAN HOORN, B. (eds) *Habitat of Palaeozoic Gas in NW Europe*. Geological Society, London, Special Publication, **23**, 73–84.

KILENYI, T. & STANDLEY, R. 1985. Petroleum prospects in the northwest seaboard of Scotland. *Oil and Gas Journal*, **84**, 100–108.

LEE, G. W. 1920. *The Mesozoic rocks of Applecross, Raasay, and North-east Skye*. Memoir of the Geological Survey of Scotland. HMSO, Edinburgh.

LOVE, L. G. & NEVES, R. 1964. Palynological evidence on the age of the Carboniferous of Inninmore. *Transactions of the Geological Society of Glasgow*, **25**, 61–71.

McCALLIEN, W. J. & ANDERSON, R. B. 1930. The Carboniferous sediments of Kintyre. *Transactions of the Royal Society of Edinburgh*, **56**, 599–619.

MACDONALD, M., ALLAN, P. M. & LOVELL, J. P. B. 1987. Geology of oil accumulation in Block 26/28, Porcupine Basin, offshore Ireland. *In*: BROOKS, J. & GLENNIE, K. W. (eds) *Petroleum Geology of North West Europe*. Graham & Trotman, London, 643–651.

MACGREGOR, M. & MANSON, W. 1934. The Carboniferous rocks of Inninmore, Morvern. *Geological Survey of Great Britain Summary of Progress for 1933*, part II, 74–84.

MEADOWS, N. S., MACCHI, L., CUBITT, J. M. & JOHNSON, B. 1987. Sedimentology and reservoir potential in the west of Shetland, UK exploration area. *In*: BROOKS, J. & GLENNIE, K. (eds) *Petroleum Geology of North West Europe*. Graham & Trotman, London, 723–736.

PARNELL, J. 1985. Hydrocarbon source rocks, reservoir rocks and migration in the Orcadian Basin. *Scottish Journal of Geology*, **21**, 321–336.

—— 1989. Hydrocarbon potential of the Lower Palaeozoic of the British Isles. *Oil and Gas Journal*, 82–86.

—— 1991. Hydrocarbon potential of Northern Ireland: 1. Burial histories and source rock potential. *Journal of Petroleum Geology*, **14**, 65–78.

——, MONSON, B. & TOSSWILL, R. J. 1990. Petrography of thoriferous hydrocarbon nodules in sandstones, and their significance for petroleum exploration. *Journal of the Geological Society*, London, **147**, 837–842.

PENN, I. E., HOLLIDAY, D. W., KIRBY, G. A., KUBALA, M., SOBEY, R. A., MITCHELL, W. I., HARRISON, R. K. & BECKINSALE, R. D. 1983. The Larne No. 2 borehole: discovery of a new Permian volcanic centre. *Scottish Journal of Geology*, **19**, 333–346.

STEIN, A. M. 1988. Basement controls upon basin development in the Caledonian foreland, NW Scotland. *Basin Research*, **1**, 107–119.

WAPLES, D. W. 1980. Time and temperature in petroleum formation — application of Lopatin's method to petroleum exploration. *AAPG Bulletin*, **64**, 916–926.

WILSON, H. E. & MANNING, P. I. 1978. *Geology of the Causeway Coast*. Memoir of the Geological Survey of Northern Ireland, HMSO, Belfast.

—— & ROBBIE, J. A. 1966. *The Geology of the country around Ballycastle*. Memoir of the Geological Survey of Northern Ireland, HMSO, Belfast.

Basin development and petroleum potential in The Minches and Sea of the Hebrides Basins

ALAN M. STEIN

Dolan & Associates, 3 Old Lodge Place, Twickenham, Middlesex TW1 1RQ, UK

The Minches and Sea of the Hebrides Basins lie within the inshore waters between the Outer Hebrides and the Northwest Highlands of Scotland. The geological history of this area is dominated by a set of linked shear zones, trending NW–SE and NE–SW, which developed in the lower crust at around 2400 Ma. The main elements of this shear zone became the focus for tectonic, metamorphic and magmatic activity throughout the development of the Precambrian basement complex and have been repeatedly reactivated as fundamental lines of weakness up to the present day (Lailey *et al.* 1989). The Minches and Sea of the Hebrides Basins are westwards-thickening half-graben which developed in the hangingwall to one of these reactivated shear zones; the NE–SW trending Outer Isles Fault (Stein 1988*a*). The Outer Isles Fault is a major convex-up fault which extends almost to the base of the crust. The overall form and internal geometry of the Minches and Sea of the Hebrides Basins can be directly related to the three-dimensional shape of the Outer Isles Fault. Compartmentalization of the basins occurs where the Outer Isles Fault is intersected by steep faults which have reactivated the NW–SE trending shear zones (Stein & Blundell 1990).

Basin development began during the Proterozoic with at least two major rifting episodes which led to the deposition of the Torridonian Supergroup. The Proterozoic sequences are up to 8000 m thick in parts of the offshore region and are thought to comprise a mostly clastic red-bed sequence that was deposited in a NE–SW trending rift basin bounded to the NW by the Outer Isles Fault. During the Caledonian Orogeny the remnants of the Proterozoic basins lay beneath the basal thrust of the Caledonian nappe complexes and as such lay within the rigid 'foreland' to the orogen. There may have been some deep inversion of the basins associated with reverse movements on the Outer Isles Fault but this part of the basin history has yet to be adequately determined by isotopic work and further field studies.

From the Carboniferous onwards, basin development appears to have been closely related to the opening history of the North Atlantic.

Sequence analysis of offshore seismic data suggests that up to 2000 m of Carboniferous sediments are present in the deepest parts of the Minches and Sea of the Hebrides Basins. Reconstructions of the Atlantic show that these basins were part of a chain of Carboniferous rifts that can be traced from the west of Ireland through western Scotland to East Greenland and beyond. The Carboniferous is unconformably overlain by a Permo-Triassic sequence of continental red-beds which achieve maximum thicknesses of up to 3000 m in places. The presence of coarse, thick, Permo-Triassic conglomerates against the Outer Isles Fault implies that the fault was actively extending at this time. There is a distinctive change of character between the Triassic and the overlying Jurassic rocks, which were deposited in a much more humid environment in a basin of variable salinity which appears to have been tectonically less active. In excess of 1000 m of Jurassic sandstones, shales and limestones outcrop on the islands of the Inner Hebrides. The earliest Cretaceous was a period of basin inversion, and most of the Upper Jurassic section is missing through erosion. A thin, fully marine, late Cretaceous sandstone was deposited upon an unconformity surface with considerable variation in the age of the sub-crop. The Minches and Sea of the Hebrides Basins are separated by a major NW–SE inversion axis which is presumed to be Cretaceous in age. The inversion axis developed as a result of transpressional reactivation of the Loch Maree Fault during Alpine compression. The Loch Maree Fault, in turn, is thought to have reactivated one of the fundamental NW–SE shear zones. Unlike major basins to the west (Rockall) and east (North Sea), the Minches and Sea of the Hebrides Basins have undergone very little Tertiary subsidence. The basins lay within the boundaries of the Tertiary Igneous Province and, during the Palaeocene, major igneous complexes were emplaced on the islands of Skye, Rhum, Mull, and on the mainland at Ardnamurchan. Piles of sub-areal basaltic lava flows up to 1800 m thick are associated with these complexes and Tertiary-age dykes are common throughout the region. Post-Palaeocene subsidence patterns display dra-

From PARNELL, J. (ed.), 1992, *Basins on the Atlantic Seaboard: Petroleum Geology, Sedimentology and Basin Evolution.* Geological Society Special Publication No 62, pp 17–20.

18 A. M. STEIN

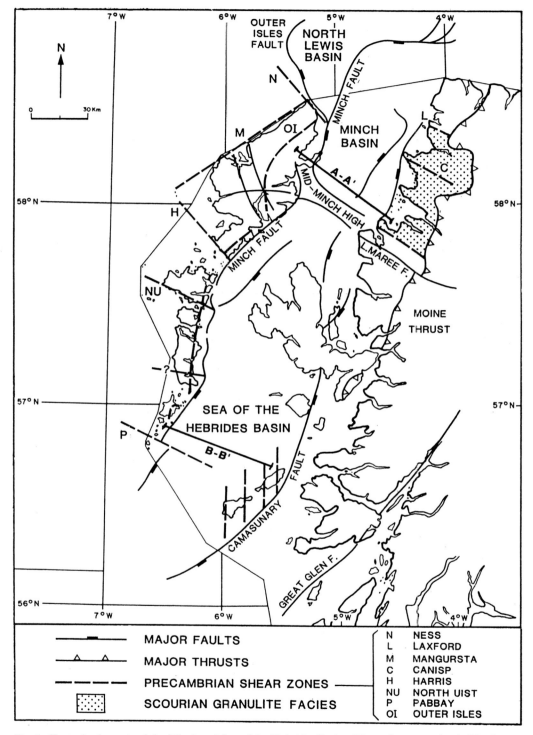

Fig. 1. Tectonic elements of the Minch and Sea of the Hebrides Basins. Lines of cross section in Fig. 2 are marked A–Á, B–Ḃ.

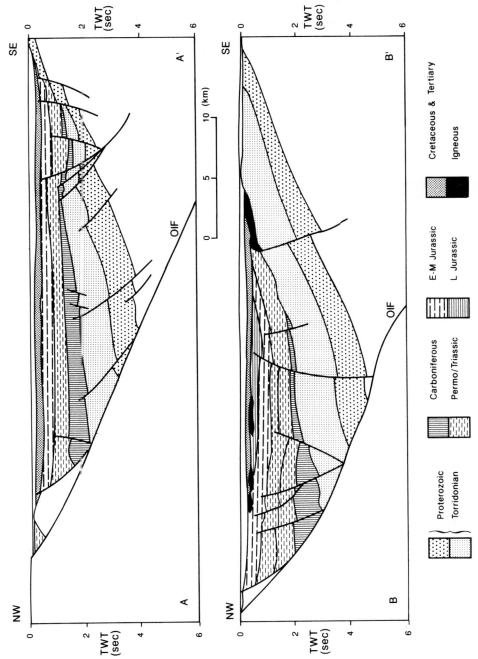

Fig. 2. Geoseismic cross sections across the Minch and Sea of the Hebrides Basins. For section locations see Fig. 1.

matic variation within the basins. Regional uplift and warping resulted in present day relief of approximately 2500 m at the base of the lava pile while in places up to 1000 m of non-marine Oligocene sediments are preserved in localised fault-bounded graben. However, over most of the Minches and Sea of the Hebrides Basins, the Mesozoic lies very close to the surface, where it is covered by a thin veneer of late Tertiary sediments.

One of the key features in an assessment of the petroleum potential of these basins is to identify an effective source rock interval. The late Jurassic Kimmeridge Clay outcrops on the Island of Skye and is known to be an excellent source rock. Unfortunately nowhere in either basin is the Kimmeridge Clay likely to have been buried deep enough to be suitably mature. The early Jurassic Pabba Shale is a moderate source rock (TOC 1–2%) which may be marginally mature over the deepest parts of the basin. Samples of this interval from the eastern margin of the basin were found to lie just above the top of the oil window (Stein 1988b). Samples collected immediately adjacent to Tertiary intrusions were found to be mature although this is not likely to be of regional significance (Thrasher, this volume).

Studies of a basin-margin Carboniferous sequence at Inninmore Bay in the Scottish Highlands clearly demonstrate the presence of a coal-bearing section of Westphalian age in these basins. Facies models based on field observations, palynological analysis, and contemporary analogues can be used to predict the distribution of source rock facies within the basin (Stein 1988b). Maturity analysis of the coals at Inninmore Bay shows them to be within the peak oil-generating zone but above the gas-generating zone. However, burial history plots for the offshore parts of the basin, where the best source rocks are predicted to occur, show the Carboniferous sequence entering the gas-generating zone during the early Jurassic. The nature of Carboniferous source rocks in these basins is likely to change progressively towards the deepest parts of the basin. Coals should be best developed in the medium–low energy parts of the hangingwall drainage system. However in the deepest parts of the basin adjacent to the fault scarp there is likely to have been very little sediment input, leading to the accumulation of low energy shales under tropical conditions in swamps and lakes with restricted circulation. Similar shales from the nearby Midland Valley Carboniferous basin are excellent oil-prone source rocks (TOC up to 30%). These source rocks could charge any of the numerous clastic reservoirs in the overlying Mesozoic section, with seals provided by intra-basinal Triassic shales or Jurassic shales and/or limestones. Tilted fault block structures are present in both basins and Middle Jurassic sandbodies in particular could provide stratigraphic exploration targets.

References

LAILEY, M., STEIN, A. M. & RESTON, T. J. 1989. The Outer Hebrides Fault: a major Proterozoic structure in NW Scotland. *Journal of the Geological Society, London*, **146**, 253–259.

STEIN, A. M. 1988a. Basement controls upon Hebridean basin development, NW Scotland. *Basin Research*, **1**, 107–119.

—— 1988b. *Northwest Scotland U.K. Evaluation of Carboniferous basin development and petroleum potential*. Non-exclusive report, JEBCO Seismic Ltd., London.

—— & BLUNDELL, D. J. 1990. Geological inheritance and crustal dynamics of the northwest Scottish continental shelf. *In*: LEVEN, J. H., FINLAYSON, D. M., WRIGHT, C., DOOLEY, J. C. & KENNETT, B. L. N. (eds) *Seismic Probing of Continents and their Margins. Tectonophysics*, **173**, 455–467.

Conodont colour maturation indices for the Carboniferous of west-central Scotland

MARK T. DEAN

British Geological Survey, Keyworth, Nottinghamshire, NG12 5GG, UK

Abstract: The colour alteration of conodont elements from Carboniferous samples from west-central Scotland is summarized, and most values fall within indices 1 to 1.5. This range corresponds to geothermal temperatures of <50°C to 90°C which lie within the immature (early dry gas) to mature (perhaps mid-oil window) stages of hydrocarbon generation. Where the index values are 1.5, and other necessary geological criteria are satisfied, support is offered here for oil generation through burial maturation.

This short contribution aims to introduce work undertaken on the thermal maturation of Carboniferous sediments in west-central Scotland using conodont colour alteration indices (CAI).

Conodonts were soft-bodied marine organisms that flourished from Cambrian to Triassic times. Each animal bore a skeletonized apparatus made up of morphologically variable microscopic elements. These elements, which became scattered after death, were composed principally of apatite with interlamellar organic matter. Unweathered and thermally unaltered conodont elements are pale yellow to light amber in colour, but when heated in a closed tube they darken (due to carbon fixing) and give off water (Ellison 1944; Lindström 1964).

Epstein *et al.* (1977) provided a new tool for palaeotemperature analysis when they showed that this heat-induced colour alteration in conodont elements could be used as a semi-quantitative index of thermal metamorphism. Based on laboratory experiment and evaluated by comparison with field data they showed that colour alteration is progressive, cumulative and irreversible; time and temperature dependent; and, in the absence of water, the CAI is unaffected by confining pressure or tectonics. Aldridge (1986) added that when the maximum temperature has been sustained for a time of the order of millions of years, the length of time makes only a small difference to the colour alteration achieved. Table 1 summarizes the six colour intervals discriminated by Epstein *et al.* (1977).

Methods, CAI values and interpretation

This study is mainly concerned with the Carboniferous outcrop in the central and western parts of the Midland Valley of Scotland (including Arran), but samples from Douglas, Thornhill and Machrihanish are also included. Dean (in prep.) referred to and gave comprehensive details of 70 samples within this area. Of these, 28 are Dinantian and 34 Namurian, all of which come from carbonates of the Lower and Upper Limestone Groups. The remaining 8 samples come from shales or bullion limestones of the Silesian Vanderbeckei (Queenslie) and Aegiranum (Skipsey's) Marine Bands.

The colour alteration of selected conodont elements extracted from these samples was determined by the use of a standard set of previously calibrated specimens, kindly supplied by Dr A. G. Harris; and element colour charts (see for example Harris *in* Robison 1981, frontispiece). Help with the calibration of the various collections was given by Dr R. D. Burnett.

Figure 1 shows the range and distribution of the conodont colour alteration indices for the Carboniferous of west-central Scotland. Closely spaced localities have been amalgamated into a single plot and precise geographical and stratigraphical details for each sample are given in Dean (in prep.). Most conodont CAI values range between 1 and 1.5, corresponding to a

Table 1. Conodont colour alteration indices (CAI). Based on Epstein *et al.* (1977). See also, for example, Burnett (1987, table 1) for a good discriminative summary of indices 1–5

Index	Colour alteration	Temperature range (°C)
1	Pale yellow	<50–80
1.5	Very pale brown	50–90
2	Brown	60–140
3		110–200
	Increasingly dark brown	
4		190–300
5	black	300–350

From Parnell, J. (ed.), 1992, *Basins on the Atlantic Seaboard: Petroleum Geology, Sedimentology and Basin Evolution.* Geological Society Special Publication. No 62, pp 21–23.

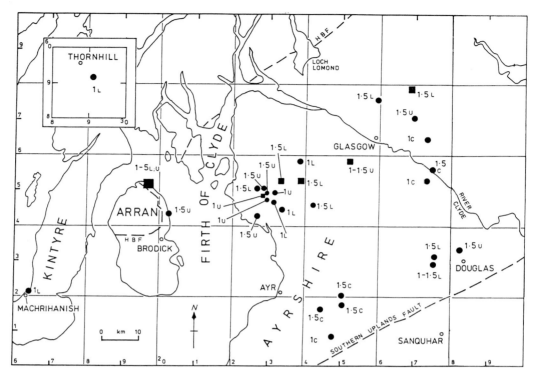

Fig. 1. Range and distribution of conodont CAI values for the Carboniferous of west-central Scotland. From Dean (in prep.). ●, Single plot (single sample locality). ■, Amalgamated plot (closely spaced sample localities). Lithostratigraphic units sampled: C: Coal Measures; L: Lower Limestone Group; U: Upper Limestone Group. HBF: Highland Boundary Fault.

temperature range of <50°C to 90°C (Epstein *et al*. 1977).

Table 2 summarizes the former stratigraphical overburden calculated from field evidence and, by implication, indicates the time of onset of major unloading by erosion. If, for the sake of simplicity, it is assumed that the average geothermal gradient during the Carboniferous was similar to that of the present day, i.e. 22.5°C km^{-1} (Browne *et al*. 1987; British Geological Survey 1988) such stratigraphical thicknesses correspond to the geothermal

Table 2. Predicted and observed conodont CAI ranges for the Carboniferous of west-central Scotland. The geothermal temperatures shown include an additional 20°C representing the ambient sea temperature at the time of deposition. From Dean (in prep.).

Region	Maximum overburden (m) Carboniferous	Permo–Trias.	Total	Corresponding geothermal temperature (°C)	Predicted CAI range	Observed CAI values
Glasgow	2062		2062	66	1–2	1–1.5
Douglas	1430		1430	52	1–1.5	1–1.5
North Ayrshire	566	750	1316	50	1–1.5	1–1.5
South Ayshire	774	750	1524	54	1–1.5	1–1.5
Thornhill	126	140	266	26	1	1
Arran	322	1000	1322	50	1–1.5	1–1.5
Machrihanish	364	1500	1864	62	1–2	1

temperatures and CAI ranges shown and the observed CAI values are seen to fit well with the field data. Dean (in prep.) suggested that the overburden thicknesses as calculated do approximate to the true maximum value, that tectonic thickening is not important, and that apart from a few isolated localities (as on Arran where the CAI range is 1 to 5 according to the proximity of Tertiary igneous dykes), local heat sources had little or no influence on the samples analysed.

Implications for hydrocarbon generation

According to Parnell (1984) the source of all hydrocarbons in the Midland Valley Basin is the Carboniferous sedimentary sequence, and whilst the Oil-Shale Groups of the Lothians have been worked in the past for oil distillation, other organic-rich shales elsewhere within the Scottish Carboniferous sequence are further possible sources.

Hydrocarbon minerals are particularly associated with igneous intrusions in the Lothians and Fife, and hence it is important to understand the differing thermal effects of the various Carboniferous (and later) intrusions in relation to the thermal conductivity of the sediments which they invaded (see Raymond & Murchison 1988).

However, not all hydrocarbon occurrences in the Midland Valley of Scotland are related to igneous intrusions, and Parnell (1984) summarized those he considered to be the products of local diagenesis. Regional and basinal studies using CAI data are valuable for hydrocarbon exploration, and the observed general range of CAI values (1 to 1.5) presented herein lies within the immature (early dry gas) to mature (mid-oil window) stages of hydrocarbon generation of Héroux et al. (1979).

Whilst significant migration of oil, naturally distilled by igneous intrusions, may have occurred in the Midland Valley, conodont colour alteration shows that it is also possible that oil could have been generated locally, solely under the influence of the geothermal gradient. CAI values of 1.5 indicate where this can reasonably be suspected. However it should be noted that the temperature range of the liquid hydrocarbon window in Palaeozoic rocks remains uncertain (see for example Héroux et al. 1979, p 2129; Burnett 1987, table 1) and the

insensitivity of conodonts to low temperatures (corresponding to CAIs 1, 1.5 and 2) limits their use as sole indicators of oil generation. Indeed thermal maturation levels are best determined using a range of methods that can be correlated (see also Dean, in prep.).

My thanks are offered to R. B. Evans, R. D. Lake and B. Owens for their criticisms of an earlier version of this paper.

References

ALDRIDGE, R. J. 1986. Conodont palaeobiogeography and thermal maturation in the Caledonides. *Journal of the Geological Society, London*, **143**, 177–184.

BRITISH GEOLOGICAL SURVEY 1988. Geothermal energy in the United Kingdom: review of the British Geological Survey's Programme 1984–1987. *Investigation of the geothermal potential of the UK*, British Geological Survey.

BROWNE, M. A. E., ROBINS, N. S., EVANS, R. B., MONRO, S. K. & ROBSON, P. G. 1987. The Upper Devonian and Carboniferous sandstones of the Midland Valley of Scotland. *Investigation of the geothermal potential of the UK*, British Geological Survey.

BURNETT, R. D. 1987. Regional maturation patterns for late Viséan (Carboniferous, Dinantian) rocks of northern England based on mapping of conodont colour. *Irish Journal of Earth Sciences*, **8**, 165–185.

ELLISON, S. P., Jr. 1944. The composition of conodonts. *Journal of Paleontology*, **18**, 133–140.

EPSTEIN, A. G., EPSTEIN, J. B. & HARRIS, L. D. 1977. Conodont color alteration — an index to organic metamorphism. *U.S. Geological Survey, Professional Paper* 995.

HARRIS, A. G. 1981. Color and alteration: an index to organic metamorphism in conodont elements. *In*: ROBISON, R. A. (ed.) *Treatise on invertebrate paleontology*, part W, supplement 2, Conodonta, W56-W60. Geological Society of America and University of Kansas Press, Lawrence, Kansas.

HÉROUX, Y., CHAGNON, A. & BERTRAND, R. 1979. Compilation and correlation of major thermal maturation indicators. *American Association of Petroleum Geologists Bulletin*, **63**, 2128–2144.

LINDSTRÖM, M. 1964. *Conodonts*. Elsevier, Amsterdam.

PARNELL, J. 1984. Hydrocarbon minerals in the Midland Valley of Scotland with particular reference to the Oil Shale Group. *Proceedings of the Geologists' Association*, **95**, 275–285.

RAYMOND, A. C. & MURCHISON, D. G. 1988. Development of organic maturation in the thermal aureoles of sills and its relation to sediment compaction. *Fuel*, **67**, 1599–1608.

Carboniferous source rocks of the Canadian Atlantic margin

DAVID J. MOSSMAN

Department of Geology, Mount Allison University, Sackville, New Brunswick, Canada E0A 3C0

Abstract: Carboniferous source rocks of relatively low to moderate maturity occur onshore along the Canadian Atlantic margin in Palaeozoic basins of western Newfoundland, New Brunswick and Nova Scotia. Coals of predominantly Westphalian age are widespread and locally abundant. In the Devono-Carboniferous Albert Formation of New Brunswick, and in equivalent Horton Group strata elsewhere in the Maritimes Basin, oil-prone type-I kerogen is predominant.

Throughout the Canadian Appalachians, the similarity of Carboniferous strata in various sedimentary basins has facilitated the recognition of four major stratigraphic cycles of deposition. Bounded in nearly every instance by unconformities, these cycles are likewise recognized offshore, where in some cases they have been the focus of commercial investigation. In the Gulf of St. Lawrence region, hydrocarbon-generating potential was early confirmed by drilling in rocks of the Windsor and Canso-Riversdale sequences. These strata may extend north from the Magdalen Basin into the Anticosti Basin, northwestward into the St. Lawrence estuary, and northeast of western Newfoundland.

Carboniferous sections south and east of Newfoundland are in most cases strongly overmature. However, recognition of equivalent Horton Group strata within the oil window in a Grand Banks well indicates the potential of Upper Palaeozoic strata to contribute to the accumulation of oil, not only within the Palaeozoic section, but also in younger strata.

Carboniferous sediments are widely distributed on the seafloor and beneath younger rocks along the Canadian Atlantic continental margin (Fig. 1). Potential source and reservoir rocks, preserved onshore and offshore in various basins, include the Horton, Windsor, Canso, Riversdale and Pictou groups (Fig. 2). Onshore, two important Late Palaeozoic source rocks have long been recognized; these are the oil shales (Macauley *et al.* 1984) of the Albert Formation (Horton Group) in southern New Brunswick, and the thick and widely distributed coal measures of the Cumberland and Pictou groups (Bell & Howie 1990).

Onshore and offshore a common stratigraphic succession is present in various depocentres and there are indications from exploration drilling that, at least in some cases, the rocks (e.g. Pictou Group) are in physical continuity from the Scotian Shelf to the Grand Banks of Newfoundland (Avery & Bell 1985). Carboniferous rocks likewise occur beneath the East Newfoundland Shelf, where there may be some potential for generating dry gas. Although source rocks have not been demonstrated thus far, Carboniferous palynomorphs, possibly reworked, are recorded from carbonates in two wells on the southern Labrador Shelf (Barss *et al.* 1979) which host significant gas/condensate reservoirs.

There are encouraging indications of hydrocarbons sourced from Carboniferous sediments in both onshore and offshore sedimentary basins along the Canadian Atlantic margin. However, substantial quantities have not thus far been proven. The objective of this contribution is to review the distribution of potential source rocks and their quality, quantity, and maturation characteristics.

Distribution of the Carboniferous sediments

Carboniferous sediments onshore eastern Canada are best known from the Appalachians (Williams 1974, 1982) where numerous basins are identified. At the base, the Horton Group (see Fig. 3 for details) consists of continental sediments with sparse volcanic rocks, resting unconformably on eroded Acadian terrain. It is overlain conformably, disconformably and rarely unconformably, by Windsor Group or younger rocks.

Regionally the Windsor Group reportedly (Howie 1988) contains the only Upper Paleozoic marine sediments in southwestern Canada. Composed of red sandstone, red and grey siltstone, limestone and minor gypsum and dolomite, it conformably to non-conformably overlies the Horton Group and pre-Carboniferous basement.

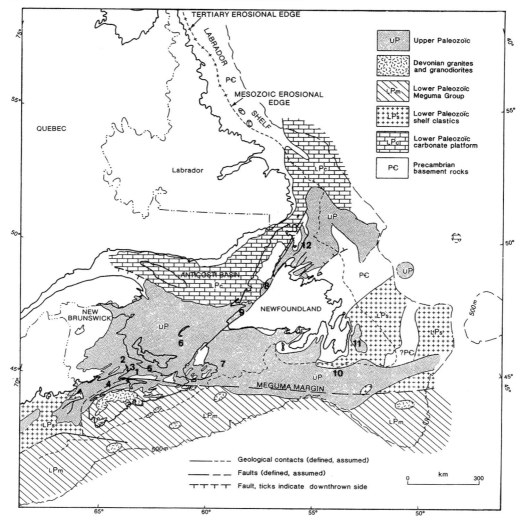

Fig. 1. Distribution of Palaeozoic rocks on the continental margin of eastern Canada (after Bell & Howie 1990, p 144). Numbered basins 1 through 12 are listed in Table 1.

Canso and Riversdale groups are commonly considered as a single unit for mapping purposes. The former consists of thinly laminated non-marine shales, sandstone and minor limestone overlying the Windsor Group or non-marine rocks of equivalent age, and unconformable with underlying older Carboniferous and pre-Carboniferous sediments. The overlying Riversdale Group (see Fig. 2) consists of red and grey sandstone, siltstone and shale with abundant plant remains and coal seams.

The Cumberland Group, localized in the fault-bounded Cumberland sub-basin, consists of non-marine red and grey conglomerates, sandstones, shale and coal. The upper beds of

this group are believed to be coeval with the lower beds of the Pictou Group (Howie 1988).

The stratigraphic succession described above is common to various depocentres onshore and offshore eastern Canada. For example, the Horton Group, well known onshore in the Atlantic provinces, has been identified in boreholes on the continental shelf off Newfoundland (Bell & Howie 1990). In western Cape Breton Island it ranges in thickness up to 3200 m, while in the Gulf of St. Lawrence at least 4000 m of Horton Group sediments have been inferred from geophysical surveys. In western Newfoundland, the Carboniferous rocks of the Bay St. George sub-basin closely resemble the

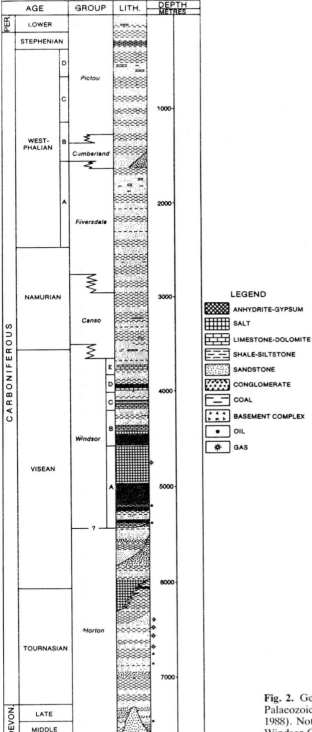

LEGEND

(anhydrite-gypsum pattern)	ANHYDRITE-GYPSUM
(salt pattern)	SALT
(limestone-dolomite pattern)	LIMESTONE-DOLOMITE
(shale-siltstone pattern)	SHALE-SILTSTONE
(sandstone pattern)	SANDSTONE
(conglomerate pattern)	CONGLOMERATE
(coal pattern)	COAL
(basement complex pattern)	BASEMENT COMPLEX
(oil symbol)	OIL
(gas symbol)	GAS

Fig. 2. Generalized stratigraphic column, Upper Palaeozoic rocks, southeastern Canada (after Howie 1988). Note presence of salt in both Horton and Windsor Groups.

Horton and Windsor Groups in Nova Scotia (Knight 1983). Overall, the Bay St. George sub-basin is part of a linear zone of horst and graben structures that persist northeastward to the limit of the continental margin east of Newfoundland. This zone is essentially an intra-continental failed rift arm that underwent extension during the early Mesozoic, followed by subsidence in late Mesozoic and the Tertiary.

Offshore, in many instances (Proctor et al. 1984), Palaeozoic sections are preserved in a strongly overmature condition beneath Mesozoic and Cenozoic sediments (Fig. 1) (e.g. in the Whale and Horseshoe sub-basins of Grand Banks South — not shown in Fig. 1). To the west, the presence of Palaeozoic rocks containing predominantly gas-prone, thermally mature terrestrial organic matter, is inferred in the Georges Bank Basin southwest of Nova Scotia at the United States—Canada border.

From the East Newfoundland Shelf, sedimentary basins trend over 5000 km NNW to Baffin Bay. Noting the presence of reworked Carboniferous palynomorphs in five wells drilled on the West Greenland Shelf, Rolle (1985) postulated that a major Carboniferous sedimentary basin existed between Canada and Greenland. Carboniferous palynomorphs, possibly reworked, are also recorded from two wells (Gudrid H-55 and Verrazano L-77) on the Labrador Shelf (Barss et al. 1979).

Source rocks

The hydrocarbon source rock potential of Carboniferous sediments along the Canadian Atlantic Margin portions of the Appalachian region has been assessed to varying degrees in different basins. Preliminary assessments for Georges Bank and the Scotian Shelf are that the Upper Palaeozoic sections are thermally mature, and likely to be gas prone (Jansa & Wade 1975; Proctor et al. 1984). A summary of source rock assessments for various basins is given in Table 1. A major area of interest is (not shown in Fig. 1) the Maritimes Basin (cf. Williams 1974; Boehner et al. 1986), which encompasses among many others, the sub-basins (see Fig. 1) Cumberland (1), Moncton (2), Sackville (3), Fundy (4), Stellarton (5), Magdalen (6), Sydney (7), Deer Lake (8) and Bay St. George (9). Approximately one third of the Maritimes Basin lies offshore; over 20 wildcat wells have been drilled but with no commercial success. The other main areas of interest are Grand Banks south of Newfoundland, and the shelf northeast of Newfoundland. Over 60 wildcat wells have been drilled on the Grand

Banks, yielding 13 significant discoveries, mainly light oil, all of them hosted in, and believed sourced from, post-Palaeozoic sediments. To the north, the extent to which the Carboniferous cycles may be represented in the sedimentary record offshore Labrador and Baffin Island is a matter of speculation.

Discussion and conclusions

Carboniferous strata throughout the Canadian Appalachians, onshore and offshore, are in most instances representative of one or more of four major tectonostratigraphic cycles of deposition. Coals are important in the last two cycles (Fig. 2) and are evidently of widespread distribution. For example, according to Hacquebard (1986), an enormous submarine coalfield beneath the Magdalen Basin could provide prolific gas at levels of maturation commensurate with a vitrinite reflectance of 0.7% (see also Bell & Campbell 1990). Certain similarities between the basins are also likely to be reflected in Carboniferous rocks on the eastern margin of the Atlantic, given the common link to the development of the early North Atlantic Ocean (Naylor & Shannon 1982; Gibling et al. 1987; Bell & Howie 1990).

In terms of source richness and total hydrocarbon-generating potential ($S_1 + S_2$) it is instructive to compare a selection of source rocks from the United Kingdom with some from the Maritimes Basin. Parnell (1991) has shown that the hydrocarbon potential of the Fermanagh shales, the Coalisland coals and the North Antrim coals and oil shales of Northern Ireland, and the Dinantian Oil Shale Group of Scotland (Parnell 1988) all rate as good to excellent (see Fig. 3). Of this selection, perhaps the lower Carboniferous Scottish samples most closely resemble the oil shales and related rocks of the Albert Formation of New Brunswick's Cumberland sub-basin. Geochemically (Fig. 3) close comparisons are also evident, including probably a matrix effect which may simulate increasing maturation in bringing about a reduction of the H/C ratio in samples with relatively low (e.g. <2%) TOC values.

In the Albert oil shales T_{max} (temperature corresponding to the maximum release of hydrocarbons during pyrolysis) ranges from 430°C to 444°C in the more organic-rich rocks; hydrogen indices (mg HC/g organic carbon) in the same samples range from 340 to 589 (Mossman et al. 1987). By comparison, hydrogen indices for the UK samples range from <100 mg/g to >300 mg/g (Coalisland coals), and >600 mg/g (North Antrim coals and oil shales, and the

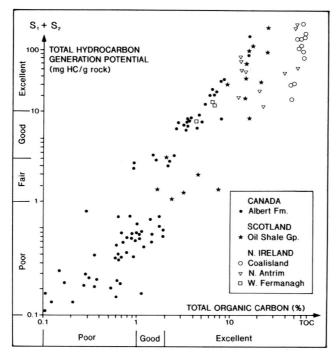

Fig. 3. Cross plot of total organic carbon content (TOC) and total hydrocarbon generation potential ($S_1 + S_2$) for: 3 shales from Fermanagh (squares), 11 coals and oil shales from North Antrim (triangles), and 11 coals from Coalisland (open circles), all from Northern Ireland (after Parnell 1991); 17 Dinantian samples from the Oil Shale Group (stars), Scotland (Parnell 1988); 71 shale and marl samples (dots) from the lacustrine facies of the Albert Formation (Cumberland sub-basin of the Maritimes Basin, New Brunswick) (after Mossman *et al.* 1987). Plot framework after Christiansen (1989).

Dinantian Oil Shale Group). This indicates not only that hydrocarbon generation is likely to have occurred in all of the respective basinal districts, but also that the oil shales represent excellent source-rock potential.

Parnell (1991) reports that vitrinite reflectance data for the Northern Ireland samples lies in the range $R_0 = 0.35$ to 0.90%. The Coalisland coals, for example, with R_0 just less than 0.5%, are immature. This contrasts with equivalent age (Westphalian C, D and Stephanian) coals of the Stellarton and Sydney sub-basins of eastern Canada (Hacquebard 1984) where R_0 ranges from 0.77 to 2.04%. Given that reflectances up to 3% represent gas potential, the upper Carboniferous strata along the north Atlantic margins are clearly attractive targets.

From Table 1 it is clear that potential source rocks of Carboniferous age occur in both onshore and offshore basins, associated with trapping mechanisms. In this latter respect, as noted by McCamis (1973), the Gulf of St. Lawrence with its numerous onshore seeps and offshore

diapiric structures, has much to recommend it. The Magdalen Basin probably contains the thickest section of Carboniferous rocks in eastern Canada. McCamis' observation is reinforced by the recent report (Sanford & Grant 1986) that potential source rocks of the Windsor and Canso-Riversdale sequences may extend farther northward into rocks of the Anticosti Basin (see Fig. 1) than previously recognized, northwestward into the St. Lawrence estuary, and to the northeast of western Newfoundland. Doubtless both stratigraphic sections and levels of maturation may be expected to vary considerably across the various structural elements of this terrane (Macauley *et al.* 1990).

Of particular interest as a potential Carboniferous source rock is the Macumber (Gays River) Formation (Giles 1983) at the base of the Windsor Group. Recognized as a blanket-type deposit of maximum thickness 25 m, the Macumber Formation is widely recognized in New Brunswick, Nova Scotia and Newfoundland (Ship Cove Formation). The lithology de-

Table 1. Carboniferous source rocks present in various offshore areas and sedimentary basins of the Canadian Atlantic Margin. Locations given on Fig. 1. Nine (1 to 9) selected sub-basins of the Maritimes Basin are

	Stratigraphy of Interest	Environment of Deposition	Basin Thickness	Source Rock Formation Thickness	Well No.
MARITIMES BASIN	Horton, Riversdale & Pictou Gps.	continental clastics coal & lacustrine shales			
1 Cumberland	Horton & Riversdale Gp. Tournaisian, Visean	alluvial-fluvial, lacustrine & minor marine evaporites	>7 km	shales, Albert Fm. 200-2000 m & Westphalian B coal	
2 Moncton	Horton Group Tournaisian	(as above)	n.d.	oil shales, Albert Fm. 200-2000 m	
3 Sackville	Horton Group Tournaisian	(as above)	n.d.	oil shales, Albert Fm. 200-2000 m	Dorchester #1 TD 2508m
4 Fundy	Mid Devonian to Early Permian	(as above)	4 to >10 km	presumed shales of Horton Gp., coal measures	
5 Stellarton	Westphalian Pictou Gp.	continental origin	n.d.	limnic coals	
6 Magdalen	Miss. to Permian Westphalian to Wolfcampian	(as above)	>12 km	clastics, evaporites and carbonates Westphalian coal	East Point E49 (uneconomic gas) TD 3529m
7 Sydney	Horton & Riversdale Tournaisian, Visean	alluvial-fluvial lacustrine & minor marine evaporites	≈4 km	Grantmire & Macumber Fm. Westphalian B coal	
8 Deer Lake (western Newfoundland)	Anguille, Deer Lake & Howley Gps. Tournaisian, Visean	dominantly non marine, lacustrine	1700 m	oil shale, Rocky Brook Fm. (<2m oil shale) mudstones etc., Anguille Gp. (gas shows)	Claybar #3 TD 580 m
9 Bay St George (western Newfoundland)	Anguille, Codroy & Barachois Gp. Tournaisian, Visean	lacustrine-fluviatile marine evaporites fluvial clastics	4 km onshore 6 km offshore	Barachois Gp. coal & oil shale	(gas) UB Anguille H98
10 GRAND BANKS SOUTH	Westphalian Pictou Gp.	continental origin	n.d.	shale with coal seams	Tern A-68 TD 4189 m; Puffin B-90 TD 4702m
11 EAST NFLD. BASIN	Visean(Up. Windsor, Canso Gps.)	shallow marine	n.d.	shale	Texaco Blue H-28 TD 6088 m
12 EAST NFLD SHELF	Westphalian Pictou Gp.	thick continental coal measures, minor carbonate & evaporite units	n.d.	shale with 12 coal seams (> 1472 m)	Hare Bay E-21 TD 4873

scribed by Schenk (1967) as an organic-rich dark grey to buff weathering carbonate, with laterally continuous flat laminae, was considered to be the result of sublittoral processes (see also McCutcheon 1981). The recent discovery of a fauna in the Macumber Formation typical of low-temperature chemosynthetic hydrothermal vent communities throws a different light on the nature and origin of this 340 Ma carbonate (von Bitter *et al.* 1990). It is now regarded as the result of relatively deep-water depositional processes. According to P. Schenk (pers. comm.

1991) organic matter in the Macumber Formation averages about 4 wt%, and may locally be an order of magnitude higher. Thus, despite its variably small thickness, it seems fair to suggest that the carbonates and shales of the Macumber Formation are prime source rocks both onshore and offshore. Almost certainly this formation can in part be held to account for the minor shows of light crude oil commonly encountered during onshore exploration drilling in the Windsor Group (e.g. Dekker 1985).

The underlying voluminous Horton Group

included. Only selected wells and sample intervals are given. TOC: total organic carbon (wt%); TAI: thermal alteration index; conventional Rock-Eval parameters are shown

Interval	Type Kerogen	TOC	Ro%	Maturity	Comments	References
	I, III				largest intermontane basin in Appalachians	McCamis, 1973; Boehner et al., 1986
	I, III	high (>10%)		within oil window		Boehner et al., 1986; Williams, 1973
	I	high (>10%)	0.5	T_{max} 430–444°C; rank = high vol. "C" bit. coal, TAI 2 to 3+	one of the oldest tectonic lake basins in the world. Small scale oil & gas production	Kalkreuth & Macauley, 1984; Mossman et al., 1985; Carter & Pickerill, 1985; Utting et al., 1989
	I	high (>10%)		within oil window	Cumberland Gp. absent; well penetrated 750 m of Albert Fm.	Martel, 1987
				no wells in Palaeozoic; presumed gas potential	folds generally parallel to fault blocks	Jansa & Wade, 1975; Boehner et al., 1986
	III	1.08 to 2.09		potential for gas	coalification is post-deformational	Hacquebard, 1984
			0.73 to 1.16	most wells end in thick continental red beds, moderate maturity	source rocks mostly untested Only 7 wells drilled	Sanford & Grant, 1990; Hacquebard, 1986; Bell & Howie, 1990
	I, II, III	high in Macumber Fm.		thick Pictou Gp within oil window	minor gas plays located (see discussion)	Giles, 1983; Gibling et al., 1987
> -600 SL	I	>5%	0.65 to 0.69	immature T_{max} 433–451°C S_1 0.34–3.44 S_2 11.3–153.8	stratigraphy = Horton, Windsor & Riversdale Gp.	Kalkreuth & Macauley, 1989; Hyde, 1981
oil shales < 1 m	III (dominant) I	to 31.9%		within oil window	oil shales tend to be lean (<90 l/t) minor oil production in early 1900s	Miller et al., 1990 Macauley, 1987
	III		0.73 to 1.25 (A-68)	reworked Penn. vitrinite within oil window in both wells	basal Pictou also encountered in Elf Hermine E-94; probably unconformably overlie older strata	Avery & Bell, 1985; M. Avery (pers. comm.)
			1.69 to 3.10	Palaeozoic rocks are strongly overmature	only one well drilled	Proctor et al., 1984
3401–4873 m	III			potential for gas, taking Ro=3% as dry gas floor	wildcat well 410 km NNE St. John's, NFLD	M. Avery (pers. comm.); Dow, 1977; D.C. Umpleby (pers. comm.)

sediments also exhibit favourable source rock characteristics (Hamblin 1989). In Newfoundland the results of CAI studies (Department of Mines and Energy, Newfoundland and Labrador 1989) of equivalent sediments are compatible with a thermal history well within the oil window. Jansa & Wade (1975) report that the Gannet 0–54 well encountered mid- to late Devonian sediments from 2395–2930 m on the Grand Banks. Certainly, Horton Group oil shale, with constituent type-I kerogen, very likely occurs in lacustrine facies buried offshore in areas hitherto unexplored. In this instance, relatively greater depths of burial may be expected to be offset by the greater temperatures required to generate hydrocarbons from type-I organic matter (Tissot & Welte 1984). The same reasoning applies to oil shale of Westphalian age associated with coals in the Pictou Group (Kalkreuth & Macauley 1987) wherever equivalent units may be present in the offshore.

North on the Labrador Shelf, the likelihood of encountering potential source rocks of Carboniferous age remains a matter for speculation.

Helpful discussions with M. Avery, A. C. Grant and P. Hacquebard (Atlantic Geoscience Centre, Bedford Institute of Oceanography) and P. Schenk (Dalhousie University) are gratefully appreciated. A. C. Grant kindly criticized constructively an early draft of this paper but is in no way responsible for any errors of omission or commission. Financial support through Natural Sciences and Engineering Research Council operating grant #A8295 is gratefully acknowledged.

References

AVERY, M. P. & BELL, J. S. 1985. Vitrinite reflectance measurements from the South Whale Basin, Grand Banks, Eastern Canada, and implications for hydrocarbon exploration: In: Current Research, Part A, Geological Survey of Canada, Paper 85−1B, 51−57.

BARSS, M. S., BUJAK, J. P. & WILLIAMS, G. L. 1979. Palynological zonation and correlation of sixty-seven wells, eastern Canada. Geological Survey of Canada Paper 78−24.

BELL, J. S. & CAMPBELL, G. R. 1990. Petroleum Resources, Ch 12 In: KEEN, M. J. & WILLIAMS, G. L. (eds) Geology of the Continental Margin of Eastern Canada, Geology of Canada, no. 2, 141−165. (also Geological Society of America, The Geology of North America, v. I-1).

—— & HOWIE, R. D. 1990. Paleozoic geology, Chapt. 4. In: KEEN, M. J. & WILLIAMS, G. L. (eds) Geology of the Continental Margins of Eastern Canada, Geological Survey of Canada, Geology of Canada, no. 2, 141−165. (also Geological Society of America, The Geology of North America, v. I-1).

BOEHNER, R. C., CALDER, J. H., CARTER, D. C., DONOHOE Jr., H. V., FERGUSON, L., PICKERILL, R. K. & RYAN, R. J. 1986. Basins of Eastern Canada: Carboniferous-Jurassic sedimentation and tectonics: Minas, Cumberland and Moncton Basins, Nova Scotia and New Brunswick. (Symposium Field Trip). Atlantic Geoscience Society Special Publication no. 4.

CARTER, D. C. & PICKERILL, R. K. 1985. Algal swamp, marginal and shallow evaporitic lacustrine lithofacies from the late Devonian-early Carboniferous Albert Formation, southeastern New Brunswick, Canada. Maritime Sediments and Atlantic Geology, 21 (Nos. 2, 3), 69−86.

CHRISTIANSEN, F. G. 1989. Petroleum geology of North Greenland. Gronlands Geol. Unders. Bull., 158, 1−92.

DEKKER, L. 1985. Potash exploration at Malagawatch Cape Breton, Nova Scotia. Bulletin of Canadian Mining and Metallurgy, 78, 27−32.

DEPARTMENT OF MINES AND ENERGY, Government of Newfoundland and Labrador 1989. Hydrocarbon potential of the western Newfoundland area.

DOW, W. G. 1977. Kerogen studies and geological interpretations. Journal of Geochemical Exploration, 7, 79−99.

GIBLING, M. R., BOEHNER, R. C. & RUST, B. R. 1987. The Sydney Basin of Atlantic Canada: an upper Paleozoic strike-slip basin in a collisional setting In: BEAUMONT, C. & TANKARD, A. J. (eds) Sedimentary Basins and Basin-Forming Mechanisms. Canadian Society of Petroleum Geologists. Memoir 12, 269−285.

GILES, P. S. 1983. The Sydney basin project. Nova Scotia Department of Mines and Energy. Mines and Minerals Branch. Report of Activities 1982, 57−70.

GRANT, A. C., McALPINE, K. D. & WADE, J. A. 1986. Offshore geology and petroleum potential of eastern Canada. Energy Exploration & Exploitation, 4, 5−52.

HACQUEBARD, P. A. 1986. The Gulf of St. Lawrence Carboniferous Basin: the largest coalfield of eastern Canada. Bulletin of Canadian Institute of Mining and Metallurgy, 79, 67−78.

—— 1984. Coal rank changes in the Sydney and Pictou coalfields of Nova Scotia; cause and economic significance. Bulletin of Canadian Institute of Mining and Metallurgy, 77, 33−40.

HAMBLIN, A. P. 1989. Basin configuration, sedimentary facies and resource potential of the Lower Carboniferous Horton Group, Cape Breton Island, Nova Scotia. Current Research Part B, Geological Survey of Canada. Paper 89−1B, 115−120.

HOWIE, R. D. 1988. Upper Paleozoic evaporites of southeastern Canada. Geological Survey of Canada Bulletin 3890.

HYDE, R. S. 1981. Geology of the Carboniferous Deer Lake Basin: Map 82−7, Mineral Development Division, Newfoundland Department of Mines.

JANSA, L. F. & WADE, J. A. 1975. Geology of the continental margin of Nova Scotia and Newfoundland. In: VAN DER LINDEN, W. J. M. & WADE, J. A. (eds) Offshore Geology of Eastern Canada, 2 Regional Geology. Geological Survey of Canada Paper 74−30, 2, 51−105.

KALKREUTH, W. & MACAULEY, G. 1984. Organic petrology of selected oil shale samples from the Lower Carboniferous Albert Formation, New Brunswick, Canada. Bulletin of Canadian Petroleum Geology, 32, 38−51.

—— & —— 1987. Organic petrology and geochemical (Rock-Eval) studies on oil shales and coals from the Pictou and Antigonish areas, Nova Scotia, Canada. Bulletin of Canadian Petroleum Geology, 35, 263−295.

—— & —— 1989. Organic petrology and Rock-Eval studies on oil shales from the Lower Carboniferous Rocky Brook Formation, Western Newfoundland. Bulletin of Canadian Petroleum Geology, 37, 31−42.

KNIGHT, I. 1983. Geology of the Carboniferous Bay St. George Subbasin, western Newfoundland: Newfoundland Department of Mines and Energy, Mineral Development Division Memoir 1.

MACAULEY, G. 1987. *Geochemical Investigation of Carboniferous Oil Shales along Rocky Brook, western Newfoundland*. Geological Survey of Canada, Open File Report 1438.

——, BALL, F. D. & POWELL, T. G. 1984. A review of the Carboniferous Albert Formation oil shales, New Brunswick. *Bulletin of Canadian Petroleum Geology*, **32**, 27–37.

——, FOWLER, M. G., GOODARZI, F., SNOWDEN, L. R. & STASIUK, L. D. 1990. Ordovician oil shale — source rock sediments in the central and eastern Canada mainland and eastern Arctic area, and their significance for frontier exploration. Geological Survey of Canada Paper **90–14**.

MARTEL, A. T. 1987. Seismic stratigraphy and hydrocarbon potential of the strike-slip Sackville subbasin, New Brunswick. *In*: BEAUMONT, C. & TANKARD, A. J. (eds) *Sedimentary Basins and Basin-Forming Mechanisms*. Canadian Society of Petroleum Geologists Memoir **12**, 319–334.

McCAMIS, J. G. 1973. The Carboniferous Basin — Land and Gulf. *Bulletin of Canadian Institute of Mining and Metallurgy*, **66**, 51–57.

McCUTCHEON, S. R. 1981. Stratigraphy and paleogeography of the Windsor Group in southern New Brunswick. *New Brunswick Geological Surveys Branch, Open File Report*, 81–31.

MILLER, H. G., KILFOIL, G. J. & PEAVY, S. T. 1990. An integrated geophysical interpretation of the Carboniferous Bay St. George Subbasin, western Newfoundland. *Bulletin of Canadian Petroleum Geology*, **38**, 320–331.

MOSSMAN, D. J., MACEY, J. F. & LEMMON, P. D. 1987. Diagenesis in the lacustrine facies of the Albert Formation, New Brunswick, Canada: a geochemical evaluation. *Bulletin of Canadian Petroleum Geology*, **35**, 239–250.

NAYLOR, D. & SHANNON, P. 1982. *Geology of Offshore Ireland and West Britain*. Graham & Trotman, London.

PARNELL, J. 1988. Lacustrine petroleum source rocks in the Dinantian Oil Shale Group, Scotland: a review in FLEET, A. J., KELTS, K. & TALBOT, M. R. (eds) *Lacustrine Petroleum Source Rocks*. Geological Society, London, Special Publication, **40**, 235–246.

—— 1991. Hydrocarbon potential of Northern Ireland. *Journal of Petroleum Geology*, **14**, 65–78.

PROCTOR, R. M., TAYLOR, G. C. & WADE, J. A. 1984. Oil and natural gas resources of Canada 1983, Geological Survey of Canada. Paper **83–31**. of St. Lawrence; *In*: *Current Research, Part B*, Geological Survey of Canada, Paper **90–1B**,

ROLLE, F. 1985. Late Cretaceous-Tertiary sediments offshore central West Greenland: lithostratigraphy, sedimentary evolution, and petroleum potential. *Canadian Journal of Earth Sciences*, **22**, 1001–1019.

SANFORD, B. V. & GRANT, A. C. 1990. Bedrock geological mapping and basin studies in the Gulf 33–42.

SCHENK, P. E. 1967. The Macumber Formation of the Maritime Provinces — a Mississippian analogue to recent strand-line carbonates of the Persian Gulf. *Journal of Sedimentary Petrology*, **37**, 365–376.

TISSOT, B. P. & WELTE, D. H. 1984. *Petroleum Formation and Occurrence*. Springer, Berlin.

UTTING, J., KEPPIE, J. D. & GILES, P. S. 1989. Palynology and stratigraphy of the Lower Carboniferous Horton Group, Nova Scotia. *Bulletin of Geological Survey of Canada*, **396**, 117–143.

VON BITTER, P. H., SCOTT, S. D. & SCHENK, P. E. 1990. Early Carboniferous low-temperature hydrothermal vent communities from Newfoundland. *Nature*, **344**, 145–147.

—— 1973. The Quebec and Maritimes basins. *In*: *Future Petroleum Provinces of Canada*, R. G. McCROSSAN (ed.) Canadian Society of Petroleum Geologists, Memoir **1**, 561–588.

WILLIAMS, E. P. 1974. Geology and petroleum possibilities in and around the Gulf of St. Lawrence. *AAPG Bulletin*, **58**, 1137–1158.

—— 1982. Geology of the Canadian Appalachians *In*: PALMER, A. R. (ed.) *Perspectives in Regional Geological Synthesis*. Geological Society of America D-NAG Special Publication **1**, 57–66.

Thermal effect of the Tertiary Cuillins Intrusive Complex in the Jurassic of the Hebrides: an organic geochemical study

JANE THRASHER (née Ambler)

Department of Geology and Petroleum Geology, Marischal College, University of Aberdeen, Aberdeen AB9 1AS, UK
Present address: BP Research Centre, Chertsey Road, Sunbury-on-Thames, TW16 7LN, UK

Abstract: The Tertiary Cuillins Intrusive Complex is partially located within the Mesozoic depositional basins of the Minch and intrudes a Jurassic sequence including a number of moderately organic-rich horizons. The thermal effect of the central intrusive activity, and related minor intrusions, on the Jurassic sediments has been assessed using organic geochemical molecular maturity parameters. Analysis of more than 60 samples, mainly from the Middle Jurassic Dun Caan and Cullaidh Shales, shows that the thermal effect of the igneous complex is very localized and that Jurassic sediments more than 15 km from the complex margin are extremely immature, except in the immediate vicinity of minor intrusions. Igneous activity similar to the Tertiary of western Britain should therefore not be invoked as an alternative maturation route for shallow-buried sediments.

The ready accessibility of the Jurassic and Tertiary rocks of the Inner Hebrides has produced a considerable body of research and a relatively good geological understanding of the area (Emeleus 1983; Hudson 1983). The presence of igneous intrusions ranging from central intrusive complexes and major sills to minor sills and dykes cutting shallow-buried sediments (Fig. 1) makes the area around the Isle of Skye an ideal location for the study of the thermal effects of igneous intrusions on a sedimentary basin. The research described here uses the technology of organic geochemical biomarker maturity parameters (Tissot & Welte 1984, pp 536–540) more generally applied, in the search for petroleum, to sediments thermally altered by burial than to geological problems such as the thermal influence of igneous intrusions. It forms part of a wider study of the effects on country rock biomarker maturity of igneous intrusions of all sizes, and the behaviour of biomarker ratios at naturally occurring high heating rates in the margins of minor intrusions (Ambler 1989).

The thermal effect of the Cuillins igneous complex has previously been assessed using the compositions of zeolite minerals in the Tertiary lavas (King 1976) and clay minerals in the Middle Jurassic Great Estuarine Series (Andrews 1987; Hudson & Andrews 1987). Clays in the immediate vicinity of the Cuillins complex in Strathaird were shown to be thermally altered, while those from Trotternish some 40 km from the complex margin were unaltered except locally by minor intrusions.

The Jurassic sediments of the Hebrides

The islands of the Inner Hebrides (particularly Skye, Raasay, Eigg and Mull) expose up to 1000 m of Jurassic sediments deposited under largely shallow marine conditions in the interconnected Permo-Triassic basins of the Hebrides (reviewed by Hudson 1983; Morton 1989). Although most of the succession comprises sandstones and muddy siltstones, the sequence does contain several moderately organic-rich horizons (Table 1), notably the Middle Jurassic Dun Caan Shale and Cullaidh Shale (Basal Oil Shale of the Great Estuarine Series prior to revision of stratigraphic nomenclature by Harris & Hudson 1980), and the poorly exposed Toarcian Portree Shale. The Lower Jurassic Pabba Shale and Upper Jurassic Staffin Shale have less petroleum potential.

The Jurassic sediments of the Inner Hebrides are unconformably overlain by thinly developed Cretaceous sediments and thick deposits of Tertiary basaltic lavas. Rapid erosion of the lava pile soon after the cessation of igneous activity meant, however, that any burial resulting from the igneous extrusion would have been on a geologically short timescale and may not have attained equilibrium.

Tertiary igneous activity on the Isle of Skye

Continued tectonic stresses related to the opening of the North Atlantic reached a critical point at 59 Ma with the onset of basaltic vol-

From PARNELL, J. (ed.), 1992, *Basins on the Atlantic Seaboard: Petroleum Geology, Sedimentology and Basin Evolution.* Geological Society Special Publication No 62, pp 35–49.

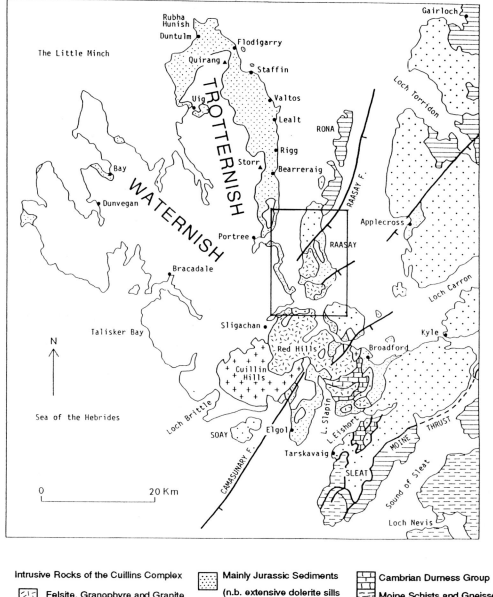

Intrusive Rocks of the Cuillins Complex

Felsite, Granophyre and Granite

Gabbro

Tertiary Basaltic Lavas

Mainly Jurassic Sediments
(n.b. extensive dolerite sills
in Jurassic of N. and N.W.
of Skye have been omitted.

Cambrian Durness Group

Moine Schists and Gneisses

Torridonian Sandstones

Lewisian Gneiss

Fig. 1. Geological map of Skye, showing principal geological features and localities mentioned in text. Inset shows position of Fig. 5.

Table 1. Total Organic Carbon contents of the argillaceous formations of the Hebridean Jurassic (from Ambler 1989)

Formation	Age	TOC[1]
Staffin Shale	Oxf./Kimm.	1.5–2.4% (7)
Duntulm Formation	Bathonian	0.3–2% (5)
Lealt Shale	Bathonian	0.4–1.7% (3)
Cullaidh Shale	Bathonian	3–15% (8)
Garantiana Clay	Bath./Baj.	1.4–1.9% (2)
Dun Caan Shale	Aalenian	Av. 2%; Max 4.7% (41)
Portree Shale	Toarcian	4% (1)
Pabba Shale	Pliens./Sin.	0.5–1% (7)
Broadford Beds	Sin./Hett.	<1% (9)

[1] Number of samples measured given in parentheses.

canism in the Hebrides (Emeleus 1983) and the extrusion of up to 1200 m of plateau lavas in Central Skye (Anderson & Dunham 1966). This was followed by the development of several high-level central intrusive complexes, notably the Cuillins complex in central Skye, each consisting of several centres containing a series of nested plutons with compositions ranging from gabbroic to granitic, probably forming the root of a complex volcanic system (Emeleus 1983). Stable isotope depletion in both plutonic and country rocks suggests that the heat from the cooling complexes initiated a hydrothermal circulation system in the surrounding rocks (Taylor & Forester 1971). Some time after the extrusion of the lavas, the sediments of north and west Skye were intruded by a major basic sill complex, the Trotternish sill complex. The final phase of igneous activity was the development of dyke swarms in a regional intrusive event. Igneous activity in the Skye Cuillins complex probably spanned about 6 Ma from 61 Ma to 55 Ma, from the first extrusion of lavas to the cessation of activity (Mussett et al. 1988).

Determination of maturity by biomarker methods

The organic matter in sediments has been found to contain some complex hydrocarbon molecules (known as biomarkers, e.g. the extended hopanes, Seifert & Moldowan 1981) that can be recognized as being derived from a biological precursor molecule (e.g. tetrahydroxybacteriohopane, Fig. 2), and can be identified by the method of GC–MS (gas chromatography–mass spectrometry) reviewed by Philp (1986). It has been recognized that the relative proportion of the different isomers (molecules with the same composition but different structural configuration) of specific biomarkers is strongly dependent on the degree of thermal stress suffered by the sediment or oil (Mackenzie 1984). Thus immature sediments contain a high proportion of biologically configured biomarkers, while mature sediments and oils contain more of the non-biological configurations stable at higher temperatures. The relative proportions of different biomarker isomers vary with the degree

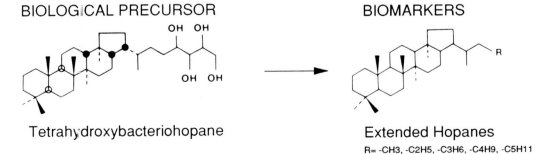

BIOLOGICAL PRECURSOR

Tetrahydroxybacteriohopane

BIOMARKERS

Extended Hopanes

R= -CH3, -C2H5, -C3H6, -C4H9, -C5H11

Fig. 2. Hopane group biomarkers and their biological precursor, tetrahydroxybacteriohopane, a bacterial cell wall constituent.

of maturation, so that measurement of a range of isomer ratios or biomarker maturity parameters allows quite precise determination of sediment maturity up to the top of the oil window (Fig. 3).

As with other organic geochemical maturity indicators, these biomarker maturity parameters cannot be used as palaeothermometers, as the changes in isomer ratios depend upon the time for which the sediment was at a high temperature as well as the maximum temperature attained. No calibration exists for the heating rates experienced in the margins of igneous intrusions. The use of biomarker maturity parameters is most valid for a determination of the relative amount of heating experienced by different outcrops containing similar kerogen, and assessment of the degree of thermal stress.

Approach

Sediments sufficiently rich in organic matter for biomarker analysis occur throughout the Jurassic succession of the Hebrides (Table 1) but exposure is limited, with the most extensive outcrops occurring where the usually soft sediments have been baked by Tertiary intrusions.

The maturation effect of the Cuillins igneous complex can, however, be assessed from the Lower and Middle Jurassic sediments exposed along the eastern coasts of mainland Skye and Raasay, where a continuous line of subcrop can be found running almost directly away from the intrusive complex (Fig. 1). The poor exposure of the shales however severely breaks up the continuity of sampling points. Samples were also collected in areas believed to be outwith the area of thermal influence of the central intrusive complexes, in order to assess the degree of maturation around the smaller sills and dykes and providing control data on the background maturity level.

Analytical methods

Outcrop samples were prepared for biomarker analysis by standard organic geochemical techniques. Clean dry sediments were crushed and solvent extractable material obtained by 48 hrs soxhlet extraction with dichloromethane. Sulphur was removed with activated copper, and the required aliphatic and aromatic hydrocarbon fractions separated by two successive stages of thin layer chromatography; dichloromethane followed by hexane. GC was per-

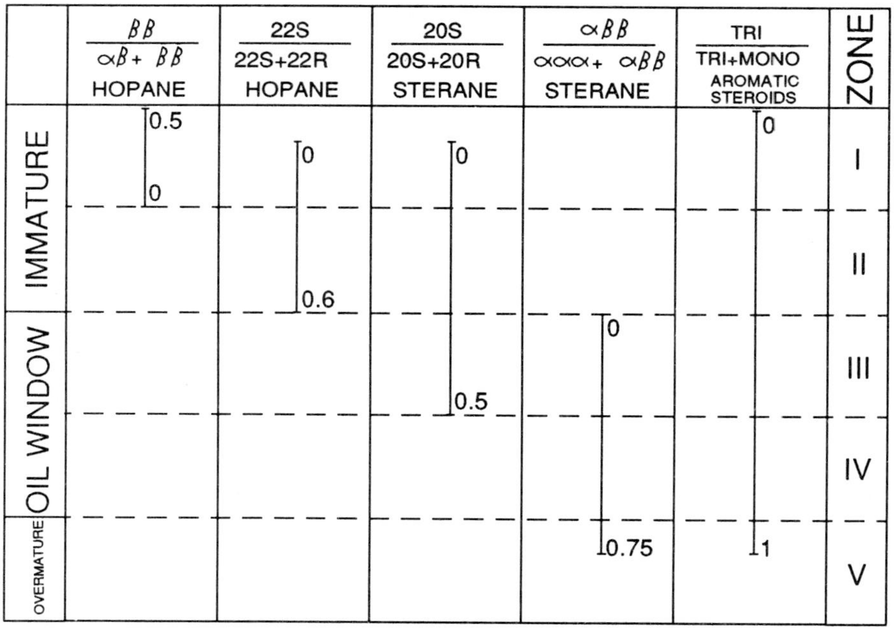

IMMATURE / OIL WINDOW / OVERMATURE	$\dfrac{\beta\beta}{\alpha\beta + \beta\beta}$ HOPANE	$\dfrac{22S}{22S+22R}$ HOPANE	$\dfrac{20S}{20S+20R}$ STERANE	$\dfrac{\alpha\beta\beta}{\alpha\alpha\alpha + \alpha\beta\beta}$ STERANE	$\dfrac{TRI}{TRI+MONO}$ AROMATIC STEROIDS	ZONE
IMMATURE	0.5 ... 0	0 ... 0.6	0 ... 0.5	0 ... 0.75	0 ... 1	I
						II
OIL WINDOW						III
						IV
OVERMATURE						V

Fig. 3. Variation of biomarker isomer ratios with maturity. The maturation zones are based on maturation by burial of the Jurassic of the North Sea and N. W. Germany (Mackenzie 1984). The numbered zones are based entirely on biomarker isomer ratios and may not relate directly to oil generation zones in rapidly heated sediments.

formed on a Carlo Erba 4160 GC equipped with 25 m × 0.3 mm OV-1 column, hydrogen carrier gas flow, temperature programmed with 2 mins at 80°C, 80−275°C at 4°C/min, and 10 min isothermal hold at 275°C, with flame ionization detection. GC−MS was performed either on a HP 5890A GC using helium carrier gas, and similar column and temperature program (but 25 mins isothermal hold at 275°C) attached by capillary direct interface to a HP 5970B MSD with electron impact ionization (at the University of Aberdeen), or on a Finnegan 4500 GC−MS (at BP Research Centre, Sunbury), using a DB-1 30 m × 0.25 mm column, helium carrier gas, and a temperature program of 3 mins at 70°C, 70−120°C at 10°C/min and 120−280°C at 3°C/min. The determination of TOC was performed on unextracted acid-decarbonated samples using a LECO GC-90 gravimetric carbon determinator.

Results

The results of the biomarker maturity determination described below are listed in Table 2 and plotted in Fig. 4. The positions of selected samples, and general biomarker maturity distributions, are illustrated in Fig. 5. Gas chromatograms and GC−MS mass fragmentograms showing typical n-alkane, hopane and sterane distributions in the Dun Caan Shales are shown in Figs 6, 7 & 8.

Sediments collected from closer than 5 km to the margin of the Cuillins intrusive complex (e.g. at Elgol and Broadford Bay, Fig. 1, and around Inverarish village on Raasay, Fig. 5) were visibly baked and indurated, and contained virtually no extractable organic matter. Several samples contained sufficient extract for gas chromatography to show mature n-alkane distributions (cf. Tissot & Welte 1984). Biomarker maturities could not be obtained for any of these samples.

Between about 5 km and 6 km from the intrusive complex margin (e.g. Inverarish Burn, Fig. 5, sample 25DCI), sediments contain biomarker distributions typical of late oil window maturity. It is normal for biomarkers to break down and decrease in absolute quantity at high maturities, but this appears to occur sooner in these relatively rapidly heated sediments than during conventional maturation. A similar effect was noted at the margins of igneous dykes (Ambler 1989). This suggests that at high temperatures the stability of the biomarker compounds is more affected than the stability of the less complex n-alkanes.

Sediments containing biomarker distributions characteristic of oil window maturity are found between 6 km and 8 km from the intrusive com-

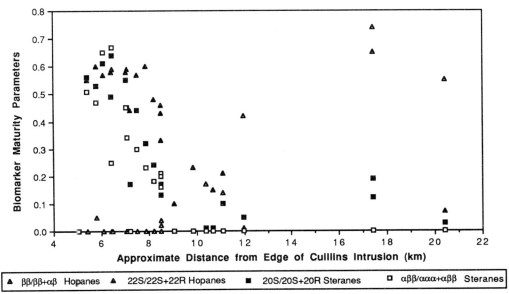

Maturation of Jurassic Sediments by Cuillins Intrusive Complex

Fig. 4. Biomarker maturity parameters of Jurassic sediments from Skye and Raasay, plotted as a function of approximate distance from the margin of the Cuillins Intrusive Complex (data in Table 2).

Table 2. Biomarker ratios in Jurassic sediments around the Cuillins Instrusive Complex, Skye and Raasay

Sample	Grid. Ref. (NG)	[1]Distance (km)	Formation Name	[2]TOC	[3]ββ αβ + ββ	[4]22S 22S + 22R	[5]20S 20S + 20R	[6]αββ αββ + ααα	[7]Tri Tri + Mono
299SSF	4675 7150	49.0	Staffin Shale	na	0.65	0.01	0.00	0.45	0.05
134DCB	5180 5240	20.4	Dun Caan Shale	0.61	0.55	0.07	0.03	0.00	0.05
446CSF	5170 4940	17.4	Cullaidh Shale	6.30	0.65	0.00	0.19	0.00	na
447CSF	5170 4940	17.4	Cullaidh Shale	15.26	0.74	0.00	0.12	0.00	na
30CSS	5755 4398	11.98	Cullaidh Shale	3.10	0.42	0.01	0.05	0.00	0.03
171DCS	5847 4312	11.12	Dun Caan Shale	1.12	0.14	0.21	0.10	0.00	0.06
289USU	5140 4270	10.7	Dun Caan Shale	na	0.00	0.15	0.01	bd	0.12
288CST	5160 4240	10.4	Cullaidh Shale	na	0.17	0.00	0.01	0.00	0.01
63CSB	5637 4184	9.84	Cullaidh Shale	4.80	0.00	0.23	0.00	0.00	na
283POT	5230 4105	9.05	Portree Shale	4.13	0.00	0.10	na	na	0.06
161DCC	5850 4050	8.5	Dun Caan Shale	0.46	0.02	0.33	0.13	0.21	0.12
162DCC	5850 4050	8.5	Dun Caan Shale	na	0.00	0.46	0.20	0.20	0.34
163DCC	5850 4050	8.5	Dun Caan Shale	2.18	0.04	0.43	0.17	0.16	na
164DCC	5850 4050	8.5	Dun Caan Shale	2.72	0.00	0.46	0.20	0.20	0.53
54DCC	5854 4023	8.23	Dun Caan Shale	3.50	0.00	0.48	0.24	0.18	0.54
56CSC	5857 3990	7.9	Cullaidh Shale	5.60	0.00	0.60	0.32	0.23	na
52CSC	5814 3949	7.49	Cullaidh Shale	14.30	0.00	0.57	0.44	0.30	0.79
281POT	5165 3920	7.2	Portree Shale	na	0.00	0.44	0.17	bd	0.61
158PSC	5902 3910	7.1	Pabba Shale	na	0.00	0.59	0.45	0.34	0.80
57DCC	5836 3904	7.04	Dun Caan Shale	1.70	0.00	0.58	0.55	0.45	0.81
58DCC	5853 3848	6.48	Dun Caan Shale	2.00	0.00	0.59	0.64	0.67	0.92
15PSH	5935 3844	6.44	Pabba Shale	0.84	0.00	0.58	0.49	0.25	0.76
59DCC	5838 3808	6.08	Dun Caan Shale	2.50	0.00	0.57	0.61	0.65	0.81
16DCH	5980 3780	5.8	Dun Caan Shale	na	0.05	0.60	0.53	0.47	0.63
67PSH	5902 3740	5.4	Pabba Shale	0.57	0.00	0.55	0.56	0.51	0.53
49DCI	5645 3704	5.04	Dun Caan Shale	2.00	bd	bd	bd	bd	bd

[1] Approximate Distance from the Margin of the Cuillins Central Intrusive Complex [2]Weight% Total Organic Carbon
[3] C30 $\beta\beta$/($\beta\beta$ + $\alpha\beta$) Hopane. $\alpha\beta$ Hopane. Hopanes measured from integrated m/z 191 mass fragmentograms.
[4] C32 22S/(22S + 22R) $\alpha\beta$ Sterane. [6] C29 $\alpha\beta\beta$/($\alpha\beta\beta$ + $\alpha\alpha\alpha$) 20S Sterane.
[5] C29 20S/(20S + 20R) $\alpha\alpha\alpha$ Sterane. Steranes measured from integrated m/z 217 (for $\alpha\alpha\alpha$) and m/z 218 (for $\alpha\beta\beta$) mass fragmentograms.
[7] Triaromatic steroids/(Triaromatic + Monoaromatic steroids). Triaromatic steroids from m/z 231, monoaromatic steroids from m/z 253 mass fragmentograms. na: not analysed. bd: below detection

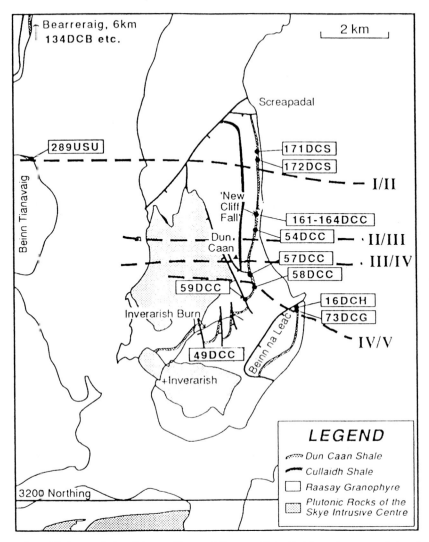

Fig. 5. Dun Caan Shale sample localities on Skye and Raasay. Maturity biomarker zones determined as described in Fig. 3 (data in Table 2).

plex margin, in an area which includes the hill Dun Caan and the former settlement of Hallaig on Raasay. As can be seen in Figs 6–8 (samples 58DCC, 59DCC), the n-alkane distributions in the gas chromatograms and the hopane and sterane distributions in the mass fragmentograms could be from conventionally matured sediments of oil window maturity.

Exposure of moderately organic-rich sediments is severely limited to the north of Dun Caan on Raasay, but those outcrops that exist show a gradual decrease in maturity from the oil generation threshold (54DCC and 171DCS),

so that at Screapadal, where the Jurassic is faulted out against Late Proterozoic Torridonian Sandstones, the Cullaidh Shale contains thermally unstable $17\beta(H),21\beta(H)$ hopanes, and at Bearreraig, 20 km from the complex margin on Skye, the saturated hydrocarbon fraction is dominated by these $17\beta(H),21\beta(H)$ hopanes and also diasterenes indicative of the absence of heating above about 50°C.

The thermal effect of the igneous intrusive complex thus reflected in the organic geochemical maturity of the surrounding sediments is very localized, restricted to within 12 km of the

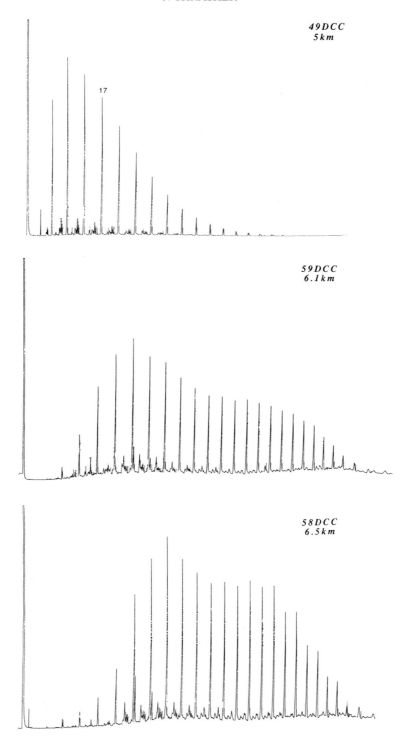

Fig. 6. Gas chromatograms of saturated hydrocarbon fractions of selected Dun Caan Shale outcrops, Isle of Raasay. Sample Localities are given in Fig. 5 and Table 2.17-C_{17} n-alkane. 27-C_{27} n-alkane. Pr, Pristane. Phy, Phytane.

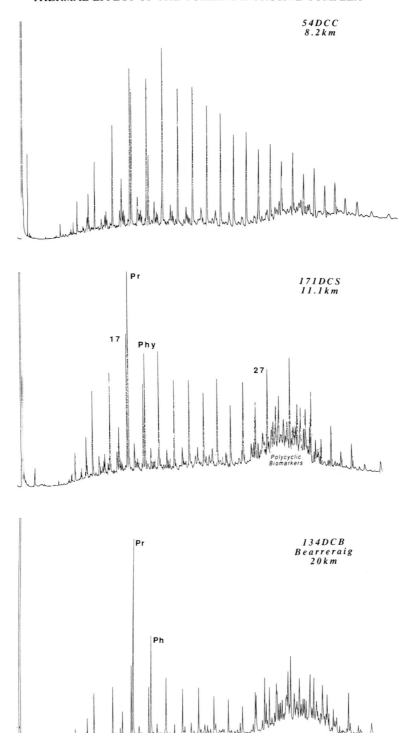

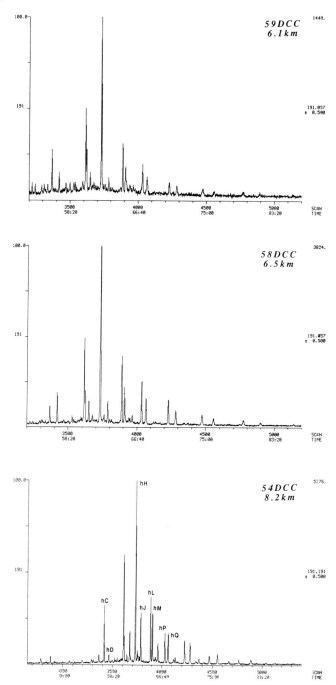

Fig. 7. Hopane biomarker distributions of selected Dun Caan Shale outcrops, Isle of Raasay. Sample localities are given in Figure 5 and Table 2. m/z 191 mass fragmentograms obtained on Finnegan GC-MS at BP Research Centre, Sunbury. Peaks identified as: hC C_{27} 17α(H) Trisnorhopane; hD C_{27} 17β(H) Trisnorhopane; hH C_{30} 17α(H), 21β(H) Hopane; hJ C_{30} 17β(H), 21α(H) Hopane; hL C_{31} 17α(H), 21β(H) Homohopane (22S); hM C_{31} 17α(H), 21β(H) Homohopane (22R); hN C_{30} 17β(H), 21β(H) Hopane; hP C_{32} 17α(H), 21β(H) Bishomohopane (22S); hQ C_{32} 17α(H), 21β(H) Bishomohopane (22R).

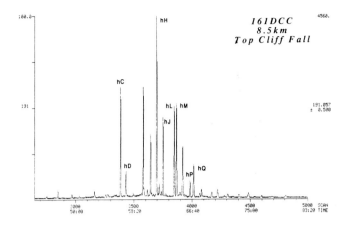

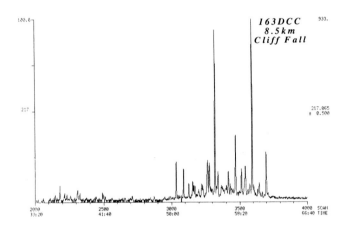

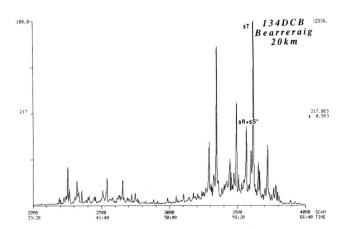

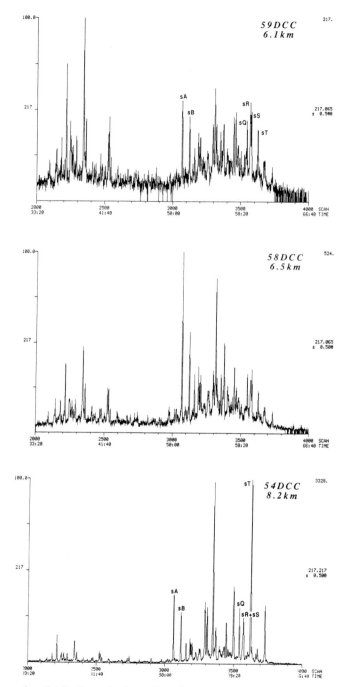

Fig. 8. Sterane biomarker distributions of selected Dun Caan Shale outcrops, Isle of Raasay. Sample localities are given in Fig. 5 and Table 2. m/z 217 mass fragmentograms obtained on Finnegan GC-MS at BP Research Centre, Sunbury. Peaks identified as: sA, C_{27} 13β(H), 17α(H) Diasterane (20S); sB, C_{27} 13β(H), 17α(H) Diasterane (20R); sQ, C_{29} 5α(H), 14α(H), 17α(H) Sterane (20S); sR, mainly C_{29} 5α(H), 14β(H), 17β(H) Sterane (20R); sS, mainly C_{29} 5α(H), 14β(H), 17β(H) Sterane (20S); sT, C_{29} 5α(H), 14α(H), 17α(H) Sterane (20R).

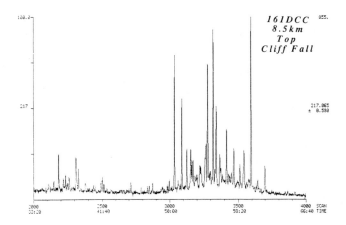

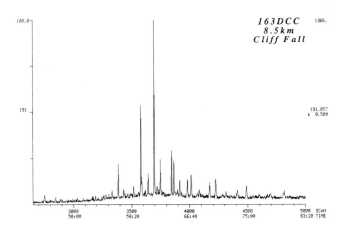

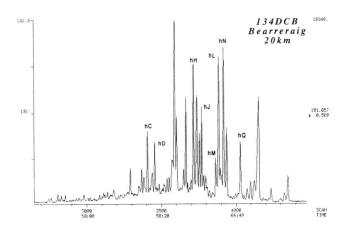

complex margin, with a general gradational decrease in maturity related more to distance from the intrusive complex than to stratigraphic horizon.

The only sediments which show any evidence of heating above 50°C further than 12 km from the margin of the Cuillins intrusive complex are close to small igneous intrusions. For example, at Bearreraig Bay the Dun Caan Shale is cut by a number of small (38 cm to 3 m) basaltic dykes. Most of the Dun Caan Shale is of extremely low maturity, but a zone directly proportional to the thickness of the dyke has been matured, with biomarker distribution analogous to the oil generation threshold found at a distance from the dyke margin equivalent to the thickness of the dyke (detailed in Ambler 1989). Similarly, near Duntulm in the north of Skye, the Duntulm Formation in Lon Ostatoin (Hudson & Morton 1969) is baked in the upper stream section close to the contact with the lower leaf of the Trotternish sill complex, but the lower section, only about 100 m below this contact with the 100 m thick sill, is of extremely low maturity.

Discussion

The maturation effect of both the central intrusive complex and the more minor intrusions is shown to be restricted to the immediate surroundings of the intrusion. The central intrusive complex has not had any thermal effect on the basin beyond what might be expected from conduction and small scale convection. There is no evidence for basin-wide thermal perturbation resulting from the igneous activity.

If there was major fluid flow in the basin resulting from the development of a hydrothermal circulation system around the igneous complex, as suggested by Taylor & Forester (1971), it might be expected that there would be some perturbation of the gradational decrease in maturity away from the central complex described above, seen around fluid conduits such as the major sandstone horizons. At the time of this research a good locality existed for the study of such an effect, where a minor landslide east of Dun Caan had exposed the gradational boundary between the Dun Caan Shale and the overlying Bearreraig Sandstone ('new cliff fall', Fig. 5). The Bearreraig Sandstone might be expected to have acted as a conduit either for superheated waters moving out from the intrusive centre, or for cool meteoric waters being drawn into the system. Biomarker analysis of Dun Caan Shales collected from the centre of the member to the contact with the sandstone (samples 161–164 DCC) showed no indubitable

evidence of a change in maturity closer to the sandstone (Figs 7 & 8), suggesting that neither localized heating nor cooling was ever important around this potential conduit.

Implications for petroleum exploration

This organic geochemical study has shown that the overall thermal effect of the Tertiary igneous activity of the Inner Hebrides was extremely localised, with heating to oil generation maturities restricted to the immediate margins of any igneous body. The principal zone of oil generation seen in the maturation aureole around the Cuillins igneous complex is only 2 km wide, covering a maximum surface area of 213 km^2. The volume of source rock that could be matured around one of the minor intrusions is even smaller. Igneous intrusive activity such as that found in the Inner Hebrides can thus not be realistically invoked as a substitute for burial in the maturation of source rocks and generation of a petroleum play.

This work was carried out under tenure of a University of Aberdeen Postgraduate Studentship under the supervision of M. J. Pearson. British Petroleum kindly provided use of GC-MS facilities at their Sunbury Research Centre. I am very grateful to N. S. Goodwin of BP for his help and advice.

References

AMBLER, J. 1989. *The Organic Geochemistry of the Minch Basin Jurassic Shales*. PhD thesis, University of Aberdeen.

ANDERSON, F. W. & DUNHAM, K. C. 1966. *The Geology of Northern Skye*. Memoir of the Geological Survey of Scotland. HMSO, Edinburgh.

ANDREWS, J. E. 1987. Jurassic clay mineral assemblages and their post depositional alteration: upper Great Estuarine Group, Scotland. *Geological Magazine*, **124**, 261–271.

EMELEUS, C. H. 1983. Tertiary igneous activity. *In*: CRAIG, G. Y. (ed.) *Geology of Scotland*. Scottish Academic Press, Edinburgh, 357–397.

HARRIS, J. P. & HUDSON, J. D. 1980. Lithostratigraphy of the Great Estuarine Series (Middle Jurassic), Inner Hebrides. *Scottish Journal of Geology*, **16**, 231–250.

HUDSON, J. D. 1983. Mesozoic sedimentation and sedimentary rocks in the Inner Hebrides. *Proceedings of the Royal Society of Edinburgh*, **83B**, 47–63.

—— & ANDREWS, J. E. 1987. The diagenesis of the Great Estuarine Group, Middle Jurassic, Inner Hebrides, Scotland. *In*: MARSHALL, J. D. (ed.) *Diagenesis of Sedimentary Sequences*, Geological Society, London, Special Publication, **36**, 259–276.

HUDSON, J. D. & MORTON, N. 1969. *Field Guide no.*

4, Western Scotland. International Field Symposium on the British Jurassic, Keele University.

KING, P. M. 1976. *The secondary minerals of the Tertiary lavas of northern and central Skye-zeolite zonation patterns, their origin and formation.* PhD thesis, University of Aberdeen.

MACKENZIE, A. S. 1984. Applications of biological markers in petroleum geochemistry. *In*: BROOKS, J. & WELTE, D. H. (eds) *Advances in Petroleum Geochemistry*, Vol 1., Academic, London, 115–215.

MORTON, N. 1989. Jurassic sequence stratigraphy in the Hebrides Basin, N. W. Scotland. *Marine and Petroleum Geology*, **6**, 243–260.

MUSSETT, A. E., DAGLEY, P. & SKELHORN, R. R. 1988. Time and duration of activity in the British Tertiary igneous province. *In*: MORTON, A. C. &

PARSON, L. M. (eds) *Early Tertiary Volcanism and the Opening of the N.E. Atlantic*. Geological Society, London, Special Publication, **39**, 337–348.

PHILP, R. P. 1986. *Fossil Fuel Biomarkers: Applications and Spectra*. Elsevier, Amsterdam.

SEIFERT, W. K. & MOLDOWAN, J. M. 1981. Palaeoreconstruction by biological markers. *Geochimica et Cosmoschimica Acta*, **45**, 783–794.

TAYLOR, H. P. & FORESTER, R. W. 1971. Low-018 igneous rocks from the intrusive complexes of Skye, Mull and Ardnamurchan, Western Scotland. *Journal of Petrology*, **12**, 465–497.

TISSOT, B. & WELTE, D. H. 1984. *Petroleum Formation and Occurrence*, 2nd edn. Springer, New York.

Introduction to Mesozoic basins on the North West Seaboard

Late Triassic to Middle Jurassic stratigraphy, palaeogeography and tectonics west of the British Isles

NICOL MORTON

Department of Geology, Birkbeck College, University of London, Malet Street, London WC1E 7HX, UK

Abstract: The Upper Triassic to Middle Jurassic stratigraphy of the Atlantic margin basins west of the British Isles (including Celtic Sea, Porcupine, Slyne, Erris, Hebrides, and west of Shetland) is summarized in terms of six major genetic sequences, defined as packages of conformable strata separated by surfaces of abrupt major facies change. They indicate common tectonic histories and are interpreted as representing episodes of evolution comprising extensional phases with laterally variable sequences (1A Late Triassic to Early Sinemurian; 2A latest Toarcian to Late Bajocian), thermal and loading sag phases (1B mid-Sinemurian to earliest Toarcian; 2B Late Bajocian to Bathonian) and stabilization phases with sequences of reduced thicknesses and hiatuses (1C Toarcian; 2C Late Bathonian to Callovian).

The basins west of Shetlands, north of the Wyville–Thomson Ridge, have a different history, especially in the Early Jurassic. Similarly, basins south of an extension of the Clare Lineament (south of Celtic Sea and Porcupine Basins) differ in having limited Middle Jurassic subsidence. These transverse elements divide the Atlantic basin system into local subsystems, each of which has a different tectonic history.

Jurassic rocks are known to occur in the western seaboard of the British Isles in a series of tilted fault-block structures (mainly half-grabens) which extend from south of Ireland to northwest of the Shetland Isles (Fig. 1). These structures are now more or less isolated from each other, but were originally part of the system of Jurassic basins on the Atlantic margins which extends from south of the Lusitanian Basin of Portugal to north of the East Greenland Basin (see papers in Tankard & Balkwill 1989 and Ziegler 1990). The northern North Sea basins, which are not included in this discussion, were also part of this system (Morton *et al.* 1987).

Stratigraphical analyses of many of the basins are hampered by a lack of detailed information, particularly concerning the biostratigraphy, and some of the offshore Jurassic has been explored by drilling to only a very limited extent. However onshore outcrops or cored boreholes in the Hebrides, northern Ireland (plus Arran in southwest Scotland), northwest England (Carlisle, Prees) and west Wales (Mochras) provide a basis for comparative studies, including the development of dynamic stratigraphical models (e.g. see Morton 1990 & this volume, for the Hebrides Basin) which can be precisely calibrated using ammonite biostratigraphy and palaeobiogeography.

It has become evident as a result of seismic exploration (e.g. Earle *et al.* 1989; Petrie *et al.* 1989; Stein & Blundell 1990; Trueblood & Morton 1991) that there are similarities of structural style in many of the basins west of the British Isles. They are half-grabens which are usually tilted to the west and have bounding faults which are downthrown to the east, although there are exceptions such as the northern Slyne Trough (Trueblood & Morton 1991) which have opposite polarity. However, the sedimentary fills of the basins can vary widely in their ages, from Devonian (e.g. West Orkney, Coward & Enfield 1987) to Cretaceous (e.g. West Shetland basins, Hitchen & Ritchie 1987), and several cycles of extension-related subsidence can be identified (Earle *et al.* 1989, p 465).

In this paper only the basins with Upper Triassic and Jurassic sedimentary fills (see Fig. 1) are discussed. Evidence from outcrops or the limited number of wells available has shown that they have in common many features of their stratigraphical evolution, especially in the uppermost Triassic to Middle Jurassic, and were tectonically linked. The genetic stratigraphical sequences recognized in the Hebrides (Morton 1989) can be correlated to most of the other basins, unless removed by subsequent erosion, and are used here as a framework for summarizing the regional stratigraphy. Exceptions include the Irish Sea and Kish Bank basins (and possibly Northern Ireland, Arran and Loch Indaal) which have very thick almost uniform Lower Jurassic successions above thick Permo-

From PARNELL, J. (ed.), 1992, *Basins on the Atlantic Seaboard: Petroleum Geology, Sedimentology and Basin Evolution.* Geological Society Special Publication No 62, pp 53–68.

53

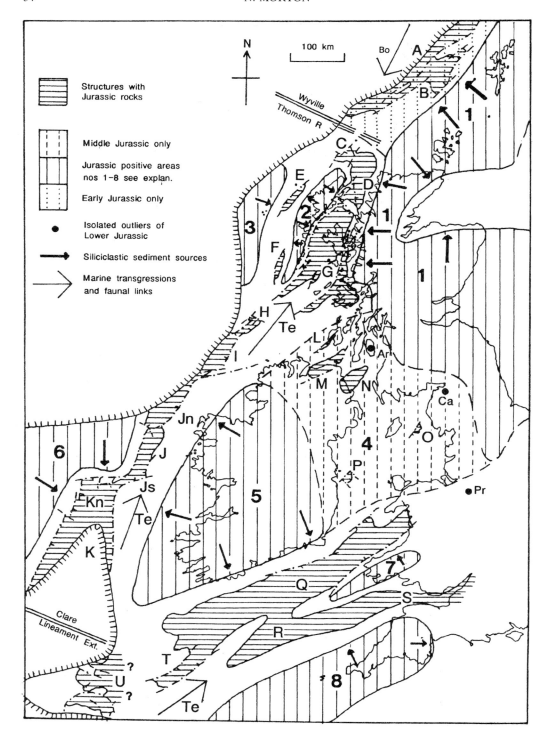

Triassic and therefore appear to have a different tectonic history. The Mochras Lower Jurassic (see Woodland 1971) is probably also of this type, but subsequent evolution of Cardigan Bay is more closely related to that of the Celtic Sea basins further southwest (Millson 1987).

The approach to recognition of genetic stratigraphical sequences used in this paper is derived from study of onshore outcrops in the Hebrides, where there is a long history of previous work (summarized in Hudson 1983, Morton 1987, 1989). For a more detailed discussion of the methodology the reader is referred to Morton (1989, 1990a, this volume). The basis is the recognition of packages of conformable strata within which Walther's Law can be applied and facies changes are gradational because of the gradual evolution through time of the depositional environments. The packages are separated by stratal surfaces across which there are abrupt major changes of facies. These are interpreted as deepening events (cf. the maximum flooding surfaces of Galloway 1989), and are sometimes associated with hiatuses. Unconformities are extremely rare and minor in the Hebrides Jurassic and from the limited seismic evidence currently available this appears to be a general feature for at least the Lower and Middle Jurassic of the basins discussed in this paper (e.g. see Trueblood this volume). It is not yet possible to establish reliable correlations between the sequences observed at outcrop and interpreted from well data and their possible seismic expression. The top of Sequence D (top of Bearreraig Sandstone Formation) can be mapped in the Slyne Trough (Trueblood & Morton 1991) and possibly in the Hebrides (Kilenyi & Stancish 1985), but identification of other sequences is uncertain at present.

In the Hebrides the genetic sequence boundaries have been interpreted (Morton 1989, 1990a, this volume) as having been caused by tectonic events in some cases and by eustatic sea level events in others. The 'Vail' approach of recognizing unconformities to correlative conformities caused by eustatic sea level changes was found to be inappropriate, and there is poor correlation between Hebrides sequence boundaries and those of Haq et al. (1987).

The purpose of this paper is to demonstrate the extent of the similarities of basin evolution, and to develop a synthesis of the stratigraphy, palaeogeography and tectonics of the western seaboard basins for the Norian to Callovian period. Stratigraphical patterns in the Upper Jurassic appear to be more complex and in part are less well known, so are not discussed in this paper.

Reconstruction of Jurassic basins

Establishing the relationship between the present-day identified structures containing Jurassic rocks and the original distribution of Jurassic depositional basins west of the British Isles is complicated by two main features of the later evolution of the area.

Post-Jurassic subsidence

Rapid subsidence during the Cretaceous and Cenozoic, associated with thinning of continental crust and eventual creation of oceanic crust, is seen in the Porcupine Trough and in the Rockall Trough, leading to the formation of the North Atlantic Ocean (Croker & Klemperer 1989; Croker & Shannon 1987; Megson 1987; Smythe 1989). The Porcupine Trough has a different orientation (N–S rather than NNE–SSW) from that of the Early Jurassic basins and appears to cut across the earlier structures (Tate & Dobson 1989). The relationship of the Cretaceous to Cenozoic evolution of the Rockall Trough to possible earlier phases of evolution is more controversial (Smythe 1989). However, the net effect in both cases is that Jurassic rocks have become deeply buried and are beyond the range of detailed examination with currently

---

Fig. 1. Map showing distribution of Jurassic rocks west of British Isles, and reconstruction of palaeogeography. Names of main basins or outliers: A, Faeroe–Shetland; B, West Shetland (A and B not subsiding during Early Jurassic); C, North Lewis; D, North Minch; E, Flannan; F, Barra; G, Hebrides; H, Donegal; I, Erris; J, Slyne (n = north, c = central, s = south); K, Porcupine (n = North Porcupine); L, Loch Indaal; M, Rathlin; N, Antrim; O, Keys; P, Kish Bank; Q, North Celtic Sea; R, South Celtic Sea; S, Bristol Channel; T, Fastnet; U, Goban Spur; Ar, Arran; Ca, Carlisle; Pr, Prees.

Positive 'land' areas: 1, Shetland Platform — Scottish Highlands — ? linking up with Mid North Sea High; 2, Outer Hebrides Platform; 3, St. Kilda Platform; 4, Irish Sea (Middle Jurassic only, subsiding basin during Early Jurassic); 5, Irish Massif; 6, Porcupine Bank — Slyne Ridge; 7, South Wales — Pembroke Ridge; 8, Cornubian Massif. Possible siliciclastic sediment sources shown by heavy arrows (see text for further details).

Long arrows show: Te → direction of late Triassic to early Jurassic marine transgression and "Tethyan" palaeobiogeographic links until late Bajocian; Bo → direction of late Bathonian to Callovian marine transgression and Boreal palaeobiogeographic links from early Callovian.

available techniques. Downfaulting of Jurassic blocks into the Rockall Trough has been documented west of Ireland (Trueblood & Morton 1991, p 197) and into the Faeroe–Shetland Trough west of the Shetlands (e.g. Duindam & van Hoorn 1987, pp 767–768). In the palaeogeographic maps discussed in a later section of this paper no attempt has been made to extend the reconstructions into the Porcupine, Rockall and Faeroe–Shetland Troughs.

Post-Jurassic erosion

The second problem is that the present isolation of the Jurassic 'basins', particularly along their projections in a NNE–SSW direction, is partly the result of subsequent uplift and erosion, for example resulting in only lowermost Jurassic rocks being preserved in the Erris and Donegal Basins. Tate & Dobson (1989) argued for the development of a Middle Jurassic uplift and formation of a crustal dome extending from North Porcupine to the southern Hebrides and the Irish Sea, and resulting in inversion of some basins and erosion of the Lower Jurassic. There was undoubtedly uplift and rejuvenation of hinterland topography immediately before the beginning of the Middle Jurassic over a very wide area from southern Ireland to at least the Shetland Platform, but there are two main lines of evidence to indicate that it was accompanied by renewed subsidence in the system of basins west of the British Isles.

1. The stratigraphical and structural evolution of the Hebrides Basin and Slyne Trough, on opposite sides of the 'crustal dome', are so similar that the same lithostratigraphical nomenclature can be applied (Trueblood this volume). It is possible that this could be due to parallel tectonic evolution of separate basins, but the virtual identity of facies and evidence of unrestricted marine connections (see also below) suggest that it is more likely that there was continuity of depositional environments. The interpretation here is that a continuous series of connected subsiding basins extended from north of the Hebrides through the Donegal and Erris Troughs to south of the Slyne Trough throughout the Early and Middle Jurassic (and probably also the Late Jurassic).

2. From the rich marine faunas (including ammonites) which occur it can be shown that marine palaeobiogeographic links between the Hebrides Basin and basins to the south, connecting eventually through to Tethys, were clearly established during the Early Jurassic and continued into the Middle Jurassic at least until the Late Bajocian (Morton & Dietl 1989; Morton

et al. 1987). No barriers to north–south faunal migration, such as would be caused by a crustal dome, can have existed throughout this time interval. The subsequent (Bathonian) widespread developments of brackish to brackish–marine conditions in the Hebrides and elsewhere were more likely to have been caused by a change in the balance of sedimentation and subsidence rates and eustatic changes of sea level, because continued marine (but restricted) marine connections are required to maintain the brackish nature of the depositional environments.

A more convincing case can be made for the post-Jurassic uplift and erosion being latest Jurassic or, more probably, Early Cretaceous. Evidence for this can be established for the Hebrides Basin, where uplift of the central ridge of basement west of the Camasunary Fault can be shown to be post-Oxfordian (and probably post–Early Kimmeridgian) and pre-Cenomanian (Morton 1990*a*, this volume). The Upper Cretaceous sediments and Palaeocene basaltic lavas rest unconformably on lowermost Jurassic or older rocks west of the fault and on Upper Jurassic rocks (here Oxfordian) east of the fault in Strathaird. The same sub-Upper Cretaceous unconformity can be recognized in Northern Ireland (and Arran), and is a widespread phenomenon west of the British Isles.

There appear to be some differences between the distributions and structural styles of the Late Triassic to Middle Jurassic basins discussed in this paper and earlier Permo-Triassic basins, many of which contain little if any Jurassic. This may be related to a major tectonic and palaeogeographic reorganisation of the basin systems during the latest Triassic and early Jurassic which is a widespread event recognizable in many circum-Atlantic regions (Ziegler 1990, pp 91–94).

Stratigraphical synthesis

Sources of information

This review is based mainly on information which is published or available in the public domain, and revision will undoubtedly be required when currently confidential information becomes available. In the stratigraphical descriptions below additional works have been cited where appropriate.

Celtic Sea basins: Ainsworth pers. comm., Ainsworth *et al.* 1987, 1989; Millson 1987; Penn & Evans 1976; Petrie *et al.* 1989.

Porcupine: Croker & Shannon 1987; Croker & Klemperer 1989; MacDonald *et al.* 1987.

Slyne: Ainsworth pers. comm.; Tate & Dobson 1989; Trueblood this volume; Trueblood & Morton 1991.

Erris (& Donegal): Ainsworth pers. comm.; Tate & Dobson 1989; Trueblood & Morton 1991.

Hebrides (? & North Minch): numerous published sources, summarized in Hudson 1983; Morton 1987, 1989.

West Shetland: Hitchen & Ritchie 1987; Meadows *et al.* 1987; Morton *et al.* 1987.

Summaries of the stratigraphy of the main basins west of the British Isles are shown in Fig. 2 for the uppermost Triassic and Lower Jurassic (Norian to Toarcian), and in Fig. 3 for the Middle Jurassic (Aalenian to Callovian). The chronostratigraphical framework for the Jurassic stages is based on detailed ammonite zonal biostratigraphy (where available) and on information from microfossil biostratigraphy (e.g. Ainsworth *et al.* 1987; Ainsworth *et al.* 1989).

Systematic review of the lithostratigraphical nomenclature is beyond the scope of this paper, and may be premature. The well established nomenclature for the Hebrides Basin can be extended to the Slyne Trough (Trueblood this

volume; Trueblood & Morton 1991). This is interpreted as indicating the former continuity of the basins and therefore the formations. Millson (1987) has provisionally named the Jurassic formations recognized in the Celtic Sea basins.

The major genetic sequences described for the Hebrides Basin (Morton 1989, 1990*a*, this volume) can generally be recognized (or interpreted) in the other basins and provide a basic framework for comparative discussion of the Upper Triassic to Middle Jurassic stratigraphy of the area.

Sequence A

At outcrops in the Hebrides the basal continental red beds of this sequence rest everywhere unconformably on pre-Mesozoic basement and show progressive onlap. They represent a new phase of basin subsidence beginning sometime in the Late Triassic but are rarely dateable. Onlapping stratigraphical relationships of the uppermost Triassic and lower Jurassic can be seen in the Slyne Trough (Trueblood pers. comm.) and at least part of the Porcupine Basin

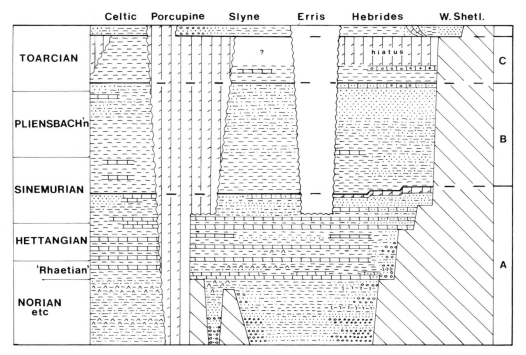

Fig. 2. Diagrammatic summary of Upper Triassic to Lower Jurassic stratigraphy in selected basins west of British Isles, with major genetic sequences (A to C) recognized in Hebrides extrapolated to other basins. Vertical lines with ticks indicate hiatuses; oblique lines indicate sediments resting on pre-Mesozoic basement.

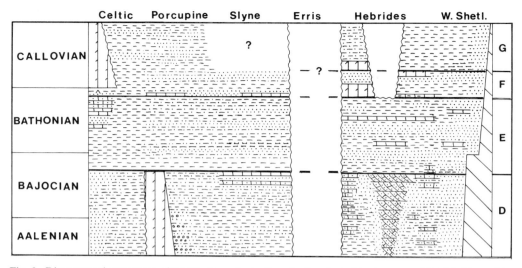

Fig. 3. Diagrammatic summary of Middle Jurassic stratigraphy in selected basins west of British Isles, with major genetic sequences (D to G) recognized in Hebrides extrapolated to other basins. Vertical lines with ticks indicate hiatuses; oblique lines indicate sediments resting on pre-Mesozoic basement.

(Croker & Shannon 1987, p 636). Elsewhere, including Northern Ireland, Irish Sea and Celtic Sea basins and possibly the deeper unexplored western part of the Hebrides Basin, the relationships of the Upper Triassic to older Triassic or possible older strata are less clear.

The oldest sediments are continental red beds which show great lateral variations in thickness and facies, from alluvial fan conglomerates and sandstones in the north and towards the margins of the basins, to mudstones in the central parts (Steel 1974, 1977). Further south, notably in the Celtic Sea basins, the marginal facies are not seen and predominantly finer-grained sediments with anhydrite occur (Ainsworth et al. 1987, p 621).

There is an upward transition from predominantly continental sediments ('New Red Sandstone') through marginal marine (brackish or hypersaline) to fully marine sediments (Lilstock Formation), and this is diachronous, being earlier (late Triassic, Rhaetian) in basins as far north as Mull, but mid-Hettangian further north in Skye and Raasay (Morton 1989). This demonstrates that the late Triassic to early Jurassic transgression came from the south.

The overlying fully marine Jurassic is also highly variable in thickness and facies laterally, with offshore shales and limestones (Blue Lias Formation in Hebrides, Woolacombe Mbr. in Celtic Sea) passing into shallow (lagoonal ?) limestones and sandstones (Broadford Beds Formation in Hebrides, Croyde Formation in

Celtic Sea) (Oates 1978; Millson 1987). A Sinemurian ammonite fragment from core no. 2 (2493–2498 m) of the Slyne Trough well 27/13–1, just below the top of Sequence A, confirms the correlation, but is too poorly preserved to be certain of more precise zonation. In many places there is an overall coarsening up of the sequence, with thick but generally fine-grained sandstones towards the top of the sequence in several areas.

Further north, in the West Shetland and Faeroe–Shetland Basins the Lower Jurassic has not been proved (though derived microfossils have been reported, Hitchen & Ritchie 1987, p 741) and appears to be missing or very limited in its development (Morton et al. 1987, p 704). It is suggested here that little or no subsidence occurred during the Early Jurassic and that Sequences A, B and C do not exist in this area. Note, however, that the sequences can be easily recognized in the northern North Sea basins (Morton et al. 1987). Available evidence from the North Minch Basin is limited to unpublished seismic surveys and shallow boreholes by the British Geological Survey (Chesher et al. 1983), but this basin appears to have the same Lower and Middle Jurassic (at least) stratigraphy as the Hebrides Basin. Further, the parallelism of seismic reflectors towards the southern margin of the North Minch Basin suggests that the Rudha Reidh High, which now separates it from the Hebrides Basin, was not a significant feature during the Jurassic.

Sequence B

Above the sandstones or limestones at the top of Sequence A there is an abrupt change of facies to shales in all areas. In the Hebrides this facies change (to the Pabba Shale Formation) usually has a strong topographic expression and this boundary could be expected to be identifiable seismically as marking at least a change of seismic facies. In some places the lowermost shales are dark and laminated with restricted benthic fauna and may be slightly organic-rich. At outcrops in the Hebrides, where detailed ammonite biostratigraphy is available, there is always a minor hiatus at the base of Sequence B, with approximately one ammonite zone missing. However this hiatus can be shown (Oates 1978; Morton 1990a, b) to be diachronous along the length of the basin, being older in the south (Mull) than in the north (Raasay). The same ammonite subzone (Birchi) is present above the hiatus in Mull and below the hiatus in Raasay.

A similar major facies change to shales can be seen in the Slyne Trough (Trueblood & Morton 1991) and Celtic Sea basins (Kilkhampton Formation) (Millson 1987; see also Petrie et al. 1989, p 439), but equivalent strata have not so far been discovered in other basins or have been removed by subsequent erosion. The hiatus seen at the base of the sequence in the Hebrides is probably below currently available biostratigraphical resolution except using ammonites.

Sequence B, compared with Sequence A, is characterized by greater lateral uniformity of thickness and facies. There is throughout the area a general overall coarsening up of the lithology, which reaches sandstone grade only in the Hebrides (Upper Pliensbachian Scalpa Sandstone Formation) and locally in the Celtic Sea (Upper Pliensbachian Saunton Member). In the Slyne Trough, only coarse siltstone grade is reached. In some localities, limestones or calcareous sandstones have been found at the top of the sequence in the basal Toarcian (Tenuicostatum Zone, Howartih 1956), and in one locality (Raasay) a chamositic ironstone occurs (which should not be confused with the overlying Raasay Ironstone, Morton 1989, p 248).

Sequence C

An abrupt facies change to much finer-grained shales or mudstones, which are sometimes very organic-rich, is present in the Hebrides, Slyne (Portree Shale Formation) and Celtic Sea basins (Stratton Formation). It is usually dated as basal Toarcian, but in the Hebrides the availability of ammonites enables more precise dating to the Falciferum Zone of the Lower Toarcian. At most of the outcrops in the Hebrides this sequence is extremely thin and the shales pass up in the Bifrons Zone into an oolitic ironstone (Raasay Ironstone Formation). However, in part of Skye (southern Trotternish) the sequence is thicker and only shales are present, and this may be more typical of the unexposed western part of the Hebrides Basin. It is certainly comparable with the much thicker shale sequences seen in the Slyne and Celtic Sea basins.

Above the ironstone in the Hebrides there is a major hiatus with much of the middle and upper parts of the Toarcian missing. There is no unequivocal evidence for a similar hiatus in the other basins, but the biostratigraphical control is poor and no clear evidence for Toarcian faunas other than from the lowermost (fauna 29 of Ainsworth et al. 1987) and uppermost Toarcian to Aalenian (fauna 28 of Ainsworth et al. 1987) has been found. This circumstantial evidence together with the abrupt change of sonic and resistivity log character seen in the Slyne well 27/13−1 at 2097 m (see Trueblood, this volume) may suggest the possible presence of a major hiatus throughout the region.

A characteristic feature of Sequence C in the Hebrides is that it is extremely thin, with a mean thickness of 5.8 m, though it may be thicker west of the outcrop areas. The strata interpreted as being equivalent in the Slyne well 27/13−1 (2176 m to log change at 2097 m) are much thicker at 79 m, but this is still much less than for the underlying (269 m) and overlying (318 m) sequences. Relatively reduced rates of subsidence and thin Toarcian successions may be a general stratigraphical feature of the area.

Sequence D

There was a widespread major change in the nature of the succession at approximately the beginning of the Middle Jurassic (summarized below) and in places an unconformity with local erosion of the Lower Jurassic and onlap. This is interpreted (see also Tate & Dobson 1989, p 56) as indicating a major tectonic event and reorganization of the basin system, and is well documented over a large area of western Europe (Ziegler 1990, p 97). In the Hebrides erosion is very limited (the thin Raasay Ironstone Formation is always preserved) and this tectonic event, which can be dated to the latest Toarcian (Aalensis Subzone), is reflected by renewed subsidence in the basin. This was accompanied by rejuvenation of hinterland topography, resulting in the influx of large quantities of coarse siliciclastic material to form the Bearreraig Sandstone Formation (Morton 1983). In some parts of the Hebrides a thick shale unit (Dun Caan Shale Member) rests on the Raasay Ironstone Formation, but where the ironstone is not developed the boundary between Sequences C and D may be difficult to correlate in the absence of independent biostratigraphical data. This is the situation in the Slyne Trough (Trueblood this volume) where the sequence boundary has been correlated with a change in the sonic and resistivity log characters in the 27/13−1 well at 2097 m within an entirely shale interval. In the Celtic Sea basins the correlative events and strata are between the Stratton Formation and the Galley Head Formation. The latter has already been compared with the Bearreraig Sandstone by Millson (1987, p 602).

Identification of Sequence D in the Porcupine basins is more difficult because there are no proven contemporaneous strata. However the oldest Middle Jurassic (Unit I of MacDonald *et al*. 1987, fig. 4, in Block 26/28), resting unconformably on pre-Mesozoic basement in the northern sub-basin of the Porcupine area, are interpreted as continental sediments deposited by high-energy fluvial systems (MacDonald *et al*. 1987, p 646). Frequent red-brown colour and association with calcrete fragments (Croker & Shannon 1987, p 636) indicate a semi-arid climate, drier than for the overlying sediments. Similar semi-arid climatic conditions have been suggested for the Bearreraig Sandstone Formation in the Hebrides, from the evidence of the high proportion of coarse sediment input into the basin and xeromorphic adaptations observed in Aalenian to Early Bajocian floras derived from the Scottish Highlands hinterland (Morton 1990*c*, and unpublished analyses by R. M. Bateman). It requires only slight adjustments in the relative subsidence and sedimentation rates to change depositional environments between marine and non-marine and therefore the north Porcupine facies into the Hebrides facies, or vice versa. The evidence for the younger Middle Jurassic, in both the Hebrides (Great Estuarine Group) and Porcupine areas, suggests that there may have been generally wetter climatic conditions (see below).

There are indications that further south in the Porcupine Basin there was passage laterally into sediments deposited in a marine environment (Croker & Shannon 1987, p 636). This is supported by evidence from the palaeobiogeography (Morton 1990*c*) which indicates that during the Aalenian and Bajocian there must have been unrestricted marine faunal links and probably therefore continuity of basin development from the Hebrides southwards through the Slyne and Porcupine Basins to the Lusitanian Basin of western Portugal and other basins of western Europe.

Throughout the region Sequence D is characterized by a return to extreme lateral variability of thickness and facies, representing a major change in the stratigraphical character of the sedimentary fill of the basins and a change in the tectonic regime (see Morton 1990*a*, this volume). Coarse siliciclastics are dominant not just near the basin margins, but also to a lesser extent towards the central part of the basin because of extensive redistribution of sand by tidal currents (Morton 1983). In the more central parts of basins, e.g. northern Skye in the Hebrides, and in the Slyne (Trueblood & Morton 1991, p 199) and Celtic Sea basins (Millson 1987, p 602) two main coarsening-up cycles can be identified. A widespread limestone unit near the top of Sequence D, which forms a useful seismic marker in the Slyne Trough (Trueblood & Morton 1991), can also be recognized at outcrop in the Hebrides, where it can be dated to the top of the Lower Bajocian or the base of the Upper Bajocian (Morton 1976).

In the West Shetland and Faeroe-Shetland Basins to the north of the Hebrides, Sequence D is the first proven unit in the Jurassic succession, though the dating of the oldest rocks as Aalenian in well 206/5−1 (Meadows *et al*. 1987, p 729) is unreliable. No evidence for the presence of significant accumulations of Lower Jurassic has yet been found in the area, and it is suggested by Morton *et al*. (1987, p 705) that the main Jurassic subsidence in this area began in the Middle Jurassic with the deposition of the equivalents of Sequence D in the basins further south.

Sequence E

At the top of the Bearreraig Sandstone Formation there is a major change in facies in the Upper Bajocian (basal Garantiana Zone, see Morton & Dietl 1989) to a dark clay which is marine at first but becomes non-marine, and sufficiently organic-rich to be a true oil shale locally, in the basal unit of the Great Estuarine Group. This Upper Bajocian to Bathonian Group, showing remarkable lateral continuity of facies and less variability of thickness, consists of a variety of sediments deposited in lagoons of variable but usually reduced salinity. This implies sufficiently increased run-off (in comparison with the Aalenian to Early Bajocian) to maintain the brackish-water conditions, though there is also evidence of seasonal aridity. There may also have been some more arid periods because algal limestones with pseudomorphs after gypsum occur (Hudson 1970), and near the top red beds with calcretes are recorded (Skudiburgh Formation, Andrews 1985). In the Hebrides three upward-coarsening or upward-regressive sequences can be recognized (Andrews 1985; Harris & Hudson 1980; Hudson 1980). The same general character can be identified in the Slyne Trough well 27/13–1, enabling correlation with Sequence E and again suggesting continuity of basin development.

Further southwest, in the northern sub-basin of the Porcupine Basin the ('Bathonian') strata interpreted here as equivalent to Sequence E are finer grained and greyer in colour (unit II of MacDonald *et al.* 1987, p 646 in block 26/28) than those interpreted above as belonging to Sequence D. They consist of fining-up sandstones, siltstones and mudstones interpreted as probably deposited in a meandering fluvial system. The facies changes imply a wetter climate, and this is consistent with an interpretation of equivalence to the Hebrides Great Estuarine Group of Sequence E. Presumably more marine or marginal-marine conditions existed to the south and east in the Porcupine Basin, to allow partial marine influence through to the basins to the northeast.

In the Celtic Sea, the transgression at the base of the Mizen Head Group is equivalent to the base of Sequence E. The succeeding argillaceous sediments remain marine, but with variable amounts of carbonaceous material and mica suggesting near-shore influence (Millson 1987, fig. 4). To the northeast there is lateral facies change to the carbonates of the Ballycotton Group.

North of the Hebrides, in the basins west of the Shetlands (West Shetland, Faeroe–Shetland etc.) the Bathonian sediments are submarine fan sandstones passing laterally into shales, and onlapping onto pre-Mesozoic basement (Meadows *et al.* 1987, p 729). However the limited information available does not at present make it possible to distinguish the Middle Jurassic sequences with confidence.

Sequence F

The base of this sequence is marked in the Hebrides by a hiatus or an abrupt facies change due to marine transgression (which appears to have been earlier in the north). The marginal-marine shales and limestones and marine sandstones (Staffin Bay Formation, Sykes 1978) represent a return to marine conditions, and the

apparently diachronous transgression together with the Early Callovian southward spread of Boreal ammonite faunas suggest that the marine transgression came from the north. There is also evidence of 'basal Callovian' transgression in the basins west of Shetland, with abrupt facies change in places from sandstones to dark shales, which is consistent with this interpretation.

The evidence in the Slyne 27/13–1 well for the presence of a marine sequence above Sequence E is circumstantial, though the change of log character from thin fining-up units to a thick coarsening-up unit in the top 100 m of the succession may suggest a comparable change of facies. Further information is required before any reliable conclusions can be drawn about the Callovian and Upper Jurassic of this basin.

In the Porcupine Basin there is again no unequivocal evidence to enable the correlation of the middle part of the Jurassic with the genetic sequences recognized in the Hebrides. However a facies change and overlap of the platform ridge at the north end of the basin may represent a sequence boundary of similar age. The indications of lacustrine sandstones, shales and occasional limestones (Croker & Shannon 1987, p 636) suggest that the Late Bathonian to Early Callovian Boreal transgression may not have reached this area.

The Celtic Sea basins show a sharp facies change in the Late Bathonian with the incoming of the red mudstones and anhydrite of the Schull Formation (Millson 1987, p 603). Although the regressive nature of this change is the opposite of the Boreal transgressive events seen in the Hebrides they may represent different responses to the same tectonic events, because both formations are thin and indicate reduced rates of subsidence with stabilization of the basins. The residual balance between subsidence and sedimentation rates would determine whether the depositional environment became more marine as in the Hebrides, or less marine as in the Celtic Sea. Also consistent with this is the marine transgression in the Early Callovian which resulted in the deposition of the thin Dungarvon Formation in only part of the Celtic Sea basins (Millson 1987).

Sequence G

The deepening event and sharp facies change to dark shales (and hiatus) seen in the Hebrides and which define the base of Sequence G in this basin can also be recognized west of Shetland, but not in the basins to the south. The Callovian and Late Jurassic genetic sequences of the western seaboard basins are complex and further information and work on the Slyne and Hebrides are required before regional patterns can be established linking the Porcupine, Celtic Sea and basins to the south (see Hiscott *et al.* 1990) with the basins west of Shetland to the north (Earle *et al.* 1989, p 467). Two common features can be pointed out at this stage.

1. *Callovian stabilization.* The Callovian has been shown to be very thin compared with the rest of the Middle Jurassic in the West of Shetland, Hebrides and Celtic Sea basins. Just as for the Toarcian (see description of Sequence C), no characteristic Callovian fossil assemblages were found in the Celtic Sea basins by Ainsworth *et al.* (1987) between their faunas 19 (Oxfordian) and 20 (Upper Bathonian). There is insufficient biostratigraphical information available to establish whether the Callovian stabilization also applies to the Porcupine Basin. In sharp contrast a thick ?Bathonian to Callovian sequence with more than 200 m of volcanic rocks is recorded by Cook (1987) in the Goban Spur immediately to the south of the area discussed in this paper.

2. *Oxfordian subsidence.* Renewed subsidence took place in all the Atlantic margin basins, including those to the south of the area discussed in this paper, and in some areas this is associated with an unconformity. The timing of renewal of subsidence varies from Early Oxfordian (e.g. Hebrides) to Middle Oxfordian (e.g. Celtic Sea and basins to the south) following a widespread Early Oxfordian hiatus (Hiscott *et al.* 1990).

Controls on sequence stratigraphy

The genetic stratigraphical sequences described above have been recognized on the basis of major abrupt changes in the nature of the sedimentary fill of the respective basins as discussed previously. Each sequence represents dynamic but gradual evolution of the depositional environments due to interaction of sedimentation, subsidence and eustatic changes of sea level. Sequence boundaries occur where this gradual evolution is disturbed by a significant event such as a tectonic episode or a rapid eustatic change of sea level, causing a sharp facies change throughout the basin.

Detailed discussions of the genetic stratigraphical sequences in the Hebrides Basin and their interpretation are given elsewhere (Morton 1989, 1990*a*, this volume). The sequence boundaries have been dated precisely using the detailed ammonite zonal and subzonal scales available for the Jurassic (Cope *et al.* 1980*a*, *b*) and can therefore be compared in

detail with the sequence boundaries tabulated by Haq *et al.* (1987) and calibrated by them against the same ammonite zones and subzones in the classical outcrops of the Jurassic in Dorset. There are very few correlations (see Morton 1989, fig. 9), indicating that eustatic sea level events were not the main causal mechanism. Most of the genetic sequence stratigraphy and stratigraphical architecture of the Hebrides Basin is therefore related to tectonic factors which are summarized below, and the similarities of stratigraphy in the other basins described above suggest that the model derived for the Hebrides can be applied more generally. However, eustatic sea level events (see Hallam 1989) causing sequence boundaries during intervals of basin stabilization and slower subsidence can be recognized in the Early Toarcian Falciferum Zone (base of Sequence C) and in the Early Callovian Jason Zone (base of Sequence G). A Late Bathonian sea-level rise (base of Sequence F) suggested for the Hebrides may be doubtful in view of the correlative regressive event seen in the Celtic Sea.

Palaeogeography

Evidence which enables the reconstruction of the palaeogeography of the western seaboard of the British Isles during the Late Triassic to Middle Jurassic shown on Fig. 1 has to be based on the limited information available concerning the sedimentary fill of the basins (see also Ziegler 1990). The best constraints on basin margins and hinterland areas are to be found in the Hebrides and are based mainly on the detrital mineralogy. The most detailed analyses so far published are by Steel (1974) for the Late Triassic to Early Hettangian (the 'New Red Sandstone'), Hudson (1964) and Harris (1984, 1989, this volume) for the Middle Jurassic. The western faulted margin of the basin was the Minch Fault zone, with the Outer Hebrides Platform to the west being a source of sediment at least to the western part of the basin. The eastern margin is unfaulted and therefore less stable through time, but must have been close to the present western coastline of the Scottish mainland because the Caledonian foreland areas west of the Moine Thrust were significant sediment source areas in the hinterland as well as the Moine and Dalradian terrains further east. Distinct source areas supplying the northern and southern areas of Skye can be recognized in the Middle Jurassic (Harris 1989, this volume), while source areas for the Late Triassic to Earliest Jurassic continental red beds were very local (Steel 1974).

For the majority of the other basins no

comparable detailed analyses of detrital mineralogy are available to identify the hinterland areas with the same confidence. In estimating the positions of basin margins and of positive areas the evidence from the Hebrides has been extrapolated to other areas. The following positive areas are tentatively identified (see Fig. 1).

1. Scottish Highlands — clear evidence from detrital mineralogy of Jurassic rocks in the Hebrides (Hudson 1964; Harris this volume) (and Moray Firth, Hurst 1985), extrapolated northwards to Shetland Platform and southwards to possibly link up with Mid-North Sea High; position of margin in southwest Scotland uncertain.

2. Outer Hebrides Platform — clear evidence from detrital mineralogy of Jurassic in Hebrides (Hudson 1964; Harris this volume), and Trias (?-Hettangian) of Stornoway (Steel & Wilson 1975).

3. St. Kilda Platform — presumed by analogy of position relative to Barra and Flannan Basins as Outer Hebrides Platform to Hebrides Basin (Stein & Blundell 1990), but no positive evidence available at present.

4. Irish Sea — strongly subsiding basin in Early Jurassic; interpreted here as a non-subsiding area during the Middle Jurassic, though possibly a submerged platform at least at times. The reasons for this interpretation are discussed below.

5. Irish Massif — no unambiguous evidence but western margin drawn by analogy with Hebrides, southern margin from facies distributions developed in Celtic Sea (Millson 1987; Petrie et al. 1989); eastern and northeastern margins very uncertain.

6. Porcupine Bank (and Slyne Ridge) — sedimentological evidence from Middle Jurassic of northern Porcupine Sub-basin (Croker & Shannon 1987; MacDonald et al. 1987), and by analogy with Outer Hebrides Platform.

7. South Wales and Pembroke Ridge — limited sedimentological evidence and from facies distributions especially in Middle Jurassic of Celtic Sea (Millson 1987; Petrie et al. 1989) and by analogy with Scottish Highlands, but existence and extent uncertain.

8. Cornubian Massif — limited evidence from facies distributions in Celtic Sea basins (Millson 1987) and from detrital mineralogy of Jurassic in neighbouring basins (Davies 1969).

Tectonic evolution of basins

The Jurassic basins of the Atlantic margins evolved in an extensional tectonic setting during the rifting phase of evolution of the North Atlantic, and tectonic models based on those of McKenzie (1978) or Wernicke (1981, 1985) can be successfully applied (see papers in Tankard & Balkwill 1989 and in Coward et al. 1987, and Stein & Blundell 1990 for discussion of the Hebridean shelf basins). Identification and dating of different phases predicted by models can be established by analyses of the stratigraphical history of the sedimentary fills of basins (see Morton 1990a). During episodes of lithospheric extension (irrespective of the precise mechanism at depth) there is differential subsidence at the surface, partly fault-controlled and possibly influenced by older structures (mainly Caledonoid in NW Scotland, Stein 1988). The resulting sedimentary successions are laterally highly variable in thickness and facies. After extension ceases, continued subsidence is driven by thermal cooling of the crust and sediment loading. This is more uniform and over a slightly larger area so that sedimentary successions deposited during these episodes are laterally more uniform in thickness and facies and may show onlap at basin margins. Subsidence and sedimentation will slow down and cease, resulting in basin fill or thin condensed successions, unless a further episode of lithospheric extension occurs. During the Late Triassic to Middle Jurassic two episodes of evolution from extension to sag and stabilization have been identified in the Hebrides Basin (Morton 1987, 1989, 1990a). The close similarities of stratigraphical evolution described in this paper suggest that the tectonic model developed for the Hebrides Basin can be applied more generally to the Jurassic basins west of the British Isles.

Tectonic history

For the Late Triassic to Middle Jurassic, six main phases of basin history can be recognized. These correspond to Sequences A to F, and are based on an integration of subsidence history analysis with an analysis of the stratigraphical architecture of the major genetic sequences.

1. *Late Triassic to Early Sinemurian (Sequence A)*. Subsidence caused by lithospheric extension, especially in the northern part of the area, resulted in Sequence A which is laterally highly variable. The surface expression of the extension was fault-controlled differential subsidence, giving variable thicknesses, and topographic irregularities within the basin and hinterland resulting in great lateral variations in facies. Superimposed on these there was gradual northward transgression of the sea into the basins, giving a diachronous transition (hence

no major sequence boundary) from continental to marine sediments.

2. *Mid-Sinemurian to Early Toarcian (Sequence B)*. Change (possibly diachronous) to a tectonic driving mechanism in which subsidence caused by thermal and loading sag resulted in the laterally more uniform thicknesses and facies typical of Sequence B. This basin sag occurred over a wider area so that onlap at the margins of the basins resulted in drowning of the sediment sources and deepening in the central part of the basin associated with a submarine hiatus and much finer grain-size of sediments. This was followed by gradual fill and progradation of coarser-grained facies.

3. *Toarcian (Sequence C)*. Stabilization of the basins resulted in slower rates of subsidence and the greatly reduced thicknesses and probable widespread hiatus seen in Sequence C, though the sharp facies change to dark shales caused by a deepening event which defines the base of the sequence must be explained by a eustatic sea level event (Hallam 1978, 1989) superimposed on the tectonic evolution of the basin. The fine grain-size of the sediments (and chamositic ironstone seen in the Hebrides) suggest that stabilization in the basins was accompanied by reduced topography and slopes in the hinterlands.

These phases of basin evolution can be established for all the basins south of the Hebrides, and almost certainly also apply to the North Minch (? and North Lewis) basins, but do not appear to have occurred in the basins further north in the area west of Shetland.

In the area of the Irish Sea (Northern Ireland, Kish Bank, Mochras, etc.) the Lower Jurassic is more uniform in facies and in rates of subsidence through time (most notable if a subsidence history curve for Mochras is constructed). The stratigraphical architecture of this area is more consistent with a prolonged basin sag after Triassic extension and differential subsidence.

4. *Latest Toarcian to Late Bajocian (Sequence D)*. A widespread tectonic event resulted in local unconformities but more significantly renewed subsidence in the basins and rejuvenation of hinterland topography. This event can be recognized in all the basins north of the Celtic Sea and Porcupine Basins and in the basins west of Shetland. It was less significant further south (e.g. Goban Spur, Cook 1987) where Masson & Miles (1986) refer to a Middle Jurassic 'quiet period'.

The existence of Middle Jurassic subsidence

in the Irish Sea area north of Cardigan Bay is also a matter for debate. It is interpreted here as *not* having occurred, for two reasons, neither of which is conclusive on its own. The first is that the closest Aalenian–Bajocian ammonite palaeobiogeographical links from the Hebrides were with basins in Portugal, western France and southwest England rather than with the Cotswolds or Midlands. The second reason is that it would be remarkable to find evidence, even from derived fossils in Cretaceous and Quaternary deposits, of only Lower Jurassic over such a wide area if significant thicknesses of younger Jurassic rocks had been deposited. The reported indications of former deep burial do not apply everywhere in the Irish Sea and can be explained by alternative events such as Tertiary intrusions and higher heat flow (see Jackson *et al.* 1987).

5. *Late Bajocian to Bathonian (Sequence E)*. The change of stratigraphical architecture from Sequence D to Sequence E is closely comparable with that between Sequences A and B described above. The same interpretation of a change from extension-driven subsidence during the Early Bajocian to broader and more uniform basin sag caused by thermal and loading factors is made for this interval. Sedimentation took place very close to sea level throughout the Great Estuarine Group, indicating a very fine balance between rates of sedimentation, subsidence and sea level change.

6. *Late Bathonian (?) to Late Callovian (Sequence F)*. This stratigraphical interval is characterized by reduced thicknesses and hiatuses, indicating slower rates of subsidence and a phase of basin stabilization comparable with that in the Toarcian.

Limits of tectonically related basins

The stratigraphical patterns described above, and the interpreted tectonic evolution, can be shown to apply to all the basins of the Atlantic margin of the British Isles from the Celtic Sea and Porcupine Basins in the south to the Hebrides and North Minch Basins in the north. They were clearly all part of the same set of tectonically related basins. Different patterns and histories can be established for basins further north and south, suggesting the recognition of more local independently evolving subsystems of basins within the Atlantic System.

To the north, the West Shetland, Faeroe–Shetland and other basins west of the Shetlands to not show evidence of the Late Triassic and

Early Jurassic subsidence (Morton *et al*. 1987), and the Middle Jurassic is similar to the Hebrides only in very general terms. These basins were part of a separate subsystem of basins with a different tectonic history.

To the south, the Goban Spur (Cook 1987) and other Atlantic margin basins (Masson & Miles 1986) are not yet well enough known for detailed comparisons of the Lower Jurassic to be made, though Late Triassic to Earliest Jurassic extension (including volcanism) has been documented (see papers in Tankard & Balkwill 1989). The differences in the Middle Jurassic are clearer, with early tectonic quiescence and later local volcanism (e.g. Goban Spur, Cook 1987). Again, a different pattern of tectonic evolution is discernable and a separate basin subsystem suggested.

The limits between the Hebrides−Porcupine Basin Subsystem, which has been described in this paper, and the independent subsystems to the north and south appear to coincide with major Atlantic transverse structures. Between the Hebrides and North Minch Basins and the Shetland−Faerøe Basins Subsystem there is a complex WNW−ESE structure, the Wyville−Thomson Ridge, which appears to mark the boundary between the two basin subsystems (and was subsequently the southern limit of the Early Cretaceous subsidence affecting the Shetland−Faerøe Basin Subsystem).

The southern end of the Porcupine Basin and the southwestern ends of the Celtic Sea (and Fastnet) Basins are less well known, but the Goban Spur and other basins to the south or southwest belong to a different subsystem. The boundary between the Hebrides−Porcupine Basin Subsystem and Iberia−Newfoundland Basin Subsystem appears to be a southeastwards extension of the Clare Lineament (and possibly the Charlie Gibbs Fracture Zone, though this may be too far north).

On the western margin of the Atlantic a similar north−south difference is evident, with the Jeanne d'Arc Basin described by Hiscott *et al*. (1990) as showing anomalously high rates of Early and Middle Jurassic subsidence compared with the other basins they discussed. These authors were more concerned with post-Middle Jurassic evolution, but the other basins for which they had information on the Lower and Middle Jurassic all belong to the Iberia−Newfoundland Basin Subsystem as envisaged here. The Jeanne d'Arc Basin may be part of the Hebrides−Porcupine Basin Subsystem.

The conclusion which follows from this analysis of basin evolution is that major transverse features, which were significant controls of sub-sequent Atlantic Ocean evolution were already important factors in the Late Triassic and Jurassic crustal evolution.

Tectonic migration

Within the Hebrides−Porcupine Basin Subsystem as defined here there are indications from the stratigraphy that the main locus of successive episodes of lithospheric extension and consequent subsidence (see Stein & Blundell 1990 for discussion of crustal dynamics) may have migrated westwards or northwestwards with time. The clearest evidence is in the Hebrides Basin. In the southeastern part of the basin (Mull and Ardnamurchan area) strong Late Triassic and Early Jurassic subsidence was followed by limited Middle Jurassic subsidence but apparently no Late Jurassic subsidence. Further northwest (Raasay and Skye area) there was also strong Middle Jurassic subsidence but possibly more limited Late Jurassic subsidence. Similar apparent tectonic migration patterns are indicated for the Celtic Sea Basins by Ruffell & Coward (this volume) and for the Slyne Basin by Trueblood (this volume).

The subsequent evolution of the basins is beyond the scope of this paper, but there are indications that Late Jurassic extension-related subsidence was mainly developed in the northern Celtic Sea Basin (Petrie *et al*. 1989, pp 439−441). Early Cretaceous extension and subsidence occurred west and northwest of the Late Triassic to Middle Jurassic basins, which became inactive or were partially inverted.

Conclusions

1. In the basins of the western seaboard of the British Isles, from the Celtic Sea and Porcupine Basins north to the Hebrides and North Minch Basins, the stratigraphy of the Upper Triassic to Middle Jurassic is sufficiently similar to enable descriptions to be summarized in terms of the same six major genetic stratigraphical sequences. The exceptions are the basins west of Shetland which do not contain Lower Jurassic, the Irish Sea area where no Middle Jurassic subsidence is postulated, and basins from the Goban Spur southwards which differ in at least the Middle Jurassic.

2. The reconstructed palaeogeography (Fig. 1) shows that the basins were bounded to the east by positive hinterland areas including the Mid-North Sea High−Scottish Highlands−Shetland Platform and smaller Irish Platform (which may have extended across the Irish Sea during the Middle Jurassic), south Wales−

Pembroke Ridge and Cornubian Massif. To the west small positive land areas included the Outer Hebrides Platform and a Porcupine—Slyne Ridge Platform.

3. The basins were tectonically linked and twice evolved from phases of lithospheric extension with sequences which were laterally variable in thickness and facies (Late Triassic to Early Sinemurian, latest Toarcian to Late Bajocian) through phases of thermal and loading sag with laterally more uniform sequences (mid-Sinemurian to earliest Toarcian, Late Bajocian to Bathonian) to phases of basin stabilization with sequences of reduced thickness (Toarcian, Late Bathonian to Callovian).

4. These basins were part of the Atlantic margin system of early Mesozoic extensional basins, but other basins to north and south have different tectonic histories. The boundaries between suggested subsystems of tectonically linked basins were major transform features of the North Atlantic, with the Wyville—Thomson Ridge separating a Shetland—Faeroe Basin Subsystem to the north from a Hebrides—Porcupine Basin Subsystem (possibly including the Jeanne d'Arc Basin of the North American margin), and the latter separated from an Iberia—Newfoundland Basin Subsystem by the Clare Lineament and its extension.

References

AINSWORTH, N. R., O'NEILL, M. & RUTHERFORD, M. M. 1989. Jurassic and Upper Triassic biostratigraphy of the North Celtic Sea and Fastnet Basins. *In*: BATTEN, D. J. & KEEN, M. C. (eds) *Northwest European Micropalaeontology and Palynology*. Ellis Horwood, Chichester 1—44.

——, ——, ——, CLAYTON, G., HORTON, N. F. & PENNEY, R. A. 1987. Biostratigraphy of the Lower Cretaceous, Jurassic and uppermost Triassic of the North Celtic Sea and Fastnet Basins. *In*: BROOKS, J. & GLENNIE, K. (eds) *Petroleum Geology of North West Europe*. Graham & Trotman, 611—622.

ANDREWS, J. E. 1985. The sedimentary facies of a late Bathonian regressive episode: the Kilmaluag and Skudiburgh Formations of the Great Estuarine Group, Inner Hebrides, Scotland. *Journal of the Geological Society, London*, **142**, 1119—1137.

CHESHER, J. A., SMYTHE, D. K. & BISHOP, P. 1983. *The Geology of the Minches, Inner Sound and Sound of Raasay*. Report of Institute of Geological Sciences 83/6.

COOK, D. R. 1987. The Goban Spur — exploration in a deep-water frontier basin. *In*: BROOKS, J. & GLENNIE, K. (eds) *Petroleum Geology of North West Europe*. Graham & Trotman, London, 623—632.

COPE, J. C. W., DUFF, K. L., PARSONS, C. F., TORRENS, H. S., WIMBLEDON, W. A. & WRIGHT, J. K. 1980a. *A correlation of Jurassic rocks in the British Isles. Part Two: Middle and Upper Jurassic*. Geological Society, London, Special Report **15**.

——, GETTY, T. A., HOWARTH, M. K., MORTON, N. & TORRENS, H. S. 1980b. *A correlation of Jurassic rocks in the British Isles. Part One: Introduction and Lower Jurassic*. Geological Society, London, Special Report **14**.

COWARD, M. P., DEWEY, J. F. & HANCOCK, P. L. (eds) 1987. *Continental Extensional Tectonics*. Geological Society, London, Special Publication **28**.

—— & ENFIELD, M. A. 1987. The structure of the West Orkney and adjacent basins. *In*: BROOKS, J. & GLENNIE, K. (eds) *Petroleum Geology of North West Europe*. Graham & Trotman, London, 687—696.

CROKER, P. F. & KLEMPERER, S. L. 1989. Structure and stratigraphy of the Porcupine Basin: Relationships to deep crustal structure and the opening of the North Atlantic. *In*: TANKARD, A. J. & BALKWILL, H. R. (eds) *Extensional Tectonics and Stratigraphy of the North Atlantic Margins*. American Association of Petroleum Geologists, Memoir, **46**, 445—459.

—— & SHANNON, P. M. 1987. The evolution and hydrocarbon prospectivity of the Porcupine Basin, offshore Ireland. *In*: BROOKS, J. & GLENNIE, K. (eds) *Petroleum Geology of North West Europe*. Graham & Trotman, London, 633—642.

DAVIES, D. K. 1969. Shelf sedimentation: an example from the Jurassic of Britain. *Journal of Sedimentary Petrology*, **37**, 1179—1188.

DUINDAM, P. & VAN HOORN, B. 1987. Structural evolution of the West Shetland continental margin. *In*: BROOKS, J. & GLENNIE, K. (eds) *Petroleum Geology of North West Europe*. Graham & Trotman, London, 765—773.

EARLE, M. M., JANKOWSKI, E. J. & VANN, I. R. 1989. Structural and stratigraphic evolution of the Faeroe-Shetland Channel and northern Rockall Trough. *In*: TANKARD, A. J. & BALKWILL, H. R. (eds) 1989. *Extensional Tectonics and Stratigraphy of the North Atlantic Margins*. American Association of Petroleum Geologists, Memoir, **46**, 461—469.

GALLOWAY, W. E. 1989. Genetic stratigraphic sequences in basin analysis I: architecture and genesis of flooding-surface bounded depositional units. *AAPG Bulletin*, **73**, 125—142.

HALLAM, A. 1978. Eustatic cycles in the Jurassic. *Palaeogeography, Palaeoclimatology, Palaeoecology*, **23**, 1—32.

—— 1989. A re-evaluation of Jurassic eustasy in the light of new data and the revised Exxon curve. *In*: WILGUS, C. K. (ed.) Sea level changes — and integrated approach. *Society of Economic Paleontologists and Mineralogists, Special Publication*, **42**, 261—273.

HAQ, B. U., HARDENBOL, J. & VAIL, P. R. 1987.

Chronology of fluctuating sea levels since the Triassic. *Science*, **235**, 1156–1167.

HARRIS, J. P. 1984. *Environments of Deposition of Middle Jurassic Sandstones in the Great Estuarine Group, N.W. Scotland*. PhD thesis, University of Leicester.

—— 1989. The sedimentology of a Middle Jurassic lagoonal delta system: Elgol Formation (Great Estuarine Group), NW Scotland, *In*: WHATELEY, M. K. G. & PICKERING, K. T. (eds) *Deltas: Sites and Traps for Fossils Fuels*. Geological Society, London, Special Publication **41**, 147–166.

—— & HUDSON, J. D. 1980. Lithostratigraphy of the Great Estuarine Group (Middle Jurassic), Inner Hebrides. *Scottish Journal of Geology*, **16**, 231–250.

HISCOTT, R. N., WILSON, R. C. L., GRADSTEIN, F. M., PUJALTE, V., GARCIA-MONDEJAR, J., BOUDREAU, R. R. & WISHART, H. A. 1990. Comparative stratigraphy and subsidence history of Mesozoic rift basins of North Atlantic. *AAPG Bulletin*, **74**, 60–76.

HITCHEN, K. & RITCHIE, J. D. 1987. Geological review of the West Shetland area. *In*: BROOKS, J. & GLENNIE, K. (eds) *Petroleum Geology of North West Europe*. Graham & Trotman, London, 737–749.

HOWARTH, M. K. 1956. The Scalpa Sandstone of the Isle of Raasay. *Proceedings of Yorkshire Geological Society*, **30**, 353–370.

HUDSON, J. D. 1964. The petrology of the sandstones of the Great Estuarine Series, and the Jurassic palaeocogeography of Scotland. *Proceedings of the Geologists' Association*, **75**, 499–527.

—— 1970. Algal limestones with pseudomorphs after gypsum from the Middle Jurassic of Scotland. *Lethaia*, **3**, 11–40.

—— 1980. Aspects of brackish-water facies and faunas from the Jurassic of north-west Scotland. *Proceedings of the Geologists' Association*, **91**, 99–105.

—— 1983. Mesozoic sedimentation and sedimentary rocks in the Inner Hebrides. *Proceedings of the Royal Society of Edinburgh*, **83B**, 47–63.

HURST, A. 1985. The implications of clay mineralogy to palaeoclimate and provenance during the Jurassic in NE Scotland. *Scottish Journal of Geology*, **21**, 143–160.

JACKSON, D. I., MULHOLLAND, P., JONES, S. M. & WARRINGTON, G. 1987. The geological framework of the East Irish Sea Basin. *In*: BROOKS, J. & GLENNIE, K. (eds) *Petroleum Geology of North West Europe*. Graham & Trotman, London, 191–203.

KILENYI, T. & STANDISH, B. 1985. Petroleum prospects in the northwest seaboard of Scotland. *Oil & Gas Journal*, **10**–7, 100–108.

MACDONALD, H., ALLAN, P. M. & LOVELL, J. P. B. 1987. Geology of oil accumulation in Block 26/28, Porcupine Basin, offshore Ireland. *In*: BROOKS, J. & GLENNIE, K. (eds) *Petroleum Geology of North West Europe*. Graham & Trotman, London, 643–651.

MASSON, D. G. & MILES, P. R. 1986. Development

and hydrocarbon potential of Mesozoic sedimentary basins around margins of North Atlantic. *AAPG Bulletin*, **70**, 721–729.

MCKENZIE, D. P. 1978. Some remarks on the development of sedimentary basins. *Earth & Planetary Science Letters*, **40**, 25–32.

MEADOWS, N. S., MACCHI, L., CUBITT, J. M. & JOHNSON, B. 1987. Sedimentology and reservoirs potential in the west of Shetland, UK, exploration area. *In*: BROOKS, J. & GLENNIE, K. (eds) *Petroleum Geology of North West Europe*. Graham & Trotman, London, 723–736.

MEGSON, J. B. 1987. The evolution of the Rockall Trough and implications for the Faeroe–Shetland Trough. *In*: BROOKS, J. & GLENNIE, K. W. (eds) *Petroleum Geology of North West Europe*. Graham & Trotman, London, 653–665.

MILLSON, J. A. 1987. The Jurassic evolution of the Celtic Sea basins. *In*: BROOKS, J. & GLENNIE, K. (eds) *Petroleum Geology of North West Europe*. Graham & Trotman, London, 599–610.

MORTON, N. 1976. Bajocian (Jurassic) stratigraphy in Skye, western Scotland. *Scottish Journal of Geology*, **12**, 23–33.

—— 1983. Palaeocurrents and palaeo-environments of part of the Bearreraig Sandstone (Middle Jurassic) of Skye and Raasay, Inner Hebrides. *Scottish Journal of Geology*, **19**, 86–95.

—— 1987. Jurassic subsidence history in the Hebrides, N.W. Scotland. *Marine and Petroleum Geology*, **4**, 226–242.

—— 1989. Jurassic sequence stratigraphy in the Hebrides Basin, NW Scotland. *Marine and Petroleum Geology*, **6**, 243–260.

—— 1990a. Tectonic and eustatic controls of Jurassic genetic sequences in the Hebrides basin, NW Scotland. *Bulletin Société Géologique de France*, série **8**, **6**, 1001–1009.

—— 1990b. The Lias of the Hebrides. Livre jubilaire R. Mouterde. *Cahiers Université Catholique de Lyon, Série sciences*, **4**, 107–119.

—— 1990c. Bearreraig (Isle of Skye, N.W. Scotland) as boundary stratotype for the base of the Bajocian Stage. *In*: CRESTA, S. & PAVIA, G. (eds) Atti del meeting sulla stratigrafia del Baiociana. *Memoria descrittiva Carta Geologica d'Italia* **40**, 23–48.

—— & DIETL, G. 1989. Age of the Garantiana Clay (Middle Jurassic) in the Hebrides Basin. *Scottish Journal of Geology*, **25**, 153–159.

——, SMITH, R. M., GOLDEN, M. & JAMES, A. V. 1987. Comparative stratigraphic study of Triassic-Jurassic sedimentation and basin evolution in the northern North Sea and north-west of the British Isles. *In*: BROOKS, J. & GLENNIE, K. (eds) *Petroleum Geology of North West Europe*. Graham & Trotman, London, 697–709.

OATES, M. J. 1978. A revised stratigraphy for the western Scottish Lower Lias. *Proceedings of the Yorkshire Geological Society*, **42**, 143–156.

PENN, I. E. & EVANS, C. D. R. 1976. *The Middle Jurassic (mainly Bathonian) of Cardigan Bay and its palaeogeographical significance*. Report Institute Geological Science 76/6.

PETRIE, S. H., BROWN, J. R., GRANGER, P. J. & LOVELL, J. P. B. 1989. Mesozoic history of the Celtic Sea Basins. *In*: TANKARD, A. J. & BALKWILL, H. R. (eds) 1989. *Extensional tectonics and stratigraphy of the North Atlantic margins*. American Association of Petroleum Geologists Memoir, **46**, 433–444.

SMYTHE, D. K. 1989. Rockall Trough — Cretaceous or Late Palaeozoic? *Scottish Journal of Geology*, **25**, 5–43.

STEEL, R. J. 1974. New Red Sandstone floodplain and piedmont sedimentation in the Hebridean Province, Scotland. *Journal of Sedimentary Petrology*, **44**, 336–357.

—— 1977. Triassic rift basins of north-west Scotland — their configuration, infilling and development. *In*: FINSTAD, F. G. & SELLEY, R. C. (eds) *Proceedings Mesozoic Northern North Sea Conference 7*.

—— & WILSON, A. C. 1975. Sedimentation and tectonism (? Permo-Triassic) on the margin of the North Minch Basin, Lewis. *Journal of the Geological Society, London*, **131**, 183–202.

STEIN, A. M. 1988. Basement controls upon basin development in the Caledonian foreland, NW Scotland. *Basin Research*, **1**, 107–119.

—— & BLUNDELL, D. J. 1990. Geological inheritance and crustal dynamics of the northwest Scottish continental shelf. *Tectonophysics*, **173**, 455–467.

SYKES, R. M. 1975. The stratigraphy of the Callovian and Oxfordian stages (Middle — Upper Jurassic) in northern Scotland. *Scottish Journal of Geology*, **11**, 51–78.

TANKARD, A. J. & BALKWILL, H. R. (eds) 1989. *Extensional Tectonics and Stratigraphy of the North Atlantic Margins*. American Association of Petroleum Geologists Memoir, **46**.

TATE, M. P. & DOBSON, M. R. 1989. Late Permian to early Mesozoic rifting and sedimentation offshore NW Ireland. *Marine and Petroleum Geology*, **6**, 49–59.

TRUEBLOOD, S. & MORTON, N. 1991. Comparative sequence stratigraphy and structural styles of the Slyne Trough and Hebrides Basin. *Journal of the Geological Society, London*, **148**, 197–201.

WERNICKE, B. 1981. Low-angle normal faults in the Basin and Range province: nappe tectonics in an extending orogen. *Nature*, **291**, 645–647.

—— 1985. Uniform-sense normal simple shear of the continental lithosphere. *Canadian Journal of Earth Science*, **22**, 108–125.

WOODLAND, A. W. (ed.) 1971. *The Llanbedr (Mochras Farm) Borehole*. Report of the Institute of Geological Sciences 71/18.

ZIEGLER, P. A. 1990. *Geological Atlas of Western and Central Europe*. 2nd edition. Shell Internationale Petroleum Maatschappij.

The Hebridean basins and adjacent areas

Petrography and diagenesis of the Permo-Triassic of Scotland

PATRICK J. McKEEVER

Department of Geology, The University, Manchester M13 9PL, UK

Abstract: Sediments considered to be of Permian or Permo-Triassic age are exposed in many areas of Scotland and within several offshore basins. These sediments were deposited within fault-bounded, intermontane basins and represent a variety of continental facies typical of arid or semi-arid areas. A major study of the diagenetic evolution of the Scottish Permo-Triassic reveals that the basins were isochemical and experienced similar patterns of diagenesis, largely controlled by the climatic aridity of the depositional environment. Depositional pore-waters in the Permo-Triassic sediments of Scotland were well oxygenated and alkaline in nature, allowing the rapid alteration of the unstable mineral assemblage. Ionic complexes released as a result of this alteration were precipitated as a suite of eodiagenetic minerals with oxygen isotope analysis on the authigenic K-feldspar phase confirming an origin from meteoric waters in an arid climate. These eodiagenetic modifications resulted in a major loss of primary porosity. Further burial resulted in minor pressure solution while further depth-related changes have been identified in the authigenic clay mineral suite. Telodiagenetic precipitation of kaolinite and minor quartz was associated with a moderate development of secondary porosity. The hydrocarbon reservoir potential of the Scottish Permo-Triassic is low, primarily due to the early destruction of porosity.

Rocks considered to be of Permian or Permo-Triassic age are exposed in many areas of the Scottish mainland and on several offshore islands. During the 1970s a series of geophysical and geomagnetic surveys, coupled with shallow offshore coring, revealed a series of offshore basins with often considerable thicknesses of Mesozoic and Permian sediments (Figs 1a, 1b). Several important works on the sedimentology of the Scottish Permian have appeared in recent years, notably those by Steel (1971, 1974*a*, *b*, 1977) on the rocks of the west coast, Brookfield (1977, 1978, 1979, 1980) on the basins of Dumfries & Galloway, and Clemmensen (1987) on the deposits at Hopeman. Although the present study is primarily concerned with those sediments of Permian age, those of uncertain Permo-Triassic age have been included. Those deposits which have conclusively been shown to be of Triassic age are not included, e.g. the rocks around Annan and Canonbie, Dumfries & Galloway and the Lossiemouth and Burghead Sandstones of Grampian. The above works were primarily concerned with depositional environments, with little attention paid to the subsequent diagenesis of the sediments.

Methodology

Sampling was concentrated on the larger areas of onshore exposure, i.e. those of Dumfries & Galloway and Grampian, although all of the

facies described by Clemmensen & Abrahamsen (1983) from Arran and by Steel (1974*a*, 1977) for the west coast were also sampled. In addition, the British Geological Survey (BGS) at Edinburgh allowed access to samples from 44 shallow boreholes that penetrated supposed Permo-Triassic sediments in the offshore areas, although only very limited access to onshore borehole samples was obtained. The distribution of these samples is shown in Fig. 1*c*. Microscope thin sections were impregnated before sectioning with blue-dyed Araldite to aid in the identification of porosity and samples were also examined using a JEOL 35CF scanning electron microscope under an accelerating voltage of 10−15 kV. They were then investigated by energy dispersive X-ray analysis using a JEOL 733 superprobe under an accelerating voltage of 15 kV and an electron beam typically 10 μm in diameter. For more precise identification of clay minerals, the samples were analysed by X-ray diffraction and a total of 96 thin sections were point-counted for rock classification; these represented a good selection of the various facies represented in the Permo-Triassic of Scotland. In addition, several samples have been examined under SEM cathodoluminescence at Manchester University and samples of authigenic K-feldspar from the Thornhill Basin of Dumfries & Galloway were analysed for their oxygen isotope values at the Scottish Universities Research and Reactor Centre, East Kilbride (Appendix).

From PARNELL, J. (ed.), 1992, *Basins on the Atlantic Seaboard: Petroleum Geology, Sedimentology and Basin Evolution*. Geological Society Special Publication No 62, pp 71−96.

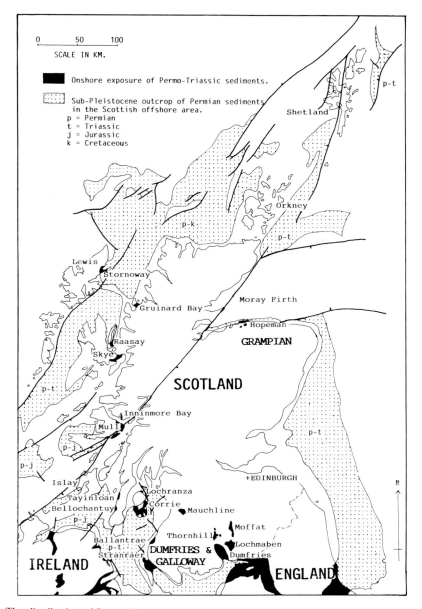

Fig. 1.(a) The distribution of Permo-Triassic sediments in Scotland and the adjacent offshore areas.

Pre-diagenetic controls

Sedimentological framework

Permian or Permo-Triassic sediments in Scotland were deposited within fault-bounded, inter-montane basins and represent a variety of continental facies typical of arid or semi-arid areas. The onshore deposits are mostly minor and include aeolian dune and minor sheetflood deposits at Hopeman (Clemmensen 1987), aeolian dune and alluvial fan deposits in Dumfries & Galloway (Brookfield 1978) and alluvial fan, floodplain and palaeosol deposits along the west coast (Steel 1971, 1974a, 1977). The distribution of the main Permo-Triassic

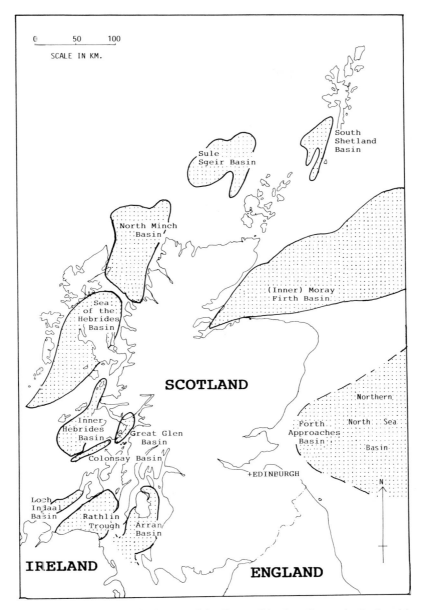

Fig. 1.(b) The distribution of offshore basins containing Permo-Triassic sediments in the Scottish area.

basins off the west coast is controlled by a number of NE—SW and NNE—SSW fault systems, including the Minch, Skerryvore, and Great Glen Faults. Typically, alluvial fan deposits drape the basin margins, the fans having been built by debris from local drainage areas, and they interfinger distally with floodplain sandstone deposits (Steel 1974a). The presence of cornstones suggests that the climate was semi-arid and that the sedimentary processes were ephemeral. Along the western boundary faults of these basins successive phases of rapid subsidence led to repeated alluvial wedge progradation. This contrasts with the more gently warped or only mildly-faulted eastern margins, where the main sedimentary response was of

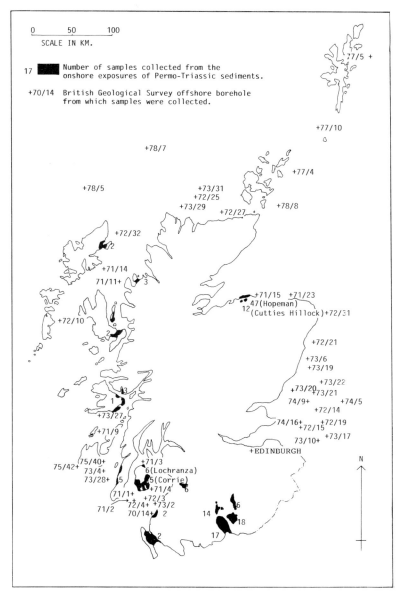

Fig. 1.(c) The distribution of samples of Permo-Triassic sediments in Scotland collected as part of the present study.

hinterland scarp retreat and a maturing of the geomorphic surface. This difference between the western and eastern margins can be understood in terms of the more rapid faulting and subsidence along the western boundary faults. Nearly 4000 m of thick fanglomerates are found along the western margin of the North Minch Basin, contrasting with only 100 m of sediment on the eastern boundary of the Sea of the Hebrides Basin. Geophysical evidence also suggests at least 1600 m of Permian sediment in the Dumfries Basin, consisting of a synclinal depression centered near the western boundary faults (Craig 1965). A full review of the sedimentological framework of the Scottish Permian is in McKeever (1990).

Detrital mineralogy

The detrital mineralogy of the Scottish Permo-Triassic sediments was strongly influenced by the local basement lithology, with individual basins being floored by material ranging from Lewisian gneiss in the North Minch Basin at Stornoway to the Westphalian D coal measures at Mauchline. Monocrystalline quartz is the predominant detrital component of the sandstones, commonly accounting for 50–60% of the whole rock and typically showing weak to strong extinction with cathodoluminescence microscopy of samples from the Thornhill Basin showing dull grey and grey-brown emission colours suggestive of a derivation from a mixed igneous–metamorphic terrain (Cowan 1989). Feldspar is the other main detrital component of these sediments and may account for over 10% of the total rock volume. The dominant feldspar is potassian, mostly orthoclase, with microcline and plagioclase being noticeably subordinate. In general, mica is a relatively minor component of these rocks and is only really abundant in the siltstones and mudrocks of the Inner Moray Firth, North Minch and Forth Approaches Basins.

Lithic fragments may constitute as much as 80% of the rock volume in some of the breccias, although amongst breccia matrices and sandstones they usually amount to 5% of the rock volume. Typically the feldspars and lithic fragments are replaced by clay or are leached to varying degrees, yielding some grain dissolution porosity. Such features are important when considering the origin of the authigenic mineral suite now found in these sediments. Opaque and heavy minerals only account for less than 2% of the total rock volume and include rutile, pyrite and zircon. Concentrations of manganese, titanium, iron, and nickel in some of the sediments strongly suggest the former presence of ferromagnesian grains that have now been totally dissolved (Burley 1984). Grain dissolution porosity typically accounts for 5–10% of the total rock volume.

The sandstones and breccia matrices are generally moderately to well sorted. This is especially obvious amongst the aeolian sandstones of southern Scotland and the Hopeman area where the rocks typically show excellent sorting within individual laminae and are usually fine to-medium grained. In several samples of sandstone from across Scotland a bimodal grain size distribution may be apparent while among the breccias there is obviously a much more varied grain size range. All the samples in this study are arenites (Pettijohn et al. 1972), most being quartz arenites (especially in the case of the Hopeman Sandstone) or subarkosic arenites. Sublithic or lithic arenites were only recorded from the breccia matrices of southern Scotland (as well as a single sample from the Cutties Hillock Sandstone). No examples of arkosic arenites were found.

Burial histories

Three main events during the burial histories of the Permo-Triassic basins of Scotland were important from a diagenetic viewpoint. The early Cimmerian Phase (Ziegler 1982) at the Triassic–Jurassic boundary resulted in a change to marine sediment deposition, while the middle Cimmerian Phase at the Lower–Middle Jurassic transition caused a break in deposition in the North Sea region, although marine deposition continued over the western area, albeit at a reduced rate. During the late Cimmerian Phase, in the latest Jurassic, rapid uplift of the Scottish region was followed by a return to marine conditions during the Upper Cretaceous characterized by deposition of the Chalk. Although the present stratigraphy of many of the offshore basins is not well known, it is possible to arrive at some idea of maximum burial depths and approximate stratigraphic columns, and burial history curves for specific areas may be compiled. The burial histories of the Sea of the Hebrides and Inner Moray Firth Basins are good representatives of the histories of basins from the western and eastern sides of Scotland respectively (Figs 2a & b). If we assume a geothermal gradient of 30°C km^{-1} (Burley 1984), then the maximum palaeotemperatures may have exceeded 120°C in the deeper parts of the basins by late Jurassic times when at least 4000 m of sediment would have accumulated. It should be remembered that given the asymmetric fill of many of these basins, burial depth maxima would have varied from very shallow (less than 1 km) in extreme cases at the passive basin margins to deep (over 3 km) at basin centres or active basin margins.

The burial history curves for the onshore basins of Dumfries & Galloway are probably similar to those of the western basins as exemplified by the Sea of the Hebrides Basin and considering that in the Dumfries Basin alone at least 1600 m of Permian sediment accumulated (Craig 1965), it is possible that they too became moderately to deeply buried by late Jurassic times and experienced palaeotemperatures in excess of 100°C at that time.

Despite the great variety of basement material the diagenetic sequences that are encoun-

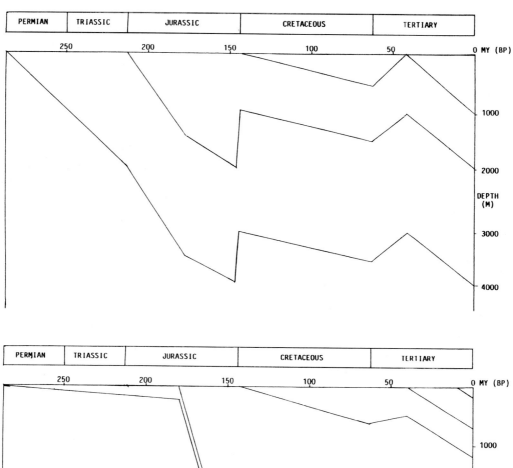

Fig. 2. (a) Burial history curve for the Sea of the Hebrides Basin. (b) Burial history curve for the Inner Moray Firth Basin.

tered amongst the Permo-Triassic sediments are generally quite similar. The same range of authigenic minerals may be found across the whole Scottish region with notable variations only in the degree of carbonate cementation and authigenic clay mineralogy. The timing of the formation of these authigenic phases was also generally similar, allowing subdivision of the diagenetic regime into three phases: the eodiagenetic, the mesodiagenetic and the telodiagenetic phases (Schmidt & McDonald 1979a). A generalized paragenetic sequence for the Scottish Permo-Triassic is illustrated in Fig. 3.

Considering that the Permo-Triassic sediments of Scotland were deposited in small, developing extensional basins where pore water circulation was largely internal it may be expected that many of the diagenetic alterations that occurred were primarily as a result of internal changes in pore water thermochemical conditions. The 'basement' rock would have been important as a source of the detrital grains; the unstable silicates whose alteration initiated diagenetic processes within these basins. Given the lack of evidence, migrating pore fluids from outside the basins are believed to have played only a minor role. The aridity of the Permian climate was important as it meant that very little chemical weathering would have occurred in the source areas of the sediments. In many areas, the source rocks were igneous or metasedimentary and an important source of ionic complexes existed in the form of unstable silicate minerals. As basinal deposition was largely continuous, although slow, the climatic aridity would mean that little surface weathering of these deposits occurred before they were buried.

Changes in the amounts and types of these detrital minerals are the driving force behind the variations in the diagenetic patterns recorded from these basins.

Eodiagenesis

Clay infiltration

During eodiagenesis, changes in the diagenetic environment are largely due to the chemistry of the depositional environment. More specifically they are influenced by the surface interstitial pore-water $Eh-pH$ conditions and the activity of dissolved ionic species. One of the first changes in the Permo-Triassic sediments of Scotland after deposition was the mechanical infiltration of clay, introduced as influent meteoric water migrated into the sediment (Walker 1976). Clay-rich laminae occur in some areas such as Dumfries and Lochmaben and are often associated with raindrop impressions and suncracked surfaces, suggesting a more intense period of rainfall or surface runoff. Although some minor infiltrated smectite was recorded from Inninmore Bay in the Great Glen Basin, most of the infiltrated clay is illite or a poorly ordered mixed-layer illite-smectite, with chlorite being common as an infiltrated clay in the Thornhill and Arran Basins. These clay coats

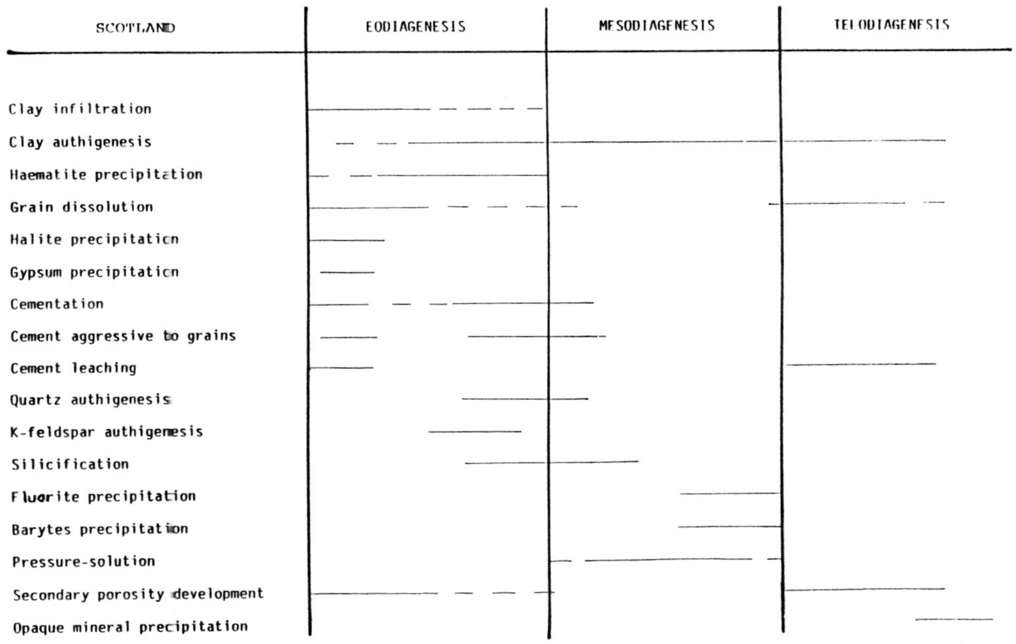

SCOTLAND	EODIAGENESIS	MESODIAGENESIS	TELODIAGENESIS
Clay infiltration			
Clay authigenesis			
Haematite precipitation			
Grain dissolution			
Halite precipitation			
Gypsum precipitation			
Cementation			
Cement aggressive to grains			
Cement leaching			
Quartz authigenesis			
K-feldspar authigenesis			
Silicification			
Fluorite precipitation			
Barytes precipitation			
Pressure-solution			
Secondary porosity development			
Opaque mineral precipitation			

Fig. 3. A paragenetic sequence for the Permo-Triassic sediments of Scotland.

would have been, more or less, continuously bathed by porewater which intermittently would have been replenished by renewed infiltration and which, given the climatic aridity, would have been well oxygenated and alkaline in nature (Walker 1976).

Haematite authigenesis

The unstable interstitial mineral assemblage would not have been in equilibrium with these surficial conditions and would soon have began to alter. Their dissolution released into the interstitial pore waters hydrated ions and other ionic complexes such as K^+, Na^+, OH^-, Ca^{2+}, Al^{3+}, Al^{4+} and Si^{4+}. More importantly, Fe^{2+} and Mg^{2+} were released in large quantities. Iron released by interstitial hydrolysis may remain in solution as ferrous iron (Fe^{2+}) or, if the Eh and pH of the water lie in the stability field of the ferric oxide Fe_2O_3, it may precipitate out as haematite or as a precursor oxide that will ultimately age to haematite. Such sediments will tend to redden with age. The Scottish Permo-Triassic is notably red in colour and given the dilute, alkaline, well oxygenated conditions of the early pore water it is not surprising that haematite is commonly recorded from these sediments. As already discussed, it precipitated on, or stained, the early infiltrated clay and in several cases whole grains were replaced by iron-stained clay. However in the Hopeman Sandstone haematite is rare and the sandstone is typically white or yellow in colour. This may suggest that although haematite may originally have formed, later during diagenesis the pH of the water was reduced and the haematite resorbed. Glennie & Buller (1983) suggest that such sediments may actually never have been reddened, with the original pore water not being suited to oxidation. However, considering the otherwise similar eodiagenetic sequence in the Hopeman Sandstone to those of other areas, including the development of a pedogenic carbonate cement, a low pH for early waters in the Hopeman Sandstone is unlikely.

Clay authigenesis

Some of the remaining ions released by this framework grain dissolution appear to have precipitated as a pore-lining authigenic clay which, in Scotland, appears to have varied from area to area. Smectite was the main early authigenic clay from Mauchline, the North Minch Basin and the Dumfries Basin, whereas chlorite precipitated out in the Thornhill, Arran and Stranraer Basins. Two morphologies of smectite

were recognized. Firstly, a cellular or boxwork structure where individual boxwork structures are usually only $4-8$ μm across (Fig. 4a). Secondly, in the Dumfries Basin, the clay is developed as a crinkly coating on the host grain with individual clay flakes about 10 μm across, and often occurring as small, thin booklets $1-5$ μm thick (Fig. 4b). Structurally, two varieties of chlorite were identified: a pure chlorite and a mixed-layer swelling chlorite. These two varieties display four individual morphological growth habits (as originally described by Wilson & Pittman 1977): stacked plates, cellular or honeycombe, rosettes and cabbagehead (Figs 4c, 4d, 4e & 4f).

However, illite—smectite is the most widely recorded early authigenic clay from the Scottish Permian and is especially common in the Dumfries and Lochmaben Basins. XRD analysis usually reveals the presence of discrete illite and smectite components, with these assemblages apparently consisting of later, authigenic illite growing as small, fibrous projections off a smectite framework. Only rarely was a true, well ordered mixed-layer clay diffraction trace observed. As far as these variations in clay chemistry are concerned it is worth noting that clays which replace basic, apparently ferromagnesian, grains exhibit a chemistry which approaches either chloritic or smectitic compositions (Burley 1984). Both the Mauchline and Thornhill Basins contain olivine-basalt lava flows while the Permian sediments of the Arran Basin are underlain, at least partially, by basalt lavas of Carboniferous and Upper Old Red Sandstone age. In addition, at Ballantrae, on the eastern periphery of the Arran Basin, the Ballantrae Igneous Complex contains several varieties of ultrabasic rocks such as picrite, pyroxenite and serpentenite (Greig 1971). Elsewhere, a poorly ordered illite—smectite was the original eodiagenetic clay but later during the diagenetic evolution of these basins, as more Al^{3+} and K^+ was released into the pore water, some of the more unstable expandable clay layers were actually replaced by illite which began to grow as a separate authigenic phase.

Grain dissolution

The precipitation of both haematite and early authigenic clays required the presence of suitable ionic complexes. These could have been introduced from outside the basins or internally by unstable grain dissolution. Evidence of such dissolution is widespread across the whole area. Very rarely were ferromagnesian minerals seen in these sediments, implying that they were

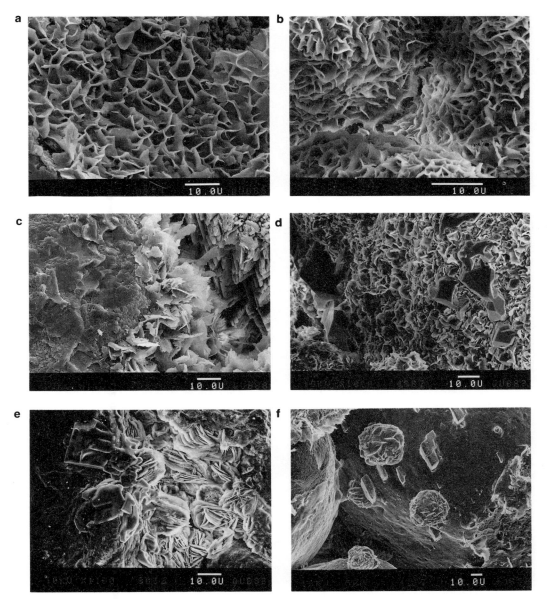

Fig. 4. SEM photomicrographs of samples from the Permo-Triassic of Scotland. (a) Authigenic smectite from the Dumfries Basin displaying a well developed boxwork structure. (b) Authigenic smectite from the Dumfries Basin developed as small, thin booklets blocking up porosity. (c) Stacked plates of authigenic chlorite from the Arran Basin. (d) Authigenic chlorite from the Sule Sgeir Basin developed as a cellular network of individual plates. (e) Rounded clusters of authigenic chlorite from the Arran Basin blocking up porosity and associated with halite. (f) Authigenic chlorite from the Arran Basin developed as rare cabbagehead-like structures.

quickly leached and/or replaced by clay, although thin pellicles of clay in these sediments may represent the compressed remnants of these grains. Partially leached grains, in various stages of dissolution, are conspicuous (Fig. 5a) with leached plagioclase being the most commonly observed. The more stable authigenic (or detrital) clay coats may remain or may eventually

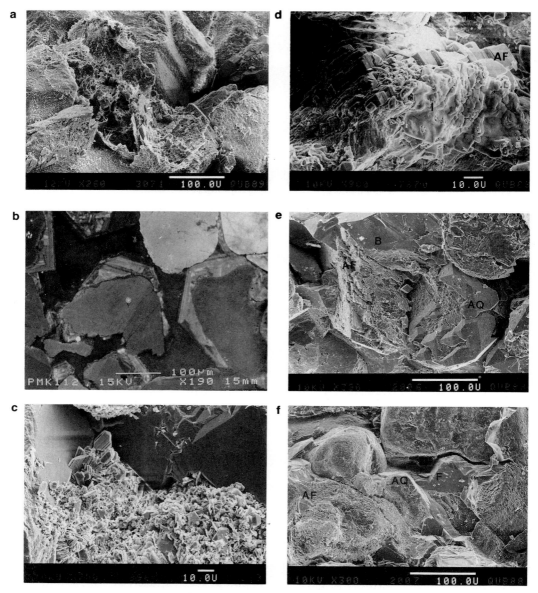

Fig. 5. SEM photomicrographs of samples from the Permo-Triassic of Scotland. (a) Authigenic illite growing off a partially leached feldspar grain from the Lochmaben Basin. (b) Zoned quartz overgrowths from the Dumfries basin as revealed under SEM-CL. (c) Extensive development of authigenic kaolinite partly engulfed by a later development of authigenic quartz from the Inner Hebrides Basin. (d) Detrital and authigenic K-feldspar (AF) partially coated by remobilised authigenic halite (H) from the Rathlin Trough. (e) A development of authigenic barytes (B) coating earlier-formed authigenic quartz (AQ) and K-feldspar (AF) from the Inner Moray Firth Basin. (f) Fluorite cement (F) coating earlier formed authigenic quartz (AQ) and K-feldspar (AF) from the Inner Moray Firth Basin.

collapse to form the thin clay pellicles. Although unstable grains were also replaced by clays, grain leaching was a much more important process in the Scottish Permo-Triassic and this is important as it provides a potentially greater source of ionic enrichment to the circulating pore waters. As these grains dissolved a greater volume of pore space became available, not only for water movement but also for the precipitation of further authigenic phases.

Cementation

Following grain dissolution and haematite and early clay authigenesis, large quantities of ionic complexes would still have been present in the early pore waters. As the activity of K^+ increased small, incipient overgrowths of K-feldspar were precipitated on detrital feldspar surfaces. Authigenic K-feldspar is very common in the Scottish Permo-Triassic although it does appear to be largely absent from the Inner Hebrides, Colonsay, Loch Indaal and South Shetland Basins. It occurs as overgrowths on detrital feldspar or feldspathic grains or as small, but individual, authigenic crystals which are pore-filling and usually display the adularia habit with quantitative electron probe analysis indicating a very good degree of uniformity in the composition of the overgrowths (McKeever 1990).

Similarly as the activity of Si^{4+} increased and the pore water became supersaturated with respect to quartz, small, incipient euhedral quartz overgrowths developed. Authigenic quartz is widespread in the Permo-Triassic of Scotland and is especially common in some samples of the Hopeman Sandstone (Inner Moray Firth Basin) where it may account for over 7% of the total rock volume in the form of syntaxial overgrowths. The authigenic quartz is generally pure silica, although minor amounts of some other elements including aluminium are commonly recorded. Textural relationships clearly show that initial feldspar authigenesis preceded that of quartz in all areas, with further growth of the two mineral phases continuing simultaneously. It is at this point that an early carbonate cement is believed to have been introduced in several areas, stunting development of feldspar and quartz overgrowths. Although calcite is very rare among the basins of southern Scotland and the Forth Approaches, it is common among the sediments along the western seaboard. The calcite is typically a coarse, poikilotopic sparite and in several cases causes total induration of the rock (Fig. 5a). The calcite not only fills interstitial pores and voids formed by the dis-

solution of unstable framework silicates but was also often aggressive to other pre-existing phases, both detrital and authigenic (Fig. 6b). The displacive manner in which some of this calcite developed is best illustrated in samples from the North Minch Basin where, in some instances, most mica flakes have been expanded apart by the displacive growth of calcite after nucleation on the mica cleavage planes (Fig. 6c). Dolomite is common in the Forth Approaches Basin and in some of the basins of southern Scotland (both onshore and offshore) and it too is non-ferroan and occurs in the form of a medium to coarse spar which is commonly poikilotopic. Again the dolomite may be replacive/displacive. Besides the stunting of early K-feldspar and quartz overgrowths, other indicators of an early or eodiagenetic origin for this cement include the limited extent of pressure solution in the sediment, indicating that very little compaction had occurred before cementation. Further, the calcite and dolomite are invariably non-ferroan in nature and a non-ferroan carbonate is generally taken as an indicator of early cementation. But could this carbonate have precipitated from a pore fluid that became supersaturated with Ca^{2+}, Mg^{2+} and CO_3^{2-} simply as a result of detrital grain dissolution? Probably it did not, and the widespread development of calcretes probably acted as a source for most of the carbonate cement.

Calcretes are widespread along the western seaboard (Steel 1974b), while calcareous concretions are found in the Hopeman Sandstone. Naylor et al. (1989) have suggested that these concretions too are pedogenic in origin. Similar, though smaller, accumulations on Arran are also likely to be of pedogenic origin. Naylor et al. (1989) analysed the Hopeman concretions and some of the calcretes from the Permo-Triassic of the Isle of Mull (Great Glen Basin) for their carbon and oxygen isotopic compositions and recorded values within the reported range for Recent calcretes, thus supporting a pedogenic origin. Given this widespread development of pedogenic carbonate it would appear to be a reasonable assumption that it was dissolution of this pedogenic carbonate that acted as the major source for the early carbonate cements seen in these sediments. There is no evidence that an external source was involved, lending further support to the isochemical basin model. Amongst the basins of Dumfries & Galloway, where pedogenic deposits have not been recorded, carbonate cementation is rare.

Where carbonate cementation did occur, porosity, both primary and secondary, was drastically reduced and often eliminated. The increase

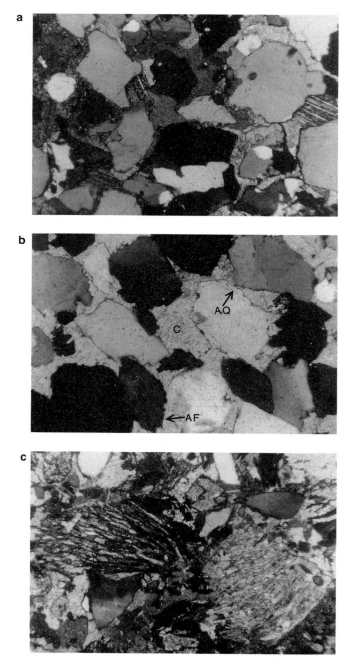

Fig. 6. Thin-section photomicrograph of **(a)** non-ferroan poikilotopic calcite cement from the Inner Moray Firth Basin, **(b)** calcite cement (C) aggressive to both authigenic and detital quartz (AQ) and feldspar (AF) grains from the Inner Moray Firth basin, and **(c)** exploded micas due to displacive calcite from the North Minch Basin. All views are under crossed polarized light with a field of view of 3 mm.

in pH that would have been associated with calcite precipitation meant that quartz (i.e. SiO_2) became unstable and began to dissolve. There is extensive evidence of quartz, and feldspar, grains with corroded edges, encased by carbonate and the etching patterns on quartz surfaces often display approximately V-shaped pits, demonstrably caused by the carbonate. In areas where carbonate cementation did not occur the eodiagenetic development of syntaxial overgrowths of quartz and feldspar continued. In some areas, such as parts of the Hopeman Sandstone uncemented by calcite, authigenic quartz itself became a major cementing mineral, and in other areas such as Dumfries & Galloway it is a locally important pore-reducing mineral. The quartz occurs mostly in the form of well developed, but usually separate, overgrowths with initial nucleation occurring randomly, but subsequent growth being concentrated on pre-existing faces. This would suggest a low degree of ionic supersaturation of the pore water with respect to silica. Authigenic feldspar is also locally important as a pore-reducing mineral, and although feldspar authigenesis is believed to be entirely eodiagenetic, quartz authigenesis was also, at least partially, a mesodiagenetic process. As porosity was reduced and the depth of burial increased the sediment would have become increasingly isolated from the influent meteoric waters that were the driving force behind the eodiagenetic modifications. Chemical reactions that owed their origin to burial-related processes would have become predominant.

Mesodiagenesis

Pressure solution

Mesodiagenesis affected the Permo-Triassic sediments of Scotland in several ways. A distinct zonation in quartz overgrowths may be seen under SEM-Cathodoluminescence (Fig. 5b). It is possible that the source of the Si^{4+} for the overgrowths may initially have come from the dissolution of unstable silicates but later, during mesodiagenesis, came from pressure solution. Although pressure solution rarely led to a major reduction in porosity, in some of the basins in Dumfries & Galloway rather spectacular pressure solution seams, or stylolites, have developed (Fig. 7a). These stylolites are preferentially developed along infiltrated clay-rich, silty laminae, a feature observed among other deposits (Turner 1980). It may be that the clay helps to increase stress and, therefore, solubility of the

quartz, or it may aid in the diffusion of ionic species away from the areas of high stress. Often 50% or more of coarse grains, complete with earlier formed overgrowth, may have dissolved during pressure solution. The released ions were then free to circulate throughout the sediment with the pore water provided that the sediment was part of an isochemical (i.e. closed) system.

Illite authigenesis

At the higher temperatures experienced during mesodiagenesis the solubility of many mineral phases rises so that pore fluids are capable of dissolving more ionic species, reaction rates increase and reaction barriers are more easily overcome (Burley et al. 1985). The most widely documented example of such temperature-related reactions are the clay mineral transformations that occur as burial depth increases. In the Permo-Triassic of Scotland illite is the common clay mineral phase that developed as a result of these mesodiagenetic processes. It can be seen not only growing off smectite but also off chlorite and, most importantly, it appears to actually replace some of the more unstable, expandable layers in the eodiagenetic mixed-layer clay, illite−smectite. Two main morphological varieties are seen: a platy (or boxwork) illite and a fibrous (or hairy) illite (Macchi 1987). Several of the illite samples show a pronounced asymmetry to the 10A reflectance which sharpens and is removed upon glycolation, indicating that there is an expandable component interlaying with the 2M illite fraction (Cowan 1989). Illite crystallinity in the Scottish Permo-Triassic is quite variable, though mostly poor, ranging from a very poorly crystalline sample from Locharbriggs in the Dumfries Basin to a highly crystalline illite from Gruinard Bay in the North Minch Basin.

The depth/temperature conversion of a precursor clay to illite (often via a mixed-layer intermediary) has been widely reported in matrix-rich sandstones undergoing shale-type diagenesis (Burley et al. 1985). But for originally clay-poor sediments such as those under discussion, this model implicitly requires the precursor clay to be an early, neoformed clay such as mixed layer illite−smectite (Macchi 1987). These reactions not only require a precursor clay but also a K-rich solution or mineral, e.g.

$$Al[Si_8O_{20}](OH)_4.nH_2O + KAlSi_3O_8 \rightarrow \quad (1)$$
$$KAl_4[Si_7AlO_{20}](OH)_4 + 4SiO_2 + nH_2O$$

i.e. pyrophyllite + K-feldspar → illite + silica + water

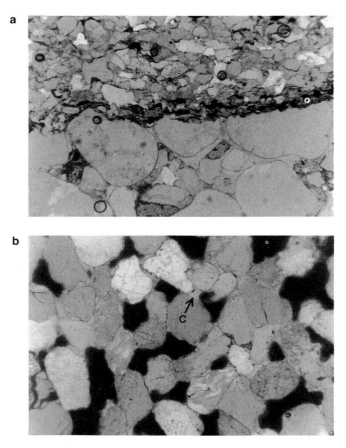

Fig. 7. Thin-section photomicrograph of (**a**) a well developed pressure solution seam from the Lochmaben Basin, and (**b**) a largely leached calcite cement (c) which has left behind secondary, cement dissolution, porosity from the Inner Moray Firth Basin. Both views are under obliquely polarised light with a field of view of 3 mm.

By substituting smectite for pyrophyllite there is a limited substitution of Mg^{2+} and Fe^{2+} for Al^{3+} in the octahedral sheets and of Al^{3+} for Si^{4+} in the tetrahedral sheets with the excess negative charge compensated by Na^+ and Ca^{2+} in the interlayer sites (Macchi 1987). The necessity of a detrital source of K^+ for the above reaction must mean that part of the detrital K-feldspar content of the sediments would be replaced or dissolved. There is evidence across the whole area of such leaching, not only of detrital feldspar but also of authigenic K-feldspar, indicating a mesodiagenetic alteration, and these grains are often associated with a development of authigenic fibrous illite (Fig. 5a). No external source need be invoked for the potassium. Glennie *et al.* (1978) have suggested that acidic pore fluids might be responsible for such leaching: the usual mechanism for produc-

ing acidic pore waters at depth is the thermal decarboxylation of kerogen in mudrocks. However, the Permo-Triassic sediments of Scotland have only limited associated mudrock sequences and they are devoid of organic matter capable of undergoing such decarboxylation. Acidic solutions generated in underlying, organic-rich sediments, such as the Coal Measures at Mauchline or on Arran, may be invoked as a source, although this would imply that the Permian basins were allochemical, whereas they have been demonstrated to have been largely isochemical. Finally, acidic solutions would have generated a widespread development of secondary porosity as carbonate cement were leached. The presence of (often) extensive poikilotopic, eodiagenetic carbonate which shows no sign of dissolution would appear to preclude the presence of widespread, pervasive acidic solutions.

No evidence of aggressive external fluids has been found. A direct, neoformed origin for the mesodiagenetic illite is more likely. Such a reaction proceeds via solutes derived from K-feldspar dissolution where the following expression may be applicable:

$$KAlSi_3O_8 + 8H_2O \rightarrow$$
$$K^+ Al(OH)_4^- + 3Si(OH)_4 \quad (2)$$

$$K^+ + 7Si(OH)_4 + 5Al(OH)^{-4} \rightarrow$$
$$KAl_4[S_{.7}AlO_{20}](OH)_4 + 4OH^- \quad (3)$$
$$+ 20H_2O.$$

The hydroxyl ions produced will cause the pore fluid solution to become more alkaline (Macchi 1987). It is clear that illite formed in this way used either the early authigenic clays or the partially leached K-feldspar as sites upon which nucleation occurred. The leaching of K-feldspar was at least partially mesodiagenetic, so a source of K^+, Al^{3+} and Si^{4+} ions was available for a direct neoformed precipitation of illite by this hypothesis. This direct precipitation of illite is believed to have occurred while these sediments were most deeply buried. This is likely to have occurred just prior to the late Cimmerian Earth Movements of latest Jurassic age. Although burial has continued in the deeper parts of some of the basins up to the present day, erosion since early Cretaceous times has exposed significant regions of the Permo-Triassic, re-introducing meteoric water into these sediments.

Telodiagenesis

Cement leaching

The Permo-Triassic sediments of Scotland were first uplifted during the early Cretaceous and since then these rocks have been repeatedly exposed to influent meteoric waters, especially in the shallower basins. Given the present-day climatic conditions and vegetation cover, influent meteoric waters into these sediments would be expected to be slightly acidic in composition and it is therefore not surprising that in many areas the early carbonate cement has been partially leached. The partial dissolution of the carbonate was important in creating secondary porosity (Fig. 7b).

Kaolinite authigenesis

The other important telodiagenetic phase is authigenic kaolinite (and dickite). Kaolinite is common as an authigenic mineral from the basins of Arran, Colonsay and those of Dumfries & Galloway as well as the Rathlin Trough, with minor amounts in parts of the North Minch Basin. Dickite is found as an authigenic mineral only from the Inninmore Bay area of the Great Glen Basin. The kaolinite is typically pore-filling rather than pore-lining and is often partially enclosed by a later phase of authigenic quartz (Fig. 5c). In most cases the kaolinite (and dickite) occurs as pseudo-hexagonal plates stacked face-to-face, giving the mineral a stacked plate or book-like appearance with individual plates up to 15 μm long. A less common growth habit is a vermicular growth where a sequence of pseudohexagonal plates may extend for 100 μm or more. Although Bjorkum & Gjelsvik (1988) demonstrated that authigenic kaolinite and K-feldspar overgrowths may form simultaneously in an isochemical system at temperatures lower than 50°C, it has already been shown that feldspar authigenesis in these sediments was eodiagenetic and kaolinite precipitation occurred after the main authigenic phases were already in place. Bjorlykke et al. (1979), however, also described euhedral quartz overgrowths partly enclosing kaolinite and have shown that an extensive breakdown of feldspar and mica to form kaolinite can occur only in pore water with low K^+/H^+ ratios. This requires large quantities of low-salinity water to pass through the sediments and meteoric water is typically of low salinity. The following reaction may then proceed:

$$2KAlSi_3O_8 + 2H^+ + 9H_2O \rightarrow Al_2Si_2O_5(OH)_4$$
$$\text{K-feldspar} \qquad \qquad \text{Kaolinite}$$
$$+ 2K^+ + 4H_4SiO_4. \quad (4)$$

Quartz precipitation will be aided if, following the reduction in K^+ content, the water remains supersaturated with respect to silica. It is therefore reasonable to associate kaolinite and a further phase of authigenic quartz precipitation in the Permo-Triassic sediments of Scotland with flushing by meteoric waters introduced as a result of uplift and/or exposure.

Regional variations in the patterns of diagenesis

Although the diagenetic cycle outlined above may be used as a generalized summary of the overall pattern of diagenesis from all areas, important regional variations do exist. Authigenic clay mineralogy is variable and has been discussed with reference to the original detrital silicate composition. However, additional cements are also present in several basins and one of the more widespread is halite, occurring as a minor cement in the North Minch, Forth Approaches, Arran and Mauchline Basins and from the Kintyre exposures of the Rathlin Trough. It is also found in samples from BGS offshore core 77/4 in what may be a northerly extension of the Inner Moray Firth Basin. In three areas (the Arran, Forth Approaches and Inner Moray Firth Basins) it is closely associated with authigenic gypsum; both of these minerals are believed to be evaporitic in origin and thus early eodiagenetic. The thick bands of gypsum and anhydrite recorded from the Forth Approaches Basin could only have formed by evaporation of highly saline waters and hopper-crystals of halite identified from the areas above are also considered to indicate an evaporitic environment (Laier & Nielsen 1989). Given that the carbonate cements of the Scottish sediments are considered to be of pedogenic, evaporitic origin, the association of gypsum and halite suggests that they too may belong to the same evaporitic cycle. Halite in modern-day sabkhas from the Middle East is generally redissolved during periods of flushing by meteoric waters and reprecipitated elsewhere (Levy 1977). Evidence from Scotland suggests that a similar redistribution of halite cement occurred and in a good example from Tayinloan, Kintyre, redistributed halite can be seen coating not only a detrital feldspar but also its well formed over-

growth (Fig. 5d). This suggests that halite dissolution and reprecipitation was a late eodiagenetic event. There is good evidence for the leaching of both halite and gypsum, with replacement by authigenic quartz and, rarely, by authigenic feldspar. The modification of the paragenetic sequence associated with these evaporitic deposits is illustrated in Fig. 8. The other main regional variation in diagenesis occurs in the Hopeman Sandstone of the Inner Moray Firth Basin where cementation by fluorite and/or barytes is common. Overgrowths of quartz and feldspar are well developed in this sandstone and there is some evidence of pressure solution prior to fluorite or barytes cementation (Figs 5e & 5f) which is, therefore, considered to have been late mesodiagenetic. Peacock et al. (1968) suggested an earlier, additional phase of fluorite cementation from the foreshore north of Greenbrae Quarry where corroded clastic grains lie in a sparse cement of euhedral, poikilotopic fluorite around which calcite concretions grew. Later shear planes cut these concretions, along which a little fluorite replacement occurred. However the textures revealed by the SEM, together with the isotopic analysis of the calcite, show that no phase of early fluorite cementation occurred and that the later fluorite replaced the calcite and was subsequently aggressive to the clastic grains. The

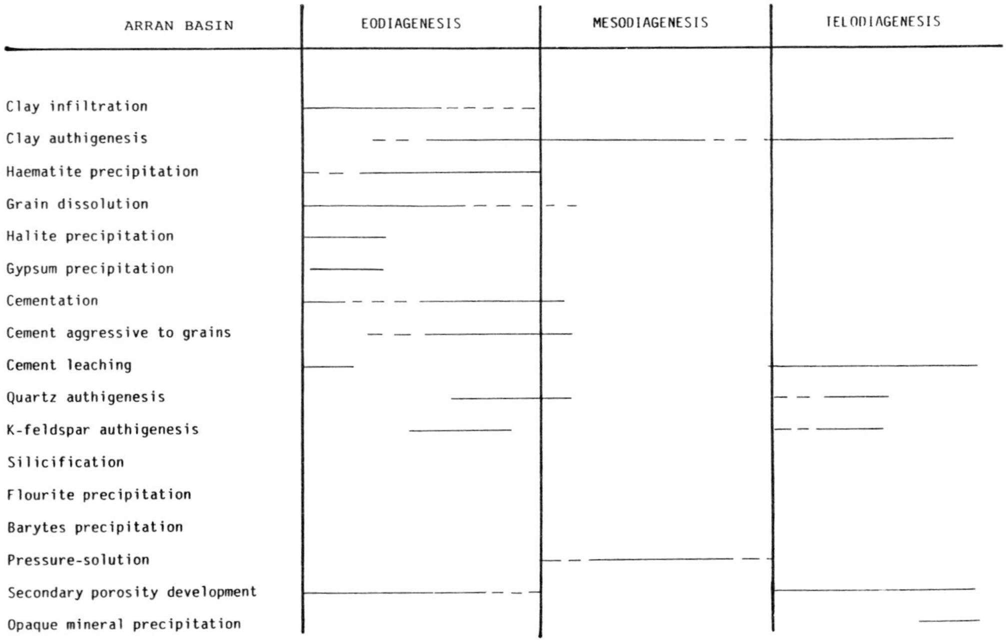

ARRAN BASIN	EODIAGENESIS	MESODIAGENESIS	TELODIAGENESIS
Clay infiltration			
Clay authigenesis			
Haematite precipitation			
Grain dissolution			
Halite precipitation			
Gypsum precipitation			
Cementation			
Cement aggressive to grains			
Cement leaching			
Quartz authigenesis			
K-feldspar authigenesis			
Silicification			
Flourite precipitation			
Barytes precipitation			
Pressure-solution			
Secondary porosity development			
Opaque mineral precipitation			

Fig. 8. A paragenetic sequence for the Arran Basin.

origin of the fluorite and barytes is unclear. Williams (1973) suggested three models by which they could have formed, although he stressed that the actual mode of emplacement may have been a combination of one or more methods. In each instance he advocated the Newer Granites as the obvious source of the mineralization. Naylor (oral pes. 1987) showed that the $\delta^{34}S$ values for the Hopeman barytes were typically $-25\permil$ whereas Zechstein evaporites from elsewhere in the Inner Moray Firth Basin had $\delta^{34}S$ values of $+10\permil$, indicating that a simple evaporitic source for the Hopeman barytes was unlikely. She demonstrated that fluid inclusions tended to be small ($<2~\mu m$) and monophase, suggesting that the barytes precipitated from cool solutions ($50-100°C$). Considering that Hopeman lies on the southern periphery of the Inner Moray Firth Basin, such temperatures may well have existed during late mesodiagenesis. A fault-related model for barytes precipitation was invoked where fluids carrying Ba^{2+} and SO_4^{2-} migrated up faults into suitable traps where simple cooling and mixing of aqueous phases caused precipitation of barytes. This is rather similar to the hydrothermal origin suggested by Williams (1973). He suggested the buried Newer Granites as being the source of the F^- and Ba^{2+} whereas Naylor suggested that the Ba^{2+} was made available after dissolution

of K-feldspar during burial. Although barytes is also quite common as very minor, authigenic inclusions in K-feldspar, not only from Hopeman but from throughout the Permo-Triassic of Scotland, it is unlikely that enough barium could have been made available from feldspar dissolution to account for the Hopeman cement. The amended paragenetic sequence for the Hopeman Sandstone is illustrated in Fig. 9.

Reservoir quality and hydrocarbon potential

Porosity values from the sediments of the Permo-Triassic basins of Scotland are quite variable as might be expected, given the range in depositional environments and the modifications related to the diagenetic evolution of the Permo-Triassic basins. Immediately following deposition, the highest porosity values would have been expected from the clean, well-sorted aeolian sandstones such as those of Dumfries & Galloway where porosity may have reached 25%. In these areas, primary porosity usually accounts for less than half the total porosity now present and quantitatively is usually less than 10%. Initially early and rapid grain dissolution would have enhanced porosity, this increase in porosity being only slightly offset by

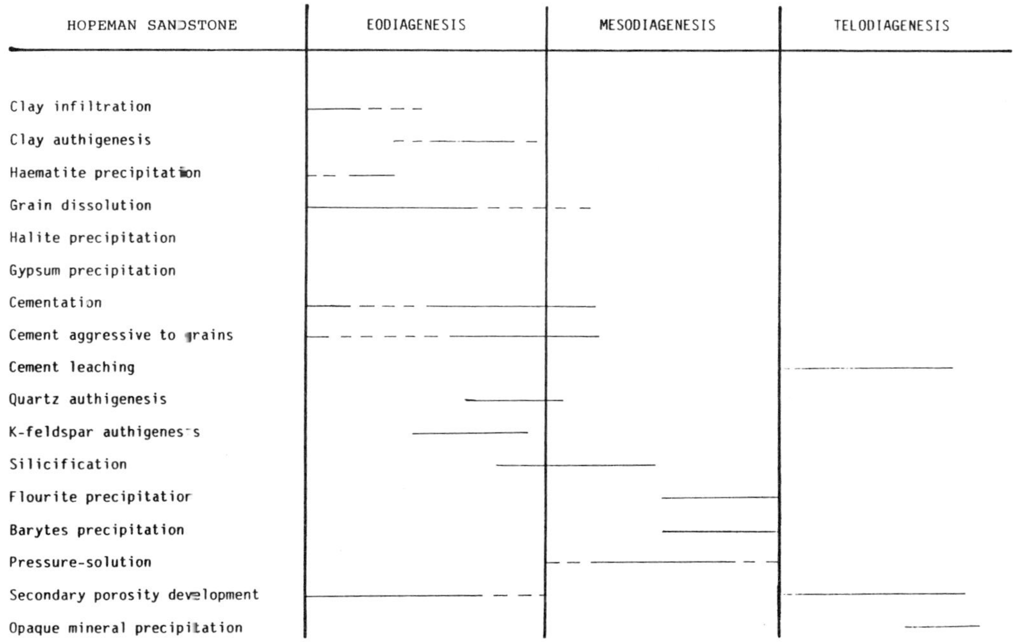

Fig. 9. A paragenetic sequence for the Hopeman Sandstone (Inner Moray Firth Basin).

clay infiltration. Clay infiltration, however, would have had a detrimental effect on permeability, especially during mesodiagenesis when clay-rich laminae acted as nucleation sites for pressure-solution seams.

Where carbonate cementation occurred, porosity values were reduced to near zero. Even in those areas where carbonate cementation was unimportant, such as parts of the basins of Dumfries & Galloway, quartz overgrowth development played a major role in reducing porosity. In the Hopeman Sandstone mesodiagenetic fluorite and barytes cements also further reduced porosity, often completely. The importance of quartz and carbonate cements in reducing porosity in Permo-Triassic sediments from elsewhere in the British Isles was stressed by Bushell (1986) in a study of the Sherwood Sandstone of the Morecambe Bay Gas Field in the northern Irish Sea. Bushell (1986) also stressed the importance of illite in reducing permeability but stated that fibrous illite, which is the important mesodiagenetic illite from Scotland, has a lesser effect on permeability than platy illite. Porosity values in the Scottish Permo-Triassic only began to recover during telodiagenetic leaching of cements, primarily of carbonate. This telodiagenetic development of secondary porosity is important and may, in some instances, represent the only porosity present in the rock. However, in some areas

where the rock is still unaffected by present-day meteoric waters, carbonate cement may still be pervasive and porosity values may still be negligible. Figure 10 illustrates the evolution of porosity in the Scottish Permo-Triassic.

Permo-Triassic sediments from elsewhere in the British Isles are important reservoir rocks for gas, notably in the southern North Sea and in the Morecambe Bay area of the Irish Sea. Although the Scottish sediments include facies similar to those of the proven hydrocarbon-bearing strata, they are unlikely to be important as a source of hydrocarbons. Maximum burial depths probably exceeded 4 km in some basins, such as the North Minch Basin, but there the underlying rock is Lewisian gneiss or Dalradian metasediments (as it is across many of the basins) with little hydrocarbon producing potential (but see Stein, this volume). However among some of the basins of southern Scotland, notably the Arran, Mauchline and Thornhill Basins, the underlying rocks are, at least partially, Coal Measures of Westphalian D age and are potential sources of hydrocarbons. Indeed it is Westphalian sediments that form the source rocks for the gas fields of the southern North Sea and Morecambe Bay (Bushell 1986). Any hydrocarbons would have been generated following the thermal decarboxylation of organic matter which would have taken place at burial depths in excess of 2500 m. Such depths, which

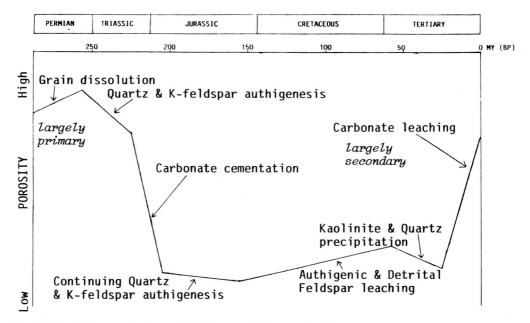

Fig. 10. Evolutionary path of porosity in the Scottish Permo-Triassic.

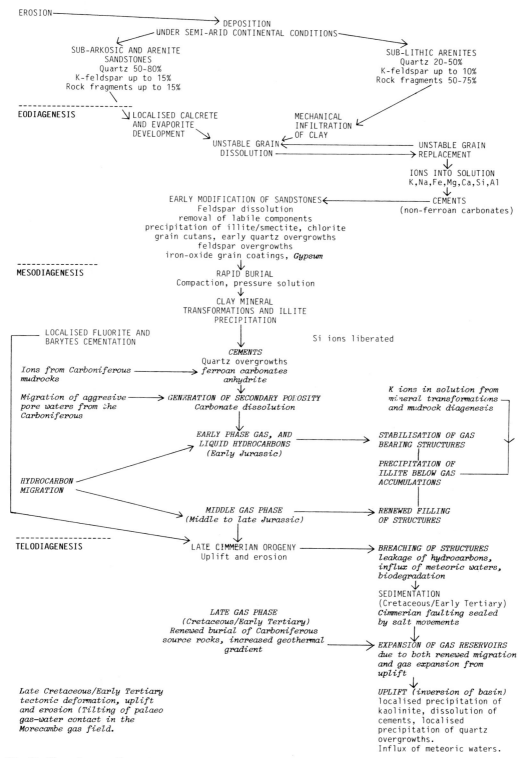

Fig. 11. Flow diagram illustrating the diagenetic evolution of the Scottish Permo-Triassic with modifications associated with the Sherwood Sandstone Group (Permo-Triassic) of England superimposed in italic (after Burley 1984; Bushell 1986).

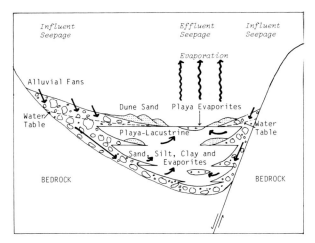

Fig. 12. Schematic representation of an isochemical desert basin (after Walker 1976). The basin may be up to several hundred kilometres across and up to several thousand metres deep.

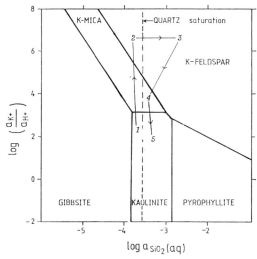

Fig. 13. A logarithmic activity diagram in the $K_2O-SiO_2-Al_2O_3-H_2O$ system at 50°C and 150 bars showing the chemical evolution of the Scottish Permo-Triassic.

may have represented burial depth maxima in some of the Scottish basins (see Dean, this volume) would have been reached just prior to late Cimmerian uplift at a time when carbonate cementation was most pervasive. The absence of any mesodiagenetic leaching of carbonate would appear to preclude the presence of acidic pore fluids that might be expected following decarboxylation and hydrocarbon generation and there is no further evidence of any mass−

solute transfer of material into these basins. Therefore it is considered unlikely that any hydrocarbons were produced and that, even if they were, the heavily cemented Permo-Triassic sediments would not have formed a good reservoir rock at the time.

Conclusion

Excluding regional variations, the patterns of diagenesis observed from the Permo-Triassic of Scotland may be summarized by the paragenetic sequence in Fig. 3 and the flow diagram in Fig. 11. This sequence is very similar to those of Burley (1984) and Bushell (1986) for the Sherwood Sandstone of England (Fig. 11), the Scottish sequence differing only in the absence of an external source of ions that, in England, was invoked as responsible for the mesodiagenetic generation of secondary porosity and hydrocarbon accumulation. In Scotland, early diagenesis was dominated by grain dissolution followed by the precipitation of new authigenic phases. Later, as burial depth increased and the activity of K^+ and Al^{3+} increased, illite not only began to replace some of the unstable expandable clay layers but also precipitated out directly. Finally, following uplift and the re-introduction of meteoric waters, the carbonate cements were partially leached and a phase of authigenic kaolinite precipitation was succeeded by a minor episode of renewed quartz authigenesis. Oxidation of various minerals under present-day atmospheric conditions has also introduced varying amounts of opaque oxides. The evidence points to an isochemical system operating throughout diagenetic evolution (Fig. 12). The changes in pore water chemistry were largely the result of the original, detrital mineralogy of the individual basins with no evidence of mass-solute transfer from an external source. This contrasts with evidence from the Sherwood Sandstone of England where Carboniferous sediments provided aggressive pore waters for secondary porosity generation. The chemical evolution of the pore water in Scotland may be illustrated using a logarithmic activity diagram in the $K_2O-SiO_2-Al_2O_3-H_2O$ system at 50°C and 150 bars, which are reasonable values given the stated burial depth maxima (Fig. 13). Following the original influent seepage of meteoric water (1), unstable silicate grain dissolution led to a rise in the K^+/H^+ ratio as the system passed into the stability field of K-feldspar which was precipitated out as an authigenic phase (2). With an increase in SiO_2 activity the system became supersaturated with respect to quartz, allowing the formation of syntaxial overgrowths (3). A subsequent decrease in the K^+/H^+ ratio allowed the formation of illite (4) and as this ratio further decreased kaolinite was precipitated (5). The water would still have been supersaturated with SiO_2 at this stage, allowing a late diagenetic precipitation of quartz.

This research was carried out during the tenure of a D.E.N.I. Natural Environment Studentship at the Queen's University of Belfast. I am indebted to J. Parnell and the technical staff of Q.U.B. Geology Department, Electron Microscope Unit; and to S. Burley and the electron microscope staff at Manchester University. The British Geological Survey is greatly acknowledged for the loan of numerous offshore borehole samples.

References

ALI, A. D. & TURNER, P. 1982. Authigenic K-feldspar in the Bromsgrove Sandstone Formation (Triassic) of central England. *Journal of Sedimentary Petrology*, **52**, 187−197.

BJORKUM, P. A. & GJELSVIK, N. 1988. An isochemical model for formation of authigenic kaolinite, K-feldspar and illite in sediments. *Journal of Sedimentary Petrology*, **58**, 506−511.

BJORLYKKE, K., ELVERHOI, A. & MALM, A. O. 1979. Diagenesis in Mesozoic sandstones from Spitsbergen and the North Sea — a comparison. *Geoligisches Rundshau*, **68**, 1152−1171.

BROOKFIELD, M. E. 1977. The origin of bounding surfaces in ancient aeolian sandstones. *Sedimentology*, **24**, 303−332.

—— 1978. Stratigraphy of the Permian and supposed Permian rocks of southern Scotland. *Geoligisches Rundshau*, **67**, 110−149.

—— 1979. Anatomy of a Lower Permian aeolian sandstone complex, southern Scotland. *Scottish Journal of Geology*, **15**, 81−96.

—— 1980. Permian intermontane basin sedimentation in southern Scotland. *Sedimentary Geology*, **27**, 176−194.

BURLEY, S. D. 1984. Patterns of diagenesis in the Sherwood Sandstone Group (Triassic), United Kingdom. *Clay Minerals*, **19**, 403−440.

——, KANTOROWICZ, J. D. & WAUGH, B. 1985. Clastic diagenesis. In BRENCHLEY, P. & WILLIAMS, B. (eds) *Sedimentology: Recent Developments and Applied Aspects*. Geological Society, London, Special Publication **18**, 189−226.

BUSHELL, T. P. 1986. Reservoir geology of the Morecambe Field. *In*: BROOKS, J., GOFF, J. C., & VAN HOORN, B. (eds) *Habitat of Palaeozoic Gas in North-west Europe*. Geological Society, London, Special Publication **23**, 189−208.

CLEMMENSEN, L. 1987. Complex star dunes and associated aeolian bedforms, Hopeman Sandstone (Permo-Triassic), Moray Firth basin, Scotland. *In*: FROSTICK, L. & REID, I. (eds) *Desert Sediments: Ancient and Modern*. Geological Society, London, Special Publication **35**, 213−231.

—— & ABRAHAMSEN, K. 1983. Aeolian stratification and facies association in desert sediments, Arran Basin (Permian), Scotland. *Sedimentology*, **30**, 311−339.

COWAN, G. 1989. Diagenesis of Upper Carboniferous sandstones: southern North Sea Basin. *In*: WHATELEY, M. K. & PICKERING, K. T. (eds) *Deltas: Sites and Traps for Fossil Fuels*. Geological Society, London, Special Publication **41**, 57−73.

CRAIG, G. Y. 1965. Permian and Triassic. *In*: CRAIG, G. Y. (ed.) *Geology of Scotland*. Oliver & Boyd, Edinburgh.

GLENNIE, K. W. & BULLER, A. T. 1983. The Permian Wiessliegend of north-west Europe; the partial deformation of aeolian sand dunes caused by the Zechstein transgression. *Sedimentary Geology*, **35**, 43−81.

——, MUDD, G. C. & NAGTEGAAL, P. J. C. 1978. Depositional environment and diagenesis of Permian Rotliegendes sandstones in Leman Bank and Sole Pit areas of the U.K. southern North Sea. *Journal of the Geological Society, London*, **135**, 25−34,

GRIEG, D. C. 1971. *British Regional Geology: the South of Scotland* (third edition). H.M.S.O., Edinburgh.

HAYES, J. B. 1979. *Sandstone Diagenesis — The Hole Truth*. Society of Economic Palaeontologists and Mineralogists Special Publication, **26**, 127−139.

HUANG, W. L., BISHOP, A. M. & BROWN, R. W. 1986. The effect of fluid/rock ratio on feldspar dissolution and illite formation under reservoir conditions. *Clay Minerals*, **21**, 585−601.

HURST, A. & IRWIN, H. 1982. Geological modelling of clay diagenesis in sandstones. *Clay Minerals*, **17**, 5−22.

LAIER, T. & NIELSEN, B. L. 1989. Cementing halite in Triassic Bunter sandstone (Tonder, south-west Denmark), as a result of hyperinfiltration of brines. *Chemical Geology*, **76**, 353–363.

LEVY, Y. 1977. Description and mode of formation of the supratidal? evaporite facies in the northern Sinai coastal plain. *Journal of Sedimentary Petrology*, **47**, 463–474.

McKEEVER, P. J. 1990. *Studies on the Sedimentology and Palaeoecology of the Permian of Scotland.* PhD thesis, Queen's University of Belfast.

MACCHI, L. 1987. A review of sandstone illite cements and aspects of their significance to hydrocarbon exploration and development. *Geological Journal*, **22**, 333–345.

PEACOCK, J. D., BERRIDGE, N. G., HARRIS, A. L. & MAY, F. 1968. The geology of the Elgin district. *Memoirs of the Geological Survey for Great Britain.*

PETTIJOHN, F. J., POTTER, P. E. & SIEVER, R. S. 1972. *Sand and Sandstone.* Springer, Berlin.

SCHMIDT, V. & McDONALD, D. A. 1979a. *The Role of Secondary Porosity in the Course of Sandstone Diagenesis.* Society of Economic Palaeontologists and Mineralogists, Special Publication, **26**, 175–207.

—— & —— 1979b. *Texture and Recognition of Secondary Porosity in Sandstones.* Society of Economic Palaeontologists and Mineralogists Special Publication, **26**, 209–225.

STEEL, R. J. 1971. *Sedimentation of the New Red Sandstone in the Hebridean province, Scotland.* PhD Thesis, University of Glasgow.

—— 1974a. New Red Sandstone floodplain and piedmont sedimentation in the Hebridean province, Scotland. *Journal of Sedimentary Petrology*, **44**, 336–357.

—— 1974b. Cornstone (fossil caliche) – its origin,

stratigraphic and sedimentological importance in the New Red Sandstone, western Scotland. *Journal of Geology*, **82**, 351–369.

—— 1977. Triassic rift basins of north-western Scotland — their configuration, infilling and development. *In*: FINSTAD, K. G. & SELLEY, R. C. (eds) *Proceedings: Mesozoic Northern North Sea Symposium 1977.* Norwegian Petroleum Society, Stavanger, Paper 7, 78–102.

—— & WILSON, A. C. 1975. Sedimentation and tectonism (?Permo-Triassic) on the margin of the North Minch Basin, Lewis. *Journal of the Geological Society, London*, **131**, 183–202.

TURNER, P. 1980. Continental red beds. *Developments in Sedimentology*, **29**. Elsevier, Amsterdam.

WALKER, T. R. 1976. Diagenetic origin of continental red beds. *In*: FALKE, H. (ed.) *The Continental Permian in Central, West and South Europe.* NATO advanced Study Institute Series C. Mathematics & Physical Sciences, **22**.

WILLIAMS, D. 1973. *The Sedimentology and Petrology of the New Red Sandstone of the Elgin Basin, Northeast Scotland.* PhD Thesis, University of Hull.

WILSON, M. D. & PITTMAN. E. D. 1977. Authigenic clays in sandstones: recognition and influence on reservoir properties and palaeoenvironmental analysis. *Journal of Sedimentary Petrology*, **47**, 3–31.

ZIEGLER, P. A. 1981. Evolution of sedimentary basins in North West Europe. *In*: ILLING, C. L. V. & HOBSON, G. D. (eds) *Petroleum Geology of the Continental Shelf of North West Europe.* Heyden, London.

Authigenic K-Feldspar in the Permo-Triassic of northwest Britain: a pilot oxygen isotope study

P. J. MCKEEVER[1], P. CAREY[2] & J. QUINN[2]

[1] Department of Geology, The University, Manchester MB 9PL, UK

[2] Department of Geology, Queen's University, Belfast BT7 1NN, UK

One of the most important authigenic precipitates found in the Permo-Triassic sediments of northwest Britain is K-feldspar. The feldspar is an extremely pure orthoclase end-member of composition Or_{99} to Or_{100} occurring as whole overgrowths on mostly fresh detrital grains or as pore-filling adularia. This phase is common in many basins in western Scotland and Northern Ireland. Petrographic studies show that the K-feldspar is an early diagenetic phase, whose precipitation commenced before compaction was completed (McKeever 1990; Parnell 1992). The K-feldspar occupies up to 4% of rock volume, and is important in inhibiting porosity and permeability in potential gas reservoirs. Pores are infilled and pore-throats are blocked within large volumes of sandstone (Fig. A1a–f). Given the abundance of the authigenic K-feldspar, it was considered plausible that it could be separated out and subjected to $^{18}O/^{16}O$ and K/Ar isotope analysis. To date, only oxygen isotope analyses have been achieved on a sample from the Permian Thornhill Sandstone Formation in Dumfries & Galloway, in which overgrowths occur on nearly all detrital feldspar grains. The Thornhill Sandstone Formation includes tabular and trough-shaped, cross-stratified sets representing aeolian dune deposits in which authigenic K-feldspar appears to be particularly common. By analysing the oxygen isotope composition of authigenic mineral phases it is possible to determine the oxygen isotope composition of the pore water from which that phase precipitated. The procedure used for the separation and isolation of the K-feldspar overgrowths from their detrital cores is described in detail in McKeever (1990). Oxygen isotope analyses were performed on a sample of the Thornhill Sandstone Formation authigenic

feldspar (Grid ref. NX 873 991) where authigenic K-feldspar represented 3.9% of the total rock volume. Following overgrowth separation, 61.4 mg of authigenic K-feldspar was obtained and the purity of this sample was checked using X-ray diffraction and electron probe analyses. Analyses were undertaken at the Scottish Universities Research and Reactor Centre yielded 14.18 and 14.14 μmoles mg^{-1} of oxygen and gave $\delta^{18}O$ values of 10.67 and 9.41‰ respectively, relative to SMOW. These results show an analytical error greater than the normal analytical error of $+/- 0.2\%$ (2σ). A similar variation in $\delta^{18}O$ values was observed by Dempsey (1987) from alkali feldspars in granitoids and he suggested that a change in temperature during feldspar precipitation may have produced the range of $\delta^{18}O$ values seen. The early diagenetic K-feldspar precipitated over a range of shallow burial depths before significant sutured grain contacts developed (<1500 m), i.e. $<50°C$ assuming a geothermal gradient of $30°C$ km^{-1}. It may be possible that the consequent range of temperatures over which the feldspar precipitated may have resulted in an analogous situation to that encountered by Dempsey, and would help explain the rather large variation in $\delta^{18}O$ values encountered. By employing the fractionation equation of O'Neill & Taylor (1967) it is possible to obtain an estimate of the $\delta^{18}O$ value of the Permo-Triassic pore waters from which the feldspar precipitated

$$10^3 \ln A = -3.41 + 2.91 \ (10^6) \ T^{-2}$$

where $10^3 \ln A = \delta^{18}O_{feldspar} - \delta^{18}O_{water}$ and T = temperature (K). Using a temperature of $T = 325$ K it can be demonstrated that $\delta^{18}O_{water}$ = -13.47 to -14.73%.

The $^{18}O/^{16}O$ ratio occurring in natural waters is highly variable (Siegenthaler 1979). In meteoric water the ratio is highly dependant on latitude, altitude and on the distance from the coast (continentality) (Dansgaard 1964). The latitude effect is reflected by temperature whereby with decreasing temperature (i.e. increasing latitude and altitude) there is a gradual decrease in concentration of the heavier isotope ^{18}O relative to the lighter isotope ^{16}O. ^{18}O in precipitation would also decrease relative to ^{16}O with distance from the coast. The driving force behind these widely observed variations is the phenomenon of isotopic fractionation during evaporation and condensation of water (Dansgaard 1964; Siegenthaler 1979). This process of isotopic fractionation is important when considering the results from the Scottish authigenic feldspars.

Limited data for authigenic K-feldspars is available from other successions. Savin &

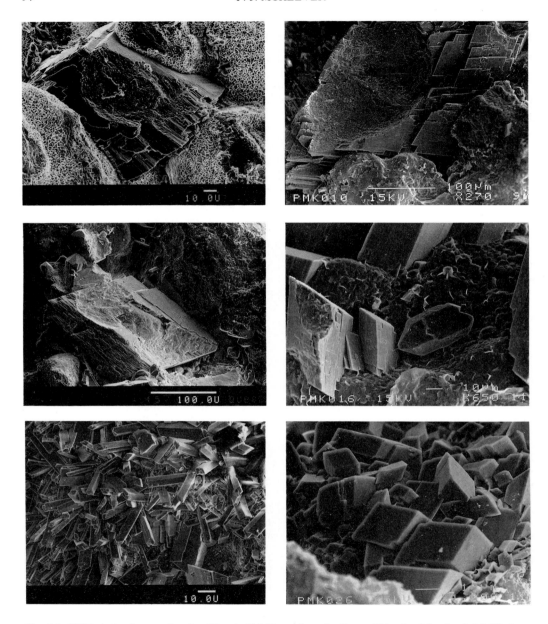

Fig. A1. SEM photomicrographs of authigenic K-feldspar from the Permo-Triassic of Scotland. (a) Whole overgrowths, British Geological Survey (BGS) Temple Bogwood borehole (NS 486 269), near Mauchline. (b) Whole overgrowth, BGS offshore core 70/14, Arran Basin. (c) Pore-filling lathes, BGS offshore core 73/28, Rathlin Trough. (d) Overgrowth left after the detrital core was plucked out, sample from Thornhill Basin. (e) Small overgrowths with a euhedral authigenic quartz crystal, sample from Thornhill Basin. (f) Intergrown rhombs, sample from Thornhill Basin.

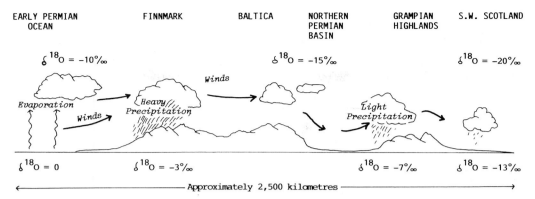

EARLY PERMIAN   FINNMARK   BALTICA   NORTHERN   GRAMPIAN   S.W. SCOTLAND
OCEAN   PERMIAN   HIGHLANDS
                                                          BASIN

$\delta^{18}O = -10\%$ $\delta^{18}O = -15\%$ $\delta^{18}O = -20\%$

Winds

Evaporation $\widehat{Heavy}$
                Precipitation   Light
Winds   Precipitation

$\delta^{18}O = 0$ $\delta^{18}O = -3\%$ $\delta^{18}O = -7\%$ $\delta^{18}O = -13\%$

←———————————————— Approximately 2,500 kilometres ————————————————→

Fig. A2. A schematic cross-section across north-western Europe in the Lower Permian showing a model of isotope fractionation used to explain the ^{18}O-isotope depletion seen in the authigenic K-feldspars of the Thornhill Basin.

Epstein (1970) indirectly determined a $\delta^{18}O$ value of +18.8‰ for K-feldspar overgrowths in the Franconia Formation of Wisconsin. Girard et al. (1989) extrapolated a value of +20.2 +/ −0.8‰ for overgrowths in Cretaceous arkoses from Angola from a suite of diagenetic K-feldspar concentrates. Diagenetic feldspars generally have $\delta^{18}O$ values in the range 18–28‰ (Kastner & Siever 1979). These values are very different from the compositions of 9.4 and 10.7‰ determined in this study. Girard et al. (1989) calculated a composition of +6 to +9 for the parent waters of the Angolan feldspar, which they interpreted to be ^{18}O-rich brines derived from evaporites in underlying sediments. Evaporitic brines are typically enriched in ^{18}O (with $\delta^{18}O$ values as high as +10‰; Holser 1979), and are not a viable precursor for the Scottish feldspars although they would be consistent with a semi-arid environment in Permian times. The oxygen isotope composition of the Scottish diagenetic feldspar and of their parent waters reflects precipitation from markedly depleted meteoric water. Present day sea water $\delta^{18}O$ values are zero but, due to the process of isotope fractionation, when sea water is evaporated the resulting water vapour would be depleted in ^{18}O and would thus have a negative $\delta^{18}O$ value. The $\delta^{18}O$ value of water vapour in an air mass would become progressively more negative each time it condenses to precipitate rain, snow or hail. The $\delta^{18}O$ value of the precipitation would therefore become increasingly negative even though the heavier isotope would be concentrated in the liquid phase. By this process precipitation falling on continental interiors may be very depleted in ^{18}O and show $\delta^{18}O$ values as low as −13 or −14‰.

During Thornhill Sandstone deposition in the Lower Permian, Scotland lay in the belt of the northeasterly trade winds but several hundred kilometres from the nearest major ocean. The moisture-laden trade winds would have already been heavily depleted in ^{18}O following evaporation of sea water at equatorial or tropical temperatures, and significant amounts of precipitation would have fallen over the Scandinavian Massif with lesser amounts falling on the windward side of the Scottish Massif. Precipitation reaching the southern Scottish area could have been very depleted in ^{18}O (Fig. A2). The greater the rainfall over the Scandanavian and Scottish massifs the greater the depletion of precipitation over southern Scotland. The value of $\delta^{18}O$ for meteoric water calculated from the analysis of the authigenic K-feldspar clearly shows that the meteoric water was indeed highly depleted in the heavier isotope of oxygen. Naylor et al. (1989) have demonstrated that even by Upper Triassic times the meteoric water responsible for micrite precipitation in northern Scotland, which at the time lay close to the edge of a major marine area, had a $\delta^{18}O$ value of −2.74‰ (relative to SMOW). The analysis from Thornhill clearly confirms that authigenic K-feldspar was eodiagenetic and that it precipitated from meteoric water markedly depleted in ^{18}O.

Additional References

DANSGAARD, W. 1964. Stable isotopes in precipitation. *Tellus*, **16**, 436–468.

DEMPSEY, C. S. 1987. *The Petrology and Geochemistry of the Caledonian Granitoids of the Barnesmore Complex, County Donegal*. PhD thesis, Queen's University of Belfast.

GIRARD, J-P., SAVIN, S. M., & ARONSON, J. L. 1989. Diagenesis of the Lower Cretaceous arkoses of the Angola margin: petrological, K/Ar dating and $^{18}O/^{16}O$ evidence. *Journal of Sedimentary Petrology*, **59**, 519–538.

HOLSER, W. T. 1979. Trace elements and isotopes in evaporites. *In*: BURNS, R. G. (ed.) *Marine minerals, Reviews in Mineralogy*. **6**, 295–346.

KASTNER, M. & SIEVER, R. 1979. Low temperature feldspars in sedimentary rocks. *American Journal of Science*, **279**, 435–479.

MCKEEVER, P. J. 1990. *Studies on the Sedimentology and Palaeoecology of the Permian of Scotland*. PhD Thesis, The Queen's University of Belfast.

NAYLOR, H., TURNER, P., VAUGHAN, D. J. & FALLICK, A. E. 1989. The Cherty Rock: a petrographic and isotopic study of a Permo-Triassic calcrete. *Geological Journal*, **24**, 205–221.

O'NEILL, J. R. & TAYLOR, H. P. 1967. The oxygen isotope and cation exchange chemistry of feldspars. *American Mineralogist*, **52**, 1414–1437.

PARNELL, J. 1992. Hydrocarbon potential of Northern Ireland: III. Reservoir potential of the Permo-Triassic. *Journal of Petroleum Geology*, **15**, 51–70.

SAVIN, S. M. & EPSTEIN, S. 1970. The oxygen isotopic compositions of coarse-grained sedimentary rocks and minerals. *Geochimica et Cosmocimica Acta*, **34**, 323–329.

SIEGENTHALER, U. 1979. Stable hydrogen and oxygen isotopes in the water cycle. *In*: JAGER, E. & Hunziker, J. C. (eds), *Lectures in Isotope Geology*. Springer, Berlin, 264–274.

Dynamic stratigraphy of the Triassic and Jurassic of the Hebrides Basin, NW Scotland

NICOL MORTON

Department of Geology, Birkbeck College, University of London, Malet Street, London WC1E 7HX, UK

Abstract: The evolution of the Hebrides Basin during the late Triassic and Jurassic has been established by integrating analyses of subsidence history, sequence stratigraphy and stratigraphical architecture. Two episodes of three-phase evolution occurred from extension-related variable sequences (1A, late Triassic to early Sinemurian; 2A, latest Toarcian to late Bajocian), through sag-related laterally more uniform sequences (1B, mid-Sinemurian to earliest Toarcian; 2B, late Bajocian to late Bathonian), to stabilization—related condensed sequences (1C, Toarcian; 2C, late Bathonian to Callovian). A final third episode of subsidence in Oxfordian to early Kimmeridgian was followed by partial basin inversion in latest Jurasic or early Cretaceous, which caused faulting, tilting and uplift of basement ridges. These structures are unconformably overlain by Upper Cretaceous sediments and Palaeocene volcanics.

There was a single Hebrides Basin during the late Triassic and Jurassic subsiding as a half-graben bounded on the west by the Minch Fault. The intrabasinal Camasunary and related faults are demonstrated not to have been significant tectonic features during the Jurassic. Occasionally they were slightly active but they did not divide the area into two sub-basins. They are largely post-Jurassic. There is evidence of a less strongly subsiding central Skye block, apparently in the area of the later Palaeocene plutonic centre.

The occurrence of Triassic and Jurassic rocks in NW Scotland has been known since the early days of geological exploration in the late 18th and early 19th centuries, so that the outcrops which occur on various islands of the Inner Hebrides and parts of the neighbouring Scottish mainland have had a long history of investigation, summarised in Hudson (1983) and Morton (1987, 1989). We now know that these 'outliers' on the northwestern edge of Europe are part of a system of basins on the Atlantic margins (Fig. 1 inset), most of which are submerged and some deeply buried beneath younger strata.

The Jurassic Hebrides Basin is unique in the British and Irish sector of the Atlantic margin system of basins, in the existence of extensive onshore outcrops [the others are a long way to the south in Portugal (Wilson *et al.* 1990), or to the north in East Greenland (Surlyk *et al.* 1981)], which enable more detailed and complete stratigraphical and sedimentological analyses. Only the western part of the basin, in the Sea of the Hebrides, cannot be observed directly and is relatively unknown. Seismic reflection surveys by commercial companies and by the British Geological Survey, who have also drilled a limited number of shallow boreholes, give an indication of structure but interpretation is complicated by the presence of numerous igneous intrusions. One exploration well has

been drilled by Pentex Oil in western Skye but the results of this remain strictly confidential at present (May 1991), while Chevron's exploration of a block in the Sea of the Hebrides to the southwest of Skye includes drilling a well (in 1991) in addition to seismic surveys.

The succession and sedimentary facies in the Hebridean islands (see Hudson 1983) are better known than those in other basins of the Atlantic system, so that the Hebrides Basin provides a model for comparison which is precisely calibrated biostratigraphically. The purpose of this paper is to summarize the Triassic and Jurassic stratigraphy and a dynamic model for the evolution of the basin during the Mesozoic. Detailed discussion of the techniques used, and the resultant derivation of the model, has been given elsewhere (Morton 1987, 1989, 1990*a*).

Structure

The present structure of the Hebrides (see Binns *et al.* 1974, 1975) is of a major westerly-tilted half-graben with the western faulted margin in the Minch Fault Zone, just east of the Outer Hebrides (Fig. 1). This set of high-angle normal faults becomes listric at depth and soles out onto the Caledonian Outer Isles Thrust (Stein 1988). The eastern margin of the basin is unfaulted and therefore its original position was likely to be more irregular and ephemeral; it is

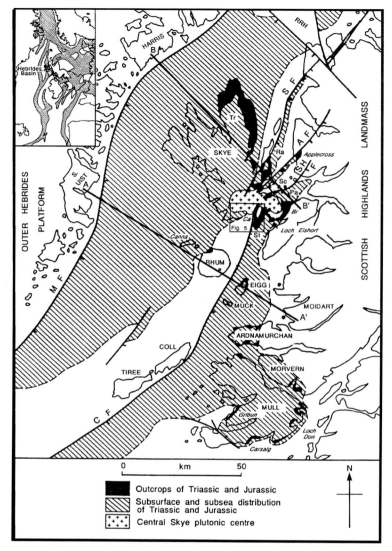

Fig. 1. Map of Hebrides Basin showing present distribution of Triassic and Jurassic rocks and basement ridges; the locations of cross sections A and B (Fig. 2) and Fig. 5 are indicated. Inset shows North Atlantic Jurassic basins. Abbreviations: AF, Applecross Fault; Br, Broadford; Ca, Camasunary; CF, Camasunary Fault; MF, Minch Fault Zone; Pa, Isle of Pabay; Ra, Isle of Raasay; RRH, Rudha Reidh High; SC, Isle of Scalpay; SHF, Scalpay House Fault; So, Sconser; St, Strathaird Peninsula; Tr, Trotternish Peninsula.

thought (see Hudson 1964) to be near the present coastline of mainland Scotland.

South of Skye there are two main tilted fault blocks (Fig. 2A). Triassic and Jurassic rocks dip WNW into the Sea of the Hebrides Fault Block from a basement ridge forming the islands of Rhum, Tiree and Coll. The eastern edge of this block is defined by the Camasunary (-Skerryvore) Fault. East of this fault the Inner

Hebrides Fault Block includes southern Skye, Eigg, Muck, Morvern and the complex areas of Ardnamurchan and Mull.

The Camasunary Fault cannot be traced through the Palaeogene Central Skye plutonic centre, and to the north its place is taken by three faults — the Screapadal, Applecross and Scalpay House Faults (see Fig. 1). These, together with the Minch Fault, define the four

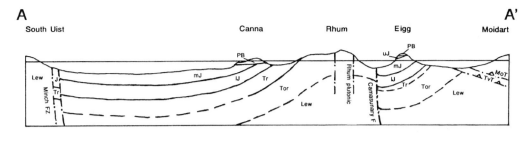

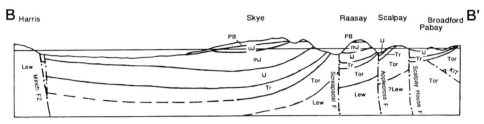

Fig. 2. Simplified cross-sections (see Fig. 1 for locations) across Hebrides Basin: A−A' south of central Skye plutonic centre, showing two main fault blocks separated by Camasunary Fault; B−B' north of central Skye plutonic centre, showing four main fault blocks. All the main faults are vertical at the surface but are presumed to sole out at depth onto the easterly-dipping Outer Isles Thrust (Stein 1988). Abbreviations: PB, Palaeocene plateau basalts (frequently underlain by thin Upper Cretaceous, not shown); uJ, Upper Jurassic; mJ, Middle Jurassic, Lower Jurassic; Tr, Triassic; Tor, Torridonian; Lew, Lewisian; KiT, Kishorn Thrust; MoT, Moine Thrust; TvT, Tarskavaig Thrust.

main WNW-tilted fault blocks of (from east to west) Broadford-Pabay, Applecross-northern Scalpay, Raasay, and the large north Skye block which has a broad synclinal structure and is an extension of the Sea of the Hebrides block (Fig. 2B).

The major NNE−SSW faults are the dominant structural features of the Triassic and Jurassic rocks with throws exceeding 1 km in places; however, they have little or no influence on the Upper Cretaceous and Palaeocene. The age and roles of the faults will be discussed in a later section of this paper. A later set of predominantly NW−SE to NNW−SSE faults also cuts the Palaeocene lavas, and is often associated with dykes, but the throws rarely exceed 100 m.

The overall simple structure of the Triassic and Jurassic rocks is disturbed near some of the major Palaeogene plutonic centres of Central Skye, Rhum, Ardnamurchan and Mull. In places the beds are steeply dipping or even overturned, but more striking are the extremely large (to more than 1 km) and poorly understood vertical movements which have sometimes resulted in unexpected juxtapositions. Examples include the presence of an easterly-dipping wedge of Upper Jurassic rocks faulted against

Torridonian in southern Scalpay (Turner 1966) [on the northern margin of the Skye granitic pluton], and Lower Jurassic in the main ring fault zone of the Rhum ultrabasic complex on southeast Rhum (Smith 1985) [downfaulted on the crest of the basement ridge of Torridonian rocks]. In the neighbourhood of the plutonic centres the Mesozoic rocks have been thermally metamorphosed, and stratigraphical or sedimentological interpretation may be difficult.

Triassic to Jurassic evolution of basin

The Mesozoic sediments seen at outcrop in the Hebrides range in age from probable Upper Triassic (or younger) continental red beds, which progressively onlap pre-Mesozoic basement, to Lower Kimmeridgian marine shales (Fig. 4). No younger Jurassic sediments have been identified anywhere. In northern Skye there may be some restricted space available under the Palaeocene lavas for preservation of slightly younger rocks, but if present these are probably very limited. Most of the 'Triassic' red beds are undated, but they are conformably overlain by dated Rhaetian (in Mull) or Hettangian (elsewhere) and this, together with the nature of the facies indicating high depositional rates, suggests that they are no older than Late Triassic in age.

Seismic reflection surveys provide evidence that the succession in the submerged western part of the basin is considerably thicker than seen at outcrop, but available results of exploration do not yet provide a unique interpretation. The existence of an older sedimentary succession (Permo-Triassic, Carboniferous or ?) has been suggested, but remains speculative at present. In any case it would not affect the present discussion, but only provide an earlier chapter in basin evolution. The extent of westward-thickening of the Upper Triassic and Jurassic also remains to be established.

Analysis of the evolution of the basin has been achieved by using an integrated approach, including geohistory and subsidence history (pioneered by van Hinte 1978), genetic sequence stratigraphy (cf. Galloway 1989 and van Wagoner et al. 1990) and interpretation of stratigraphical architecture. The techniques used here are in part modified from those based mainly on seismic stratigraphy. Detailed discussions of the methodology are given elsewhere (Morton 1987, 1989, 1990a); only brief summaries and the main results and conclusions are brought together here.

Subsidence history

The purpose of subsidence history analysis is to establish in quantitative terms (e.g. by reference to a linear timescale) the history of subsidence through geological time of the basement surface on which the sedimentary fill of the basin rests (or a convenient stratigraphical datum as substitute). It is necessary to separate as far as possible the effects of sediment loading, eustatic changes of sea level over the time interval of interest, and the subcrustal tectonic driving mechanisms. The methods used here (see Morton 1987) differ only slightly from those described by van Hinte (1978), mainly in modified parameters for decompaction and progressive compaction of different lithologies, and in attempting to make corrections for estimated eustatic sea level changes (after Hallam 1981, 1989).

The technique involves making several assumptions, notably in converting from a chronostratigraphical scale (stages and chronozones) to a linear chronological scale (in Ma) (which is not well established for the Jurassic), in quantifying decompaction and progressive compaction (so-called 'backstripping'), and in estimating depths of deposition and the magnitude of eustatic sea-level changes. These all limit the resolution of the technique and care

must be taken not to overinterpret the data.

The results for three areas in the Hebrides are shown in Fig. 3, which is derived from cumulative sediment thicknesses, corrected for compaction, palaeobathymetry, estimated eustatic sea level changes and sediment loading (see Morton 1987 for details). Analysis of the Jurassic palaeobathymetry of the Hebrides indicates that most of the main changes through time can be correlated with short-term eustatic changes of sea level identified by Hallam (e.g. 1981, 1989), and are therefore not significant in analysing subsidence rates. Similarly lateral changes in palaeobathymetry interpreted from lateral facies changes are interpreted as being too small to require compensation in reconstructing basement subsidence in the Hebrides Basin during the Jurassic.

The changes of slope of the basement subsidence curves (Fig. 3) can therefore be interpreted as indicating the thermo-tectonic history. Three main episodes of basin evolution can be established.

1. *Late Triassic and Early Jurassic.* The oldest Mesozoic sediments seen at outcrop in the area are continental red beds which cannot be directly dated in the absence of biostratigraphical data. They are interpreted as being Upper Triassic because they are rapidly-deposited alluvial fan to flood-plain sediments (Steel 1974) conformably overlain by dated Rhaetian (Mull), basal Hettangian (Morvern, Ardnamurchan) or upper Hettangian (Skye, Applecross) (Oates 1978, Morton 1990b). Therefore subsidence began in the Late Triassic, but sedimentation did not begin at the same time everywhere because there was progressive (diachronous) onlap (see below and Fig. 4) from Late Triassic until early Sinemurian. Subsidence and sedimentation rates remained more or less in balance and varied only slightly relative to each other until the end of the Pliensbachian or very earliest Toarcian, so that there were only minor changes of depth during this time interval.

In the lower Toarcian there is a thin condensed succession and a major hiatus in the Middle and Upper Toarcian (see below and Morton 1987, 1989, 1990b) so that the rate of sedimentation had decreased. There is no evidence of deepening during the Toarcian or of uplift and erosion, so that this time interval is interpreted as representing a phase of tectonic stabilisation. If estimates of eustatic sea level rise in the Toarcian are taken into account (see Morton 1987, p 239) the curves suggest that some minor uplift or basement rebound occurred.

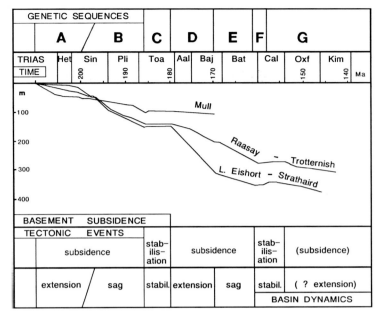

Fig. 3. Boundaries of major genetic sequences recognised in the Hebrides (see Fig. 4) plotted against linear time scale (from Snelling 1986) and basement thermo-tectonic subsidence curves (from Morton 1987) corrected for sediment loading and long-term eustatic sea level changes (based on Hallam 1978, 1981). The interpreted tectonic phases in the evolution of the basin are also shown.

This episode of basin evolution was strongly developed throughout the area.

2. *Middle Jurassic.* Renewed subsidence after the Toarcian hiatus began in the latest Toarcian, immediately before the Early–Middle Jurassic boundary, and continued until the Late Bathonian. Evidence for an intrabasinal unconformity is extremely limited, with slight unconformity in southern Strathaird (south Skye), but the thin Toarcian formations are never removed by erosion in any part of the basin. Throughout the Aalenian, Bajocian and Bathonian there were only slight variations in the palaeobathymetry above or below sea level, indicating an approximate balance of subsidence and sedimentation rates. During the Late Bathonian and, more especially, Callovian there were again reduced rates of sedimentation and subsidence. These (as in the Toarcian) indicate that a second phase of stabilisation occurred, and correcting the curves for estimated eustatic sea-level rise during the Callovian (see Morton 1987) shows even clearer evidence for basement rebound. Net sedimentation occurred only because sea level was rising faster than the basement.

This episode of subsidence was strongest in the area of Raasay and Skye, but was much weaker further south in the Mull and Ardnamurchan area.

3. *Late Jurassic.* Outcrops of Upper Jurassic rocks in the Hebrides are limited so that there is less regional information available. Renewed subsidence occurred in the Oxfordian, but the timing of the greatest change of rate varied from early Oxfordian in northern Skye to middle Oxfordian in southern Skye. This episode of subsidence continued into the early Kimmeridgian, but subsequent evolution is unknown.

This episode of subsidence appears from the thicknesses and facies of sediments deposited to have been less pronounced than the earlier episodes, and in the Mull area it may not have taken place until there was early Kimmeridgian onlap (see Morton 1989).

Genetic sequence stratigraphy

Concepts of genetic sequence stratigraphy have evolved from various approaches. These include the following.

1. Interpretation and correlation of sedimentary cycles identified at outcrops (for example Einsele & Seilacher 1982 for general discussion,

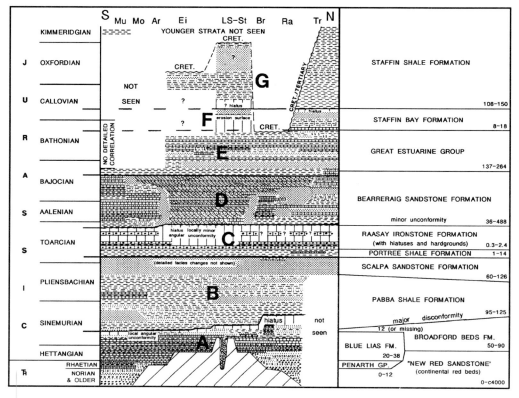

Fig. 4. Upper Triassic and Jurassic stratigraphy of the Hebrides Basin showing major sequence boundaries, lateral facies variations, lithostratigraphical nomenclature and ranges of thicknesses (in m). Localities: Mu, Mull; Mo, Morvern; Ar, Ardnamurchan; Ei, Eigg; LS, Loch Slapin; St, Strathaird; Br, Broadford; Ra, Raasay; Tr, Trotternish. Horizontal axis not to accurate scale; vertical axis is time with stages allocated durations according to Snelling (1986).

and Hallam 1978, 1989 for analyses of Jurassic stratigraphy; see also Miall 1984).

2. Recognition of unconformities and their correlative conformities, identified using the techniques of seismic stratigraphy pioneered by the Exxon group (described in Bally 1987).

3. Identification of transgressive maximum flooding surfaces, also based on seismic stratigraphy and well correlations (e.g. Galloway 1989).

Some of the approaches were developed in the context of a specific palaeogeographical setting and causal mechanism. For example the Exxon method of recognising sequences related to coastal onlap/offlap patterns is based on eustatic falls and rises of sea level affecting a coast-shelf-basin setting. Subsequent discussions about integration of seismic stratigraphy and interpretation of outcrops (van Wagoner et al. 1990) have been based on the presumption of eustatic sea-level changes as the prime controlling mechanism. However, other authors (e.g. Cloetingh et al. 1987) have argued that similar apparent sea-level patterns could result from purely tectonic mechanisms without input of eustatic sea-level influences.

Irrespective of the technique used and assumptions about palaeogeographical setting and causal mechanism, all the approaches have in common the recognition of packages of strata which are genetically related because they were deposited in a system of gradually evolving environments. Walther's Law is applicable to strata within the package. They are separated by surfaces of discontinuity across which the strata are not genetically related because there was an abrupt change in depositional environment. This may be associated with a hiatus or unconformity. The development of the concept which has been applied to the Jurassic of the Hebrides is described in detail in Morton (1989) and is summarized below.

The sedimentary fill of a basin will evolve through time according to the dynamic interaction of subsidence, sedimentation and eustatic changes of sea level. The nature of the succession will depend on whether:

(a) There is gradual ('steady state') interaction resulting in evolution of the depositional environment so that facies changes are progressive and Walther's Law can be applied. The stratigraphical changes can include transgressive or regressive cycles and progressive onlap or offlap. There is a genetic relationship within the succession and this constitutes a genetic stratigraphical sequence.

(b) A major perturbation of one of the controlling mechanisms is superimposed on the basin so that there is an abrupt change in the depositional environments. These may be caused by a rapid change of eustatic sea level, a tectonic event (such as a change in the mechanism driving subsidence) or a climatic event (such as a glacial episode, though this does not apply for the British Jurassic). The result is a sharp facies change, possibly associated with a hiatus or unconformity, and this can be used to identify a genetic sequence boundary.

This approach has enabled the recognition of six major basin-wide genetic sequence boundaries in the Jurassic of the Hebrides. They are interpreted to be abrupt deepening events, as described below, and this is the usual case in the Jurassic of most areas (Hallam 1978, 1989).

The Triassic and Jurassic stratigraphy of the Hebrides Basin is summarized in Fig. 4. The seven major genetic sequences which have been recognized are briefly described below and will be further discussed later.

1. *Sequence A [Upper Triassic to Lower Sinemurian (Semicostatum to Turneri Zones)].* The basal Mesozoic, resting unconformably on basement and showing progressive onlap, consists of continental red beds ('New Red Sandstone') grading upwards through 'Passage Beds' into normal marine sediments, the change being diachronous — Late Triassic in Mull but Hettangian in the Raasay and Skye area. The Jurassic passes laterally from offshore limestones and shales (Blue Lias Fm.) into nearshore sandstones and limestones (Broadford Beds Fm.).

2. *Sequence B [mid-Sinemurian (Turneri to Oxynotum Zones) to earliest Toarcian (Tenuicostatum Zone)].* The abrupt facies change to shales which defines the base of this sequence is everywhere associated with a small hiatus which is diachronous from south to north along the length of the basin. There is gradual overall coarsening-up from shales (Pabba Shale Fm.)

to sandstones (Scalpa Sandstone Fm.).

3. *Sequence C [Toarcian (Falciferum and Bifrons Zones, hiatus in Variabilis to Levesquei Zones)].* The deepening event and abrupt facies change which defines the base of this sequence is isochronous throughout the basin and not associated with a hiatus (within the limits of biostratigraphical resolution at ammonite zonal level). In most areas the Portree Shale Fm. passes up into the Raasay Ironstone Fm. The sequence is very thin and there is a large hiatus with most of the Middle and Upper Toarcian missing.

4. *Sequence D [uppermost Toarcian (Aalensis Subzone) to Upper Bajocian (Subfurcatum Zone)].* Above the Toarcian hiatus there is evidence of slight erosion only in southern Strathaird. Renewal of subsidence and sedimentation (Bearreraig Sandstone Fm.) was associated with the influx of large quantities of coarse siliciclastic material indicating rejuvenation of hinterland topography and renewed erosion.

5. *Sequence E [Upper Bajocian (Garantiana Zone) to probable Upper Bathonian].* A basin-wide deepening event and abrupt facies change to marine clay marks the base of this sequence. There is then upward gradation into a succession of brackish-lagoonal sediments (Great Estuarine Group) which show three upward-regressive cycles.

6. *Sequence F [Upper Bathonian (probable Discus Zone) to Lower Callovian (Calloviense Zone)].* An abrupt facies change as a result of marine transgression in northern Skye and a hiatus in southern Skye mark the base of this thin sequence consisting of shallow marine sediments (Staffin Bay Fm.).

7. *Sequence G [Middle Callovian (Jason Zone) to Lower Kimmeridgian (Mutabilis Zone)].* The base of this sequence is marked by a deepening event and abrupt facies change to shales (Staffin Shale Fm.) after a minor hiatus in northern Skye and a longer hiatus in southern Skye. The Callovian part of the sequence is very thin, but zonally complete, while the Oxfordian and Lower Kimmeridgian are much thicker.

Stratigraphical architecture and basin evolution

The genetic stratigraphical sequences described above represent the main evolutionary stages in the sedimentary fill of the basin. Each sequence is characterized by three principal stratigraphical properties:

(a) time interval represented and the

completeness of the sedimentary record;

(b) geometry, measured by thickness and its lateral variability (or described as sheet, wedge, etc.);

(c) composition, described by the facies and its lateral variability.

These properties of each genetic stratigraphical sequence, and the relationships between successive sequences, describe the stratigraphical architecture of the basin fill (see also Miall 1984, pp 277–279).

The time interval represented by each sequence and the completeness of the succession are described above and shown in Fig. 4. The geometry of a sequence can be expressed by the range of thicknesses (shown on Fig. 4 for the Formations) but more useful in understanding basin evolution are the means (M) and coefficients of variation (V). The latter are used because they provide a measure of lateral variability which is independent of the value of the mean. Ideally these should be based on decompacted and progressively compacted thicknesses, but most compaction takes place in the very early stages of burial (see Morton 1987 for detailed calculations) and the differences would not be significant at this level of analysis of basin evolution. The geometries of the sequences (or successive parts of sequences) are summarised below, but it must be acknowledged that the available database is sometimes limited. The compositions are summarized by the lateral facies variations shown in Fig. 4 and briefly described below. For more detailed descriptions and interpretations of depositional environments the reader is referred to Morton (1989) and references therein.

The three stratigraphical properties can be used to interpret the evolution of the surface on which sedimentation has taken place and therefore the succession of events in the subsidence of the basement. In certain circumstances a fourth parameter would need to be taken into account, which is the net change in palaeobathymetry from the beginning to the end of each sequence corrected for eustatic change of sea level. However, it has been shown (see Morton 1987) that for the Jurassic of the Hebrides this is a minor factor.

The stratigraphical architecture and evolution of the basin can be summarised in terms of seven phases based on integrating information from the subsidence history with interpretation of the genetic sequences and their stratigraphical properties (see Fig. 3).

1. *Late Triassic to Early Sinemurian*. Sequence A is highly variable in thickness and facies, indicating that subsidence was strongly

differential within the basin. There is some evidence of fault control of subsidence, especially on the western margin Minch Fault Zone by analogy with the Stornoway Beds further north (see Steel 1977). Within the basin, faulting was mostly relatively minor (e.g. at Mingary Pier, Ardnamurchan; the role of the Camasunary and other faults is discussed below) but the topographic expression of the differential nature of the subsidence is clearly indicated by the frequent locally-derived conglomerates, very rapid lateral facies changes in both the 'New Red Sandstone' and the Broadford Beds Fm., and stratigraphical overlaps which are not confined to the basin margins (e.g. in central Skye).

This interval is interpreted as a phase of differential subsidence related to lithospheric extension which was strongest in the Late Triassic and earliest Jurassic. It continued into the Sinemurian with diminishing differential effects indicated by decreasing coefficients of thickness variation from the Late Triassic to early Hettangian ('New Red Sandstone', $M = 29.5$ m; $V = 112.4$; $N = 23$) into the Late Hettangian to earliest Sinemurian (lower Broadford Beds equivalent, $M = 39.5$ m; $V = 63.0$; $N = 10$) and the early Sinemurian (upper Broadford Beds equivalent, $M, = 68.3$ m; $V = 44.4$; $N = 7$).

2. *Mid-Sinemurian to earliest Toarcian*. From Sequence A to Sequence B there is marked change in stratigraphical architecture to greater lateral uniformity of facies and thickness. The coefficients of thickness variation (V) are further reduced to 38.1 for the Pabba Shale Fm. ($M = 145.5$ m; $N = 8$) and 34.7 for the Scalpa Sandstone Fm. ($M = 100.6$ m; $N = 11$) [adjusted to allow for the diachronism of the lithostratigraphical boundary].

These changes, together with sharp reduction in grain size, evidence of onlap at basin margins (Morvern) and submarine hiatus, indicate a change of tectonic regime. The evidence is consistent with a diachronous change (from south to north along the length of the basin) to a broader post-rift sag caused by sediment loading and thermal cooling of the crust.

3. *Toarcian*. During the early Toarcian, subsidence and sedimentation rates became greatly reduced resulting in the condensed nature of Sequence C ($M = 5.8$ m; $V = 60.3$; $N = 12$) and the major hiatus in the middle and upper Toarcian. The widespread development of the Raasay Ironstone is interpreted as the result of starvation of siliciclastic input into the basin in a shallow near-shore depositional environment. There is some evidence to indicate that the

slowing of subsidence rate happened at the beginning of the Toarcian, because the uppermost Pliensbachian Hawskerense Subzone is 31 m thick on Raasay while the basal Toarcian Tenuicostatum Zone is only 2 m thick (Howarth 1956).

These features are interpreted as indicating a phase of stabilization in the basin (and also in the hinterland to give reduced sediment input). The subsequent deepening event which caused the facies change at the base of Sequence C is isochronous within the basin and is also correlative with similar events elsewhere (Hallam 1989). It is therefore interpreted as due to a global eustatic sea level rise.

4. *Latest Toarcian to Late Bajocian*. Renewed strongly differential subsidence within the basin and rejuvenation of hinterland topography resulted in the deposition of the much thicker Sequence D, which is dominated by coarse siliciclastics and shows spectacular lateral changes of facies and thickness ($M = 205.2$ m; overall $V = 60.8$, but even higher locally, see Morton 1965 fig. 7; $N = 12$) over short distances. Remarkably, subsidence and sedimentation rates were almost exactly matched so that the depositional environment did not change much in depth and there is little evidence of emergence except in one locality (Torvaig, southern Trotternish, Morton 1965, p 197). Palaeocurrent patterns (Morton 1983) indicate some submarine topographic influence of the Camasunary and Screapadal Faults.

This second rift phase of basin evolution is interpreted as due to another episode of lithospheric extension causing strongly differential subsidence of basins and uplift of hinterland.

5. *Late Bajocian to Late Bathonian*. The change in stratigraphical architecture from Sequence D to Sequence E is similar to that between Sequences A and B. Lateral uniformity of facies is striking, with some thin algal beds being recognised over a very wide area (Hudson 1980). Thickness variability was also progressively reduced, to $V = 38.0$ in the lower part of the sequence ($M = 24.2$ m; $N = 4$) then $V = 21.7$ ($M = 123.3$ m; $N = 4$) and $V = 25.4$ ($M = 66.0$ m; $N = 4$) in higher parts. In this interval also the subsidence and sedimentation rates remained in balance so that the depositional environment remained very close to sea level (Hudson 1980).

The change to Sequence E is interpreted in the same way as for Sequence B, as a change to a post-rift phase of broader sag-type subsidence caused by sediment loading and thermal cooling following the lithospheric extension phase of Sequence D.

6. *Late Bathonian to Callovian*. A marine transgression and/or hiatus marks a change in stratigraphical architecture to thin condensed successions in Sequence F ($M = 8.6$ m; $V = 83.7$; $N = 4$) and the lower (Callovian) part of Sequence G ($M = 7.1$ m; $V = 66.2$; $N = 4$). These indicate reduced rates of subsidence during a phase of stabilisation of the basin. The deepening events which mark the beginnings of each Sequence appear to be related to eustatic sea level rises (cf. Hallam 1989).

7. *Early Oxfordian to Early Kimmeridgian*. Upper Jurassic rocks are very limited in their outcrop distribution in the Hebrides, which restricts interpretation of the dynamic evolution of the basin during this Epoch. Sedimentation rates increased again during the Early Oxfordian ($M = 20.3$ m; $V = 55.7$; $N = 6$) and Middle to Late Oxfordian ($M = 92.8$ m; $V = 42.6$; $N = 3$), but these are apparently not reflected in the genetic sequence stratigraphy. A third phase of lithospheric extension and renewed subsidence has been suggested (Morton 1987), but on the basis of limited available evidence its effects were less marked than those of previous extension events.

The youngest known Jurassic rocks in the Hebrides are Lower Kimmeridgian shales at outcrops in northern Skye (thickness = 24.0 m) and in Mull. The former are in stratigraphical continuity with Oxfordian strata and indicate merely continuing subsidence, but the isolated faulted outlier in Mull (where the youngest Jurassic otherwise known is the base of the Great Estuarine Group) may suggest an unconformity between the Lower Kimmeridgian and older Jurassic. The significance of this is not clear, but it is possible that Late Jurassic subsidence did not occur in the southeastern part of the Hebrides until the early Kimmeridgian onlap (see Morton 1989, p 255).

Post-Jurassic inversion and uplift of basement ridges

The youngest Jurassic rocks known in the Hebrides Basin belong to the Lower Kimmeridgian Mutabilis Zone (Arkell & Callomon 1963: Sykes & Callomon 1979; Wright 1973). The rest of the Upper Jurassic and the whole of the Lower Cretaceous are missing throughout the area. Thin Upper Cretaceous sandstones and chalks occur as widely scattered, but mostly very small, isolated outcrops, with the thickest successions and best outcrops occurring in Morvern (see Lowden *et al.* This vol.) The oldest sediments are dated as Cenomanian.

The Upper Cretaceous outcrops are so widespread that, though now apparently isolated, there must originally have been a continuous cover resting with angular unconformity on the older Mesozoic. The Cretaceous is overlain by Palaeogene tuffs and lavas with no apparent angular unconformity, although there is a major hiatus and presumably local erosion. Structurally the Upper Cretaceous is more closely related to the Palaeogene, and post-dates the formation of the intrabasinal basement ridges.

The clearest evidence for dating the uplift of the basement ridges is to be found in central Skye, especially in the Strathaird—Camasunary area (Fig. 5). East of the Camasunary Fault, in Strathaird, the Upper Cretaceous rests on Oxfordian and there is a low-angle unconformity between the Jurassic and the overlying Upper Cretaceous sediments and Palaeocene lavas. To the west of the Camasunary Fault the Upper Cretaceous rests unconformably on lowermost Jurassic or older strata, again with low angular discordance.

Therefore the main structure of the Jurassic

rocks, the NNE—SSW major faults and westerly tilting is post-Oxfordian pre-Upper Cretaceous in age (see also Peach et al. 1910). Extrapolating evidence from elsewhere in the Hebrides, this age can be stated more precisely as post-Early Kimmeridgian and pre-Cenomanian. An Early Cretaceous age for the partial basin inversion and uplift of the intrabasinal basement ridges is the most likely.

Role of Camasunary and related faults

The occurrence of the Hebridean Triassic and Jurassic rocks in two main tilted fault-block structures separated by the Camasunary—Rhum—Tiree basement ridge has been the basis for the recognition of two separate Sea of the Hebrides and Inner Hebrides basins (Binns et al. 1974, 1975 and other authors). The main uplift of the basement ridges has been established above as post-Jurassic, but there remain some doubts about the role of the bounding faults (Camasunary, Screapadal, Applecross,

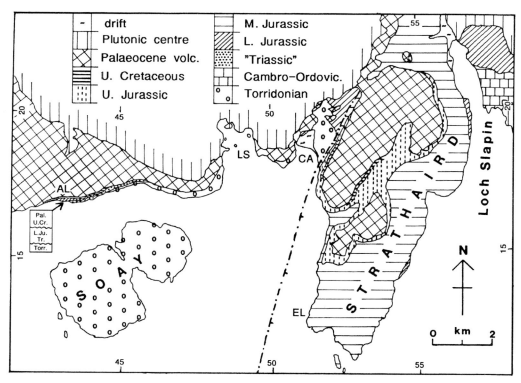

Fig. 5. Simplified geological map of Soay-Camasunary-Strathaird area showing outcrops east and west of the Camasunary Fault. Details of plutonic intrusions, minor intrusions and faults are omitted. Locality abbreviations: AL, Allt nan Leac; CA, Camasunary; LS, Loch Scavaig; EL, Elgol.

Scalpay House) during the late Triassic and Jurassic.

Steel (1977) proposed a model for the Triassic development of the basin as two asymmetrical half-grabens bounded on the west by the Minch and Camasunary Faults respectively. There is convincing evidence for the role of the Minch Fault Zone as an active syndepositional structure by extrapolation from its onshore outcrop in the Stornoway area. Here, Steel & Wilson (1975) have interpreted the (?) Triassic Stornoway Formation ('New Red Sandstone'), which has an apparent thickness of some 4000 m, as formed by deposition of alluvial fans stacked against a series of retreating fault scarps. Their interpretation is consistent with the seismic evidence of the nature of the western margin of the Hebrides Basin (Stein 1988), and detrital mineralogical evidence in northwest Skye of sediment derivation from the Lewisian of the Outer Hebrides (Hudson 1964). Steel's (1977) model for the role of the Minch Fault Zone is almost certainly correct.

The role of the Camasunary Fault is more controversial. 'Triassic' rocks are present in some parts of central Skye but in other localities in the same region they are absent, for example they are overlapped by the Broadford Beds Formation in the area east of Loch Slapin. This area lies east of the Camasunary Fault and therefore should have been in the subsiding part of a half-graben according to Steel's model. In fact the area of overlap is related to the outcrop of the carbonates of the Cambro-Ordovician Durness Group, and can be explained by the resistance of these rocks to weathering and erosion in the semi-arid climate of the area during the late Triassic. The same stratigraphical relationships between Triassic rocks and resistant carbonates are well known elsewhere, for example with the Carboniferous Limestone in the Mendips (S. W. England) where spectacular wadi-fills can be seen on the British Geological Survey one-inch map sheet 280 (Wells) (Green & Welch 1965).

There are several other lines of evidence to suggest that the Camasunary Fault was not controlling deposition during the late Triassic and Jurassic.

1. 'Triassic' sedimentary rocks occur on the north side of Soay Sound, west of Camasunary (Clough & Harker 1904, pp 8–9) (see Fig. 5). They are highly variable but include conglomerates dominated by large blocks of Durness Group limestones derived from east of the Camasunary Fault. Therefore this fault cannot have been active and forming an east-facing scarp of Torridonian rocks separating 'down-faulted' Durness Limestone source areas to the east from 'upfaulted' depositional areas to the west of the fault at that time.

2. The Broadford Beds Formation outcrops in Skye west of the Camasunary Fault, not only on the north side of Soay Sound (Clough & Harker 1904, pp 9–10) but also together with the Pabba Shale Formation in the Camasunary area west of the Fault (Peach et al. 1910, pp 108–110). No recent work has been done on the Jurassic of this area, and no estimate of the thickness of the Pabba Shale Formation is given by the Survey because the beds are faulted and metamorphosed. The thickness of the Broadford Beds Formation (apparently complete from the description) was estimated as 300 feet; as c. 90 m this is comparable with 96 m east of Broadford, Wedd (in Peach et al. 1910, p 109) specifically comments 'that no greater thickness of Lower Lias obtains on the east than on the west side of Blath-bheinn', i.e. across the Camasunary Fault.

3. Further south on the basement ridge which extends from Skye to Rhum, Tiree and Coll there are no in situ outcrops of Mesozoic except for 'Triassic' on the northwest corner of Rhum. However, the presence of metamorphosed sediments of the Broadford Beds Formation overlain by Palaeocene basalt lavas in the Main Ring Fault of the Tertiary plutonic centre in southeast Rhum has been proved (Smith 1985), and indicates the former extension of Mesozoic rocks across the basement ridge.

4. There is continuity of Jurassic stratigraphy across the various faults from southern Skye (Broadford–Loch Eishort–Strathaird) to Raasay and northern Skye (Trotternish), including thin units such as the Raasay Ironstone Formation and algal beds in the Great Estuarine Group.

5. The sedimentary facies distributions and detrital mineralogy of sandstones in the Great Estuarine Group (Harris 1989, this volume) indicate the development of separate lagoon delta systems in north Skye (Trotternish–Raasay) and south Skye (Strathaird–Eigg). However the outcrop areas are widely separated and the differences can be explained equally well by separate source river systems flowing from different areas of the hinterland into the basin.

6. Commercial seismic reflection surveys by Merlin Geophysical and other companies in the area south of Skye show that there are no lateral variations in the Mesozoic succession from the Sea of the Hebrides towards the Camasunary–Rhum–Tiree basement ridge. There was former continuity of strata which

were subsequently tilted and eroded. A composite reconstructed cross section is shown in Fig. 6.

It must be concluded that there was only one depositional basin in the Hebrides during the late Triassic and Jurassic. There is some evidence of thinning of formations towards central Skye (e.g. Bearreraig Sandstone Formation, see Morton 1965) and of facies changes in some formations (e.g. in the upper Broadford Beds Formation from sandstones in Broadford and eastern Raasay to carbonates in southwest Raasay and Sconser in Skye). However these indicate only slightly slower rates of subsidence in an area which cannot yet be delineated with confidence, but is not affected by the Camasunary and other faults. It appears to be possibly related to the position of the later Skye Tertiary plutonic centre.

The only evidence for syndepositional activity on the Camasunary, Screapadal and Applecross Faults is found in the tidal palaeocurrent directions described for the Bearreraig Sandstone Formation (Morton 1983). During the latest Toarcian to early Bajocian phase of lithospheric extension and differential subsidence the faults may have been sufficiently active to have enough topographic expression to influence tidal flow regimes but not otherwise the depositional environment.

Summary

1. During the late Triassic and Jurassic subsidence phase of the evolution of the Hebrides Basin seven phases can be identified.

(i) Late Triassic to early Sinemurian lithospheric extension and differential subsidence resulting in a rift sequence which is laterally highly variable in thickness and facies.

(ii) Mid-Sinemurian to earliest Toarcian change to thermal and loading sag which is broader and more uniform so that post-rift sequence thicknesses and facies are laterally much less variable.

(iii) Toarcian stabilisation with greatly reduced subsidence and sediment input from the hinterland so that there is a condensed sequence with a major hiatus.

(iv) Latest Toarcian to Late Bajocian lithospheric extension causing renewed subsidence in the basin and rejuvenation of hinterland topography resulting in the influx of large quantities of coarse siliciclastics and a second rift sequence which is laterally highly variable.

(v) Late Bajocian to Bathonian change to thermal and loading sag and a second post-rift sequence which is laterally more uniform in thickness and facies.

(vi) Late Bathonian to Callovian stabilisation and reduced rates of subsidence resulting in a second condensed sequence with hiatuses.

(vii) Oxfordian to at least early Kimmeridgian renewed subsidence, presumably related to a third episode of lithospheric extension, but limited data available precludes more detailed analysis at present.

2. Important flooding events related to eustatic sea level rises can be identified in the early Toarcian (Falciferum Zone), late Bathonian (probably Discus Zone) and early Callovian (Jason Zone).

3. Partial basin inversion, with tilting of blocks, intrabasinal faulting and uplift of basement ridges, occurred between early Kimmeridgian and Cenomanian, most likely in the early Cretaceous.

4. The Hebrides Basin evolved as a single half-graben bounded on the west by the Minch Fault during the late Triassic and Jurassic. With the exception of the Aalenian and Bajocian extension phase when they may have had suf-

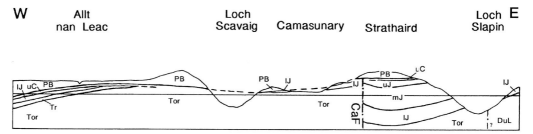

Fig. 6. Simplified cross section across the Camasunary Fault in southern Skye. The section is composite, based on evidence from various localities indicated (see Fig. 5). Abbreviations: PB, Palaeocene plateau basalts; uC, Upper Cretaceous; uJ, Upper Jurassic; mJ, Middle Jurassic; lJ, Lower Jurassic; Tr, New Red Sandstone (Trias — ? lower Hettangian); DuL, Durness Limestone (Cambro-Ordovician); Tor, Torridonian; CaF, Camasunary Fault.

ficient submarine topographic expression to influence tidal current directions, the Camasunary and related Faults were not significantly active during this time and did not divide the area into two subsiding basins. They are post-depositional structures.

References

ARKELL, W. J. & CALLOMON, J. H. 1963. Lower Kimmeridgian ammonites from the drift of Lincolnshire. *Palaeontology*, **6**, 219–245.

BALLY, A. W. 1987. *Atlas of seismic stratigraphy, vol. 1*. American Association of Petroleum Geologists Studies in Geology 27.

BINNS, P. E., McQUILLIN, R., FANNIN, N. G. T., KENOLTY, N. & ARDUS, D. A. 1975. Structure and stratigraphy of the Sea of the Hebrides and the Minches. *In*: WOODLAND, A. W. (ed.) *Petroleum Geology and the Continental Shelf of Northwest Europe. 1. Geology*. Applied Science, Barking, 93–102.

——, —— & KENOLTY, N. 1974. *The Geology of the Sea of the Hebrides*. Report of the Institute of Geological Sciences 73/14.

CLOETINGH, S., LAMBECK, K. & McQUEEN, H. 1987. Apparent sea-level fluctuations and a palaeo-stress field for the North Sea region. *In*: BROOKS, J. & GLENNIE, K. (eds) *Petroleum Geology of North-West Europe*. Graham & Trotman, London. 49–57.

CLOUGH, C. T. & HARKER, A. 1904. *The Geology of West-Central Skye, with Soay*. Memoirs of Geological Survey Scotland.

EINSELE, G. & SEILACHER, A. (eds) 1982. *Cyclic and Event Stratification*. Springer, Berlin.

GALLOWAY, W. E. 1989. Genetic stratigraphic sequences in basin analysis I: architecture and genesis of flooding-surface bounded depositional units. *AAPG Bulletin*, **73**, 125–142.

GREEN, G. W. & WELCH, F. B. A. 1965. *Geology of the Country around Wells and Cheddar*. Memoirs of Geological Survey of Great Britain.

HALLAM, A. 1978. Eustatic cycles in the Jurassic. *Palaeogeography, Palaeoclimatology, Palaeoecology*, **23**, 1–32.

—— 1981. A revised sea-level curve for the early Jurassic. *Journal of The Geological Society, London*, **138**, 735–743.

—— 1989. A re-evaluation of Jurassic eustasy in the light of new data and the revised Exxon curves. *In*: WILGUS, C. K. (ed.) *Sea Level Changes — an Integrated Approach*. Society of Economic Paleontologists and Mineralogists Special Publication, **42**, 261–273.

HARRIS, J. P. 1989. The sedimentology of a Middle Jurassic lagoonal delta system: Elgol Formation (Great Estuarine Group), NW Scotland. *In*: WHATELEY, M. K. G. & PICKERING, K. T. (eds) *Deltas: Sites and Traps for Fossil Fuels*. Geological Society, London, Special Publication **41**, 147–166.

HOWARTH, M. K. 1956. The Scalpa Sandstone of the Isle of Raasay, Inner Hebrides. *Proceedings of the Yorkshire Geological Society*, **30**, 353–370.

HUDSON, J. D. 1964. The petrology of the sandstones of the Great Estuarine Series, and the Jurassic palaeogeography of Scotland. *Proceedings of the Geologists Association*, **75**, 499–527.

—— 1980. Aspects of brackish-water facies and faunas from the Jurassic of north-west Scotland. *Proceedings of the Geologists Association*, **91**, 99–105.

—— 1983. Mesozoic sedimentation and sedimentary rocks in the Inner Hebrides. *Proceedings of the Royal Society of Edinburgh*, **83B**, 47–63.

MIALL, A. D. 1984. *Principles of Sedimentary Basin Analysis*. Springer, New York.

MORTON, N. 1965. The Bearreraig Sandstone Series (Middle Jurassic) of Skye and Raasay. *Scottish Journal of Geology*, **1**, 189–216.

—— 1983. Palaeocurrents and palaeo-environment of part of the Bearreraig Sandstone (Middle Jurassic) of Skye and Raasay, Inner Hebrides. *Scottish Journal of Geology*, **19**, 87–95.

—— 1987. Jurassic subsidence history in the Hebrides, N. W. Scotland. *Marine and Petroleum Geology*, **4**, 226–242.

—— 1989. Jurassic sequence stratigraphy in the Hebrides Basin, NW Scotland. *Marine and Petroleum Geology*, **6**, 243–260.

—— 1990a. Tectonic and eustatic controls of Jurassic genetic sequences in the Hebrides basin, NW Scotland. *Bulletin Société géologique de France*, série, **8**, 6, 1001–1009.

—— 1990b. *The Lias of the Hebrides*. Livre jubilaire R. Mouterde. Cahiers Université Catholique de Lyon, Série sciences, **4**, 107–119.

OATES, M. J. 1978. A revised stratigraphy for the western Scottish Lower Lias. *Proceedings of the Yorkshire Geological Society* **42**, 143–156.

PEACH, B. N., HORNE, J., WOODWARD, H. B., CLOUGH, C. T., HARKER, A. & WEDD, C. B. 1910. *The Geology of Glenelg, Lochalsh and South-east part of Skye*. Memoirs of Geological Survey of Scotland.

SMITH, N. J. 1985. The age and structural setting of limestones and basalts on the Main Ring Fault in southeast Rhum. *Geological Magazine*, **122**, 439–445.

SNELLING, N. J. (ed.) 1986. *The Chronology of the Geological Record*. Geological Society, London Memoir **10**.

STEEL, R. J. 1974. New Red Sandstone floodplain and piedmont sedimentation in the Hebridean Province, Scotland. *Journal of Sedimentary Petrology*, **44**, 336–357.

—— 1977. Triassic rift basins of north-west Scotland — their configuration, infilling and development. *In*: FINSTAD, F. G. & SELLEY, R. C. (eds) *Proceedings Mesozoic Northern North Sea Symposium* (MNNS) 7.

—— & WILSON, A. C. 1975. Sedimentation and tectonism (? Permo-Triassic) on the margin of the North Minch Basin, Lewis. *Journal of The Geological Society, London*, **131**, 183–202.

STEIN, A. 1988. Basement controls upon basin development in the Caledonian foreland, N. W. Scotland. *Basin Research*, **1**, 107–119.

SURLYK, F., CLEMMENSEN, L. B. & LARSEN, H. C. 1981. Post-Palaeozoic evolution of the East Greenland continental margin. *Memoir of Canadian Society of Petroleum Geologists*, **7**, 611–645.

SYKES, R. M. & CALLOMON, J. H. 1979. The *Amoeboceras* zonation of the Boreal Upper Oxfordian. *Palaeontology*, **22**, 839–903.

TURNER, J. 1966. The Oxford Clay of Skye, Scalpay and Eigg. *Scottish Journal of Geology*, **2**, 243–252.

VAN HINTE, J. E. 1978. Geohistory analysis — application of micropaleontology in exploration geology. *AAPG Bulletin*, **62**, 201–222.

VAN WAGONER, J. C., MITCHUM, R. M., CAMPION, K. M. & RAHMANIAN, V. D. 1990. *Siliciclastic Sequence Stratigraphy in Well Logs, Cores, and Outcrops*. American Association of Petroleum Geologists Methods in Exploration Series **7**.

WILSON, R. C. L., HISCOTT, R. N., WILLIS, M. G. & GRADSTEIN, F. M. 1990. The Lusitanian Basin of West-Central Portugal: Mesozoic and Tertiary tectonic, stratigraphic, and subsidence history. *In*: TANKARD, A. J. & BALKWILL, H. (eds) *Extensional Tectonics and Stratigraphy of the North Atlantic Margins*. American Association of Petroleum Geologists Memoir **46**, 341–361.

WRIGHT, J. K. 1973. The Middle and Upper Oxfordian and Kimmeridgian Staffin Shales at Staffin, Isle of Skye. *Proceedings of the Geologists Association*, **84**, 447–457.

Mid-Jurassic lagoonal delta systems in the Hebridean basins: thickness and facies distribution patterns of potential reservoir sandbodies

J. P. HARRIS

Department of Geology, University of Leicester, University Road, Leicester LE1 7RH, UK

(Present address: Simon-Robertson, Llandudno, Gwynedd, N Wales LL30 1SA)

Abstract: In the Inner Hebrides the facies distribution patterns and mineralogy of outcropping Great Estuarine Group (Bathonian) sandbodies indicate SSW progradation of copiously supplied lagoonal deltas in two sub-basins (Sea of the Hebrides Basin and Inner Hebrides Basin). These were both westerly tilted half graben and were probably separated by a slowly subsiding basement ridge known as the mid-Skye palaeohigh. In the Bathonian these basins had an intermittent connection with the open sea and were supplied with clastic sediment from mineralogically distinct source areas in the Scottish Landmass to the east and an Outer Hebrides Landmass to the west. Fluvial-dominated and fluvial-wave interaction deltas supplied by low sinuosity rivers form successive sandbodies intercalated with lagoonal mudstones. The facies distribution patterns and mappable depositional limits of these sandbodies are dependent on the style and rate of fluvial supply, the configuration of the basins, variations in wave energy and salinity fluctuations. This demonstrates concepts which are probably applicable to the prediction of reservoir thickness and facies patterns in related sedimentary basins.

This paper concerns the stratigraphy, sedimentology and distribution pattern of potential reservoir sandbodies in the Bathonian Valtos Sandstone Formation of the Sea of the Hebrides and adjacent Inner Hebrides basins, NW Scotland. The Mesozoic sediments of these two Hebridean basins include potential reservoir targets at various horizons. The three most important of these are: fluvial channel sandbodies in the Triassic; thick, laterally extensive, marine sandstones in the Bajocian Bearreraig Sandstone Formation; and the more complex, lagoonal delta and lagoon shoreline sediments of the Bathonian Valtos Formation. This formation includes the most important potential reservoir sandbodies within the Great Estuarine Group. At outcrop on the islands of Skye, Raasay, Eigg and Muck in the Inner Hebrides (Fig. 1), the Valtos Formation is up to 110 m thick. It comprises sandstones, mudstones and shell debris limestones with a potential net reservoir/gross stratigraphic thickness ratio of between 0.5 and 0.7. In the subsurface these potential reservoir sandbodies would be effectively sealed by the overlying mudstones of the Duntulm and Kilmaluag Formations (see Fig. 2) and occur in association with potential hydrocarbon source rocks within the Great Estuarine Group (Cullaidh Shale Formation) and in the overlying Staffin Bay and Staffin Shale Formations (Callovian–Kimmeridgian).

The Great Estuarine Group represents an important paralic episode within an otherwise marine Jurassic section in the Hebridean Basins (Hudson 1983). During the Bathonian the basins were characterized by rapid and frequent salinity fluctuations (see Fig. 2). These had a profound influence on the fauna and on sedimentation in the basins such that no age diagnostic macrofaunas have been documented and the Great Estuarine Group includes some unique salinity-controlled facies assemblages. The salinity fluctuations have been interpreted by Hudson (1963a, b), Tan & Hudson (1974), Harris (1989) and Andrews & Walton (1990) as recording varying rates of fresh water run-off into semi-enclosed sedimentary basins with partial or intermittent connections with the open sea. The marked similarities in the stratigraphy of the Bathonian in the two Hebridean basins (Sea of the Hebrides Basin and Inner Hebrides Basin) and the equivalent sediments in the Slyne Basin to the west of Ireland (Trueblood & Morton 1991; Morton this volume) probably demonstrates that this set of controls was not unique to the Hebrides and that these outcropping sediments may provide the key to the interpretation of age-equivalent sediments in the subsurface offshore of western Britain and Ireland.

Valtos Formation sediments are illustrated here by means of graphic logs representing seven

From PARNELL, J., (ed.), 1992, *Basins on the Atlantic Seaboard: Petroleum Geology, Sedimentology and Basin Evolution.* Geological Society Special Publication No 62, pp 111–144.

111

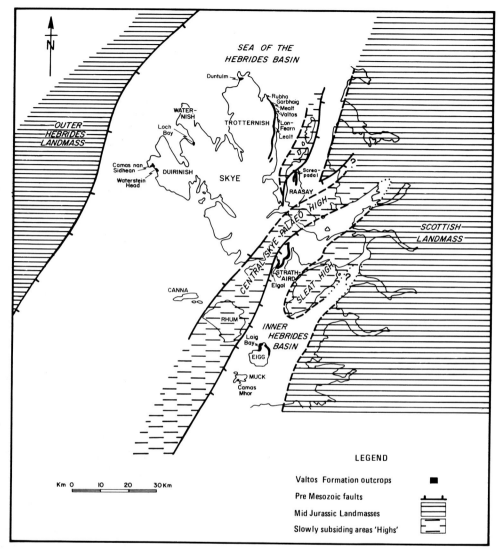

Fig. 1. Major Mid-Jurassic structural controls on basin configuration (based on Binns *et al.* 1975; Steel 1976).

facies which occur in five distinct facies sequences. These sequences are interpreted as
representing axial and lateral parts of lagoonal
deltas and interdeltaic lagoon shorelines together with intradeltaic and offshore/pro-delta
environments. The logs record a virtually completely exposed stratigraphic section in the Sea
of the Hebrides Basin (outcrops in Trotternish
and Waternish on Skye and on Raasay) and the
Inner Hebrides Basin (outcrops in Strathaird in
south Skye and on Eigg and Muck).

Interpretation of the facies and facies se-

quences are based on grain size profiles, sedimentary structures, biogenic structures and
macro-fossils. Interpretations are constrained
by previous work on the nature of the hinterland
and palaeoclimate (Tan & Hudson 1974;
Hudson 1970; Harris 1989) and the salinity of
water in the receiving basins (Hudson 1963*a*, *b*;
Hudson & Harris 1979; Hudson 1980; Andrews
& Walton 1990).

The configuration of the basins (Fig. 1) and
nature of the basin margin faults can be defined
by combining the structural mapping of Binns

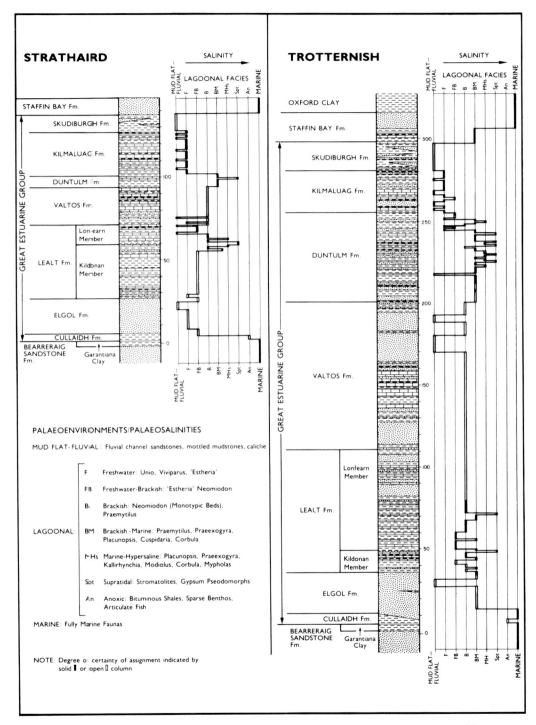

Fig. 2. Great Estuarine Group, Strathaird and Trotternish composite stratigraphic sequences with palaeoenvironmental-palaeosalinity plots (modified from Hudson & Harris 1979; from Harris 1989).

et al. (1975) with the Triassic palaeogeography established by Steel *et al.* (1975) and Steel (1976) cf. Evans *et al.* (1982). Palaeogeographic reconstructions for the Middle Jurassic have been interpreted using elements of these maps as a template (Harris 1984, 1989). The presence, in the Mid-Jurassic, of the structural elements used in this palaeogeographic scheme has been substantiated by the recently published seismic interpretations (Brewer & Smythe 1984; Stein 1988; Earle *et al.* 1989; Stein & Blundell 1990) and is elaborated here. The seismic interpretations demonstrate that the Mesozoic basins were parts of a series of linked extensional basins. They were controlled in their position and extent by the extensional reactivation of pre-existing, largely Caledonide thrusts to create major, down to the east, normal faults at the margins of westerly-tilted half graben (Brewer & Smythe 1984; Stein 1988). In the Hebrides the most important of these Mesozoic normal faults are the Camasumary−Skerryvore Fault which bounds the Inner Hebrides Basin and the Minch Fault which bounds the Sea of the Hebrides Basin (Fig. 1).

Some controversy surrounds the presence in the Mesozoic of the Camasunary−Skerryvore fault and the associated mid Skye palaeohigh which today separates the two Hebridean basins. It is possible that in the mid-Jurassic two separate Valtos Formation delta systems (see discussion below) were deposited in a single Hebridean basin. However seismic interpretations demonstrate that Mesozoic sediments thin across the mid-Skye palaeohigh (Stein, pers. comm.). This thickness distribution pattern is consistent with sedimentological findings for the Triassic (Steel *et al.* 1975, 1976) and the mid-Jurassic (Andrews 1985; Harris 1989; Andrews & Walton 1990). Facies, thickness and mineralogy of the Valtos Formation described here indicate that a narrow slowly subsiding basement ridge, known as the mid Skye palaeohigh probably separated the two subbasins in the mid-Jurassic (Fig. 1). This feature was probably topographically subdued such that it was not an important sediment source. The striking similarities in stratigraphy and facies of both sub-basins is probably attributable to the synchronous subsidence histories of these linked extensional basins.

Lithostratigraphy

The Valtos Formation comprises sandstones with unusually large ferroan calcite concretions (Hudson & Andrews 1987; Wilkinson & Dampier 1990; Wilkinson, this volume) and

shell debris (*Neomiodon*) limestones intercalated with siltstones and mudstones. This sandstone-dominated formation intervenes between the lagoonal mudstones and lagoon shoreline sediments of the Lealt Formation and Duntulm Formation (see Fig. 2). The Lealt Shale Formation records fresh-brackish with subordinate brackish marine salinities and the Duntulm Formation records marine-brackish salinities with occasional fresh water and hypersaline episodes (Hudson & Harris 1979; Andrews & Walton 1990).

In the type section in north Trotternish the Valtos Formation is 110 m thick and is divided into three lithostratigraphic units (Harris & Hudson 1980). These are a lower sandstone-dominated unit, a middle limestone-shale unit and an upper sandstone-dominated unit (see Fig. 3).

Outcrops elsewhere in the Sea of the Hebrides Basin (Waternish and Raasay) demonstrate the basin wide extent of these three units. In the Inner Hebrides Basin (see Fig. 4) the formation is thinner (up to 73 m) and in Strathaird (in the Inner Hebrides Basin), close to the basin margin, it exhibits major thickness and facies variations. Here the formation is only 24 m thick, and the major sandbodies which dominate the formation elsewhere are replaced by shell debris limestones, desiccation-cracked limestones and shales.

The recognition of distinct facies and facies sequences (see discussion below) has allowed the formation to be subdivided into a series of genetically related, correlatable lithostratigraphic divisions (see Figs 3 & 4). These are termed divisions I-XII in the main outcrop area in north Trotternish, Skye (Sea of the Hebrides Basin) and A-E in the main outcrop area on Eigg (Inner Hebrides Basin).

Petrography and provenance

Both the sedimentary basins have similar burial and diagenetic histories (Hudson 1964; Harris 1984; Hudson & Andrews 1987) and the Valtos Formation in both basins represents the same range of grain size so that differences in detrital mineralogy are attributed to differences in the mineralogy of the rocks exposed in the hinterlands of the basins rather than to the post-depositional alteration (cf. Hudson & Andrews 1987). Valtos Formation sandstones in the Sea of the Hebrides Basin are subfeldspathic− feldspathic with 5−26% feldspar. These contrast with the feldspar poor, quartzose sandstones with less than 5% feldspar of the Valtos Formation in the Inner Hebrides Basin.

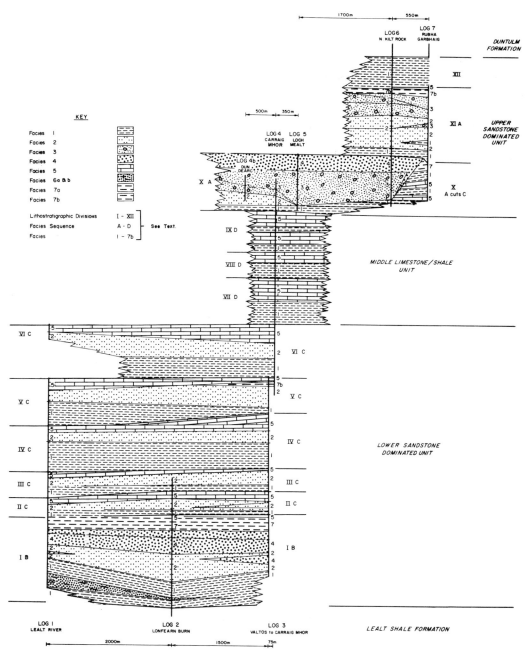

Fig. 3. Lithostratigraphic correlation of the Valtos Formation in North Trotternish, Skye.

Heavy mineral assemblages from the two basins are also different. These differences were first established by Hudson (1964) on the basis of entire heavy mineral separations. In order to examine these differences further, heavy mineral separations in the 1.5−3.0∅ size fraction were prepared from all the main Valtos Formation outcrops (Harris 1984). This tech-

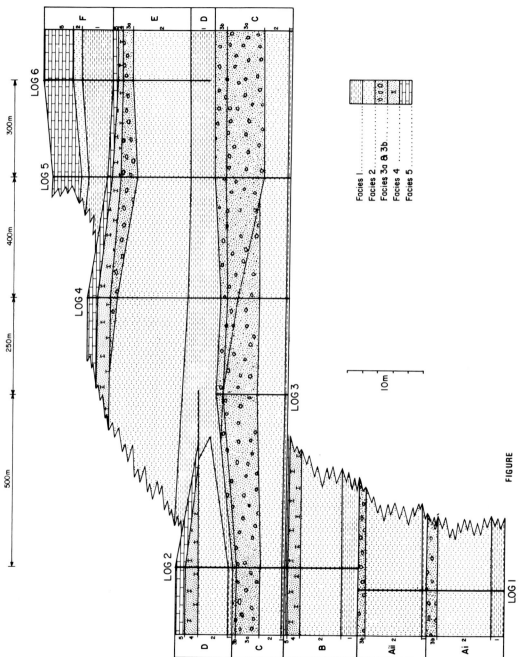

Fig. 4. Lithostratigraphic and facies correlation of the Valtos Formation, Bay of Laig, Eigg.

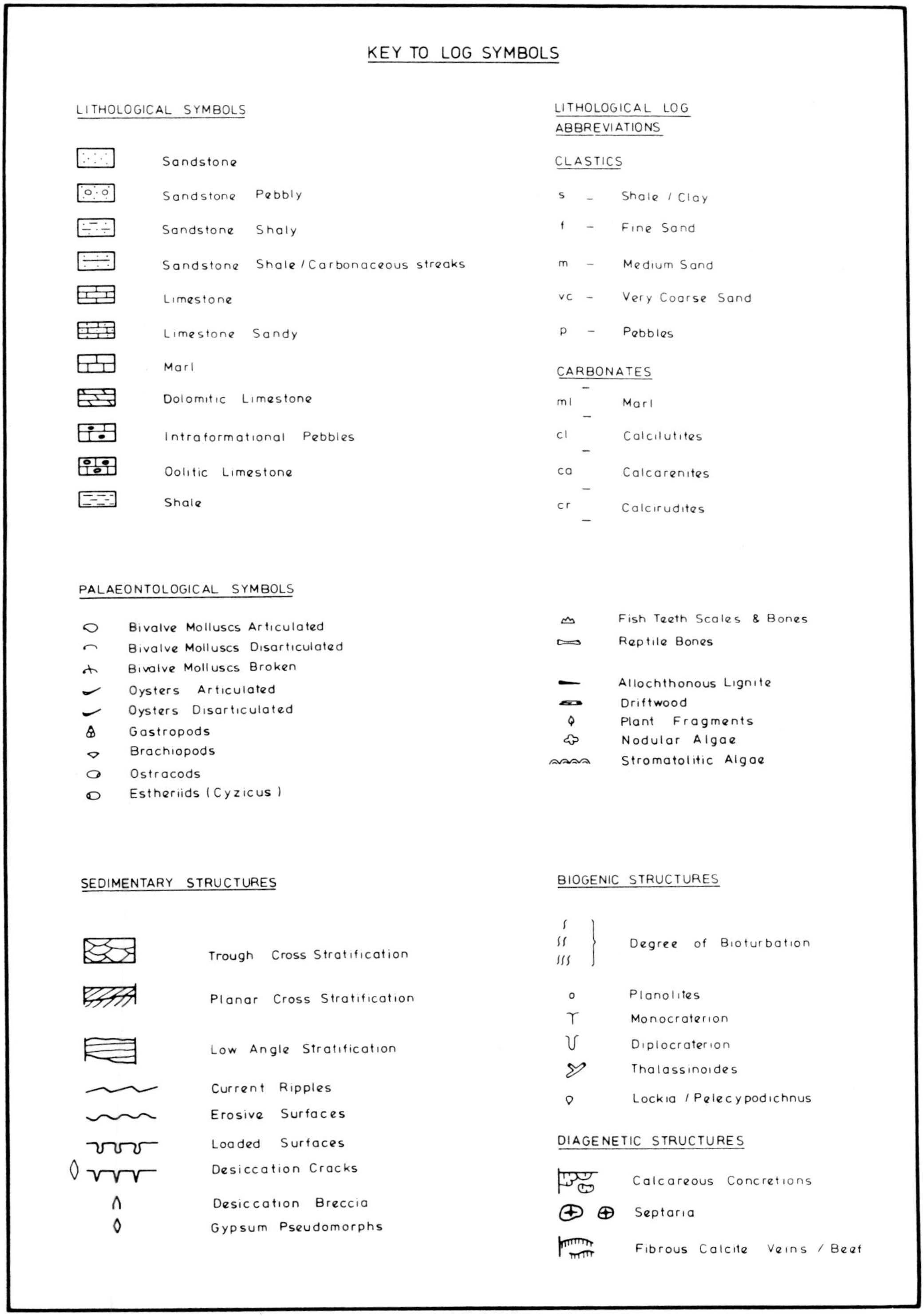

KEY TO LOG SYMBOLS

LITHOLOGICAL SYMBOLS

- Sandstone
- Sandstone Pebbly
- Sandstone Shaly
- Sandstone Shale/Carbonaceous streaks
- Limestone
- Limestone Sandy
- Marl
- Dolomitic Limestone
- Intraformational Pebbles
- Oolitic Limestone
- Shale

LITHOLOGICAL LOG ABBREVIATIONS

CLASTICS

- s — Shale / Clay
- f — Fine Sand
- m — Medium Sand
- vc — Very Coarse Sand
- p — Pebbles

CARBONATES

- ml — Marl
- cl — Calcilutites
- ca — Calcarenites
- cr — Calcirudites

PALAEONTOLOGICAL SYMBOLS

- Bivalve Molluscs Articulated
- Bivalve Molluscs Disarticulated
- Bivalve Molluscs Broken
- Oysters Articulated
- Oysters Disarticulated
- Gastropods
- Brachiopods
- Ostracods
- Estheriids (Cyzicus)

- Fish Teeth Scales & Bones
- Reptile Bones

- Allochthonous Lignite
- Driftwood
- Plant Fragments
- Nodular Algae
- Stromatolitic Algae

SEDIMENTARY STRUCTURES

- Trough Cross Stratification
- Planar Cross Stratification
- Low Angle Stratification
- Current Ripples
- Erosive Surfaces
- Loaded Surfaces
- Desiccation Cracks
- Desiccation Breccia
- Gypsum Pseudomorphs

BIOGENIC STRUCTURES

- Degree of Bioturbation
- Planolites
- Monocraterion
- Diplocraterion
- Thalassinoides
- Lockia / Pelecypodichnus

DIAGENETIC STRUCTURES

- Calcareous Concretions
- Septaria
- Fibrous Calcite Veins / Beef

nique was adopted to remove the flood of tiny
zircon grains which typified Hudson's (1964)
analyses and thereby allow the further examination of the larger, more provenance sensitive
mineral grains (see Table 1 and Fig. 5).

The Valtos Formation in the Inner Hebrides
Basin contains garnet-poor, staurolite-rich,
rutile-rich assemblages, probably indicating
a significant although indirect contribution of
sediment from the Dalradian of the Southern
and Eastern Highlands (possibly via the Old
Red Sandstone which may have extended into
the hinterland of this basin). In the Sea of the
Hebrides Basin the formation contains garnet-
rich heavy mineral assemblages with consistent
amounts of kyanite and epidote, probably indicating a greater contribution of sediment from
the Moines (cf. Hudson 1964). In west Skye,
Valtos Formation sandstones contain an average
of 69% green epidote, probably derived from
the Lewisian of the Outer Hebrides Landmass.
This local dominance of Lewisian epidote
is attributable to the close proximity of the
Waterstein outcrops to the Minch Fault and
coincides with easterly palaeoflow directions.

Pebbles in the Valtos Formation in both sedimentary basins are predominantly vein quartz
but also include Moinian 'granulites', probable
Cambrian quartzites, red jasper pebbles from
the Torridonian and cherts, probably from the
Durness Group. All of these could be derived
from the Caledonian fold/thrust belt and
Caledonian foreland of the Scottish Landmass
immediately to the east or north east of both
basins.

The petrographic provinces defined here (by
reference to both the light and heavy mineralogy
of the sandstones) demonstrate the derivation
of sediment from two distinct hinterland areas
in the Scottish Landmass to the east of the
Hebridean basins and derivation from a single
hinterland area in the Outer Hebrides Landmass
to the west. These petrographic provinces correspond directly with the palaeogeographic
elements defined in Fig. 1 (see discussion below
and Fig. 19).

Facies description and interpretation

Seven genetically related facies (three of which
are divided into two subfacies) can be defined in
the Valtos Formation. These are based on distinct associations of lithology, grain size profile,
sedimentary structures, trace fossils and macro-
fossils. The distribution of these facies in the
main outcrops of the Valtos Formation is shown
on Figs 3 & 4, they are illustrated graphically in

Figures 6–10 and described in Table 2 (detailed
descriptions in Harris 1984). These facies
comprise the following:

(1) *Neomiodon* mudstone–siltstone facies,
    representing offshore lagoonal mudstones
    at the base of each facies sequence.
(2) Coarsening-upward sandstone facies, rep-
    resenting delta front and lower–middle
    lagoon shoreface sands in the lower part of
    each of the Valtos Formation sandbodies.
(3) Coarse–'pebbly' sandstone facies, rep-
    resenting distributary channel and sand flat
    environments. Locally this can be split into
    3a; a pebbly facies and 3b; a thin bedded,
    trough cross stratified coarse sandstone
    facies.
(4) Wave formed sandstone facies, represent-
    ing wave reworked (fluvially supplied),
    mid–upper shoreface, foreshore and
    backshore sandstones.
(5) *Neomiodon* debris limestone facies, rep-
    resenting transgressive deposits capping
    abandoned lagoonal delta and lagoon
    shoreline sequences and shallow lagoonal,
    shell debris, sheets and shoals intercalated
    with facies-1 mudstones–siltstones.
(6) Thin bedded sand sheet facies, representing
    storm or flood generated shallow offshore/
    sublittoral sands intercalated with facies-1
    mudstones. Locally this can be subdivided
    into 6a; a load cast facies and 6b; a ripple
    drift cross laminated facies, representing a
    distinctive type of storm-generated waning
    flow sandstone also intercalated with facies
    1 mudstones.
(7) Desiccation crack facies, representing
    periodically emergent lagoon shoreline
    mud flats. Locally this facies can also be
    subdivided into 7a; the desiccation-cracked
    facies and 7b; rootlet-penetrated facies,
    representing emergent vegetated areas of
    the delta plain, mudflats and sand flats.

The fauna of the Valtos Formation, is dominated by the bivalve *Neomiodon*. It records
rapid and wide salinity fluctuations (Hudson
1963a; 1980), probably controlled by varying
rates of fluvial run off (see discussion below).
The fauna also includes the fresh water snail
Viviparus and locally abundant fish debris including shark teeth and fin spines. Finely divided
plant debris is common in all the sandstone
facies and there are also local accumulations of
coniferous driftwood.

The Sea of the Hebrides Basin was larger
than the Inner Hebrides Basin and therefore
had a greater fetch. Water depths in the distal
parts of this basin were probably also greater.
Consequently wave-formed structures and

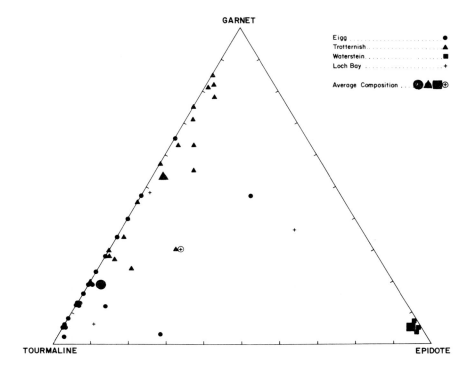

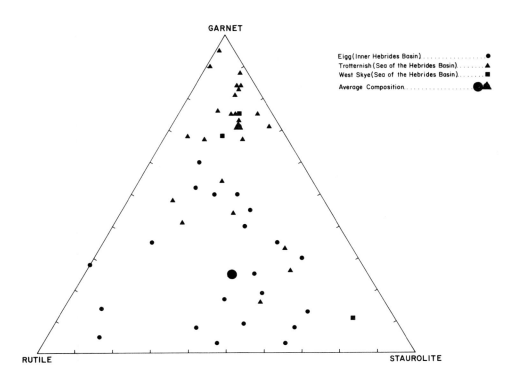

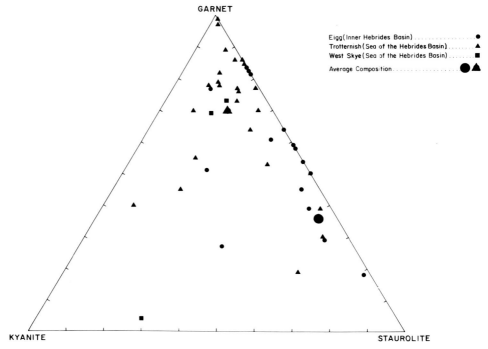

Fig. 5. Triangular plots to illustrate heavy mineral distribution patterns in the three petrographic provinces (see Table 1).

sequences (see facies 4) are more important here than in the Inner Hebrides Basin.

The palaeocurrent pattern (recorded by means of rose diagrams and vector arrows included alongside the field logs) in both basins is dominated by southerly flow directions. This is interpreted as demonstrating an axial sediment dispersal pattern. Occasional northerly flow directions record palaeocurrent reversals. This pattern could represent southerly, fluvial and ebb currents with a subordinate northerly flood tidal component. Alternatively the northerly palaeoflow directions can be attributed to wind/storm driven currents. This is the more likely control on palaeocurrent reversals, given the salinity fluctuations (recorded by the *Neomiodon*-dominated fauna) which indicate that the basins were isolated or semi-enclosed (lagoons) and probably only had a partial connection with the open sea (see discussion below).

Facies sequences and depositional model

Facies interpretation and the identification of genetic relationships between facies have allowed the definition of five facies sequences. These are applicable to both sedimentary basins. Facies shown in brackets in the following descriptions of the sequences are rare or laterally impersistent elements within otherwise consistent sequences. These sequences are as follows.

Facies sequence A is a coarsening-upward sequence representing the axial part of the lagoonal delta systems (see Figs 11 & 12). It includes proximal mouth bar sands truncated by fining-upward distributary channel sands. The facies sequence is 1→2→3→(4)→(7b).

Facies sequence B differs from A in that it does not include mouth bar or distributary channel facies (see Figs 13–15). It represents lagoonal delta shoreline progradation in the form of a wave-dominated beach face with a backshore or delta plain lagoon. The facies sequence is 1→2→4→(7)→5.

Facies sequence C represents simple, interdeltaic lagoon shoreline progradation. Like B, the sequence is capped by transgressive erosively based coquinas (see Fig. 16). The facies sequence is 1→2→(7b)→5.

Table 1. *Average heavy mineral composition (%) of Valtos Formation Sandstones 1.5–3.00 φ micron fraction, opaque grains omitted, full analytical results in Harris (1984)*

	Zircon	Tourmaline	Rutile	Garnet	Staurolite	Kyanite	Epidote	Apatite	Sphene	Monazite	Hornblende	Brookite	Tremolite
Inner Hebrides Basin Eigg and Muck (21 samples analysed)	23	38	12	8	13	1	1	P	–	P	P	–	–
Sea of the Hebrides Basin Trotternish and Raasay (23 samples analysed)	13	26	7	35	9	6	2	1	P	P	P	–	–
Sea of the Hebrides Basin Loch Bay (3 samples analysed)	8	26	4	20	9	16	12	P	1	–	2	–	–
Sea of the Hebrides Basin Waterstein (3 samples)	7	2	P	4	2	3	69	2	1	3	2	3	4

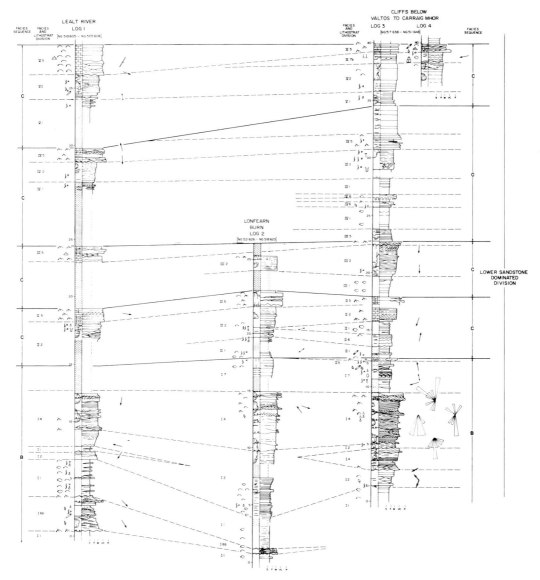

Fig. 6. Graphic logs (1–4) of divisions I–V, lower sandstone dominated unit of the Valtos Formation, North Trotternish.

Facies sequence D comprises shallow lagoonal shell debris sheets and shoals and lagoonal muds deposited during a period characterized by low rates of clastic supply. The facies sequence is a simple alternation of 1→5.

Facies sequence E only occurs in west Skye and on Raasay. It probably represents the off-

shore or distal parts of successive lagoonal delta progradation sequences. The facies sequence is a simple alternation of 1→2.

In addition to these distinct sequences, certain facies are simply interbedded. Facies 6 sandstones (probably representing storm-generated clastic influxes) are intercalated with facies 1 mudstones at various horizons to give this type

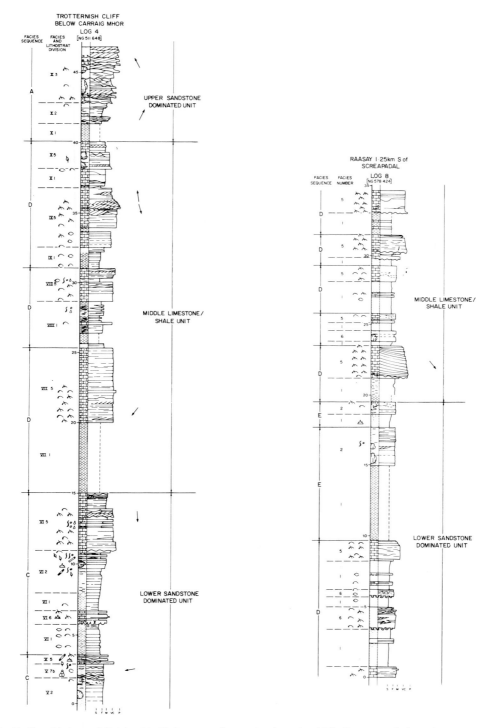

Fig. 7. Graphic logs of division V−X, lower sandstone dominated, middle limestone shale and upper sandstone dominated units of the Valtos Formation, North Trotternish and the equivalent rocks of Raasay.

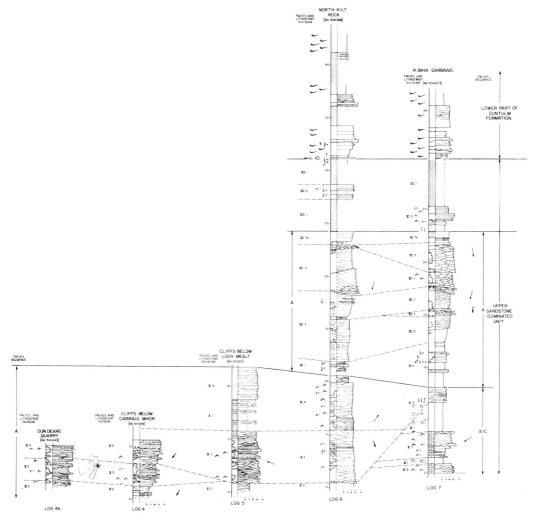

Fig. 8. Graphic logs (4–7) of divisions X–XII, upper sandstone dominated unit of the Valtos Formation and the basal Duntulm Formation, North Trotternish.

of alternation. Certain facies also occur in isolation. In Strathaird, close to the margin of the Inner Hebrides Basin the formation is anomalously thin (24 m) and facies 7 (desiccation-cracked limestone facies) occurs in isolation at the base of the formation.

The block diagrams (Figures 18.1–18.4) illustrate the probable genetic relationships of facies in the most important facies sequences (A-B-C-D). These are discussed in stratigraphic

sequence (B-C-D-A) in order to account for the evolution of the Valtos lagoonal delta system as recorded in the main-north Trotternish outcrops. Very similar facies relationships are identified in the Valtos Formation on Eigg and Muck in the Inner Hebrides Basin (similar to Figure 18.1 and 18.4 although waves were probably less important in this smaller and probably also shallower basin). Figure 18 forms the basis of the following summary.

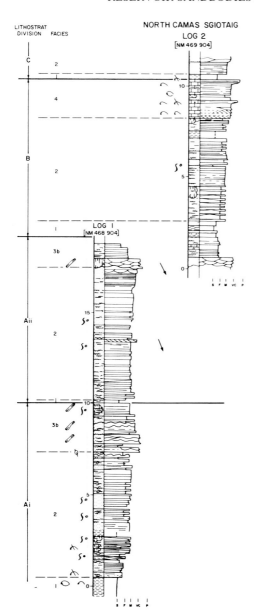

Fig. 9. Graphic log of divisions Ai, Aii and B, Valtos Formation, North Camas, Sgiotaig and Eigg.

coastal mudflats represented by the top of the Lealt Formation, resulting in the establishment of a shallow brackish lagoon in which mudstones—siltstones were deposited.

Copious clastic supply to the basin is recorded by the southerly progradation of a lagoonal delta system. This delta is represented by facies sequence B (see Fig. 18.1). It records high wave energies which generated a beach spit system (facies 2 and 4) with shoreface bars (ridge and runnel topography), storm generated scour and fill structures and a well defined foreshore zone with swash cross stratification. The system was actively supplied with sediment, reworked by waves, probably from near-by fluvial distributaries.

Landward of the beach spit (Fig. 18.1) was a delta plain lagoon or bay bordered by wave-rippled (flaser-bedded) mudflats (facies 7) cut locally by ephemeral channels. The lagoon was infilled by muds and washover lobe sands, the top surfaces of which were occasionally sub-aerially exposed and desiccation cracked.

Storms which generated the washover lobes and scour and fill structures in the shoreface sands are also the presumed origin of the sublittoral ('turbidite like') beds (facies 6b) in division I. It is unclear how these sandstones equate with the hummocky cross stratified sublittoral sandstones in marine sedimentary systems (cf. Swift 1985; Swift & Niedorada 1985).

The facies sequence (B) is capped by a thin *Neomiodon* limestone (facies 5) and is overlain by the facies 1 lagoonal mudstones of the next shoreline progradational sequence. The limestone is interpreted as recording abandonment (cessation of clastic supply) of the delta, continued subsidence and a consequent brackish transgression of the delta plain. Deposition of transgressive facies 5 limestones is not illustrated in any of the diagrams in Fig. 18.

Facies sequence B in the base of the Valtos Formation is thicker and more complex than the facies sequence C, shoreline sandbodies which characterize the rest of the lower sand-dominated unit in north Trotternish. It probably represents the reworking by waves of fluvially-supplied sediment in a relatively axial position with respect to fluvial supply.

North Trotternish, lower sandstone dominated unit

Facies sequence B (1→2→4→7→5)
(Fig. 18.1)

Deposition of the Valtos Formation in Trotternish commenced with the inundation of the

Facies sequence C (1→2→(7b)→5)
(Fig. 18.2)

The shoreline progradational sequences which make up the rest of the lower sandstone dominated unit in Trotternish represent repeated simple shorelines without shoreface bars. (Divisions II, III, IV, V, VI).

Table 2. *Valtos Formation, facies description and interpretation. The localities and log numbers included after the facies name are intended to provide good or typical illustrations of each facies*

Facies	Description	Interpretation
1) Neomiodon mudstone-sandstone facies. (Division I, north Trotternish, see Figure 6, log 1)	Silty, greenish grey, bioturbated-siltstones with thin (<10 cm) wave and or current-rippled very fine grained sand beds: contains *Neomiodon* as intact single valves and articulated specimens, mostly randomly orientated (i.e. few imbricate or convex up). Passes up gradationally into facies 2, or is intercalated with facies 5 limestones or 6a and 6b sandstones.	Deposition in shallow brackish lagoons. The lagoon floor was colonized by *Neomiodon* and periodic storms caused wave-formed concentrations of shells (subsequently bioturbated) and the emplacement of thin sand beds.
2) Coarsening upward sandstone facies (Division E, Laig, Eigg, see Figure 10).	Gradational coarsening-upward sequences passing down into facies 1. Bioturbated, with mudstone partings passing up into wave-rippled, locally current-rippled sandstones. Locally includes low angle (2–8°) inclined surfaces with depositional dip directions to S and SE (Figure 17). Truncated by facies 3 or capped by facies 4. Includes Pelecypodichnus and Teichichnus.	Progradation of delta shoreline and interdeltaic lagoon shoreline systems. Where current-rippled and truncated by facies 3 represents mouth bar progradation. Low angle inclined surfaces record progradation of broad lobate delta front probably indicating density-controlled underflow in reduced salinity receiving basins (cf. Elgol Formation, Harris 1989).
3) Coarse pebbly sandstone facies (Division XI and XIII, north Trotternish see Figure 8, log 7).	Includes three main types of sand body: – Major channel form, fining-upward sandbodies forming multistorey multilateral sequences (Figures 11 and 12). These have pebbly basal lags contain trough cross stratified cosets, large planar cross bed sets (up to 50 cm high) and some complex lateral accretion surfaces at the flanks of channel form units. Palaeoflow directions are predominantly S or SW. This facies truncates facies 2 coarsening-upward sequences and is capped by facies 4 or 7. – Thinner pebbly trough cross stratified sandstones capping facies 2 coarsening-upward sequences (termed facies 3a). – Finer grained, thinner bedded sandstones with mudstone partings (termed facies 3b).	Major delta distributary channels and their associated channelized mouth bars. Channels probably contained in-channel dunes and traverse bar bed forms. The S and SW palaeoflow directions mean that this was an axial sediment dispersal system in both basins. The coarse grain size and channelized character of bar crest sandstones probably means that they were friction-dominated (cf. Wright 1977). The thinner sandstones facies 3a probably represent broad delta plain sandflats. The 3b sandstones were probably a lateral equivalent deposited away from the main fluvial distributaries (where rootlet-penetrated this facies would be termed 7b).
4) Wave formed sandstone facies (Division E Bay of Laig, Eigg see Figure 10 and Division I Valtos, Trotternish see log 3 Figure 6).	Facies varies from sandstones with *Neomiodon* debris and low angle planar cross lamination with low-angle discordances between sets (probably swash cross lamination, Figure 15) to thicker more complex sandbodies. The facies contains distinctive large scale calcite concretions (Figure 13) which preserve *Neomiodon* debris. The thicker facies 4 sandbodies	The swash cross laminated sandstone capping distributary channel fill sequences probably represent the wave reworking of fluvially supplied sand at the delta shoreline. The thicker more complex sandbodies are interpreted as the upper shoreface-foreshore of prograding delta shoreline systems (cf. Kumar and Sanders, 1976).

coarsen upwards, contain planar laminated, granule-pebble lined scour-and-fill structure and *Neomiodon* escape structures (Figure 14). Towards the top the facies includes swash cross stratification with distinctive textural alternations. The facies is capped by calcite-cemented, pebbly, *Neomiodon* debris sandstones and is usually overlain by facies 7.

Where this facies intervenes between progradational sandbodies and lagoonal mudstones it represents brackish transgressions of the lagoon shoreline. Commonly the underlying sequences are incomplete and the sharp base of the facies demonstrates erosion of shoreline and delta/coastal plain sediments during transgression. The imbricate stacks of shells may represent wave-generated shell concentrations (cf. Futterer 1982). The red-weathering limestones with vertebrate debris are not true bone beds but may represent condensed sequences including pre-phosphatized material derived from delta/coastal plain sediments (cf. Aepler 1974). Where intercalated with offshore lagoonal mudstone (facies 1) the facies probably represents shell debris sheets and shoals.

5) *Neomiodon* debris limestone facies (division V Lealt River and Valtos, see logs 1 and 3, Figure 6).

Neomiodon debris in rock-forming abundance with pebbles and granules cemented by poikilotopic calcite. Locally the facies is reddish brown and contains reptile bones, fish debris large numbers of shark teeth and rare shark fin spines (Figure 16). *Neomiodon* debris commonly forms imbricate stacks of shells and sedimentary structures are indistinct. The facies is usually sharp or erosively-based. It overlies some coarsening-upward sandbodies and is either overlain by facies 1 mudstones or is intercalated with facies 1 mudstones. Locally the facies has wedge geometries and contains truncation surfaces.

6) Load cast and ripple drift cross laminated sandstone facies (Division IV Valtos see log 3, Figure 6 and Division I Lealt, see log 1, Figure 3).

10 cm-1 m thick fine or very fine-grained sandstones occurring as single beds or groups of beds intercalated with facies 1 mudstones. The beds are sharp-based and graded. Usually planar lamination is subordinate to type A and type B ripple drift cross lamination (facies 6b in Figures 3, 6, 7 and 8) and the facies is often disrupted by large scale load casts (facies 6a). Lenticular concentrations of *Neomiodon* are presented in the top of some beds.

Waning current velocities to give graded 'turbidite like' sand beds deposited offshore from prograding delta and lagoon shorelines. These are similar to the sub-littoral sheet sandstones of Hamblin and Walker (1979) but do not contain hummocky cross stratification. They are interpreted as sand sheets deposited on the lagoon floor.

7) Desiccation crack and rootlet-penetrated facies.

A group of rock types all exhibiting evidence of subaerial emergence. The facies includes limestones and shales with desiccation cracks usually associated with crustacean burrows (Facies 7a) and sandstones and thin mudstone-siltstone with rootlets (Facies 7b). This facies often also includes the fresh water snail *Viviparus*.

Lagoon margin mudflats subject to periodic emergence and desiccation. The facies also associated with progradational lagoon shoreline sandbodies. Locally these were colonized by plants and rootlet penetrated. The *Viviparus*-bearing mudstones probably represent pools of fresh water on the delta/coastal plain.

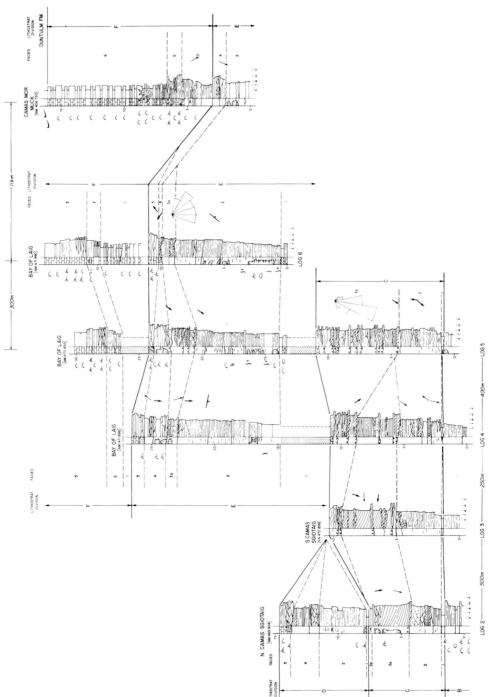

Fig. 10. Graphic logs of divisions C, D, E and F Valtos Formation, Camas Sgiotaig and Bay of Laig, Eigg and Cmas Mor, Muck.

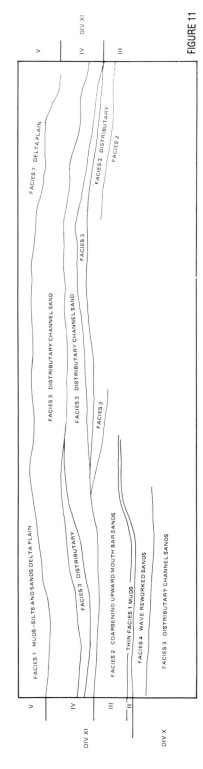

Fig. 11 Panoramic photomontage of multistorey-multilateral distributary channel and mouth bar sandstones in division X and XI, north, Kilt Rock Trotternish, cliff is 22 m high. Cliff section comprises:

I   Multistorey distributary channel sandstone of (facies 3) capped by *Neomiodon* bearing beach face sandstones (facies 4);

II   Thin lagoonal mudstones (facies 1) at base of division XI;

III   Coarsening upward mouth bar sandstones (facies 2);

IV   Multilateral and multistorey distributary channel sandstones (facies 3); basal truncation surfaces define channel-form sandbodies, but oblique section makes these and low angle-lateral accretion surfaces indistinct;

V   Delta plain mudstones and flood derived sandstones (facies 7).

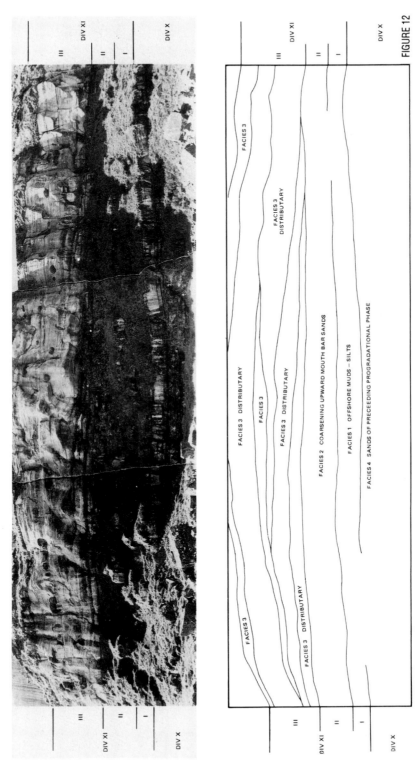

Fig. 12. Panoramic photomontage of a single lagoonal delta progradation sequence, division XI, south Rubha Garbhaig, Trotternish. Cliff is ca 18 m high. Cliff section includes:

I   Offshore lagoonal mudstones — siltstones (facies 1);
II   Coarsening upward mouth bar sandstones (facies 2);
III Multistorey — multilateral distributary channel sandstones (facies 3).

Fig. 13. Large, botryoidal calcite concretions developed in planar laminated and low angle planar cross laminated sandstones with pebble lined scours of a progradational delta shoreline sequence. Division I, Valtos, North Trotternish.

Offshore-lower and middle shoreface, regressive sediments (facies 1 and 2) are recognized in each sequence but most are truncated by transgressive facies 5 limestones (delta-destructive) so that delta plain sediments are only rarely preserved (e.g. division V, Figure 6). The sequence is repeated five times in the outcrops of the lower sand-dominated unit.

The depositional model for facies sequence C (Fig. 18.2) functions in a similar way to facies sequence B. Waves impinging on the shoreline redistributed sediment and caused southerly shoreline progradation by accretion of the beach face. Occasionally storm waves generated offshore directed currents which caused the rapid deposition of sub-littoral sandsheets (facies 6).

Sandbodies formed by facies sequence C are all thinner and finer grained than the facies sequence B sandbody. They probably indicate deposition during a period of localized low subsidence rate and are interpreted as representing deposition further alongshore from the locus of clastic supply than facies sequence B. The sequences are therefore interpreted as simple, interdeltaic lagoon shorelines.

The truncation of these regressive shoreline sequences at the base of the facies 5 transgressive limestones is possibly also a function of local, low subsidence rate. This would also account for the occurrence of limestones with fish debris (occupying pockets on the truncation surfaces) probably derived from the erosion of lagoon shoreline or coastal plain sediments.

North Trotternish middle limestone-shale unit

Facies sequence D (1→4) (Fig. 18.3)

Facies sequence D represents a major change in depositional style and in north Trotternish is the only facies sequence type in the middle limestone-shale unit. It represents a period characterized by low rates of clastic supply and high organic productivity, leading to the abundant availability of *Neomiodon* shell debris.

Wave- and storm-generated currents probably concentrated shell debris into shoals which

Fig. 14. Laminated pebbly sandstones with probable *Neomiodon* escape structures recording storm events in the middle shoreface (facies 4), division I, Valtos, Trotternish. Scale is a 10 p coin, diameter 28 mm.

Fig. 15. Pebbly, *Neomiodon* bearing sandstones interbedded with planar laminated and low angle planar cross laminated sands with low angle discordances between sets. Structures interpreted as swash cross lamination, top of facies 4, division I, Valtos, Trotternish. Scale is 50 mm across.

Fig. 16. Probable shark fine spine in *Neomiodon* debris limestone, facies 5, division V, Lealt River, Trotternish. Scale is 55 mm in diameter.

Fig. 17. Dvisions C, D and E, south of Camas Sgiotaig, Eigg. The lower cliff comprises a thin pro-delta muddy siltstone of facies 1 (in the wave cut notch) and coarsening upward delta front sandstones of facies 2 truncated by distributary channel sandstones of facies 3a. The unexposed section corresponds to pro-delta/offshore mud-silts. The upper cliff comprises a coarsening upward sequence with low angle offshore inclined delta front sandstones. These are overlain by probable shallow channel (facies 3a) and delta shoreline sandstones (facies 4). The cliff is capped by transgressive shell debris limestones of facies 5. Cliff is *c.* 27 m high.

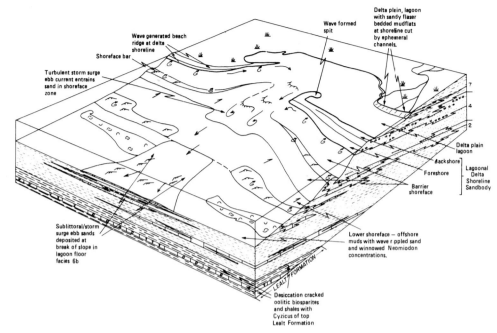

Fig. 18.1 Delta shoreline progradation represents wave redistributed sediment forming a barred high energy beach face in a relatively axial position with respect to fluvial supply
Facies sq. B
Lower Sandstone Dominated Unit
Division I

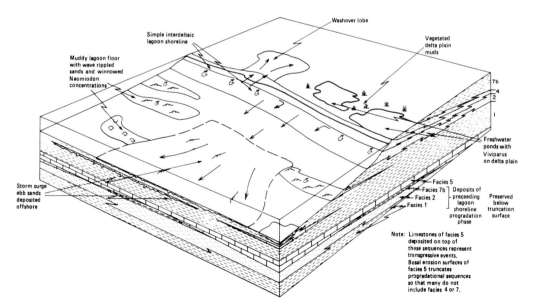

Fig. 18.2 Simple interdeltaic lagoon shoreline progradation phases represent wave redistributed sediment forming simple beach face sequences in a lateral position, distant from the contemporary fluvial supply.
Facies sq. C
Lower Sandstone Dominated Unit
Division II, III, IV, V and VI

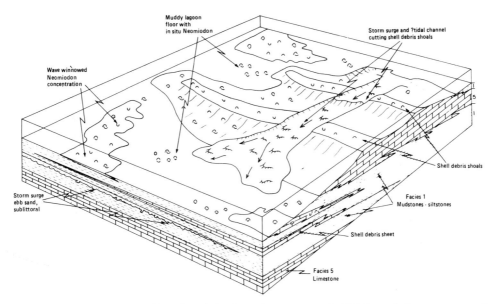

Fig. 18.3 Shell debris sheets (sublittoral) and shoals cut by storm surge? tidal channel. Represents a period characterized by low rates of clastic supply to the basin. Shoreline sediments exposed in W. Skye comprise desiccation cracked micritic limestones and dark shales.
Facies sq. D
Middle Limestone Shale Unit
Divisions VII, VIII and IX

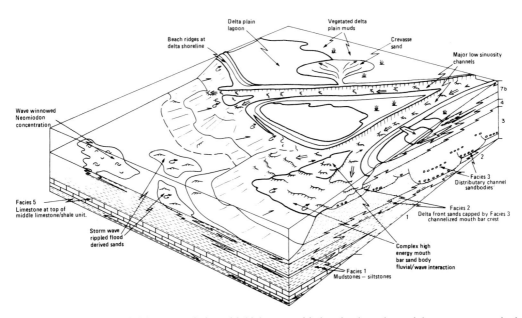

Fig. 18.4 Lobate lagoonal delta progradation with high energy friction dominated mouth bars, wave reworked delta front beach ridges, low sinuosity distributaries and vegetated delta plain.
Represents the axial portion of each lagoonal delta progradation phase.
Facies sq. A
Upper Sandstone Dominated Unit
Divisions X and XI

contain truncation surfaces and shallow channel structures. These are locally draped by thin mud laminae or include bioturbated horizons. This system was probably similar to the shallow marine 'blanket sandstone' model of Anderton (1976) and is similar to the crinoidal grainstones and coquinas discussed by Jeffrey & Aigner (1982).

Sand intercalations in the middle limestone-shale unit are all assigned to facies 6a and are interpreted as distal storm-generated, sub-littoral sheets.

North Trotternish upper sand dominated unit

Facies sequence A (1→2→3→(4)→(7b))

(Fig. 18.4)

Division X and XI in the upper sand-dominated unit comprise lagoonal delta progradation sequences and record the resumption of clastic supply to the basin. These sequences are dominated by S or SW-orientated bed load-dominated distributary channels. The texture of these channel sandstones together with the suite of in-channel bedforms demonstrates the existence of an energetic fluvial system with major fluctuations in river stage. These characteristics probably also indicate the interaction of fluvial and basinal processes close to the distributory mouth.

On the delta plain periodic flood events are the origin of the crevasse splay or sheet flood sands which are intercalated with carbonaceous and occasionally rootlet-penetrated muds. These represent delta plain lakes or lagoons with vegetated banks. The lateral migration of low sinuosity distributaries probably accounts for the small amounts of overbank, delta plain sediment preserved.

It is proposed that high rates of bedload transport and high outflow velocities in combination with shallow-water in the receiving basin (lagoon) resulted in the dominance of frictional processes at the distributary mouths (cf. Wright 1977). These outflow dynamics have also been invoked for lagoonal deltas of the Elgol Formation at the base of the Great Estuarine Group (Harris 1989). Like the Valtos Formation these deltas were deposited in a reduced salinity or fresh water-receiving basin. Because of these outflow dynamics distributary mouth bar sandstones in both formations are coarse-grained, contain high current velocity structures in the bar crest and are probably broadly lenticular in form. This geometry means

that sedimentation occurred very close to the delta shoreline so that sand could be readily reworked by waves into beach face sequences.

Depending on the extent of lateral migration of distributaries, the beach face sandstones may overly channel fill sequences (e.g. division X) or form complete beach face sequences (e.g. division I) defining the delta shoreline. Laterally these sequences should pass into finer-grained, simple, interdeltaic lagoon shorelines (e.g. divisions II, III, IV, V, VI).

Basinward of the delta front/distributary mouth, low current energies resulted in the deposition of lagoonal muds which are interrupted by occasional sharp-based current-rippled sandstones. These could be interpreted as the result of high discharge at the river mouths but are indistinguishable from the storm-derived facies 6a sands discussed above. Shallow water depths in the lagoon are indicated by wave ripples on the top surface of thin lenticular sands.

Facies sequence A is repeated twice in the upper sand-dominated unit (Fig. 8) with the establishment of rootlet-penetrated (Rubha Garbhaig log 7) or desiccation-cracked (Cairidh Ghlumaig, Duntulm) delta plain sands and muds close to the top of the formation. The occurrence of oyster-dominated faunas marking the base of the Duntulm Formation corresponds with a reduction in clastic supply to the basin and a marked increase in salinity of the basin water which allowed brackish-marine faunas to become established.

Depositional model: discussion

The facies sequences defined above are interpreted as genetically related elements of a lagoonal delta-lagoon shoreline system (see Fig. 18), in which a set of proximal–distal and axial–lateral relationships can be defined.

Proximal–distal relationships are illustrated where individual sequences 'pinch-out' in the direction of progradation (see Figs 4 & 10) as occurs in the Eigg outcrop. Similarly, the series of subdued coarsening upward sequences (facies sequence E) on Raasay and in west Skye are interpreted as the offshore equivalents of lagoonal delta/shoreline progradation sequences and therefore probably approximate to the depositional limits of those sequences. These could be interpreted as representing muddy lagoon shoreline progradation but do not contain any evidence of subaerial emergence.

Axial–lateral facies relationships are not observed directly. In Strathaird in the Inner Hebrides basin the progradational sandbodies are replaced by an anomalously thin strati-graphic section comprising desiccation-cracked and burrowed limestones (facies 7) and shell debris limestones (facies 5). This demonstrates low subsidence rates and low rates of clastic supply to the area.

The distributary channel and mouth bar sand-stones of facies sequence A (Fig. 18.4) are inferred to pass laterally via facies sequence B (Fig. 18.1) into thin, simple lagoon shoreline sequences (facies sequence C, Fig. 18.2) re-cording the redistribution of fluvially supplied sediments by waves. The importance of waves as a major control on lateral facies variation differentiates the Valtos Formation in the Sea of the Hebrides Basin from the equivalent rocks in the Inner Hebrides Basin and corresponds with the greater size of the Sea of the Hebrides Basin.

The character of delta plain sediments in the two basins is also different. In the Inner Hebrides Basin facies 3b records sheet flood processes which together with low-sinuosity fluvial channel sandstones (facies 3) makes the delta plain analogous to the sand flats of some fan deltas (e.g. McGowan 1970). In this type of system wave reworking of sediments is limited to restricted abandoned sections of the delta shoreline. The dominance of in-channel sands over sheet flood sand-flat deposits in the Sea of the Hebrides Basin and the evidence for exten-sive redistribution of sand by waves indicates that the Sea of the Hebrides lagoonal delta system is more closely analogous to fluvial-wave interaction systems e.g. the Copper River delta of Alaska (Galloway 1976). The Copper River delta is supplied by a low sinuosity river and is fronted by a wave-formed barrier shoreface and therefore shares some characteristics with the Valtos Formation model (Fig. 18). However, there are important differences; the receiving basin for the Valtos Formation deltas was a non-marine lagoon and tides were probably negligible.

The characteristics of distributary mouth bar sandstones (see Table 2) indicate shallow water depths and, during phases of delta progradation, low basin water salinities. These were the prob-able controls on the deposition of friction-dominated mouth bars (cf. Wright 1977) with low-angle, offshore-inclined surfaces (see Fig. 17). Directly analogous mouth bar sedi-ments also occur in the Elgol Formation at the base of the Great Estuarine Group (Harris 1989). These sediments record copious fluvial runoff (possibly seasonal) which probably caused rapid salinity reductions in the shallow lagoons. In the Valtos Sandstone Formation these salinity fluctuations probably allowed the opportunistic bivalve *Neomiodon* to colonize the shallow lagoons in huge numbers (see Hudson 1980). In the absence of predators and/or competition this organism dominated the fauna and provided shell debris in rock-forming abundance.

Ancient analogues of the Valtos Formation deltas occur in the Eocene Green River For-mation, Wyoming (Surdam & Stanley 1979). However, this lacustrine system includes true Gilbert-type delta lobes which are not rep-resented in the Valtos Formation. The Green River Formation does exhibit the lateral tran-sition from fluvially dominated delta lobes to interdeltaic shoreline deposits in the same way as proposed for the Valtos Formation.

The Valtos Formation also has some similar-ities with the Late Jurassic–Early Cretaceous fan deltas discussed by Sykes & Brand (1976) from East Greenland but better analogues are probably represented in the Wealden rocks of the Hastings area described by Stewart (1981).

Fan delta analogues are applied by Stewart (1981) in the interpretation of Wealden lagoonal deltas. These have similarities with the sandy fringes of Recent, Red Sea fan deltas described by Sneh (1979). However, the Valtos Formation in the Sea of the Hebrides Basin does not fit readily into a fan delta classification (cf. Nemec & Steel 1988) because there is no evidence of true alluvial fans although these may have been small and limited to the margins of the basins. The Valtos Formation is therefore classified here as a fluvial-wave interaction lagoonal delta system, but is similar in many respects to the braid deltas defined by Nemec & Steel (1988), Orton (1988) and Nemec (1990).

Palaeogeography

The main conclusions drawn from the facies analysis of the Valtos Formation in the Sea of the Hebrides and Inner Hebrides Basins are embodied in a series of maps (Figs 19.1–19.4). They are constructed for each of the main stratigraphic units assuming the lagoonal delta — lagoonal shoreline depositional model discussed above, and structural controls based on the maps of Binns *et al.* (1975) and Steel (1976, 1978) cf. Evans *et al.* (1982). Some questions remain regarding some of the facies interpretations and the validity of using a combi-nation of Triassic palaeogeographic elements and present-day structural information for Middle Jurassic time. Some of these questions are discussed below.

The distribution of the facies sequence types

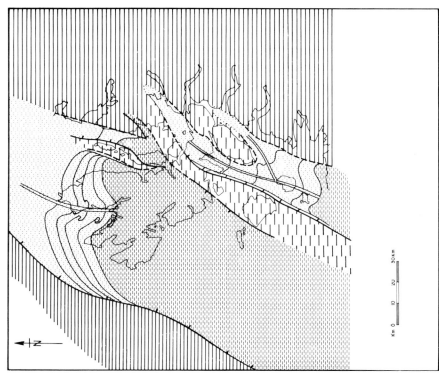

Fig. 19.2 Probable maximum extent of 5 successive lagoonal delta/shoreline progradational phases, lower sandstone dominated unit. Division II, III, IV, V and VI.

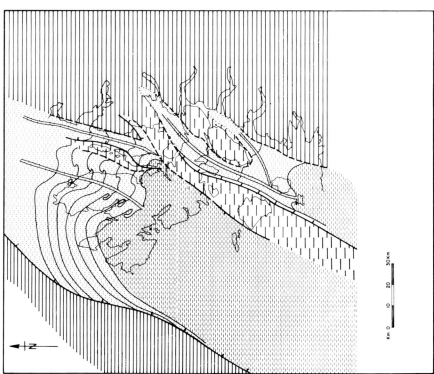

Fig. 19.1 Probable maximum extent of a 1st lagoonal delta/shoreline progradation phase, lower sandstone dominated unit.

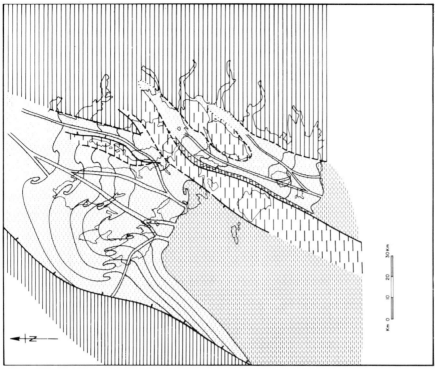

Fig. 19.4 Possible maximum extent of 2 lagoonal delta progradation phases, upper sandstone dominated unit. Divisions X and XI.

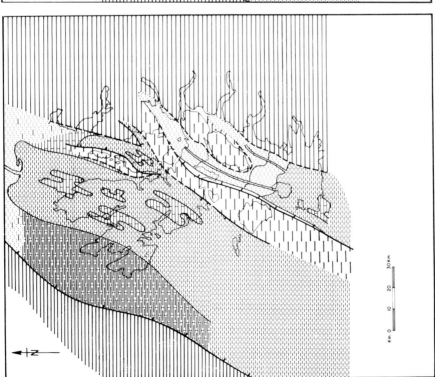

Fig. 19.3 Possible shoreline configuration in the middle Limestone/Shale Unit. Divisions VII, VIII and IX with sublittoral shell debris shoals.

defined above indicates that the most important controlling factors were probably subsidence rate (controlled by the contemporary structure) and the rate of clastic supply. The distribution of facies sequence types within any one lithostratigraphic unit also indicates that proximity to an active fluvial system supplying clastic sediment (controlled largely by subsidence rate) was the main control on facies development. The following discussion makes references to lithostratigraphic division I-XII in the Sea of the Hebrides Basin and divisions A1−F in the Inner Hebrides Basin.

Lower sandstone-dominated unit, division I/Ai (Fig. 19.1)

This lithostratigraphic interval in north Trotternish comprises a relatively thick, coarse-grained lagoon shoreline sequence indicating southerly shoreline progradation. Thickness, grain size and sedimentary structures indicate that the sequence (an example of facies sequence B) probably represents a near axial position with respect to fluvial supply. A major NNE−SSW trending distributary system just to the west of the north Trotternish outcrop is therefore inferred (Fig. 19.1).

The presence of thin offshore lagoonal sands and muds (facies sequence E) in west Skye (c. 5 m) is used to define the approximate depositional limits of this delta shoreline system.

On Raasay the outcrop of this lithostratigraphic interval is poor but probably comprises a thin (<10 m) lagoon shoreline sequence (facies sequence C). This places the progradational limit of the division I lagoonal delta with its associated interdeltaic lagoon shoreline south of the Raasay outcrop.

Lagoonal delta sandbodies at this horizon on Eigg (facies sequence B) are well exposed but there are no outcrops of this horizon on Muck. The depositional limit mapped in Fig. 19.1 is therefore conjectural. This horizon is represented by thin desiccation-cracked limestones in Strathaird. This is surprising given the close proximity of these outcrops to the Camasunary Fault and may record onlap of the Central Skye palaeohigh, possibly by deposition on a complex basin margin terrace.

Lower sandstone-dominated unit, divisions II, III, IV, V and VI/Aii, B, C (Fig. 19.2)

In the Sea of the Hebrides Basin the rest of the lower sandstone-dominated unit comprises five E−W orientated interdeltaic lagoon shoreline sequences (facies sequence C) indicating a lateral shift in the locus of distributary channel and mouth bar deposition away from the area of the north Trotternish outcrop. The channel system in Fig. 19.2 has therefore been drawn further to the west than indicated in Fig. 19.1, (i.e. closer to the axis of the Sea of the Hebrides Basin). The repetition of five similar lagoon shoreline progradational episodes in north Trotternish demonstrates the long term establishment of this palaeogeographic scheme.

The mapping of depositional or progradational limits of these successive lagoonal deltas and associated lagoon shorelines (seen at outcrop), is constrained by the occurrence of offshore lagoonal mudstones and storm-derived sandstones in western Skye and Raasay. The differences between the Raasay and north Trotternish sequences over this lithostratigraphic interval are probably supporting evidence for the existence of the small 'high' separating the Raasay area from the main basin. This structure possibly also accounts for some of the differences in stratigraphy of the Bajocian Bearreraig Sandstone Formation discussed by Morton (1965).

Thin carbonates at this horizon in Strathaird demonstrate a lack of clastic supply and continued low rates of subsidence at this basin margin. A lack of outcrops south of Eigg means that the depositional limit mapped in the Inner Hebrides Basin at this horizon (Fig. 19.2) is conjectural.

Middle limestone-shale unit, divisions VII, VIII, IX/D (Fig. 19.3)

In the Sea of the Hebrides Basin the middle limestone-shale unit records a period characterized by low rates of clastic supply so that lagoonal deltas and sandy lagoon shoreline sequences are not seen at outcrop. This lithostratigraphic interval is dominated by shell debris shoals with intervening offshore lagoonal muds. However, evidence of subaerial exposure in west Skye (desiccation-cracked lagoon shoreline limestones at Loch Bay) demonstrates the existence of the sand-starved lagoon shoreline tentatively drawn in Fig. 19.3.

In the Inner Hebrides Basin the sand starved basin margin (terrace) persisted in the area of the Strathaird outcrop while a single delta progradation sequence occupied the axis of the basin. Continued sand supply to this basin contrasts with the reduced sediment supply rate documented from the Sea of the Hebrides Basin. However, this sandbody (Division D) is less persistent than the rest and reaches the depositional limit mapped in Fig. 19.3 within the Eigg outcrop (see also Figs 4 & 10).

Upper sandstone-dominated unit, divisions X, XI, XII/E, F (Fig. 19.4)

In the Sea of the Hebrides Basin S and SW orientated distributary channel and proximal mouth bar sandstones occur at outcrop in Trotternish and represent the axial parts of two lagoonal delta progradation sequences. The renewal of clastic supply to this area is marked by the truncation of facies 1 mudstones and facies 5 limestones at the base of distributary channel sandstones in Division X.

Coarse-grained delta shoreline and distributary channel sandbodies (18 m) outcropping in west Skye (An Stac, Waterstein) have a very distinctive heavy mineralogy, probably derived from the Lewisian of the Outer Hebrides. These rocks represent two minor eastwardly prograding lagoonal delta systems sourced from the Outer Hebrides Landmass to the west of the Sea of the Hebrides Basin.

The upper sandstone-dominated unit in the Sea of the Hebrides Basin therefore represents two major phases of lagoonal delta progradation. None of the outcrops (not exposed on Raasay) provide any evidence of depositional or progradational limits so that the line shown in Fig. 19.4 is arbitrary.

Desiccation-cracked (Duntulm) and rootlet-penetrated delta plain sands (south Rubha Garbhaig, log 7) occur at the top of Division XI in north Trotternish. These record a reduction in clastic supply and probably indicate reduced fluvial run-off. This reduction in clastic supply is associated with a distinct change in fauna which defines the base of the overlying Duntulm Formation. The basal Duntulm Formation comprises oyster-bearing muds with stromatolitic and nodular algal limestones representing marine-brackish salinities and shallow water depths on the inundated delta plain. The reduction in the rate of clastic supply indicated by these sediments and the increased (almost marine) salinities were probably associated and may have been climatically controlled.

In the Inner Hebrides Basin the same faunal change occurred and was presumably contemporaneous with events in the Sea of the Hebrides Basin. In this basin a single delta progradation sequence was deposited in division E of the Valtos formation. It crops out on both Eigg and Muck such that the depositional limit mapped on Fig. 19.4 is conjectural. The narrow basin

margin zone persisted in the Strathaird area. The final stratigraphic division in the Inner Hebrides Basin comprises *Neomidon* shell debris limestones and lagoonal mudstones, indicating a reduction in the rate of clastic supply to the Eigg–Muck area before palaeosalinities increased and the faunal change marking the base of the Duntulm Formation had occurred.

Hinterland characteristics and controls on palaeosalinity

In the area of Wester Ross to the east and northeast of the Hebridean basins, the hinterland was probably an intermittently uplifted area with a partial cover of weathered sediments overlying the Moines, and the rocks of the Caledonian foreland. To the west of the Sea of the Hebrides Basin the hinterland was probably similar topographically, although composed of Lewisian gneiss, possibly with a partial locally derived sedimentary cover. Palaeosalinity interpretations (Hudson 1963a, b, 1980) and palynofloral interpretations (Andrews & Walton 1990) indicate that these areas probably had seasonal rainfall and a vegetation dominated by conifers. The mineralogy of the sediment source rocks exposed in the Scottish landmass to the east and northeast of the two basins probably differed. The more feldspathic sands of the Sea of the Hebrides Basin were probably derived ultimately from Moinian granulites and Torridonian arkoses whereas the Valtos Formation in the Inner Hebrides Basin was probably derived from sediments originally sourced in part from Dalradian Quartzites. Low sinuosity-braided rivers with widely fluctuating discharge probably supplied the Valtos Formation lagoonal delta system.

On entering the basin these rivers could have generated a type of fan delta (cf. Sneh 1979; Nemec & Steel 1988) but the distance of progradation of the successive delta sequences S and SW into the basin, the nature of the distributary channels and the importance of waves in reworking fluvially-supplied sediment into lagoon shoreline sequences precludes the application of a fan delta classification. The system is more closely analogous to some of the braid deltas described by Nemec & Steel (1988) and Nemec (1990).

Widely fluctuating salinities within the basin (cf. Hudson 1963a, b, 1980; Tan & Hudson 1974; Andrews & Walton 1990) were probably controlled by seasonally fluctuating runoff from the hinterland leading to the predominance of *Neomiodon* in the fauna of the Valtos Formation). During the two episodes of repeated lagoonal delta progradation (lower and upper sandstone-dominated units), facies sequences like that of the middle limestone shale unit were probably established in the basin to the SW of Skye. This hypothesis is used to establish the relationship shown in Fig. 19.3 where a lagoonal delta system is proposed in the area NE of Skye during deposition of the middle limestone shale unit.

Given a marine connection to the SW, fluvial discharge into the basin could have displaced salt water seawards (SW) so that it would be possible to establish more saline brackish-marine facies like those of the overlying Duntulm Formation to the SW of Skye. Although there is no direct evidence, these rocks could be transitional to normal marine facies to the SW of the Sea of the Hebrides Basin in the area of Berneray and Hawes Bank.

The absence of the middle limestone/shale unit in the Inner Hebrides Basin is probably attributable to differing subsidence histories in so far that the Eigg outcrops are in a more proximal position in the Inner Hebrides Basin than are the Trotternish outcrops in the Sea of the Hebrides Basin.

The major difference between the facies developed in the two basins is in the dominance of wave-generated lagoon shoreline and wave-dominated delta shoreline sequences in the Sea of the Hebrides Basin (compare Figs 6, 7 & 8 with Figs 9 & 10). Although wave-generated beach ridges have been identified in the Valtos Formation in the Inner Hebrides Basin they are relatively unimportant. This corresponds with the relative size of the two basins and is reflected in the general form of the shorelines shown in Fig. 19.

Conclusions

The stratigraphic correlation, facies analysis and palaeogeographic interpretations outlined here can be used to establish the following set of conclusions. Some of these may be more broadly applicable such that they could provide the key to the interpretation of age equivalent sediments in related sedimentary basins of the northwest seaboard.

(1) The distribution patterns of thickness, facies and mineralogy demonstrate the southerly progradation of delta systems in two adjacent basins (Sea of the Hebrides Basin and Inner Hebrides Basin). These were both westerly-tilted half graben defined at their western margins by major down-to-the-east normal faults (Minch Fault and Camasunary—

Skerryvore Fault). The two basins were probably separated by a narrow slowly subsiding basement ridge, known as the mid-Skye palaeohigh.

(2) The Valtos Formation deltas represent three distinct petrographic provinces.

(i) An epidote-dominated province which is restricted to the western part of the Sea of the Hebrides Basin. It comprises sandstones derived from the Lewisian of the Outer Hebrides landmass to the west of the basin.

(ii) A subfeldspathic—feldspathic arenite province with garnet-rich heavy mineral assemblages which also contain consistent amounts of epidote and kyanite. This province occupied the rest of the Sea of the Hebrides Basin and comprises sandstones largely derived from the Scottish landmass to the east and northeast of the basin.

(iii) A quartzose sandstone province with garnet-poor, staurolite-rich, rutile-rich heavy mineral assemblages. This province was restricted to the Inner Hebrides Basin and comprises sandstones derived from a mineralogically distinct area of the Scottish landmass to the east and northeast of the basin.

(3) The Valtos Formation deltas were copiously supplied with clastic sediment from large scale, low-sinuosity distributaries. These rivers drained two distinct hinterland areas in the Scottish landmass to the east of the basins and one hinterland area in the Outer Hebrides landmass to the west. These hinterland areas were hilly, they had a seasonal climate (rainfall) and a vegetation cover dominated by conifers.

(4) Rivers which supplied the Valtos Formation deltas entered the basins from both the east and west flanks and were deflected to the SSW to form axial sediment dispersal systems. Successive progradational sequences reached southerly depositional limits in both basins such that the formation will have higher net reservoir:gross reservoir thickness ratios in the north of each basin than in the south.

(5) Outflow dynamics at the distributary mouths and the form of these lobate lagoonal deltas was controlled by a combination of fluctuations in the rate of clastic supply (probably seasonal), shallow water depths in the basins (<10 m and often <5 m), generally high wave energies and widely fluctuating basin water salinities (probably also seasonal and reflecting seasonal run-off).

(6) These lobate lagoonal deltas were fluvial-dominated and fluvial-wave interaction systems. Wave fetch was greater in the Sea of the

Hebrides Basin than in the Inner Hebrides Basin such that wave formed delta and inter-deltaic lagoon shoreline sequences are more important in the larger of the two basins.

(7) Rapid salinity fluctuations allowed the colonization of the shallow lagoon floor and the lagoon shorelines by the non-marine (probably highly opportunistic) bivalve *Neomiodon*. This organism dominated the fauna throughout the deposition of the Valtos Sandstone Formation and provided shell debris in rock forming abundance. This accumulated in beach ridges at delta and interdeltaic lagoon shorelines and, in areas of reduced clastic supply, it accumulated in shell debris shoals and sheets on the lagoon floor.

Most of this work was undertaken during the tenure of a NERC research studentship at the University of Leicester. I am indebted to John Hudson for critically reviewing an earlier version of this paper, for introducing me to the Great Estuarine Group and for his much valued supervision of my work during my three years at Leicester. I am also grateful to John Parnell and two anonymous references for their comments on the manuscript. Tony Stephens (Robertson Group) draughted the figures. The directors of the Robertson Group, North Wales are thanked for providing reprographic, word processing and photographic facilities.

References

AEPLER, R. 1974. Der Rhatsandstein von Tubingen — Ein Kondensiertes Delta (the Rhaetic Sandstone of Tubingen — a condensed delta). *N. Jahrbuch fur Geologie und Palaeontologie, Abhandlungen,* **147.2**, 113–162.

ANDERTON, R. 1976. Tidal shelf sedimentation: An example from the Scottish Dalradian. *Sedimentology,* **23**, 429–458.

ANDREWS, J. E. 1985. The sedimentary facies of a late Bathonian regressive episode: the Kilmaluag and Skudiburgh Formations of the Great Estuarine Group, Inner Hebrides, Scotland. *Journal of the Geological Society, London,* **142**, 1119–1137.

—— & WALTON W. 1990. Depositional environments within Middle Jurassic oyster-dominated lagoons: an integrated litho-, bio- and palynofacies study of the Duntulm Formation (Great Estuarine Group, Inner Hebrides. *Transactions of the Royal Society of Edinburgh: Earth Sciences,* **81**, 1–22.

BINNS, P. E., McQUILLIN, R., FANNIN, N. G. T., KENOLTY, N. & ARDUS, D. A. 1975. Structure and Stratigraphy of Sedimentary Basins in the Sea of the Hebrides and the Minches. *In:* WOODLAND, A. W. (ed.) *Petroleum and the Continental Shelf of North West Europe,* 93–102.

BREWER, M. D. & SMYTHE, D. K. 1984. MOIST and the continuity of crustal reflector geometry along the Caledonian — Appalachian orogen. *Journal of the Geological Society, London,* **141**, 105–120.

EARLE, M. M., JANKOWSKI, E. J. & VANN, I. R. 1989. Structural and stratigraphic evolution of the Faeroe-Shetland Channel and Northern Rockall Trough. *In:* TANKARD, A. J. & BALKWILL, H. R. (eds) *Extensional Tectonics and Stratigraphy of North Atlantic Margins.* American Association of Petroleum Geologists, Memoir 46.

EVANS, D., CHESHER, J. A., DEEGAN, C. E. & FANNIN, N. G. T. 1982. *The Offshore Geology of Scotland in Relation to the IGS Shallow Drilling Programme.* 1970–1978. Report of the Institute of Geological Sciences No. 81/12.

FUTTERER, E. 1982. Experiments on the distinction of wave and current influenced shell accumulations. *In:* EINSELE, G & SEILACHER, A. (eds) *Cyclic and Event Stratification.* Springer, Berlin, 175–179.

GALLOWAY, W. E. 1976. Sediments and stratigraphic framework of the Copper River fan delta, Alaska. *Journal of Sedimentary Petrology,* **46**, 726–737.

HAMBLIN, A. P. & WALKER, R. J. 1979. Storm dominated shallow marine deposits of the Fernie — Kootenay (Jurassic) transition, southern Rocky Mountains. *Canadian Journal of Earth Sciences,* **16**, 1673–1689.

HARRIS, J. P. 1984. *Environments of deposition of Middle Jurassic sandstones in the Great Estuarine Group, N.W. Scotland.* PhD thesis, Leicester University.

—— 1989. The sedimentology of a Middle Jurassic lagoonal delta system: Elgol Formation (Great Estuarine Group), N.W. Scotland. *In:* WHATELEY, M. K. G. & PICKERING, K. T. (eds) *Deltas: Sites and Traps for Fossil Fuels.* Geological Society, London, Special Publication, **41**, 147–166.

—— & HUDSON, J. D. 1980. Lithostratigraphy of the Great Estuarine Group (Middle Jurassic), Inner Hebrides. *Scottish Journal of Geology,* **16**, 231–250.

HUDSON, J. D. 1963a. The recognition of salinity-controlled mollusc assemblages in the Great Estuarine Series (Middle Jurassic) of the Inner Hebrides. *Palaeontology,* **6**, 313–326.

—— 1963b. The ecology and stratigraphical distribution of the invertebrate fauna of the Great Estuarine Series. *Palaeontology,* **6**, 327–348.

—— 1964. The petrology of the sandstones of the Great Estuarine Series, and the Jurassic palaeogeography of Scotland. *Proceedings of the Geologists' Association,* **75**, 499–528.

—— 1970. Algal limestones with pseudomorphs after gypsum from the Middle Jurassic of Scotland. *Lethaia.* **3**, 11–40.

—— 1980. Aspects of brackish-water facies and faunas from the Jurassic of north-west Scotland. *Proceedings of the Geologists' Association,* **91**, 99–105.

—— 1983. Mesozoic sedimentation and sedimentary rocks in the Inner Hebrides. *Proceedings of the Royal Society of Edinburgh,* **83b**, 47–63.

—— & ANDREWS, J. E. 1987. The diagenesis of the

144   J. P. HARRIS

Great Estuarine Group, Middle Jurassic, Inner Hebrides Scotland. *In*: MARSHALL, J. D. (ed.) *Diagenesis of Sedimentary Sequences*. Geological Society, London, Special Publication, **36**, 259–276.

—— & HARRIS, J. P. 1979. Sedimentology of the Great Estuarine Group (Middle Jurassic) of North-West Scotland. *In*: *Symposium Sedimentation Jurassique. W. European, Paris, 9–10 May 1977*. Association des Sediments Francaise, Publication Speciale 1, 1–13.

JEFFREY, D. & AIGNER, T. 1982. Storm sedimentation in the Carboniferous limestones near Weston-Super-Mare (Dinantian, SW-England). *In*: EINSELE, G. & SEILACHER, A. (eds) *Cyclic and Event Stratification*. Springer, Berlin, 240–247.

KUMAR, N. & SANDERS, J. E. 1976. Characteristics of shoreface deposits: modern and ancient. *Journal of Sedimentary Petrology*, **46**, 145–162.

McGOWAN, J. H. 1970. *Gum Hollow fan-delta, Neuces Bay, Texas*. Bureau of Economic Geology, University of Texas at Austin. Report of Investigation, 69.

MORTON, N. 1965. The Bearreraig Sandstone Series (Middle Jurassic) of Skye and Raasay. *Scottish Journal of Geology*, **1**, 189–216.

NEMEC, W. 1990. Deltas — remarks on terminology and classification. *In*: COELLA, A. & PRIOR, D. B. (eds) *Coarse grained deltas*. International Association of Sedimentologists, Special Publication, **10**, 3–12.

—— & STEEL, R. J. 1988. What is a fan delta and how do we recognize it? *In*: NEMEC, W. & STEEL, R. J. (eds) *Fan Deltas: Sedimentology and Tectonic Settings*. Blackie, Glasgow.

ORTON, G. R. 1988. A spectrum of middle Ordovician fan deltas and braidplain deltas, North Wales: a consequence of varying fluvial clastic input. *In*: NEMEC, W. & STEEL, R. J. (eds) *Fan Deltas: Sedimentology and Tectonic Settings*. Blackie, Glasgow.

SNEH, A. 1979. Late Pliestocene fan-deltas along the Dead Sea Rift. *Journal of Sedimentary Petrology*, **49**, 451–552.

STEEL, R. J. 1976. Triassic rift basins of northwest Scotland — their configuration, infilling and development. *In*: *Mesozoic of the Northern North Sea Symposium 7/8*, 1–18. Norwegian Petroleum Society.

——, NICOLSON, R. & KALANDER, L. 1975. Triassic palaeogeography in central Skye. *Scottish Journal of Geology*, **11**, 1–13.

STEIN, A. 1988. Basement controls upon Hebridean basin development. N.W. Scotland. *Basin Research*, **1**(2), 107–119.

—— & BLUNDELL, D. J. 1990. Geological inheritance and crustal dynamics of the northwest Scottish continental shelf. *Tectonophysics*, **173**, 455–467.

STEWART, D. J. 1981. A field guide to the Wealden Group of the Hastings area and Isle of Wight. *In*: T. ELLIOTT (ed.) *Field Guides to modern and ancient fluvial systems in Britain and Spain*. University of Keele, September, 1981.

SURDAM, R. C. & STANLEY, K. D. 1979. Lacustrine sedimentation during the culminating phase of Eocene Lake Gosiute, Wyoming (Green River Formation). *Bulletin of the Geological Society of America*, **90**, 93–110.

SWIFT, D. J. P. 1988. Response of the shelf floor to flow. *In*: TILLMAN, R. W., SWIFT, D. J. P. & WALKER, R. G. (eds) *Shelf Sands and Sandstone Reservoirs*. Society of Economic Paleontologists and Mineralogists, Short Course No. 13.

—— & NIEDORADA, A. W. 1988. Response of the shelf floor to flow fluid and sediment dynamics on continental shelves. In: TILLMAN, R. W., SWIFT, D. J. P. & WALKER, R. G. (eds) *Shelf Sands and Sandstone Reservoirs*. Society of Economic Paleontologists and Mineralogists, Short Course No. 13.

SYKES, R. M. & BRAND, R. D. 1976. Fan-delta sedimentation: an example from the Late Jurassic — Early Cretaceous of Milne Land, Central East Greenland. *Geologie en Mijnbouw*, **55**, 195–203.

TAN, F. C. & HUDSON, J. D. 1974. Isotopic studies on the palaeoecology and diagenesis of the Great Estuarine Series (Jurassic) of Scotland. *Scottish Journal of Geology*, **10**, 91–128.

TRUEBLOOD, S. & MORTON, N. 1991. Comparative sequence stratigraphy and structural styles of the Slyne Trough and Hebrides Basin. *Journal of the Geological Society, London*, **148**, 197–201.

WILKINSON, M. & DAMPIER, M. D. 1990. The rate of growth of sandstone-hosted calcite concretions. *Geochemica et Cosmochemica Acta*, **54**, 3391–3399.

WRIGHT, L. D. 1977. Sediment transport and deposition at river mouths: A synthesis. *Bulletin of the Geological Society of America*, **88**, 856–868.

Concretionary cements in Jurassic sandstones, Isle of Eigg, Inner Hebrides

MARK WILKINSON

Department of Geology, Leicester University, University Road, Leicester, LE1 7RH, UK
(Present address: Department of Geology and Applied Geology, Glasgow University,
Glasgow G12 8QQ, UK

Abstract: Minor element and stable isotope data are presented for calcite cements within seven decimetre-scale concretions from a single bedding plane within the Middle Jurassic Valtos Sandstone Formation of Eigg. Stable oxygen isotope data ($\delta^{18}O = -9.3$ to $-11.1‰$) suggest precipitation at burial depths of between 200 and 300 m at temperatures of $31-45°C$, within static pore waters of meteoric origin. Mg/Ca and Mn/Ca ratios (2.5 ± 1.2 and 0.062 ± 0.008 mole percent respectively) imply that growth was predominantly transport-controlled. An average sized concretion from the horizon ($r = 11.8$ cm) is predicted to have grown in $0.36-0.84$ Ma. Stratigraphic constraints show concretion growth to have been delayed by at least 15 Ma after the deposition of the sediments.

The concretions are shown to be clustered within the bedding plane; concretion nucleation is interpreted to have been controlled by the availability of suitable substrates within the sediment. The concretions probably nucleated upon aragonitic *Neomiodon* shells which had previously transformed to calcite.

Several of the Jurassic sandstone-dominated formations of the Inner Hebrides contain well developed calcite concretions. These are a product of burial diagenesis, and generally consist of a single generation of blocky calcite cement, precipitated from meteoric waters (Hudson & Andrews 1987; Wilkinson 1989, 1991). Although much is known about the growth of concretions located within shales (e.g. Irwin *et al.* 1977; Raiswell 1987), sandstone-hosted concretions are less well understood. The recognition that concretions are important features within some petroleum reservoirs (e.g. Kantorowicz *et al.* 1987; Bryant *et al.* 1988) has given fresh impetus to the study of the sandstone-hosted examples. This paper presents the results of a study of a single concretionary horizon within the Valtos Sandstone Formation from the Isle of Eigg, Inner Hebrides, Scotland.

Geological setting

The Bathonian (Middle Jurassic) Valtos Sandstone Formation is a part of the Great Estuarine Group of the Inner Hebrides, Scotland (Figs 1 & 2). The formation comprises the deposits of a tidally influenced near-shore lagoon complex, the major sandbodies recording delta progradation (Hudson & Andrews 1987). Because the lagoons into which the deltas prograded were of reduced and/or variable salinity (Hudson 1980) the macrofauna was mainly restricted to the opportunistic aragonitic-shelled bivalve *Neomiodon*.

The burial of the Eigg sediments was a two stage process. Subsidence and sporadic sedimentation during the Middle and Upper Jurassic buried the sediments to approximately 300 m depth, while little burial took place during the Cretaceous (Morton 1987). The extrusion of approximately 600 m of plateau basalts buried the sediments to around 900 m depth (Emeleus 1991, p 457). All the studied sediments are currently exposed close to sea level.

Methods

Sampling and petrography

Seven decimetre-scale concretions (denoted E2 to E8, Fig. 3) were sampled from a single concretionary horizon (Fig. 1) from Division E of the Valtos Sandstone Formation (Harris & Hudson 1980). The concretions were drilled vertically from top to centre to lower margin, and the cores subdivided into between 8 and 26 subsamples, depending upon core length. The spatial distribution of the concretions was determined by compass-tape survey.

Carbonate cement mineralogy was determined by staining thin sections (Dickson 1966), and by X-ray diffraction studies of powdered samples. All thin-sections were examined by cathodo-luminescence microscopy.

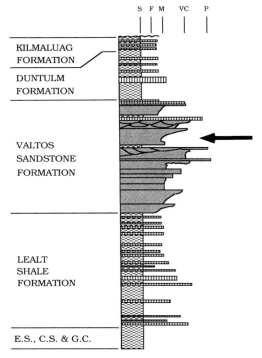

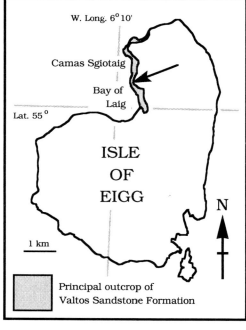

Fig. 1. Simplified graphic log of the Great Estuarine Group of Eigg, redrawn from Hudson & Harris (1979). The arrow marks the concretionary horizon which forms the subject of this paper. ES, CS and GC indicate the Elgol Sandstone Formation, the Cullaidh Shale Formation and the Garantiana Shale Member. Note that the latter is within the Bearreraig Sandstone Formation, which underlies the Great Estuarine Group, and that the uppermost formation of the Great Estuarine Group, the Skudiburgh Formation, is not developed on Eigg (Harris & Hudson 1980). Dashed lines denote shale, fine stipple denotes sand and vertical lines denote limestone.

Fig. 2. Map of Eigg showing the approximate extent of the principal outcrop of the Valtos Sandstone Formation. The arrow marks the outcrop of the concretions described in this paper.

Geochemistry of carbonates

Elemental analyses of the carbonates were made by ICP analysis after leaching from whole-rock samples using 1.0 M HCl. The reaction time was minimized to prevent the leaching of cations from alumino-silicate phases. Two sigma values are approximately ± 10% of any result. Data are tabulated in Table 1 for concretions E3 and E6.

For stable isotopic analysis, samples containing between 2.5 and 3.5 mg of calcite were digested in anhydrous phosphoric acid under vacuum and the CO_2 collected and cleaned. The gas was analysed at Liverpool University on a V.G. Sira-12 triple-collector, dual-inlet mass spectrometer against a Lincolnshire Lime-stone internal laboratory standard. The results were corrected using standard techniques (Craig 1957) and an alpha value of 1.01025 (for calcite–CO_2 fractionation for reaction with phosphoric acid). They are presented in standard delta notation in per mil difference from the PDB standard. Analyses are reproducible to within ±0.1‰.

Temperatures of precipitation for the measured calcites are derived from equation (1) (Craig 1957, modified by Anderson & Arthur 1983):

$$T(°C) = 16.0 - 4.14(\delta c - \delta w) + 0.13\ (\delta c - \delta w)^2 \tag{1}$$

where δw and δc are $\delta^{18}O$ for the water and the calcite respectively. The former is expressed relative to SMOW, the latter to the international PDB isotopic standard. Results are tabulated in Table 1 for concretions E2, E3 and E6 to E8.

Results

Concretion geometry

Figure 4 shows the spatial arrangement of concretions within horizon A. No orientation data

Fig. 3. Typical concretions from the horizon described in this paper.

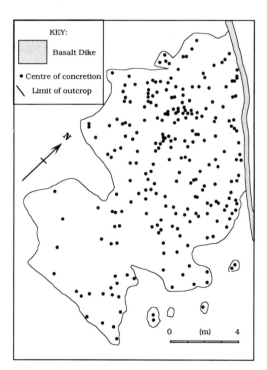

KEY:

Basalt Dike

• Centre of concretion

\ Limit of outcrop

Fig. 4. Plan view of concretionary horizon showing centre points of concretions. No orientation data is shown as >95% of the concretions were too spherical for a reliable elongation direction to be measured.

is shown as >95% of the concretions were so spherical (in plan view) that no visual estimate of the direction of elongation could be made. The spatial distribution of the concretions was analysed by quadrat sampling as described by Raiswell & White (1978); the results are tabulated in Table 2. The distribution of the concretions is compared to a Poisson (random) distribution, and the differences compared using a χ^2 test (Table 3). For quadrat sizes of 0.5 and 0.75 m, the concretion distribution is found to be random, while for larger quadrat sizes, significant deviations from a random distribution are found.

The nature of the deviation from a random distribution can be assessed by calculating variance/mean (for each quadrat size) and comparing this to the value expected from a random distribution, i.e. 1.00 (Kershaw & Looney 1985). A Student's t-test is then used to assess the significance of the deviation (Table 3). The variance/mean describes the degree of clustering; values below 1.0 indicate even spacing relative to a random distribution, while values above 1.0 indicate clustering. The concretions of horizon A show significant clustering (at the 95% confidence level) when examined on scales of 1.0 m and above (Table 3). Fig. 5 shows the size distribution of the concretions.

Table 1. *Stable isotope and minor element chemistry of Eigg concretionary calcites*

Concretion E2 (diameter = 15 cm) Sample	$\delta^{13}C$	$\delta^{18}O$	Concretion E3 (diameter = 10 cm) Sample	$\delta^{13}C$	$\delta^{18}O$	$MnCO_3$	$FeCO_3$	$MgCO_3$	$SrCO_3$
M88118−8	−4.66	−7.48	M88119−2	−	−	0.042	0.47	2.8	0.051
M88118−9	−3.69	−9.79	M88119−3	−	−	0.044	0.60	3.2	0.054
M88118−10	−4.35	−9.80	M88119−4	−	−	0.045	0.57	3.3	0.056
M88118−11	−4.99	−9.78	M88119−5	−	−	0.044	0.47	3.0	0.057
M88118−12	−5.71	−9.62	M88119−6	−	−	0.047	0.45	2.9	0.061
M88118−13	−5.41	−9.75	M88119−7	−	−	0.048	0.47	3.1	0.063
M88118−14	−5.66	−9.98	M88119−8	−4.83	−9.78	0.044	0.44	3.0	0.061
			M88119−9	−5.09	−9.85	0.047	0.46	3.0	0.063
Concretion E7 (diameter = 7.5 cm)			M88119−10	−5.09	−9.71	0.048	0.45	3.0	0.059
Sample	$\delta^{13}C$	$\delta^{18}O$	M88119−11	−5.64	−9.75	0.043	0.42	2.7	0.059
M88123−5	−4.50	−10.54	M88119−12	−5.43	−9.70	0.041	0.40	2.6	0.056
M88123−6	−3.69	−10.90	M88119−13	−5.38	−9.70	0.042	0.44	2.6	0.056
M88123−7	−4.45	−11.05	M88119−14	−6.02	−9.51	0.041	0.45	2.7	0.056
M88123−8	−5.07	−10.98	M88119−15	−6.19	−9.36	0.040	0.55	3.0	0.053
M88123−9	−5.22	−10.73							

Concretion E8 (Diameter = 9 cm)			Concretion E6 (diameter = 12.2 cm) Sample	$\delta^{13}C$	$\delta^{18}O$	$MnCO_3$	$FeCO_3$	$MgCO_3$	$SrCO_3$
Sample	$\delta^{13}C$	$\delta^{18}O$	M88122−1	−	−	0.061	0.71	3.0	0.047
M8638−1	−5.09	−10.79	M88122−2	−	−	0.056	0.63	3.1	0.058
M8638−2	−5.32	−10.28	M88122−3	−	−	0.052	0.48	2.6	0.061
M8638−3	−5.33	−10.11	M88122−4	−	−	0.050	0.43	2.5	0.063
M8638−4	−6.16	−9.94	M88122−5	−	−	0.053	0.38	2.3	0.063
M8638−6	−5.87	−10.32	M88122−6	−	−	0.069	0.39	1.9	0.054
M8638−7	−5.30	−9.83	M88122−7	−5.12	−10.04	0.050	0.38	2.2	0.061
M8638−8	−6.24	−9.45	M88122−8	−5.60	−10.39	0.048	0.33	2.2	0.065
			M88122−9	−5.77	−10.06	0.047	0.33	2.2	0.062
Tertiary cements*			M88122−10	−5.52	−9.93	0.050	0.40	2.4	0.061
Sample	$\delta^{13}C$	$\delta^{18}O$	M88122−11	−6.02	−9.83	0.047	0.44	2.6	0.060
MTR8/1	−0.07	−17.18	M88122−12	−4.29	−13.99	0.362	0.66	3.1	0.044
MTR8/2	−0.21	−13.81							

* Collected and analysed by J. D. Marshall of Liverpool University
All minor element data are expressed as mole % carbonate, isotopic data are expressed as ‰ relative to the PDB standard. All samples are from NGR NG472888.

Table 2. *Distribution of concretions as a function of quadrat size*

	Number of quadrats containing N_0 concretions												Total
N_0	0	1	2	3	4	5	6	7	8	9	10	>10	
Quadrat size (m)													
0.5	241	124	27	9	−	−	−	−	−	−	−	−	401
0.75	68	71	33	11	4	2	−	−	−	−	−	−	189
1.0	15	27	28	17	7	1	1	1	2	−	−	−	99
1.5	4	2	7	5	4	5	7	3	0	2	2	−	41
2.0	2	0	0	1	2	2	3	1	2	3	1	5	22

Table 3. *Statistical data for χ^2 analysis of goodness of fit to Poisson series*

	Quadrat size (m)				
	0.5	0.75	1.0	1.5	2.0
No. concretions counted	205	196	196	173	159
χ^2	3.11	3.30	49.8	42.3	257
Degrees of freedom	2	3	6	8	11
Probability (of concretions being randomly distributed)	0.21	0.35	<0.001	<0.001	<0.001
Varience/mean	1.018	1.091	1.309	1.423	1.936
t	0.257	0.884	2.163	1.793	3.034
Probability (of concretions being randomly distributed)	0.60	0.81	<0.05	<0.05	<0.001

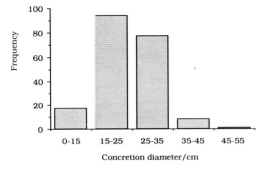

Fig. 5. Histogram of concretion diameter ($n = 251$).

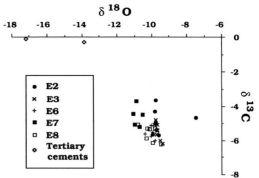

Fig. 6. Stable isotope cross-plot of cement samples from concretions E2, E3 and E6 to E8. Also shown are two analyses from cements associated with Tertiary dykes. Both $\delta^{13}C$ and $\delta^{18}O$ are measured versus PDB. See Hudson & Andrews (1987) for a discussion of the effects of the Tertiary volcanism upon calcite isotopic values within the Jurassic sediments of the Inner Hebrides.

Cement petrography and geochemistry

All sampled concretions comprise a single generation of ferroan calcite which luminesces orange, but shows no zoning under cathodoluminescence. Cement crystal sizes are uniform (5–50 mm), with a poikilotopic texture commonly developed. There is no elongation or preferential orientation of cement crystals as has been observed from concretions from the same formation at Valtos, Skye (Wilkinson 1989).

Figure 6 shows stable isotopic data for concretions E2, E3 and E6 to E8, which have, with a single exception, $\delta^{13}C$ values from -3.6 to $-6.2‰$ and $\delta^{18}O = -9.3$ to $-11.1‰$. For comparison, two analyses from calcites from the cemented margins of a Tertiary dyke (Hudson & Andrews 1987, Fig. 7a) are also plotted. Minor element contents within the concretionary calcites are shown in Fig. 7 for concretions E3 and E6. These data are representative of all the concretions studied. The calcite of concretion E3 has approximately constant minor element contents, while those of E6 are more variable, with increasing Fe and Mg contents radially outwards.

Discussion

Pore water origin and depth of formation

Isotopically, the concretionary calcites of Eigg differ significantly from calcites that are spatially associated with Tertiary dykes (Fig. 6, and Hudson & Andrews 1987). The concretions are interpreted to pre-date the Palaeocene igneous episode, and to have been unaffected by any ground water mobilised at this time. Pre-Palaeocene calcites within the Great Estuarine Group which are interpreted to have re-equilibrated with heated waters during the Palaeocene are restricted to Strathaird, on Skye (Hudson & Andrews 1987) and to a small number of locations associated with minor intrusions (J. E. Andrews, pers comm.). The concretionary calcites of Eigg do not display the anomalously light oxygen isotopic signatures

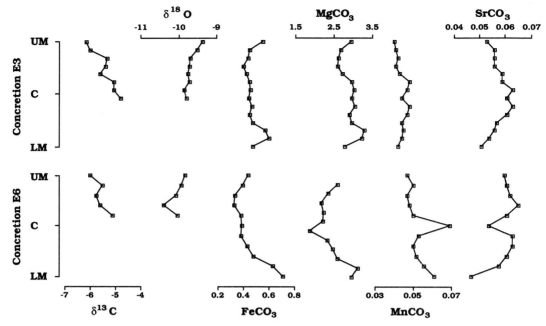

Fig. 7. Geochemical data for concretions E3 and E6. Both concretions were sampled from upper margin (UM) to centre (C) to lower margin (LM). Stable isotope data is measured relative to PDB. Minor element data is expressed as mole % carbonate.

found within the same formation on Skye (Wilkinson 1989).

Hudson & Andrews (1987) discussed the origin of the Valtos Sandstone Formation concretions, and showed that they formed after initial burial of the host-sediments. The stratigraphy of the Inner Hebrides Basin suggests that the maximum burial depth of the Valtos Sandstone Formation (prior to burial by the Tertiary plateau basalts) was little more than 300 m (Morton 1987). The oxygen isotopic compositions of the concretionary cements can be most simply explained by precipitation from pore waters of meteoric origin (-5 to $-6‰$ SMOW, Hudson & Andrews 1987) at temperatures of between 31 and 46°C. With a surface temperature of between 15 and 25°C, and an assumed geothermal gradient of 30°C/km, this corresponds to a burial depth range of 200–1000 m. The shallower burial depths (and hence lower temperatures, 31–34°C) are preferred on stratigraphic grounds.

The present-day stratigraphy of the area suggests that the Valtos Sandstone Formation would not have been buried to greater than 200 m depth before the middle Oxfordian (Morton 1987), implying a minimum time span of approximately 15 Ma between deposition of

the host-sediment and concretion formation. A corresponding interval of 8 Ma has been estimated for the Bajocian concretions of the Bearreraig Sandstone Formation, Skye (Wilkinson 1991).

Rate of formation

Wilkinson & Dampier (1990) presented models for concretion growth by diagenetic redistribution and applied these to the growth of concretions within the Valtos Sandstone Formation of Valtos, Skye. To apply the models to the Eigg concretions, an assessment of the conditions under which growth took place must be made.

The Mg/Ca and Mn/Ca ratios of the pore fluids from which concretions E2 to E8 were precipitated can be estimated from the mean calcite composition ($MgCO_3 = 2.5 \pm 1.2$ mol%, $MnCO_3 = 0.062 \pm 0.008$ mol%, $n = 96$) and a distribution coefficient appropriate to the temperature of precipitation. The distribution coefficient for magnesium has been measured at 25°C as between 0.013 and 0.06 (Veizer 1983 and references therein), at 90°C as 0.12 (Katz 1973) and at 100°C as 0.25–0.33 (Boles & Ramseyer 1987). Using a value of between 0.01

and 0.05, the Mg/Ca ratio of the pore fluids would be between 1.3 and 0.26. This is in broad agreement with the modern ground water composition data of Veizer (1983). Calcite precipitation rates are relatively unaffected by the Mg content of the pore waters for Mg/Ca < 1.0 (Walter 1986), though specific data are only available for Mg/Ca values of 0.0, 1.0 and 5.0. The rate constants for Mg/Ca = 0.0 and 1.0 are henceforth adopted as the most suitable of those available. A similar treatment of the Mn/Ca ratio (distribution coefficients from Veizer 1983 and references therein) yields pore fluid ratios between 1.3×10^{-4} and 2×10^{-5}. The inhibition effect of Mn at these low ratios is probably insignificant (Dromgoole & Walter 1990). Both surface reaction constants and diffusion constants are temperature-dependent. As precipitation is constrained to have occurred at between 31 and 46°C, and the lower end of this range is more consistent with present-day stratigraphy, values determined at 25°C are used.

Concretion growth rates and shapes are dependent upon the rate of pore fluid flow; growth rates and elongation increase as flow rate increases (Berner 1968, 1980; Johnson 1989; Nielsen 1961). The high degree of sphericity of the concretions of Eigg (>95% proved to be too spherical to determine a direction of elongation) suggests that either pore fluid flow rates were low, or that surface reaction effects overcame the effects of flow. As the Mg/Ca ratio within the pore waters has been determined to be below 1.3 (see above), surface reaction would not be important relative to solute transport processes (see Wilkinson & Dampier 1990 Fig. 5), from which it may be concluded that pore fluid flow rates were low. However, minor element concentrations within some of the concretions are approximately constant (concretion E3, Fig. 7), suggesting precipitation under open system conditions. Other concretions show more variable minor element contents (concretion E6, Fig. 7), which suggest precipitation in a more closed system. As the minor element patterns do not assist in constraining pore fluid flow rates, these are assumed to have been low (≪1 m/a).

Concretion growth times are also dependent upon the concentration of soluble calcium carbonate (i.e. shell material) within the host sandbody. As little shell material is preserved within the concretions, this factor can only be estimated by assessing the amount of calcite within the formation at the present day, and assuming that this was all derived by the dissolution of shell material. Wilkinson (1989) estimated that approximately 5.7% of the concretionary

horizon was cemented, hence the ratio of volume fraction of dissolving mineral within the host-rock to volume fraction of precipitating mineral within the concretion (F_d/F_p of Wilkinson & Dampier 1990) is 0.057. Concretion growth times for these conditions are plotted in Fig. 8 for Mg/Ca ratios of 0.0 and 1.0. An average sized concretion from this bed (radius = 11.8 cm) is predicted to have taken 0.36−0.84 Ma to form.

Spatial distribution and concretion nucleation

Previous work concerning the spatial distribution of concretions within a bedding plane is limited. Raiswell & White (1978) showed that concretions from the Jurassic Jet Rock of N.E. England were randomly distributed. This was interpreted to indicate that growth was surface reaction controlled (Raiswell 1988). Pirrie (1987) showed that concretions from the Marambio Group of James Ross Island, Antarctica, were distributed in two distinct, non-random fashions. The concretions were either aligned in parallel rows or were at the maximum spacing possible for the observed density. Pirrie (1987) interpreted the latter distribution to indicate that the growth of one concretion would inhibit the formation of another within a certain range. Bjørkum & Walderhaug (1990) determined concretion spacing from outcrops oriented perpendicular to bedding within the Bridport Sands, and came to the same conclusion.

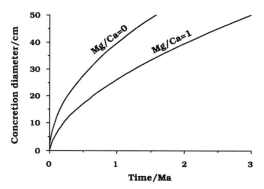

Fig. 8. Model growth times for concretions, Eigg. The assumptions made in the calculations are discussed in the text. A typical concretion (diameter = 11.8 cm) would have taken between 0.36 and 0.84 Ma to grow, depending upon the Mg/Ca ratio of the porefluids.

The clustered distribution of the concretions from Eigg can be interpreted to indicate that the nuclei upon which the concretions formed were clustered. The alternative explanation, that the formation of a single concretion increases the probability of others forming close by, is clearly untenable as the formation of one concretion decreases the degree of pore fluid supersaturation around it (Bjørkum & Walderhaug 1990) and hence reduces the probability of another concretion nucleating. It is more probable that, within the Valtos Sandstone Formation of Eigg, the formation of one concretion had no influence upon the probability of another forming close by. Hence the arrangement of the concretions was controlled by the arrangement of suitable nuclei; these nuclei must have had a clustered distribution.

Previous studies concerning the nature of the nuclei for sandstone-hosted concretions have concluded as follows.

(1) The concretions formed around sedimentary accumulations of organic matter. These accumulations raise the degree of calcite supersaturation as decay of the organic matter proceeds (e.g. Deegan 1971; Pirrie 1987).

(2) The concretions nucleated upon detrital shell material (e.g. McBride 1988), with the differing solubilities of the shells and the calcite precipitate driving nucleation and precipitation (Bjørkum & Walderhaug 1990).

(3) The concretionary nuclei were early diagenetic ferroan calcite cements formed by sulphate reduction within burrows at very shallow depths of burial. Early cements were recorded within the concretions of the Bearreraig Sandstone Formation of Skye (Wilkinson 1991), where they are thought to control not only concretion location but also shape. The early cements are found preferentially within horizons representing periods of low sedimentation rate, which subsequently became layers of stratabound concretions. The burrow-fills were formed from porewaters of marine origin, though precipitation caused modification of the porewater chemical composition leading to a wide range of cement compositions. A subsequent sparry calcite cement phase (petrographically similar to the cements of the Eigg concretions) precipitated from meteoric or mixed marine/meteoric waters upon the burrow-fill cements and formed metre-scale concretions (Wilkinson 1991).

None of the above explanations are completely satisfactory for the Eigg concretions. Stable isotope data can be interpreted to suggest that most of the carbon within the concretionary cements of Eigg is derived from the dissolution of shell material, while the organic-nucleated concretions described by Pirrie (1987) have been interpreted to contain significantly higher contributions from organic carbon (Pirrie & Marshall 1991). The principal problem with the second theory (above) is that it predicts that the formation of one concretion should have inhibited the formation of others close by (Bjørkum & Walderhaug 1990), whereas the distribution data presented above suggests that this was not the case. Early diagenetic ferroan calcites have not been observed, though their presence in low concentrations cannot be ruled out.

It is proposed, in the case of the Eigg sandbody, that the number of potential nuclei within the sediments were limited and each potential nucleus became a concretion. There are few potential nuclei within the Valtos Sandstone Formation, as the preservable macrofauna was limited to the aragonite-shelled bivalve Neomiodon. Discounting the possible role of rare detrital calcite, it is concluded that the Neomiodon shells themselves were the most likely nuclei. The extent to which aragonite can act as a nucleus to calcite in the subsurface is limited by the low degrees of supersaturation encountered (e.g. De Boer 1977). However, as burial proceeds, temperatures increase, and as the original porewaters are displaced by meteoric fluids, the probability of an aragonitic fossil recrystallising to calcite increases. This is especially true if the aragonite crystals within the shell are damaged, e.g. by current action. It is suggested that the concretions nucleated upon detrital aragonite as it underwent spontaneous recrystallisation to calcite under the influence of increasing burial temperatures.

The results of this paper were derived from a single outcrop on the Isle of Eigg. Hence one must be cautious about extending the conclusions either basinwide or to other sedimentary basins. However, the cementation phenomena observed here can be important, and may need to be recognised in a basin if the diagenesis or hydrology is to be fully understood. The cementation phase described in this paper was shallow (in terms of petroleum production), yet before the host-rock was buried to more than 300 m, cementation had locally reduced porosity from 15–20% (pointcounted from impregnated thin-sections) to effectively zero. While only around 6% of the study bedding plane is cemented, other horizons from Eigg show almost complete cementation, and similar cements of the Bearreraig Sandstone Formation of Skye occupy up to 75% of the surface of individual bedding planes (Wilkinson 1991).

Conclusions

(1) The concretions upon which this study is based grew at burial depths of between 200−300 m, at temperatures inferred from stable oxygen isotope data of 31−46°C, in pore waters of meteoric origin.

(2) There was a significant delay between the deposition of the host-sandstone and the onset of concretion growth, of 15 Ma or longer.

(3) An average concretion (radius = 11.8 cm) grew in approximately 0.36−0.84 Ma. Growth was predominantly transport-controlled, though the uncertainty in the growth time estimate is the effect of the poorly constrained Mg/Ca ratio upon the value of the surface reaction rate constant.

(4) The concretions show a clustered distribution when examined on a scale of 1 m or greater.

(5) The most likely nucleus for the concretions are detrital *Neomiodon* shells. These were originally aragonite, though they would have altered to calcite prior to the onset of concretion growth. The distribution of suitable nucleation sites controlled the spatial arrangement of concretions.

The author wishes to thank Shell Expro U.K. for funding the study upon which this paper is based and J. D. Hudson for his valuable assistance with the project. Thanks also to Mark Allan for help with the survey, to J. D. Marshall for reading and improving the manuscript and to J. E. Andrews and T. R. Astin for helpful reviews The stable isotope laboratory at Liverpool University is funded jointly by the University and the NERC though J. D. Marshall.

References

ANDERSON, T. F. & ARTHUR, M. A. 1983. Stable isotopes of oxygen and carbon and their application to sedimentologic and paleoenvironmental problems. *In*: ARTHUR, M. A. (ed.). *Stable Isotopes in Sedimentary Geology*, SEPM Short Course, Tulsa, 10, 1.1−1.151.

BERNER, R. A. 1968. Rate of concretion growth. *Geochimica et Cosmochimica Acta*, 32, 477−483.

—— 1980. *Early Diagenesis, a Theoretical Approach*. Princeton University Press, New York.

BJØRKUM, P. A. & WALDERHAUG, O. 1990. Geometrical arrangement of calcite cementation within shallow marine sandstones. *Earth-Science Reviews*, 29, 145−161.

BOLES, J. R. & RAMSEYER, K. 1987. Diagenetic carbonate in Miocene sandstone reservoir, San Joaquin Basin, California. *AAPG Bulletin*, 71, 1475−1487.

BRYANT, I. D., KANTOROWICZ, J. D. & LOVE, C. F. 1988. The origin and recognition of laterally continuous carbonate-cemented horizons in the Upper Lias Sands of southern England. *Marine and Petroleum Geology*, 5, 108−133.

CRAIG, H. 1957. Isotopic standards for carbon and oxygen factors for mass-spectrometric analysis of carbon dioxide. *Geochimica et Cosmochimica Acta*, 12, 133−149.

DE BOER, R. B. 1977. Influence of seed crystals on the precipitation of calcite and aragonite. *American Journal of Science*, 277, 38−60.

DEEGAN, C. E. 1971. The mode of origin of some late diagenetic sandstone concretions from the Scottish Carboniferous. *Scottish Journal of Geology*, 7, 357−365.

DICKSON, J. A. D. 1966. Carbonate identification and genesis as revealled by staining. *Journal of Sedimentary Petrology*, 36, 491−505.

DROMGOOLE, E. L. & WALTER, L. M. 1990. Inhibition of calcite growth rates by Mn^{2+} in $CaCl_2$ solutions at 10, 25 and 50°C. *Geochimica et Cosmochimica Acta*, 54, 2991−3000.

EMELEUS, C. H. 1991. Tertiary Igneous Activity. *In*: CRAIG, G. Y. (ed.) *Geology of Scotland*. Geological Society, London, 455−502.

HARRIS, J. P. & HUDSON, J. D. 1980. Lithostratigraphy of the Great Estuarine Group (Middle Jurassic), Inner Hebrides. *Scottish Journal of Geology*, 16, 231−250.

HUDSON, J. D. 1980. Aspects of brackish-water facies and fauna from the Jurassic of north-west Scotland. *Proceedings of the Geologists' Association*, 91, 99−105.

—— & ANDREWS, J. E. 1987. The diagenesis of the Great Estuarine Group, Middle Jurassic, Inner Hebrides, Scotland. In: MARSHALL, J. D. (ed.). *Diagenesis of Sedimentary Sequences*. Geological Society, London, Special Publication, 36, 259−276.

—— & HARRIS, J. P. 1979. Sedimentology of the Great Esturine Group (Middle Jurassic) of North-west Scotland. *In*: *Sedimentation Jurassique W. Européen*. Association des Sedimentologistes Français, Publ. Speciale no 1, 1−13.

IRWIN, M., CURTIS, C. D. & COLEMAN, M. L. 1977. Isotopic evidence for source of diagenetic carbonates formed during burial of organic-rich sediments. *Nature*, 269, 209−213.

JOHNSON, M. R. 1989. Paleogeographic significance of oriented calcareous concretions in the Triassic Katberg Formation, South Africa. *Journal of Sedimentary Petrology*, 59, 1008−1010.

KANTOROWICZ, J. D. BRYANT, I. D., & DAWANS, J. M., 1987. Controls on the geometry and distribution of carbonate cements in Jurassic sandstones: Bridport Sands, southern England and Viking Group, Troll Field, Norway, *In*: MARSHALL, J. D. (ed.). *Diagenesis of Sedimentary Sequences*. Geological Society, London, Special Publication, 36, 103−118.

KATZ, A. 1973. The interaction of magnesium with calcite during crystal growth at 25−90°C and one atmosphere. *Geochimica et Cosmochimica Acta*, 37, 1563−1586.

KERSHAW, K. A. & LOONEY, J. H. H. 1985. *Quantitative and Dynamic Plant Ecology*, Edward Arnold,

London, 3rd Edition.

McBRIDE, E. F. 1988. Contrasting diagenetic histories of concretions and host-rock, Lion Mountain Sandstone (Cambrian), Texas. *Geological Society of America Bulletin*, **100**, 1803–1810.

MORTON, N. 1987. Jurassic subsidence history in the Hebrides, N.W. Scotland. *Marine and Petroleum Geology*, **4**, 226–242.

NIELSON, A. E. 1961. Diffusion controlled growths of a moving sphere. The kinetics of crystal growth in potassium perchlorate precipitation. *Journal of Physical Chemistry*, **74**, 309–320.

PIRRIE, D. 1987. Oriented calcareous concretions from James Ross Island, Antarctica. *British Antarctic Survey Bulletin*, **75**, 41–50.

—— & MARSHALL, J. D. 1991. Field relationships and stable isotope geochemistry of concretions from James Ross Island, Antarctica. *Sedimentary Geology*, **71**, 137–150.

RAISWELL, R. 1987. Non-steady state microbiological diagenesis and the origin of concretions and nodular limestones. *In*: MARSHALL, J. D. (ed.) *Diagenesis of Sedimentary Sequences*, Geological Society, London, Special Publication, **36**, 41–54.

—— 1988. Evidence for surface reaction-controlled growth of carbonate concretions in shales. *Sedi-*

mentology, **35**, 571–575.

—— & WHITE, N. J. M. 1978. Spatial aspects of concretionary growth in the Upper Lias of northeast England. *Sedimentary Geology*, **20**, 291–300.

VEIZER, J. 1983. Chemical diagenesis of sediments: theory and application of trace element technique: *In*: ARTHUR, M. A. (ed.). *Stable Isotopes in Sedimentary Geology*, SEPM Short Course, Tulsa, 10, 3.1–3.100.

WALTER, L. M. 1986. Relative efficiency of carbonate dissolution and precipitation during diagenesis: A progress report on the role of solution geochemistry. In: GAUTIER, D. L. (ed.) *Roles of Organic Matter in Sediment Diagenesis*. SEPM Special Publication 38, 1–11.

WILKINSON, M. 1989. *Sandstone-Hosted Concretionary Cements of the Hebrides, Scotland*. PhD Thesis, Leicester University, U.K.

——, 1991. The concretions of the Bearreraig Sandstone Formation: geometry and geochemistry. *Sedimentology*, **38**, 899–912.

—— & DAMPIER, M. D. 1990. The rate of growth of sandstone-hosted calcite concretions. *Geochimica et Cosmochimica Acta*, **54**, 3391–3399.

Middle Jurassic clay-minerals from the Minch Basin: isotopic tracing of provenance and post-depositional alteration

P. J. HAMILTON[1], A. E. FALLICK[2], J. E. ANDREWS[3] AND D. J. WHITFORD[1]

[1] CSIRO Division of Exploration Geoscience, P.O. Box 136, North Ryde New South Wales 2113, Australia

[2] Isotope Geology Unit, Scottish Universities Research and Reactor Centre, East Kilbride, Glasgow G75 0QU, UK

[3] School of Environmental Sciences, University of East Anglia, Norwich NR4 7TJ, UK

Although clay-mineralogical studies can potentially yield information on depositional palaeoclimate, sediment provenance, thermal (burial) history and fluid-sediment interactions of basin fills, clay-mineralogy used alone is often difficult to interpret unequivocally. However, over the last twenty years it has been demonstrated that mineralogical information, combined with isotopic data can be a powerful means of understanding the origins and evolution of the clay component of basin fills.

The mudrocks of the upper part of the Bathonian Great Estuarine Group of the Inner Hebrides, Scotland (Hudson 1983), part of the Jurassic sedimentary fill of the Minch Basin, *sensu* Hudson (1964), contain a highly variable suite of clay-minerals (Andrews 1987). These are interpreted to have had both depositional and post-depositional-alteration origins. This study (reported fully in Hamilton *et al.* (1992)) was intended to constrain and improve the ideas discussed by Andrews (1987) by using both radiogenic (Rb−Sr, Sm−Nd) and stable (O, H) isotope tracers on the less than 2 μm clay fractions.

The mudrocks of these marine-brackish-lagoonal (Duntulm Formation; Andrews & Walton 1990) to low-salinity closed lagoonal (Kilmaluag Formation; Andrews 1985) palaeoenvironments are characterized by four typical clay-mineral assemblages (Andrews 1987). Assemblage 1 is dominated by illite/smectite mixed-layer clays and illite and is interpreted as representing primary Jurassic clay deposition. The smectite component is probably the product of argillization of Jurassic volcanic dust, whilst the illite is a weathering product. Assemblage 2 is dominated by smectite (>80%) and found in a stratigraphically thin band (about 5 cm thick) (see Fig. 1). This band probably represents a secondary bentonite layer (i.e. a redeposited volcanic ash), the smectite having formed by alteration of volcanic glass. Potassium saturation (Weaver 1958) confirms that the parent

material to this smectite (and that of assemblage 1) was predominantly mafic volcanic minerals. Assemblage 3 is characterized by illite and poorly expandable illite−smectite, whilst as-

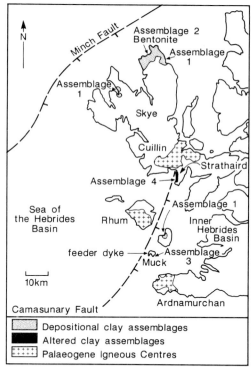

Fig. 1. Localities of clay mineral assemblages 1−4 (Duntulm and Kilmaluag Formations of the Great Estuarine Group). Note that assemblage-4 clays are found within a few kilometres of the Cuillin Igneous Centre and that assemblage-3 clays are mainly from the Isle of Muck, close to a gabbroic feeder dyke. The Minch and Camasunary faults mark the western margins of the Sea of the Hebrides and Inner Hebrides Basins respectively. These basins were collectively termed the Minch Basin by Hudson (1964). Diagram after Andrews (1987).

From PARNELL, J. (ed.), 1992, *Basins on the Atlantic Seaboard: Petroleum Geology, Sedimentology and Basin Evolution.* Geological Society Special Publication No 62, pp 155−158.

155

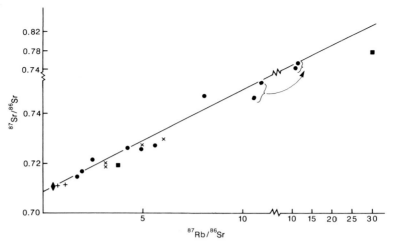

Fig. 2. Plot of $^{87}Sr/^{86}Sr$ versus $^{87}Rb/^{86}Sr$ data. The regression line is fitted to the nine assemblage-1 (unaltered) samples (dots). The slope yields an apparent age of 290 Ma. An alternative interpretation is that the array represents a mixing line of components with various Rb/Sr values. The assemblage-2 samples (diamonds) appear to have low Rb/Sr ratios, which suggests that weathering-derived clays have higher Rb/Sr ratios (see text). Altered samples (assemblage-3 = crosses and assemblage-4 = squares) also plot close to the line. Diagram after Hamilton *et al.* (1992).

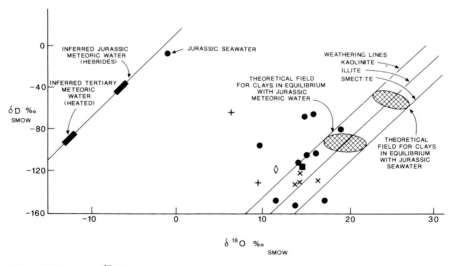

Fig. 3. Plot of δD versus $\delta^{18}O$ data (same symbols as Fig. 2) relative to theoretical isotopic compositions for clay minerals formed at surface temperatures, shown as 'weathering lines'. (Justification for these lines is given in Hamilton *et al.* 1992). The two hatched areas represent weathering values for clays in equilibrium with Jurassic seawater and meteoric water respectively. Most of the samples are depleted in δD which suggests equilibration with Tertiary meteoric water. However, the altered samples do not show the expected oxygen depletion (temperatures around 200°C are inferred for assemblage-4 samples) which may mean final equilibration with younger, cooler Tertiary meteoric water. Diagram after Hamilton *et al.* (1992).

semblage 4 is dominated by illite with variable amounts of kaolinite and chlorite. Assemblages 3 and 4 are found close to major Tertiary igneous intrusions, particularly the Cuillins pluton (Fig. 1): they are interpreted as the products of post-depositional alteration of the clays by reaction with convecting meteoric waters, heated by the igneous centres (see Taylor & Forester 1971). The main effect was illitization of the smectite component, this being most marked in assemblage 4. Temperatures of around 180–200°C would have caused illitization, consistent with vitrinite reflectivity (Hudson & Andrews 1987) and spore coloration data (Riding 1984) for the Strathaird area (Fig. 1).

The Rb/Sr ratios for the unaltered clay-mineral assemblages plot in a linear array relative to $^{87}Sr/^{86}Sr$ values. The regression line for these data has a slope which, if taken as of geochronological significance, yields an apparent age of 290 Ma (Fig. 2). This could be interpreted as the age of the hinterland regolith from which the Bathonian sediments were derived. However, plots of initial $^{87}Sr/^{86}Sr$ versus Sr content and versus reciprocal Sr content for these data define hyperbolic and rectilinear trends respectively, consistent with a two-component mixing model (Faure 1977). The data might thus be explained by the mixing of material with both high and low Rb/Sr values. The assemblage 2 (volcanic-derived) data plot in the low Rb/Sr position (Fig. 2) and are thus the best candidate for the low Rb/Sr material. However, it is unclear what the high Rb/Sr material is. The Rb/Sr ratio does not simply increase with increasing illite or illite-smectite content, so the notion of a high Rb/Sr weathering-sourced illite is not wholly correct. It is probable that more than two high Rb/Sr end-members are implicated.

The Sm–Nd data were used to calculate model ages (when the crustal precursor to the sediment was differentiated from the mantle). The ages range between 1.49 to 1.95 Ga, compatible with a weathering source dominated by Dalradian age lithologies (see also Andrews et al. 1987) with an admixed younger component derived from penecontemporaneous volcanic ash (now altered to smectite).

The δD and $\delta^{18}O$ values for these clay assemblages (Fig. 3) imply that isotopic exchange last occurred with meteoric waters that were D and ^{18}O depleted, (e.g. Tertiary meteoric waters (Taylor & Forester 1971)) and are therefore not indicative of provenance. Most of the samples in this study show clear effects of H-isotope exchange (values range from −64 to −153‰ SMOW). Thus the altered assemblages were probably affected by high temperature (>70°C) sediment-water interaction followed by lower temperature reactions as the hydrothermal waters cooled, whereas the unaltered clays were only affected by lower temperature (<70°C) isotopic exchange, insufficient to have caused clay mineral alteration. The $\delta^{18}O$ values (6–19‰ SMOW) indicate less extensive O-isotope exchange with partial retention of a depositional $\delta^{18}O$ signal.

References

ANDREWS, J. E. 1985. The sedimentary facies of a late Bathonian regressive episode: the Kilmaluag and Skudiburgh Formations of the Great Estuarine Group, Inner Hebrides, Scotland. *Journal of the Geological Society, London*, **142**, 1119–1137.

—— 1987. Jurassic clay-mineral assemblages and their post-depositional alteration: upper Great Estuarine Group, Scotland. *Geological Magazine*, **124**, 261–271.

——, HAMILTON, P. J. & FALLICK, A. E. 1987. The geochemistry of early diagenetic dolostones from a low-salinity Jurassic lagoon. *Journal of the Geological Society, London*, **144**, 687–698.

—— & WALTON, W. 1990. Depositional environments within Middle Jurassic oyster-dominated lagoons: an integrated litho-, bio-, and palyno-facies study of the Duntulm Formation (Great Estuarine Group, Inner Hebrides). *Transactions of the Royal Society of Edinburgh, Earth Sciences*, **81**, 1–22.

FAURE, G. 1977. *Principles of Isotope Geology*. Wiley, New York.

HAMILTON, P. J., FALLICK, A. E., ANDREWS, J. E. & WHITFORD, D. J. 1992. Isotopic constraints on the provenance and post-depositional alteration of clay minerals: an example from the Jurassic of Scotland. *Earth and Planetary Science Letters*, in press.

HUDSON, J. D. 1964. The petrology of the sandstones of the Great Estuarine Series, and the Jurassic palaeogeography of Scotland. *Proceedings of the Geologists' Association*, **75**, 499–527.

—— 1983. Mesozoic sedimentation and sedimentary rocks in the Inner Hebrides. *Proceedings of the Royal Society of Edinburgh*, **83B**, 47–63.

—— & ANDREWS, J. E. 1987. The diagenesis of the Great Estuarine Group, Middle Jurassic, Inner Hebrides, Scotland. *In*: MARSHALL, J. D. (ed.) *Diagenesis of Sedimentary Sequences*. Geological Society, London, Special Publication, **36**, 259–276.

RIDING, J. B. 1984. The palynology of the Tobar Ceann Siltstone Member, Staffin Shale Formation (Jurassic: Callovian/Oxfordian), Strathaird, Southern Skye. *Reports of the British Geological*

Survey, **16**, No. 10, 1−5.

TAYLOR, H. P. Jr. & FORESTER, R. W. 1971. Low-^{18}O igneous rocks from the intrusive complexes of Skye, Mull and Ardnamurchan, Western Scotland. *Journal of Petrology*, **12**, 465−487.

WEAVER, C. E. 1958. The effects and geologic significance of potassium "fixation" by expandable clay minerals derived from muscovite, biotite, chlorite and volcanic material. *American Mineralogist*, **43**, 839−861.

Sedimentological studies of the Cretaceous Lochaline Sandstone, NW Scotland

BEN LOWDEN[1], SHARON BRALEY[2], ANDREW HURST[3] &
JONATHAN LEWIS[4]

[1] *Department of Mineral Resources Engineering, Imperial College, London SW7 2BP, UK*

[2] *Department of Geology, Polytechnic South West, Plymouth PL4 8AA, UK*

[3] *Unocal UK Ltd., 32 Cadbury Road, Sunbury-on-Thames TW16 7LU, UK*

[4] *Department of Petroleum Engineering, Heriot-Watt University, Edinburgh EH14 4AS, UK*

Sediments of Cretaceous age in northwest Scotland outcrop in small, often isolated exposures throughout the Inner Hebrides and Morvern. Despite limited exposure, a range of sedimentary facies are recognized which potentially influence the interpretation of offshore data, in particular with respect to the hydrocarbon potential of offshore Cretaceous sections.

The Mid–Late Cretaceous development of the Inner Hebrides basin includes two periods of marine transgression. The first began in the latest Albian and continued through the early Cenomanian with the deposition of the marginal clastic facies of the Morvern Formation (Fig. 1). In the Late Cenomanian, a minor period of regression occurred during which the Lochaline Sandstone Member (the White Sandstone of Humphries 1961) was deposited.

Sedimentology

In and around the Lochaline sand mine (Grid Ref. NM 680450) extensive fresh exposures afford considerable potential for sedimentological and petrophysical studies of a large siliciclastic sand body (Lewis *et al.* 1990), further detail of which is reported here. Regional sedimentological and palaeoenvironmental data, including description and interpretation of the late Cenomanian and Turonian strata, are reported in Braley (1990).

Within the mine, between 3 and 8 metres of the Lochaline Sandstone Member are exposed, the workings generally lying between a lower silty horizon and an upper quartz-cemented horizon. Along the east shore of Loch Aline the sandstone is approximately 12 metres thick. Thicker, cleaner sandstone units are often located in fault footwalls. Small-scale syndepositional faulting is also seen with evidence of

sand draping. Slump structures provide additional evidence of sediment failure.

An idealized vertical sequence through the mined section (Fig. 2) reveals a general fine to medium sand coarsening-upwards sequence. However, the coarsening-up transition varies in thickness, in some places representing less than a metre of the overall sequence. Bioturbation is abundant near the base of the mine exposure.

Above this finer-grained, bioturbated interval is a scoured horizon about 1 metre thick con-

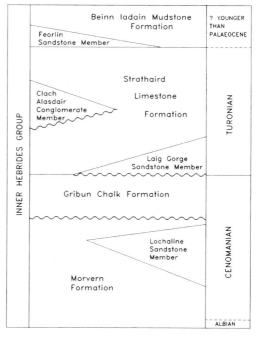

Fig. 1. Lithostratigraphy for the Cretaceous of NW Scotland.

From PARNELL, J. (ed.), 1992, *Basins on the Atlantic Seaboard: Petroleum Geology, Sedimentology and Basin Evolution*. Geological Society Special Publication No 62, pp 159–162.

159

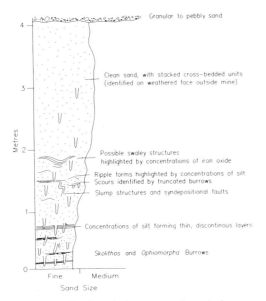

Fig. 2. Idealized vertical sequence through the Lochaline Sandstone Member from the sand mine.

taining ripples (which are highlighted by silty drapes), rare swaley structures, and soft sediment deformation. Scoured surfaces are also present, and usually mark the appearance of cleaner sands with occasional isolated *Ophiomorpha* and very rarely, approximately 0.5 metre thick trough cross-beds. Above this, at the top of the sequence exposed in the mine, rare granular, occasionally conglomeratic sands are found. These are quartzitic, sub-rounded to rounded, with an undulose base. In some areas large pebble-sized sandstone clasts occur.

On close inspection, and with suitable lighting in the mine, bedforms are visible and trough cross-bedding, planar cross-bedding, (?)current-ripples, slump structures and scours are identified (Lewis *et al.* 1990). Flaser-bedding has been recorded from sandstone exposures at Beinn Iadain, 10 km to the north of the mine (Braley 1990), where a plant-rich (coal) horizon is also reported (Judd 1878). Foreset orientations record a unidirectional, northwesterly current flow. The boundaries between cross-bedded units are sharp and, in most cases, horizontal. A number of units can be traced horizontally over tens of metres from within the mine to the exposure outside. Cross-bed thickness and dip remain approximately uniform over this distance, from which it is postulated that the cross-bedded units may have lateral extents of the order of 100 metres.

Although the internal structure of the ripples is difficult to discern, the morphology of the ripple drapes appears slightly asymmetric. The wavelength of the ripples averages 40 cm and the distance between clay drape horizons (i.e. ripple set thickness) averages 18 cm. Clay ripple drapes are not laterally extensive over more than 1.2 metres and reach a maximum thickness of 4 mm in the ripple troughs. Where thickest, silt grade partings are visible within the clay drapes. The partings are generally lighter in colour than the clay itself, and have normal grading.

The sandstone comprises very well sorted, fine to medium grained sand. Sieve analyses of sand samples from a vertical profile confirm the presence of an overall coarsening-upwards sequence, but also show that fine-grained sediment, although decreasing in abundance, continued to be deposited throughout the unit. This fine-grained sediment, and a small amount of clay material, where most common, probably constitutes burrow linings.

Sieved samples from different outcrops and various locations within the mine have approximately log-normal grain size distributions (Humphries 1961; Lewis *et al.* 1990). It has been estimated that 70% of the sand is between 0.2 and 0.3 mm, 10% is coarser than 0.3 mm and only 3% is less than 0.08 mm (Smith 1989). A small fraction of silt- to clay-sized grains and coarse to medium pebble-sized particles are also present, though they are rare. Grain roundness varies from angular to rounded, with a strong positive correlation between grain size and roundness (Humphries 1961).

Mineralogy and diagenesis

The sandstone unit is characteristically little altered by diagenesis, consolidation largely being caused by compaction (Fig. 3a). Apart from two hard ribs of quartz-cemented sandstone and localized contact metamorphic effects immediately adjacent to dykes, there is little evidence of diagenesis. Quartz comprises between 99.65% and 99.85% of the sand extracted from the mine by weight (Highley 1977), with the remaining fraction consisting of a heavy mineral fraction, including opaque minerals and tourmaline, and a light fraction, including glauconite and clay minerals (Humphries 1961). Clay minerals occur as pellets of silt-sized quartz grains and aggregates of clay particles.

'Hard bands', approximately 0.5 metres thick, are developed towards the bottom and top of the Lochaline Sandstone Member. The bases of the hard bands are planar towards the outcrop

 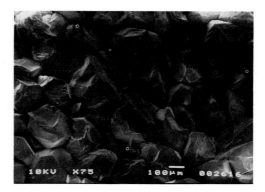

Fig. 3. (A) SEM micrograph typical of sandstones from the Lochaline Sandstone Member with no discernable diagenesis. Scale bar 100 μm. (B) SEM micrograph from the 'hard band' in the roof of the mine showing well developed quartz overgrowths. Scale bar 100 μm.

and more mammary in form further into the sub-crop. Close examination of the hard bands reveals that many of the grains have frosted surfaces (Bailey 1925). The frosting occurs on grains of all sizes and in some cases is seen to transform into larger, quartz overgrowths. It is implied that the frosting is a diagenetic process, where quartz overgrowth has produced the faceting (Lewis *et al.* 1990). Within the hard bands, syntaxial quartz overgrowths are common (Fig. 3b). As sandstones between the hard bands have little evidence of grain frosting, it is implied that the quartz cementation process was very localized. Decalcification is inferred from the absence of calcareous fossils in a sandstone which otherwise has abundant evidence of faunal activity, including burrowing. This contrasts with the underlying glauconitic sandstones, which contain abundant calcareous fossils.

The coarsening-up sequence and regional setting make a wave-dominated, prograding shoreface a possible interpretation. The fine grained, intensely bioturbated sandstones at the base of the sequence may represent an offshore-transition zone. The transition from offshore facies to shoreface facies would be represented by the upward increase in mean grain size, which correlates with a reduction in the occurrence of bioturbation. Alternatively, scour structures, small ripples, and possible swaley/hummocky cross stratification (HCS) identified in the middle of the sequence may represent a lower shoreface facies. The lack of preservation of sedimentary structures may be attributed to storm reworking. After deposition of the sand-

stone a major sea-level rise occurred which terminated with the deposition of the Gribun Chalk Formation. Therefore, a prograding delta or shoreline would require that the sedimentation rate was greater than this relative sea-level rise. The absence of any identifiable hiatus, such as intensely bioturbated horizons, concentrations of fines, or hard grounds, supports that sand deposition was rapid and may well have exceeded the rate of sea-level rise.

Quartz cementation

The silicification of the Lochaline sandstones has been associated with the silicification of the overlying chalks at Beinn Iadain (MacLennan 1949). Silicification of the chalk occurred during the Cenomanian (fragments of silicified chalk are found within the Turonian clastic units; Braley 1990), thus quartz cementation may be associated with the circulation of ground waters synchronous with a period of uplift and erosion. Cementation can be demonstrated to be unrelated to the igneous activity (Lewis *et al.* 1990). Whether of Cretaceous or later age, it seems most likely that quartz cementation is related to primary depositional variations, either concentrating along highly permeable levels, or related to possible concentrations of biogenic silica. No evidence has been found for the pre-existence of a siliceous fauna. Similar cemented horizons have been described from the Oligocene Fontainbleau Sand (Thiry *et al.* 1988) and are attributed to cementation caused by fluctuations in the water table over the last few thousand years.

Economic significance

The Lochaline Sandstone Member has excellent
reservoir characteristics. Within the mine, the
average permeability is 2.1D and the average
porosity is 19.5%, with very low permeability
anisotropy (Lewis *et al.* 1990). Offshore,
Cretaceous rocks are interpreted to be well
developed and extensive on the West Shetland
Platform and in the Faroe Basin (Naylor
& Shannon 1982). Thick accumulations of
Mesozoic sediments (1200 m) are present in the
Colonsay Basin, and may be present in the
Malin, Inner Hebrides, and Outer Hebrides
basins, with possible thin accumulations in the
North Minch Basin. The thick pre-Tertiary
strata may contain hydrocarbon source rocks,
and faulting associated with Mesozoic subsidence may have produced significant structural
and, synsedimentary tectonically induced
stratigraphic traps. Differentiation between
pre-Cretaceous and Cretaceous sediments on
seismic data is difficult because of their similar
velocity characteristics. Whether the Lochaline
Sandstone Member, or a similar sandstone, is
present offshore NW Scotland will only be
resolved by drilling. The presence of mature,
hydrocarbon-prone source rocks offshore is a
further unknown with regard to hydrocarbon
potential. Liassic shales, examples of which
outcrop around Loch Aline, are a possible
source rock. Potential top seals are provided by
the Gribun Chalk, Strathaird Limestone and
Beinn Iadain Mudstone formations.

Tilcon (Scotland) Ltd. and their employees at the
sand mine are thanked for their co-operation.

References

BAILEY, E. B. 1924. The desert shores of the chalk
seas. *Geological Magazine*, **61**, 102–116.

BRALEY, S. 1990. *Sedimentology, Palaeoecology and
Stratigraphy of the Cretaceous Rocks of Northwest
Scotland*. PhD Thesis, Polytechnic South West.

HIGHLEY, D. 1977. *Silica*. Mineral Dosier No. 18.
Mineral Resource Consultancy Communications,
London HMSO.

HUMPHRIES, D. W. 1961. The Upper Cretaceous
White Sandstone of Lochaline, Argyll, Scotland.
Proceedings of the Yorkshire Geological Society,
33, 47–76.

JUDD, J. W. 1878. The sedimentary rocks of Scotland
3rd paper. The strata of the western coast and
islands. *Quarterly Journal of the Geological
Society*, **34**, 660–741.

LEWIS, J. J. M., LOWDEN, B. D. & HURST, A. 1990.
Permeability distribution and measurement of
reservoir-scale sedimentary heterogeneities in
sub-surface exposures of a shallow-marine sandbody. *In: Excursion Guides. 13th International
Sedimentological Congress, Nottingham,
England, September 1990*.

MACLENNAN, R. M. 1949. A starfish from the glass
sand of Lochaline. *Geological Magazine*, **86**,
94–96.

NAYLOR, D. & SHANNON, P. 1982. The geology of
offshore Ireland and Western Britain. *In: Geology of Offshore Ireland and Western Britain*.
Graham & Trotman, London, 103–114.

SMITH, C. G. 1989. *Scottish Highlands and Southern
Uplands mineral portfolio. Silica Sand And Silica
Rock Resources*. British Geological Survey
Technical Report WF/89/6.

THIRY, M., AYRAULT, M. B. & GRISONI, J. 1988.
Ground-water silicification and leaching in sands:
example of the Fontainbleau Sand (Oligocene)
in the Paris Basin. *Geological Society of America
Bulletin*, **100**, 1283–1290.

The role of Palaeocene magmatism in the tectonic evolution of the Sea of the Hebrides Basin: implications for basin evolution on the NW Seaboard

RICHARD W. ENGLAND

Department of Geological Sciences, University of Durham, Durham, DH1 3LE, UK
(Present address: BIRPS, Bullard Laboratories, Madingley Road, Cambridge, CB3
0EZ, UK)

Abstract: Major, trace element and isotope geochemistry of the magmas of the British Tertiary Volcanic Province suggests they rose through the lithosphere in dykes and ponded as sills at the Moho and within the upper crust. In the Sea of the Hebrides basin a linked system of discrete dyke swarms, sills and normal faults record rapid NE−SW extension at the near surface. The presence of a similar system of dykes and sills within the upper crust and at the Moho could have influenced mechanisms of lithospheric extension by dissipating vertical variations in strain laterally, eliminating space problems associated with depth dependant stretching. The addition of large thicknesses of magma to basins along the NW seaboard would have resulted in local burial, but subsidence would be offset by uplift resulting from isostatic effects and thermal expansion of the lithosphere during melting. Heat loss from rising magma would have a negligible effect on the maturation history of the sediments.

The study of magmatism in the British Tertiary Volcanic Province (BTVP) has occupied geologists since the beginning of this century. What has only recently been established is that the BTVP is only a minor, marginal part of a massive phase of magmatic activity which accompanied the opening of the NE Atlantic above a mantle plume (White 1988; Upton 1988; White *et al.* 1987; White & McKenzie 1989). As a result, many of the long lived basins in the Norwegian−Greenland Sea region which had developed during protracted rifting from the late Carboniferous onward (Ziegler 1988) were covered by sub-aerial lavas which accumulated to form the oceanward-dipping reflector sequences during the earliest phases of sea floor spreading (Parson *et al.* 1988). Subsequent subsidence has left these basins buried beneath a thick layer of lavas and up to 2 km of water (Wood *et al.* 1987; Mudge & Rashid 1987; Duindam & van Hoorn 1987) (Fig. 1). This contribution discusses the influence of BTVP magmatism on the early Tertiary evolution of the Sea of the Hebrides basin (SOHB) where the best exposed onshore sections for study of the style of Palaeocene magmatism on the NE Atlantic margins occur. A number of conclusions are drawn which may be applicable to the Tertiary evolution of the margins of the N Atlantic and to the role of magma in basin development in general.

Magma migration within the lithosphere

In the upper elastic layer of the lithosphere, most basic low viscosity magmas migrate in dykes which develop normal to the axis of the minimum principal stress, or exploit existing fractures within the extensional field of the stress ellipsoid (Delaney *et al.* 1986). If dykes are to form at deeper levels, where the rheology of the lithosphere is dominantly plastic, magma pressure must exceed the tensile strength of the rock and migration must occur at a rate at which the behavior of the lithosphere is brittle. If these conditions are not satisfied, magma will rise under its own bouyancy as a diapir (Marsh & Kantha 1978).

Two further lines of evidence obtained from studies of magmas erupted at the surface can also be used to constrain their migration mechanism. Basic magmas frequently contain evidence of contamination resulting from partial melting of the rocks believed to form the walls of the conduits through which they ascended. This effect is most notable where basalts traverse large thicknesses of leucocratic rocks or readily fusible lithospheric mantle (McKenzie 1989; Thompson *et al.* 1989) with significantly lower melting points than the temperature of the rising magma. Basalts containing high concentrations of large ion lithophile elements (e.g. K, Ba, Rb, Th) and light rare earth elements coupled with

From PARNELL, J. (ed.), 1992, *Basins on the Atlantic Seaboard: Petroleum Geology, Sedimentology and Basin Evolution.* Geological Society Special Publication No 62, pp 163−174.

163

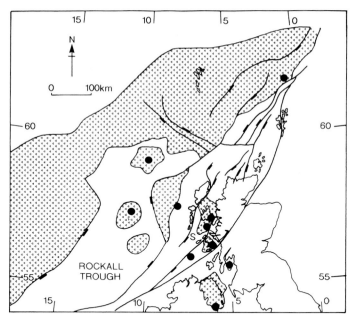

Fig. 1. Map of the NW seaboard illustrating the known extent of lavas and sills (stippled pattern) and central complexes (filled circles) both onshore and offshore. (S — Sea of the Hebrides Basin.)

isotopic ratios significantly different from the mantle reservoir result from contamination by partial melts of specific types of lithosphere. Consequently the ascent path of the magma may be deduced, providing that supporting knowledge of the structure and composition of the lithosphere is available (e.g. from xenoliths, surface geology and deep seismic data). Patchett (1981) noted that such a contamination process is only effective if the magma passes through sheet-like conduits which have a large surface area (area of partial melting) to volume ratio. Turbulent flow within the conduit would also enhance the heat transfer/melting/mixing process. Broad conduits or diapiric bodies would have low surface area to volume ratios and hence the effects of contamination will be diluted. In addition to this, petrography and fractionation trends of major and trace elements can be used to demonstrate that magmas occurring at the surface crystallized phases which are stable at higher pressures but which are not on the liquidus at low pressures. It is concluded that crystallization of these phases occurred at a level at which the magmas had been temporarily trapped and had to change density (by fractionating) before they could rise further. Such levels are likely to occur where there is a rapid decrease in density such as at the Moho (Cox

1980). The actual depth at which fractionation occurred can be estimated from experimental data for crystallization in the basaltic system over a wide range of temperatures and pressures (Thompson 1974).

Magmatism in the British Tertiary Volcanic Province

The magmatic plumbing system

Magmatism in the BTVP began at around 63 Ma and ceased at about 52 Ma, with the most intense activity occurring around 59 Ma immediately prior to the opening of the NE Atlantic (Mussett *et al.* 1988). Magmas were erupted sub-aerially into the SOHB and the Inner Hebrides basin over a peneplaned surface exposing Lewisian, Torridonian and Mesozoic through to latest Cretaceous rocks. The extensive lava fields which developed were intruded by major central igneous complexes (Fig. 2). Sills, which post-date the lower lavas, were intruded into the well-stratified Mesozoic sediments filling the basins. The lavas, sills and central complexes are cut by complex swarms of dykes, striking NW–SE, and a set of swarm parallel normal faults. Cross cutting evidence indicates that the dykes were emplaced

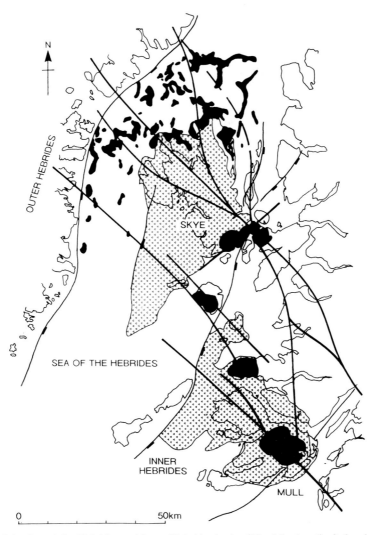

Fig. 2. Map of the Sea of the Hebrides and Inner Hebrides basins (Fig. 1 for location) showing the preserved extent of Palaeocene magmatism within the basin. Lava fields are indicated by the triangular pattern; sills and central complexes in black; thick lines indicate axes of discrete dyke swarms.

throughout the period of igneous activity. The faulting also spans the igneous activity.

Thompson & Morrison (1988) noted that magmas showing little evidence of crustal contamination have compatible (Ni, Cr, Y, Nb) to moderately-incompatible element (Ti, P, Zr, Hf, Sr, MREE) concentrations similar to those of Icelandic (mantle derived) tholeiitic to mildly alkalic ocean island basalts (OIB). However, their incompatible element concentrations resembled the ranges shown by mid-ocean ridge basalts. They reconciled these contrasting characteristics by postulating that all the BTVP magmas were ultimately derived by partial melting of asthenospheric mantle but that their elemental OIB characteristics had been modified by substantial contamination by partial melts of lower lithosphere (thermal boundary layer) which had already lost a small fraction of melt during a phase of late Carboniferous to early Permian extension (Morrison et al. 1980). Thompson et al. (1982, 1986) demonstrated, using major, trace and Pb isotope data, that the lower tholeiitic parts of the lava pile (members of the Staffa magma type) fractionated olivine and plagioclase at low pressures while assimilating large volumes of upper crustal rocks. Pb isotope data also indicate that these lavas had been contaminated by small amounts of acidic partial melts from the lower crust. The alkali basalts which form the bulk of the lava pile (the Skye main lava series or Mull plateau group) can be shown to have equilibrated at the Moho (at around 25 km), fractionating the high pressure assemblage of olivine and subcalcic clinopyroxene with plagioclase. These magmas rose into the crust where they absorbed their high-pressure phenocrysts and mixed with acidic partial melts of granulite facies gneiss before rising toward the surface. Alternatively they could have assimilated partial melts of upper mantle rocks with isotopic compositions similar to that of Lewisian granulite gneiss prior to fractionation at the Moho (Thompson & Morrison 1988). Similarly Dickin *et al.* (1984) used Pb isotope data to demonstrate that the Preshal Mhor magma type, which forms the uppermost preserved part of the lava succession on Skye, the core of the Cuillin complex and a substantial component of the dyke swarm, contained a significant amount of upper crustal contaminant. However, ponding and contamination of these magmas in the lower crust cannot be excluded. Thompson (1982) noted

that the late occurrence of these magmas in the Skye lava pile suggests they may not have acquired Pb from partial melts of lower crustal rocks because either the dykes within the lower crust were already lined with refractory alkali basalt of Skye main lava series type, or most of the fuseable material had already been removed by the passage of earlier batches of magma.

The chemistry and contamination patterns of the Hebridean magmas suggests that they rose through the lithosphere in relatively narrow conduits with a large surface area to volume ratio (i.e. dykes) and variously ponded in the upper mantle, at the Moho, in the lower crust or within the upper crust, where they fractionated and assimilated partial melts of leucocratic wall rocks. This suggests that an interconnected system of dykes and sills existed beneath the SOHB, which fed the fissures feeding the lava pile, the central complexes, dykes and sills (Fig. 3).

Evolution of the Sea of the Hebrides Basin

Before considering the distribution of the Tertiary magmas in the SOHB it is necessary to review the structure and stratigraphy of the basin. The stratigraphic record contains evidence for a late-Triassic rifting event which resulted in the accumulation of a relatively thin

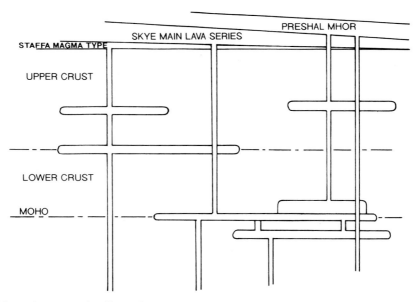

Fig. 3. Schematic cross section illustrating the geometry of the magmatic plumbing system beneath the Sea of the Hebrides basin as deduced from geochemical data (after Morrison *et al.* 1985).

sequence of Jurassic sediments (Morton 1987, 1989). Recent interpretations of the basin history based on seismic and gravity data (O'Neill & England in prep.) conclude that there is little evidence for late Carboniferous subsidence as proposed by Stein (1988). A maximum of 500 m of Carboniferous sediments lying in the deeper parts of the basin can be incorporated into gravity models but there is no unequivocal evidence in the seismic data, such as a Triassic sequence overstepping Carboniferous onto Torridonian basement, to confirm this. O'Neill & England (in prep.) view the subsidence history described by Morton (1987) as representing a single late-Triassic rifting event (producing 500 m of subsidence) followed by Jurassic thermal subsidence (resulting in the preservation of 1.5 to 2.0 km of sediment). During this latter phase the basin reached thermal equilibrium (after 70 Ma) and subsidence ceased. There appears to have been little or no subsidence in the SOHB following the late Jurassic, in contrast to many of the basins on the NW seaboard which contain thick accumulations of late Jurassic to early Cretaceous sediments preserved by a major phase of extension, e.g. in the West Shetland and Faeroes basins (Duindam & van Hoorn 1987). In the SOHB only a thin sequence of Cretaceous greensands and chalk are locally preserved within the basin. Late Cretaceous uplift, probably related to dynamic uplift above the N Atlantic plume, resulted in peneplanation and erosion of much of the thin chalk sequence to yield fluviatile early Tertiary flint conglomerates (Hallam 1982).

Distribution of lavas at the near surface

The early Tertiary lavas were erupted over the late Cretaceous—early Tertiary erosion surface. The lavas are cut by a series of parallel NW—SE trending major dyke swarms linked by sigmoidal secondary swarms (Speight *et al.* 1982; England 1988) (Fig. 2). Parallel to the dykes are a series of extensional faults of the same age. Both the faults and the dykes cut dolerite sills (Fig. 4) which are locally intruded into the base of the lava pile but most commonly lie within middle and upper Jurassic shales. Where they are observed, transgressive steps in the sills strike parallel to the dykes and the faults, indicating that there is a component of extension across the transgressive steps parallel to the direction of extension across the dykes and the faults. Locally faults detach into the bases of the sills (Fig. 4). These observations record a component of horizontal NE—SW-directed extensional displacement across the faults, dykes and surfaces of the sills. The absence of consistent cross-cutting relationships between the faults and minor intrusions suggests that all three components were active during the same period of time and as such constitute a relatively simple interconnected or linked extensional system (Fig. 4). It is contended that the dykes, sills and

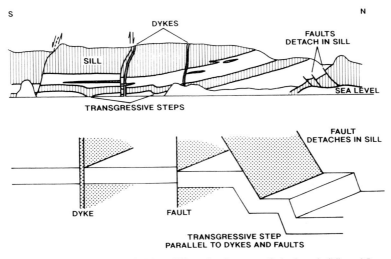

Fig. 4. The upper figure is a sketch of a 2.5 km cliff section between Culnaknock (N) and Inver Tote (S), (vertical scale exaggerated). The lower figure illustrates the major structures associated with sill emplacement.

faults form a relatively simple inter-connected or linked extensional system through which the crust stretched in a NE–SW direction.

The evolution of this linked extensional system is a direct record of how the upper crust responded to the NE–SW orientated tensional stresses. The field observations indicate that the sills play an important role in this system by transferring extensional strains laterally, either concentrating extension into one particular zone (Fig. 5) or dissipating it over a wide area, and by acting as detachment surfaces for faults permitting the amount of extension in a vertical section to vary (Fig. 5). Variations in the amount of extension with depth at the near surface due to dyke emplacement or faulting appears to be dissipated by horizontal movements along the surfaces of sills permitted by transgressive steps accompanied by faults detaching into the top or floor of the intrusion (Fig. 5). This may occur directly in an open system where sills and dykes are connected and emplaced synchronously, or each component of the system may be active at different times in order to dissipate extensional stresses by small increments of extension. The latter would result in complex cross-cutting relationships between dykes, sills and faults, as are typically observed in the field. Concentration of movements along the margins of the minor intrusions and across faults would reduce internal deformation of the sediments by minor faulting, joint development

and stretching (boudinage), which is again consistent with the field observations.

Dyke emplacement: implications for extension rate and crustal deformation

The geometry of the dyke swarms (Fig. 2) provides further important data on the mechanism of crustal extension. Speight *et al.* (1982) demonstrated that the swarms of the BTVP occur as groups of closely spaced dykes recording between 4% and 20% extension of the crust, separated by areas of sparse dyke intrusion and little extension due to faulting. Hence the swarms are discrete structures representing localized deformation of the crust (Fig. 5). Palaeomagnetic evidence and ^{40}Ar–^{39}Ar dating (Musset *et al.* 1988) indicates that the bulk of the dykes within the swarms were emplaced over a period of 5 Ma. Speight *et al.* (1982) indicated local finite extensions due to dyke emplacement of 20%, which indicates a relatively rapid strain rate of 10^{-15}s^{-1} (Carter & Tsenn 1987). These observations support the numerical models of Kusznir & Park (1987) and Sonder & England (1989) who noted that rapid stretching (strain rate $> 5 \times 10^{-15}$s^{-1}) caused localized extension as a result of strain softening (weakening) of the lithosphere due to an elevated geothermal gradient. In the SOHB this elevated gradient would have been enhanced by

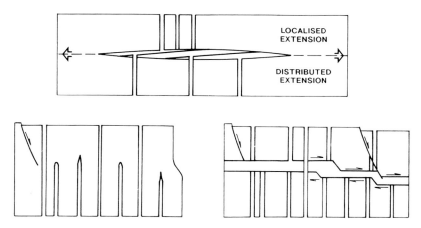

Fig. 5. The upper figure illustrates the role sills may play in localizing extension by transferring magma laterally to regions of active extension. Both the upper and lower layers extend equally, the upper layer by localized extension and the lower layer by distributed extension. The lower figures illustrate the role of sills in dissipating strains resulting from different amounts of extension with depth by acting as detachment surfaces. The lower left-hand figure illustrates variable extension with depth resulting from faulting and dyke emplacement which results in a volume deficit near the surface. The lower right-hand diagram illustrates how structures illustrated in Fig. 4 can accommodate equal amounts of stretching above and below the intruding sill.

rising magma. Heat released from cooling intrusions would locally maintain elevated crustal temperatures, thus favouring ductile deformation of the crust and permitting high strain rates to be maintained. As the magmatic activity waned the crust would cool and increase in strength. At this point the low magnitude stress field responsible for the orientation of the dykes (England 1988) would have been insufficient to cause further extension and stretching of the Hebridean crust ceased.

The role of magmatism in crustal extension

Current models for extension of the continental lithosphere account for the observed 'steers head' geometry of sedimentary basins by assuming that stretching of the lithosphere occurs over a wider area with increasing depth (Rowley & Sahagian 1986; White & McKenzie 1988). This requires the lithosphere to have rheological properties which enable it to dissipate different finite strains at progressively lower strain rates with increasing depth beneath the rift axis. Hence the upper crust could be expected to deform largely by brittle processes and the lower crust and lithospheric mantle by ductile processes (Kuznir & Park 1986, 1987; Rutter & Brodie 1991). The field observations described above indicate that the migration of magma (when present) may play an important role in accommodating variations in strain with depth (Fig. 5), at least at the near surface.

The geochemical evidence presented above (Fig. 3) suggests that a linked system of dykes and sills similar to that observed at the present surface extends down to at least the Moho beneath the BTVP. Similar sill complexes have also been identified from seismic and well core data in the Rockall Trough (Wood et al. 1988) and the Faeroes basin (Gibb & Kanaris-Sotiriou 1988). Development of sills at different levels in the crust can be explained by trapping magmas at density interfaces which they cannot cross before fractionating to compositions of lower density. Such density interfaces frequently reflect changes in rock composition and, more importantly, rheological behaviour. Different strains could develop across these interfaces either as a result of different volumes of magma migrating to different depths, by analogy to the near surface, or as a result of different deformation mechanisms operating in adjacent layers. Such differences in strain, which constitute discontinuous depth-dependent stretching (Royden & Keen 1980; Beaumont et al. 1982) could either be maintained by magma migration (Fig. 5 top), or dissipated by magma migration (Fig. 5 lower) which would constitute continuous depth-dependent stretching. Consequently the generation of magma during extension could influence the way in which the lithosphere deforms. White & McKenzie (1988) demonstrated that the style of lithospheric extension is reflected in the aerial extent and magnitude of the post-rift thermal subsidence. However, uplift resulting from underplating the crust with basaltic magma, discussed by Cox (1980) and quantified by White & McKenzie (1989), could significantly modify patterns of thermal subsidence and sedimentation, making this hypothesis difficult to test.

Discussion

The interconnected network of dykes, sills and lava flows described (Fig. 2) affects the evolution of the SOHB on both local and regional scales. While the investigation of the magnitude of these effects is the subject of continuing work, some general comments will be made here.

It is unclear exactly how much magma was added to the crust during the phase of Palaeocene volcanism because there are uncertainties in our knowledge of the thickness of the sill complexes within the middle and upper crust and at the Moho, and much of the lava pile has been eroded. A conservative estimate of 1.5 km (1 km of lavas exposed in Mull, Bailey et al. 1924; an aggregate of 1200 m of lava in Skye (England unpublished) and an aggregate of 250 m for the sills (Chesher et al. 1983)) still exceeds the thickness predicted by the stretching model of McKenzie & Bickle (1988) for the small amount of stretching indicated by the regional dyke swarms, even accounting for the elevated mantle temperatures due to the proximity of the North Atlantic plume (White & McKenzie 1989). No good estimate of β is available for Tertiary extension in the SOHB. Regional extension due to dyke emplacement is less than 1% (England 1988). Deep seismic profiles suggest that the crust thins from 30 km to 25 km beneath the SOHB (Meissner et al. 1986), indicating a β of 1.2. However the age of this thinning is not known. While it is probably of late Triassic age the β of 1.025 determined by Morton (1987), from the thickness of the Jurassic post rift sediments, for this stretching event is clearly not in agreement with the observed change in crustal thickness. If stretching equal to $\beta \approx 1.2$ occurred during the early Tertiary, the McKenzie & Bickle (1988) model predicts that only 0.5 km of melt would have been generated by thinning the lithosphere over mantle with an asthenospheric temperature of between 1380 and 1480°C. This discrepancy between the theoretical prediction of 0.5 km of melt and the observed thickness of 1.5 km could be resolved by depth-dependent stretching of the lithosphere. Strictly, volumes of melt should be considered rather than thicknesses. Extension of the lithosphere over a wider area than the crust, a process which could be enhanced by the higher heat flux from anomalously hot mantle, could result in upwelling of the asthenosphere over a broader area than if the lithosphere had stretched over the same area as the crust (Fig. 6). Consequently a much larger volume of asthenosperic mantle would suffer decompressive melting. This could account for the much larger volume of magma observed at the surface. However the amount of upwelling would be less and hence the degree of partial melting lower, such that the compositions of the magmas generated would be more alkaline than those observed. This could be resolved by invoking lateral migration of magmas from areas of greater upwelling. At present there is insufficient data on the amount of extension across the North Atlantic margins during the early Tertiary and the size of the area over which the base of the lithosphere is stretched to attempt to reconcile the observed volume and composition of melts generated beneath the SOHB with the theoretical models for melt generation. There is clearly a need for a more thorough investigation of the nature of this problem on a regional scale, which could encompass models for extension of the continental margin during the Palaeocene based on basin structure and stratigraphy, combined with models for magma generation.

The effect of adding partial melts to the lithosphere is to lower its density, thus raising the depth at which it is isostatically compensated relative to sea level. This is a partial cause of uplift of the surface. Further uplift, which decays with time, results from thermal expansion of the asthenosphere during melting. These two factors combine to produce a small amount of uplift ($\approx$250 m, from White & McKenzie 1989). This uplift would have gradually decayed due to cooling of the lithosphere once ocean floor spreading was initiated and the Hebridean lithosphere moved away from the N Atlantic plume. This slow subsidence may explain the preservation of Tertiary (Oligocene) sediments (Smythe & Kenolty 1975) within the Canna basin. Alternatively subsidence may result from NW−SE stretching of the lithosphere following the opening of the NE Atlantic (England 1988; O'Neill & England in prep.).

Of greater significance, particularly further west on the continental margin where the oceanward-dipping reflector sequences are well developed, is the rapid burial of the sediments beneath the accumulating piles of early Tertiary

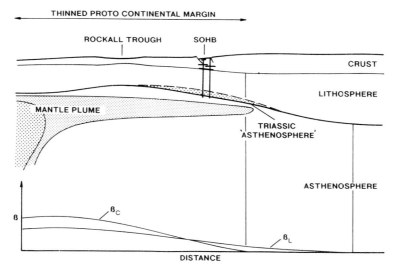

Fig. 6. NW−SE orientated schematic cross section (not to scale) across the continental margin showing the location of the Sea of the Hebrides basin relative to the North Atlantic plume prior to the opening of the North Atlantic. The lower part of the figure shows the variation in β for the crust (β_C) and lithosphere (β_L) (following White & McKenzie 1988).

lavas and to a certain extent the intrusion of the sills. This would have resulted in at least 1 km of burial in the SOHB (this study), 1 km along the western margin of the Faeroes basin (Hitchen & Ritchie 1987) and between 1 and 1.5 km in the northern parts of the Rockall Trough (Wood *et al.* 1987, 1988) and a minimum of 3 km in the region of the Faeroes (Waagstein 1988). The amount of burial would have increased rapidly where basins are overstepped by the oceanward dipping reflector sequences which locally reach 6 km in thickness (White 1988).

In addition to the tectonic effects of Palaeocene magmatism the large input of magma into the crust may have resulted in changes in the heat flux within the SOHB, causing changes in the geothermal gradient and consequently the maturation history of any organic matter present. However it would appear from available data that the additional heat flux due to stretching (taking $\beta = 1.2$) would be negligible (McKenzie 1978) and only a small increase in heat flux, of the order of 5 mWm^{-2} (Courtney & White 1986), would have resulted from the spread of the margins of the N Atlantic plume beneath the area. Field data indicates that locally the effects of magma migration, emplacement and eruption were more extensive. Due to the incremental nature of sill and dyke emplacement, there would be a cooling period between successive injections of magma, allowing the rocks immediately adjacent to the intrusion to cool. This would result in significant heating of the rocks only over a distance equal to the thickness of the intrusion from its margin (Jaeger 1959). Hence the thermal effects of sill and dyke emplacement would be minimal except where the sills are very thick and very extensive, for example in the Trotternish area of northern Skye and in the Little Minch (Fig. 2). In these areas rapid heating of the organic-rich shales of the Great Estuarine series (Middle Jurassic), into which the bulk of the sills are emplaced, has lead to limited generation of hydrocarbons (Parnell this volume). Recently, Raymond & Murchison (1991) have emphasized the role of pore waters and lack of sediment consolidation in decreasing the width of thermal aureoles around minor intrusions determined from vitrinite reflectance measurements. While similar work on the Hebridean minor intrusions is currently being completed (A. Bishop pers. comm.) field observations of the margins of minor intrusions reveal evidence of magma/wet sediment interaction, as described by Walker & Francis (1987), in the form of peperites produced by the explosive mixing of magma and vapourising pore waters derived from unconsolidated sediment. These observations suggest that the effects of the magma on the thermal and maturation history of the sediments would be limited.

Heat loss from the lavas would have been largely to the surface and hence would have had little effect on temperatures within the basin. The most significant effects of heat loss from magmas are seen around the central volcanic complexes. Continual emplacement of large intrusive bodies into these centres over a period of about 9 Ma resulted in continual loss of heat to the surrounding rocks. This resulted in the generation of hydrothermal convection systems circulating heated groundwaters through the complexes and surrounding sediments, causing alteration of $\delta^{18}O$ ratios (Taylor & Forester 1971) and the development of concentric zones of zeolites around the centres (Walker 1971). The effects of these hydrothermal systems on organic material contained in the sediments surrounding the complexes is discussed elsewhere in this volume (Thrasher), but the direct result of heat loss from the centres was to generate concentric zones of overmature, mature and undermature rocks at increasing distances from the complexes. These zones do not appear to be distinctly modified by the local intrusion of sills or particularly intense swarms of dykes, which confirms the conclusions drawn above that the minor intrusions within the basin have had little effect on its thermal evolution.

Conclusions

Palaeocene stretching of the lithosphere across the north Atlantic plume resulted in the generation of large volumes of magma which were emplaced into the SOHB, the northern parts of the Rockall Trough and the West of Shetland/Faeroes basins.

The magmas migrated through the lithosphere in a series of narrow dykes. Geochemical data from the SOHB suggests that the magma ponded in sills at the Moho and in the upper crust. Comparison with structures exposed at the surface suggests that the sills could have formed detachment surfaces permitting local discontinuous depth-dependent stretching of the lithosphere. It is contended that the migration of magma may locally modify the mechanism of crustal extension, thus eliminating the finite strain (space) problems associated with some models of depth-dependent stretching. The style of dyke emplacement within the SOHB reflects rapid extension over a short period of time, which resulted in elevation of the geotherm in the vicinity of the dyke swarms. This extensional system would have remained stable as long as there was magma present. Once the flow of magma declined, the local geothermal gradients would decay and the dykes would be emplaced over a broader area. Magmatic activity ceased as the locus of melting concentrated on the developing mid-Atlantic ridge, and the SOHB and basins further west drifted away from the centre of the plume and over cooler asthenosphere.

Extrusion of thick lava flows over the NW continental margin would have resulted in rapid burial and preservation of basin sediments. However subsidence and consequently rising temperatures would have been buffered by the isostatic effects of emplacing magma into the crust and thermal expansion of the asthenosphere during melting. The basin would have experienced little change in heat flux and hence the effects of igneous activity on hydrocarbon generation would be minimal. The emplacement of minor intrusions such as dykes and sills was too intermittent to cause significant changes in temperatures within the basin and the additional heat flux from the plume would only have been between 5 and 15 mWm^{-2}, depending upon the distance from the centre of the plume. The only effective source of heat within the basins would appear to be the central volcanic complexes.

This paper describes the initial results of a study of the interaction between magmatism and basin development within the Sea of the Hebrides funded by NERC Special Topic award GST/02/354. A thoughtful review by Nicky White and discussions with Rob Butler, Bob Thompson, Henry Emeleus, Sally Gibson, Simon Day and Andy Kerr of earlier drafts of this paper are gratefully acknowledged.

References

BAILEY, E. B., CLOUGH, C. T., WRIGHT, W. B., RICHEY, J. E. & WILSON, G. V. 1924. *The Tertiary and post Tertiary geology of Mull, Lochaline and Oban*. Memoir of the Geological Survey (Scotland), HMSO.

BEAUMONT, C., KEEN, C. E. & BOUTILIER, R. 1982. On the evolution of rifted continental margins: comparison of models and observations from the Nova Scotian margin. *Geophysical Journal of the Royal Astronomical Society*, **70**, 667–715.

CARTER, N. L. & TSENN, M. C. 1987. Flow properties of the continental lithosphere. *Tectonophysics*, **136**, 27–63.

CHESHER, J. A., SMYTHE, D. K. & BISHOP, P. 1983. *The Geology of the Minches, Inner Sound and Sound of Raasay*. Report of the Institute of Geological Sciences 83/6, HMSO.

COURTNEY, R. C. & WHITE, R. S. 1986. Anomalous heat flow and geoid across the Cape Verde rise: evidence for dynamic support from a thermal plume in the mantle. *Geophysical Journal of the Royal Astronomical Society*, **87**, 815–67 (microfiche GJ 87/1).

COX, K. G. 1980. A model for flood basalt volcanism. *Journal of Petrology*, **21**, 629–50.

DELANEY, P. T., POLLARD, D. D., ZIONY, J. I. & McKEE, E. H. 1986. Field relations between dikes and joints: emplacement processes and palaeostress. *Journal of Geophysical Research*, **91B**, 4920–4939.

DICKIN, A. P., BROWN, J. L., THOMPSON, R. N., HALLIDAY, A. N. & MORRISON, M. A. 1984. Crustal contamination and the granite problem in the British Tertiary Volcanic Province. *Philosophical Transactions of the Royal Society of London*, **A310**, 755–780.

DUINDAM, P. & VAN HOORN, B. 1987. Structural evolution of the West Shetland continental margin. *In*: BROOKS, J. & GLENNIE, K. W. (eds) *Petroleum Geology of North West Europe*, Graham & Trotman, London, 765–773.

ENGLAND, R. W. 1988. The early Tertiary stress regime in NW Britain: evidence from the patterns of volcanic activity. *In*: MORTON, A. C. & PARSON, L. M. (eds) *Early Tertiary Volcanism and the Opening of the NE Atlantic*. Geological Society, London, Special Publication, **39**, 381–389.

GIBB, F. G. F. & KANARIS-SOTIRIOU, R. 1988. The geochemistry and origin of the Faeroe-Shetland sill complex. *In*: MORTON, A. C. & PARSON, L. M. (eds) *Early Tertiary Volcanism and the Opening of the NE Atlantic*. Geological Society, London, Special Publication, **39**, 241–252.

HALLAM, A. 1982. Jurassic, Cretaceous and Tertiary sediments. *In*: CRAIG, G. Y. (ed.) *Geology of Scotland*. Scottish Academic Press, Edinburgh 343–356.

HITCHEN, K. & RITCHIE, J. D. 1987. Geological review of the West Shetland area. *In*: BROOKS, J. & GLENNIE, K. W. (eds) *Petroleum Geology of North West Europe*. Graham & Trotman, London, 677–685.

JAEGER, J. C. 1959. Temperatures outside a cooling intrusive sheet. *American Journal of Science*, **257**, 44–54.

KUSZNIR, N. J. & PARK, R. G. 1986. Continental lithosphere strength: the critical role of lower crustal deformation. *In*: DAWSON, J. B., CARSWELL, D. A., HALL, J. & WEDEPOHL, K. H. (eds) *The Nature of the Lower Continental Crust*. Geological Society, London, Special Publication, **24**, 79–93.

—— & —— 1987. The extensional strength of the continental lithosphere: its dependance on geothermal gradient, and crustal composition and thickness. *In*: COWARD, M. P., DEWEY, J. F. & HANCOCK, P. L. (eds) *Continental Extensional Tectonics*. Geological Society, London, Special Publication, **28**, 35–53.

McKENZIE, D. 1978. Some remarks on the development of sedimentary basins. *Earth and Planetary Science Letters*, **40**, 25–32.

—— 1989. Some remarks on the movement of small

melt fractions in the mantle. *Earth and Planetary Science Letters*, **95**, 53−72.

—— & BICKLE, M. J. 1988. The volume and composition of melt generated by extension of the lithosphere. *Journal of Petrology*, **29**, 625−679.

MARSH, B. D. & KANTHA, L. H. 1978. On the heat and mass transfer from an ascending magma. *Earth and Planetary Science Letters*, **39**, 435−443.

MEISSNER, R., MATTHEWS, D. & WEVER, T. 1986. The Moho in and around Great Britain. *Annales Geophysicae*, **4**,B,6, 659−664.

——, —— & DICKIN, A. P. 1985. Geochemical evidence for complex magmatic plumbing during development of a continental volcanic centre. *Geology*, **13**, 581−584.

——, ——, GIBSON, I. L. & MARRINER, G. F. 1980. Lateral chemical heterogeneity in the Palaeocene upper mantle beneath the Scottish Hebrides. *Philosophical Transactions of the Royal Society of London*, A297, 229−244.

MORTON, N. 1987. Jurassic subsidence history in the Hebrides, NW Scotland. *Marine and Petroleum Geology*, **4**, 226−242.

—— 1989. Jurassic sequence stratigraphy in the Hebrides basin, NW Scotland. *Marine and Petroleum Geology*, **6**, 243−260.

MUDGE, D. C. & RASHID, B. 1987. The geology of the Faeroe basin area. *In*: BROOKS, J. & GLENNIE, K. W. (eds) *Petroleum Geology of North West Europe*. Graham & Trotman, London, 751−763.

MUSSET, A. E., DAGLEY, P. & SKELHORN, R. R. 1988. Time and duration of activity in the British Tertiary Igneous Province. *In*: MORTON, A. C. & PARSON, L. M. (eds) *Early Tertiary Volcanism and the Opening of the NE Atlantic*. Geological Society, London, Special Publication, **39**, 337−348.

PARSON, L. M. & the ODP Leg 104 Scientific Party. 1988. Dipping reflector styles in the NE Atlantic Ocean. *In*: MORTON, A. C. & PARSON, L. M. (eds) *Early Tertiary Volcanism and the Opening of the NE Atlantic*. Geological Society, London, Special Publication, **39**, 57−68.

PATCHETT, P. J. 1981. Thermal effects of basalt on continental crust and crustal contamination of magmas. *Nature*, **283**, 559−561.

RAYMOND, A. C. & MURCHISON, D. G. 1991. The relationship between organic maturation, the widths of thermal aureoles and the thicknesses of sills in the Midland Valley of Scotland and Northern England. *Journal of the Geological Society, London*, **148**, 215−218.

ROWLEY, D. B. & SAHAGIAN, D. 1986. Depth − dependant stretching: a different approach. *Geology*, **14**, 32−35.

ROYDEN, L. & KEEN, C. E. 1980. Rifting processes and thermal evolution of the continental margin of eastern Canada determined from subsidence curves. *Earth and Planetary Science Letters*, **51**, 343−361.

RUTTER, E. H. & BRODIE, K. H. 1991. Lithosphere rheology − a note of caution. *Journal of Structural Geology*, **13**, 363−367.

SMYTHE, D. K. & KENOLTY, N. 1975. Tertiary sediments in the Sea of the Hebrides. *Journal of the Geological Society, London*, **131**, 227−233.

SONDER, L. J. & ENGLAND, P. C. 1989. Effects of a temperature dependant rheology on large scale continental extension. *Journal of Geophysical Research*. **94B**, 7603−7619.

SPEIGHT, J. M., SKELHORN, R. R., SLOAN, T. & KNAAP, R. J. The dyke swarms of Scotland. *In*: SUTHERLAND, D. S. (ed.) *Igneous Rocks of the British Isles*. Wiley, Chichester, 449−459.

STEIN, A. M. 1988. Basement controls upon basin development in the Caledonian forehand, NW Scotland. *Basin Research*, **1**, 107−119.

TAYLOR, H. P. & FORESTER, R. W. 1971. Low ^{18}O igneous rocks from the intrusive complexes of Skye, Mull and Ardnamurchan, western Scotland. *Journal of Petrology*, **12**, 465−497.

THOMPSON, R. N. 1974. Primary basalts and magma genesis. I. Skye, North West Scotland. *Contributions to Mineralogy and Petrology*, **45**, 317−341.

—— 1982. Magmatism in the British Tertiary Volcanic Province. *Scottish Journal of Geology*, **18**, 49−107.

——, DICKIN, A. P., GIBSON, I. L. & MORRISON, M. A. 1982. Elemental fingerprints of isotopic contamination of Hebridean Palaeocene mantle-derived magmas by Archean sial. *Contributions to Mineralogy and Petrology*, **79**, 159−168.

——, LEAT, P. T., DICKIN, A. P., MORRISON, M. A., HENDRY, G. L. & GIBSON, S. A. 1989. Strongly potassic mafic magmas from lithospheric mantle sources during continental extension and heating: evidence from Miocene minettes of northwest Colarado, USA. *Earth and Planetary Science Letters*, **98**, 139−153.

—— & MORRISON, M. A. 1988. Asthenopheric and lower lithospheric mantle contributions to continental extensional magmatism: an example from the British Tertiary Province. *Chemical Geology*, **68**, 1−15.

——, ——, DICKIN, A. P., GIBSON, I. L. & HARMON, R. S. 1986. Two contrasting styles of interaction between basic magmas and continental crust in the British Tertiary Volcanic Province. *Journal of Geophysical Research*, **91B**, 5985−5997.

UPTON, B. G. J. 1988. History of Tertiary igneous activity in the north Atlantic borderlands. *In*: MORTON, A. C. & PARSON, L. M. (eds) *Early Tertiary Volcanism and the Opening of the NE Atlantic*. Geological Society, London, Special Publication, **39**, 429−454.

WAAGSTEIN, R. 1988. Structure, composition and age of the Faeroe basalt plateau. *In*: MORTON, A. C. & PARSON, L. M. (eds) *Early Tertiary Volcanism and the Opening of the NE Atlantic*. Geological Society, London, Special Publication, **39**, 225−238.

WALKER, B. H. & FRANCIS, E. H. 1987. High level of emplacement of an olivine-dolerite sill into Namurian sediments near Cardenden, Fife. *Transactions of the Royal Society of Edinburgh, Earth Sciences*, **77**, 295−307.

WALKER, G. P. L. 1971. The distribution of amygdale minerals in Mull and Morvern (western Scotland). *In*: MURTY, T. V. V. G. R. K. & RAO,

S. S. (eds) Studies in Earth Sciences, West commemoration volume, 181–194.

WHITE, N. & McKENZIE, D. 1988. Formation of the "steers head" geometry of sedimentary basins by differential stretching of the crust and mantle. *Geology*, **16**, 250–253.

WHITE R. S. 1988. A hot-spot model for early-Tertiary volcanism in the North Atlantic. *In*: MORTON, A. C. & PARSON, L. M. (eds) *Early Tertiary Volcanism and the Opening of the NE Atlantic*. Geological Society, London, Special Publication, **39**, 3–14.

—— & McKENZIE, D. 1989. Magmatism at rift zones: the generation of volcanic continental margins and flood basalts. *Journal of Geophysical Research*, **94B**, 7685–7729.

——, SPENCE, G. D., FOWLER, S. R., McKENZIE, D. P., WESTBROOK, G. K. & BOWEN, A. N. 1987. Magmatism at rifted continental margins. *Nature*, **330**, 439–44.

WOOD, M. V., HALL, J. & DOODY, J. J. 1988. Distribution of early-Tertiary lavas in the NE Rockall Trough. *In*: MORTON, A. C. & PARSON, L. M. (eds) *Early Tertiary Volcanism and the Opening of the NE Atlantic*. Geological Society, London, Special Publication, **39**, 283–292.

——, —— & VAN HOORN, B. 1987. Post-Mesozoic differential subsidence in the north east Rockall Trough related to volcanicity and sedimentation. *In*: BROOKS, J. & GLENNIE, K. W. (eds) *Petroleum Geology of North West Europe*. Graham & Trotman, London, 677–685.

ZIEGLER, P. A. 1988. *Evolution of the Arctic–North Atlantic and the Western Tethys*. American Association of Petroleum Geologists Memoir, **43**.

Low-temperature effects of the Skye Tertiary intrusions on Mesozoic sediments in the Sea of Hebrides Basin

CHERRY L. E. LEWIS[1], ANDREW CARTER & ANTHONY J. HURFORD

University of London Fission Track Research Group, Department of Geological Sciences, University College London, Gower Street, London WC1E 6BT, UK

(Present address: Geotrack International Pty Ltd, 30 Upper High St, Thame, Oxfordshire, UK)

Abstract: Fission track analysis of samples from the Sea of Hebrides Basin and surrounding regions demonstrates two very distinct age groups around 50 Ma and 300 Ma, regardless of the stratigraphic age. Apatite fission track results from sediments within 8 km of the Tertiary igneous complex on Skye were totally reset by temperatures >110°C during intrusion of the centres, but now yield ages younger than the granites. Zircon fission track results from the granites also demonstrate ages significantly younger than their hosts. Mean track lengths in apatites of <13.5 μm, and reduced apatite and zircon ages, suggest that temperatures remained elevated throughout the 6 Ma during which intrusive activity occurred, but were hotter within the granite bodies than the surrounding sediments.

Prior to intrusion of the complex, temperatures in the basin sediments presently at outcrop were unlikely to have been higher than 50°C, and beyond the effects of the Tertiary intrusions from northern Skye, the Isle of Lewis and the west coast of Scotland illustrate that the area is unlikely to have been buried beneath more than 2 km of sediment at any one time since the end of the Devonian. North of the Highland Boundary Fault, Tertiary uplift and erosion in Scotland is considered to have been between 1−1.5 km. This is consistent with a regional pattern of Tertiary erosion identified across the British Isles, but considerably less than that recognised in Northern England.

The Sea of Hebrides Basin is one of a series of NE−SW orientated, fault bounded basins that lie off the west coast of Scotland (Fig. 1). The western margin of the basin is bounded by the Minch Fault, while to the east the Moine Thrust divides the Caledonian orogenic belt, which suffered extreme deformation during the Lower Palaeozoic, from the Lewisian gneisses of the Hebridean Craton that are locally overlain by thick Torridonian sediments (Upper Proterozoic). This cratonic area remained relatively unaffected by Caledonian disturbances, the last major thermo-tectonic event occurring *c.* 1800 Ma (Watson 1985). The basin contains a relatively shallow fill of Mesozoic sediments that outcrop on several of the Hebridean islands, and during the Early Tertiary these sediments were intruded by major igneous centres and multiple dyke and sill swarms. Up to 800 m of basalt was erupted onto the surface, possibly covering an area as large as that represented by the dyke swarms (Preston 1982), although little evidence of it now remains.

In order to evaluate the lateral extent to which intrusion of the igneous complex thermally affected sediments in the basin, outcrop samples from sediments of various ages were taken from the islands of Skye and Raasay and subjected to apatite fission track analysis. Fission track ages of zircons extracted from the Tertiary granites and two Jurassic sediments on Skye were also measured. Finally, apatite fission track results from Torridonian sediments and Lewisian gneisses of the Hebridean craton outcropping on the west coast of Scotland and the Isle of Lewis were modelled, in order to constrain the thermal structure of the region prior to Tertiary activity.

Fission track analysis

Apatite

Using AFTA it is possible to determine palaeo-temperatures up to 110°C and to identify the time at which maximum temperatures last occurred. The principles of applying the technique to thermal history analysis have been discussed in detail by Green (1989), but interpretation of the data depends on an assessment of the degree of annealing (track shortening) that has occurred since deposition, which is manifested in the sample by a reduction in the length of confined tracks (Green *et al.* 1986). As tem-

From PARNELL, J. (ed.), 1992, *Basins on the Atlantic Seaboard: Petroleum Geology, Sedimentology and Basin Evolution.* Geological Society Special Publication No. 62, pp 175−188.

175

peratures increase, track lengths shorten and this results in a reduction in the density of tracks occurring at the surface of a crystal, thus the measured fission track age also becomes reduced. Gleadow *et al.* (1986) have shown that all apatite fission track 'ages' are only *apparent* ages unless the mean track length associated with that age is greater than 14.5 μm and has a standard deviation of less than one.

When temperatures exceed 110°C over time-scales of 1–10 Ma, tracks are not retained in the crystal lattice until it cools again below this temperature. If cooling is rapid then the mean confined track length will be long (>14.5 μm) and the standard deviation less than one, but if cooling is protracted and temperatures remain elevated, tracks will be annealed during cooling and the resulting distribution will be shorter and wider. Little track annealing occurs below temperatures of 50°C.

Zircons

Recent laboratory experiments (Tagami *et al.* 1990) demonstrate that, like apatites, track shortening in zircons is predominantly controlled by temperature, but due to the higher temperatures at which zircons anneal a suitable geological situation with which the laboratory experiments can be compared has not yet been located. As a result of this the annealing kinetics of zircons are still poorly understood and track lengths are not usually measured. At the present time, the 'closure' temperature for fission tracks in zircons has been qualitatively assessed by interpolating a temperature between 300°C for the Rb–Sr closure temperature in biotite, and 100°C for fission tracks in apatite, from the age given by the zircon. Using this method Hurford (1986) obtained a closure temperature for zircon of 240 ± 50°C, but Harrison *et al.* (1979) placed it much lower at 175 ± 25°C. These differences may reflect a difference in cooling rates or the fact that, like apatites, the annealing rates in zircons are affected by their chemical composition as suggested by Lewis *et al.* (in press). In this study, a temperature of 200°C was taken to be a reasonable estimate of the temperature at which tracks in zircons are totally annealed over geological timescales, thus partial annealing probably starts to occur between temperatures of 160–170°C.

Data presentation

At the time of deposition, each apatite grain in a sediment will contain an inherited track distribution which records the thermal history pre-

viously experienced by that grain. The result is that a range of single grain ages can be found within any one sample. If the sediment is then subjected to elevated temperatures subsequent to deposition, differential annealing rates in grains with varying Cl contents (Green *et al.* 1989*a*) further enhances this spread of single ages. 'Central' ages (Lewis *et al.* in press) are therefore used for estimating the modal fission track age in a sample which displays a large spread of single grain ages, and the dispersion of single grain ages about the modal age is expressed as a percentage variation which is quoted in addition to the standard error, i.e. 60 ± 4 Ma (20%), where ±4 indicates the precision (standard error at the 1 s level) of the Central age estimate and (20%) describes the variation (relative standard deviation) about that Central age.

Single grain ages within any one sample are presented on histograms as well as radial plots (Galbraith 1990), which are a graphical method of comparing several estimates that have differing precisions. Arranged radially around the edge of the plot are fission track ages in millions of years, and the approximate age of any one grain can be read by drawing a line from the origin on the *y* axis, through that point to the edge of the plot, as demonstrated in Fig. 4a. For inter-sample comparison, the length of the *x* axis in all plots throughout this paper is kept constant for both apatites and zircons, and grains with the highest precision plot furthest from the *y* axis. The display of data in this manner allows instant assessment of both age variation and precision, and provides considerable information regarding the samples' thermal history. Those grains with a higher Cl content that are more resistant to annealing represent the minimum source age of a sample, while grains that are less Cl-rich and more sensitive to annealing constrain the maximum age of any heating event.

Modelling apatite fission track data

Since the degree of annealing is primarily determined by temperature, comparison of the Central age with the stratigraphic age of a sample provides a qualitative assessment as to whether that sample has experienced post-depositional annealing. Sediments with a Central fission track age younger than the stratigraphic age have clearly been annealed, and must therefore have experienced elevated temperatures since deposition, but a more quantitative evaluation of maximum palaeo-temperatures can be determined by comparing measured age and track length data with modelled distributions. The programme involves the forward modelling of parameters resulting from likely thermal histories using the quantitative description of annealing outlined by Laslett *et al.* (1987), Duddy *et al.* (1988) and Green *et al.* (1989*b*). The modelling programme predicts parameters in apatites with an average Cl content of about 0.4 wt% (Durango apatite).

Results and interpretation

Table 1 records the localities from which outcrop samples were collected, and Tables 2 and 3 present full analytical data for apatites and zircons respectively. The zircons were extracted from the Tertiary granites on Skye (which did not yield apatite) as well as from two samples of Jurassic sediments, while the apatites were de-

Table 1. *Sample type and location details*

Sample No.	Rock type	Grid ref	Locality	Formation	Stratigraphic/ Formation Age
Apatites					
Mainland					
SKY 166	Sandstone	NG 753 440	Carn Breac	Torridonian	Precambrian
SKY 167	Sandstone	NG 707 438	Milton	Torridonian	Precambrian
SKY 171	Sandstone	NG 705 457	Cruarg	Torridonian	Precambrian
SKY 175	Gneiss	NG 775 560	Inverbain	Lewisian	Precambrian
SKY 178	Sandstone	NG 798 540	Rhutoin	Torridonian	Precambrian
SCOT 300	Sandstone	NC 198 601	Kinlochbervie	Torridonian	Precambrian
SCOT 302	Grit	NC 300 562	Gualin House	Torridonian	Precambrian
SCOT 304	Grit	NC 410 675	Durness		Ordovician
Isle of Raasay					
SKY 161	Sandstone	NG 582 462	North Raasay	Torridonian	Precambrian
SKY 315	Sandstone	NG 593 375	Beinn na Leac	Bearreraig	Jurassic
SKY 317	Sandstone	NG 599 382	Rubha na Leac	Stornoway	Triassic
SKY 318	Sandstone	NG 570 361	Fearns Road	Scalpa	Jurassic
SKY 319	Conglomerate	NG 575 342	Eyre	Stornoway	Triassic
SKY 320	Sandstone	NG 574 341	Eyre	Torridonian	Precambrian
Skye					
SKY 308	Sandstone	NG 520 540	Bearreraig Bay	Bearreraig	Jurassic
SKY 327	Sandstone	NG 702 248	Ob Lusa	Torridonian	Precambrian
SKY 329	Sandstone	NG 671 122	Skulamus	Torridonian	Precambrian
SKY 330	Sandstone	NG 672 160	Drumfearn	Torridonian	Precambrian
SKY 331	Sandstone	NG 700 150	Loch na Dal	Torridonian	Precambrian
SKY 337	Conglomerate	NG 639 196	Loch Buidhe	Torridonian	Precambrian
SKY 341	Sandstone	NG 639 178	Beinn nan Charn	Stornoway	Triassic
SKY 350	Sandstone	NG 516 188	Camasunary	Torridonian	Precambrian
SKY 358	Sandstone	NG 528 113	Strathaird	Bearreraig	Jurassic
Lewis/Harris					
LEW 292	Tonalite	NF 994 907	Northton, Harris		Precambrian
LEW 294	Gneiss	NG 182 062	N of Tarbert, Harris	Lewisian	Precambrian
LEW 298	Conglomerate	NB 488 327	Eye Peninsula	Stornoway	Triassic
Zircons					
GE	Granite	NG 538 300	Western Red Hills	Glamaig	Tertiary
MG	Granite	NG 561 316	Western Red Hills	Maol na Gainmhich	Tertiary
BDME	Granite	NG 534 288	Western Red Hills	Beinn Dearg Mhor	Tertiary
LAE1	Granite	NG 565 298	Western Red Hills	Loch Ainort	Tertiary
LAE2	Granite	NG 534 268	Western Red Hills	Loch Ainort	Tertiary
NPF	Felsite	NG 562 307	Western Red Hills	Northern Felsite	Tertiary
GBMDE	Granite	NG 585 281	Eastern Red Hills	Glas Bheinn Mhor	Tertiary
AFE	Granite	NG 614 234	Eastern Red Hills	Allt Fearna	Tertiary
BADE	Granite	NG 606 198	Eastern Red Hills	Beinn an Dubhaich	Tertiary
BNC	Granite	NG 610 232	Eastern Red Hills	Beinn na Caillich	Tertiary
CSE	Granite	NG 603 266	Eastern Red Hills	Creag Strollamus	Tertiary
BERR/AS	Sandstone	NG 590 257	Creag Strollamus	Bearreraig	Jurassic
BERR/ELG	Sandstone	NG 513 131	Elgol	Bearreraig	Jurassic

Table 2. *Full analytical data for apatite samples*

Sample number	Locality	Number of crystals	Dosimeter ρd	Dosimeter Nd	Spontaneous ρs	Spontaneous Ns	Induced ρi	Induced Ni	$P(\chi^2)$	Age variation %	Central age (Ma) ±1σ	Length (μm) ±1σ	Std. Dev.	No of lengths
Apatites														
Mainland														
SKY 166	Carn Breac	17	2.416	10665	1.196	1269	1.796	1905	<1	17	288.87 ± 17.44	11.41 ± 0.24	1.07	21
SKY 167	Milton	18	2.410	10665	0.935	360	1.312	505	<1	26	303.69 ± 25.84	11.80 ± 0.27	1.30	24
SKY 171	Cruarg	20	2.412	10665	0.746	617	1.201	993	<1	24	286.16 ± 24.17	10.57 ± 0.30	1.70	34
SKY 175	Inverbain	22	2.416	10665	1.943	1736	2.886	2578	<1	12	279.39 ± 11.62	11.93 ± 0.15	1.54	100
SKY 178	Rhutoin	9	2.418	10665	1.580	55	2.211	781	<1	30	306.07 ± 30.32	11.19 ± 0.26	1.86	52
SCOT 300*	Kinlochbervie	10	1.322	9158	0.892	536	0.780	496	98	0	263.47 ± 17.66	12.13 ± 0.39	1.94	26
SCOT 302*	Gualin House	20	1.322	9158	2.146	2675	1.498	1867	<1	16	320.18 ± 17.40	12.67 ± 0.15	1.47	100
SCOT 304*	Durness	4	1.322	9158	2.211	536	1.349	327	49	0	374.62 ± 27.58	11.66 ± 0.93	2.29	7
Isle of Raasay														
SKY 161	North Raasay	20	2.407	10665	0.637	822	0.942	1216	<1	20	293.06 ± 19.64	11.99 ± 0.30	1.89	41
SKY 315	Beinn na Leac	5	1.464	2535	0.272	98	1.286	463	32	9	52.60 ± 6.00	14.12 ± 0.23	1.34	34
SKY 317	Rubha na Leac	20	1.523	6412	0.243	271	1.264	1413	57	0	47.01 ± 3.22	12.03 ± 1.39	2.77	5
SKY 318	Fearns Rd	20	1.464	2535	0.450	263	2.099	1227	89	0	53.30 ± 3.90	13.46 ± 0.31	1.08	13
SKY 319	Eyre	20	1.464	2535	0.385	300	1.375	1071	5	18	69.80 ± 6.20	12.94 ± 0.32	2.56	65
SKY 320	Eyre	20	1.536	6412	0.265	357	1.362	1837	88	0	47.87 ± 2.88	12.61 ± 0.60	2.94	25
Skye														
SKY 308	Bearrcraig Bay	20	1.530	6412	3.368	3167	2.267	3132	<1	29	357.12 ± 27.21	12.16 ± 0.15	1.52	100
SKY 327	Ob Lusa	20	1.563	6412	0.413	376	1.972	1794	10	19	53.49 ± 4.35	12.30 ± 0.64	2.22	13
SKY 329	Skulamus	18	1.464	2535	0.407	493	2.298	2782	<1	19	47.20 ± 3.70	13.50 ± 0.30	1.56	29
SKY 330	Drumfearn	20	1.464	2535	0.827	418	4.211	2129	4	19	49.70 ± 3.80	13.18 ± 0.23	1.87	68
SKY 331	Loch na Dal	19	1.464	2535	0.722	210	2.438	709	46	11	72.80 ± 6.60	13.05 ± 0.63	1.68	8
SKY 337	Loch Buidhe	20	1.543	6412	0.434	267	1.990	1224	95	0	53.85 ± 3.75	10.58 ± 0.99	3.44	13
SKY 341	Beinn nan Charn	20	1.464	2535	0.214	327	1.129	1721	23	5	47.10 ± 3.30	14.21 ± 0.65	1.83	9
SKY 350	Camasunary	20	1.556	6412	0.244	362	2.010	1801	15	13	52.37 ± 3.91	13.15 ± 0.35	1.89	30
SKY 358	Strathaird	21	1.555	6412	0.312	318	1.397	1424	2	22	56.93 ± 5.13	13.47 ± 0.66	0.94	3
Lewis/Harris														
LEW 292*	Northton, Harris	20	1.322	9158	1.778	1197	1.474	992	4	15	281.86 ± 16.83	13.31 ± 0.11	1.12	100
LEW 294*	Tarbert, Harris	20	1.322	9158	1.681	2700	1.330	2137	<1	22	290.57 ± 18.20	13.05 ± 0.16	1.27	64
LEW 298*	Eye Peninsula, Lewis	20	1.322	9158	1.406	1636	1.141	1328	<1	16	292.42 ± 17.95	12.48 ± 0.30	2.00	47

Dosimeter and induced track densities ($\times 10^6$ cm^{-2}) measured on external mica detectors (g = 0.5).

Spontaneous track densities ($\times 10^6$ cm^{-2}) measured on internal mineral surfaces.

Ages for apatites calculated by Lewis using $\zeta = 341 \pm 7$ and *Hurford using $\zeta = 361 \pm 8$ for dosimeter glass CN5.

Lengths measured by Carter.

$P(\chi^2)$ indicates the probability of the single grain ages representing a homogeneous population.

Table 3. *Full analytical data for zircon samples*

Sample Number	Locality	Number of crystals	Dosimeter		Spontaneous		Induced		$P(\chi^2)$	Age variation %	Central Age (Ma) $\pm 1\sigma$
			ρd	Nd	ρs	Ns	ρi	Ni			
Skye											
GE*	Western Red Hills	16	1.072	2031	4.249	1172	5.022	1385	15	10	51.90 ± 2.70
MG*	Western Red Hills	20	1.005	2031	2.698	1189	3.179	1401	15	9	48.40 ± 2.50
BDME	Western Red Hills	13	1.049	2030	1.952	467	1.208	593	50	0	51.00 ± 3.40
LAE1	Western Red Hills	15	0.740	5175	1.113	247	0.894	247	30	7	45.80 ± 4.30
LAE2	Western Red Hills	14	0.761	5175	1.151	418	1.165	423	50	9	45.90 ± 3.50
NPF	Western Red Hills	20	0.753	5175	1.685	710	1.590	670	25	9	49.60 ± 3.00
GBMDE*	Eastern Red Hills	14	1.094	2031	2.724	808	3.166	939	<1	16	53.10 ± 3.70
AFE	Eastern Red Hills	20	0.964	3020	2.964	1131	3.548	1354	60	1	49.70 ± 2.20
BADE	Eastern Red Hills	20	0.735	2036	1.869	887	1.785	847	30	7	47.50 ± 2.60
BNC	Eastern Red Hills	20	0.968	3020	1.818	730	2.216	890	95	0	49.00 ± 2.60
CSE*	Eastern Red Hills	11	0.983	2016	1.554	485	1.631	509	85	0	53.60 ± 3.60
BERR/AS	Creag Strollamus	7	0.958	3020	1.587	330	2.115	440	70	0	44.40 ± 3.30
BERR/ELG	Elgol	16	0.740	5175	5.436	1680	4.199	1267	<1	18	62.70 ± 3.90

Dosimeter and induced track densities ($\times 10^6$ cm^{-2}) measured on external mica detectors (g = 0.5).
Spontaneous track densities ($\times 10^6$ cm^{-2}) measured on internal mineral surfaces.
Ages measured by Carter using $\zeta = 115 \pm 5$ for dosimeter glass *CN1 and $\zeta = 124 \pm 7$ for dosimeter glass CN2.
$P(\chi^2)$ indicates the probability of the single grain ages representing a homogeneous population.

rived from sedimentary and metamorphic rocks ranging in age from Lewisian to Jurassic, and collected over a much wider area than the zircons (Fig. 1). It should be noted however, that all apatite samples were collected from west of the Moine Thrust and are thus representative of either the Hebridean craton or the Mesozoic basin.

As can be seen from Fig. 2, which plots fission track age against age variation, results from both apatites and zircons fall into two very distinct categories: apatites and zircons that gives ages younger than 100 Ma, clustering around 50 Ma, and apatites that are within error of 300 Ma. On Skye and Raasay both age groups were observed, but elsewhere only apatite ages in the older group have been found. In Fig. 3 the relationship between the mean track length and the measured fission track age of apatites for all samples in this study is shown,

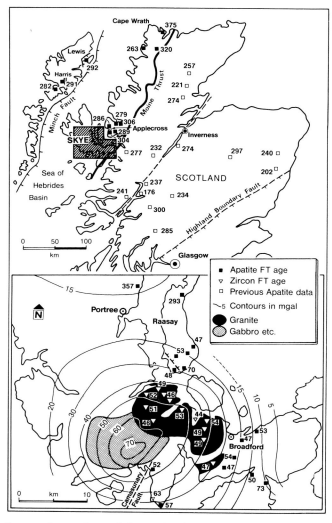

Fig. 1. Sample location map for apatites and zircons showing ages obtained from each locality sampled in this study (filled squares and triangles, respectively). The enlarged area on Skye demonstrates the relationship of the reset apatite ages to Bott & Tuson's (1973) Bouger anomaly map. Also included for comparison are apatite fission track ages of the 'newer and last granites' from Hurford (1977) (open squares). The similarity of all apatite fission track ages, outside the effects of the Tertiary intrusions, suggests a similar post-Devonian history for the whole region north of the Highland Boundary Fault.

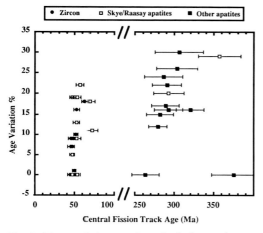

Fig. 2. Measured zircon and apatite fission track ages are plotted against the percent age variation within each sample. They illustrate two distinct age groups: zircons and apatites that cluster around 50 Ma, and a much older group of apatites only that lie within error of 300 Ma.

and representative track length distributions are displayed around the edge of this plot. For comparative purposes the Late Cretaceous annealing curve for rocks from Northern and Central England is superimposed upon the data from this study (Green 1986 and Lewis *et al.* in press). This curve presupposes that the source age of the apatites was around 300 Ma (i.e. that all apatites were totally annealed at 300 Ma) and that all samples have been affected to some extent by elevated temperatures during the Late Cretaceous, which was followed by cooling and erosion in the Tertiary. While these Scottish data fit well onto the younger end of the trend, there is considerable scatter at the older end suggesting that in this region the source age is less clearly defined and probably somewhat older than in Northern England. Furthermore, these samples do not appear to have been significantly affected by Late Cretaceous burial.

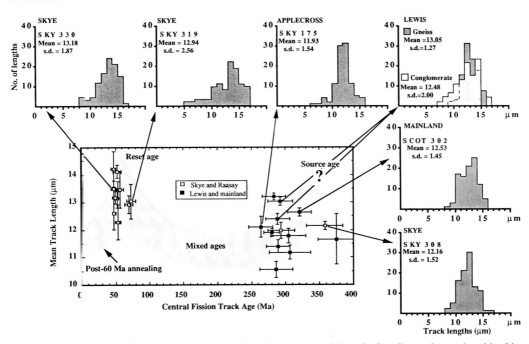

Fig. 3. Measured apatite fission track ages plotted against mean track lengths for all samples analysed in this study. The data are superimposed upon the pre-60 Ma annealing curve (shaded) identified by Green (1986). Samples which display old ages but long track lengths have not seen significant post-depositional annealing temperatures, and are therefore most representative of the apatite 'source' age. Samples with young ages and long track lengths have been totally reset and are therefore most representative of the age of cooling. Samples with ages between these values are mixed ages resulting from a component of short tracks inherited from the source age, and a component of long tracks formed after cooling from elevated temperatures. Representative track length distributions are shown around the edge to illustrate how lengths shorten and distributions widen with increasing temperatures. The relatively short mean length and wide distribution from SKY 330 supports evidence from the age which suggests that annealing continued after intrusion of the granites.

182   C. L. E. LEWIS *ET AL.*

The older group: apatites

All samples within this group demonstrate apatite fission track ages within error of 300 Ma, with peaks of single grain ages occurring between 200 and 300 Ma (Fig. 4), and it is interesting to note that Hurford (1977) also recognised apatite fission track ages of 200–300 Ma in his study of the 'newer and last granites' from the Highlands of Scotland. For comparison, ages from his data set have been added to Fig. 1, but it should be recognized that

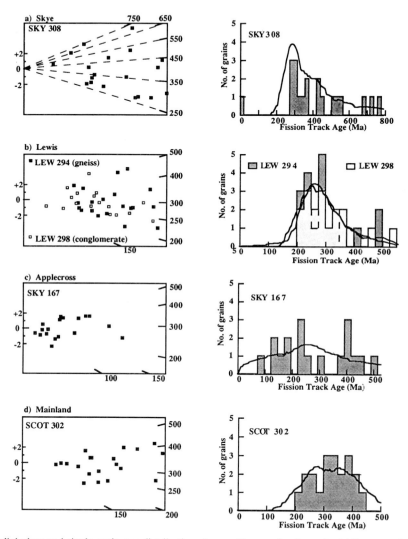

Fig. 4. Radial plots and single grain age distributions for apatite samples from the 'old' group of ages. (a) A Jurassic sample from Skye displays a wide range of single grain ages from 730–270 Ma. Dashed lines are drawn from the origin on the y axis, through the crystal to the edge of the plot where the approximate age of the crystal can be estimated. (b) A boulder of Lewisian gneiss from a Triassic conglomerate on the Isle of Lewis displays an almost identical single grain age distribution to that from the Lewisian basement on Harris, with a single grain age peak between 200–300 Ma. This suggests that neither sample has experienced temperatures higher than 60°C since the Devonian. (c) A sample from Raasay demonstrates weak effects of Tertiary heating by the presence of single grain ages younger than 200 Ma. (d) A slightly older peak in a sample from Durness on the Scottish mainland indicates earlier cooling.

neither track length measurements nor single grain age estimates were made at that time and thus these ages are less readily interpreted.

All Torridonian sandstone and Lewisian gneiss samples from the older group in this data set contain a tail of single grain ages up to 500 Ma (Fig. 4), indicating a minimum age at which this level of exposure last saw temperatures higher than 100°C. However, since the majority of grains peak in the 200–300 Ma range it suggests that moderate annealing has occurred subsequent to 500 Ma. This is further confirmed by the mean track lengths in these samples that are generally shorter than 13 μm (Fig. 3). At Bearreraig Bay on Syke the Mid-Jurassic sandstones are considered to have been derived from erosion of both the Northern Highlands and the Hebridean craton (Hudson 1964), thus the retention of grains older than 700 Ma in a sample from this horizon (SKY 308), coupled with the lack of grains much younger than 300 Ma (Fig. 4a) and a track length distribution very similar to that seen in samples both from the mainland and the Isle of Lewis (Fig. 3), indicates that these sediments have largely retained the grain age and track distribution inherited at the time of deposition, and are therefore unlikely to have experienced temperatures higher than 50°C since that time.

On the Isle of Lewis a similar situation is observed when comparing samples of Lewisian gneiss from Harris (LEW 294) and a Lewisian gneiss boulder (LEW 298) taken from the Triassic Stornoway conglomerate which is comprised almost entirely of detritus from the Hebridean craton (Hall 1991). These display an almost identical range of grain ages as can be seen from Fig. 4b, where data from the two samples are superimposed upon each another. Both also demonstrate a peak of ages around 200–300 Ma, with a tail of older grains up to 500 Ma, although the conglomerate displays a slightly shorter mean track length and a wider standard deviation on the track distribution than the gneiss (Fig. 3), indicative of having experienced somewhat higher temperatures than the gneiss. Locally the Stornoway Formation is considered to have reached 4 km thick (Steel & Wilson 1975), although this sample is unlikely to have been buried more than 2 km.

At Applecross evidence of post-Triassic heating is demonstrated by the presence of single grain ages less than 200 Ma in all the Torridonian sandstones collected from this locality. Those grains that are less than 100 Ma (Fig. 4c) constrain the timing of this heating event to being younger than 100 Ma. Dyke intrusions associated with the Tertiary igneous

centres are found in this area, and although care was taken to sample well away from dykes it is possible that annealing of these younger grains is associated with intrusive activity. Alternatively the young grains and short mean track lengths (all less than 12 μm) found in these samples could reflect greater burial depths at this locality which may have underlain the Tertiary lava field. Elsewhere on the mainland the age distribution (Fig. 4d) is similar to that on Lewis, although a slightly older peak suggests less annealing.

The younger group: apatites and zircons

Figure 2 plots the Central age for both apatites and zircons against percent age variation and demonstrates that, except for one sedimentary zircon and two apatites, both zircon and apatite fission track ages from the young group are within error of each other around 50 Ma, regardless of their stratigraphic age and the age of the intrusions (see below). In other studies where concordant apatite and zircon ages have been identified the apatites have mean track lengths of 14.5 μm which demonstrates fast cooling in a region of rapid uplift (e.g. Fitzgerald & Gleadow 1988). In this study however, the mean track lengths in the apatites are demonstrably shorter than 14.5 μm, having a mean value for the 11 totally annealed apatites of only 13 μm, thus these apatites have clearly experienced some annealing as a result of temperatures remaining elevated during cooling. However, short lengths in the apatites initially appear to be inconsistent with the fact that both apatites and zircons record essentially the same ages, since in other regions demonstrated to have experienced slow cooling (e.g. Lewis 1990) it is generally assumed that apatite ages will be younger than zircon ages due to the fact that zircons start to accumulate tracks at higher temperatures than apatites.

Figure 5 illustrates the age relationship between the Rb–Sr intrusion age ($\pm$2s) of individual plutons on Skye (Dickin 1981) and the zircon fission track ages ($\pm$1s) from those plutons. These Rb–Sr intrusion ages range from 59.3 $\pm$ 1.4 Ma for the Coire Uaigneich Granophyre (Dickin 1981), believed to be the oldest Skye granite (Richey 1932), to 53.4 $\pm$ 0.8 Ma for the Beinn an Dubhaich Epigranite (Dickin 1981), considered by Bell (1976) to represent one of the youngest intrusions on Skye. It can be seen that, except for the Creag Strollamus Epigranite, all zircon ages are reduced from the intrusion age, although at the 2 σ level this would not be so evident, and there is no obvious relationship between the age of the granite and

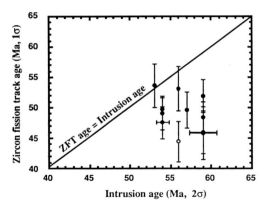

Fig. 5. Zircon fission track ages from the Tertiary granites on Skye are plotted against intrusion ages of the host granite. The majority of zircon ages fall below the 1:1 age line demonstrating that temperatures remained sufficiently high to partially anneal the zircons after intrusion of the granites. Closed circles, zircons from granites; open circles, zircons from sediments.

the amount by which the zircon fission track ages are reduced. One sedimentary zircon from Jurassic sediments that directly overlie the Bein na Cro Epigranite (BERR/AS) is also shown to be considerably reduced from the intrusion age and consistent with those from the granites. The other sedimentary zircon (BERR/ELG), from Jurassic sediments adjacent to a small undated intrusion near Elgol on the Strathaird Peninsular, yields an age of 63 ± 4 Ma (18%) (Table 3), which is somewhat older than the other zircons but within error of a single Rb/Sr date from the Cuillin peridotite (Dickin 1981).

Correlation of the apatite data with Bott & Tuson's (1973) Bouger anomaly map (Fig. 1) shows that all samples lying within the 15 mgal contour interval were totally reset, thus intrusion of the Tertiary igneous centres on Skye and Raasay had a significant impact on the surrounding sediments, totally annealing apatites up to 8 km away from present-day exposures of the intrusions. On the southeast coast a sample lying on the 10 mgal contour (SKY 331) yields an apatite fission track age of 73 ± 7 Ma (11%), and examination of the single grain ages (Fig. 6a) illustrates an older and wider spread of ages than its neighbour (SKY 330, Fig. 6b) which lies just within the 15 mgal contour. On Fig. 3, SKY 331 is seen to lie apart from the main group falling on the partially annealed section of the curve and has not been totally reset. Thus temperatures experienced by this sample only reached about 100°C which

constrains the maximum distance at which total annealing occurred to approximately 8 km from the intrusions.

One other partially annealed apatite sample (SKY 319, Fig. 6c) that also experienced temperatures around 100°C lies on the downthrown (easterly) side of a NW−SE trending fault in the south of the Isle of Raasay (Fig. 1). The direction of the fault is coincident with that of the main Palaeocene dyke swarm, and it is considered that faults orientated in this direction represent a phase of extension associated with dyke intrusion (Morton 1990). On the westerly side of the fault a sample from the Torridonian Sandstone (SKY 320) is totally annealed, therefore movement on this fault must have occurred *subsequent* to intrusion of the granites in order to juxtapose partially and fully annealed samples against each other. The amount of throw on the fault is considered not to have been more than 300 m (England, pers. comm.), which gives an indication of the vertical distance above the intrusion to which temperatures up to 100°C extended.

SKY 330 is typical of the totally annealed apatite samples, demonstrating a fairly tight single grain age distribution and a marked peak in the 40−50 Ma interval (Fig. 6b). However, the short mean track length of 13.18 ± 0.23 μm and standard deviation of 1.87 μm (Fig. 3) strongly suggest that temperatures remained elevated after intrusion, during which time ages reduced as the tracks lengths were shortened. For comparison, the single grain age distribution of a representative zircon (BNC) is included in Fig. 6d. The radial plot shows that, unlike the apatites, track densities in each zircon grain were very similar, therefore the spread is much smaller, but in the single grain age histogram a peak of ages in the 40−50 Ma interval is identical to that seen in the apatites. These young zircon ages further indicate that subsequent to intrusion temperatures remained elevated both within the granites and the surrounding sediments.

Regional implications

Throughout the Devonian the Hebridean region was supplying great thicknesses of sediment to the Clye area, Welsh borders and SE Ireland, indicating a period of extensive erosion that lasted into the Lower Carboniferous (Watson 1985). At the same time the Caledonian mountains were being eroded to levels that unroofed the Newer Granites, such that granite clasts were incorporated into Old Red Sandstone conglomerates, and Old Red Sandstone over-

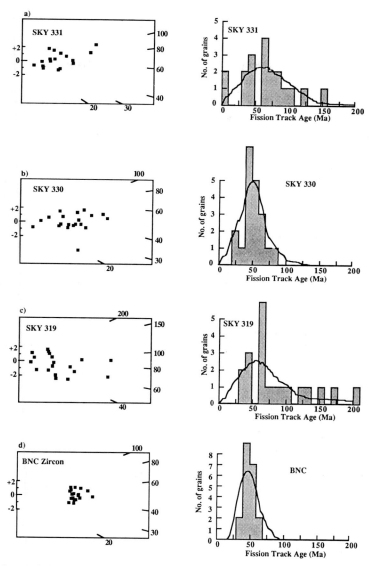

Fig. 6. Radial plots and single grain age distributions from the young group of apatites and zircons illustrate: (a) a wide range of apatite grain ages for SKY 331 that lies outside the 15 mgal gravity contour (Fig. 1), indicating that this sample has not been totally annealed; (b) SKY 330, which lies within the 15 mgal contour and shows a much tighter distribution than SKY 331 as a result of having been totally annealed; (c) another partially annealed sample (SKY 319) is found on the downthrown side of a NW–SE trending fault on Raasay, and illustrates that movement occurred subsequent to intrusion of the igneous complex; (d) the distribution on the radial plot from a representative zircon is much tighter than the apatites, but illustrates the same age peak as the totally reset apatite in (b).

stepped onto the granites (Hall 1991). Given the remarkable similarity of apatite fission track ages seen across the region from the Highland Boundary Fault to the Outer Hebrides (Fig. 1), as well as Orkney and the Shetland Isles (Hurford unpublished data), it appears probable that by the end of the Devonian the whole area was eroded to similar levels of moderate relief, and that on a regional scale it has subsequently experienced a fairly uniform history and never been covered by any great thickness of sediment.

Both Watson (1985) and Hall (1991) cite a list of geomorphological features to support arguments that favour very limited post-Devonian erosion across the region. They suggest that the Scottish massif remained low-lying thoughout the Mesozoic, although phases of moderate uplift and erosion obviously have occurred. During the Triassic, uplift of the Outer Hebrides resulted in the Stornoway Formation, and in the Moray Firth Permo-Triassic sediments up to 500 m thick (Frostick *et al.* 1988) indicate uplift in the Highlands. Moderate thicknesses (>300 m) of the Great Estuarine Group on Skye, containing detritus derived from both the Highlands and the Hebridean craton (Hudson 1964), imply continued denudation during the Jurassic. Indeed, Hudson comments on how similar the Jurassic paleogeography of Scotland must have been to that of the present day.

Two apatite samples from Mesozoic sediments yield fission track ages much older than their stratigraphic ages, immediately indicating that these sediments have not seen significantly elevated temperatures since deposition. Furthermore, the close similarity of the single grain ages seen in these samples to those measured in the Lewisian and Torridonian basement from which they were derived further supports the suggestion that these horizons have experienced very moderate burial depths since deposition and are thus relatively immature. Modelling of the apatite fission track data predicts that present-day exposure levels of the Lewisian and Torridonian basement started to cool below 110°C at the beginning of the Devonian. Therefore, assuming normal geothermal gradients of 25–30°C, they must have been buried beneath 3–4 km of overburden at that time. However, the presence of single grain ages up to 500 Ma suggests that temperatures had previously not been much higher than 120°C, thus this depth of burial probably represents the maximum for this level of exposure since at least the beginning of the Devonian. This is in reasonable agreement with estimates of 5 km of overburden present in this region during the Silurian, as indicated by petrographic features seen in fault rocks along the Moine and Outer Hebrides thrusts which are known to have been active between 430–400 Ma (Coward 1983).

Continued erosion throughout the Late Palaeozoic and Mesozoic is consistent with the apatite data, although the peaks of single grain ages in the 200–300 Ma range seen in almost all samples implies that temperatures at the end of the Triassic were still in the 60–70°C range and thus at least 2 km of overburden probably existed at that time. Furthermore, in order to reduce the mean track lengths to those observed in the samples from around Applecross, it is necessary to invoke approximately 2 km of burial in the Early Tertiary for this region, unless heating of these samples resulted from slightly raised geothermal gradients associated with igneous activity at this time.

Tertiary effects

Musset *et al.* (1988) suggest that igneous activity on Skye spanned a period of 6 Ma, and evidence that large hydrothermal systems existed during this time was demonstrated by Forester & Taylor (1977) who showed that almost all rocks within a 4 km radius of the intrusive complexes were depleted in ^{18}O due to extensive interaction with heated meteoric groundwaters. The presence of totally and severely annealed apatites up to 10 km away from the centres further extends the area over which interaction must have occurred, and indicates that temperatures at this distance were at least 100°C throughout the period of intrusive activity. Within the granites themselves, zircon fission track ages around 50 Ma demonstrate either that cooling below 200°C did not occur until this time, or that subsequent heating sufficiently reduced the intrusion ages to the measured values.

Rapid uplift of the Tertiary intrusions is suggested by George (1966), who proposed that as much as 2 km is missing from above the igneous centres on Skye, and rapid unroofing is confirmed by the presence of granite clasts in inter-basaltic conglomerates (Emeleus 1983). Therefore it would be reasonable to anticipate that cooling both of the granites and the surrounding sediments occurred very rapidly after intrusion. However, Taylor & Forester (1971) suggest that large amounts of heat may have been transferred upwards from underlying magma chambers, thus keeping rocks hot for unusually long periods. Indeed, the later intrusion of igneous bodies at depth may well have contributed to the significant uplift. If the granites acted as 'thermal funnels' through which this heat was directed, the higher temperatures in the granites would shorten tracks in the zircons, and the age would be reduced accordingly. Modelling of the apatite data from the sediments predicts that cooling from 110°C around 52 Ma would result in the measured values seen here if erosion occurred fairly continuously until the present time. The net result is that both minerals now demonstrate reduced ages that are indistinguishable from each other, within error.

Conclusions

The relationship of the fission track results to gravity contours and the subsurface structure of the igneous bodies on Skye, believed to extend to some 14 km at depth (Bott & Tuson 1973), suggests that for at least 8 km away from the complex, temperatures in the sediments currently at outcrop were elevated to >110°C during intrusion. The shortened track lengths in the apatites indicate that temperatures remained around 100–110°C, despite evidence for rapid uplift at this time, for at least the 6 Ma during intrusive activity. Within the granites themselves, temperatures must have been somewhat higher than in the sediments in order to partially anneal the zircons.

From these fission track data it is not possible to estimate the amount of erosion that occurred during intrusion of the igneous centre since everything has been reset, but apatite fission track analysis of Jurassic sediments from Bearreraig Bay on Skye and a Torridonian sandstone on Raasay illustrate that heating effects related to the intrusions, and any accompanying uplift, must have been extremely localized and limited to approximately a 10 km radius around the centre. The Jurassic sediments in particular contain Precambrian-aged grains, so are thus unlikely to have experienced temperatures higher than 50°C since deposition. But on the mainland around Applecross, apatite fission track age and length distributions suggest that almost 2 km of overburden may have existed during the Late Cretaceous.

Elsewhere on the Hebridean craton, ages and track length distributions are consistent with cooling from temperatures around 110°C at the beginning of the Devonian, but by the end of the Cretaceous maximum temperatures of samples from Lewis were unlikely to have been more than 30°C, and 40°C for Cape Wrath samples, indicating that 1–1.5 km of erosion has occurred since that time. Elsewhere in Scotland previous apatite fission track ages suggest that similar depths of cover existed at this time across the whole region north of the Highland Boundary Fault. Tertiary uplift in Scotland has previously been established (e.g. Hall 1991; Watson 1985; Knox et al. 1981) and the 1–1.5 km of erosion identified in this study is consistent with the regional pattern of Tertiary uplift and erosion now recognized across the whole of the British Isles, although it is con-

siderably less than the 2–3 km identified by fission track analysis in Northern England (Green 1986, Lewis et al. in press).

We are particularly grateful to BP Research for funding this project. We also acknowledge support from the NERC Special Topic Grant GST/02/354 and NERC grant GR3/7068. Samples from Skye were collected by Rob Butler and Richard England, and technical assistance given by Marc Davies and Susie Garnish.

References

BELL, J. D. 1976. The Tertiary intrusive complex of the Isle of Skye. *Proceedings of the Geologists' Association*, **87**, 247–271.

BOTT, M. H. P. & TUSON, J. 1973. Deep Structure beneath the Tertiary Volcanic Regions of Skye, Mull and Ardnamurchan, North-west Scotland. *Nature*, **242**, 114–116.

COWARD, M. P. 1983. The thrust and shear zones of the Moine thrust zone and the NW Scottish Caledonides. *Journal of the Geological Society, London*, **140**, 795–812.

DICKIN, A. P. 1981. Isotope Geochemistry of Tertiary Igneous Rocks from the Isle of Skye, N.W. Scotland. *Journal of Petrology*, **22**, 155–189.

DUDDY, I. R., GREEN, P. F. & LASLETT, G. M. 1988. Thermal annealing of fission tracks in apatite. 3. Variable temperature behaviour. *Chemical Geology (Isotope Geoscience Section)* **73**, 25–38.

EMELEUS, C. H. 1983. Tertiary Igneous Activity. *In*: CRAIG, G. Y. (ed.) *Geology of Scotland*. Edinburgh, Scottish Academic Press, 357–397.

FITZGERALD, G. & GLEADOW, A. J. W. 1988. Fission-track geochronology, tectonics and structure of the Transantarctic Mountains in Northern Victoria Land, Antarctica. *Chemical Geology (Isotope Geoscience Section)*, **73**, 169–198.

FORESTER, R. W. & TAYLOR, H. P. 1971. Low-O[18] Igneous Rocks from the Intrusive Complexes of Skye, Mull and Ardnamurchan, Western Scotland. *Journal of Petrology*, **12**, 465–497.

FROSTICK, L., REID, I., JARVIS, J. & EARDLY, H. 1988. Triassic sediments in the Inner Moray Firth, Scotland: early rift deposits. *Journal of the Geological Society, London*, **145**, 235–248.

GALBRAITH, R. F. 1990. The radial plot: graphical assessment of spread in ages. *Nuclear Tracks and Radiation Measurements*, **17**, 207–214.

GEORGE, T. N. 1966. Geomorphic evolution of Hebridean Scotland. *Scottish Journal of Geology*, **2**, 1–34.

GLEADOW, A. J. W., DUDDY, I. R., GREEN, P. F. & HEGARTY, K. A. 1986. Fission track lengths in the apatite annealing zone and interpretation of mixed ages. *Earth and Planetary Science Letters*, **78**, 245–254.

GREEN, P. F. 1986. On the thermo-tectonic evolution of Northern England: evidence from fission track analysis. *Geological Magazine*, **123**, 493–506.

—— 1989. Thermal and tectonic history of the East Midlands shelf (onshore UK) and surrounding regions assessed by apatite fission track analysis. *Journal of the Geological Society, London.* **146**, 755–773.

——, DUDDY, I. R., GLEADOW, A. J. W., TINGATE, P. R. & LASLETT, G. M. 1986. Thermal annealing of fission tracks in apatite. 1. A qualitative description. *Chemical Geology (Isotope Geoscience Section)*, **59**, 237–253.

——, ——, & LOVERING, J. F. 1989a. Apatite Fission-Track Analysis as a Paleotemperature Indicator for Hydrocarbon Exploration. *In:* NAESER, N. D. & McCULLOH, T. H. (eds) *Thermal History of Sedimentary Basins-Methods and Case Histories,* **X**, 181–195.

——, ——, LASLETT, G. M., HEGARTY, K. A., GLEADOW, A. J. W. & LOVERING, J. F. 1989b. Thermal annealing of fission tracks in apatite. 4. Quantative modelling techniques and extension to geological timescales. *Chemical Geology (Isotope Geoscience Section)*, **79**, 155–182.

HALL, A. M. 1991. Pre-Quaternary landscape evolution in the Scottish Highlands. *Transactions of the Royal Society of Edinburgh: Earth Sciences,* **82**, 1–26.

HARRISON, T. M., ARMSTRONG, R. L., NAESER, C. W. & HARAKAL, J. E. 1979. Geochronology and thermal history of the Coast Plutonic Complex, near Prince Rupert, British Columbia. *Canadian Journal of Earth Sciences,* **16**, 400–410.

HUDSON, J. D. 1964. The petrology of the sandstones of the Great Estuarine Series, and the Jurassic palaeogeography of Scotland. *Proceedings of the Geologists Association,* **75**, 499–528.

HURFORD, A. J. 1977. A preliminary fission track dating survey of Caledonian 'newer and last granites' from the Highlands of Scotland. *Scottish Journal of Geology,* **13**, 271–274.

—— 1986. Cooling and uplift patterns in the Lepontine Alps, South Central Switzerland and an age of vertical movement on the Insubric fault line. *Contributions to Mineralogy and Petrology,* **92**, 413–427.

KNOX, R. W. O'B., MORTON, A. C. & HARLAND, R. 1981. Stratigraphical Relationships of Palaeocene Sands in the UK Sector of the Central North Sea. *In:* ILLING, L. V. & HOBSON, G. D. (eds)

Petroleum Geology of the Continental Shelf of North West Europe, 267–281.

LASLETT, G. M., GREEN, P. F., DUDDY, I. R. & GLEADOW, A. J. W. 1987. Thermal annealing of fission tracks in apatite. 2. A quantitative analysis. *Chemical, Geology, (Isotope Geoscience Section)*, **65**, 1–13.

LEWIS, C. L. E. 1990. Thermal history of the Kunlun batholith, N. Tibet and implications for uplift of the Tibetan plateau. *Nuclear Tracks and Radiation Measurements,* **17**, 301–307.

——, GREEN, P. G., CARTER, A. C. & HURFORD, A. J. 1991. Elevated palaeotemperatures throughout Northern England: three kilometres of Tertiary erosion? *Earth and Planetary Science Letters* (in press).

MORTON, N. 1990. Bearreraig (Isle of Skye, N.W. Scotland) as boundary stratotype for the base of the Bajocian Stage. *Memorie Descrittive della Carta Geologica D'Italia,* **XL**, 23–48.

MUSSET, A. E., DAGLEY, P. & SKELHORN 1988. Time and duration of activity in the British Tertiary Igneous Province. *In:* MORTON, A. C. (ed.) *Early Tertiary Volcanism and the Opening of the NE Atlantic,* Geological Society, London, Special Publication, **39**, 337–348.

PRESTON, J. 1982. Eruptive Volcanism. *In:* SUTHERLAND, D. S. (ed.) *Igneous rocks of the British Isles,* Wiley, Chichester, 351–368.

RICHEY, J. E. 1932. Tertiary ring structures in Britain. *Transactions of the Geological Society of Glasgow,* **19**, 42–140.

STEEL, R. J. & WILSON, A. C. 1975. Sedimentation and tectonism (?Permo-Triassic) on the margin of the North Minch Basin, Lewis. *Journal of the Geological Society, London,* **131**, 183–202.

TAGAMI, T., ITO, H. & NISHIMURA, S. 1990. Thermal annealing characteristics of spontaneous fission tracks in zircon. *Chemical Geology (Isotope Geoscience Section),* **80**, 159–169.

TAYLOR, H. P. & FORESTER, R. W. 1977. $^{18}O/^{16}O$, D/H and $^{13}C/^{12}C$ studies of the Tertiary igneous complex of Skye, Scotland. *American Journal of Science,* **277**, 136–177.

WATSON, J. 1985. Northern Scotland as an Atlantic-North Sea divide. *Journal of the Geological Society, London,* **142**, 221–243.

Onshore and offshore North of Ireland

The origin of Upper Palaeozoic sedimentary basins in Northern Ireland and relationships with the Canadian Maritime Provinces

W. I. MITCHELL

Geological Survey of Northern Ireland, 20 College Gardens, Belfast BT9 6BS, UK

Abstract: The evolution of Carboniferous and early Permian sedimentary basins in Northern Ireland is related to a rapidly changing pattern of tectonic episodes. Character- istic sedimentary assemblages and facies changes are associated with discrete phases of basin formation and were related to tectonic events that can be correlated with events in a wide zone of dextral strike-slip in the Canadian Maritime Provinces. Small, localized non- marine basins developed during late Asbian−early Brigantian and Westphalian B times. These data support the extension of the Canadian Maritime transform fault system into Northern Ireland in late Silesian times.

Transatlantic correlation of Carboniferous lithostratigraphical units in Northern Ireland, Scotland and the Canadian Maritime Provinces (Fig. 1) was demonstrated by Belt (1969). He concluded that early Dinantian (Tournaisian) sediments in northeast Canada (Horton Group), and Ireland (Tyrone Group), were deposited in rifts that were subsequently inundated by an early Viséan marine transgression. Correlation is not, however, now confined to the early Dinantian rocks, but encompasses Carbonifer- ous strata of all ages, in the North Atlantic area. Dating of major Carboniferous tectonic events in Northern Ireland (Mitchell & Owens 1990) has emphasised the remarkable similar- ities between the Carboniferous successions there and in northeast Canada.

The main lithostratigraphical divisions of Carboniferous basins fringing the northern North Atlantic (Fig. 1) are reviewed and recent theories regarding the timing and nature of tectonic episodes in the Canadian Maritime Provinces are applied in an analysis of the history of basin subsidence, and the relationship between tectonics and sedimentation, in Northern Ireland.

Lithostratigraphy and tectonic history of the Carboniferous in the North Atlantic area

Canadian Maritime Provinces

The interaction of tectonics, basin formation and sedimentation has been intensively studied in the Maritime Provinces of northeast Canada (Bradley 1982). During Carboniferous and early Permian times this area was a dextral strike-slip plate boundary zone, and basins subsided in a transtensional tectonic regime. Dextral offsets ranging from a few kilometres to 225 km are estimated for major faults in Newfoundland and Nova Scotia. The areal distribution of sedi- ments of alluvial fan, fluvial and lacustrine facies has been used to determine the positions of, and the relative rates of subsidence along, basin marginal faults for all lithostratigraphical groups (Fig. 2).

The total thickness of Carboniferous and Permian rocks in the Maritime Provinces is estimated at 19 km, but the maximum thickness recorded in any one basin does not exceed 9.1 km (Howie & Barss 1975). Six lithostrati- graphical groups are recognized in this area (Fig. 2), each consisting largely of non-marine sediments, which are arranged in facies belts that are both diachronous and partially laterally equivalent. The subsidence history of Carbon- iferous basins in the Maritime Provinces con- forms to McKenzie's (1978) model for basin formation, whereby an initial rift phase of rapid, localized, fault-controlled subsidence is fol- lowed by regional thermal subsidence and the deposition of sediments over former basin margins and basement features.

(i) *Horton Group.* The Horton Group (Fig. 2) and its lateral equivalents were deposited during Middle Devonian to early Viséan times and are over 4000 m thick in the Magdalen Basin (Howie & Barss 1975). They consist of red and grey non-marine sediments with evap-

From PARNELL, J. (ed.), 1992, *Basins on the Atlantic Seaboard: Petroleum Geology, Sedimentology and Basin Evolution.* Geological Society Special Publication No. 62, pp 191−202.

191

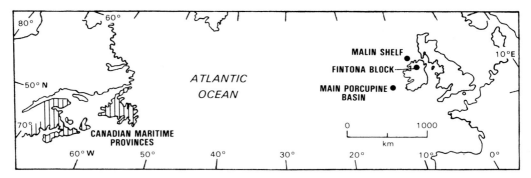

Fig. 1. Sketch map of the northern North Atlantic Ocean showing the Canadian Maritime Provinces and areas offshore and onshore Ireland referred to in the text.

orites, volcanic rocks and a few coal seams. Deposition was periodically influenced by rapid basement uplift and fault control of basin margins. Tectonically quiescent periods permitted the development of fluvio-lacustrine environments and the establishment of peat swamps. Clastic sediments of the Horton Group were deposited in pull-apart basins located between dextral strike-slip faults (Bradley 1982).

(ii) *Windsor Group.* These rocks were deposited over much of Maritime Canada by a mid-Viséan to early Namurian regional marine transgression. Rapid lateral and vertical lithological changes reflect the importance of contemporaneous tectonic activity on these sediments which were deposited in terrestrial, shallow and open marine environments. Thick deposits of salt, gypsum and anhydrite that accumulated in restricted basins responded to tectonism with the formation of diapirs or salt domes. Although Bradley (1982) identified the Windsor transgression as the first expression of Carboniferous thermal subsidence in northeast Canada, downwarping did not develop as a simple regional sag since the presence of separate units of alluvial fanglomerates indicates the existence of multiple fault line scarps bounding internal basement horsts.

(iii) *Canso-Riversdale Groups.* These lithologically similar groups, which are at least 3000 m thick (Howie & Barss 1975) were originally defined at separate stratotypes in Nova Scotia and each was assigned a restricted age range; Namurian A for the Canso Group and Westphalian A for the Riversdale Group, although there is now known to be a considerable overlap in their ages (Fig. 2). Both consist of non-marine, fine-grained clastic sediments, with conglomerates forming only a minor component. Field recognition of the two groups depends largely on colour differences, though

transitional units occur. Fluvio-lacustrine sediments of the Canso Group are predominantly red and were deposited in a semi-arid environment. In contrast, the coal-bearing sediments of the Riversdale Group are mainly grey and were deposited under predominantly fluvial conditions, in a warm temperate climatic regime.

Deposition of Canso Group sediments occurred during a tectonically quiescent period at a time of low topographic contrast between basins and clastic source areas. Uplift during Riversdale Group times led to the accumulation of thick fluvial sands in local pull-apart basins in eastern Nova Scotia but coincided with regional thermal subsidence in the west (Bradley 1982).

(iv) *Cumberland Group.* This group (Fig. 2) consists of over 3300 m of late Westphalian A− Westphalian B red and grey, non-marine clastic sediments with coal seams. After deposition of the Riversdale Group tectonic uplift and deformation of earlier Carboniferous strata occurred over much of Maritime Canada. Contemporaneous subsidence of localized dextral pull-apart basins resulted in the accumulation of thick fanglomerates during Westphalian B times. The penetrative deformation and low grade metamorphism of some Riversdale-Canso strata (Yeo 1985) is thought to be associated with this tectonic episode.

(v) *Pictou Group.* A decline in tectonic activity after Westphalian B times continued through the late Westphalian, Stephanian and early Permian. Pictou Group sediments reflect this declining influence of faulting on basin margins. They commence with thin conglomerates and thick, but local coarse-grained, feldspathic fluvial sands that are succeeded by coarse, mature sands and coals deposited during a late Carboniferous and early Permian phase of thermal subsidence. The new enlarged basin

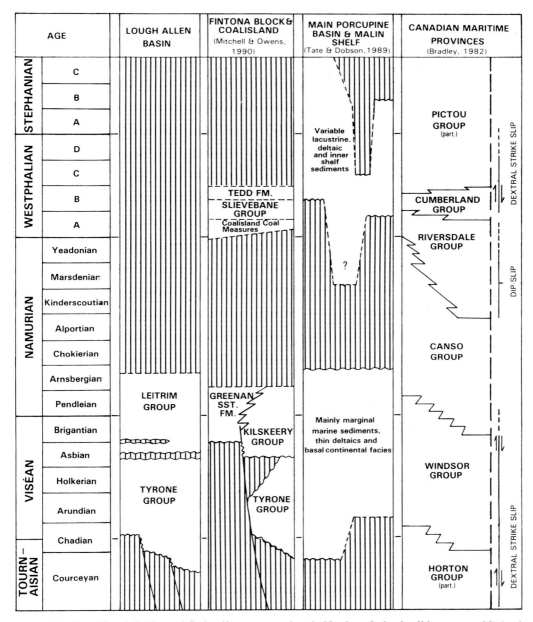

Fig. 2. Stratigraphic subdivisions of Carboniferous successions in Northern Ireland, offshore west of Ireland and the Canadian Maritime Provinces.

incorporated all former basin areas and basement blocks in the Maritime Provinces.

Main Porcupine Basin and Malin Shelf

Offshore seismic surveys and drilling west and northwest of Ireland (Fig. 1) proved a Permo-

Carboniferous section up to 3.7 km thick (Robeson *et al.* 1988; Tate & Dobson 1989). A mid-Namurian hiatus divides late Tournaisian-early Namurian basal clastic, peritidal and marine sediments that pass up into cyclical clastic and carbonate rocks, from overlying Namurian C-Westphalian A coal-bearing deltaic rocks succeeded by Westphalian B-Stephanian and Early Permian (Autunian) deltaic, brackish and freshwater sediments (Fig. 2). Carboniferous sediments of the alluvial fan red-bed association (Besly 1988) are not recorded in offshore basins west of Ireland.

Northern Ireland

Dinantian and early Silesian rocks (Tyrone and Leitrim groups) that crop out west and south of Lower Lough Erne (Figs 2 & 3) represent the northern part of the Lough Allen Basin. In northwest Ireland the Lough Allen Basin is one of several sub-basins that together constitute the Northwest Carboniferous Basin (See Philcox et al., this volume). Carboniferous sedimentation patterns in the Lough Allen Basin reflect, and were profoundly influenced by, regional tectonic events.

(i) *Late Tournaisian-Viséan rifting.* In the Lough Allen Basin Tyrone and Leitrim Group sediments, up to 3.7 km thick, were deposited in an epicontinental sea. The earliest sediments consist of red fanglomerates and sandstones, and fluvio-deltaic sediments of late Courceyan to late Chadian age. These were onlapped by transgressive peritidal carbonates followed by a fully marine late Chadian and Arundian sequence in which successive units overlap northwards onto the Dalradian basement in the Kesh−Omagh area (Fig. 3B). A similar succession is present in County Armagh (Fig. 3A), where there is evidence of southward overstep of late Courceyan−late Chadian lithostratigraphical units onto the Lower Palaeozoic rocks that form the northern part of the Down−Longford massif (GSNI 1984). Progressive submergence of this and the Kesh−Omagh basement high was the consequence of extensional faulting and expansion of the depositional rift basin. The Down−Longford high was finally breached in late Asbian−early Brigantian times (Smith et al. 1991), but whether as a result of regional submergence or more localized rift-controlled incursion is not known.

Relative tectonic quiescence during mid-Arundian to early Asbian times was accompanied by the deposition of marine mudstones and siltstones over much of Northern Ireland. Southward thickening of the sediments indicates that basin subsidence may still have been influenced by extensional faults.

(ii) *Late Viséan tectonics in the Lough Allen Basin.* The late Viséan sediments of the Lough Allen Basin contain abundant evidence of tectonic instability and of the importance of syn-depositional fault control of localized depocentres. The first indications of increased tectonic activity are found in the Dartry Limestone Formation (Fig. 4). Enhanced carbonate production accompanied the formation of in-basin ramps and platforms, with examples of slumped horizons and debris flows, and rapid thickness variations and facies changes over relatively short distances. An erosional hiatus occurs between the Tyrone and Leitrim groups (Fig. 2). Regional marine regression accompanied by uplift and erosion of limestones of the Dartry Formation was followed by deposition of supratidal (sabkha), marine, deltaic and fluvial sediments of the Meenymore Formation (Fig. 4) in the late Asbian (B_2a Subzone). Though fault control of local depocentres is evident in the latter formation, the great variety of apparently random facies variations which characterizes the unit is considered to reflect principally the multiplicity of depositional environments that existed on an extensive coastal plain. Late Asbian tectonic activity in the Lough Allen Basin, which resulted in uplift and development of the hiatus between the Tyrone and Leitrim groups, is contemporaneous with the onset of fault-controlled subsidence of the non-marine basin that was infilled by red-beds of the Kilskeery Group (Fig. 2).

In the Clogher Valley−Slieve Beagh areas (Fig. 3B), evidence of tectonic instability is found in late Asbian sediments (Mitchell & Owens 1990). However, the presence of B_1 Subzone goniatites in these sediments suggests that Asbian sedimentation was not interrupted by significant uplift, and that an erosional hiatus was not developed in these areas.

Overlying the Meenymore Formation in the Lough Allen Basin, the coarse-grained to pebbly, feldspathic Glenade Sandstone Formation (Fig. 4) is about 300 m thick in the north of its outcrop, on the south side of Lower Lough Erne, and 4 m thick at Aghagrania, County Leitrim, 45 km to the south (Brandon & Hodson 1984, p 12). Sediment, derived from the north, was deposited in a strongly asymmetric half-graben. Continuous movement on the northern basin-bounding normal fault caused active uplift of the footwall, erosion of older Carboniferous strata (Higgs 1984, p 185), unroofing of metamorphic rocks and the production of a virtually horizontal top surface to the sandstone wedge. Minor subsidence on this fault also continued during deposition of the lower members of the succeeding Bellavally Formation (Fig. 4), and marine bands, such as the Larkfield and Lugasnaghta Shale members (B_2b Subzone), thin southwards and were not deposited in southern parts of the outcrop (Brandon & Hodson 1984, Fig. 3).

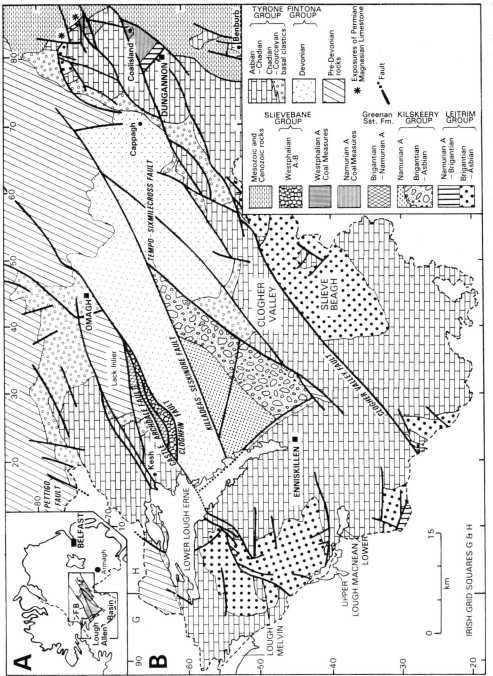

Fig. 3. General geological map of southwest Northern Ireland showing the principal stratigraphical divisions of the Carboniferous. Abbreviations: FB – Fintona Block. Modified from Geological Survey of Northern Ireland (1977).

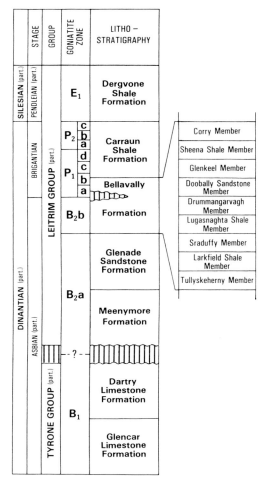

Fig. 4. Lithostratigraphy of the late Dinantian-early Silesian rocks in the Lough Allen Basin (modified from Brandon & Hodson 1984); hatched ornament denotes non-sequence.

In the upper part of the Bellavally Formation the Glenkeel and Sheena Shale members contain P_1b goniatites (Brandon & Hodson 1984 and GSNI unpublished information). The absence of P_1a faunas in the unfossiliferous succession betwen the Larkfield Shale – Lugasnaghta Shale and Glenkeel – Sheena Shale members may be an indication either of hostile depositional environments, represented by sabkha facies in the Drummangarvagh Member and pebbly sandstones in the Doobally Sandstone Member (Brandon & Hodson 1984), or of a depositional hiatus. That this level correlates with the tectonic event that resulted in the onset of subsidence of the non-marine basin in which

the Greenan Sandstone Formation was deposited (Fig. 2), suggests that the non-sequence reflects the effect of tectonism, not eustatically driven regression, on the depositional cycles in the Bellavally Formation.

(iii) *Late Viséan non-marine basin formation.* Dinantian basin evolution in Northern Ireland was catastrophically interrupted in mid- to late Asbian times by uplift of a southwestern extension of the Tyrone Igneous Complex (GSNI 1977; Hutton 1987). Marine regression that affected the entire region is reflected in the late Asbian sediments of the Tyrone and Leitrim groups in the Lough Allen Basin (Figs 4 & 5). Widespread uplift of the northern part of this basin led to the erosion of at least 1000 m of Tyrone Group sediments that covered the metamorphic rocks of the Lack Inlier (Fig. 3B) and an unknown, but probably greater, thickness of sediments in the upper part of the same group in the south of the Fintona Block (Fig. 3A; Mitchell & Owens 1990) before the Kilskeery Group started to accumulate there (Figs 2, 3B).

Rapid subsidence of two new, localized non-marine basins occurred at the margins of the rising Tyrone Igneous Complex in the area of the Fintona Block. At least 2500 m of late Asbian–Pendleian red-beds of the Kilskeery Group (Figs 2, 3B) accumulated in the fault-bounded southern basin. On Slieve Beagh (Fig. 3B) fine-grained Asbian red-beds of the Leitrim Group, which are equivalent to the coarse sandstones in the lower part of the Kilskeery Group, are interbedded with fine-grained fossiliferous marine sediments and were deposited in a strandline environment (Mitchell & Owens 1990). The base of the Kilskeery Group is not exposed in the Fintona Block. Coarse-grained sandstones, up to 1000 m thick, represent the early sediment-fill but conglomerates, about 300 m thick and of probable Brigantian age, indicate the timing of maximum uplift on marginal faults and of basin subsidence. Within the conglomerates are clasts of Lower Palaeozoic greywacke and fresh to deeply weathered rhyolite. Similar volcanic rocks exposed at Cappagh (Fig. 3B) are of Middle or Upper Devonian age (Mitchell & Owens 1990) but are not the source of the volcanic clasts in the late Viséan conglomerate. The occurrence of rhyolite blocks, up to 30 cm diameter, in this conglomerate suggests instead that the volcanic clasts originated by the erosion of contemporaneous lava flows. Declining subsidence rates in late Brigantian–Pendleian times led to a decrease in sediment grain size and to a northward migration of fluvio-lacustrine facies across older fault lines and possibly the metamorphic basement.

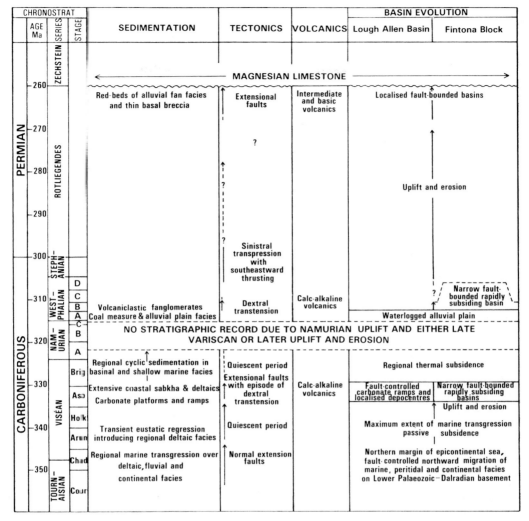

Fig. 5. Summary of the principal events in the Upper Palaeozoic history of Northern Ireland. The estimates of the absolute time for the various subdivisions are based upon radiometric dates from the work of Hess & Lippolt (1986) and Odin & Odin (1990).

The sediment-fill of the northern basin comprises the Greenan Sandstone Formation of Brigantian–Pendleian age (Figs 2, 3B), which consists of a thin basal epiclastic breccia and over 500 m of purple-red sandstones with thin conglomerates, and correlates with the middle and upper formations of the Kilskeery Group (Fig. 2; Mitchell & Owens 1990). In the Kesh–Omagh area marine and deltaic sediments of the Tyrone Group were uplifted, deeply eroded and slightly deformed prior to, and during, the subsidence of this northern basin.

Many of the effects that movement along

strike-slip fault systems produce on contemporaneous sediments and successions (Reading 1980), are now recognized in the late Viséan rocks of Northern Ireland. These include the rapid subsidence of new non-marine basins, associated calc-alkaline volcanism, and the formation of carbonate ramps and localized depocentres in the Lough Allen Basin.

The profound influence of contemporaneous dextral strike-slip faulting on Carboniferous sedimentation is particularly well illustrated in the Maritime Provinces of northeast Canada. Similar stratigraphical units and facies sequences there and in Northern Ireland include the coarse fanglomerates of the Kilskeery Group, which correlate with late Windsor Group and early Canso Group fanglomerates in New Brunswick (Howie & Barss 1975) and Nova Scotia (Belt 1968; Bradley 1982; Yeo 1985). These indicate that late Viséan sedimentation in Northern Ireland was also influenced by contemporaneous tectonism and that non-marine basins formed adjacent to major faults, probably with a dextral displacement but certainly with a large element of extension.

(iv) *Late Viséan-early Silesian thermal subsidence.* Mitchell & Owens (1990) recognised the effects of regional thermal subsidence on early Brigantian (P_1b) to Arnsbergian (E_2b) Leitrim Group sediments in the north of Ireland (Fig. 2), although there is evidence that sporadic tectonic activity persisted at this time. Leitrim Group strata of this age crop out over an area of almost 1400 km^2 (Fig. 3B pars; Brandon & Hodson 1984). The influence of this episode of thermal subsidence may also have extended eastwards to the Dungannon area where Brigantian–Namurian A mudstones of the Leitrim Group are exposed (Fig. 3B).

(v) *The mid-Namurian unconformity.* Evidence for the existence of a mid-Namurian unconformity in the north of Ireland is tenuous and is based only on the age differences between two Namurian sections some 100 km apart. There are no exposures of Namurian rocks representing the time between the Arnsbergian (E_2b_1 Subzone; *Cravenoceratoides edalensis*) of the Connaught Coalfield, County Leitrim (Yates 1962) and the undated, presumably Yeadonian, strata that are overlain conformably by the Subcrenatum Marine Band (Westphalian A) at Coalisland (Figs 2, 3B; Fowler & Robbie 1961). Although it is recognized that late Variscan or Mesozoic-Cenozoic erosion may have artificially extended the chronostratigraphical gap represented by this hiatus in the north of Ireland, it is worth noting that an erosional hiatus with similar well constrained limits is also known from west Cumbria (Ramsbottom *et al.* 1978) and offshore west of Ireland (Fig. 1; Robeson *et al.* 1988; Tate & Dobson 1989).

(vi) *Westphalian sediments and tectonics.* Until recently all Westphalian strata in Ireland were assigned to the coal measures facies and were regarded as not younger than Westphalian A (Sevastopulo 1981). The Slievebane Group (Fig. 2) of the Fintona Block comprises two formations (Mitchell & Owens 1990). These are the late Westphalian A–early Westphalian B Tullanaglare Mudstone Formation, comprising

50–80 m of grey-green sediments of the alluvial plain facies association with a 0.5 m bed of pink pedogenic limestone at the top, and the succeeding Drumlish Conglomerate Formation, consisting of 1000 m of volcaniclastic fanglomerates and pebbly sandstones. The age of the conglomerate is not known precisely. Therefore, although there is no angular discordance between it and the underlying formation, and no erosion of the pink limestone at the top of that formation, it is possible that the boundary is a surface of nondeposition (Mitchum *et al.* 1977). Clasts of fresh trachytoid rhyolite up to 0.5 m diameter are very common in the conglomerate, often in a matrix composed largely of angular fragments of weathered rhyolite. The size and relative abundance of these volcanic clasts, in the lower part of the formation, compared with metamorphic lithologies suggests that they originated in a source area close to the basin margin, in which successive lava flows replenished the supply of fresh debris to the alluvial fans.

The youngest Carboniferous strata in Northern Ireland may be the 450 m of predominantly fine-grained red-beds of the Tedd Formation (Fig. 2). Although the Slievebane Group and Tedd Formation outcrop in separate fault-bounded segments between the Cloghfin and Castle Archdale faults (Fig. 3B), sediments at their top and base respectively are very similar and are part of a 1.5 km thick fining-upward cycle that exhibits a progressive change from sediments of alluvial fan facies, in the Drumlish Conglomerate Formation of the Slievebane Group (Fig. 2) (Westphalian B), to fluvial and lacustrine facies at the top of the Tedd Formation. The episode of tectonic activity (Fig. 5) responsible for the rapid subsidence of the fault-bounded basin and accumulation of this conglomerate occurred in Westphalian B times and is contemporaneous with a period of dextral strike-slip (transtension) in the Maritime Provinces (Bradley 1982), and with rapid subsidence of pull-apart basins and deposition of the Cumberland Group in Nova Scotia (Yeo 1985). Although volcanic rocks are not associated with Cumberland Group sediments in northeast Canada, basalt and rhyolite lavas, of Westphalian B age, are interbedded with conglomerates in the Narragansett Basin in Rhode Island and Massachusetts (Skehan *et al.* 1979).

Lower Permian rocks in Northern Ireland

In northeast Ireland red-beds that occur below the Upper Permian Magnesian Limestone, and above either Dinantian or Lower Palaeozoic rocks, are traditionally assigned an early Permian age. Though cropping out only in a small area in east County Tyrone (Fig. 3B) and a narrow strip extending 20 km SW and 8 km NE of Belfast (GSNI 1977), these rocks are also present in the subsurface and have been encountered in deep boreholes (Wilson 1983).

Exposures in east County Tyrone consist of between 0.1 and 7.74 m of red pebbly sandstones and conglomerates that rest unconformably on late Viséan marine limestones of the Tyrone Group and are overlain by the Magnesian Limestone (Fowler & Robbie 1961). On the northwest side of the Down−Longford Massif, near Belfast (Fig. 3A), Ordovician rocks are overlain unconformably by between 3.3 and 21 m of breccia and up to 23 m of coarse-grained, red sandstones (Manning et al. 1970; Smith 1986). The boundary between these clastic sediments and the succeeding Magnesian Limestone, and its lateral equivalent in the Belfast Harbour Borehole Formation, is a disconformity (Smith 1986). To the southwest of Belfast the combined outcrop of the basal clastics and Magnesian Limestone is attenuated by the successive overstep of the Permo-Triassic Belfast Mudstones (Wilson 1981) and the Lower Scythian Sherwood Sandstone Group, onto Silurian rocks (GSNI 1977; Smith 1985). At Cultra, northeast of Belfast, the Magnesian Limestone is underlain by 1.5 m of breccia that rests unconformably on late Tournaisian (Courceyan) shales, peritidal carbonates and evaporite beds (Clayton 1986). These occurrences of relatively thin clastic sediments beneath the Magnesian Limestone probably represent a residual regolith.

Active subsidence at the fault-bounded northern margin of the Newtownards Trough, some 15 km E of Belfast, resulted in the accumulation of alluvial fan breccias and coarse sandstones, which are at least 245 m thick in the north, but 3 km further south are only 1 m thick (Smith et al. 1991). The absence of the Magnesian Limestone in this narrow basin casts doubt on the Permian age assigned to these clastic sediments which are overlain, instead, by blanket sands of the Sherwood Sandstone Group.

The thickest succession of pre-Magnesian Limestone (Permian ?) rocks recorded in Northern Ireland occurs in the Larne No 2 Borehole and consists of three main units comprising 62.5 m of unbottomed, very coarse breccio-conglomerates and sandstones at the base, overlain by 554 m of heavily altered intermediate and basic volcanic rocks, tuffs and tuffaceous sediments with 440 m of purple to red-brown sandstones and pebble conglomerates at the top (Penn et al. 1983). Deposition may have been from braided streams or on alluvial fans in a location proximal to the sediment source. While the lavas have yielded K−Ar ages ranging from 220 ± 5 Ma (Norian-Carnian Stages of the late Triassic) to 268 ± 6 Ma (Kungurian Stage of the Permian; Forster & Warrington 1985) there is no biostratigraphical evidence for the age of the strata.

End-Variscan tectonic history of Northern Ireland

The timing and nature of late Carboniferous tectonism in Northern Ireland can now be determined more accurately than hitherto. The recognition of post-Westphalian B faulting allows a simplified strain model to be deduced for this region (Fig. 5). Strata particularly affected by these movements belong to the Greenan Sandstone Formation, Slievebane Group and Tedd Formation (Fig. 2) and the Siegenian Shanmullagh Formation (Mitchell & Owens 1990). Anticlockwise rotation of these Devonian strata located south of the Cloghfin Fault (Fig. 3B) is attributed to an early phase of sinistral strike-slip on this fault (Mitchell & Owens 1990). Between the Cloghfin and Castle Archdale faults (Fig. 3B) the segmented Carboniferous outcrop represents the eroded remnant of a series of imbricate rock slices, each resting on a northwesterly inclined thrust plane. Southward or southeasterly directed thrusting on the Castle Archdale Fault occurred after the initial episode of sinistral strike-slip and superimposed Dalradian metamorphic rocks (Lack Inlier) and Tyrone Group sediments (Kesh−Omagh area; Chadian−Holkerian age), located north of the fault, on the Greenan Sandstone Formation in the footwall. These latter strata are also overthrust southwards and now rest on the Westphalian A−B sediments of the Slievebane Group.

This combination of strike-slip and thrusting (Fig. 5) may indicate that transpressional deformation was responsible for regional uplift during late Westphalian, Stephanian and, possibly, earliest Permian times, and would account for the absence of sediments of this age in Northern Ireland. The thickness variations of early Permian (pre-Magnesian Limestone) strata in different parts of Northern Ireland are the result of the formation of new fault-bounded, non-marine basins during an episode of crustal extension. Thin basal clastic sediments exposed in east County Tyrone and near Belfast thus accumulated on elevated ground when the thick red-beds, which include alluvial fanglomerates, and volcanic rocks encountered at Larne (Penn *et al.* 1983) and in the Ballymacilroy Borehole (276 m +), County Antrim (Thompson 1979) were deposited in localized basins. The orientation of these basins in Northern Ireland may be parallel to the NW—SE trending structures described by Hall *et al.* (1984) from the western part of the Midland Valley of Scotland and the adjacent offshore areas.

Conclusions

Many similarities exist between the Carboniferous successions that fringe the North Atlantic region. In northeast Canada and Northern Ireland, local and regional unconformities occur that have similar timing and duration and there is evidence, in both areas, of contemporaneous fault control of basin initiation and subsidence. Information from the late Palaeozoic of the Canadian Maritime Provinces had aided resolution of some of the complexities of the Variscan orogeny in Northern Ireland. Although the stratigraphical data accurately delimits the Carboniferous tectonic episodes in Northern Ireland and thus compares well with the Canadian Maritime Provinces, there is no hard data for fault kinematics. The latter is drawn from a comparison with the Canadian geology.

The effects of rifting, dextral strike-slip (transtension), transpression and thermal subsidence are evident in the Carboniferous and early Permian rocks of Northern Ireland. Extensional rift faults controlled the initial expansion of the early Carboniferous epicontinental sea in late Tournaisian—early Viséan times. Localized subsidence, in excess of 2.5 and 1.5 km, of small non-marine basins occurred adjacent to major faults in late Viséan and Westphalian B times respectively. These syn-depositional faults may have been parallel to pre-existing NE—SW trending Caledonide lineaments and were probably dextral. Regional N—S extension acting upon these pre-existing faults would result in dextral transtension, the formation of normal-slip faults with an E—W orientation, and rapid subsidence of small pull-apart basins. From early Brigantian to mid-Arnsbergian times thermal subsidence was the dominant influence on sedimentation although minor contemporaneous faulting persisted. The causes of the mid-Namurian hiatus in Northern Ireland are not known. The end-Variscan deformation is now thought to coincide with a period of transpression that was responsible for the uplift of earlier sedimentary basins and for the non-deposition of late Westphalian, Stephanian and

earliest Permian sediments. Early Permian crustal extension and basin formation may be related to an early phase of North Atlantic rifting.

Current views on the timing of North Atlantic rifting and formation of ocean crust are expressed in two contrasting theories. Russell (1972, 1976) and Haszeldine (1984, 1988) argue that proto-rifting of the North Atlantic, between northeast Canada-Greenland and the British Isles, was evident in Westphalian C—D times and continued into the early Permian. Leeder, however, concluded that spreading only commenced in the early Permian and envisaged an extension of the Maritime Canadian crustal shear zone into the North Atlantic between the British Isles and Greenland (1988, Fig. 9 Inset). The new data presented here does not bear directly on the precise timing of proto-Atlantic rifting but provides new evidence supporting the northeasterly continuation of this shear zone into Northern Ireland. There is evidence for a tectonic episode in Westphalian B, and possibly later, times and by comparison with the Canadian Maritime Provinces it is likely to be dextral. Sinistral transpression associated with N—S compression, affected the Province in the late Westphalian-Stephanian period and resulted in thrusting and strike-slip along the NE—SW Caledonide faults.

The main Carboniferous shear zone in Northern Ireland was located at different times either under or to the north of the Fintona Block (Mitchell & Owens 1990) and is the northeasterly continuation of the Canadian Maritime Provinces plate boundary zone of dominantly dextral strike-slip. It marks the locus of significant palaeogeographical changes and, as the major facies divide, imparted a strong influence on the marine and terrestrial sediments that accumulated adjacent to this zone from late Viséan into Westphalian times.

I thank A. Brandon, A. Chadwick, G. Warrington and two independent referees for their constructive comments on an earlier draft of the manuscript. Publication is by permission of the Director, British Geological Survey (NERC).

References

BELT, E. S. 1968. Carboniferous continental sedimentation, Atlantic Provinces, Canada. *In*: KLEIN, G. de V. (ed.) *Symposium on Late Paleozoic and Mesozoic continental sedimentation, northeastern North America.* Geological Society of America Special Paper, **106**, 27—176.
—— 1969. Newfoundland Carboniferous stratigraphy and its relations to the Maritimes and Ireland.

In: KAY, M. (ed.) *North Atlantic — Geology and Continental Drift*. American Association of Petroleum Geologists Memoir, **12**, 734–753.

BESLY, B. M. 1988. Palaeogeographic implications of late Westphalian to early Permian red beds in Central England. *In*: BESLY, B. M. & KELLING, G. (eds) *Sedimentation in a Synorogenic Basin Complex: the Upper Carboniferous of Northwest Europe*. Blackie, Glasgow, 200–221.

BRADLEY, D. C. 1982. Subsidence in Late Paleozoic basins in the northern Appalachians. *Tectonics*, **1**, 107–123.

BRANDON, A. 1977. *The Meenymore Formation — an extensive intertidal evaporitic formation in the Upper Viséan (B2) of north-west Ireland*. Institute of Geological Sciences Report, 77/23.

—— & HODSON, F. 1984. *Stratigraphy and Palaeontology of the Connaught Coalfield*. Geological Survey of Ireland Special Paper, **6**.

CLAYTON, G. 1986. Late Tournaisian miospores from the Ballycultra Formation at Cultra, County Down, Northern Ireland. *Irish Journal of Earth Sciences*, **8**, 73–79.

FORSTER, S. C. & WARRINGTON, G. 1985. Geochronology of the Carboniferous, Permian and Triassic. *In*: SNELLING, N. J. (ed.) *The Chronology of the Geological Record*. Geological Society Memoir, **10**, 99–113.

FOWLER, A. & ROBBIE, J. A. 1961. *Geology of the country around Dungannon*. Memoir of the Geological Survey of Northern Ireland, **35**, HMSO, Belfast.

GEOLOGICAL SURVEY OF NORTHERN IRELAND (GSNI) 1977. *1:250 000 Geological Map of Northern Ireland*. Belfast.

—— 1984. *1:50 000 Solid Geology of Sheet 47 (Armagh)*. Belfast.

HALL, J., BREWER, J. A., MATTHEWS, D. H. & WARNER, M. R. 1984. Crustal structure across the Caledonides from the WINCH seismic reflection profile: influences on the evolution of the Midland Valley of Scotland. *Transactions of the Royal Society of Edinburgh, Earth Sciences*, **76**, 97–109.

HARLAND, W.B. 1971. Tectonic transpression in Caledonian Spitsbergen. *Geological Magazine*, **108**, 27–42.

HASZELDINE, R. S. 1984. Carboniferous North Atlantic palaeogeography: stratigraphic evidence for rifting, not megashear or subduction. *Geological Magazine*, **121**, 443–463.

—— 1988. Evidence against crustal stretching, north-south tension and Hercynian collision, forming British Carboniferous basins. *In*: ARTHURTON, R. S., GUTTERIDGE, P. & NOLAN, S. C. (eds) *The Role of Tectonics in Devonian and Carboniferous Sedimentation in the British Isles*. Yorkshire Geological Society Occasional Publication, **6**, 25–35.

HESS, J. C. & LIPPOLT, H. J. 1986. ^{40}Ar/^{39}Ar ages of tonstein and tuff sanidines: new calibration points for the improvement of the Upper Carboniferous time scale. *Chemical Geology*, **59**, 143–154.

HIGGS, K. 1984. Stratigraphic palynology of the Carboniferous rocks in northwest Ireland. *Bulletin of the Geological Survey of Ireland*, **3**, 171–196.

HOWIE, R. D. & BARSS, M. S. 1975. Upper Paleozoic rocks of the Atlantic Provinces, Gulf of St. Lawrence and adjacent continental shelf. *Geological Survey of Canada Paper*, **74–30**, 35–50.

HUTTON, D. H. W. 1987. Strike-slip terranes and a model for the evolution of the British and Irish Caledonides. *Geological Magazine*, **124**, 405–425.

LEEDER, M. R. 1988. Recent developments in Carboniferous geology: a critical review with implications for the British Isles and N. W. Europe. *Proceedings of the Geologists' Association*, **99**, 73–100.

McKENZIE, D. P. 1978. Some remarks on the development of sedimentary basins. *Earth and Planetary Science Letters*, **40**, 25–32.

MANNING, P. I., ROBBIE, J. A. & WILSON, H. E. 1970. *Geology of Belfast and the Lagan Valley*. Memoir of the Geological Survey of Northern Ireland, **36**, HMSO, Belfast.

MITCHELL, W. I. & OWENS, B. 1990. The geology of the western part of the Fintona Block, Northern Ireland: evolution of Carboniferous basins. *Geological Magazine*, **127**, 407–426.

MITCHUM, R. M., VAIL, P. R. & THOMPSON, S. 1977. The depositional sequence as a basic unit for stratigraphic analysis. *In*: PAYTON, C. E. (ed.) *Seismic stratigraphy — applications to hydrocarbon exploration*. American Association of Petroleum Geologists Memoir, **26**, 53–62.

ODIN, G. S. & ODIN, C. 1990. Echelle numerique des temps geologiques. *Geochronique*, **35**, 12–21.

PENN, I. E., HOLLIDAY, D. W., KIRBY, G. A., KUBALA, M., SOBEY, R. A., MITCHELL, W. I., HARRISON, R. K. & BECKINSALE, R. D. 1983. The Larne No. 2 Borehole: discovery of a new Permian volcanic centre. *Scottish Journal of Geology*, **19**, 333–346.

RAMSBOTTOM, W. H. C., CALVER, M. A., EAGAR, R. M. C., HODSON, F., HOLLIDAY, D. W., STUBBLEFIELD, C. J. & WILSON, R. B. 1978. *A correlation of Silesian rocks in the British Isles*. Geological Society, London, Special Report, **10**.

READING, H. G. 1980. Characteristics and recognition of strike-slip fault systems. *In*: BALLANCE, P. F. & READING, H. G. (eds) *Sedimentation in oblique-slip mobile zones*. Special Publication of the International Association of Sedimentologists, **4**, 7–26.

ROBESON, D., BURNETT, R. D. & CLAYTON, G. 1988. The Upper Palaeozoic geology of the Porcupine, Erris and Donegal Basins, offshore Ireland. *Irish Journal of Earth Sciences*, **9**, 153–175.

RUSSELL, M. J. 1972. North-south geofractures in Scotland and Ireland. *Scottish Journal of Geology*, **8**, 75–84.

—— 1976. A possible Lower Permian age for the onset of ocean floor spreading in the northern North Atlantic. *Scottish Journal of Geology*, **12**, 315–323.

SEVASTOPULO, G. D. 1981. The Upper Carboniferous. *In*: HOLLAND, C. H. (ed.) *A Geology of Ireland*.

Scottish Academic Press, Edinburgh, 173–187.

SKEHAN, J. W., MURRAY, D. P., HEPBURN, J. C., BILLINGS, M. P., LYONS, P. C. & DOYLE, R. G. 1979. The Mississippian and Pennsylvanian systems in the United States — Massachusetts, Rhode Island and Maine. *United States Geological Survey Professional Paper*, **1110–A**, A1–A30.

SMITH, A. 1985. Geological results of the Lagan Valley groundwater development programme 1977–1984. *Geological Survey of Northern Ireland Open File Report*, No. 71.

SMITH, R. A. 1986. Permo-Triassic and Dinantian rocks of the Belfast Harbour Borehole. *Report of the British Geological Survey*, **18**, No. 6.

——, JOHNSTON, T. P. & LEGG, I. C. 1991. *Geology of the country around Newtownards*. Memoir of the Geological Survey of Northern Ireland, **37**, HMSO, Belfast.

TATE, M. P. & DOBSON, M. R. 1989. Pre-Mesozoic geology of the western and north-western Irish continental shelf. *Journal of the Geological Society, London*, **146**, 229–241.

THOMPSON, S. J. 1979. Preliminary report on the Ballymacilroy No. 1 Borehole, Ahoghill, Co. Antrim. *Geological Survey of Northern Ireland Open File Report*, No. 63.

WILSON, H. E. 1981. Permian and Mesozoic. *In*: HOLLAND, C. H. (ed.) *A Geology of Ireland*, Scottish Academic Press. Edinburgh, 201–212.

—— 1983. Deep drilling in Northern Ireland since 1947. *Irish Naturalists Journal*, **21**, 160–163.

YATES, P. J. 1962. The palaeontology of the Namurian rocks of Slieve Anierin, Co Leitrim, Eire. *Palaeontology*, **5**, 355–443.

YEO, G. M. 1985. Upper Carboniferous sedimentation in northern Nova Scotia and the origin of Stellarton Basin. *In*: *Current Research, Part B, Geological Survey of Canada Paper*, **85–1B**, 511–518.

Evolution of the Carboniferous Lough Allen Basin, Northwest Ireland

M. E. PHILCOX, H. BAILY, G. CLAYTON & G. D. SEVASTOPULO

Department of Geology, Trinity College, Dublin 2, Ireland

Abstract: The Lough Allen Basin contains approximately 2.9 km of Dinantian (Courceyan) to Silesian (Arnsbergian) limestone, mudstone and sandstone, mostly of marine origin. The basin was initiated during the Courceyan Stage as a result of movement of the basin margin fault complex along the southeast side of the Ox Mountains inlier. The main rifting phase, during the late Courceyan, resulted in the deposition of a southeasterly thinning, initially non-marine, clastic wedge. The intrabasinal Dowra−Macnean High and Slisgarrow Trough developed during the Chadian Stage. Movement on the Curlew fault, which bounds the basin to the south, may have begun in the Courceyan but culminated in the Arundian. There is little direct evidence of fault-controlled sedimentation in the Holkerian and much of the Asbian, although the distribution of carbonate mudmounds of Asbian age in part coincides with earlier structural elements. During the late Asbian, there appears to have been renewed tectonic activity, which led to substantial regional differences of thickness of the lower formations of the Leitrim Group. There is little evidence of tectonic control on sedimentation from the Brigantian to the Arnsbergian.

Vitrinite reflectance determinations show that the Carboniferous rocks in the basin are supra-mature for the generation of oil but are mature with respect to the generation of gas. The maturation values for the youngest preserved rocks suggest that they have been buried under 3−5 km of Upper Palaeozoic cover.

Carboniferous (Dinantian and Silesian) rocks occur widely in northwest Ireland (Fig. 1), surrounding inliers of varied pre-Carboniferous rocks. These include Precambrian metamorphic basement in the Ox Mountains; Lower Palaeozoic slates and greywackes in the Longford−Down inlier; and Lower Devonian shales, sandstones and conglomerates in the Fintona Block and Curlew Mountains. The inliers resulted from uplift on segments of several of the long northeast trending faults which traverse the region. The Carboniferous rocks, which consist of mixed carbonates, terrigenous sandstones and shales, of Dinantian age, and Silesian shales, sandstones and thin coals, have been the target for the exploration for hydrocarbons.

Drilling programmes in the Lough Allen Basin (Fig. 1) were carried out by Ambassador Irish Oil Company in 1963−1966 (Sheridan 1977) and by a consortium led by Aran Energy plc in 1984−1985. The Dowra-1 well, drilled in the earlier phase of exploration, flowed gas at 31 000 cfd (Sheridan 1977). Cores from boreholes drilled by mineral exploration companies and the Geological Survey of Ireland (GSI) have provided stratigraphical information in areas marginal to the basin. The locations of the wells and boreholes discussed below are shown in Fig. 1.

The purpose of this paper is to outline the depositional, structural and maturation histories of the basin, based mainly on new subsurface information. This information is derived mostly from cuttings and interpretation of wireline logs of the deep wells, and from diamond drill cores from the shorter, mineral exploration boreholes. The hydrocarbon wells have been dated mainly by means of palynology, with additional information from foraminifera. Because the wells were originally logged in feet, down-hole depths are also recorded in feet in this account.

The Lough Allen Basin, named after the lake near its centre (Fig. 1; Sheridan 1977), contains rocks of late Courceyan (Dinantian) to Arnsbergian (Silesian) age. Successions proved by the drilling within the basin are generally thicker than elsewhere in northwest Ireland (Fig. 2). The northwest margin of the basin is sharply defined by a contemporaneous fault complex southeast of the Ox−Ballyshannon High. The southern margin is sharply demarcated by the Curlew Mountains fault on the north side of the Curlews inlier in the west, but its position further east is not known. Although the succession in the Ballymote syncline (Fig. 1) is known to be relatively thin (Dixon 1972 and unpublished borehole information), no distinct western margin of the basin has been identified. To the east, the present extent of the Dinantian is controlled by the Lower Lough Erne fault (Mitchell & Owens 1990), but it is not clear whether this formed the basin margin. Most

From PARNELL, J. (ed.), 1992, *Basins on the Atlantic Seaboard: Petroleum Geology, Sidementology and Basin Evolution*. Geological Society Special Publication No 62, pp 203−215.

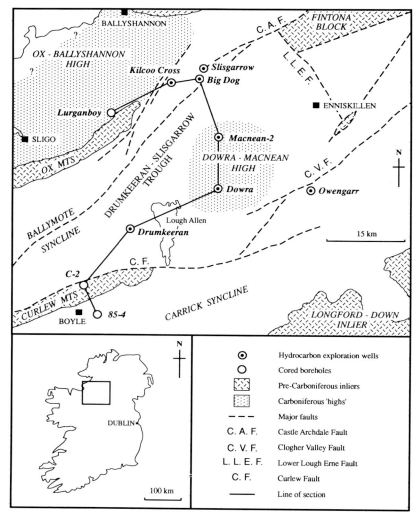

Fig. 1. Outline geology of northwest Ireland, showing the location of wells and other names referred to in the text.

formations recognized within the basin extend beyond the margins identified above. However, the margins can be recognized from thickness changes and, in some cases, from facies changes.

Within the Lough Allen Basin, two intra-basinal features, the Dowra–Macnean High and the Drumkeeran–Slisgarrow Trough (Fig. 1), are postulated here from subsurface information. Mapped folds and faults in the basin (Sheridan 1972; Price & Max 1988; Mitchell & Owens 1990) are mostly the product of Variscan tectonism, post-dating the preserved basin fill, but some faults were active during sedimentation.

Stratigraphy

The successions in the gas exploration wells (Figs 2 & 3) are based on wireline and litho-logical logs completed by one of us (M.E.P.), except for Dowra-1 and Big Dog-1, which were described by Sheridan (1972, 1977). Thicknesses of formations shown in the figures are 'down-hole'; dips are typically 5–20°. Successions in areas marginal to the basin are based on outcrop data (Oswald 1955; Caldwell 1959; Dixon 1972), supplemented by boreholes drilled by the Geological Survey of Ireland and mineral exploration companies (unpublished logs). The

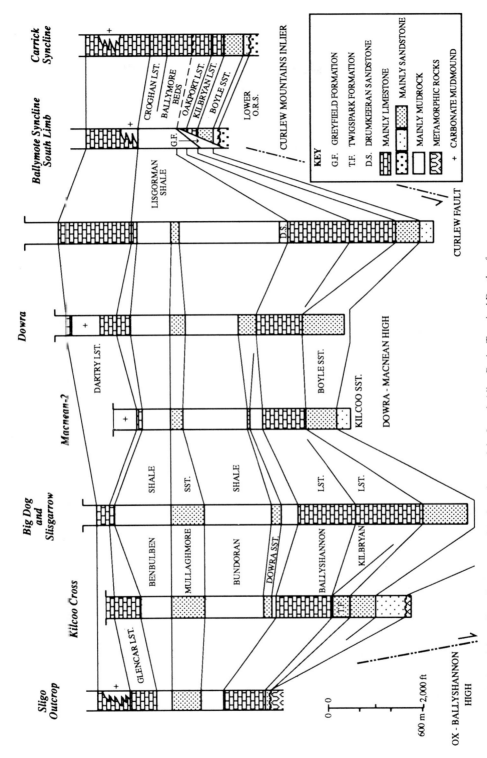

Fig. 2. Correlation of the wells and outcrop sections in and around the Lough Allen Basin. Terminal Depths of the gas exploration wells are as follows: Kilcoo Cross, 6269 ft; Big Dog, 6569 ft; Slisgarrow, 6557 ft; Macnean No. 2, 4968 ft; Dowra, 6005 ft; Drumkeeran, 8236 ft. Well locations are shown in Fig. 1. Sligo section after Oswald (1955); Ballymote Syncline section from Philcox *et al.* (1989); Carrick Syncline section after Caldwell (1959).

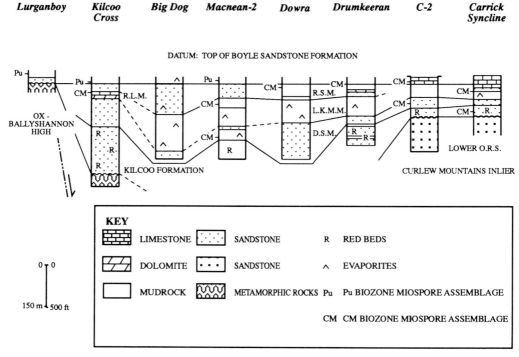

Fig. 3. Facies and thickness variation of the Kilcoo Sandstone and Boyle Sandstone Formations. D.S.M., Drumbrick Sandstone Member; L.K.M.M., Lough Key Mudstone Member; R.S.M., Rockingham Sandstone Member; R.L.M., Rosskit Limestone Member. Well locations are shown in Fig. 1.

stratigraphical terms used here are mainly those in George *et al.* (1976), which have been amended to conform with modern stratigraphical practice. In addition, several new formations and members are defined in this paper: the Kilcoo Sandstone Formation; the Boyle Sandstone Formation (redefined), containing the Drumbrick Sandstone, Lough Key Mudstone, Rockingham Sandstone, and Rosskit Limestone Members; the Twigspark Formation; and the Drumkeeran Sandstone Member. The stratigraphical units are described briefly below.

Kilcoo Sandstone Formation (new name)

This name replaces the Upper Old Red Sandstone of Sheridan (1972). The type section of the formation is designated in Kilcoo Cross-1 from 5590 to 6170 ft (1704–1881 m). This interval consists mainly of pink to red, fine to very coarse sandstone and conglomerate. The formation here rests on metamorphic basement. The top contact, which is sharp, is placed at the top of the pink- and red-dominant succession.

Seismic sections (unpublished, except for the line illustrated by Price & Max (1988) and made available to us by Aran Energy plc) show that the formation in this well forms the lower part of a large clastic wedge, which thins southeastward towards the basin centre.

In Macnean-2, the predominant lithology is pink, green and grey silty mudstone, with common caliche carbonate. In Drumkeeran-1, the formation, while predominantly red, includes some pale grey sandstone and a higher proportion of mudstone than at Kilcoo. In C-2 and GSI-85-4, the formation consists of stacked cycles, each grading from coarse, pale grey or greenish sandstone to a thin cap of red mudstone. The formation is absent on the Ox–Ballyshannon High.

There is no direct palaeontological evidence for the age of this formation. Because it is conformably overlain by rocks containing late Courceyan miospore assemblages and because late Devonian rocks have not been found north of the Irish Midlands (Higgs *et al.* 1988), it is likely to be of Courceyan rather than Devonian age.

Boyle Sandstone Formation (redefined)

The name 'Boyle Sandstone Formation' is proposed for the succession of predominantly pale grey sandstones and mudstones with occasional beds of micrite, dolomicrite and evaporitic sulphate, which occurs between the Kilcoo Sandstone Formation and the fully marine carbonate sequence in the Lough Allen Basin and around the Curlew Mountains inlier. The name is derived from 'Boyle Sandstone Group' (Caldwell 1959), but the interval containing red sandstones in the lower part of Caldwell's lithological unit is here specifically excluded. 'Boyle Sandstone Formation' replaces 'Basal Clastics' (Brunton & Mason 1979) and 'Basal Sandstones, Limestones and Shales' (Sheridan 1972).

The designated type section is in the Geological Survey of Ireland borehole 85−4 (Fig. 1) at 188.5−256.4 m. The base of the formation is placed at the base of the lowest dark grey mudstone, which is approximately 1.2 m above the highest red mudstone and 3 m below the lowest dolomicrite. In the underlying Kilcoo Formation in GSI-85−4, red beds, mainly mudstone, are subordinate to pale grey and pink sandstone. In the deep gas exploration wells the two formations contrast more sharply, because red beds predominate in the lower formation. However, GSI-85−4 is preferred as a type section, because it was drilled in the type area of Caldwell's Boyle Sandstone and because it was cored throughout.

Schopfites claviger−Auroraspora macra. (CM) Biozone miospore assemblages have been recorded from the Boyle Sandstone Formation in several sections (see Fig. 3). These indicate a late Courceyan age (Clayton et al. 1978).

The formation is divided into three members that extend across most of the Lough Allen Basin; their names are derived from localities around the Curlew Mountains; a fourth member is recognized only in Kilcoo Cross-1.

Drumbrick Sandstone Member. This member, whose type section is from 233.3−256.4 m in GSI-85−4, typically consists of pale grey sandstone with varying but subordinate amounts of pale pink and green beds in the lower part. It exhibits considerable lateral variation in lithology. In Kilcoo Cross-1 the sandstone is mainly coarse and pebbly; it forms the upper part of the clastic wedge noted on seismic sections. In Macnean-2, nearer the basin centre, the member is thinner and consists of silty mudstone with scattered evaporitic sulphates and rare sandstone. In Dowra-1 (Fig. 3), an exceptionally thick sequence of pale pink, green and grey sandstone and mudstone (mainly silty) was reported by Sheridan (1972). The relative thicknesses suggest interfingering with the Kilcoo Formation in this area. In Drumkeeran-1, pale grey, fine to medium sandstone predominates. The greater proportion of sandstone in comparison to Macnean-1, Macnean-2 and Dowra-1 suggests a location closer to the basin margin. In C-2, the member consists of units 3 to 4.5 m thick, grading upwards from pale grey sandstone into greenish mudstone. In GSI-85−4, the member is similar, but the mudstones are dark grey. Rare dolomicrite and micrite beds in both C-2 and GSI-85−4 reflect sporadic development of marginal marine environments.

Lough Key Mudstone Member. In most of the wells in the Lough Allen Basin this member consists of grey, green and tan mudstone, with minor amounts of sandstone, micrite, dolomicrite and evaporitic sulphate. In the type section in GSI-85−4, (205.6−233.3 m), it consists mainly of units of black mudstone less than 3.5 m thick, with thin interbeds of burrowed sandstone, micrite, shell bands and evaporites. The member is not present in Kilcoo Cross-1.

Rockingham Sandstone Member. In the type section, GSI-85−4, this member is 17 m thick (188.5−205.6 m) and consists of burrowed, light grey, fine sandstone, overlain by sandy biosparite. In Dowra-1 and Drumkeeran-1, the member is c. 50 m thick and consists of mudstone and both silty and crinoidal limestone, with subordinate fine sandstone. Further north the member is an easily distinguished, pale grey sandstone. In Macnean-2, it consists of 47 m of very fine to medium sandstone. In Slisgarrow-1 and Big Dog-1, the sandstone is c. 106 m thick and is locally very coarse and pebbly. It thins towards Kilcoo Cross (30 m), where it is finer grained. The overall thickness and lithofacies trends suggest derivation of sand from the north or northeast, rather than from the direction of the Ox−Ballyshannon High. Palynofacies evidence indicates a non-marine environment in Slisgarrow-1 and a marine environment in Kilcoo Cross-1, which is consistent with the facies pattern.

In C-2, Member 3 has not been identified, but whether this reflects facies change or non-deposition is not clear.

Rosskit Limestone Member. In Kilcoo Cross-1, the Drumbrick and Rockingham Members are separated by 21 m of sandy, crinoidal limestone (5190−5256 ft), which is partly dolomitized. The Lough Key Member is absent in this well.

Kilbryan Limestone Formation

Caldwell (1959) proposed this formation based on scattered exposures in the Carrick syncline. He did not specify a type section. The interval from 89.2 to 188.5 m in GSI-85−4 is here designated as the type section. In GSI-85−4, the formation consists of argillaceous, commonly bioturbated limestone and subordinate mudstone. In Drumkeeran-1, Slisgarrow-1 and Big Dog-1, the formation is much thicker and more argillaceous. It is absent in Macnean-1, Dowra-1 and Kilcoo Cross-1, and on the Ox−Ballyshannon High. Whether the Kilbryan Formation passes laterally into the lower part of the Ballyshannon Limestone in these areas or has been removed by erosion is not known.

CM Biozone miospore assemblages have been recorded from the base of the Kilbryan Limestone in C-2 (McPhilemy 1988). In several other sections (see Fig. 3), *Lycospora pusilla* (Pu) Biozone miospore assemblages have been obtained from horizons low in the formation. The CM/Pu zonal boundary is considered to correlate approximately with the Courceyan/Chadian boundary (Clayton *et al.* 1978; Higgs *et al.* 1988).

Twigspark Formation (new formation)

The Twigspark Formation consists of sandstone, sandy limestone, and mudstone with minor amounts of micrite and evaporitic sulphate. The name is derived from the townland near Lurganboy, County Leitrim (Fig. 1), where boreholes which include the type section were drilled. The cores are stored by the Geological Survey of Ireland. The type section is designated in core LIT.70−10 at 39.6−90.4 m (T.D.), which is structurally undisturbed, but which terminated without reaching basement. The bottom part of the formation is more completely represented in LIT.70−9 below 90 m, but is partly faulted; the contact with underlying basement quartzite is at 110.4 m. The top of the formation is placed at the sharp top of a black, unfossiliferous mudstone *c.* 3 m thick, which is overlain by coarse crinoidal limestone of the Ballyshannon Limestone. The full thickness of the formation here is *c.* 65 m. The Twigspark Formation is known only from the type area, which is a few kilometres northwest of the basin margin, and in Kilcoo Cross-1, where it is lithologically similar but thicker (Fig. 2).

Pu Biozone miospore assemblages from the Twigspark Formation indicate a Chadian (or younger) age (Higgs 1984).

Ballyshannon Limestone Formation

Oswald (1955) described this formation from exposures around Ballyshannon on the Ox−Ballyshannon High (Fig. 1) where it consists of pale grey, crinoidal limestone of shallow-water origin (referred to below as 'shelf' facies). In the Lough Allen Basin, the formation consists of dark grey, argillaceous, crinoidal limestone with subordinate mudstone (Sheridan 1972), which is referred to below as 'basinal' facies.

Foraminifera are rare in the basinal successions encountered in the deep wells, but diagnostic Arundian microfaunas were identified in the upper half of the Ballyshannon Formation in Drumkeeran-1. The shelf sequences of the Ballyshannon Formation range from Chadian at the base to Arundian (George *et al.* 1976). Pu Biozone miospore assemblages, indicating a Chadian to Arundian age, have been recorded from the Ballyshannon Limestone Formation, and the younger Bundoran Shale Formation, and the Dowra Sandstone and the Drumkeeran Sandstone Members, described below.

Oakport Limestone Formation

This formation was described by Caldwell (1959) and occurs in the Carrick and Ballymote synclines (Fig. 1). It consists of skeletal and peloidal packstone and grainstone deposited in shallow water environments and is the lateral equivalent of part of the Ballyshannon Formation. In the Carrick syncline it is of Chadian age (Philcox *et al.* 1989).

Bundoran Shale Formation

This formation, described by Oswald (1955), consists of dark grey, calcareous mudstone with thin limestones. Two sandstone members are distinguished in the lower part of the formation (Fig. 2). Faunas from the type area of the Bundoran Shale Formation indicate an Arundian age (George *et al.* 1976). No diagnostic microfaunas were found in the deep gas exploration wells.

Dowra Sandstone Member. Sheridan (1972) described the Dowra Sandstone from Dowra-1, where it consists of silty mudstone with subordinate sandstone. In Kilcoo Cross-1 and Big Dog-1, it consists of *c.* 53 m of sandstone, which at some horizons is coarse grained and locally is pebbly. In Macnean-2, it is thinner (*c.* 25 m) and generally finer grained. Variations in the grain size and the proportion of sandstone in these wells is consistent with derivation from the north (Sheridan 1972). The Dowra Member has not been identified on the Ox–Ballyshannon High or elsewhere at outcrop.

Drumkeeran Sandstone Member (new member)

The type section for the Drumkeeran Sandstone Member is between 5215–5320 ft (1589.5–1621.5 m; 56 m thick) in Drumkeeran-1. It consists of pale grey, mainly fine, but locally coarse, sandstone and silty mudstone. The bottom contact with the Ballyshannon Formation is sharp. The top contact is gradational through c. 6 m into overlying mudstone. Well preserved spores and coarse vascular plant debris in one sample from this Member suggest proximity to land. The Drumkeeran Member is generally coarser grained than the Dowra Member in Dowra No. 1. It is tentatively interpreted as a southerly derived, basin-equivalent of the Greyfield Formation.

Greyfield Formation

This formation, described by Philcox et al. (1989) from the north side of the Curlew Mountains inlier, consists of a complex sequence of locally derived sandstone breccia, carbonate mudmound, polymict conglomerate and graded sandstones. The formation overlies a local unconformity where as much as 360 m of Oakport Limestone and underlying beds have been eroded. Erosion was a consequence of Arundian uplift on the Curlew Mountains fault (Fig. 1).

Mullaghmore Sandstone Formation

This formation was described by Oswald (1955) from coastal exposures west of the Ox Mountains inlier. In Kilcoo Cross-1, Big Dog-1 and Slisgarrow-1, it is between 195 and 217 m thick and consists of pale grey sandstone (rarely coarser than medium grained) and silty mudstone, with subsidiary limestone. In Macnean-2, it is thinner (87 m) and has a lower proportion of sandstone. In Dowra-1, it is 93 m thick and consists mainly of silty mudstone. In Drumkeeran-1, it is represented only by silty mudstone, but it is still easily recognized on wireline logs. The pattern of thickness and grain size changes indicate that the sandstone was derived from between northwest and northeast (Sheridan 1972).

A Knoxisporites triradiatus — K. stephanephorus (TS) Biozone miospore assemblage, indicating an Arundian–Holkerian age, was recorded from the Mullaghmore Formation in Slisgarrow-1. Higgs (1984) recorded TS Biozone assemblages from the Mullaghmore Sandstone Formation at outcrop at several localities in northwest Ireland.

Benbulben Shale Formation

This formation was described by Oswald (1955) from outcrops in County Sligo on the Ox–Ballyshannon High. It is similar to the Bundoran Shale Formation, but is more calcareous and fossiliferous. Its thickness varies substantially in the northern part of the basin (Fig. 2). Lithological and wireline log correlations show that the relatively thin succession in Macnean-2 is laterally equivalent to only the lower half of the formation in Slisgarrow-1 (and probably Big Dog-1). The formation in Kilcoo Cross-1, Drumkeeran-1 and Dowra-1 is similar to that in Macnean-1 and Macnean-2. At Slisgarrow, the upper half of the formation includes several distinct limestone tongues up to 6 m thick, which appear from wireline logs to correlate with similar thick, limestones within the Glencar Limestone Formation in Kilcoo Cross-1. The upper part of the Benbulben Shale Formation in the Slisgarrow-Big Dog area is therefore interpreted as interfingering with the Glencar Limestone Formation on a large scale, which explains the thickness variations of the two formations.

A Perotrilites tesseletus — Schulzospora campyloptera (TC) Biozone miospore assemblage was obtained from a single sample in the middle of the Benbulben Shale Formation in Slisgarrow-1, indicating a Holkerian-Asbian age. Higgs (1984) recorded TC Biozone assemblages from the formation at several localities, and a TS Biozone assemblage from low in the formation in Macnean-1 (559.7 m).

Glencar Limestone Formation

This formation, described by Oswald (1955), consists of argillaceous limestone and calcareous mudstone, and is cyclic in some areas (Schwarzacher 1964). The lithological succession within the formation varies widely between the wells. The Glencar Formation in the Lough Allen Basin is believed to be a diachronous transitional facies between the Benbulben Shale and the Dartry Limestone Formations.

Dartry Limestone Formation

Two main facies are present in this formation, first described by Oswald (1955): carbonate mudmounds ('reefs') and well bedded, dark, cherty limestone (Schwarzacher 1961; Brunton & Mason 1979). The formation thins towards the Slisgarrow–Big Dog area (Fig. 2). However, the thickness of the interval 'top-Mullaghmore to top-Dartry' does not change in this area and the thickness pattern apparently reflects lateral passage from Dartry Limestone through Glencar into Benbulben Shale. In Drumkeeran-1, the formation consists of pale cherty limestone similar to the Bricklieve Limestone Formation which crops out in the Ballymote syncline (Caldwell & Charlesworth 1962; Dixon 1972).

A *Raistrickia nigra* – *Triquitrites marginatus* (NM) Biozone miospore assemblage was recorded from the Dartry Limestone Formation in Slisgarrow-1, indicating a late Asbian age.

Leitrim Group

The Leitrim Group, comprehensively reviewed by Brandon & Hodson (1984), overlies the Dartry Limestone Formation, and is preserved in the upland area surrounding Lough Allen and between Lough Macnean and Lough Erne in County Fermanagh. Strata within the Leitrim Group were intersected in three wells. Dowra-1 and Slisgarrow-1 spudded in the Meenymore Formation; and Drumkeeran-1 spudded in the Dergvone Shale Formation.

The preserved succession (Fig. 4) is at most 520 m thick (Brandon & Hodson 1984) and ranges from late Asbian to Arnsbergian in age. The Meenymore Formation (Brandon 1977), of late Asbian age, consists of a complex, cyclical succession of rare, thin, marine, goniatite-bearing shales; stromatolitic limestones, dolomicrites and evaporites; and barren, greenish grey mudstone with thin, flaggy sandstone of fluviatile origin. The basal contact is typically sharp, and locally probably disconformable, but in some areas it is transitional through tens of metres. The Glenade Sandstone Formation is a southward-thinning wedge of coarse to medium-grained sandstone, which has been interpreted as being of deltaic origin. The Bellavally Formation is lithologically similar to the Meenymore Formation, but contains more numerous goniatite-bearing mudstones; the higher part of the formation contains goniatites of the P1b Zone, so that the Asbian/Brigantian boundary probably lies within it (cf. Brandon & Hodson 1984). The Carraun Shale Formation

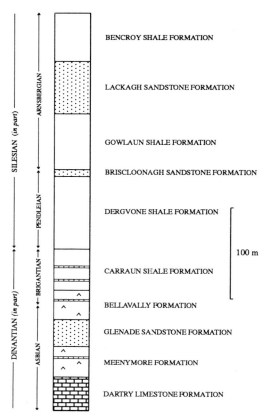

Fig. 4. Outline stratigraphy of the Dartry Limestone Formation and the Leitrim Group in the Lough Allen Basin. Data from Brandon & Hodson (1984). Ornament as in Fig. 2.

represents a change from the carbonate and evaporite-rich facies of the lower formations to the mudstone-dominated facies of the Dergvone Shale (E1), Gowlaun Shale (E2a) and Bencroy Shale (E2b) Formations. The latter contain goniatite-bearing, commonly calcareous shale; barren silty shale; and rare sandstones, some of which are turbidites. They are interpreted as having been deposited in deeper water than the lower part of the Leitrim Group. The Briscloonagh Sandstone Formation consists mostly of northerly derived turbidites, and the Lackagh Sandstone Formation, which contains thin coals in the region around Lough Allen, has been interpreted as being of deltaic origin.

Most of the thickness variation recorded by Brandon & Hodson (1984) is related to north-to-south thinning of the sandstone formations. They found little evidence of control by the major faults, except across the line of the Clogher

Valley fault (Fig. 1), where the Meenymore Formation is five times thicker on the southern side. Some thickness variation appears to reflect relict topography of carbonate mudmounds in the Dartry Limestone Formation.

Summary of Basin Evolution (Fig. 5)

Courceyan

Non-marine phase. This is represented by the Kilcoo Formation and the Drumbrick Sandstone Member of the Boyle Sandstone Formation.

Evidence for the initial phase of evolution of the basin is available only near its margins (Fig. 3). The oldest rocks are of non-marine, red bed facies (Kilcoo Formation). The basin was bounded on its northwest side by an active, northeast-trending fault complex. The Kilcoo Formation, interpreted as Courceyan in age, formed the lower part of a southerly thinning wedge and is coarser in the northwest than in the basin centre and along the southern margin. Thickness and facies trends are consistent with the development of alluvial fans along the northwest margin of an active half graben. There is no evidence (Fig. 5A) that the intra-basinal Dowra–Macnean High and Slisgarrow Trough had been differentiated. The change from red beds to grey sandstone of the Boyle Sandstone in CM Miospore Biozone times heralded a marine transgression from the south (Philips & Sevastopulo 1986).

Marginal marine phase. This is represented by the Lough Key Mudstone and Rosskit Limestone Members of the Boyle Sandstone Formation (CM miospore Biozone).

A reduced influx of coarse clastic sediment was accompanied across most of the basin by intermittent marine incursions, which resulted in the formation of micrite, dolomicrite and evaporitic sulphate (Boyle Sandstone Formation, Lough Key Mudstone Member). The relationship with the clastic wedge along the northwest margin of the basin is unknown; the evaporitic sequence, assumed to be younger, may partly overlap the wedge. Alternatively, the evaporitic environment may not have extended to this part of the basin, as outlined below.

The Lough Key Member is not present in Kilcoo Cross-1, in which the Rosskit Limestone Member directly overlies the Drumbrick Member. It is not known whether the Rosskit Member is the time-equivalent of the Lough Key Member. The fully marine conditions represented in Kilcoo Cross-1 were apparently confined to a narrow gulf along the downthrown side of the basin-margin fault. This must reflect differential subsidence. A possible explanation is that the Kilcoo Cross area was at the deeper-water end of a tilted, hanging wall block. The marine connection between Kilcoo Cross and the established shelf sea to the south must have been along the western margin of the basin.

Marine phase. This is represented by the Rockingham Sandstone Member of the Boyle Sandstone Formation and, in the south, by the lower part (which yields CM Biozone miospore assemblages) of the Kilbryan Limestone Formation.

Renewed influx of sand, derived now from the northeast rather than northwest, reflects uplift outside the basin. The sandstone passes south into finer-grained clastic facies with inter-tonguing limestone (Drumkeeran-1); the upper part of the Rockingham Member may be the time-equivalent of the lower part of the muddy limestone (Kilbryan Limestone Formation) in the Curlew Mountains area. There was now marine deposition across most of the basin. Palynofacies analysis suggests that the shoreline lay between Slisgarrow (non-marine) and Kilcoo Cross. The Ox–Ballyshannon High remained emergent.

Chadian-Arundian (part)

During the deposition of the Kilbryan and Ballyshannon Limestone Formations (Pu Miospore Biozone) there was an important phase of differential subsidence within the basin, which gave rise to the Dowra–Macnean High and the Drumkeeran–Slisgarrow Trough (Fig. 5B). A thick sequence of muddy marine sediments accumulated in the trough (basinal facies of the Kilbryan Limestone), but much less, if any, on the Dowra–Macnean High. During the Chadian, the sea transgressed the Ox–Ballyshannon High. The Twigspark Formation, of Chadian age, represents the initial transgressive facies on the edge of the High, extending as an apron along the basin margin. During deposition of the Ballyshannon Limestone, there was further transgression and the area of marine deposition expanded well beyond the Lough Allen Basin. The precise timing of the initial transgression in relation to differential subsidence within the basin is uncertain.

The main phase of differential subsidence within the basin terminated before the end of Ballyshannon Limestone deposition (Arundian). However, the limits of the basin are reflected in the distribution of the basin and shelf facies of the Ballyshannon Limestone. The Curlew Mountains area (Fig. 1) was a high

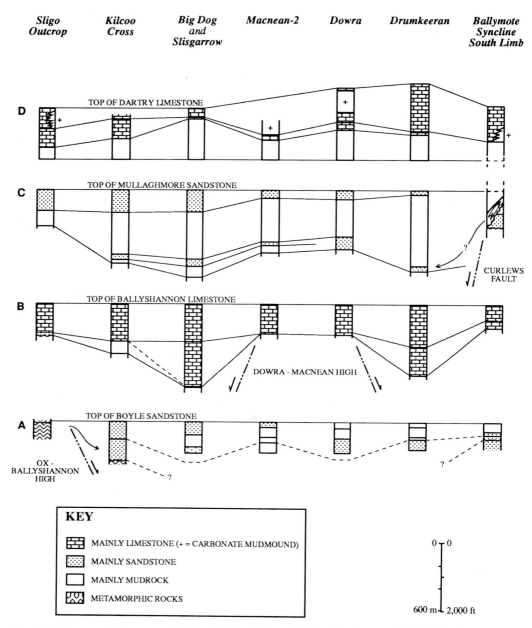

Fig. 5. Thickness variation across the Lough Allen Basin: A, Kilcoo Sandstone and Boyle Sandstone Formation; B, Kilbryan Limestone Formation. Twigspark Formation (unornamented) and Ballyshannon Limestone Formation; C, Bundoran Shale Formation and Mullaghmore Sandstone Formation (upper unit with stipple). D, Benbulben Shale to Dartry Limestone Formations. See Fig. 1 for location of wells and Figs 2 & 3 for details of stratigraphy.

and only a thin sequence of shelf facies limestone (Oakport Limestone) was deposited on it.

Arundian (part) — Holkerian (part)

During the deposition of the Bundoran Shale Formation (Pu Miospore Biozone), the Lough Allen Basin continued to subside. The Dowra—Macnean High affected sediment thickness less than in the preceding period. The Dowra and Drumkeeran Sandstone Members are restricted to the basin and may reflect uplift around the margin. Philcox *et al.* (1989) have described major uplift and erosion of the northern margin of the Curlew Mountains High during the Arundian. In contrast, the Mullaghmore Sandstone (TS and TC Miospore Biozones) is widely distributed in northwest Ireland. It is likely to reflect tectonic uplift in source areas far removed from the Lough Allen Basin. Its geometry in the basin (Fig. 5C) is a wedge that thins to the south; the thinning is accompanied by a reduction in grain size.

Holkerian (part) — Asbian (part)

This interval is represented by the deposition of the Benbulben Shale, Glencar and Dartry Limestone Formations (TS, TC & NM Miospore Biozones).

The top of the Mullaghmore Sandstone Formation is sharp, reflecting an abrupt cessation of the transport of sand into the basin. Widespread mud deposition, represented by the Benbulben Shale, resumed, both within and to the northwest of the basin. Wireline and lithological log correlations suggest that subsidence throughout the basin at this time was uniform; the thick development of Benbulben Shale in the Big Dog and Slisgarrow area (Fig. 5D) is a result of its diachronous boundary with the overlying Glencar Limestone.

The Dartry Limestone Formation occurs in both carbonate mudmound and bedded facies. There does not appear to be a simple relationship between the distribution of mudmounds and the basin architecture. However, it is noteworthy that the Dowra-Macnean High was the site of extensive mudmound development; and several areas of the basin margin also are characterized by mudmounds. The thin development of the Dartry Formation in the Big Dog—Slisgarrow area, attributed by Sheridan (1972) to the influence of the Ox—Ballyshannon High, actually occurs within the basin and seems to be a consequence of lateral facies changes between the Benbulben, Glencar and Dartry Formations. The aggregate thickness of these

three formations varies very little in this part of the basin.

Asbian (part) — Arnsbergian

This interval corresponds to the deposition of the Leitrim Group. The Meenymore Formation reflects widespread regression which resulted in shallower water, evaporitic facies of variable thickness across the Lough Allen Basin and Ox—Ballyshannon High. At the same time there was substantial erosion on the Fintona Block (Michell & Owens 1990). Significant syn-sedimentary fault movement is indicated by a fivefold thickness increase of the Meenymore Formation southwards across the Clogher Valley fault (Fig. 1; Brandon & Hodson 1984). Further northeast, on approximately this trend, thick conglomerates accumulated in a basin on the southern margin of the uplifted Fintona Block (Mitchell & Owens 1990). Mitchell (this volume) has argued that the pronounced thinning of the late Asbian Glenade Sandstone Formation (which overlies the Meenymore Formation) from 300 m in the north to 4 m south of Lough Allen is evidence that it was deposited in an active half graben.

In the younger part of the Leitrim Group, mudstones, sandstones and subsidiary limestones (Fig. 4) accumulated across the Lough Allen Basin. In general the sandstones thin southwards away from their northern source, and the mudstones thicken in the same direction. On the Fintona Block, substantial fault-controlled uplift, erosion and deposition of conglomerates took place, mainly between the Arnsbergian and Westphalian B, younger than the preserved succession in the Lough Allen Basin. The northwest-trending Lower Lough Erne fault (Fig. 1) was an important structural boundary; some of the syn-sedimentary faults on the Fintona Block cannot be recognized to the southwest.

Post-Arnsbergian Cover

It is clear from the maturation studies, discussed below, that as much as 3—5 km of Silesian cover has been removed from the Lough Allen Basin.

Maturation

Organic maturation of the Lough Allen Basin sediments has been established on the basis of mean random vitrinite reflectance (%Rm), spore colour, and, where applicable, spore fluorescence. Vitrinite reflectance (Rm) in the well sections ranges from 0.9% to just over 4%.

The level of maturity appears to be governed largely by depth of burial. Vitrinite reflectances of samples from the same stratigraphical horizons vary laterally, with lower reflectances over structural highs. Some local variation in maturation values has been observed close to small-scale igneous intrusions of presumed Tertiary age in the Arigna Coalfield immediately west of Lough Allen.

Maturation is interpreted as being the product of Upper Carboniferous, rather than Mesozoic burial. Vitrinite reflectance from Permian rocks, which unconformably overlie the Carboniferous in the adjacent offshore Erris Trough, are low, at around 0.3% Rm (Robeson 1989), indicating that there has not been substantial post-Permian burial in the latter area. This is believed also to be the case in the Lough Allen Basin.

The rocks of the Lough Allen Basin are generally supra-mature with respect to oil generation, although some samples close to the present-day surface fall within the oil window. Most of the Dinantian succession penetrated by the exploration wells is mature with respect to gas generation, but the deepest levels in the walls are supra-mature.

Discussion

The fault complex along the southern margin of the Ox Mountains was a major basin-bounding structure in the Courceyan, but its effect was much reduced after the Chadian transgression across the Ox Mountains. The Curlew Mountains fault may have been active in the Courceyan. It clearly influenced Chadian thickness and facies, but its activity culminated in the Arundian. The Dowra–Macnean High developed rapidly during the Chadian, but was much less active thereafter. Some of the major faults in and around the basin have thus had an important controlling influence on sedimentation, but their main movements have been out of phase with each other. They were variously reactivated during the Hercynian, together with other faults that appear to have been nearly dormant since the Devonian. Although the controlling faults were clearly quiescent for long periods, the main pulses of movement were not synchronous across the basin.

We thank Aran Energy plc, in particular Mr T. Earls, for access to data and samples, and for permission to publish; Mr J. F. Kenny, Northwest Exploration, Ltd for facilitating our study; the Department of Energy (Petroleum Affairs Division), in particular Dr K. Robinson, for access to samples; the Geological Survey of Ireland, in particular Dr R. Horne, for access to borehole cores. We are especially grateful to Mr C. V. MacDermot (Geological Survey of Ireland) for helpful discussion.

References

BRANDON, A. 1977. *The Meenymore Formation — an extensive intertidal evaporite formation in the Upper Viséan (B2) of northwest Ireland.* Institute of Geological Sciences Report No. 77/23.

—— & HODSON, F. 1984. *The Stratigraphy and Palaeontology of the late Viséan and Early Namurian Rocks of North-east Connaught.* Geological Survey of Ireland Special Paper No. 6.

BRUNTON, C. H. C. & MASON, T. R. 1979. Palaeoenvironments and correlations of the Carboniferous in west Fermanagh, Ireland. *Bulletin of the British Museum (Natural History)*, **32**, 91–108.

CALDWELL, W. G. E. 1959. The Lower Carboniferous rocks of the Carrick-on-Shannon syncline. *Quarterly Journal of the Geological Society of London*, **115**, 163–188.

—— & CHARLESWORTH, H. A. K. 1962. Viséan coral reefs in the Bricklieve mountains of Ireland. *Proceedings of the Geologists' Association*, **73**, 359–382.

CLAYTON, G., HIGGS, K., KEEGAN, J. B. & SEVASTOPULO, G. D. 1978. Correlation of the palynological zonation of the Dinantian of the British Isles. *Palinologia, num. extraord*, **1**, 137–147.

DIXON, O. A. 1972. Lower Carboniferous rocks between the Curlew and Ox Mountains, Northwestern Ireland. *Quarterly Journal of the Geological Society, London*, **128**, 71–102.

GEORGE, T. N., JOHNSON, G. A. L., MITCHELL, M., PRENTICE, J. E., RAMSBOTTOM, W. H. C., SEVASTOPULO, G. D. & WILSON, R. B. 1976. *A correlation of Dinantian Rocks in the British Isles.* Geological Society, London Special Report, **7**.

HIGGS, K. 1984. Stratigraphic palynology of the Carboniferous rocks in northwest Ireland. *Geological Survey of Ireland Bulletin*, **3**, 171–202.

——, CLAYTON, G. & KEEGAN, J. B. 1988. *Stratigraphic and systematic palynology of the Tournaisian rocks of Ireland.* Geological Survey of Ireland Special Paper No. 7.

McPHILEMY, B. 1988. The value of fluorescence microscopy in routine palynofacies analysis: Lower Carboniferous successions from Counties Armagh and Roscommon, Ireland. *Review of Palaeobotany and Palynology*, **56**, 345–359.

MITCHELL, W. I. & OWENS, B. 1990. The geology of the western part of the Fintona Block, Northern Ireland: evolution of Carboniferous basins. *Geological Magazine*, **127**, 407–426.

OSWALD, D. H. 1955. The Carboniferous rocks between the Ox Mountains and Donegal Bay. *Quarterly Journal of the Geological Society*,

London, **111**, 167–186.

PHILCOX, M. E., SEVASTOPULO, G. D. & MACDERMOT, C. V. 1989. Intra-Dinantian tectonic activity on the Curlew Fault, north-west Ireland. *In*: ARTHURTON, R. S., GUTTERIDGE, P. & NOLAN, S. C. (eds) *The Role of Tectonics in Devonian and Carboniferous Sedimentation in the British Isles*. Yorkshire Geological Society Occasional Publication, **6**, 55–66.

PHILLIPS, W. E. A. & SEVASTOPULO, G. D. 1986. The stratigraphic and structural setting of Irish mineral deposits. *In*: ANDREW, C. J., CROWE, R. W. A., FINLAY, S., PENNELL, W. M. & PYNE, J. F. (eds) *Geology and Genesis of Mineral Deposits in Ireland*. Irish Association for Economic Geology, Dublin, 1–30.

PRICE, C. & MAX, M. D. 1988. Surface and deep structural control of the NW Carboniferous Basin of Ireland: seismic perspectives of aeromagnetic and surface geological interpretation. *Journal of Petroleum Geology*, **11**, 365–388.

ROBESON, D. 1989. *Palynostratigraphy and Thermal Maturity of Carboniferous Strata Offshore Western Ireland*. PhD thesis, University of Dublin.

SCHWARZACHER, W. 1961. Petrology and structure of some Lower Carboniferous reefs in north-western Ireland. *AAPG Bulletin*, **45**, 1481–1503.

—— 1964. An application of statistical time-series analysis of a limestone-shale sequence. *Journal of Geology*, **72**, 195–213.

SHERIDAN, D. J. R. 1972. *Upper Old Red Sandstone and Lower Carboniferous of the Slieve Beagh syncline and its setting in the northwest Carboniferous basin, Ireland*. Geological Survey of Ireland Special Paper No. 2.

—— 1977. The hydrocarbons and mineralization proved in the Carboniferous strata of deep boreholes in Ireland. *In*: GARRARD, P. (ed.) *Proceedings of the Forum on Oil and Ores in Sediments* (Imperial College, 1975) Department of Geology, Imperial College, London, 113–144.

Palaeoenvironment of a Lower Carboniferous sandstone succession northwest Ireland: ichnological and sedimentological studies

J. O. BUCKMAN

Department of Geology, School of Geosciences, Queen's University, Belfast, BT7 1NN, UK

Abstract: The shallow-marine deltaic sandstones and shales of the Lower Carboniferous Mullaghmore Sandstone, northwest Ireland, contain abundant trace fossils. A twenty-five metre thick measured section of Mullaghmore Sandstone from the northwest corner of Mullaghmore Head contains a minimum of twenty-eight ichnogenera and four informally named trace fossils. At least four coarsening-upward sequences occur within the measured section, with a possible total of six. Sedimentary structures and trace fossils indicate that each sequence represents deposition in a shallow-marine deltaic environment; prodelta-interdistributary bay passing upwards into a subaqueous channel environment. These represent a *Cruziana*-type ichnofacies, with an interbedded tempestite-associated *Arenicolites* ichnofacies, and a *Skolithos*-type ichnofacies respectively. The ichnogenus *Neonereites*, more typical of the *Nereites* ichnofacies, also occurs within the *Cruziana* ichnofacies, but only in limited numbers, and is atypical of the ichnofauna. Local lateral variation in ichnogenera and their sporadic occurrence along bedding planes indicates the need for extensive investigation, if trace fossils are to be used for detailed environmental reconstruction.

The Mullaghmore Sandstone forms an arenaceous deltaic complex (Sheridan 1972), within the Lower Carboniferous limestone and shale-dominated succession of the Sligo syncline, northwest Ireland. It is stratigraphically bounded by the Bundoran Shale below, and the Benbulben Shale above (Fig. 1). The type locality at Mullaghmore Head has been dated as Holkerian from palynological data (Higgs 1984; Higgs *et al.* 1988), and is believed to have been deposited by a delta complex migrating southwards and south eastwards (Sheridan 1972) from a landmass to the north (see Leeder 1988, Fig. 5). Previous work on the Mullaghmore Sandstone from its type area has included that by Oswald (1955), and two unpublished theses by Avbovbo (1973) and Chandra (1974); the latter two on sedimentological and ichnological aspects respectively. Work on the trace fossils from the Mullaghmore Sandstone, undertaken as part of a more extensive ichnological survey of the clastic facies of central and northern Donegal Bay, indicates the presence of around 40 ichnogenera within the Mullaghmore Sandstone.

The present paper describes a 25 m thick measured section from the northwest corner of Mullaghmore Head (Fig. 2), which gently dips (10−20°) in a westerly direction, and is well exposed in a series of cliff and platform sections. A minimum of four major sedimentary sequences can be recognized, with a possible maximum of six (Fig. 3). At least 28 ichno-

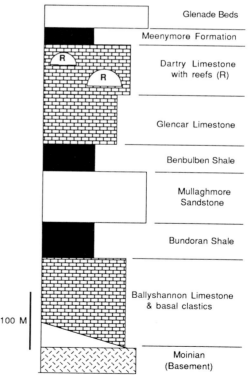

Fig. 1. Lower Carboniferous stratigraphy of the Sligo syncline, northwest Ireland. Scale approximate only. Based on Oswald (1955), and Parnell *et al.* (1990).

From PARNELL, J. (ed.), 1992, *Basins on the Atlantic Seaboard: Petroleum Sidementology and Basin Evolution.* Geological Society Special Publication No 62, pp 217−241.

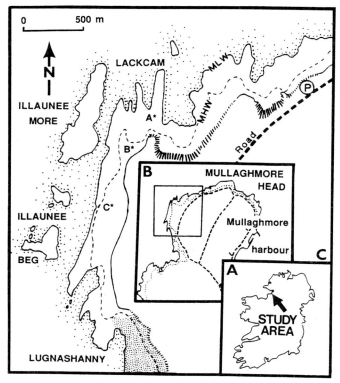

Fig. 2. Locality map, (A) Ireland, (B) Mullaghmore Head, (C) northwest Mullaghmore Head, measured section from Lackcam to Lugnashanny. A*–C* refer to bedding planes indicated on Figure 3. In part after Parnell *et al.* (1990).

genera, and a further four informally named trace fossils, occur within this section. The sequences are characterized by the decreasing importance of siltstones and shales upwards (coarsening upwards), the increasing size and occurrence of channels, and the decreasing diversity and abundance of ichnogenera. Each sequence represents a change from interdistributary bay/shallow prodelta deposits, with intercalated storm sands, to thick channelized sands (questionably fluviatile in part).

The ichnofauna exhibit marked vertical changes, and are consistent with a shallow-water *Cruziana* ichnofacies, with an intercalated *Arenicolites* ichnofacies, passing up into a *Skolithos*-style ichnofacies. The majority of deposits are interpreted as deposited above storm wavebase and fairweather wavebase, as indicated by the common occurrence of hummocky cross-stratification/swaley cross-stratification (HCS/SCS), and wave-rippled surfaces.

Sedimentology

The sedimentology of the northwest corner of Mullaghmore Head is here subdivided into three broad sedimentary facies; siltstones and shales, with varying degrees of generally minor intercalated sandstones (facies 1), well-bedded sandstones with minor shales (facies 2), and massive typically channel-forming sandstones (facies 3). Subfacies can be identified within facies 1 and 3: Subfacies 1A, a thick laminated-sandstone unit; 1B, small isolated channels; and 3A, a clay-rich trough cross-bedded erosively based coarse sandstone. The distribution of the facies is indicated in Figure 3.

Trace fossils are most abundant in facies 1. This may be a reflection of outcrop bias, as facies 1 is more amenable to the preservation and exposure of trace fossils, and readily accessible (e.g. unit F). However, not all differences can be attributed to such factors, and there is a definite positive relationship between facies type and ichnodiversity.

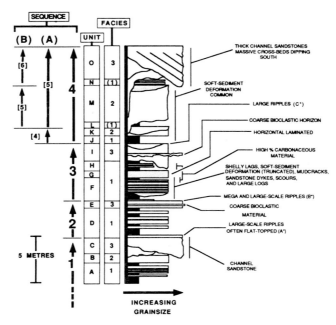

Fig. 3. Sedimentary log of northwest Mullaghmore Head, indicating positions of units, facies, and sequences described in the text. A*–C* refer to positions on Fig. 2. Alternative sequence interpretation for units J–O indicated under (A) and (B). Facies numbers in brackets tentative. Modified after Parnell *et al.* (1990).

The measured section can be subdivided into four major coarsening-upwards sequences, although the fourth may be divisible into two or three smaller sequences (Fig. 3), depending on the interpretation of the poorly exposed units at the top of the section (i.e. units L–O). Each sequence is composed of a lower shale-rich unit, with generally minor sandstones (facies 1), and is either overlain by facies 2 sandstones (erosive or conformable base), or erosively overlain by coarse channel-sandstones (facies 3). In only one case is a complete sequence from facies 1, through facies 2, to facies 3 definitely observed (sequence 1, see Fig. 3).

Facies 1; siltstones and shales (units A, D, F, G, H, J, (L, N))

This facies is dominated by siltstone and shales, with subordinate amounts of sandstone, which are variable in thickness and importance; sandstones in some cases becoming more numerous towards the top of each unit. Sandstone beds are 10–400 mm thick, and highly variable in thickness laterally. Cross-bedding within the sandstone beds is shallow-angle, or more typically trough cross-bedded (Fig. 4b). Hummocky cross-stratification (HCS)/swaley cross-stratification (SCS) is common within these

sandstones, as is typical of the Mullaghmore Sandstone on the whole. The sandstones commonly are erosively based with scours and tool marks a common feature, indicating a transportation direction towards the south. Ball and flame structures also occur, and are commonly truncated (Fig. 4c). Shelly lags composed of crinoid, gastropod, bivalve and brachiopod debris are locally present. Evidence of emergence occurs in the form of sand-filled desiccation cracks (Fig. 4d). Small-scale sandstone dykes are also present. Large-scale flat-topped ripples occur near the base of unit D. The siltstones and shales are commonly laminated, or contain streaks or lenticular lenses of sandstone. Carbonaceous debris is common, occurring as large flattened logs (pyritized and carbonized), small 'twigs', or more finely disseminated material. This facies contains the most diverse and abundant ichnofauna; trace fossils occurring in epirelief, hyporelief, and as full reliefs, in both sandstones and shales/siltstones.

Subfacies 1A; Massive parallel-laminated sandstone (unit G). A single laterally persistent parallel-laminated sandstone occurs within typical facies 1 sediments, and forms a useful marker horizon. This sandstone body is tabular in form, and consistent in thickness throughout its ob-

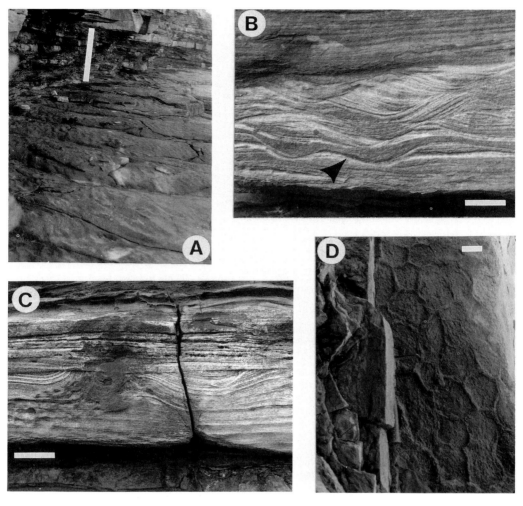

Fig. 4. (A) Mega-ripped platform (top of unit E), with superimposed large ripples, scale 2 m. (B) Trough cross-bedding, and HCS/SCS (arrowed) from unit F, scale 100 mm. (C) Truncated ball and flame, from unit F, scale 100 mm. (D) Desiccation cracks (hyporelief), from unit F, scale 70 mm.

served outcrop (approximately 0.8 m thick). No trace fossils are recorded, the primary sedimentary structures remaining intact.

Subfacies 1B; small channel-form sandstones (within unit F). Small channel-form sandstones infrequently occur within the siltstone/shale-rich horizons which comprise facies 1. These are comparatively rare and are not observed within every occurrence of facies 1. The channels are typically no wider than several metres, and are generally slightly wider than deep. They are composed of structureless medium-grained sandstone, with no apparent trace fossils or bioclastic material. One of the channel-form

sandstones has a large log just above it (see facies 1 above).

Facies 2; well-bedded sandstones (units B, K, M)

This facies is composed of typically well bedded medium-grained sandstones, with occasional and variable amounts of interbedded shale. The beds are generally planar, although occasional channels with erosive bases are also known. The channels are intermediate in size between those in facies 1 and facies 3, and are typically shallow in nature. Sedimentary structures other than channels are generally not observed because of poor outcrop access. However, units K and M commonly exhibit large-scale soft-sediment deformation structures, which are visible within the cliff sections.

Ichnodiversity and density is generally low, and is intermediate between facies 1 and facies 3. As with facies 1, this facies is dominated by bedding-parallel trace fossils, and most closely resembles facies 1 in its ichnological content. Unit K is notable for its high density of bivalve resting marks (*Lockeia*), and 'branched burrows', which are observed halfway through the unit.

Facies 3; massive, channelized sandstones (units C, E, I, O)

Facies 3 comprises medium-grained or coarse-grained sandstones, with erosive bases that commonly cut down by up to several metres. Individual channels are up to 10 m wide and are commonly observed to cross-cut in a complex manner, and are most clearly observed in unit O. Large-scale cross-bedding within channels occasionally occurs, although the channels are more commonly massive and structureless. The upper surface of this facies may be either sharp or transitional over about 0.2 m.

Trace fossils are generally rare or non-existent, with the vertical ichnogenera *Skolithos* and *Diplocraterion* occurring sparsely and typically in association with gritty lags (comprising shelly debris, crinoidal and goniatitic material). Limited numbers of predominantly bedding-parallel trace fossils occasionally occur within the upper parts of this facies (e.g. units C and I), at the transition with facies 1 sediments.

Subfacies 3A; Trough cross-bedded, erosive based, coarse-sandstone (unit E). A 1.10 m thick clay-rich coarse-grained sandstone, with an irregular erosive base, but apparently not channelized. The upper surface is irregular, and commonly mega-rippled (Fig. 4a) with superimposed large-scale ripples. This unit is divided into two halves by a coarse bioclastic horizon. Trough cross-bedding occurs in the upper half, and ladder ripples are a common feature along the northern section. The vertical ichnogenera *Arenicolites* and *Diplocraterion* are common within the basal half, whereas horizontal trace fossils occur in the upper half (e.g. *Taenidium*).

Trace fossils

A total of 28 ichnogenera (with approximately 34 ichnospecies), and four informally named trace fossils, are recognized from the measured section. One of the informally named trace fossils is clearly assignable to a new ichnogenus (the 'branched burrows'). A new ichnogenus is not erected for this at the present time as no representative material has as yet been collected. Ichnogenera are described in alphabetical order, with informally named forms at the end. Their vertical distribution is indicated in Fig. 5, and their relative abundance in Fig. 6. Ethologically the trace fossils cover a wide spectrum (Fig. 7), which is dominated by fodinichnia, reflecting the greater ichnodiversity within the facies 1 shales and siltstones.

All collected material has been deposited at the Ulster Museum (BELUM), Belfast, Northern Ireland.

Systematic Palaeontology

Ichnogenus *ARCHAEONASSA* Fenton & Fenton, 1937
Archaeonassa fossulata Fenton & Fenton, 1937
Figs 8a, b, f.
Occurrence. Units F and I, particularly abundant towards the top of unit F.
Material. Blocks BELUM K13558, BELUM K13559, BELUM K13574, and BELUM K13578 from the top of unit F; with approximately six, one, two, and one specimens respectively.
Description. Convex epireliefs 15 mm wide (exceptionally 2 mm wide), up to 900 mm long, bedding-parallel following rippled surfaces. Comprising a pair of lateral ridges of low relief, typically 4 mm wide. Ridges obliquely lobed, or smooth. Central region flat, or slightly raised, and either smooth or marked by transverse ribs which are straight or curved. Gently curving, sinuous, or rarely looped (Fig. 8b). Cross-cutting common. Examples parallel to ripple crests typically having only one lateral ridge, the missing ridge always that nearest to the ripple crest.

Discussion. These represent the surface expression of either near surface or surface movement, probably of gastropods (cf. Abel 1935; Fenton & Fenton 1937b), and are typical of shallow-water intertidal environments (Knox & Miller 1985). Variations in ornamentation are caused by different degrees of sand cohesion/water saturation, and depth of burrowing (Knox & Miller 1985).

Ichnogenus *ARENICOLITES* Salter, 1857.
Arenicolites ichnosp. type-A Fig. 8c.
Occurrence. Unit F, within sandstone beds.
Description. Endogenic full relief U-shaped burrows, seen in vertical cross-section. Burrows 5–10 mm wide, with a 1–2 mm thick lining composed of sand-grade material. Maximum length observed in the horizontal plane 160 mm. The exact shape of the U-burrow is variable, occurring either in the form of a smooth

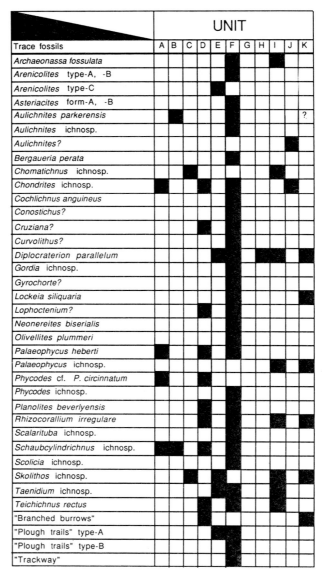

Fig. 5. Distribution of the main trace fossils, from the measured section. No trace fossils observed within units L–O.

curve, or with near vertical limbs and a flat base. Always much broader than deep.

Discussion. These burrows are referred to *Arenicolites* because of their simple U-shape (without a spreite). Although *Arenicolites* is generally unlined (Häntzschel 1975), lined forms are known (Fürsich 1974*a*; (?) Bjerstedt 1987, Fig. 6a; Dam 1990, p. 123). The presence of a lining reflects local sediment consistency,

and the permanent nature of the domicile (Dam 1990).

Arenicolites ichnosp. type-B Figs 8d, e.
Occurrence. Unit F, from the base, and near the top.
Material. On blocks BELUM K13558, BELUM K13561, and BELUM K13574 displaying vertical entrance burrows. From near the top of unit F, at the northwest corner of the locality.
Description. Endogenic full reliefs, comprising verti-

COMMON	MODERATELY COMMON	RARE	VERY RARE
Archaeonassa fossulata Arenicolites type-A Asteriacites lumbricalis form-A Aulichnites parkerensis Chondrites ichnosp. Diplocraterion parallelum Olivellites plummeri Palaeophycus heberti Rhizocorallium irregulare Schaubcylindrichnus ichnosp. Skolithos ichnosp. Taenidium ichnosp. Teichichnus rectus "Branched burrows"	Asteriacites lumbricalis form-A Arenicolites type-B Cruziana? Lockeia siliquaria Lophoctenium? Phycodes cf. P. circinnatum Planolites beverlyensis "Plough trails" type-A	Arenicolites type-C Bergaueria perata Cochlichnus anguineus Conostichus? Chomatichnus ichnosp. Gordia ichnosp. Gyrochorte? Neonereites biserialis Palaeophycus ichnosp. Scalarituba ichnosp. "Plough trails" type-B	Aulichnites ichnosp. Aulichnites? Curvolithus? Scolicia ichnosp. Phycodes ichnosp. "Trackway"

Fig. 6. Relative abundance of trace fossils.

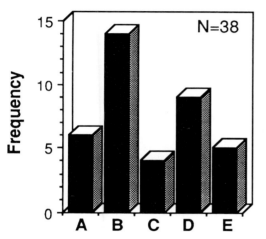

Fig. 7. Ethological classification of trace fossils; (A) domichnia, (B) fodinichnia, (C) pascichnia, (D) repichnia, (E) cubichnia.

cal U-shaped, mud-filled, unlined burrows, of variable morphology. Burrows 1−3 mm wide, both limbs within the same plane. Broad shallow forms, forms of approximately equal depth and width, and presumably (?) long narrow forms. The latter only seen as concave epireliefs, some of which are joined by a spindle-shaped depression. Burrows typically originate from low-amplitude wave rippled surfaces.

Discussion. The shallow spindle-shaped depression exhibited by many of the burrows represents the collapse of the U-burrow, rather than a spreite (Osgood 1970, p. 317).

Arenicolites ichnosp.
type-C

Occurrence. Known from the lower half of unit E, where it is moderately common.
Description. Paired vertical sand-filled burrows

observed in vertical section. Burrows 3−7 mm wide, with a maximum observed burrow depth of 200 mm.

Discussion. This type of *Arenicolites* is difficult to differentiate from *Skolithos*, particularly given that no U-shaped terminations are observed. However, it is assigned to *Arenicolites* based on its apparent paired nature. This material has similar hydrodynamic implications as *Skolithos*, and therefore the above taxonomic problem is of minor environmental importance.

Ichnogenus *ASTERIACITES* von Schlotheim, 1820
Asteriacites lumbricalis von Schlotheim, 1820 form-A Figs 8j, 11a.

Occurrence. From the base of unit F, occurring at both ends of the section, approximately half a dozen examples seen.
Description. Concave epireliefs, pentameral, 10−15 mm wide. Comprising a central depression 4−5 mm wide, with concave rays that rapidly taper to a point and have a maximum length of 5 mm.

Discussion. Considered to represent the resting traces of ophiuroids (Seilacher 1953; Häntzschel 1975), although difficulties in differentiating between ophiuroid and asteroid resting marks do exist (see Seilacher 1953, Fig. 1). The Mullaghmore material is of similar size, or smaller, to *Asteriacites* described by Hakes from Kansas (Hakes 1985), such small forms cited as possible indicators of decreased salinity shallow-water marine environments (Hakes 1976, 1985).

Asteriacites lumbricalis von Schlotheim, 1820 form-B Figs 8f, g, 16a.

Occurrence. From near the top of unit F, where this form of *Asteriacites lumbricalis* is extremely common (upwards of thirty examples counted).
Material. Occurring on blocks BELUM K13558, BELUM K13559, BELUM K13562, and BELUM

224   J. O. BUCKMAN

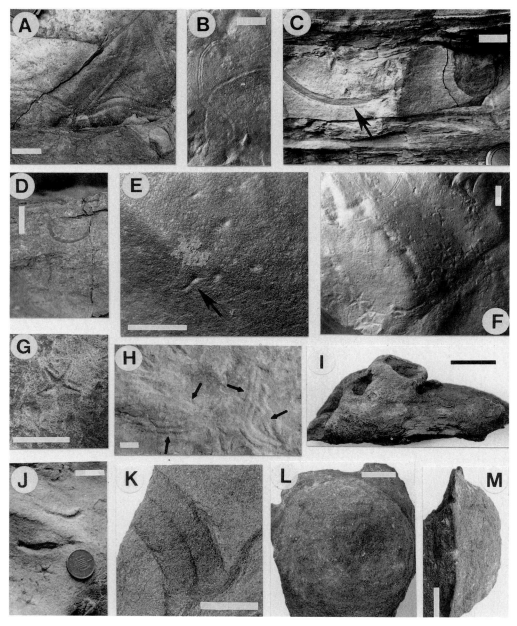

Fig. 8. *Archaeonassa fossulata*, epirelief, scale 30 mm. (B) *Archaeonassa fossulata* passing into 'plough trail' type-A, BELUM K13558, epirelief, scale 10 mm. (C) *Arenicolites* type-A (arrowed), and *Diplocraterion* (right hand side), vertical section, scale 20 mm. (D, E) *Arenicolites* type-B, vertical section and epirelief (BELUM K13561) respectively, spindle-form (arrowed in E), scale 30 mm and 20 mm. (F) *Asteriacites lumbricalis* form-B, 'plough trail' type-A, and *Archaeona ssa fossulata*, BELUM K13558, epirelief, scale 10 mm. (G) *Asteriacites lumbricalis* form-B, epirelief, scale 20 mm. (H) *Aulichnites parkerensis* (arrowed), epirelief, scale 20 mm. (I) *Chomatichnus* (with funnel-shaped entrances), BELUM K13566, side view, scale 20 mm. (J) *Asteriacites lumbricalis* form-A on rippled surface, epirelief, scale 20 mm. (K) *Aulichnites* ichnosp., BELUM K13563, epirelief, scale 15 mm. (L, M) *Bergaueria perata*, BELUM K13570, basal view, and side view, scales 10 mm.

K13578; with eight, five, one, and two/three specimens respectively.

Description. 10–15 mm wide concave epireliefs, pentameral; five rays radiating from a central depression. Individual rays 1–2 mm wide at their base, and tapering to a point, or more commonly petering out distally. Petal-shaped rays (lanceolate or tear-shaped) also occasionally occur. Individual rays are bordered by lateral ridges, which run parallel to the rays and comprise arcuate mounds between neighbouring rays. A central raised knob may occur, which in some cases isolates the individual rays. Occurring in closely associated groups, commonly cross-cutting.

Discussion. The differences observed between the two forms of *A. lumbricalis* are interpreted as reflecting differences in grain-size and substrate consistency between the two *Asteriacites* bearing horizons.

Ichnogenus *AULICHNITES* Fenton & Fenton, 1937
Aulichnites parkerensis Fenton & Fenton, 1937 Fig. 8h.

Occurrence. Units B, F, and ?K; several dozen observed at outcrop, but uncollectable. Most abundant at the base of unit F.

Description. Bedding-parallel convex epireliefs, 7–12 mm wide (maximum 15 mm), and a maximum of 5 mm in relief. Unilobed concave-up base. Upper surface subdivided into two parallel lobes, separated by a shallow median groove. Lobes not always of equal width. Some examples transitional to 'plough trails', with a much wider central groove (4 mm wide). Faint fine transverse ribbing occasionally visible, which gently curves towards the margins; although normally smooth in appearance. Maximum observed length 0.5 m. Shallow-angle entrance and exit ramps occur, but are rare. Typically straight, curved, or slightly sinuous, with occasional hairpin bends. Guided meanders as in *Helminthoida* are not developed. Commonly associated with rippled surfaces, and exhibiting a positive relationship to ripple crest orientations (Fig. 9a).

Discussion. This trace fossil occurs in association with *Olivellites* at the base of unit F, both of which were put into synonymy with *Psammichnites* by D'Alessandro and Bromley (1987, p. 749). However, the two ichnogenera are maintained here.

Aulichnites ichnosp Fig. 8k.

Occurrence. Found only in the lower half of unit F, above *Aulichnites parkerensis*.

Material. Known from only one example, BELUM K13563.

Description. A convex epirelief, 15 mm wide, 4 mm deep, exposed for 35 mm along its length. Both upper and lower surfaces are bilobed, the upper surface displaying sub-millimetre arcuate transverse backfill.

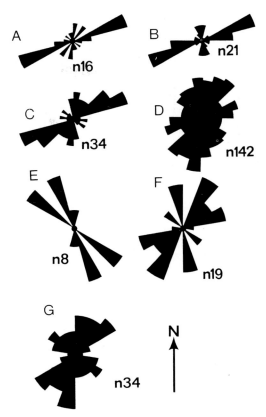

Fig. 9. Orientation diagrams of ichnogenera; (A) *Aulichnites parkerensis*, (B) *Olivellites*, (C) *Taenidium*, (D) *Diplocraterion*, (E–G) *Rhizocorallium*.

Discussion. This trace fossil is similar to *Aulichnites parkerensis*, in most respects, apart from its bilobed lower surface.

Aulichnites? ichnosp. Fig. 10.

Occurrence. Top of unit, known from one example.

Description. Bilobed convex epirelief, in the form of a convex-up arc (as viewed parallel to trace fossil axis). 30 mm long, 16 mm wide, and approximately 10 mm high. Each lobe is smooth and 7 mm wide, a slight depression occurring between lobes.

Discussion. Similar in appearance to some forms of smooth *Rusophycus* (Bjerstedt 1988a, Pl.11.3). However, differing from *Rusophycus* in its convex epirelief form. The short length and nature of terminations (coffee-bean shape) appears to preclude inclusion in the ichnogenus *Aulichnites* (However, cf. the terminations of *Aulichnites* ichnosp., Frey 1990, Fig. 12a). This structure may have an inorganic origin.

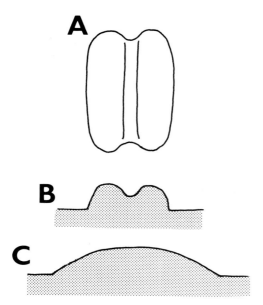

Fig. 10. *Aulichnites?* ichnosp. (A) plan view, (B) transverse cross section, (C) longitudinal cross section. Scale as in text.

Ichnogenus *BERGAUERIA* Prantl, 1945
Bergaueria perata Prantl, 1945 Figs 8l, m.
Occurrence. Five closely associated examples in the upper half of unit F, on a loaded sandstone base.
Material. BELUM K13570, a single specimen of the ichnogenus
Description. Convex hyporeliefs, bowl-shaped, with a central basal concavity. Orientated perpendicular to bedding, but with slight lateral distortion. Roughly circular in horizontal cross-section, 35 mm wide (15–18 mm at the base) by 15 mm deep. Faint concentric laminae, and even fainter narrow (millimetre wide) radial ornamentation.

Discussion. The size, shape, occurrence of an apical depression, and faint radial ornamentation indicate that this trace fossil is assignable to *Bergaueria perata*, as recently reviewed by Pemberton *et al.* (1988), and Pemberton and Magwood (1990).
    Representing the resting traces of anemones (Pemberton *et al.* 1988), these trace fossils are believed to represent shallow-water marine environments (Chamberlain 1971; Bjerstedt 1987; Pemberton *et al.* 1988; Martino 1989). They are therefore of environmental significance.

Ichnogenus *CHOMATICHNUS* Donaldson
& Simpson, 1962
Chomatichnus ichnosp. Fig. 8i.
Occurrence. Units C and I, rare, generally found in closely associated groups.

Material. BELUM K13565 and BELUM K13566 from units C and I respectively.
Description. Convex epireliefs comprising small solitary cones or rounded mounds, up to 30 mm high by a maximum of 100 mm wide, with a central opening 2–10 mm wide. Rare examples with funnel-shaped openings occasionally occur (Fig. 8i).

Discussion. These trace fossils may represent shallow-water conditions, such as those in which lug-worm casts are produced on modern beaches. However, *Chomatichnus* cannot be used to indicate water-depth with any accuracy, as many other organisms (e.g. crustaceans and holothurians) are capable of producing similar mounds over a wide range of depths. These structures are unlikely to represent sand volcanoes, as elsewhere where *Chomatichnus* occurs in abundance, no water-escape structures are associated. Instead *Skolithos* and *Arenicolites* occur in association.

Ichnogenus *CHONDRITES* von
Sternberg, 1883
Chondrites ichnosp.
Occurrence. Unit D and F, rare, probably more common than noted.
Material. Some small *Chondrites* occurring on the base of BELUM K13581, and BELUM K13587, from within unit F.
Description. Endogenic full reliefs, and occasional convex hyporeliefs. Comprising branching networks, with individual burrows 1–3 mm wide (some submillimetre scale). Flattened in the horizontal plane, and sand-filled within a finer-grained matrix. Individual burrow segments typically appear straight. However, preservation precludes determination of the precise network form.

Discussion. This material is assigned to *Chondrites* on the basis of size and branched form. It is not identified to ichnospecies level because of poor exposure, mainly in vertical cross-section. The ichnogenus *Chondrites* is known from a wide range of marine environments, and thus is of limited environmental use.

Ichnogenus *COCHLICHNUS* Hitchcock, 1858
Cochlichnus anguineus Hitchcock,
1858 Fig. 11a.
Occurrence. Base of unit F, only known from one complete example, and several smaller segments.
Description. Concave epirelief surface trail, comprising a smooth sine-wave pattern in the horizontal plane (wavelength 50–60 mm). V-shaped in cross section, and cut to a reasonably consistent depth (several millimetres), 5 mm wide, 110 mm long (parallel to trail direction). Discontinuous lateral ridges (several millimetres high) preferentially developed on the outsides of bends, the surface otherwise smooth. Cross-cutting a rippled surface at right angles.

Fig. 11. (A) *Cochlichnus anguineus*, and *Asteriacites lumbricalis* form-A, epirelief, scale 20 mm. (B, C, F) *Conostichus?* ichnosp., BELUM K13567, BELUM K13569, BELUM K13568, in vertical section, side-view, and from above, scale 20 mm, 10 mm, and 20 mm. (D, E) *Cruziana?* ichnosp., BELUM K13572, BELUM K13571, hyporeliefs (Light from top right in D), coffee-bean form (arrowed in D), scale 15 mm and 20 mm. (G) *Diplocraterion parallelum*, vertical section, scale 30 mm. (H) *Gyrochorte?*, BELUM K13561, epirelief, scale 3 mm. (I) *Lophoctenium?*, BELUM K13577, epirelief, scale 10 mm. (J) *Gyrochorte?*, epirelief, scale 10 mm. (K) *Neonereites biserialis*, BELUM K13580, hyporelief, scale 6 mm. (L) *Olivellites plummeri*, epirelief, truncated backfilled section arrowed, scale 30 mm.

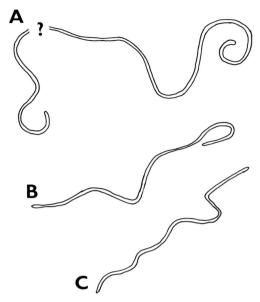

Fig. 12. *Gordia* ichnosp., field sketches to show variation in morphology, (A) coiled at both ends, (B) at one end only, and (C) at neither end. All exhibit a sinuous meandering section of variable complexity. Occurrence of terminating coils is probably a preservational feature. Scale as in text.

Discussion. Similar to other simple V-shaped exogenic plough trails, but differentiated on the basis of its sine-wave morphology. It compares with *C. anguineus* described by Dam (1990, Fig. 6a), although the Mullaghmore material is larger. *Cochlichnus* is generally found in deeper water flysch deposits (Häntzschel 1975), but also occurs in shallow-water deposits (cf. Hitchcock 1858; Dam 1990).

Ichnogenus CONOSTICHUS Lesquereux, 1876
Conostichus? Ichnosp. Figs 11b, c, f.

Occurrence. Unit F (lower half), three examples known.
Material. BELUM K13567, BELUM K13568, and BELUM K13569.
Description. Smooth cone-shaped (apex down) endogenic full reliefs, with a rounded or flattened base. Cone walls diverge at about 45 degrees. 50–55 mm wide (15 mm at the base), by 25–30 mm deep. Upper surface circular in cross section, and exhibiting concentric laminae.

Discussion. These lack an apical disc, central subcylindrical core, or distinctive ornamentation, as is normal for *Conostichus* (Pemberton et al. 1988). The ichnogenus *Bergaueria*,

although of similar dimensions, and smooth, is not conical, and is usually walled (Pemberton et al. 1988), and therefore differs from this material. Bjerstedt (1987, Fig. 10.8–10), and Martino (1989, Figs 4.7–4.8) figure material similar to that under discussion as *Conostichus* or *?Conostichus* respectively. This material is therefore only tentatively assigned to *Conostichus*.

As with *Bergaueria*, *Conostichus* is believed to be the product of anemones, and to represent shallow-water conditions (see *Bergaueria* discussion). The observed concentric laminae may represent cone-in-cone structure, reflecting upward movement during periods of active sedimentation (Pemberton et al. 1988).

Ichnogenus CRUZIANA d'Orbigny, 1842
Cruziana? ichnosp. Figs 11d, e.

Occurrence. Units D and F, best exposed at the top of unit F, approximately one dozen examples.
Material. BELUM K13571, and BELUM K13572, collected from the top of unit F.
Description. Low relief smooth convex hyporeliefs comprising two equidimensional parallel lobes. Total width mainly between 7–16 mm (maximum 23 mm), ribbon form, maximum observed length 200 mm. Variable in morphology from gently curving to straight, bedding-parallel, occasionally curving upwards. Cross-cutting at both high and low angles, sometimes overlapping to a high degree. One coffee-bean form example (Fig. 11d).

Discussion. This material is tentatively assigned to *Cruziana*, although the scratch marks of that ichnogenus are not apparent. Comparison to other material within the Mullaghmore Sandstone suggests that this material be assigned to *Cruziana* rather than the morphologically similar *Didymaulichnus*.

Ichnogenus CURVOLITHUS Fritsch, 1908
Curvolithus? ichnosp.

Occurrence. Unit F, one example, uncollected.
Description. A trilobed 8 mm wide convex epirelief, with lateral ridges 1.5 mm wide. Lateral ridges and central lobes are smooth and convex-up. Occurring at a shallow angle to bedding, passing through a rippled surface. Length of trail 20 mm.

Discussion. This compares favourably with *Curvolithus* illustrated in Häntzschel (1975, p.W57, Fig. 3b.), and Hakes (1976, Pl. 2, Fig. 2a). Only tentatively assigned to *Curvolithus* because of its singular occurrence, and poor preservation. Known from the *Cruziana* and *Skolithos* ichnofacies (Martino 1989), and occurring in intertidal deposits (Chamberlain 1978).

Ichnogenus *DIPLOCRATERION* Torell, 1870
Diplocraterion parallelum Torell, 1870
Figs 8c, 11g, 13f, 16f.

Occurrence. Units E, F, I, and K; very common, several hundred observed, none collected.
Description. Full reliefs, with burrow widths 4–10 mm wide (maximum 15 mm), total widths 22–45 mm (maximum 65 mm), and observed depths typically of 40–65 mm (100 mm maximum). The U-closure is in the form of a smooth curve, or more rarely with a flat base. Laminae within the spreite are of the same shape as the U-closure, and 1–2 mm thick. Protrusive and retrusive forms occur, one form dominating within any given bed. Retrusive forms with funnel apertures on both limbs occur. Funnels comprise concentric laminae (horizontal section), with a maximum diameter of several tens of millimetres. A few examples have a 1–2 mm thick mud-rich lining around the burrow. Some examples exhibit a preferred direction of orientation (Fig. 9d).

Discussion. The mode of life attributed to the maker of *Diplocraterion* is usually that of a suspension-feeder (Fürsich 1974c), typically in high-energy shallow-water environments. Possession of two funnels may indicate an ability to circulate water bi-directionally, thus supporting a shallow-water intertidal environment of deposition for *Diplocraterion* in units I and K. Preservation of the funnel apertures as concentric laminae indicates active sedimentation and upwards migration.

Ichnogenus *GORDIA* Emmons, 1844
Gordia ichnosp. Fig. 12.

Occurrence. Unit F, occurring in small numbers on the sole of only one sandstone bed; the same as for *Neonereites.*
Material. Possible examples on the base of BELUM K13580
Description. Smooth convex thread-like hyporeliefs typically less than 1 mm wide, and up to 60 mm in length. Comprising loose meanders in the horizontal plane (meander belt width typically 25 mm or less), and commonly terminating in a coil or hook.

Discussion. Similar to *Spirophycus*, but smaller in diameter and without the rugose ornamentation typical of *Spirophycus*. Also similar to *Mermia* (cf. Walker 1985, Fig. 8a), but this is generally smaller, and preferentially develops coils rather than sinuous sections. The Mullaghmore material is assigned to the ichnogenus *Gordia*, given its similarity with *Gordia* illustrated by Häntzschel (1975, Fig. 39.1a, b).

Ichnogenus *GYROCHORTE* Heer, 1865
Gyrochorte? ichnosp. Figs 11h, j.

Occurrence. Unit F, sparsely occurring at the base of the unit, and from one example near the top.

Material. BELUM K13561 from the upper horizon.
Description. Bedding-parallel low relief convex epi-reliefs, 3–7 mm wide, and up to 80 mm long. Transversely ribbed on a millimetre scale. Curved or tortuous in the horizontal plane.

Discussion. Tentatively placed in the ichnogenus *Gyrochorte*, based on size and bilobed convex epirelief form. Oblique plaited surface ornamentation, and typical internal structure not observed (see Heinberg 1973).

Ichnogenus *LOCKEIA* James, 1879
Lockeia siliquaria James, 1879

Occurrence. Units F and K; several hundred examples.
Description. Convex hyporeliefs, length 5–35 mm, width 2–15 mm, variable relief. Usually vertical in orientation, a small number inclined to one side. Shape either boat-hulled or almond-like, with or without a sharp well-defined keel.

Discussion. Representing the resting traces of bivalves (Seilacher 1953). Reported from a variety of environments from within the *Cruziana* and *Skolithos* ichnofacies, and also from fluviatile environments (Broadhurst *et al.* 1980). The Irish examples were probably produced by marine bivalves, given their close association with known marine ichnogenera (*Diplocraterion*). *Lockeia* is observed to cross-cut other trace fossils (the 'branched burrows'), indicating that in this case the *Lockeia* represent true burrows rather than surface resting traces. The name *Lockeia* is used here in preference to *Pelecypodichnus* following Maples & West (1989).

Ichnogenus *LOPHOCTENIUM* Richter, 1850
Lophoctenium? ichnosp. Fig. 11i.

Occurrence. Units D and F.
Material. BELUM K13577, from near the top of unit F.
Description. Endogenic cleavage reliefs, and concave epireliefs. Comprising shale-filled burrow segments, which are arcuate in form, and 1–2 mm wide by 10–20 mm long. More commonly occurring as concave troughs with raised margins. Individual segments commonly do not intersect each other, and are arranged in a number of styles; nested and radiating from a central point, or nested and occurring in two parallel (commonly divergent) rows, or rarely in a random fashion. A preference for ripple troughs is apparent.

Discussion. An example of *Chondrites recurvus* illustrated by Chamberlain (1971, Fig. 6d, and 1978, p. 51) is similar to this trace fossil, but is less complex. This trace fossil bears some similarity to some of the forms of *Lophoctenium* illustrated by Chamberlain (1978), but not to those illustrated by Häntzschel (1975, Fig. 50.1b). The Mullaghmore examples lack the 'comb'-like structure that is typical of *Lophoctenium*, therefore they are only tentatively assigned to this ichnogenus. These burrows represent three-dimensional complex mining structures, feeding on concentrated organic material within ripple troughs (cf. *Rhizocorallium irregulare* Fürsich 1974*b*).

Ichnogenus *NEONEREITES* Seilacher, 1960
Neonereites biserialis Seilacher, 1960. Fig. 11k.

Occurrence. Unit F, sparse, and restricted to one sandstone bed.

Material. Occurring on blocks BELUM K13580, BELUM K13581, and BELUM K13582.

Description. Convex and concave hyporeliefs, 5 mm or less in width, and up to 200 mm long. Biserial pustules approximately 2 mm wide, occur on upper and lower surfaces, and are occasionally separated by a basal central groove. Sinuous in the horizontal plane, and may be sharply bent. Some examples have three, or possibly more, pellets across their width.

Discussion. Assigned to *N. biserialis* rather than *N. uniserialis* owing to the biserial row of 'pellets' seen in these examples. Forms with more than two pellets appear similar to *Neonereites* illustrated by Ekdale *et al.* (1984, Fig. 18.5 bottom), whereas the more typical form closely resembles *Neonereites* of Bjerstedt (1988b, Fig. 5b). Normally associated with the deep-water *Nereites* ichnofacies, but demonstrated as facies-crossing, also occurring in shallow-water deposits (Hakes 1976; Turner & Benton 1983).

Ichnogenus *OLIVELLITES* Fenton & Fenton, 1937
Olivellites plummeri Fenton & Fenton, 1937 Fig. 11l.

Occurrence Unit F; abundant within the basal 100 mm, but sporadic in occurrence, not known from the northern end of the headland. Also rarely from the top of unit F at the north end of the section.

Material. One or two specimens on BELUM K13557, and one on BELUM K13562, both from the top of unit F.

Description. Convex epireliefs, 10−20 mm wide, up to 500 mm long, and approximately 5 mm high. Characterized by a central groove, or more rarely a ridge (typically 2 mm wide). Comprising long sinuous straights, tight smooth curves, and describing a semimeandering pattern. Typically not self cross-cutting, although parallel sections are common. Bedding-parallel, and exhibiting a strong positive relationship between burrow axis and ripple crest orientation (Fig. 9b). Surface either smooth or slightly undulatory, occasionally exhibiting faint, fine, millimetre scale transverse ornamentation (backfill).

One example (on BELUM K13562) has 1 mm wide pimples along its mid-line, spaced approximately every 10 mm along the axis. These occur either instead of, or in association with the central ridge, which is poorly developed and faint.

Discussion. This material resembles the 'annelid' trail *Cymaderma* (= congeneric with *Olivellites*), described by Duns (1877), which also lacks a central ridge, having instead a discontinuous central groove. Given that the Mullaghmore material in part has a central ridge, it is assigned to *Olivellites plummeri* (cf. Fenton & Fenton 1937*a*).

Ichnogenus *PALAEOPHYCUS* Hall, 1847
Palaeophycus heberti (Saporta, 1872)

Occurrence. Units A, B, D, and F; moderately common.

Material. BELUM K13587, BELUM K13588, from unit F.

Description. Thickly lined convex hyporeliefs, and endogenic full reliefs within the shales. Width 5−10 mm, up to 100 mm in length, and predominantly horizontal, with cross-cutting common. The undersides of the burrows may exhibit a rough transverse ornamentation, with individual ribs 1−3 mm thick, and chevron−arcuate in shape.

Discussion. These burrows are identified as *Palaeophycus heberti* on the basis of their thick lining, horizontal form, and lack of collapse structures. They compare with *Arenicolites* type-A and *Schaubcylindrichnus* in the nature of their lining; *Palaeophycus heberti* representing basal sections of these ichnogenera in many cases, although this is not always possible to confirm.

Palaeophycus ichnosp. Fig. 13a.

Occurrence. Sparse within units I and K.

Material. BELUM K13596, collected from strata just above the measured section.

Description. Generally flat or concave epireliefs, on sandstone beds. Width 10−20 mm, and up to approximately 80 mm in length. This ichnospecies is characterized by its distinct transverse annulations, which are straight, curved or sinuous in nature, and 1−2 mm in width. Bedding-parallel, straight, curved or sinuous in morphology.

Discussion. Material from other parts of the Mullaghmore Sandstone appear to represent flattened, transversely annulated, distinctly sand-lined burrows. Therefore these burrows are assigned to *Palaeophycus*, although not concurring with any known ichnospecies of *Palaeophycus* (see Pemberton & Frey 1982).

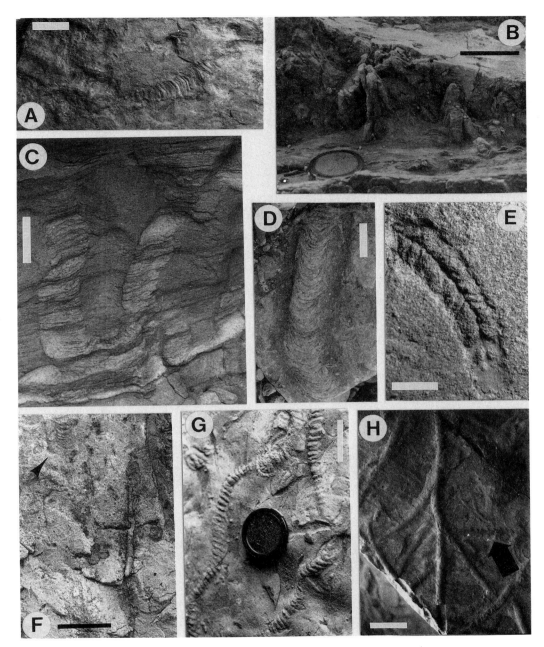

Fig. 13. (A) *Palaeophycus* ichnosp., BELUM K13596, epirelief, Scale 20 mm. (B) *Phycodes* ichnosp. (cf. *Phycodes circinnatum*), full reliefs (viewed from below), scale 30 mm. (C) *Rhizocorallium irregulare* (vertical-retrusive phase), vertical section, scale 20 mm. (D) *Rhizocorallium irregulare* (protrusive phase), epirelief, scale 50 mm. (E) *Scolicia* ichnosp., BELUM K13573, epirelief, scale 10 mm. (F) *Skolithos* and *Diplocraterion* (arrowed), vertical section, scale 80 mm. (G) *Taenidium* ichnosp. (cf. *Taenidium serpentinum*), epirelief, scale 55 mm. (H) 'Branched burrow', ornamentated section arrowed, hyporelief, from north of Classie Bawn Castle (G 695 570), scale 30 mm.

Ichnogenus *PHYCODES* Richter, 1850
Phycodes ichnosp.
(cf. *Phycodes circinnatum* Richter, 1853)
Fig. 13b.

Occurrence. Units B and D; common in the former.
Description. Horizontal convex hyporeliefs and full
reliefs, comprised of a vertically-retrusive spreite,
composed of concave-up gutter-shaped stacked
lamellae. Spreite up to 50 mm in height. Width of
lamellae 10−15 mm, each 1−2 mm thick. Total observed length 80 mm (incomplete). Occurring in
bundles, which branch at acute angles. Individual
branches straight or slightly curved. No tube preserved
on top of spreite.

Discussion. Assigned to *Phycodes*, although
some forms of *Teichichnus* are also known to be
branched (Seilacher 1955), or to radiate from a
central point (Baldwin 1977, Fig. 7, *T. stellatus*).
In this paper, the use of *Teichichnus* is restricted
to spreite burrows which are non-branched,
Whereas similar, but branched forms are
referred to *Phycodes*.

These examples of *Phycodes* are similar in
character to the proximal portion of *Phycodes
circinnatum*, illustrated in Häntzschel (1975,
Fig. 59.2b), but differ in size and lack the distal
section characteristic of *Phycodes circinnatum*.

Phycodes ichnosp.

Occurrence. Unit F; one example.
Description. A 20 mm wide horizontal convex hyporelief. Comprised of a vertically−retrusive spreite
composed of a stack of concave-up gutter-shaped
lamellae. Lamellae 1−2 mm thick. Sinuous in the
horizontal plane, with occasional acute branches alternating from side to side. Maximum observed length
300 mm.

Discussion. This form of *Phycodes* is readily
confused with *Teichichnus* when occurring in
small sections. Differing from *P. circinnatum* by
its nature of branching.

Ichnogenus *PLANOLITES* Nicholson, 1873
Planolites beverleyensis (Billings, 1862)

Occurrence. Abundant in the base of unit D, and
sporadic in unit F.
Description. Convex hyporeliefs, and endogenic full
reliefs, comprising simple sand-filled horizontal cylinders, less than 10 mm in diameter and of consistent
width along their length. Less than 100 mm long.

Discussion. *Planolites* is used to describe predominantly horizontal, unbranched, sand-filled
cylinders with no obvious internal structure.
Because the majority of these trace fossils are
only seen in vertical cross section, identification
to the specific level is difficult, but those seen as
hyporeliefs appear to fit the criteria for *Planolites beverleyensis*. The existence of other ichnospecies of *Planolites* cannot be overlooked.

Ichnogenus *RHIZOCORALLIUM*
Zenker, 1836
Rhizocorallium irregulare Mayer, 1954
Figs 13c, d.

Occurrence. Units D, F, I and K; occurring in dense
masses, which dominate bedding planes.
Material. Part of a specimen on the top of block
BELUM K13587, from unit F.
Description. Concave epireliefs and endogenic full
reliefs. Comprising U-shaped burrows with individual
limbs 5−25 mm wide (constant for any given burrow),
total width 15−90 mm, and 600 mm maximum observed length. Horizontal or slightly inclined (maximum 25 degrees), arms parallel or more commonly
diverging towards the U-closure. Long axis of the
burrow straight or curved to a variable degree. Generally much longer than wide, with the exception of one
'rectangular' example. A protrusive spreite is generally developed between the arms, composed of a
series of arcuate lamellae which stand out as ridges,
and are generally on a millimetre scale. The protrusive
phase is followed by a vertically retrusive one of up to
95 mm in height (Fig. 13c). The retrusive phase
comprises a series of stacked gutter-shaped concave-
up lamellae, which occur along the perimeter of the
trace fossil. The lamellae are delicate (millimetre
scale) and typically continuous features, with dark
faecal pellets scattered along their surface. Pellets
appear bacilliform in shape, and are up to 2 mm long
and 0.5 mm wide. The final burrow is generally not
preserved. Burrows commonly exhibit a preferred
orientation in a north−south direction (Fig. 9c-g),
with no apparent preference for direction of closure.

Discussion. Assigned to *Rhizocorallium irregulare* on the basis of its overall morphology;
long and horizontal. It represents a sediment-
feeding mode of life in a normally quiet water
environment. The occurrence of a substantial
vertically-retrusive spreite may represent an
escape/equilibrium structure, caused by sediment influx. However, this may also represent a
modification to sediment-feeding, and need not
necessarily be a reflection of sedimentation.
Normally considered as good marine indicators,
Rhizocorallium is also known from non-marine
deposits (Fürsich & Mayr 1981; Pollard 1981).
The Irish *Rhizocorallium* are most probably of
marine origin, given their association with other
typical marine trace fossils. The occurrence of a
vertically retrusive wall structure, in association
with *Rhizocorallium irregulare*, indicates that
this cannot be used as a diagnostic tool at
ichnospecific level for *Rhizocorallium* or for
simple ethological classification (cf. Fürsich
1974b, p. 20−21, 24).

Ichnogenus *SCALARITUBA* Weller, 1899
Scalarituba ichnosp.

Occurrence. Unit F, sparse, approximately half-way
through the unit.
Description. Full reliefs in vertical cross section, within a sandstone bed. Total width 6 mm, with a 1 mm

thick 'lining' or zone of disturbance. A crescentic backfill is occasionally observed, with 0.5–1 mm thick sandstone ridges, and 1 mm thick (or greater) shale packets.

Discussion. Assigned to *Scalarituba* on the basis of its thin crescentic sandstone menisci, and the presence of a disturbance halo (cf. Rodriguez & Gutschick 1970, Pl. 6d). *Helminthopsis* illustrated by Bromley (1990), although similar, is not meniscate. Other meniscate burrows such as *Taenidium* and *Rutichnus* are excluded by their generally larger size and their different nature of backfill (see D'Alessandro & Bromley 1987).

Ichnogenus *SCHAUBCYLINDRICHNUS* Frey & Howard, 1981
Schaubcylindrichnus ichnosp. Fig. 14.

Occurrence. Units B, D, and F.
Material. Along a cut section of block BELUM K13587. Block BELUM K13588, and BELUM K13589, with burrows observed in basal section. Block BELUM K13593, which contains a number of associated specimens occurring in epirelief. All from unit F, at the north end of the section.
Description. Endogenic full reliefs viewed in vertical section, in sandstone and shales, and also as epireliefs and hyporeliefs. Generally 10 mm wide, with a 1–3 mm thick sand-grade lining. Variable in cross section from circular to ovoid (laterally compressed), the burrow orifice in some cases keyhole, or hourglass-shaped. Two major morphologies occur (Fig. 14); closely associated penetrating bundles of tubes, or as single rows of interpenetrating tubes. Both appear to comprise half U-shaped burrows. However, the true burrow shape may be U-shaped, with only one tube on the second limb, as indicated in a small number of examples.

Discussion. In bedding plane section these burrows appear identical to *Schaubcylindrichnus coronus* (Frey & Howard 1981). However, they differ in their vertical morphology, by the incongruent nature of the tube bundles, and their apparent U-shaped vertical plan. This trace fossil is here considered to represent *Schaubcylindrichnus*; its relationship to *Schaubcylindrichnus coronus* and other ichnogenera (*Arenicolites* type-A, *Palaeophycus heberti*), along with its ethological implications will be discussed in a future paper. This material is very similar to modern burrows produced by *Arenicola* illustrated by Schäfer (1972, Fig. 217), to which it may well have a similar ethological relationship.

Ichnogenus *SCOLICIA* de Quatrefages, 1849
Scolicia ichnosp. Fig. 13e.

Occurrence. One example in the bottom half of unit F.
Material. BELUM K13573.
Description. Gently convex bilobed epirelief, with a

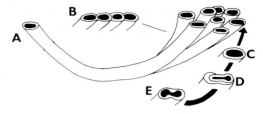

Fig. 14. Reconstruction of *Schaubcylindrichnus* ichnosp., (A) typical bundled form (cf. *Arenicola* burrow, Schäfer 1972, Fig. 217), (B) alternative tube arrangement. (C) Standard oval tube cross-section, (D) keyhole tube cross-section, also exhibiting high degree of tube overlap, and (E) hourglass tube cross-section.

sharp medial groove, and a convex-down unilobed base. Width 10 mm, by 45 mm long, and only a few millimetres in relief. Surface covered with oblique lobes, on a millimetre scale which form a transverse chevron pattern. Slightly curved in the horizontal plane, and at a slight angle to bedding.

Discussion. Assigned to the ichnogenus *Scolicia* by similarity to *Scolicia* sp. illustrated by Fürsich (1974a, Fig. 35). The ichnogenus *Scolicia* is applied here in the widest sense of the *Scolicia* 'group' of trace fossils.

Ichnogenus *SKOLITHOS* Haldemann, 1840
Skolithos ichnosp. Fig. 13f.

Occurrence. Units C and I, abundant.
Description. Endogenic full reliefs, 5–10 mm wide, up to 200 mm long, and in some cases longer. Vertical, or near vertical, straight, and with a distinct or indistinct boundary. Occasionally occurring in clumps, infrequently appearing to occur in pairs.

Discussion. Comparable to the deep *Skolithos* of Bjerstedt (1987, Fig. 6d), and also to *Diplocraterion habichi* (Heinberg & Birkelund 1984, Fig. 5a; Dam 1990); the latter examples possibly assignable to *Arenicolites* according to Dam (1990). These burrows are difficult to differentiate in the field, although they probably have similar environmental implications (high-energy stable substrates (Dam 1990)). Examples with indistinct boundaries represent weathered material.

Ichnogenus *TAENIDIUM* Heer, 1877
Taenidium ichnosp.
(cf. *T. serpentinum* Heer, 1877) Fig. 13g.

Occurrence. Units E, F, and I, occurring in dense masses.
Material. BELUM K13592, BELUM K13594, and BELUM K13595 from the basal part of unit F.
Description. Bedding-parallel convex and flat epireliefs, circular in cross section, 7–14 mm wide (commonly 10 mm), and up to 500 mm long. Straight or sinuous (bends rounded or angular), sharp changes in direction common (angle of change commonly

around 60 degrees), occasionally recurved. Commonly observed with a preferred orientation parallel to ripple crests (Fig. 9c). Comprised completely of sand-grade material, and having a distinctive transverse rugose ornamentation of typically 2–5 mm thick ridges, although one example has a structureless patch approximately 15 mm long. Internally apparently backfilled, although the details are unclear.

Discussion. These trace fossils resemble *Taenidium serpentinum*, as redescribed by D'Alessandro & Bromley (1987). However, they are not serpentiform and have sediment packets much thinner than those of *T. serpentinum*. They are also similar in form to *T. serpentinum* illustrated by Dam (1990). A lack of internal contrast prohibits definite assignment to *T. serpentinum*.

Ichnogenus *TEICHICHNUS* Seilacher, 1955
Teichichnus rectus Seilacher, 1955
Occurrence. Units D, F, and I, reasonably abundant.
Description. Concave or flat epireliefs, 7–15 mm wide (occasionally 20 mm), maximum length 400–500 mm. Sinuous to tortuous horizontals, or straight to curved inclined forms. The former in unit I, the latter at the base of D. Both comprise a vertically retrusive spreite composed of parallel vertically stacked lamellae, that are gutter-shaped, and concave-up. Spreite up to 70–80 mm high (20 mm wide examples from unit F). Sandstone-filled burrow on top of the spreite generally not present.

Discussion. The two morphological forms of *Teichichnus*, represent different levels of the same burrow system, and can be assigned to *Teichichnus rectus* (cf. Frey & Howard 1990).

'BRANCHING BURROWS' Figs 13h, 15.
Occurrence. Units D, F, and K. Sparse to prolific, concentrated vertically and laterally.

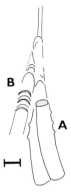

Fig. 15. Field sketch of 'Branched burrow', hyporelief, with (A) ornamentation on base of burrow, and (B) inclined plates above lower burrow. Scale 10 mm.

Material. BELUM K13576, a part of one branch, from unit D.
Description. Convex hyporeliefs, on the base of sandstone beds, comprising a series of branching horizontal burrows (generally three of four), dividing at acute angles at the distal end. Branches 8–15 mm wide, and up to 400 mm in length. Branches ornamentated along their sides by 1–3 mm wide pimples, spaced at 8–10 mm intervals. Burrow overlain by dipping plates (inclined towards proximal end), which are up to 30 mm high, 2–4 mm thick, and exhibit evidence of collapse.

Discussion. These burrows cannot be assigned to any known ichnogenus. A full description and assignment to a new ichnogenus will be published at a later date. Apparently representing a sediment-feeding mode of life, by an as yet unknown organism.

'PLOUGH TRAILS'
type-A Fig. 16a.
Occurrence. Units E and F.
Material. On blocks BELUM K13562 and BELUM K13564, from the top of unit F.
Description. Bedding-parallel concave exogenic epireliefs, 2–20 mm wide, and 20–500 mm in length. Cross section V-shaped (rarely U-shaped), angle of 'V' variable along and between individual examples. Lateral ridges typically developed, which are up to 5 mm in relief. Straight, curved, sinous or tortuous (occasionally looped) in morphology. Examples parallel to ripple crests commonly lack a ridge on the side closest to the crest (cf. *Archaeonassa*). Ridges either smooth or variably lobed; transverse or oblique.

Discussion. The taxonomic position of simple V-shaped plough trails is complex. Although sometimes placed in the ichnogenus *Scolicia* (Turner 1978), other authors prefer to name these trace fossils informally, for example as 'furrows' (Wright & Benton 1987) and this latter convention is followed here. These plough trails may have been produced by a variety of organisms, for example gastropods (Fig. 16c), and bivalves (Fig. 16d), at or near the surface. Highly facies-crossing, and therefore of limited environmental significance, although their preservation indicates low-energy or sheltered conditions.

'PLOUGH TRAILS'
type-B Fig. 16e, f.
Occurrence. Unit F, relatively rare, and poorly preserved.
Description. Convex exogenic epireliefs, comprising V-shaped grooves, with lateral ridges. Width 10 mm, and up to 150 mm in length. Maximum relief of 4 mm. Ridges ornamentated by transverse or oblique lobes, rarely smooth. The surface groove is underlain by a series of transverse hollows, which are dumbbell-shaped. These are straight to variably curved, up to 2

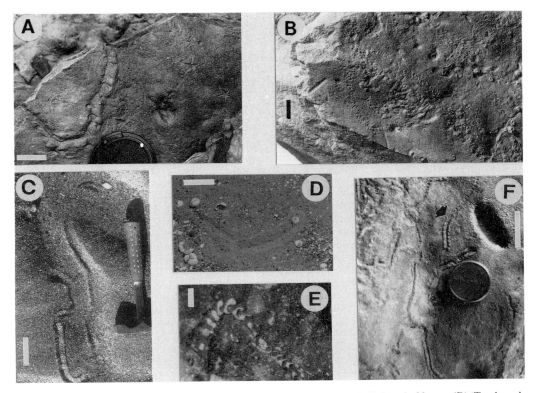

Fig. 16. (A) 'Plough trail' type-A, and *Asteriacites lumbricalis* form-B, epirelief, scale 20 mm. (B) 'Trackway', epirelief, scale 20 mm. (C) Modern gastropod trail, scale 70 mm. (D) Modern bivalve trail, scale 100 mm. (E) Lower section through 'plough trail' type-B, epirelief, scale 10 mm. (F) 'Plough trail' type-B, arrowed example exhibiting both upper and lower sections. *Diplocraterion* top right, epirelief, scale 55 mm.

or 3 mm wide (measured parallel to trail axis), and typically swollen at their margins. Material from other localities indicates that these trails have a variable morphology; straight, curved, sinuous, and looped.

Discussion. These are similar to the type-A 'plough trails', but, differ from them in their possession of transverse dumbbell-shaped depressions. The exact ethological significance of these depressions is uncertain, although their presence does appear to be of taxonomic significance. These trails will be further discussed in a later paper.

'TRACKWAY' Fig. 16b.

Occurrence. One poorly preserved example, from the base of unit F, uncollected. Apparently also near the top of unit F, from the *Archaeonassa* horizon.
Description. Concave epirelief, comprising a narrow trackway less than 6 mm wide, with concave dactyli imprints 1 mm or less in width. Exact nature and form of imprints unclear.

Discussion. Similar trackways (Fig. 16b), occur between Blackrocks and Skerrydoo (G 731 565

to G 743 574), from a similar environmental setting (intertidal). Such dactyli impressions also appear to occur from the *Archaeonassa* bearing horizon near the top of unit F, but are poorly preserved and inconspicuous. These are here interpreted as representing the activity of arthropods, although they are unlike other known forms (e.g. those in Häntzschel 1975). The producer of these trackways need not be restricted to crustaceans, but may also include a variety of insects (cf. Hitchcock 1858). Preservation prohibits a more precise diagnosis.

Bioturbational fabric

Most units exhibit some degree of bioturbation, with the notable exception of the laminated sandstone (unit G), and possibly the massive channel sandstone of unit O. Bioturbation within the measured section varies from highly reworked to limited bioturbation with primary sedimentary structures clearly preserved, or unbioturbated. Bioturbation exhibits vertical variation in intensity, even on a bed-scale, and considerable variation laterally. Because of the high degree of lateral variability in amount of bioturbation, no bioturbation index has been applied to this section (cf. Drosser & Bottjer 1986). However, the most bioturbated fabrics always occur in facies 1, and then notably to a greater extent within the finer-grained component (shales and siltstones). This positively reflects rates of sedimentation, the more slowly accumulated mud-rocks of facies 1 exhibiting the highest degree of bioturbation, and highest diversity of ichnogenera present.

Tiering

Tiering within this section, and other parts of the Mullaghmore Sandstone is not commonly observed. The recognition of palaeotiering requires plentiful examples of cross-cutting between ichnogenera (in vertical section) which is rarely observed within the present section. The endobenthic depth and relationships of most ichnogenera are unknown, and difficult to calculate with any reliability. Therefore no tiering model is presented here.

Colonization

Colonization is recognized, and clearly observed within the section. Both *Diplocraterion* and *Arenicolites* type-A are frequently observed as opportunistic colonisers of the thin tempestite sandstone horizons within facies 1. These ichnogenera represent the colonization of the sandstone after rapid deposition, or in some cases post-hydrodynamic reworking, both caused by storm events. Similar examples of colonization, and subsequent modification with changing energy levels is also observed within the lower half of subfacies 3A (unit E).

Trace fossil usage: environmental use, problems, pitfalls

Trace fossils are commonly used for environmental elucidation, particularly where sedimentological details are lacking. Seilacher's bathymetry of trace fossils (Seilacher 1967) has since its conception been regularly expanded and updated (e.g. Frey *et al.* 1990; Bromley & Asgaard 1991; and references therein). Some authors, such as Ekdale (1988), have pointed out contributing factors which affect the zonation of trace fossils, other than depth, which include oxygen levels, substrate condition, and salinity. However, the general ichnological facies concept still remains pertinent as a tool for environmental reconstruction.

The ichnogenera recovered from any given section will depend on the type of outcrop. For example, vertical sections and bedding plane surfaces will yield different ichnogenera (see Bromley 1990, p 222 and p 236, for relevance to work with cores); each on its own will not fully reflect the environment of deposition. Such an example occurs within the upper part of unit F, on the north side of the measured section. Here *Rhizocorallium* occurs on a large bedding plane surface at one locality, with apparently barren beds above (beds observed in vertical section only). Near-by (exposed in a stepped vertical section) the *Rhizocorallium* is not observed, but the sandstones above clearly exhibit a rich ichnofauna that includes; *Archaeonassa*, *Arenicolites* (types A and B), *Asteriacites*, *Olivellites*, and *Schaubcylindrichnus*. Similar results may also result from variably weathered sections.

Examination of the section presented in this paper indicates that many trace fossils have a somewhat sporadic or clustered lateral distribution, and commonly exhibit lateral changes in ichnogeneric composition and numbers. This is observed along the basal part of unit F, where *Taenidium* dominates and occurs in sporadic clusters, whereas the distribution of other ichnogenera is highly variable along the section (Fig. 17). This may represent only local variability in the concentration of particular ichnogenera, caused by differences in degree of weathering and quality of exposure; but also possibly reflecting an environmental gradient (at least in the case of *Olivellites*). A single vertical log through this horizon would result in a misleading and incomplete picture of the vertical distribution of the ichnogenera present, and accordingly a less precise environmental diagnosis. The omission of such details in lateral variation would also result in the loss of more subtle information on environmental gradients.

Another example of information that can be extracted by careful lateral trace fossil distribution mapping is seen halfway through unit F at the north end of the section. Here a general increase in the size of *Diplocraterion* is observed (Fig. 18); with size increasing towards the east. As no *Diplocraterion* occur to the west this may indicate an increase an energy levels eastwards (? local shoaling).

Therefore, even if the exposure is good in terms of type (both bedding plane and vertical section exposure) and degree of weathering, limitations to lateral continuity may distort the full ichnological picture and lead to erroneous environmental evaluation.

COMMON TO BOTH PARTS OF THE SECTION	ONLY OBSERVED AT THE SOUTH END	ONLY OBSERVED AT THE NORTH END
Asteriacites lumbricalis form-A *Aulichnites parkerensis* *Diplocraterion parallelum* *Taenidium* ichnosp. "Plough trails" type-A	*Gyrochorte?* *Olivellites plummeri* "Trackway"	*Archaeonassa fossulata* "Plough trails" type-B

Fig. 17. Lateral distribution of trace fossils along the section, at the base of unit F.

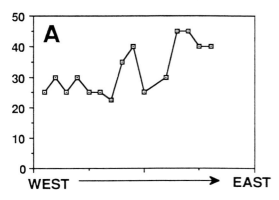

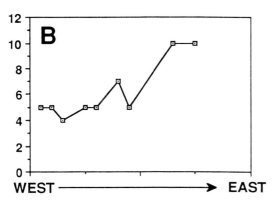

Fig. 18. Graphs showing relationship of *Diplocraterion* total width (A), and burrow width (B), along an easterly traverse. From the upper half of unit F at the north end of the measured section. Vertical scales in millimetres.

Environmental overview

At least four coarsening-upwards sequences occur, the lower three of which comprise alternations of facies 1 overlain by either facies 2 or facies 3; the lowest of which passes from facies 1, through facies 2, into facies 3 (Fig. 3). The uppermost sequence (sequence 4) is capped by facies 3, and is underlain by a series of facies 2 sandstones (unit K and M) interbedded with shales of facies 1 (unit J), or probable facies 1 type (units L and N). If unit L is considered to represent a distinct phase of facies 1 sedimentation, then sequence 4 could be subdivided into two separate sequences (sequence 4 and 5 of Fig. 3a). Additionally, the shale unit (unit N) is of unknown lateral extent, being cut-out by the overlying sandstone. If this shale unit where originally of appreciable lateral extent, and also equivalent to facies 1, then sequence 5 could be further divided into two sequences (sequence 5 and 6 of Fig. 3b). Unfortunately access problems do not allow for a more precise diagnosis for units L-O.

Each sequence reflects a shift in the locus of maximum sediment transportation and deposition (delta progradation). These represent a change from shallow-water marine/brackish conditions (prodelta or interdistributary bay) to that of subaqueous delta channel deposits (possibly in part non-marine fluviatile). Not all sequences are complete; either lacking a capping of facies 3 because of distance (lateral or axial) from the delta front, or missing in facies 2 because of erosion by facies 3.

Facies 1 (prodelta/interdistributary bay environment)

This facies contains the most diverse ichnofauna, comprising errant and static feeding burrows, resting/dwelling structures, and dwelling/suspension-feeding burrows. These trace fossils are typical of a shallow-water *Cruziana*-type ichnofacies, with an interbedded *Arenicolites* ichnofacies in association with thin tempestite sandstones (see Bromley & Asgaard 1991). The occurrence of *Neonereites* does not imply the presence of the *Nereites* deep-water ichnofacies, occurring as it does in small numbers and in restricted outcrop. This interpretation is supported by the sedimentary structures, with small-scale wave ripples the dominant feature. The occurrence of desiccation cracks indicates intertidal conditions, with periods of emergence; this is further indicated by the rare occurrence of flat-topped ripples, a common feature of intertidal waters (see Tanner 1958). Hummocky cross-stratification (HCS) and swaley cross-stratification (SCS) are noted from the section. These features are generally taken to be indicative of deposition between storm and fairweather wavebase, but as noted by Allen & Underhill (1989), the latter are more an indicator of high sediment load unidirectional flows, rather than restricted to any one depth or mechanism.

Shallow water is particularly indicated by the ichnogenera *Olivellites*, *Aulichnites*, and *Archaeonassa*, all well known from shallow-water environments above wavebase. Traces similar to *Archaeonassa* in particular have been recorded from modern intertidal deposits (Knox & Miller 1985). Also *Curvolithus*, although not common, is indicative of the *Skolithos–Cruziana* ichnofacies (Martino 1989), and is common in tidal flat environments (Chamberlain 1978). The occurrence of anemone resting structures (*Bergaueria* and *Conostichus?*) is again indicative of shallow-marine conditions, interdistributary bay or back barrier lagoonal environments (see Chamberlain 1971; Martino 1989). The small size of *Asteriacites* may indicate reduced salinities (brackish conditions) for part of the time (see Hakes 1976, 1985).

The majority of ichnogenera from this facies are bedding-parallel, particularly those within the shale and siltstone horizons. This indicates a generally low-energy environment, with low rates of sedimentation. The prolific occurrence of surface trails, such as *Archaeonassa* and 'plough trails', indicates that sedimentation was slow and sporadic.

Subfacies 1A (unit G), composed of parallel-laminated sandstone, contains neither body nor trace fossils, and the primary sedimentary structures are therefore undisturbed. The exact nature and mechanism of deposition of this unit is unclear. Unit G is thicker, and of more widespread distribution compared to other sandstone bodies within facies 1. The parallel-laminated nature of unit G, and its consistent thickness over a wide area (0.8 m) indicates a high-energy sustained unrestrained flow (sheet-flood) over a number of hours or days. This unit is therefore considered to represent flood-discharge deposition into a prodelta or interdistributary bay environment.

The small channel-form sandstone bodies

(subfacies 1B), occasionally found within facies 1, represent small prodelta subaqueous extensions to the delta drainage system. Such channels are common throughout the Mullaghmore Sandstone, and the laterally equivalent Kildoney Sandstone, and have also been recorded from other delta environments (see Elliott 1986, Fig. 6.38).

Therefore, facies 1 is interpreted as representative of a quiet water *Cruziana*-type ichnofacies, in a prodelta or interdistributary bay setting, with generally low rates of sedimentation and a high degree of bioturbation. The occurrence of suspension-feeding burrows (*Diplocraterion*, *Arenicolites* type-A) in association with thin sandstone beds does not imply any radical water-depth change, but rather the rapid influx of sand-laden waters, associated with storm events, or periods of higher river discharge. The majority of the thin sandstone beds represent tempestite deposits, and/or storm reworked horizons, as indicated by the occurrence of HCS, SCS, and shelly lags. Larger storms or river flood events produced the more continuous thick laminated-sandstones (unit G), and small isolated channels represent the subaqueous continuation of the delta drainage system.

Facies 2 (Intermediate environment)

The general lack of detail on sedimentary structures, and limited numbers of available trace fossils, make this facies difficult to interpret in terms of its environment. However, its stratigraphical occurrence indicates that this facies was deposited in an intermediate environment between facies 1 and facies 3. The dominance of sandstone over shale indicates deposition closer to the active delta margin, as does the greater size of observed channels in comparison to facies 1. The continued dominance of bedding-parallel trace fossils indicates that although nearer to the locus of deposition, and presumably shallower, the environment was still essentially that typified by the *Cruziana* ichnofacies (relatively low-energy).

Facies 3 (subaqueous delta channel environment)

This facies is characterized by medium and coarse-grained sandstones, which are typically feldspathic in nature. Facies 3 units have sharp erosional bases, and are generally composed of a series of multiply stacked channel-form beds. This facies is characterized by low trace fossil diversity, typically with only occasional

Skolithos / Arenicolites type-C and *Diplocraterion* which are commonly truncated by coarser-grained bioclastic horizons. The occurrence of these ichnogenera represents the opportunistic colonization of a high-energy environment; *Skolithos / Arenicolites* type-C in a high-energy stable substrate, and *Diplocraterion* in a high-energy mobile substrate.

Units E and I also have predominantly horizontal trace fossils within their upper part which are more characteristic of facies 1. The horizontal ichnogenera either represent periods of quiescence as within unit E ('plough trails' in particular associated with mud-drapes), or as with unit I, represent the transition from facies 3 to facies 1.

This facies represents subaqueous delta channel deposits. Examples of this facies from other localities within the Mullaghmore Sandstone may partially by non-marine in origin, but no clear evidence for this exists within the present section. High-energy conditions are indicated by the occurrence of mega-ripples (unit E), and shallow-water by ladder-ripples (unit E) (see Wright & Benton 1987). Subfacies 3A (unit E) is interpreted as representing the margins of a more extensive facies 3 complex, the higher mud content resulting from the admixture of facies 1 muds during initial deposition. This subfacies has undergone subsequent hydrodynamic reworking, particularly in the upper part, and is atypical of the facies as a whole. The occurrence of mega-ripples with superimposed large-scale ripples indicates the shallow-water nature of the environment (cf. Klein 1963, p 848).

Conclusions

The 25 m thick section of Mullaghmore Sandstone exposed on the northwest corner of Mullaghmore Head contains a diverse ichnofauna, which along with the observed sedimentary structures, are indicative of a shallow-water marine environment. The measured section contains at least four (and possibly as many as six) coarsening-upwards sequences, interpreted as representing a shift from a prodelta or interdistributary bay environment to that of a more proximal subaqueous delta channel environment.

In terms of ichnofacies the environment can be interpreted as that of a *Cruziana* ichnofacies, with an interbedded *Arenicolites* ichnofacies, passing up into a higher energy *Skolithos* ichnofacies. However, not all sequences are complete.

Examination of the section indicates that the ichnogenera present have a highly sporadic lateral distribution. This, along with type of available section and state of weathering, must be taken into account where trace fossils are used for environmental elucidation.

This paper represents part of work carried out under a research studentship from the Department of Education for Northern Ireland, which is gratefully acknowledged. M. J. Benton, P. F. Carey, A. J. Newell, P. J. Orr and A. D. Wright are thanked for their constructive comments on the manuscript, as are R. G. Bromley and R. Goldring for critical review. The Department of Geology, Bristol University, is acknowledged and thanked for the use of facilities. The Moran family of the Bella Vista, Bundoran, Co. Donegal are thanked for accommodation during fieldwork.

References

ABEL, O. 1935. Vorzeitliche Lebensspuren. Gustav Fischer, Jena.

ALLEN, P. A. & UNDERHILL, J. R. 1989. Swaley cross-stratification produced by unidirectional flows, Bencliff Grit (Upper Jurassic), Dorset, UK. *Journal of the Geological Society, London*, **146**, 241–252.

AVBOVBO, A. A. 1973. *Sedimentological analysis of Viséan clastics in northwestern Ireland*. PhD thesis, Imperial College, London.

BALDWIN, C. T. 1977. The stratigraphy and facies associations of trace fossils in some Cambrian and Ordovician rocks of north western Spain. *Geological Journal* Special Issue, **9**, 9–40.

BJERSTEDT, T. W. 1987. Trace fossils indicating estuarine deposystems for the Devonian-Mississippian Cloyd Conglomerate Member, Price Formation, central Appalachians. *Palaios*, **2**, 339–349.

——— 1988a. Trace fossils from the early Mississippian Price Delta, southeast West Virginia. *Journal of Paleontology*, **62**, 506–519.

——— 1988b. Multivariate analyses of trace fossil distribution from an early Mississipian oxygen-deficient basin, central Appalachians. *Palaios*, **3**, 53–68.

BROADHURST, F. M., SIMPSON, I. M. & HARDY, P. G. 1980. Seasonal sedimentation in the Upper Carboniferous of England. *Journal of Geology*, **88**, 639–651.

BROMLEY, R. G. 1990. *Trace Fossils: Biology and Taphonomy*. Unwin Hyman, London.

——— & ASGAARD, U. 1991. Ichnofacies: a mixture of taphofacies and biofacies. *Lethaia*, **24**, 153–163.

CHAMBERLAIN, C. K. 1971. Morphology and ethology of trace fossils from the Ouachita Mountains, southeast Oklahoma. *Journal of Paleontology*, **45**, 212–246.

——— 1978. *A Guidebook to the Trace Fossils and Paleoecology of the Ouachita Geosyncline*. Society of Economic Paleontologists and Mineralogists, Tulsa.

CHANDRA, A. 1974. *Ichnology of Viséan sandstones in northwestern Ireland. A study of trace fossils in their palaeoecological and sedimentological context.* PhD thesis, Imperial College, London.

D'ALESSANDRO, A. & BROMLEY, R. G. 1987. Meniscate trace fossils and the *Muensteria-Taenidium* problem. *Palaeontology*, **30**, 743–763.

DAM, G. 1990. Taxonomy of trace fossils from the shallow marine Lower Jurassic Neill Klinter Formation, East Greenland. *Bulletin of the Geological Society of Denmark*, **38**, 119–144.

DROSSER, M. L. & BOTTJER, D. J. 1986. A semiquantitative field classification of ichnofabric. *Journal of Sedimentary Petrology*, **56**, 558–559.

DUNS, J. 1877. On an unnamed Palaeozoic annelid. *Proceedings of the Royal Society of Edinburgh*, **9**, 352–359.

EKDALE, A. A. 1988. Pitfalls of paleobathymetric interpretations based on trace fossil assemblages. *Palaios*, **3**, 464–472.

——, BROMLEY, R. G. & PEMBERTON, S. G. 1984. Ichnology. The use of trace fossils in sedimentology and stratigraphy. Society of Economic Paleontologists Mineralogists, Short Course, 15.

ELLIOTT, T. 1986. Deltas. *In*: READING, H. G. (ed.) *Sedimentary environments and facies.* Blackwell Scientific Publications, Oxford, 113–154.

FENTON, C. L. & FENTON, M. A. 1937a. *Olivellites*, a Pennsylvanian snail burrow. *American Midland Naturalist*, **18**, 452–453.

—— & —— 1937b. *Archaeonassa*, Cambrian snail trails and burrows. *American Midland Naturalist*, **18**, 454–456.

—— & —— 1937c. Burrows and trails from Pennsylvanian rocks of Texas. *American Midland Naturalist*, **18**, 1079–1084.

FREY, R. W. 1990. Trace fossils and hummocky cross-stratification, Upper Cretaceous of Utah. *Palaios*, **5**, 203–218.

—— & HOWARD, J. D. 1981. *Conichnus* and *Schaubcylindrichnus*: redefined trace fossils from the Upper Cretaceous of the western interior. *Journal of Paleontology*, **55**, 800–804.

—— & —— 1990. Trace fossils and depositional sequences in a clastic shelf setting. Upper Cretaceous of Utah. *Journal of Paleontology*, **64**, 803–820.

——, PEMBERTON, S. G. & SAUNDERS, D. A. 1990. Ichnofacies and bathymetry: a passive relationship. *Journal of Paleontology*, **64**, 155–158.

FÜRSICH, F. T. 1974a. Corallian (Upper Jurassic) trace fossils from England and Normandy. *Stuttgarter Beiträge zur Naturkunde, Serie B (Geologie und Paläontologie)*, **13**, 1–52.

—— 1974b. Ichnogenus *Rhizocorallium. Paläontologische Zeitschrift*, **48**, 16–28.

—— 1974c. On *Diplocraterion* Torell 1870 and the significance of morphological features in vertical spreiten-bearing, U-shaped trace fossils. *Journal of Paleontology*, **48**, 952–962.

—— & MAYR, H. 1981. *Non-marine Rhizocorallium* (trace fossil) from the upper freshwater molasse (Upper Miocene) of southern Germany. *Neues Jahrbuch für Geologie und Palaöntologie, Monatshefte*, **6**, 321–333.

HAKES, W. G. 1976. Trace fossils and depositional environment of four clastic units upper Pennsylvanian megacyclothems, northeast Kansas. The University of Kansas Paleontological Contributions, Article 63, 46 pp.

—— 1985. Trace fossils from brackish-marine shales, upper Pennsylvanian of Kansas, U.S.A. *In*: CURRAN, H. A. (ed.) *Biogenic structures: Their use in interpreting depositional environments.* Society of Economic Paleontologists and Mineralogists, Special Publication, **35**, 21–35.

HANTZSCHEL, W. 1975. Trace fossils and problematica. *In*: TEICHERT, C. (ed.) *Treatise on invertebrate paleontology, part W, miscellanea, supplement 1.* Geological Society of America and University of Kansas Press, Colorado and Lawrence, Kansas.

HEINBERG, C. 1973. The internal structure of the trace fossils *Gyrochorte* and *Curvolithus. Lethaia*, **6**, 227–238.

HEINBERG, C. & BIRKELUND, T. 1984. Trace-fossil assemblages and basin evolution of the Vardekløft Formation (Middle Jurassic, central East Greenland). *Journal of Paleontology*, **58**, 362–397.

HIGGS, K. 1984. Stratigraphic palynology of the Carboniferous rocks in northwest Ireland. *Geological Survey of Ireland, Bulletin*, **3**, 171–201.

——, MCPHILEMY, B., KEEGAN, J. B. & CLAYTON, G. 1988. New data on palynological boundaries within the Irish Dinantian. *Review of Palaeobotany and Palynology*, **56**, 61–68.

HITCHCOCK, E. 1858. *Ichnology of New England. A report on the sandstone of the Connecticut Valley, especially its footprints.* W. White, Boston.

KLEIN, G.deV. 1963. Bay of Fundy intertidal zone sediments. *Journal of Sedimentary Petrology*, **33**, 844–854.

KNOX, L. W. & MILLER, M. F. 1985. Environmental control of trace fossil morphology. *In*: CURREN, H. A. (ed.) *Biogenic structures: their Use in Interpreting Depositional Environments.* Society of Economic Paleontologists and Mineralogists, Special Publication, **35**, 167–176.

LEEDER, M. R. 1988. Devono-Carboniferous river systems and sediment dispersal from the orogenic belts and cratons of NW Europe. *In*: HARRIS, A. L. & FETTES, D. J. (eds) *The Caledonian–Appalachian Orogen.* Geological Society, London, Special Publication, **38**, 549–558.

MAPLES, C. G. & WEST, R. R. 1989. *Lockeia*, not *Pelecypodichnus. Journal of Paleontology*, **63**, 694–696.

MARTINO, R. L. 1989. Trace fossils from marginal marine facies of the Kanawha Formation (middle Pennsylvanian), West Virginia. Journal of Paleontology, **63**, 389–403.

OSGOOD, R. G. 1970. Trace fossils of the Cincinnati area. *Palaeontographica Americana*, **6**, 281–444.

OSWALD, D. H. 1955. The Carboniferous rocks between the Ox Mountains and Donegal Bay. *Quarterly Journal of the Geological Society,*

London, **111**, 167–186.

PARNELL, J., MONSON, B. & BUCKMAN, J. 1990. *Excursion guide: Basins and Petroleum Geology in the North of Ireland.* School of Geosciences, Belfast.

PEMBERTON, S. G. & FREY, R. W. 1982. Trace fossil nomenclature and the *Planolites-Palaeophycus* dilemma. *Journal of Paleontology*, **56**, 843–881.

——, FREY, R. W. & BROMLEY, R. G. 1988. The ichnotaxonomy of *Conostichus* and other plug-shaped ichnofossils. *Canadian Journal of Earth Sciences*, **25**, 866–892.

—— & MAGWOOD, J. P. A. 1990. A unique occurrence of *Bergaueria* in the Lower Cambrian Gog Group near lake Louise, Alberta. *Journal of Paleontology*, **64**, 436–440.

POLLARD, J. E. 1981. A comparison between the Triassic trace fossils of Cheshire and south Germany. *Palaeontology*, **24**, 555–588.

RODRIGUEZ, J. & GUTSCHICK, R. C. 1970. *Late Devonian-Early Mississippian ichnofossils from western Montana and northern Utah.* Geological Journal Special Issue, **3**, 407–438.

SCHÄFER, W. 1972. *Ecology and Palaeoecology of Marine Environments.* Oliver and Boyd, Edinburgh.

SEILACHER, A. 1953. Studien zur Palichnologie. II. Die fossilen Ruhespuren (Cubichnia). *Neues jahrbuch Geologie und Paläontologie, Abhandlungen*, **98**, 87–124.

—— 1955. Spuren und Fazies im Unterkambrium. *In:* SCHINDEWOLF, O. H. & SEILACHER, A. Beiträge zur kenntnis des Kambriums in der Salt Range (Pakistan). *Akademie der Wissenschaften und der Literatur zu Mainz, mathemtisch-naturwissenschaftliche Klasse, Abhandlungen*, **10**, 11–143.

—— 1967. Bathymetry of trace fossils. *Marine Geology*, **5**, 413–428.

SHERIDAN, D. J. R. 1972. Upper Old Red Sandstone and Lower Carboniferous of the Slieve Beagh syncline and its setting in the northwest Carboniferous basin. Geological Survey of Ireland, Special Paper No. 2.

TANNER, W. F. 1958. An occurrence of flat-topped ripple marks. *Journal of Sedimentary Petrology*, **28**, 95–96.

TURNER, B. R. 1978. Trace fossils from the Upper Triassic fluviatile Molteno Formation of the Karoo (Gondwana) Supergroup, Lesotho. *Journal of Paleontology*, **52**, 959–963.

—— & BENTON, M. J. 1983. Paleozoic trace fossils from the Kufra Basin, Libya. *Journal of Paleontology*, **57**, 447–460.

WALKER, E. F. 1985. Arthropod ichnofauna of the Old Red Sandstone at Dunure and Montrose, Scotland. *Transactions of the Royal Society of Edinburgh, Earth Sciences*, **76**, 287–297.

WRIGHT, A. D. & BENTON, M. J. 1987. Trace fossils from Rhaetic shore-face deposits of Staffordshire. *Palaeontology*, **30**, 407–428.

Origin of reddening and secondary porosity in Carboniferous sandstones, Northern Ireland

W. H. WANG

School of Geosciences, The Queen's University of Belfast, Belfast BT7 1NN, UK

Abstract: Carboniferous sandstones in the Ballycastle district of Northern Ireland were deposited in fluvio-deltaic environments. Significant secondary porosity was generated in the sandstones, particularly in red-coloured sandstones, due to the dissolution of carbonate cement. Minor secondary porosity was also created by the leaching of feldspar grains. Virtually all the observed porosity in the Carboniferous sandstones has a secondary origin. Subsequently, the precipitation of kaolinite reduced the porosity. The red-coloured sandstones are important in showing the depth of invasion of oxidising meteoric fluids following late Carboniferous–Permian uplift. The red colour is due to iron oxides liberated during the dedolomitization of a ferroan dolomite cement. Several instances of reddened Carboniferous strata across the UK probably have a similar origin and are potential oil and gas reservoirs as reddened sandstones may have a high secondary porosity.

Much of the secondary porosity in ancient sandstones is a result of the mesogenetic leaching of carbonate mineral cements, including calcite, dolomite and siderite. Most mesogenetic decarbonatization results from the decarboxylation of organic matter in strata adjacent to the sandstone during the course of organic maturation (Schmidt & McDonald 1979a). However, some workers suggest that the organic-rich strata do not yield enough CO_2 to generate significant secondary porosity. Carbonate and framework grain leaching by meteoric water during relatively shallow burial may also create some secondary porosity (Bjørlykke 1983; Giles & Marshall 1986). This paper gives an account of the generation of secondary porosity by the leaching of carbonate and feldspar during telodiagenesis.

Red-coloured sediments have for many years been interpreted as being predominantly of continental origin. Furthermore, the cause of the red coloration has been well documented as due to the presence of ferric oxide, particularly hematite (Berner 1969). However, the origin of the hematite has been the subject of considerable debate. The earliest suggestion was that the red coloration was caused by iron liberated during the decomposition of hornblende and mica (Lyell 1852). Subsequently, workers considered the hematite to form in lateritic soils in tropical, humid climates under deep weathering conditions (Krynine 1949). In the oxidizing environment of the hot desert, iron rapidly becomes ferric and either enters the lattice of newly forming clay minerals, or forms a fine coating on individual clay particles (McBride 1974; Walker *et al.* 1978; Besly & Turner 1983).

Other studies show that hematite and other iron oxides such as goethite are commonly associated with dedolomite and are generally interpreted as by-products of the dedolomitization of ferroan dolomite (e.g. Katz 1971; Al-Hashimi & Hemingway 1973; Frank 1981). This study documents iron oxides in sandstones as by-products of the dedolomitization of a ferroan dolomite cement.

The study area at Ballycastle is located in the northeast of Northern Ireland (Fig. 1). The Carboniferous succession is a conformable sequence of mixed marine and non-marine strata which mainly consists of sandstones, mudrocks, conglomerates, limestones and coal seams. The sandstones, including a series of red-coloured sandstones which are cemented by ferroan dolomite, are the predominant rocks in the succession. The objective of this paper is to interpret the origin of reddening and secondary porosity in the sandstones.

Review of secondary porosity in sandstones

The concept of relating secondary porosity generation to the generation of oil through a decarboxylation–decarbonatization process was first developed by Chepikov *et al.* (1961). Subsequently, several workers have described occurrences of secondary porosity from the subsurface where the porosity originated after burial (e.g. Schmidt & McDonald 1979a, b; Bjørlykke 1983; Shanmugam 1985; Parnell 1987).

Secondary porosity is an important factor, not only in improving reservoir quality but also in modifying the original composition and tex-

From PARNELL, J. (ed.), 1992, *Basins on the Atlantic Seaboard: Petroleum Geology, Sedimentology and Basin Evolution.* Geological Society Special Publication No 62, pp 243–254.

243

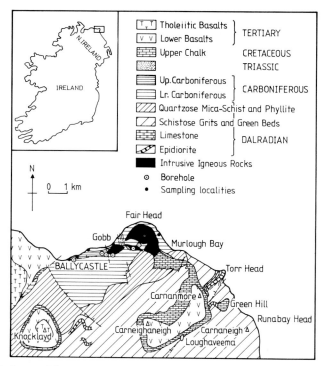

Fig. 1. Geological map of the Ballycastle area showing borehole and surface sample locations (after Wilson & Robbie 1966).

ture of sandstones by the dissolution of framework grains and cements. Schmidt & McDonald (1979b) distinguished five genetic classes of secondary porosity in sandstones according to their origin and pore texture: fracturing, shrinkage, dissolution of sedimentary grains and matrix, dissolution of authigenic pore-filling cement and dissolution of authigenic replacive minerals. Porosity originating from the dissolution of authigenic cement is probably the most common type of secondary porosity. It results from the selective dissolution of soluble cements such as calcite, dolomite and siderite. Porosity resulting from the dissolution of authigenic replacive minerals commonly forms a significant percentage of secondary porosity, and is formed by the selective dissolution of soluble minerals (predominantly calcite, dolomite and siderite) that previously replaced sedimentary constituents and/or authigenic cements.

Chepikov et al. (1961) introduced the first criteria for the recognition of secondary porosity in sandstones, including corroded grains, adjacent porous and less-porous zones, sinuous pores, remnant cement, and inhomogeneous packing. Schmidt & McDonald's (1979b)

petrographic criteria for recognising secondary porosity additionally include: partial dissolution, molds, oversized pores, elongate pores, intra-constituent pores, and fractured grains. In fact, recognition of secondary porosity should be based on multiple evidence because some non-fractured secondary pores mimic primary pores. Generally, secondary pores are larger in size, more irregular in shape, and more random in distribution than primary pores (Schmidt & McDonald 1979b). Understanding the origin of pores is critical in the recognition of secondary porosity. Shanmugam (1985) proposed 20 criteria for recognising secondary porosity according to the origin of pores in sandstones: fracturing of grains (diagenetic) and rock (tectonic); dissolution of framework grains, cement, cleavage planes, fossils (molds), inclusions and matrix; remnants of twin lamellae, replacive cement, clay rims, quartz veins, overgrowths and grains; corroded grains; oversized pores; elongate pores; insoluble residues; shrinkage voids; and adjacent porous and nonporous sand beds. In most cases, more than one criterion can be recognized.

Sampling and analytical techniques

Sandstone samples were obtained from both surface exposures and borehole cores (Fig. 1). Outcrop samples were collected from Gobb and Murlough Bay, east of Ballycastle. Thin sections were prepared from samples of sandstone impregnated with blue resin. Selected samples were examined by scanning electron microscopy (SEM), electron microprobe analysis and cathodoluminescence microscopy, to investigate and identify authigenic minerals and make a detailed analysis of secondary porosity.

Stratigraphy and depositional environments

A generalized stratigraphy for the Ballycastle area is shown in Fig. 2. The palaeontological evidence indicates that the Main Limestone is of Visean age and the uppermost beds of the succession are Namurian. The base of the Main Coal horizon is possibly the boundary between the Visean and Namurian (Wilson & Robbie 1966; Whitaker 1978). Carboniferous sediments were deposited predominantly within fluvio-deltaic environments. The sandstones are distributary channel deposits, which exhibit medium-angle cross-bedding, convolute bedding and plant debris. Mudrocks were deposited in both marine and non-marine environments. The non-marine mudrocks represent delta-top deposits and contain siderite nodules. The Main Limestone is the most important marker rock in the area, deposited in shallow marine environments and containing abundant marine fossils. The coal seams represent interdistributary swamp conditions. At least four marine transgressive events are represented in the succession.

Sandstone petrography

Most of the sandstones are quartz arenites, according to the classification of Folk (1974) and include just four subarkoses among 26 representative sandstone samples. Earlier studies showed that the Carboniferous sandstones were derived from pre-existing sediments or metamorphosed sediments, noting particularly the unusually small proportion of heavy minerals and scarcity of garnet grains (Adamson & Wilson 1933). Most of the sandstone samples have high porosities, especially the red-coloured samples (Fig. 3a). Point counts of impregnated thin sections show that porosity values reach 29%.

Quartz

Quartz grains account for 92–99% of the detrital framework constituents. The quartz is predominantly monocrystalline and shows weak to strong strain extinction, with quartz overgrowths in most samples. The relative proportion of polycrystalline quartz grains is generally greater in the coarser-grained sandstones. Most detrital quartz grains exhibit subangular to subrounded original grain boundaries and moderate sphericities. Both quartz grains and quartz overgrowths exhibit replacement by authigenic carbonate which may have been partially or completely removed during later diagenesis, to leave irregular grain margins (Fig. 3a).

Feldspar

Plagioclase and K-feldspar are present in minor to trace amounts, and in similar quantities. Some twinned plagioclase grains exhibit fracturing due to compaction and framework collapse, but appear relatively fresh compared to the K-feldspars. All feldspars exhibit at least partial alteration, being replaced by clays or carbonate. Dissolution of feldspars occurred to varying degrees, often producing honeycombed grains (Fig. 3b).

Rock fragments

A limited quantity of sandstone clasts are observed in some samples. Dissolution of feldspar also occurred within these rock fragments.

Authigenic minerals

A number of authigenic minerals were formed during diagenesis. The deduced diagenetic sequence is shown in Fig. 4.

Authigenic quartz

Authigenic quartz occurs to varying degrees in most of the studied samples. Since dust rims are not preserved in most samples, it was generally impossible to quantify the amount of authigenic quartz using a polarising microscope. However, by using cathodoluminescence, the authigenic quartz can be distinguished. SEM studies show that there are two stages of quartz overgrowth: An early cement which exhibits partial corrosion (Fig. 3a,c), and a later cement that precipitated in secondary pores, which do not exhibit any corrosion (Fig. 3d). Moreover, the earlier quartz overgrowth crystals are gen-

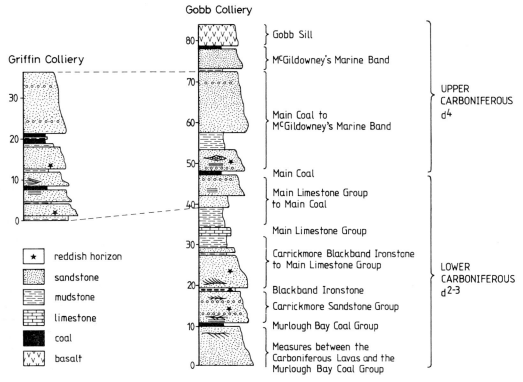

Fig. 2. Schematic vertical sections in Carboniferous at Colliery Bay, Ballycastle, showing the stratigraphy and reddened horizons.

erally larger than those of the later stage, since the earlier crystals were precipitated in the primary pores and the later crystals were precipitated in the secondary pores which were generated from dissolution of carbonate.

Ferroan dolomite

Ferroan dolomite is an important authigenic cement in the sandstones. The size of the dolomite rhombs is variable, ranging from 20 μm up to 50 μm. Electron microprobe analysis showed that the iron content of the dolomite crystals steadily increases outwards, and that there are also minor fluctuations in the Ca/Mg ratio. Significant secondary porosity was achieved by dissolution of the ferroan dolomite. SEM photographs clearly show a selective dissolution of ferroan dolomite. There are two patterns of selective dissolution. In some cases, dissolution proceeded outwards from the centre of the crystal to the rhombohedral margin (Fig. 3e); in other cases dissolution proceeded from the rhombohedral margin towards the centre of the crystal (Fig. 3f). Clearly, the selective dis-

solution is controlled by the chemical zoning in the crystals. Evamy (1967) proposed that the rhombohedral pores concerned result from the selective leaching of mineralogically unstable high-magnesian calcite or aragonite, in many cases the initial product of dedolomitization. This suggests that the Ca/Mg ratio is the critical control over the selective dissolution.

Calcite

Calcite occurs within the dolomite rhombs and is interpreted as a product of dedolomitization. Most of the calcite was probably leached out during later diagenesis to yield secondary porosity.

Kaolinite

Kaolinite was identified in most samples, using the SEM. Early kaolinite occurs as the replacement of feldspars. Subsequently, relatively small kaolinite crystals were precipitated within dolomite crystals after the selective dissolution of the dolomite (Fig. 5a,b). At a late stage,

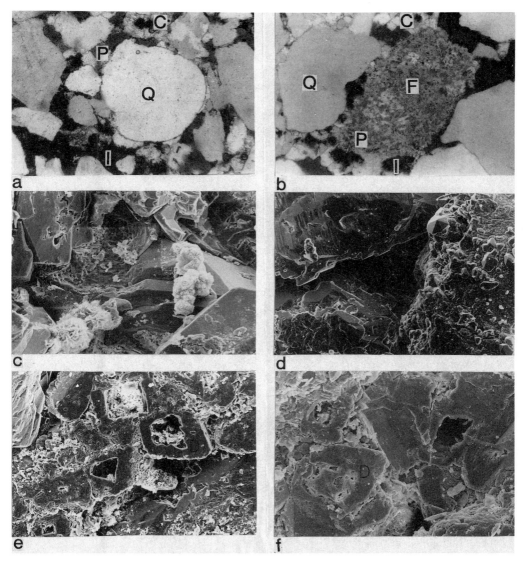

Fig. 3. Photomicrographs of sandstone samples from Colliery Bay. (a) Secondary porosity in red-coloured sandstone after dissolution of carbonate cement. P, secondary porosity; Q, quartz grains and quartz overgrowths; C, carbonate cement; I, iron oxide; cross-polarized (field width 2.4 mm). (b) Honeycombed dissolution of feldspar grain and dissolution of carbonate cement. P, secondary porosity; Q, quartz grains; F, feldspar; C, carbonate cement; I, iron oxide; cross-polarized (field width 2.4 mm). (c) SEM photomicrograph showing early stage quartz overgrowths which exhibit partial corrosion and later stage hematite precipitation (field width 0.118 mm). (d) SEM photomicrograph showing later stage quartz overgrowths (field width 0.179 mm). The later stage quartz overgrowth crystal is much smaller than that of the early stage. (e) & (f) SEM photomicrographs, showing selective dissolution of ferroan dolomite. (e) Dissolution occurred outwards from the centre of the crystal to the rhombohedral margin (field width 0.164 mm); (f) Dissolution occurred from the rhombohedral margin towards the centre of the crystal (field width 0.118 mm).

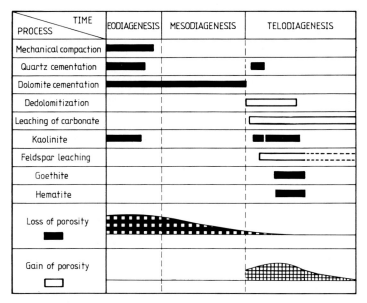

Fig. 4. Diagenetic sequence for the Carboniferous sandstones in the Ballycastle district.

relatively large booklets of kaolinite were precipitated in large secondary pores following the further dissolution of carbonate (Fig. 5c,d).

Iron oxides

Iron oxides occur in red-coloured sandstones, and display two crystal habits. One occurrence is as thin, circular plates of hematite, grouped in rosettes (Fig. 5e); the other is as prismatic bundles and prismatic radiating aggregates of goethite crystals (Fig. 5f). Both of them are relatively late-stage authigenic minerals, and hematite is predominant. The iron oxides are commonly associated with dedolomite and are interpreted as the products of dedolomitization of ferroan dolomite.

Diagenetic history

Diagenetic processes are clearly related to the burial history. Figure 6 shows a generalized burial history in the Ballycastle district and adjacent areas. The burial history was constructed using data from the Port More borehole to the west of Ballycastle (Wilson & Manning 1978) and the Rathlin Trough immediately offshore (Evans *et al.* 1980). The maximum burial depth is nearly 4000 m at the present day. However, there was no significant later burial after the late Carboniferous−Permian uplift onshore in the Ballycastle district (McCann 1988, Fig. 2). Most sandstone samples contain a

significant secondary porosity, interpreted as a product of telodiagenesis. Figure 4 shows the diagenetic processes which occurred in quartz arenites that contain diagenetic carbonate cement and replacement.

Eodiagenesis and mesodiagenesis

Eodiagenesis includes all reactions between the mineral phases of the sandstone and the pore-water from the time of deposition to effective burial (Schmidt & McDonald 1979a). These diagenetic processes are very important in sandstones because the porosity can be significantly changed at that stage by early cementation, compaction or dissolution and also because these processes strongly influence the later mesodiagenetic processes during deeper burial. Early minor quartz overgrowths can be seen in the sandstones. Following the minor quartz overgrowths, abundant ferroan dolomite cement was precipitated and partially replaced the detrital grains. The carbonate can account for up to 30% of the composition of the rock and exhibits replacive boundaries with the framework grains. Primary porosity was reduced by the carbonate cement, quartz overgrowths and compaction.

Telodiagenesis

Late Carboniferous−Permian uplift and erosion resulted in the telodiagenesis of Carboniferous

Fig. 5. SEM photomicrographs of Carboniferous sandstones. (a) & (b) Small kaolinite booklets precipitated within the dolomite crystals in which selective dissolution occurred (field width: a, 0.066 mm; b, 0.074 mm). (c) & (d) Larger kaolinite booklets precipitated in larger secondary pores due to further carbonate dissolution (field width: c, 0.054 mm; d, 0.079 mm). (e) & (f) Iron oxides in red-coloured sandstones. (e) Thin, circular plates of hematite, grouped in rosettes (field width 0.039 mm); (f) Prismatic bundles and prismatic radiating aggregates of goethite (field width 0.044 mm).

strata. The uppermost Carboniferous rocks were exposed to meteorically derived oxidizing fluids which caused the visible reddening of the Carboniferous. There was widespread reddening of the Carboniferous strata in the Ballycastle district and elsewhere across the central British Isles (Fig. 7). The depth of reddening is variable, ranging from a few decametres to over 500 m (Table 1, Fig. 8). SEM studies show that the iron oxides are the latest diagenetic minerals. Therefore dedolomitization of ferroan dolomite must have occurred prior to the formation of the iron oxides. It has been suggested by several authors that ferroan dolomite is preferentially replaced under near-surface, oxidizing conditions (Katz 1971; Al-Hashimi &

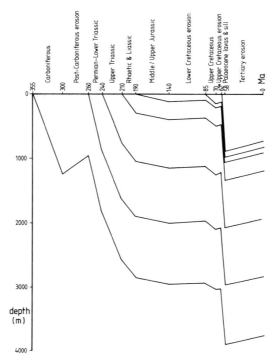

Fig. 6. Generalized burial history plot for Ballycastle and adjacent areas (data from Wilson & Manning 1978 and Evans *et al*. 1980).

Hemingway 1973; Frank 1981). Moreover, other well documented reports of near-surface dedolomitization have led to the general conclusion that most dedolomite occurrences are indicative of telodiagenetic weathering (Scholle 1971; Mossler 1971). However, several studies document dedolomitization under a variety of diagenetic conditions. For instance, calcitization of dolomite within a fresh water zone along a major fault system has been reported by Longman & Mench (1978). Therefore, the Tow Valley Fault (McCann 1988, Fig. 1) may have significantly influenced the diagenetic processes. Petrographic studies have shown that dedolomitization and carbonate dissolution in Carboniferous sandstones reached more than 70 metres beneath the land surface, probably because of the penetration of oxidizing meteoric fluids during the late Carboniferous–Permian period of uplift and erosion (see below), and that significant secondary porosity was generated as a result. Pore-filling kaolinite clearly reduced the porosity but still exhibits an effective microporosity. Permeability between the pores is relatively unrestricted. Leaching of feldspar grains may also have occurred at this time. The

dissolution and leaching of carbonate and feldspar may also have continued to the present time.

Discussion

Secondary porosity in sandstones

Of the five textural origins of secondary porosity in sandstones distinguished by Schmidt & McDonald (1979*b*), four types are recognized in the studied sandstone samples. Dissolution of authigenic pore-filling and replacive carbonate cement made a major contribution to the secondary porosity in the sandstones. Dissolution of unstable framework grains such as feldspar is also common. The dissolution and leaching of feldspar occurred to varying degrees and produced honeycombed grains in the sandstone samples. However, this kind of porosity makes just a minor contribution to the secondary porosity in the Ballycastle samples because most of the sandstones are quartz arenites. Fracture porosity is limited because the compaction was reduced by early carbonate cementation. In fact, individual pores often have a

Fig. 7. Localities of reddened Carboniferous rocks in the central British Isles (for sources see text).

complex origin; many are composed of several genetic classes of secondary porosity. For example, replacement of the margins of sand grains frequently occurred simultaneously with the cementation of the adjacent intergranular spaces by the same mineral. Complete dissolution of an authigenic mineral would create hybrid pores because both pore cement and grain replacement cement are removed.

The generation of secondary porosity requires certain physico-chemical conditions, particularly a suitable fluid to leach away unstable components in the sandstones. During the late Carboniferous–Permian, the uppermost Carboniferous rocks were exposed to meteorically derived oxidizing fluids which caused the reddening of Carboniferous strata following uplift and erosion. Significant secondary porosity resulted from the dissolution of carbonate. The presence of kaolinite within the secondary porosity caused by carbonate dissolution suggests dissolution by an acidic fluid. Carbonate dissolution by an acidic fluid would cause the pH of the fluid to rise to the point where it is supersaturated and the mineral kaolinite is precipitated (Curtis 1983; Parnell 1987).

Distribution and significance of red-coloured sandstones

Red-coloured Carboniferous strata occur across the central British Isles. The relationship between the red coloration of Carboniferous strata and Permo-Triassic desert conditions in Scotland was first discussed by Goodchild (1896). He suggested that the red colour is due to the deposition of ferric oxide from a percolating solution of ferrous bicarbonate which he believed was derived from Permo-Triassic lakes and penetrated to a depth of 183 m below the land surface. Bailey (1926) described the reddening of the Carboniferous beds of Arran to considerable depths. Bailey considered that the red colour in these rocks was formed in situ through oxidation of Carboniferous iron by air and water during the Permo-Triassic, and not by the introduction of iron from outside. Trotter (1953) described the reddening of Carboniferous strata in northwest England where both the Carboniferous Limestone and the Coal Measures are reddened where they are unconformably overlain by Permo-Triassic rocks, the maximum depth of reddening below the unconformity being 518 m. The reddening is considered to be the result of the oxidation of ferrous carbonate to ferric oxide before the Permo-Triassic rocks were deposited. In the east Irish Sea Basin, the Carboniferous succession was secondarily reddened to a considerable 250 m depth (Jackson *et al.* 1987). In northeast Northern Ireland, the reddening of Carboniferous rocks is highly variable, ranging from a few decametres to hundreds of metres, and the maximum depth is 430 m recorded in the Cross Borehole (Wilson & Robbie 1966). This suggests that meteoric fluids penetrated rocks to depths of hundreds of metres. Cowan (1989) reported similar observations in the southern North Sea Basin.

The red colour is due to the presence of iron oxide such as hematite and goethite which were formed as by-products of dedolomitization. The red colour occurs in ferroan-dolomite cemented sandstones which suggests that the diagenetic iron oxides probably precipitated directly when Fe^{2+} was released from ferroan dolomite during dedolomitization and oxidized to Fe^{3+}, rather than by the introduction of iron from outside. Alternatively, the hematite may have dehydrated from a precursor ferric oxyhydroxide such as goethite (Elmore 1985). All red-coloured sandstones in the Ballycastle district have abundant secondary porosity, suggesting that much reddened Carboniferous sandstone elsewhere in the UK also contains a significant secondary porosity since they have the same origin. Oil and gas may be trapped in these sandstones as a result. For instance, the source of gas discovered in the Rotliegendes and Sherwood Sandstone Groups in the southern North Sea Basin is in deeply buried organic-rich

Table 1. *Depth of reddening of Carboniferous in the central British Isles*

District	Age of overlying rocks	Depth of reddening	Reference
Ballycastle (N. Ireland)	Triassic	22−430 m	Wilson & Robbie (1966)
East Irish Sea Basin	Lower Permian	69−546 m	Jackson *et al.* (1987)
Arran	Permian	?−250 m +	Macgregor (1965)
Northwest England	Permian−Triassic	?−518 m	Trotter (1953)
Ayrshire	Permian	?−400 m	Smith *et al.* (1974)
Solway Basin	Permian	?	Barrett (1988)

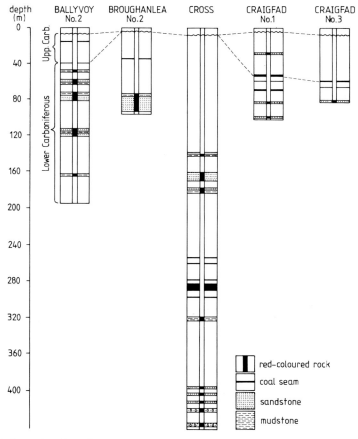

Fig. 8. Borehole sections in Ballycastle district, showing the relative position of red-coloured rocks and coal seams (data from Wilson & Robbie 1966).

mudrocks and coals of Carboniferous age, and gas shows have frequently been recorded from intervening Carboniferous sandstones (Cowan 1989). However, there are no oil/gas shows in the Ballycastle district because the source rocks are not mature (Parnell 1991).

Conclusion

There is significant secondary porosity in red-coloured sandstones of the Ballycastle district. The secondary porosity was created by carbonate dissolution, and to a lesser extent by the leaching of feldspar grains. Virtually all the porosity preserved in the Carboniferous sandstones is secondary in origin. The formation of significant secondary porosity necessitates not only abundant authigenic carbonate cement but also a suitable fluid for carbonate dissolution. The late Carboniferous–Permian uplift allowed access to such a fluid. Dedolomitization of ferroan dolomite and the dissolution of carbonate occurred during this time.

The reddening of Carboniferous rocks was due to the penetration of oxidizing meteoric fluids following the late Carboniferous–Permian uplift. All red-coloured sandstones have a significant secondary porosity. There are abundant reddened Carboniferous sandstones across the northern UK, and these sandstones may also exhibit a significant secondary porosity. Oil and gas may have taken advantage of this porosity in some areas. There are no hydrocarbon shows in the Ballycastle Carboniferous sandstones because of their inadequate burial history. However, in other regions of eastern Northern Ireland where the Carboniferous succession has been buried more deeply (Illing & Griffith 1986), there is a prospect of finding hydrocarbons within this porosity.

I thank Dr J. Parnell who supervised this study, W. Allingham for preparing the impregnated thin sections and all the staff of The Queen's University Electron Microscopy Unit for their support in this work. I also acknowledge receipt of a Visiting Studentship from the Academic Council, The Queen's University of Belfast.

References

ADAMSON, J. H. & WILSON, G. F. 1933. Petrography of the Lower Carboniferous rocks of N.E. Ireland. *Proceedings of the Royal Irish Academy*, **41**, 179–190.

AL-HASHIMI, W. S. & HEMINGWAY, J. E. 1973. Recent dolomitization and origin of rusty crusts of Northumberland. *Journal of Sedimentary Petrology*, **43**, 82–91.

BAILEY, E. B. 1926. Subterranean penetration by a desert climate. *Geological Magazine*, **63**, 276–280.

BARRETT, P. A. 1988. Early Carboniferous of the Solway Basin: A tectonostratigraphic model and its bearing on hydrocarbon potential. *Marine and Petroleum Geology*, **5**, 271–281.

BERNER, R. A. 1969. Goethite stability and the origin of red beds. *Geochimica et Cosmochimica Acta*, **33**, 267–273.

BESLY, B. M. & TURNER, P. 1983. Origin of red beds in a moist tropical climate (Etruria Formation, Upper Carboniferous, U.K.). *In*: WILSON, R. C. L. (ed.) *Residual Deposits: Surface Related Weathering Processes and Materials*. Geological Society, London, Special Publication, **11**, 131–147.

BJØRLYKKE, K. 1983. Diagenetic reactions in sandstones. *In*: PARKER, A. & SELLWOOD, B. W. (eds) *Sediment Diagenesis*. Reidel, Dordrecht, 169–213.

CHEPIKOV, V. P., YERMOLOVA, Y. P. & ORLOVA, N. A. 1961. Corrosion of quartz grains and examples of the possible effect of oil on the reservoir properties of sandy rocks. *Doklady of the Academy of Sciences, USSR, Earth Science Sections*, **140**, 1111–1113.

COWAN, G. 1989. Diagenesis of upper Carboniferous sandstones: Southern North Sea Basin. *In*: WHATELEY, M. K. G. & PICKERING, K. T. (eds) *Deltas: Sites and Traps for Fossil Fuels*. Geological Society, London, Special Publication, **41**, 57–73.

CURTIS, C. D. 1983. Geochemical studies on development and destruction of secondary porosity. *In*: BROOKS, J. (ed.) *Petroleum Geochemistry and Exploration of Europe*. Geological Society, London, Special Publication, **12**, 113–125.

ELMORE, R. D. 1985. Absolute dating of dedolomitization by means of paleomagnetic techniques. *Geology*, **13**, 558–561.

EVAMY, B. D. 1967. Dedolomitization and the development of rhombohedral pores in limestones. *Journal of Sedimentary Petrology*, **37**, 1204–1215.

——, KENOLTY, N., DOBSON, M. R. & WHITTINGTON, R. J. 1980. *The Geology of the Malin Sea*. Report of the Institute of Geological Sciences **79/15**.

FOLK, R. L. 1974. *Petrology of sedimentary rocks*. Hemphills, Austin, Texas.

FRANK, J. R. 1981. Dedolomitization in the Taum Sauk Limestone (Upper Cambrian). Southeast Missouri. *Journal of Sedimentary Petrology*, **51**, 7–18.

GILES, M. R. & MARSHALL, J. D. 1986. Constraints on the development of secondary porosity in the subsurface: re-evaluation of processes, *Marine and Petroleum Geology*, **3**, 243–255.

GOODCHILD, J. G. 1896. Desert conditions in Britain. *Transactions of the Geological Society of Glasgow*, **11**, 71–104.

ILLING, L. V. & GRIFFITH, A. E. 1986. Gas prospects in the 'Midland Valley' of Northern Ireland. *In*: BROOKS, J., GOFF, J. C. & VAN HOORN, B. (eds)

Habitat of Palaeozoic Gas in N.W. Europe. Geological Society, London, Special Publication, **23**, 73–84.

JACKSON, D. I., MULHOLLAND, P., JONES, S. M. & WARRINGTON, G. 1987. The geological framework of the East Irish Sea Basin. *In:* BROOKS, J. & GLENNIE, K. (eds) *Petroleum Geology of North West Europe.* Graham & Trotman, London, 191–203.

KATZ, A. 1971. Zoned dolomite crystals. *Journal of Geology*, **79**, 38–51.

KRYNINE, P. D. 1949. The origin of red beds. *Academy of Sciences Transactions, New York*, **11**, 60–68.

LONGMAN, M. W. & MENCH, P. A. 1978. Diagenesis of Cretaceous limestones in the Edwards aquifer system of south-central Texas: a scanning electron microscope study. *Journal of Sedimentary Geology*, **21**, 241–276.

LYELL, C. 1852. *Manual of Elementary Geology..* Murray, London.

MACGREGOR, M. 1965. *Excursion Guide to the Geology of Arran.* Geological Society of Glasgow, The University, Glasgow.

MCBRIDE, E. F. 1974. Significance of colour in red, green, purple, olive-brown and grey beds of Difunta Group, Northwestern Mexico. *Journal of Sedimentary Petrology*, **44**, 760–773.

MCCANN, N. 1988. An assessment of the subsurface geology between Magilligan Point and Fair Head, Northern Ireland. *Irish Journal of Earth Sciences*, **7**, 71–78.

MOSSLER, J. H. 1971. Diagenesis and dolomitization of Swopw Formation (Upper Pennsylvanian), south-east Kansas. *Journal of Sedimentary Petrology*, **41**, 962–970.

PARNELL, J. 1987. Secondary porosity in hydrocarbon-bearing transgressive sandstones on an unstable Lower Palaeozoic continental shelf, Welsh Borderland. *In:* MARSHALL, J. D. (ed.) *Diagenesis of Sedimentary Sequences.* Geological Society, London, Special Publication, **36**, 297–312.

—— 1991. Hydrocarbon Potential of Northern Ireland: Part 1. Burial histories and source-rock potential. *Journal of Petroleum Geology*, **14**, 65–78.

SCHMIDT, V. & MCDONALD, D. A. 1979a. The role of secondary porosity in the course of sandstone diagenesis, *Society of Economic Paleontologists and Mineralogists Special Publication*, **26**, 175–207.

—— & —— 1979b. *Texture and Recognition of Secondary Porosity in Sandstones.* Society of Economic Paleontologists and Mineralogists Special Publication, **26**, 209–225.

SCHOLLE, P. A. 1971. Diagenesis of deep-water carbonate turbidites, Upper Cretaceous Monte Antola Flysh, Northern Appennines, Italy. *Journal of Sedimentary Petrology*, **41**, 233–250.

SHANMUGAM, G. 1985. Significance of secondary porosity in interpreting sandstone composition. *AAPG Bulletin*, **69**, 3, 378–384.

SMITH, D. B., BRUMSTROM, R. G. W., MANNING, P. I., SIMPSON, S. & SHOTTON, F. W. 1974. *A Correlation of Permian Rocks in the British Isles.* Geological Society, London, Special Report, 5.

TROTTER, F. M. 1953. Reddened beds of Carboniferous age in north-west England and their origin. *Proceedings of the Yorkshire Geological Society*, **29**, 1–20.

WALKER, T. R., WAUGH, B. & CRONE, A. J. 1978. Diagenesis in first-cycle desert alluvium of Cenozoic age, southwestern United States and northwestern Mexico. *Bulletin of the Geological Society of America*, **89**. 19–32.

WHITAKER, M. F. 1978. Palynology of Carboniferous strata from the Ballycastle area, Co. Antrim, Northern Ireland. *Palynology*, **2**, 147–158.

WILSON, H. E. & MANNING, P. I. 1978. *Geology of the Causeway Coast.* Memoirs of the Geological Survey, N. Ireland. Belfast, H.M.S.O.

—— & ROBBIE, J. A. 1966. *Geology of the Country around Ballycastle.* Memoirs of the Geological Survey, Great Britain. Belfast, H.M.S.O.

The post-Variscan history of Ireland

DAVID NAYLOR

Department of Geology, Trinity College, Dublin 2, Republic of Ireland

Abstract: Permian and Mesozoic rocks are of limited distribution in Ireland, except for the Ulster Basin in the northeast of the island. This contrasts with the offshore basins, the widespread Mesozoic and Tertiary sequences of which are briefly reviewed. Onshore Permo-Triassic red-bed rocks occur in the Kingscourt Graben and in Wexford. Jurassic red clays are recorded in karstic solution hollows in Carboniferous limestones in south County Cork, and Upper Cretaceous chalk in a karstic collapse feature at Ballydeenlea, near Killarney. A growing number of Tertiary non-marine fissure and collapse deposits are being found, and where dated are of Oligocene and Neogene age. The stratigraphy and setting of the post-Carboniferous outliers are discussed. Published organic maturation data suggest that high maturation values in the Carboniferous over much of the country can be attributed to high heat flows during the Variscan episode, and to a cover of Silesian rocks. Post-Variscan burial depths appear to have been modest.

Available evidence suggests that Ireland has been a positive and largely emergent feature for much of post-Variscan time. Permo-Triassic deposits were probably never widespread onshore. The Early Jurassic and Late Cretaceous were periods of marine submergence, although rocks of this age were subsequently largely removed by erosion. Low topographic relief and the protective layers of Lias and Chalk have combined to restrict the amount of erosion of the landscape, the essential elements of which had been etched out by the end of the Triassic. The scattering of Mesozoic and Tertiary deposits at low topographic levels argue against the traditional view of the Irish landscape as a product of erosion of a high-level peneplain.

Post-Carboniferous rocks are in little evidence over onshore Ireland, except in the northeastern part of the island. This is in direct contrast to Britain where Mesozoic and Tertiary rocks cover much of southern and eastern England. Work during the past three decades has shown that Ireland is in fact ringed offshore by linear Mesozoic–Tertiary basins, forming part of the network of basins which crosses northwestern Europe (Ziegler 1982). The published stratigraphic information on the Irish offshore basins, together with improved knowledge of the fragmentary onshore outcrops, now allows more informed speculation on the post-Carboniferous history of the island.

Permian to Tertiary rocks onshore

Ulster Basin

The Rathlin Trough and Lough Neagh–Larne Basin, together with the offshore North Channel Basin, constitute the Ulster Basin (Figs 1 & 2). This basin contains rocks ranging from Permian to Tertiary in age. The Permian and Mesozoic rocks have been protected from erosion by the cover of Tertiary plateau basalts, but their preservation is probably also due to the existence of thicker sequences in this region than elsewhere. The onshore stratigraphy of north-

eastern Ireland has been summarized by a number of authors (Wilson 1972; Naylor & Shannon 1982; Illing & Griffith 1986; McCann 1988, 1990), and Penn (1981 & Fig. 2), who described the stratigraphy of the Larne-2 geothermal well.

The major accumulations of post-Carboniferous sediments in northeast Ireland are within two fault-bounded basins, the Rathlin Trough and the Lough Neagh–Larne Basin. The two basins are separated by the Dalradian metamorphic rocks of the Highland Border Ridge, which also contains complex areas of Carboniferous, Mesozoic and Tertiary igneous rocks. To the south, the Larne–Lough Neagh Basin extends towards Belfast and the line of the Southern Upland Fault forming the northern margin of the Ordovician and Silurian rocks of the Longford–Down Massif. Inland the basin extends west of Lough Neagh. To the north, the Rathlin Trough is contained between the Tow Valley Fault, forming the northern margin of the Highland Border Ridge, and the Foyle Fault in the northwest. The structural setting of the Lough Neagh–Larne Basin is discussed by McCaffrey & McCann (this volume).

Deep boreholes at Magilligan and Port More in the Rathlin Trough (Fig. 2A) encountered more than 2000 m of Mesozoic strata (McCann 1988 & Table 1). Deep drilling in the larger Lough Neagh–Larne Basin has demonstrated

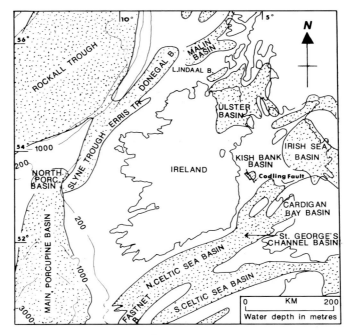

Fig. 1. Mesozoic–Tertiary basins around Ireland.

Table 1. *Deep boreholes in the Rathlin Trough*

	Thickness (m)	Base (m)
Magilligan Borehole		
Recent	52.4	52.4
Tertiary sill	58.6	111.0
L. Jurassic: L. Liassic	89.9	200.9
Triassic: Penarth Group	7.9	208.8
Triassic: Mercia Mudstone Group	371.5	580.3
Triassic: Sherwood Sandstone		
Group Permian	396.0	976.3
Carboniferous	370.3	1346.6 TD
Port More Borehole		
Tertiary basalt	77.1	77.1
Cretaceous	91.3	168.4
L. Jurassic: L. Liassic	269.4	437.8
Tertiary sill	222.9	660.7
Triassic: Penarth Group	4.1	664.8
Triassic: Mercia Mudstone Group	652.5	1317.3
Triassic: Sherwood Sandstone Group	51.3	1797.7
Permian	66.3	1864.0 TD

more than 3000 m of post-Carboniferous strata in the deeper part of the basin near the coast, thinning towards the basin margins (Wilson 1972; Thompson 1979; McCann 1990). The Newmill-1 and Larne-2 wells in the basin centre (Fig. 2B) failed to penetrate the full Permian section and terminated in brockram and Lower

Permian conglomerates respectively (Penn 1981; Downing *et al.* 1982; McCann 1990). The Lower Permian clastic sequences are overlain by the marine Magnesian Limestone and the Upper Permian Marls.

The succeeding Sherwood Sandstone Group strata overstep northwards onto the long-

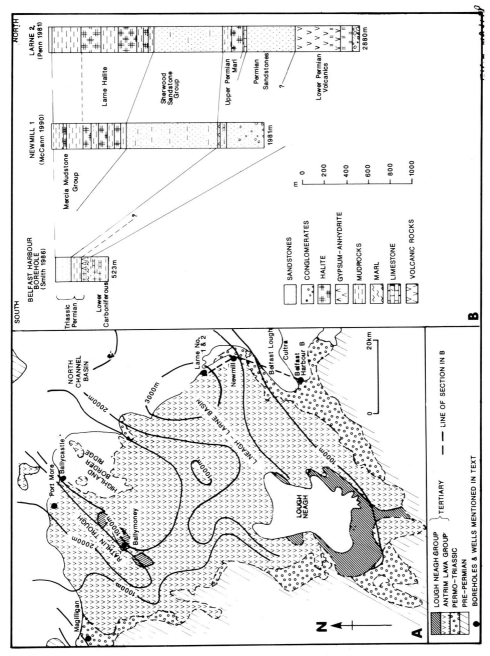

Fig. 2. A. The Ulster Basin, northeast Ireland (modified after Thompson 1979). B. Section across the southern part of the Lough Neagh—Larne Basin (modified after McCann 1990)

standing positive element of the Highland Border Ridge and are overlain by the Mercia Mudstone succession containing several major evaporite horizons. The Mercia Mudstone is 976 m thick in the Larne-1 borehole in the basin centre but thins markedly towards the basin margin. The onshore succession continues with marine mudrock-dominant Rhaetic and Lower Liassic beds. The remainder of the Jurassic and the Lower Cretaceous is not represented, although derived Middle and Upper Liassic fossils have been recorded in basal Cretaceous conglomerates in north Antrim and Middle Liassic fossils in drift boulders near Ballycastle (Wilson 1972). Rhaetian and Liassic strata were deposited in the Lough Neagh–Larne and Rathlin Trough basins. The rocks are known from coastal outcrops (Wilson 1972) and have also been described from boreholes (McCann 1988, 1990). The thickness of the Lower Lias sediments is greatly variable due to pre-Cretaceous erosion, but the thickest development was found in the Rathlin Trough where the Port More borehole (Fig. 2A) penetrated almost 250 m of Sinemurian to Lower Pliensbachian rocks. Generally, however, only the Rhaetian and the Hettangian–lowest Sinemurian are preserved.

The Upper Cretaceous sequence in the Ulster Basin ranges from lower Cenomanian to lower Maastrichtian. Two main facies are developed (Reid 1971; Fletcher 1977); the Hibernian Greensand Formation, and the Chalk or Ulster White Limestone Formation which overlies, or is in part laterally equivalent to, the Greensand. Upper Cretaceous sedimentation began with a marine invasion in the southeast, and glauconitic beds followed by yellow weathering sandstones were deposited. There then followed a period of non-deposition and erosion which lasted into the early Senonian when renewed transgression eventually extended deposition to the whole of the Ulster Basin. Marginal glauconitic chalks were deposited up to earliest Campanian time. There was progressive transgression of the Highland Border Ridge, but the whole structure was not submerged until the late Santonian. There was further inundation during the Campanian, extending chalk deposition to its present outcrop limits. Maastrichtian chalk is known and was probably originally extensive, but now has a restricted distribution due to pre-basalt erosion. The maximum thickness of the Ulster White Limestone is more than 120 m in the Ballycastle area of the Rathlin Trough, where the succession is almost complete.

There followed a period of emergence and erosion in latest Cretaceous and earliest Tertiary time. A differentially eroded but generally low relief surface developed which was then covered by Paleocene basaltic lavas more than 500 m thick. The basalts became weathered, and in the Lough Neagh region are overlain by interbedded lithomarge, pyroclastics and lacustrine deposits, of possible Eocene age (Parnell et al. 1989).

Subsequently, probable fault-related subsidence in the Lough Neagh area allowed the accumulation of thick siliciclastic and lignitic deposits which constitute the Lough Neagh Group. A range of environments associated with a freshwater lacustrine system are represented. The sediments are of Upper Oligocene age (Wilkinson et al. 1980) and after further faulting and later erosion were finally buried beneath Quaternary deposits. A number of separate small fault-related basins containing Lough Neagh Group sediments also developed on the north flank of the Highland Border Ridge near Ballymoney (Parnell et al. 1989 & Fig. 2).

Variscan deformation in northeast Ireland probably caused reactivation along Caledonian northeast–southwest trends, and brockrams appear to have been deposited at fault controlled scarps which were active during latest Carboniferous to early Permian time. Mesozoic tectonism was dominated by ENE–WSW extension, resulting in the formation of NNW–trending extensional faults. Further reactivation of Caledonian structures may also have occurred at this time. The presence of active NNW trending faults during Upper Triassic deposition is implied by the thickness variations in rocks of this age, as on the northern side of Belfast Lough. Major gaps in the Jurassic–Cretaceous sequences imply periods of uplift and tectonism during the Late Mesozoic. The Lough Neagh Group sedimentation was probably controlled by NE–SW and NNW–SSE fractures in an extensional or strike-slip setting.

Kingscourt Graben

With the exception of the Ulster Basin there are only limited occurrences of post-Carboniferous strata over the remainder of the island. The largest of these is near Kingscourt in County Cavan (Fig. 3) where a Permo-Triassic red-bed sequence is located within a north–south trending half-graben that is faulted on its western margin (Gardiner & Visscher 1971; Visscher 1971). The Permo-Triassic rocks rest unconformably on synclinally folded Upper Carboniferous rocks (Namurian–Lower Westphalian; Jackson 1965). The whole area is poorly

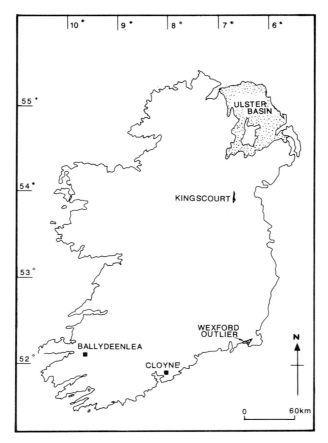

Fig. 3. Location of Permian and Mesozoic outliers, onshore Ireland.

exposed and the geology is known chiefly from borings and from the workings for gypsum. The Permo-Triassic sequence has a maximum thickness of 550 m and consists of two formations, namely the Kingscourt Gypsum Formation and the overlying Kingscourt Sandstone Formation. The lower formation comprises a basal conglomerate overlain by red and grey mudstone and gypsum cycles. There is an apparently conformable passage upwards into the Kingscourt Sandstone Formation which consists of a basal sequence of red siltstones (80–100 m) overlain by red and grey fine-grained sandstones (+400 m). Visscher (1971) recognized distinct palynological assemblages of Thuringian and Scythian (early Triassic) age, the latter being restricted to the Kingscourt Sandstone Formation. The Permian–Triassic boundary probably coincides with the junction between the two formations.

Wexford outlier

In County Wexford more than 200 m of red siltstones, sandstones and conglomerates (Killag Formation) of probable Permo-Triassic age (Clayton *et al.* 1986; Burnett *et al.* 1990) rest unconformably on Carboniferous rocks. Major NE–SW faults in the area have probably controlled the deposition and preservation of this small outlier. The lack of proven Permian strata in the immediate offshore area of the southern Irish Sea and Celtic Sea make a Triassic age more likely, but the onshore rocks have not been dated.

Cloyne Syncline

Reddened clay deposits of Jurassic age (Higgs & Beese 1986) occur within karstic solution hollows on Lower Carboniferous reef limestones near Cloyne (Bishopp & McCluskey 1948 & Fig. 3). The silica-rich clays are 1.8 to 4.0 m thick and rest on an irregular, cavernous and altered limestone surface. Higgs & Beese (1986) record a microflora with a possible age range from late Lower Jurassic (Toarcian) to Middle Jurassic, with a Middle Jurassic age more likely. They suggest that the clays were deposited in a lacustrine environment on carbonate lowlands. The clays infilled shallow solution cavities, and present-day steep bed attitudes suggest that there was later solution subsidence or collapse.

Ballydeenlea outlier, Killarney

The Ballydeenlea outlier (Walsh 1966 & Fig. 3) in the Gweestin valley, north of Killarney, is the only recorded occurrence of Upper Cretaceous rocks in Ireland, other than those of the Ulster Basin described above. The Ballydeenlea occurrence was interpreted by Walsh as resulting from the submarine collapse of karstic caverns in Lower Carboniferous limestones. The chalk forms the matrix of a breccia containing Namurian shale fragments that occurs in the surrounding Namurian bedrock a short distance above the contact with the Carboniferous Limestone. The surface of the bedrock at the deposit is at about 125 m O.D. and the breccia extends to a depth of at least 40 m. The minimum areal extent of the breccia is 100 m × 30 m. Foraminiferal evidence (Walsh 1966) suggests a Campanian (*mucronata* Zone) age for the chalk matrix. The regional observations made by Walsh in the light of the discovery of the outlier, are considered below.

Tertiary deposits

Several small Tertiary deposits have been discovered on the Carboniferous limestone surface of Ireland. In addition, other undated deposits are presumed by their lithologies and geological setting to be Tertiary in age. Undoubtedly others remain to be found, as indicated by the evidence of gravity surveys (Murphy 1962, 1966). Davies (1970) and Mitchell (1980) have summarized many of the known occurrences, most of which are shown on Fig. 4.

A non-marine pipeclay containing plant material and pollen at Ballymacadam, discovered by the Geological Survey (Wynne 1857) and reexamined by Watts (1957), is Oligocene in age (Watts 1970; Boulter 1980). The clay lies in Carboniferous limestones at an altitude of about 100 m O.D. (Mitchell 1980). Walsh (1966) recorded breccias of presumed Tertiary age at 43 m O.D. near Listry (Fig. 4), 7 km west of the Ballydeenlea chalk deposit. He considered these to be terrestrial deposits resulting from collapse of karstic limestone caverns.

Upper Pliocene (Boulter 1980) dark coloured non-marine clays and sands also occur in a pipe deposit at Hollymount (Fig. 4) and extend from the limestone surface at about 62 m O.D. to a minimum depth of 50 m (Mitchell 1980).

At Poulnahallia (Fig. 4), near Headford, non-marine silica sands occur within gorges and caves in Carboniferous limestones (Coxon & Flegg 1987). Analysis of pollen from an organic deposit some 5 m thick suggests either a late Pliocene or early Pleistocene age. Karstification of the limestone surface in this area (about 50 m O.D) had thus taken place by the Late Tertiary and subsequent denudation, particularly by Pleistocene glaciers, appears to have been minimal.

At Tynagh, County Galway, site of an abandoned lead−zinc mine, the rich near-surface ores consisted of complex hydrated compounds that were derived from alteration of the sulphide ores and were redeposited in solution hollows on the limestone surface. The altered ore contained a log of *Cupressus* wood, and Mitchell (1980) suggested that solution of the limestone and alteration of the ore took place under different climatic conditions, in Tertiary time.

Other pipe deposits of probable Tertiary age (Mitchell 1980) occur in Carboniferous limestones at Tullyallen and Drybridge (Fig. 4). The latter deposit (at 15 m O.D.) is more than 50 m thick. At Ballyellin a 15 m diameter conical pipe is filled with micaceous clays to a minimum depth of 15 m.

Beese *et al.* (1983) describe a silica clay with chert of inferred Tertiary age at Ballygaddy (Fig. 4). The deposit is at an elevation of 133 m and test borings and gravity data are interpreted by the authors as suggesting a diameter of some 60 m and a depth of about 40 m. The location of the solution pipe in the Dinantian carbonates appears to be fault-controlled and the authors suggest that the deposit may have suffered several hundreds of metres of subsidence. This is considerably more than is indicated in the case of the other Tertiary deposits.

The nature of the Tertiary in Ireland was reviewed by Davies (1970) who highlighted the conflict between new evidence regarding Cretaceous and Tertiary deposits and the traditional concepts of widespread high-level Carboniferous, Cretaceous or Tertiary erosion surfaces. Superimposition of the present river system in southern Ireland from these older high-level surfaces had traditionally been used by geomorphologists to explain its discordance with

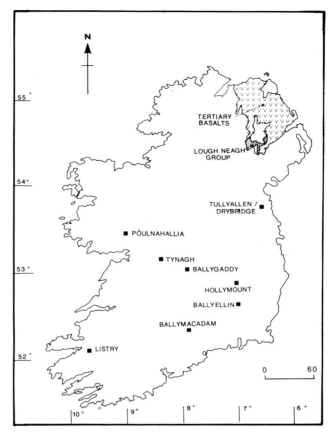

Fig. 4. Location of Tertiary deposits, onshore Ireland.

respect to the structural grain of the exposed rocks.

In northeast Ireland, intra-Cretaceous and Tertiary and folding and faulting are demonstrable (George 1967). Evidence from the offshore points to significant strike-slip movement on faults, e.g. the NNW–SSE Codling Fault in the Kish Bank Basin (Fig. 1), which Jenner (1981) suggests, on the basis of outcrop displacement, had a dextral movement of several km. The Codling Fault is of the same trend and age as the Sticklepath and related faults in southwest England. Off the west coast of Ireland the Porcupine Basin accomodated 5 km of Tertiary sediments during the thermal sag phase of basin development. The Celtic Sea was affected by early Tertiary inversion and Oligocene–Miocene compression (Tucker & Arter 1987). The Tertiary therefore cannot be envisaged as a quiescent period in the development of the island.

Kerr (1987) produced a detailed study of Tertiary stress systems in northeast Ireland. He defined four phases of Tertiary fracturing that affected the Carboniferous rocks there and demonstrated a long history of activity on the faults. He was not able, however, to identify a significant phase of tectonic activity at the end of the Cretaceous or early in the Tertiary, and supporting evidence for this is provided by the widespread preservation of Upper Cretaceous rocks beneath the Eocene basalts.

Permian to Tertiary rocks offshore

Celtic Sea Basins

A blanket of Upper Cretaceous and Tertiary strata extends throughout most of the Celtic Sea area, with the exception of the southern Irish Sea, Cardigan Bay and Bristol Channel area (Blundell 1979). Underlying this cover is a thick Lower Cretaceous sequence, a variable, but thick, Jurassic layer (Millson 1987), and a Triassic sequence which rests unconformably on Palaeozoic rocks (Fig. 5). Major inversion (post-Maastrichtian and pre-Middle Eocene) affected the central portion to the North Celtic Sea Basin, with perhaps 1 km of uplift (Tucker & Arter 1987).

Permian strata have not been drilled in either of the Celtic Sea Basins (Naylor & Shannon 1982) or in the Fastnet Basin (Robinson et al. 1981). However, the existence of possible Late Permian sub-basins in the South Celtic Sea Basin and the Crediton Cuvette (Devon), and possibly in the other Celtic Sea basins, has been suggested by Van Hoorn (1987) and Petrie et al. (1989), in part from seismic evidence. The position is much the same in the Cardigan Bay Basin, where Permian rocks are unproved but may still be found in the undrilled axial parts of the basin (Barr et al. 1981). In the Bristol Channel Basin Upper Triassic rocks rest unconformably on deformed Devonian and Carboniferous strata; Permian and Lower Triassic rocks being absent (Kamerling 1979). Permian strata are thus unproven on the shelf south of Ireland, and if undrilled pockets of Permian strata exist they are clearly of limited extent.

The Triassic rocks of the Celtic Sea Basins are divided into the Sherwood Sandstone Group at the base, which is probably restricted to the main fault-bounded depocentres, and the overlying evaporite-bearing Mercia Mudstone Group, which has a basinwide distribution. There is a conformable transitional sequence into the fully marine Jurassic succession above. The marine trangression was of Rhaetian to Hettangian age. A number of transgressions and regressions in the Lower Jurassic produced a variable sequence of argillaceous and calcareous sediments. Regressive clastics of late Sinemurian age are thought by Petrie et al. (1989) to have been sourced from exposed Old Red Sandstone in southwest Ireland and from the Leinster massif. Inundation followed in the Pliensbachian, although derivation of sediment may have continued from the Leinster area. Late Pliensbachian regression was followed by transgression in the Toarcian, when maximum coverage of the onshore area can be assumed.

The variations of lithology in the succeeding Middle Jurassic are a reflection of the uplift and facies changes which accompanied Mid-Cimmerian tectonism (Naylor & Shannon 1982). Bathonian and older marine mudrocks are succeeded (Ainsworth et al. 1987) by latest Bathonian freshwater-brackish marine strata and then by presumed Callovian beds. Petrie

et al. (1989) suggest that the massifs surrounding the Celtic Sea, and in particular the Leinster massif, were uplifted in late Bathonian–early Callovian time, giving rise to prograding red-bed clastics on the northern margin of the North Celtic Sea Basin. A complex non-marine and marginal marine sequence then developed in the St. Georges Channel and Cardigan Bay Basins. Callovian and Lower Oxfordian strata are lacking in the west of the North Celtic Sea Basin, probably due to erosion. The succeeding Middle–Upper Oxfordian sequence is mainly non-marine and is followed in the North Celtic Sea Basin by a sharply defined marine pulse in the Late Oxfordian (Colin et al. 1981). A variable Kimmeridgian–Tithonian non-marine sequence with marine intercalations then developed over much of the region, with Upper Jurassic fluvio-lacustrine clastic deposits along the northern margin of the North Celtic Sea Basin.

In the Celtic Sea region the Late Cimmerian unconformity is well developed only at the basin margins. Lower Cretaceous rocks have been intersected by most of the exploration wells drilled in the basins and are divisible into a lower continental sandy (Wealden) section overlain by a marine sand and shale sequence. The marine transgression reached its maximum extent in the Aptian (Petrie et al. 1989). A thick accumulation of chalk was deposited from Cenomanian time onwards in the Celtic Sea and Fastnet basins. The Celtic Sea Chalk (Cenomanian to ?Maastrichtian) is up to 1000 m thick (Naylor & Shannon 1982) and crops out over a large area of the sea floor. Turonian to Late Santonian marginal facies along the northern margin of the North Celtic Sea Basin suggest that the basin margin may not have been much further north than the present outcrop limit. Expansion of the basin is suggested by the establishment of uniform chalk deposition throughout the remainder of the Late Cretaceous (Petrie et al. 1989).

Tertiary sediments are limited to an elongate outcrop in the eastern part of the North Celtic Sea Basin and attain a thickness of 800 m.

West Coast Basins

The Porcupine Basin is subdivided into the Main Porcupine Basin and the smaller North Porcupine Basin (Fig. 1). A chain of relatively complex, narrow sedimentary troughs, the Slyne and Erris Troughs and the Donegal Basin (Fig. 1), extends northeastwards from the North Porcupine Basin, roughly parallel to the Irish coast (Naylor & Shannon 1982; Tate & Dobson

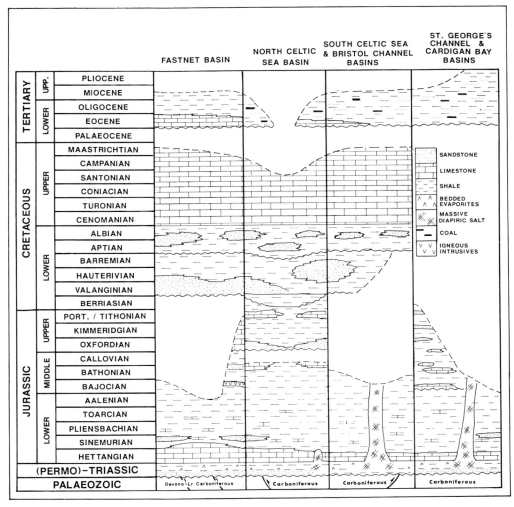

Fig. 5. Generalized stratigraphy of the major basins in Celtic Sea region (modified after Shannon 1991*b*).

1989*b*; Trueblood & Morton 1991; Trueblood this volume). A generalized stratigraphy for the Porcupine Basin is shown in Fig. 6.

The history of deposition in the west coast offshore basins during latest Carboniferous and Permian times contrasts with that of the Celtic Sea region. Stephanian sediments are well documented in the Porcupine Basin (Ziegler 1982; Croker & Shannon 1987; Robeson *et al.* 1988). Drilling in the northern part of the Main Porcupine Basin has shown that sedimentation continued without break from Upper Carboniferous sandstones and shales into continental Autunian (Lower Permian) claystones and sandstones. Younger Permian strata have not been encountered in drilling, and elsewhere in this

area the Triassic rests unconformably on the eroded Carboniferous surface.

The Triassic of the Porcupine Basin is little known, since only two of the published wells have penetrated Triassic rocks. Seismic evidence suggests that more than 2000 m of Triassic rocks may occur. Undifferentiated Permo-Triassic continental sequences have been drilled in the Northwest offshore basins. The succession is 288 m thick in the Erris Trough (Amoco 19/5−1), and 655 m in the Donegal Basin (Amoco 12/13−1A; Tate & Dobson 1989*a*). The Erris sequence comprises undated red−brown poorly sorted and argillaceous sandstones resting conformably on an evaporitic Upper Permian sequence. Rhaetian strata in marginal facies

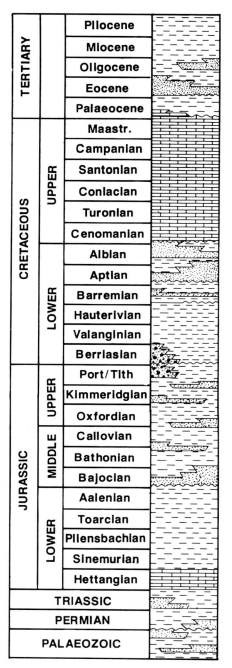

Fig. 6. Generalized stratigraphy of the Porcupine Basin (modified after Shannon 1991a)

follow conformably upon the continental deposits.

Liassic rocks are known in the North Porcupine Basin (Croker & Shannon 1987) where they appear to onlap irregular pre-Jurassic topography. A Liassic succession was encountered by the two exploration wells in the Erris (218 m) and Donegal Basins (Tate & Dobson 1989a). Here the Rhaetian is conformably overlain by Hettangian to early Sinemurian limestones with claystone, siltstone and sandstone interbeds, probably deposited in freshwater to shallow marine conditions. The upper zones of the Liassic in these wells are missing and the sequence is unconformably overlain by Cretaceous or Tertiary sediments.

Middle Jurassic, dominantly non-marine, sequences in the northern part of the Porcupine Basin rest unconformably on Liassic and older strata (Naylor & Shannon 1982; Croker & Shannon 1987). Drilling in the Slyne Trough (Trueblood & Morton 1991) has revealed a very thick shallow marine and estuarine Middle Jurassic sequence. A thin non-marine to marginal marine Middle Jurassic succession may also occur in the Erris and Donegal Basins (Naylor & Shannon 1982; Tate & Dobson 1989a) but has not yet been drilled.

Upper Jurassic (Oxfordian to Portlandian) strata occur in most of the Porcupine Basin wells. Sedimentation was apparently continuous through Middle and Late Jurassic times. Nevertheless, latest Middle and Late Jurassic time was a period of differential subsidence in the basin and this is reflected by the varied continental sandstone and shale sequences which are interrupted by intercalations of shallow marine strata. Upper Jurassic sediments may not be preserved in the Northwest Irish Basins, but if preserved are likely to be of varied facies, reflecting the strongly fault-dominated nature of this province.

The faulted nature of the Late Cimmerian erosion surface in the Porcupine Basin has been documented by Naylor & Anstey (1987). At the centre of the basin the overlying Lower Cretaceous is a thick and uniform sequence, but towards the basin margins it separates into several seismo-stratigraphical units bounded by unconformities and overlain by Cenomanian to Maastrichtian Chalk. Lower Cretaceous rocks have been identified on published seismic sections of the Northwest basins and a thick unspecified Cretaceous section has been encountered in drilling of the Donegal Basin (Tate & Dobson 1989a).

About 400 m of Upper Cretaceous is preserved near the margins of the Porcupine Basin, while in excess of 1000 m occurs towards the central axis. A reduced Upper Cretaceous succession is also anticipated in parts of the Northwest offshore basins (Naylor & Shannon 1982), but may be absent in places due to subsequent erosion.

Northern Ireland Offshore Basins

A number of younger basins of Caledonian trend have been mapped between Ireland and western Scotland. The dominant northeast-southwest trend is controlled by the major faults extending from the Scottish coast. North of the Highland Border Ridge, the Rathlin Trough (Fig. 2A) extends offshore northeastwards towards Scotland into the southern part of the Sound of Jura. The bulk of the 2.4 km thick fill of the offshore Rathlin Basin is probably composed of Triassic redbeds. Seabed boreholes in the area (Evans et al. 1980) encountered probable Upper Triassic gypsiferous marls overlain by Rhaetic marls and mudstones. Middle and Upper Jurassic and Cretaceous rocks are unknown in the basins off the north coast of Northern Ireland.

Further northwest (Fig. 1) the narrow Loch Indaal Basin (Dobson & Evans 1974) contains Triassic redbeds, but Permian rocks are unproven in the graben. In the northeastern portion of the basin there is a transition from the Mercia Mudstone Group to ammonitic black mudstones of the overlying Penarth Group (Westbury Formation; Rhaetian to early Jurassic).

A thin layer of basal sand and chalk was laid down unconformably across the denuded surface of Jurassic, Triassic and older rocks of the Inner Hebrides, Malin Shelf, Firth of Clyde and Ulster regions. Much of this chalk layer has subsequently been removed by erosion. Upper Cretaceous rocks are only preserved over parts of the basins of western Scotland, in the Ulster Basin (described above), and in the Firth of Clyde (as blocks within a volcanic centre on Arran). Younger Mesozoic sequences are not preserved in the basins of the Malin Shelf.

Irish Sea Basins

The geology of the Irish Sea Basin, east of the Isle of Man, is well summarized in papers by Colter & Barr (1975) and Jackson et al. (1987). In the Kish Bank Basin (Fig. 1 & Jenner 1981), seismic interpretation suggests that the Carboniferous is overlain unconformably by 3000 m of Permo–Triassic rocks. These are likely to resemble the onshore sequence at Kingscourt and

that of the Irish Sea Basin. Triassic rocks crop out in the southern Irish Sea within, and around the margins of, the Cardigan Bay Basin and probably form some part of the undifferentiated areas of mapped offshore Mesozoic outcrop (I.G.S. Cardigan Bay Sheet 1982). It is everywhere conformably overlain by the Rhaetic.

Broughan et al. (1989) suggest that up to 2700 m of Lower Jurassic strata may occur on the western flank of the Kish Bank Basin against the western bounding faults. Lower Liassic rocks have been sampled from the sea bed at the northern margin of the basin. A surprisingly thick section of Liassic sediments within the Cardigan Bay Basin was also proved by the Mochras (Llanbedr) borehole on the Welsh coast (Woodland 1971). A total section of 1305 m was drilled in marine Lower Jurassic of Hettangian to Upper Toarcian age. The sequence comprises grey, locally silty, calcareous mudstones with some darker mudstone intercalations, particularly in the Lower Liassic. Seabed coring on the flank of the St. George's Channel Basin (Whittington et al. 1981) proved Liassic shales and limestones.

The Liassic of the Irish Sea and Ulster Basins in uniformly fine-grained and thin-bedded, and is indicative of relatively shallow, quiet marine conditions. More varied marine conditions obtained on the Celtic Sea shelf, with deepening environments further west.

Middle and Upper Jurassic sediments are unknown along the northern and eastern coasts of Ireland and over much of the Irish Sea. Available evidence also suggests that Middle Jurassic rocks may be absent or very thin in the Kish Bank Basin. However, in the Cardigan Bay Basin (Barr et al. 1981 & Fig. 5) exploration drilling has revealed an almost complete Lower Lias to Lower Purbeckian succession. The Lias is succeeded with apparent conformity by 760 m of Middle Jurassic mudstone and calcareous mudstone with thin limestone interbeds, the products of shallow marine neritic to carbonate shelf environments. Sedimentation continued in the Cardigan Bay Basin throughout the Jurassic and a continuous sequence of shales, mudstones and calcareous mudstones (1498 m) up to the Lower Purbeckian is preserved. Depositional conditions were probably shallow marine.

The Lower Cretaceous is not represented in the basins around Northern Ireland or in the Irish Sea. Similarly, Upper Cretaceous rocks are not known in the Kish Bank and Irish Sea Basins, and are absent from the floor of the St. George's Channel and Cardigan Bay Basins. Upper Cretaceous rocks, exceeding 1000 m

thick, unconformably succeed Lower Cretaceous strata in the western part of the Bristol
Channel (Fig. 5), but thin eastwards and are
absent over the eastern part of that basin.

Evidence from maturation

Vitrinite reflectance and spore coloration data
have been published which have a bearing on
interpretations of the Mesozoic history of the
region. The Thermal Maturation map of Ireland
(Clayton et al. 1989) shows that much of the
southern and central part of Ireland has been
subjected to high heat flows. Data for the Upper
Devonian–Carboniferous sequence on the
south coast of County Cork are indicative of
meta-anthracite coal rank (Clayton 1989). No
correlation between vitrinite reflectance and
stratigraphic position is observed in this area
through 2 km of section across large-scale folds.
The inference is that high temperatures were
maintained until after the Variscan Orogeny.
Clayton (1989) points out that, even allowing
for high palaeogeothermal gradients, a substantial thickness of strata would have been required
to produce the high maturation levels.

Lower Carboniferous correlatives of the south
coast rocks in the North Celtic Sea Basin have
comparably high maturation values (Clayton
1989). In this case the Lower Carboniferous
strata (Rm 4.52–4.93%) are overlain by
Jurassic beds with Rm values of 0.62%. In the
case of the Cloyne deposits (Fig. 3) described
above, mean reflectance data from the Lower–
Middle Jurassic suggest limited post-Middle
Jurassic burial (0–1.25 km maximum, G.
Clayton, pers. comm.). There is thus a major
disconformity of the maturation profile in the
region, probably at the base of the Mesozoic,
although this cannot be tightly constrained in
the region due to the lack of Silesian and Permo-
Triassic rocks. The uniformity of maturation in
the Upper Devonian to Lower Namurian rocks
suggests that this maturation episode pre-dates
the Variscan erosion surface. Clayton (1989)
suggests that the 5–7 km thick sedimentary
sequence required to explain the maturation of
the Carboniferous rocks was provided by a thick
Silesian section eroded after the Variscan orogeny, rather than that great thicknesses of
Permo-Triassic rocks were deposited and
eroded.

Maturation levels in the Silesian rocks of the
Wexford outlier (Burnett et al. 1990) suggest
that post-Variscan burial probably played a part
in increasing the maturation levels, thus implying Triassic and possibly younger cover rocks
in the area. Further north, at Kingscourt,

Visscher (1971) has noted that the Permo-
Triassic palynomorphs show a range of colour
from yellow to black; the latter he attributes to
the influence of the frequent Tertiary intrusions
in the area. The significantly higher coalification
levels in the Carboniferous of the region again
suggests a marked change in the maturation
profile at the Variscan erosion surface.

Maturation data for the Northwest Carboniferous Basin (Clayton & Baily in press &
Philcox et al. this volume) suggest uplift and
erosion of up to 4.2 km of post-Lower Carboniferous cover. Although most of this can be
explained in terms of the Silesian section, the
area is along strike from the Ulster Basin and
may have had some Permo-Triassic cover (Fig.
7B). Recent evidence from the Fintona Block
(Mitchell & Owens 1990) demonstrates that
Silesian rocks are more widespread and varied
than had previously been suspected.

The conclusion to be drawn from the maturation evidence onshore in Ireland is that an
extensive, and in places thick, Silesian section,
combined with a high pre-Permian heat input
over the south of the island, afford the best
explanation of the observed data.

Discussion

Permo-Triassic

There is little evidence to support the view that
thick Permo-Triassic successions were widespread onshore across Ireland outside of the
Ulster Basin and have subsequently been removed by erosion. The preserved Permo-
Triassic outliers are in fault-dominated settings.
This is particularly the case in northeast Ireland
where thick successions accumulated within a
distinct structural province in basins bordered
by the major faults extending southeastwards
from Scotland. However, the Kingscourt and
Wexford deposits are also fault-controlled.
Where the lower contact is seen, at Kingscourt,
a Thuringian evaporitic sequence rests on the
Carboniferous without intervening Lower
Permian strata.

Red karstic deposits of proven Permo-Triassic
age have not been recorded on the Carboniferous surface in southern Ireland. This is in contrast to the widespread karstic caves and
deposits of this age found in southern England
and in Wales. This difference cannot be attributed entirely to the more widespread cover
of glacial deposits in Ireland. Similarly, reddened Carboniferous surfaces are relatively rare
in Ireland, although some reddening beneath
the unconformity is found in the vicinity of the

Kingscourt outlier (Jackson 1965). These facts suggest that Permo-Triassic deposits were of limited extent onshore; although it could be argued that subsequent deep erosion of the Carboniferous surface removed all evidence of widespread Permo-Triassic cover. Where younger post-Triassic deposits are seen (Cloyne & Killarney; Fig. 3) they are in direct contact with the Carboniferous. The evidence from the offshore basins points to gradual marine encroachment during the Rhaetian, without significant intervening erosion. Furthermore, there is little evidence of aggressive erosion of thick Triassic sequences, or of rapid deposition into the Early Jurassic seas around Ireland.

The balance of evidence therefore appears to point to much of Ireland remaining positive during Permian and Triassic times, with continued erosion and deflation of the Variscan surface in arid conditions. There is no proven Permian deposition offshore around the southern coastline, or in the Irish Sea up to the latitude of Anglesey. Deposition during the Permian along the northern and eastern coasts of Ireland was in dominantly non-marine depositional conditions. Volcanic activity extended at this time from Scotland across into the Ulster Basin, as evidenced by the Larne-2 borehole. The Ulster Basin was clearly a depositional centre during the Permo-Triassic (Fig. 2), probably containing more than 3000 m of sediment in the east coast area. Deposition persisted without break from Carboniferous through into Early Permian time in the Porcupine Basin. During Late Permian time (Fig. 7A) the Bakevellia Sea extended into the Irish Sea and Ulster Basins, giving carbonate and evaporite deposition. The offshore basins around Ireland then subsided rapidly during the Triassic and a thick standard sequence was widely deposited, with the Sherwood Sandstone and Mercia Mudstone Groups readily discernible.

Onshore, outside of the Ulster Basin, there was only limited deposition. Erosion had probably etched out the main physiographic form of the island by the end of the Triassic, with strong Caledonian influence in the north and east, and Variscan influence in the south. Rising sea levels in the late Triassic gave rise to a widespread development of sabkha facies evaporites and marls in the Celtic Sea, Irish Sea and Ulster Basins (Fig. 7B).

The Triassic was brought to a close by a widespread marine incursion across the subdued Rhaetian topography of the offshore basins, where only a few structural intra-basinal highs persisted as areas of non-marine deposition. The basin margin faults show little indication of movement during this period (Woodland 1971; Broughan et al. 1989). Fine-grained and thin-bedded marine sequences are typical of the Liassic in the Malin Shelf, Ulster and Irish Sea basins.

Liassic

Onshore the Lower Liassic of the Ulster Basin is variably thick due to pre-Cretaceous erosion. The maximum preserved thickness is 250 m at the Port More borehole in the Rathlin Trough, whilst 51 m (Hettangian) were penetrated in the Larne-1 borehole in the Larne–Lough Neagh Basin. The fragmentary evidence of previously existing Middle and Upper Liassic beds suggests that the Lower Jurassic succession was once thicker. Whilst the thin Liassic (and Lower Cretaceous) sequences may owe their preservation in part to the protective cover of basalt, it can be argued that the Early Jurassic seas did not transgress much beyond the currently defined basinal areas. This minimum incursion limit is depicted on Figure 7C.

The same problem presents itself with respect to the Kish Bank Basin, where possibly up to 2700 m of Liassic rocks are preserved against the western boundary faults of the half graben (Broughan et al. 1989). Did the Liassic seas transgress these faults and extend onto the Irish mainland? Cope (1984) has convincingly argued, with respect to the Cardigan Bay Basin, that a considerable portion of the Welsh Massif was submerged at this time and was further inundated later in the Jurassic (but see Ziegler 1990 for an alternate view). On the west side of the Irish Sea the Leinster Massif, which was upstanding and a source of sediment as early as late Devonian time and was onlapped in the early Carboniferous, may not have constituted much of a physical barrier to incursion by Lower Jurassic time. The present topography of Leinster probably results from Tertiary (Neogene?) adjustments and the existence of roof pendants on the batholith also suggests that the area has not suffered deep erosion and may have had a protective cover of younger strata (Davies 1960, 1970). There is, however, a total absence of recorded Liassic rocks onshore south of the Ulster Basin, despite the fact that Liassic lithologies should be distinctive and easy to recognize over much of the limestone terrain of the Irish Midlands. Tate & Dobson (1989a) have suggested that a broad E–W axis of uplift developed across Ireland at the end of the Early Jurassic. It seems likely that if such a positive axis existed then it trended from the Erris Trough eastwards across Ireland towards the

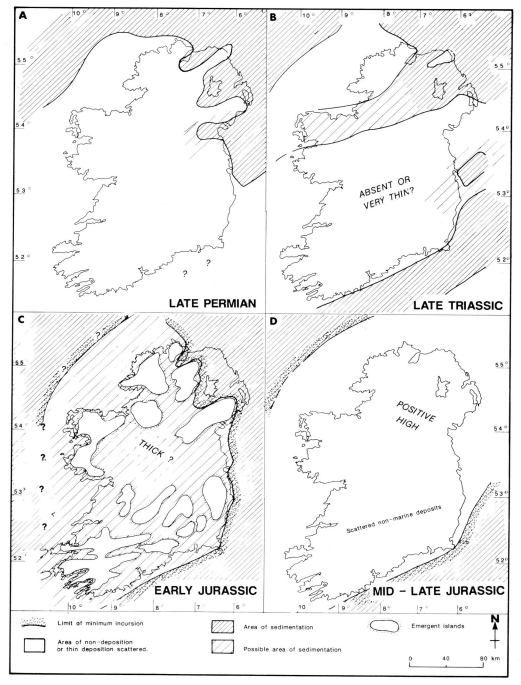

Fig. 7. Palaeogeography of Ireland in (A) Late Permian time; (B) Late Triassic time; (C) Early Jurassic time; (D) Middle-Late Jurassic time.

central part of the Irish Sea (Fig. 7D). This high may have extended (Tate & Dobson 1989*a*) across the Irish Sea to link with a proposed extension of the North Sea rift dome (Sellwood & Hallam 1974; Penn & Evans 1976). Inversion of this axis in Ireland would explain the complete removal of the (?thicker) Liassic from the central area by active erosion with, at the same time, only partial erosion of the Liassic on the northern flank of the arch in the Ulster Basin.

Clastic input into the North Celtic Sea Basin (Petrie *et al.* 1989) suggests that emergent source areas were available in the south of the country, at least for part of the time interval, with the maximum transgression in the Toarcian. Two pictures of Liassic palaeogeography are presented on Fig. 7C. The first envisages marine incursion only in the northeast region, with minimal encroachment elsewhere. This is the picture presented by Naylor & Shannon (1982) and Ziegler (1990). The alternate view, preferred here, is that most of Ireland was covered by (?late) Liassic sediments which were subsequently uplifted and subjected to erosion. The island areas within the Liassic sea in Fig. 7C are intended to give a general indication of the palaeogeography rather than a precise picture. Temporal constraints on the subsequent period of erosion of the Liassic are provided in the Ulster Basin and in County Kerry (Ballydeenlea) by Upper Cretaceous sediments, and over the Irish Midlands by Tertiary deposits. In the south at Cloyne, however, if any marine Liassic (or non-marine Triassic) was deposited it must have been eroded prior to the formation of the red karstic clays of probable Middle Jurassic age.

Middle and Upper Jurassic

In Middle Jurassic time there was intermittent subsidence in the offshore region around the southern part of Ireland. Relatively thick sequences accumulated within the basins, probably with generally westwards deepening conditions. The northwestern, northern and eastern offshore areas appear to have been more positive, with the lack of preserved rock sequences indicating either non-deposition or thin marginal facies subsequently removed by erosion. No Middle Jurassic rocks are present onshore in Ireland, even in the Ulster Basin, nor are there reworked fossils or other evidence to suggest the prior existence of rocks of this age. Jurassic fossils recovered from the drift near Dublin, and believed to be derived from the Kish Bank Basin (Broughan *et al.* 1989), are also restricted to Liassic species. It can be argued

that erosion has removed any Middle Jurassic which had been deposited, but it seems more likely that the positive arch initiated in Early Jurassic time persisted, and that onshore Ireland was an area of non-deposition in the Middle Jurassic (Fig. 7D). Evidence for a persistent high in the area of the Erris Trough is provided by maturation data for the Upper Permian of the Amoco 19/5–1 well (Robeson *et al.* 1988). Vitrinite reflectance figures of around 0.3% (Philcox *et al.* this volume) suggest that the section has never been buried substantially deeper than at present. Regionally, as Tate & Dobson (1989*a*) have pointed out, Bajocian–Bathonian sediments on the flanks of this high show derivation from the north and south and are unusually thick: *c.* 850 m in Cardigan Bay Basin (Penn & Evans 1976), *c.* 600 m in the Sea of Hebrides Basin (Morton 1987), in excess of 1500 m in the Slyne Trough (Trueblood & Morton 1991), and more than 700 m in the Main Porcupine Basin (Croker & Shannon 1987). Non-marine and marginal marine facies are commonly developed in the Middle Jurassic of the west coast offshore basins, and basin margin facies can be identified in the North Celtic Sea Basin (Petrie *et al.* 1989). With this picture of near emergence in the offshore it is unlikely that the onshore massif was submerged.

Marine conditions persisted intermittently through Late Jurassic time along the southwestern and southern seaboards of Ireland. However, the Late Jurassic is marked by generally regressive regimes. Non-marine sediments are again seen over parts of the North Celtic Sea Basin and the Porcupine Basin. Quiet shallow marine conditions persisted in Cardigan Bay. There is no evidence that Late Jurassic sediments were deposited in the offshore region around the northern portion of Ireland, which probably remained positive, together with the onshore region, as in Middle Jurassic time. Figure 7D depicts the emergent onshore area and serves as a general picture for the Middle and Late Jurassic.

Cretaceous

There was a gradual build-up of tectonic activity towards the close of the Late Jurassic which culminated in the Late Cimmerian episode of the offshore basins, with a period of general emergence. Following upon widespread erosion of the Late Cimmerian surface, deposition in Berriasian to Aptian time, associated with rifting of the Atlantic margins, resumed within the southern and western offshore basins, with non-marine to marginal facies dominant. However, Lower Cretaceous rocks are not represented throughout the offshore basins of the Malin Sea and Minches (Evans *et al*. 1980), the Ulster Basin, or the Irish Sea basins. George (1967) ascribed the folding of pre-Cretaceous rocks in Ulster beneath the Upper Cretaceous overstep to Mid-Cretaceous folding, but it is more likely to belong to the Cimmerian phases. It seems probable that Lower Cretaceous rocks were never deposited onshore in Ireland and the pattern of Early Cretaceous palaeogeography was probably similar to that depicted in Fig. 7D for the Mid–Late Jurassic.

The Late Cretaceous was a time of worldwide sea-level rise (Vail *et al*. 1977). Global sea levels began to rise during the Albian, leading to widespread transgression. Around Ireland the basin margins were progressively overstepped and the Late Cretaceous seas spread onto the surrounding positive massifs. Thick accumulations of chalk were deposited in the Celtic Sea and Porcupine Basins. In the north a layer of chalk extended into the Ulster Basin, but none is now preserved in the Irish Sea basins.

The extent to which the present Irish landmass was covered by the Chalk remains conjectural. In his discussion of the significance of the Ballydeanlea chalk outlier Walsh (1966) postulates that the distinctive topography of southwest Ireland, with the high ground on the Old Red Sandstone anticlines and the lower ground on synclinal Carboniferous rocks, was already formed in Late Cretaceous time. He argues that present day topography essentially represents an exhumed land surface and that Late Cretaceous sea level was probably 300 m higher than at present, thus flooding most of southern Ireland. Evidence from the Celtic Sea Basins (Petrie *et al*. 1989) suggests that the maximum extent of the chalk sea was in Campanian–Maastrichtian time, as in the Ulster Basin (Reid 1971), and this is supported by the Campanian date for the preserved remnant at Ballydeenlea. However, although it seems likely that much of southern Ireland was inundated at this time, a simple extrapolation of proposed water depth and present topography is too simplistic. It is probable that there has been some subsequent warping and faulting of the land surface, together with possible rejuvenation and erosional modification of the upland areas (see below). On the other hand, George (1967, and Discussion in Walsh 1966) preferred to view the Ballydeenlea chalk as a synclinal remnant resulting from end Cretaceous–early Tertiary folding, with the southern Irish landscape as the product of later erosion of a widespread high-

level Neogene peneplain. Walsh (1966) had discussed and rejected the concept of preservation of the Ballydeenlea outlier as a synclinal remnant. No other evidence has been presented of post-Cretaceous folding in southern Ireland on this scale.

The question is whether an Irish Midlands arch existed in the Late Cretaceous and effectively separated a southern basin of chalk deposition from the Ulster Basin in the north. This pattern of palaeogeography was favoured by Naylor & Shannon (1982), Ziegler (1990) and Shannon (1991). An alternate concept deserves consideration, in which the Midlands arch foundered and chalk deposition spread across lowland Ireland. The thickest deposits may indeed have been in the Midlands area. Renewed uplift along the axis, extending eastwards into the Irish Sea, at the end of the Cretaceous may then have produced active erosion and removal of the chalk cover. In this view the absence of Upper Cretaceous in the central part of the Irish Sea is due to erosion rather than to non-deposition. The two views of Cretaceous palaeogeography are given in Fig. 8.

Tertiary and Quaternary

Towards the end of the Cretaceous period the first major pulses of the Alpine Orogeny (Laramide) were felt throughout the region, causing uplift. The Chalk sea retreated from the rising landmass of Britain and Ireland towards the marginal depressions of the North Sea and the Rockall Trough. Ireland became emergent, together with large tracts of the surrounding continental shelf.

In the northeast of Ireland Cretaceous rocks were eroded and locally removed from areas such as the Highland Border Ridge and the flank of the Longford–Down Massif. This took place before the onset of Eocene igneous activity. The plateau basalts generally rest upon the Chalk, but also overstep the Chalk onto older rocks.

The importance of Tertiary tectonism and erosion in shaping the present landscape of Ireland was stressed by George (1967) and Mitchell (1980). There is no general agreement as to the origin of various Tertiary platforms and peneplains, or even whether these are wavecut or of subaerial origin. The preservation of Jurassic (Cloyne), Cretaceous (Ballydeenlea), and Tertiary (Ballymacadam etc.) sediments at low altitude within collapse features on the Carboniferous surface suggests that the land surface of the southern part of the country has not been much reduced by erosion during

Mesozoic and Tertiary time. The Tertiary deposits are all non-marine and it is difficult to conceive that widespread Neogene marine bevelling, as advocated by George (1967), could have taken place. Other than in Ulster there are as yet no proven Paleocene or Eocene deposits, and it was possibly during this interval that the protective Upper Cretaceous cover was eroded. Walsh (1966) has argued that the collapsed chalk breccia at Ballydeenlea may be about 40–140 m below the original depositional surface. Higgs & Beese (1986) and Beese et al. (1983) have also noted collapse features suggesting a lowering of the deposits into the cavities from above; but it is difficult to envisage that the deposits were laid down more than a few tens of metres above their present position. This is not to deny the possibility of adjustments of the terrain by warping or faulting. The younger deposits at Cloyne and Ballydeenlea are in synclinal settings within the Carboniferous; but this is to be expected both in terms of the existence of water bodies on topographically lower ground and the existence of soluble Carboniferous limestone in the synclinal cores. The explanation for the indicated small amount of post-Variscan erosion may be found in the protection afforded by a layer of Chalk over much of the lower ground. Erosional modification will undoubtedly have been greater over the higher ground of the Old Red Sandstone and Lower Palaeozoic inliers. To this must be added the effects of upland glaciation and for this reason the emergent areas on Figs 7C & 8, which are form lines based on the present topography, cannot be viewed as providing an accurate picture.

The threads of evidence presented above suggest that the structural framework of Ireland, established in the Variscan orogeny, had given rise, by the end of the Triassic, to a topographic outline similar to that of today. The major tectonic influences onshore since that time appear to have been large scale warps giving rise to regional highs. Some areas, such as the Longford–Down massif, probably were generally positive throughout the Mesozoic and Tertiary, and received only a thin cover of younger beds (see McCaffrey & McCann, this volume). The influence of post-Variscan faulting is harder to discern in the Carboniferous terrain, but younger extensional and wrench movements must have taken place. Isostatic adjustments have undoubtedly occurred over areas such as the Leinster and Donegal granites. Thick Permo-Triassic deposits were deposited only within the Ulster Basin and possibly its westward extension, and were probably largely absent or thin over the remainder of the country. Of the younger sequences the Liassic and particularly the Upper Cretaceous Chalk are the most likely horizons to have seen widespread development. Shannon (1991a) points out in the context of the offshore basins that the Hettangian and Cenomanian transgressions are the two regional eustatic events which clearly outweighed the general domination of the offshore depositional regimes by local tectonic control. It is reasonable to anticipate that this was also true for the onshore region. Maturation evidence and interval velocity studies have indicated a possible 2–3 km of post-Triassic uplift and erosion in parts of the Irish Sea Basin (Colter 1978; Ziegler 1987), with Jurassic and Upper Cretaceous strata being suggested as the missing section. Similarly, Jenner (1981) suggested that 3 km of burial and uplift is required to explain the maturation evidence in the Kish Bank Basin. If future maturation, fission track and other studies demonstrate a similar requirement for uplift across the central onshore part of Ireland, then it is suggested that the Liassic and Upper Cretaceous may have provided most of the missing section. The evidence from the scattered post-Carboniferous outliers is that both topographic relief and erosion of the onshore region has apparently been relatively modest for long periods of time, particularly in the Tertiary. This suggests that the land surface has been low-lying since Triassic time and may have been afforded some protection for part of that time by a cover of Liassic and Upper Cretaceous strata. Preservation of roof pendants on the higher parts of the Leinster batholith (Davies 1960, 1970) indicates the lack of deep erosion and may suggest that this protection extended over the batholith and that the islands depicted on Figs 5C & 6 may have become submerged during part of those time intervals. The younger cover was subsequently removed by erosion following Tertiary rejuvenation of the batholith.

Mention has been made of the modification of upland areas by Pleistocene glaciation. In many valleys and lowland areas also there are spectacular examples of glacial action. However, the evidence of the Tertiary deposits suggests that general erosion and lowering of the land surface by glacial action may have been relatively small. One of the main effects of glaciation was probably the removal of protective erosion products from the limestone surface, which is now open to solution and erosion. It seems unlikely that Pleistocene modification of the land surface was great enough to radically change the palaeogeographic outlines presented in Figs 7 & 8.

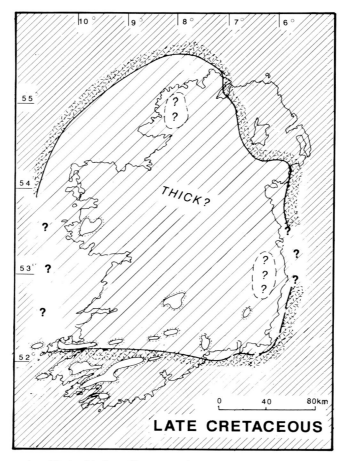

Fig. 8. Palaeogeography of Ireland in Late Cretaceous time.

There has been little reference here to the discordant river system of southern Ireland which in places markedly cuts across the Caledonian and Variscan structural grain, and which was the starting point for much of the speculation regarding the post-Carboniferous history of Ireland. We are not much nearer to having an answer to this problem because of the number of variables involved. If the main part of the speculation above is correct then it is unlikely that the topography and drainage pattern of Ireland has been carved from a high level erosion surface. The overall form of the landscape has probably been in existence since the end of the Triassic. However, drainage patterns established on lower level, and possibly domed, mid-Jurassic and end-Cretaceous surfaces between inliers of older rocks forming the higher ground, may have provided the origins of the present river system. Tertiary warping and faulting may also have played a significant role. When more data are available with respect to these several controlling factors, then it may be possible to throw more light on the problems posed by the present-day drainage system.

The author wishes to express his thanks to Professor G. D. Sevastopulo, Dr. G. Clayton and Professor G. L. Herries Davies for helpful discussion and critical comment on the manuscript.

References

AINSWORTH, N. R., O'NEILL, M., RUTHERFORD, M. M., CLAYTON, G., HORTON, N. F. & PENNY, R. A. 1987. Biostratigraphy of the Lower Cretaceous, Jurassic and Late Triassic of the North Celtic Sea and Fastnet Basins. *In*: BROOKS, J. & GLENNIE, K. W. (eds) *Petroleum Geology of North West Europe*, Volume 2, Graham & Trotman, London, 611–622.

BARR, K. W., COLTER, V. S. & YOUNG, R. 1981. The geology of Cardigan Bay-St. George's Channel Basin. *In*: ILLING, L. V. & HOBSON, G. D. (eds) *Petroleum Geology fo the Continental Shelf of North-West Europe*. Heyden, London, 432–443.

BEESE, A. P., BRUCK, P. M., FEEHAN, J. & MURPHY, T. 1983. A silica deposit of possible Tertiary age in the Carboniferous Limestone near Birr, County Offaly, Ireland. *Geological Magazine*, **120**, 331–340.

BISHOPP, D. W. & McCLUSKEY, J. A. G. 1948. Sources of industrial silica in Ireland. Geological Survey in Ireland, Emergency Period Pamphlet No. 3.

BLUNDELL, D. J. 1979. The geology and structure of the Celtic Sea. *In*: BANNER, F. T., COLLINS, M. B. & MASSIE, K. S. (eds) *The North-West European Shelf Seas: The Sea Bed and the Sea in Motion 1, Geology and Sedimentology*, Elsevier, Amsterdam, 43–60.

BOULTER, M. C. 1980. Irish Tertiary plant fossils in a European context. *Journal of Earth Sciences, Royal Dublin Society*, 3, 1–14.

BROUGHAN, F. M., NAYLOR, D. & ANSTEY, N. A. 1989. Jurassic rocks in the Kish Bank Basin. *Irish Journal of Earth Sciences*, **10**, 99–106.

BURNETT, R. D., CLAYTON, G., HAUGHEY, N., SEVASTOPULO, G. D. & SLEEMAN, A. G. 1990. The organic maturation levels of Carboniferous rocks in south County Wexford, Ireland. *Irish Journal of Earth Sciences*, **10**, 145–155.

CLAYTON, G. 1989. Vitrinite reflectance data from the Kinsale Harbour-Old Head of Kinsale area, southern Ireland and its bearing on the interpretation of the Munster Basin. *Journal of the Geological Society, London*, **146**, 611–616.

—— & BAILY, H. (in press). Organic maturation levels of pre-Westphalian Carboniferous rocks in Ireland, and in the Irish offshore. *Proceedings of International Deep Gas Workshop*, Federal Institute for Geosciences and Natural Resources, Hannover, Germany, 1990. International Energy Agency, Paris.

——, HAUGHEY, N., SEVASTOPULO, G. D. & BURNETT, R. D. 1989. *Thermal maturation levels in the Devonian and Carboniferous of Ireland*. Geological Survey of Ireland.

——, SEVASTOPULO, G. D. & SLEEMAN, A. G. 1986. Carboniferous (Dinantian and Silesian) and Permo-Triassic rocks in South County Wexford, Ireland. *Geological Journal*, **21**, 366–374.

COLTER, V. S. 1978. Exploration for gas in the Irish Sea. *Geologie en Mijnbouw*, **57**, 503–516.

—— & BARR, K. W. 1975. Recent developments in the geology of the Irish Sea and Cheshire Basins. *In*: WOODLAND, A. W. (ed.) *Petroleum and the Continental Shelf of North-West Europe, 1, Geology*. Applied Science, London, 61–75. 61–75.

COLIN, J. P., LEHMANN, R. A. & MORGAN, B. E. 1981. Cretaceous and Late Jurassic biostratigraphy of the North Celtic Sea Basin. *In*: NEALE, J. W. & BRAZIER, M. D. (eds) *Microfossils from Recent and Fossil Shelf Seas*. Ellis Horwood, Chichester, 122–155.

COPE, J. C. W. 1984. The Mesozoic history of Wales. *Proceedings of the Geologists' Association*, **95**, 373–385.

COXON, P. & FLEGG, A. M. 1987. A Late Pliocene/Early Pliestocene deposit at Pollnahallia, near Headford, County Galway. *Proceedings of the Royal Irish Academy*, **87B**, 2–42.

CROKER, P. F. & SHANNON, P. M. 1987. The evolution and hydrocarbon prospectivity of the Porcupine Basin, offshore Ireland. *In*: BROOKS, J. & GLENNIE, K. W. (eds) *Petroleum Geology of North West Europe*, Volume 2, Graham & Trotman, London, 633–642.

DAVIES, G. L. 1960. The age and origin of the Leinster mountain chain. *Proceedings of the Royal Irish Academy*, **61B**, 79–107.

—— 1970. The Enigma of the Irish Tertiary. *In*: STEPHENS, N. & GLASSOCK, R. E. (eds) *Irish Geographical Studies*. The Queen's University of Belfast, 1–16.

DOBSON, M. R. & EVANS, D. 1974. The geological structure of the Malin Sea. *Journal of the Geological Society, London*, **130**, 475–478.

DOWNING, R. A., BURGESS, W. G., SMITH, I. F., ALLEN, D. J., PRICE, M. & EDMUNDS, W. M. 1982. *Geothermal aspects of the Larne No. 2 Borehole*. Institute of Geological Sciences, London.

EVANS, D., KENOLTY, N., DOBSON, M. R. & WHITTINGTON, R. J. 1980. *The Geology of the Malin Sea*. Report, Institute of Geological Sciences, London, 79/15.

FLETCHER, T. P. 1977. *Lithostratigraphy of the Chalk (Ulster White Limestone Formation) in Northern Ireland*. Report, Institute of Geological Sciences, London, 77/24.

GARDINER, P. R. R. & VISSCHER, H. 1971. The Permian-Triassic Transition sequence at Kingscourt, Ireland. *Nature*, **299**, 209–210.

GEORGE, T. N. 1967. Landform and structure in Ulster. *Scottish Journal of Geology*, 3, 413–448.

HIGGS, K. & BEESE, A. P. 1986. A Jurassic microflora from the Colbond Clay of Cloyne, County Cork. *Irish Journal of Earth Sciences*, 7, 99–110.

INSTITUTE OF GEOLOGICAL SCIENCES & GEOLOGICAL SURVEY OF IRELAND 1982. Cardigan Bay, Sheet 52 N-06 W, 1:250 000 Series, Solid geology. Institute of Geological Sciences, London.

ILLING, L. V. & GRIFFITH, A. E. 1986. Gas prospects in the Midland Valley of Northern Ireland. *In*: BROOKS, J., GOFF, J. C. & VAN HOORN, (eds) *Habitant of Palaeozoic Gas in NW Europe*. Geological Society, London, Special Publication, **23**, 73–84.

JACKSON, D. I., MULHOLLAND, P., JONES, S. M. & WARRINGTON, G. 1987. The geological framework of the East Irish Sea Basin. *In*: BROOKS, J. & GLENNIE, K. W. (eds) *Petroleum Geology of North West Europe*, Volume 1, Graham & Trotman, London, 191–204.

JACKSON, J. S. 1965. The Upper Carboniferous Namurian and Westphalian) of Kingscourt, Ireland. *Scientific Proceedings of the Royal Dublin Society*, **A2**, 131–152.

JENNER, J. K. 1981. The structure and stratigraphy of the Kish Bank Basin. In: ILLING, L. V. & HOBSON, G. D. (eds) Petroleum Geology of the Continental Shelf of North West Europe, Heyden, London, 426–431.

KAMERLING, P. 1979. The geology and hydrocarbon habitat of the Bristol Channel Basin. Journal of Petroleum Geology, 2, 75–93.

KERR, I. D. V. 1987 Basement/cover Structural Relationships in the North Antrim Area, Ireland. PhD thesis, The Queen's University of Belfast.

McCANN, N. 1988. An assessment of the subsurface geology between Magilligan Point and Fair Head, Northern Ireland. Irish Journal of Earth Sciences, 9, 71–78.

—— 1990. The subsurface geology between Belfast and Larne, Northern Ireland. Irish Journal of Earth Sciences, 10, 157–173.

MILLSON, J. A. 1987. The Jurassic evolution of the Celtic Sea Basins. In: BROOKS, J. & GLENNIE, K. W. (eds) Petroleum Geology of North West Europe, Vol. 2, Graham & Trotman, London, 599–610.

MITCHELL, G. F. 1980. The search for the Tertiary in Ireland Journal of Earth Sciences, Royal Dublin Society, 3, 13–33.

MITCHELL, W. I. & OWENS, B. 1990. The geology of the western part of the Fintona Block, Northern Ireland: evolution of Carboniferous basins. Geological Magazine, 127, 407–426.

MORTON, N. 1987. Jurassic subsidence history in the Hebrides, N.W. Scotland. Marine and Petroleum Geology, 5, 226–242.

MURPHY, T. 1962. Some unusual low Bouguer anomalies of small extent in central Ireland and their connection with geological structure. Geophysical Prospecting, 10, 258–270.

—— 1966. Deep alteration of Carboniferous strata in the Midleton, Co. Cork district as detected by gravity surveying. Proceedings of the Royal Irish Academy, 64B, 323–334.

NAYLOR, D. & SHANNON, P. M. 1982. The Geology of Offshore Ireland and West Britain, Graham & Trotman, London.

—— & ANSTEY, N. A. 1987. A reflection seismic study of the Porcupine Basin, offshore West Ireland. Irish Journal of Earth Sciences, 8, 187–210.

PARNELL, J., SHUKLA, B. & MEIGHAN, I. G. 1989. The lignite and associated sediments of the Lough Neagh Basin. Irish Journal of Earth Sciences, 10, 67–88.

PENN, I. E. 1981. Larne No. 2 Geological well completion report. Report of the Institute of Geological Sciences, London, 81/6.

—— & EVANS, C. D. R. 1976. The Middle Jurassic (mainly Bathonian) of Cardigan Bay and its palaeogeographical significance. Report of the Institute of Geological Sciences, London, 76/6.

PETRIE, S. H., BROWN, J. R., GRANGER, P. J. & LOVELL, J. P. B. 1989. Mesozoic History of the Celtic Sea Basins. In: TANKARD, A. L. & BALKWILL, H. R. (eds) Extensional tectonics and stratigraphy of the North Atlantic Margins.

American Association of Petroleum Geologists, Memoir 46, 433–444.

REID, R. E. H. 1971. The Cretaceous rocks of North-Eastern Ireland. Irish Naturalists Journal, 17, 105–139.

ROBESON, D., BURNETT, R. D. & CLAYTON, G. 1988. The Upper Palaeozoic geology of the Porcupine, Erris and Donegal Basins, offshore Ireland. Irish Journal of Earth Sciences, 9, 153–175.

ROBINSON, K. W., SHANNON, P. M. & YOUNG, D. G. G. 1981. The Fastnet Basin: an integrated analysis. In: ILLING, L. G. & HOBSON, G. D. (eds) Petroleum Geology of the Continental Shelf of North West Europe, Heyden, London, 444–454.

SELLWOOD, B. W. & HALLAM, A. 1974 Bathonian volcanicity and North Sea rifting. Nature, 252, 27–28.

SHANNON, P. M. 1991a. The development of the Irish offshore sedimentary basins. Journal of the Geological Society, London, 148, 181–189.

—— 1991b. Tectonic framework and petroleum potential of the Celtic Sea, Ireland. First Break, 9, 107–122.

SMITH, R. A. 1986. Permo–Triassic and Dinantian rocks of the Belfast Harbour Borehole. Report of the British Geological Survey, 18, No. 6.

TATE, M. P. & DOBSON, M. R. 1989a. Late Permian to early Mesozoic rifting and sedimentation offshore NW Ireland. Marine and Petroleum Geology, 6, 49–59.

—— 1989b. Pre-Mesozoic geology of the western and north-western Irish continental shelf. Journal of the Geological Society, London, 146, 229–240.

THOMPSON, S. J. 1979. Preliminary report of the Ballymacilroy No. 1 borehole, Ahoghill, Co. Antrim. Geological Survey of Northern Ireland, Open File Report 63.

TRUEBLOOD, S. & MORTON, N. 1991. Comparative sequence stratigraphy and structural styles of the Slyne Trough and Hebrides Basin. Journal of the Geological Society, London, 148, 197–201.

TUCKER, P. M. & ARTER, G. 1987. The tectonic evolution of the North Celtic Sea and Cardigan Bay basins. Tectonophysics, 137, 191–307.

VAIL, P. R., MITCHUM, JR, R. M., TODD, R. G., WIDMIER, J. M., THOMPSON, S., SANGREE, J. B., BUBB, J. N., HATFIELD, W. G. 1977. Seismic stratigraphy; application to hydrocarbon exploration. American Association of Petroleum Geologists Memoir 26, 42–212.

VAN HOORN, B. 1987. The South Celtic Sea-Bristol Channel Basin: origin, deformation and inversion history. Tectonophysics, 137, 309–334.

VISSCHER, H. 1971. The Permian and Triassic of the Kingscourt outlier, Ireland. Geological Survey of Ireland, Special Paper, 1.

WALSH, P. T. 1966. Cretaceous outliers in South West Ireland and their implications for Cretaceous palaeogeography. Quarterly Journal of the Geological Society, London, 122, 63–84.

WATTS, W. A. 1957. A Tertiary deposit in County Tipperary. Scientific Proceedings of the Royal Dublin Society, 27, 309–311.

—— 1970. Tertiary and interglacial floras in Ireland. *In*: STEPHENS, N. & GLASSOCK, R. E. (eds) *Irish Geographical Studies*, The Queen's University of Belfast, 17–33.

WHITTINGTON, R. J., CROKER, P. F. & DOBSON, M. R. 1981. Aspects of the geology of the south Irish Sea. *Geological Journal*, **16**, 85–88.

WILKINSON, G. C., BAZLEY, R. A. B. & BOULTER, M. C. 1980. The geology and palynology of the Oligocene Lough Neagh Clays, Northern Ireland. *Journal of the Geological Society, London*, **137**, 65–75.

WILSON, H. E. 1972. *Regional geology of Northern Ireland*. H.M.S.O., Belfast.

WOODLAND, A. W. 1971. *The Llanbedr (Mochras Farm) borehole*. Report of the Institute of Geological Sciences, 71/18.

WYNNE, A. B. 1857. *On the Tertiary Clay and Lignite at Ballymacadam*. Report of the British Association, Dublin, 94–95.

ZIEGLER, P. A. 1982. *Geological Atlas of Western and Central Europe*. 1st Edition. Shell Internationale Petroleum Maatschappij, B. V.

—— 1987. Manx-Furness Basin. *Tectonophysics*, **137**, 389–440.

—— 1990. *Geological Atlas of Western and Central Europe*. 2nd Edition. Shell Internationale Petroleum Maatschappij B. V.

Post-Permian basin history of northeast Ireland

ROBERT J. McCAFFREY[1] & NOEL McCANN[2]

[1] School of Geosciences, The Queen's University of Belfast, Belfast BT7 1NN, UK
[2] 3 Drumlea View, Downpatrick, Co. Down, BT30 6SZ, UK

Abstract: Basin histories and major structures for Mesozoic and Cenozoic strata in northeast Ireland have been constrained with the help of computer-contoured isopach maps. Hand-drawn maps are included for comparison. The Highland Border Ridge, a well defined structural element since at least Lower Carboniferous times, separates the Rathlin Trough from the Lough Neagh–Larne Basin. The development of these basins was controlled by the pre-existing structures of the area, fault reactivation during late Hercynian movements and also Pangean rifting. A long-lived structural high in the Lough Neagh–Larne Basin, the Knockagh axis, is inferred to be a major block detached from the adjacent Longford–Down Massif.

The Lough Neagh–Larne basin of northeast Ireland is bounded to the southeast by the Lower Palaeozoic rocks of the Longford–Down Massif and to the northwest by the Dalradian metasediments of the Highland Border Ridge (McCann 1991). To the north of this ridge is the smaller Rathlin Trough. The northwest margin of this largely off-shore basin extends from County Donegal to Islay, Scotland (Evans et al. 1983). In simple terms, the basins are the areas on Fig. 1 with gravity values of less than 15 mGal, and the Highland Border Ridge is the northeast-trending gravity feature of more than 15 mGal which lies between them.

Upper Palaeozoic rocks occur in both basins but as there is insufficient information to prepare isopachs for them, they are discussed only briefly below.

Devonian Old Red Sandstone (ORS) rocks crop out at a small coastal exposure just south of the Highland Border Ridge and also beyond the western margin of the area of interest (Wilson 1972). Coal exploration boreholes west of Lough Neagh bottomed in Carboniferous strata. However, both ORS and Carboniferous rocks are absent in the Langford Lodge borehole (Manning et al. 1970) on the east side of Lough Neagh. This hole, on a northeast-tending gravity ridge, proved 72 m (unbottomed) of Lower Palaeozoic grit and mudstone below 1453 m drilled depth (Fig. 1). Dinantian carbonates crop out immediately west of the coal exploration holes and at very small exposures near the Belfast Harbour and Haw Hill boreholes (Fig. 1).

The Belfast Harbour borehole cored 200 m (unbottomed) of probable Chadian carbonates, mudstones and siltstones immediately beneath the Hercynian unconformity (Smith 1986).

Coals, and some Brigantian mudrocks which might also be potential hydrocarbon sources for the Lough Neagh–Larne Basin, are known only from the worked out mining area to the west of Lough Neagh. However, downfaulted blocks of these rocks may have survived Hercynian erosion anywhere within the basin (Wright 1919). Unfortunately the deep boreholes in this basin at Ballymacilroy, Newmill and Larne did not reach Carboniferous strata; they all bottomed in Permian red bed facies of sandstones, conglomerates, breccias and tephra (McCann 1991). Information from Ballytober, drilled during November 1990, is confidential at the time of writing.

In the east of the Lough Neagh–Larne Basin the Hercynian unconformity is known at depth only from the Belfast Harbour borehole. It is likely to have been extensively faulted due to later Hercynian movements, based on seismic evidence of faulting in younger reflectors (Papworth 1982). Considerable variations in both the lithology and the thickness of the immediately overlying Permian sediments are known from the boreholes as shown in Fig. 2. Vibroseis results indicate the presence of a much faulted gentle upfold between Larne and the Newmill well, while a gas show was recorded from Lower Permian sandstone at 1829 m in the Larne No. 2 geothermal test.

In the Rathlin Trough the Portmore borehole (Fig. 1) failed to reach Carboniferous strata and bottomed at 1897 m in Permian conglomeratic sandstone (Wilson & Manning 1978). However coal was mined to the southeast of this basin, on the margin of the Highland Border Ridge. 40 km west of the Portmore borehole, close to the northwest margin of the Rathlin Trough, the Magilligan borehole encountered two thin coals.

From PARNELL, J. (ed.), 1992, *Basins on the Atlantic Seaboard: Petroleum Geology, Sedimentology and Basin Evolution.* Geological Society Special Publication No 62, pp 277–290.

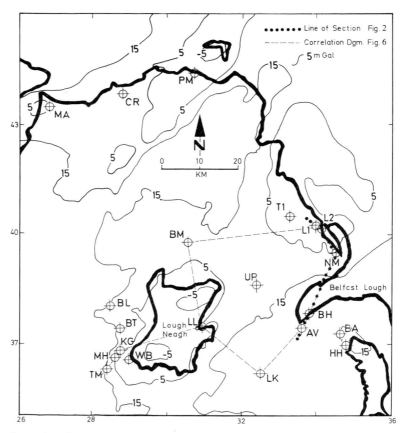

Fig. 1. Location and gravity anomaly map of northeast Ireland (after G.S.N.I. 1984), showing section (Fig. 2), and correlation diagram (Fig. 6). Borehole codes and total depths are as follows: MA Magilligan (1347 m), CR Corbally Reservoir (276 m), PM Portmore (1897 m), BM Ballymacilroy (2272 m), L1 Larne No. 1 (1284 m), L2 Larne No. 2 (2280 m), NM Newmill No. 1 (1981 m), BH Belfast Harbour (523 m), AV Avoniel (183 m), BA Ballyalton (552 m), HH Haw Hill (183 m), LK Long Kesh (91 m), Up Upton Park (129 m), LL Langford Lodge (1525 m), BL Ballyloughan Bridge (555 m), BT Ballytrea (611 m), KG Killary Glebe (1159 m), MH Mire House (1231 m), WB Washing Bay (600 m), AD Aughrimderg (507 m), T1 Ballytober, and TM Twyfords Mill (499 m). See also Table 2

These strata were found above 182 m of Namurian sandstones which were unbottomed at 1347 m (McCann 1988).

Following the pioneering work of J. J. Hartley in the 1940s, based mainly on coal exploration boreholes and water wells, Wilson (1972) used the earliest gravity and aeromagnetic information to help explain the subsurface geology of northeast Ireland. The drilling results and complete suites of wireline logs for the Newmill, Ballymacilroy and Larne No 2 boreholes, along with improved aeromagnetic and gravity information, and some seismic results became available in the early 1980s.

Objectives and methodology

The pre-Tertiary geology of the Lough Neagh–Larne Basin is rather poorly constrained due to lack of suitable outcrop and a paucity of deep boreholes. This is especially the case in the areas covered by Tertiary basalt.

The present work presents computer-interpolated isopach maps for the strata shown in Table 1, as the limited deep drilling data makes effective interpolation for pre-Permian rocks problematic. It is proposed that the production of post-Permian isopach maps gives an impression of the 3D arrangement of these

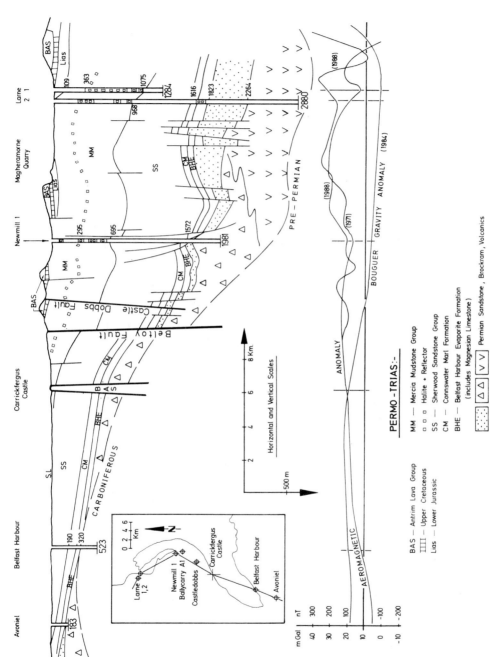

Fig. 2. Geological cross section of the rocks between Larne and Avoniel (after McCann 1990). See Fig. 1 for location and text for discussion.

Table 1. *Stratigraphic summary of the major post-Carboniferous basins of Northern Ireland (after Evans et al. 1983). Strata presented in Figs 3 & 4 are marked with an asterisk. Major unconformities are marked u/c*

Epoch	Stratum	Lithology
Palaeogene	Antrim Lava Group	Basalts, rhyolites, laterites.
	u/c	
Cretaceous	Ulster White Limestone Formation*	Chalk with flint horizons.
	Hibernian Greensand Formation*	Glauconitic calcareous sandstone.
	u/c	
Jurassic	Liassic*	Mudstone with thin limestones.
Triassic	Rhaetic*	Shale, mudstone and limestone.
	Mercia Mudstone Group*	Marls, mudstone and siltstone with locally thick anhydrite.
Permo-Triassic	Sherwood Sandstone Group*	Sandstone with mudstone partings.

strata. Post-Permian maps, along with sea bed and geophysical mapping should allow constraints to be placed on the limits and morphology of the sedimentary basins of northeast Ireland.

A simplified litho- and chronostratigraphy, as shown in Table 1, was used to select data for each of the maps. This information, concerning the *present-day* thickness of post-Permian rocks, has been compiled from published maps, reports and papers. Only data for units which have had their total thickness proved have been used. The UNIRAS program UNIMAP (using the 'fault' interpolation method) was used to process the data. The area of the map was divided into a regular grid and the data values within each grid cell averaged. The data values at the nodes of the grid were used in quadratic interpolation and the results smoothed. The program recognizes faults and trends, and interpolates to areas where there is no present-day outcrop, and hence no data, and these areas have been masked out. This method for drawing computer-generated isopach maps does not involve gravity modelling, but major faults known to have existed (see below) during the corresponding period of deposition have been included, and the interpolation routine takes these into account. The computer-drawn maps by RJM (Figs 3a–e) may be compared to hand-drawn isopach maps by NMcC (Figs 4a–d), in which gravity (GSNI 1984), aeromagnetic (GSNI 1988) and the small amount of local seismic information is considered.

Faulting

The naming and location of the various faults in the area has generated considerable discussion (Fig. 5a). Three long-lived and well-documented faults are included in the computer-drawn isopach maps, and are discussed below.

Tow Valley fault

Carboniferous sediments are known to thin against the northern margin of the Highland Border Ridge and the *en echelon* intraformational and possibly synsedimentary trace of the Tow Valley fault (TVF) may be identified from the WINCH reflection profile across the Rathlin Trough (Hall *et al.* 1984; Fig. 5b). The TVF is clearly a fault with a long history of activity. Since the Eocene it has offset the Upper and Lower Basalt Formations of the Antrim Lava Group, which provide the fault's very pronounced magnetic signature. As far as is known, the Highland Boundary fault (HBF) (see below) in Scotland has not been active during the Paleocene–Eocene. If the TVF ever shared the history of movement of the HBF, it has not done so recently. The TVF is at the eastern end of the Fair Head–Clew Bay Linear (FCL) (Max *et al.* 1983; Hutton 1987), which has been equated with the HBF (Klemperer *et al.* 1991). However, continuation of the eastern end of the FCL to link with the Scottish segment of the HBF is not proven. Hall *et al.* (1984) continue the TVF up the western side of Kintyre, partly on the basis of seismic evidence, and this line is used in the current paper.

Highland Boundary fault

It is clear that both the TVF and the Cushendall fault to the south east have been major lineaments bounding the Dalradian block in north Antrim and many workers (Sanderson 1970; Curry *et al*. 1984; Hall *et al*. 1984; Illing & Griffith 1986; Klemperer *et al*. 1991) have indicated the Cushendall fault as the along-strike correlative of the HBF in Scotland. The Cushendall fault, like the HBF, forms the southern boundary of an area of Dalradian rocks. The fault may have had oceanic remnants emplaced along its strike (i.e. the Tyrone Igneous Complex; Hutton 1987) and is known to have had a complex history of movement (Sanderson 1970). Hutton (1987) has indicated that the Cushendall fault is the southern boundary of an extension of the Grampian Terrane south of the end-Silurian/early Devonian HBF. The Tyrone Igneous Complex was thought by Hutton (1987) to have been partly obscured by the southerly directed thrusting of the Dalradian, although there is no evidence to continue this style of faulting to the east along either the TVF or Cushendall fault. Variation in fault behaviour may be accounted for by several phases of activity, of different styles. Palaeomagnetic studies (Trench & Haughton 1990) in Scotland have shown that there was probably very little displacement of the HBF after Lower Old Red Sandstone deposition. However, the Cushendall fault became inactive *after* the deposition of ORS conglomerates on the flanks of the Highland Border Ridge, since these strata contain fractured pebbles indicative of movement on a local fault (cf. Ramsay 1964). Constraints are placed on the movement of the Cushendall fault by unfaulted Upper Cretaceous sediments, which thin onto the Highland Border Ridge and which lie unconformably on the Dalradian rocks. The line of the Cushendall fault and its presumed continuation in pre-Triassic rocks towards the northern boundary of the Tyrone Igneous Complex is taken as the correlative of the HBF in this paper.

Southern Uplands fault (SUF)

The trace of the SUF in northeast Ireland is more problematic than the HBF and TVF. Anderson (1964) observed that 'It is not necessary, or even perhaps desirable, to think in terms of a single master fault, which has no proven outcrop in Ireland and has yet to be precisely located.' Since no convincing outcrop exists, attempts have been made to place the fault upon the computer-generated isopach maps using geophysical evidence. The northwestern edge of the Longford–Down Massif, presumably bounded by the SUF, is the pronounced lineament where Mesozoic and Cenozoic basin-fill sediments abut against the Palaeozoic meta-sediments of the Southern Uplands block. Anderson (1964) and Max *et al*. (1983) indicate that the line of the steepest magnetic gradient comes ashore on the north side of Belfast Lough where it is coincidental with a pronounced gravity lineament (GSNI 1984). This combined magnetic and gravity anomaly lineament led Max *et al*. (1983) to propose a Southern Uplands Linear, and prompted Hutton (1987) and Illing & Griffith (1986) to suggest positions for the SUF. The line of Hutton (1987) is used here, although it should be noted again that there are other possible fault correlatives of the SUF in northeast Ireland, and that this line is only the most obvious.

Results

A computer-generated isopach map has been generated for each of the five stratigraphic intervals chosen (Fig. 3). Also, a correlation ribbon diagram (Fig. 6) and a computer-generated isopach map totalling all post-Permian strata (Fig. 7) are included. The individual stratigraphic intervals are described below.

Sherwood Sandstone Group (SSG)

The SSG (Figs 3a, 4a) is the primary potential hydrocarbon reservoir for both basins, with the overlying Mercia Mudstone Group acting as the caprock. The limited amount of drilling in the Rathlin Trough does not allow a detailed appraisal of the morphology of the basin-fill. However, seismic profiling (Hall *et al*. 1984, Fig. 5b) and gravity modelling (Kerr 1987) indicate a half-graben deepening towards the Highland Border Ridge. The Lough Neagh–Larne Basin is larger, asymmetric and, as indicated in Fig. 4a, is probably in two parts. The Newmill wildcat well proved nearly 900 m of SSG rocks, and off-shore seismic reflection profiling (Hall *et al*. 1984) along a line about 20 km east of the Newmill well has shown the presence of about 1000 m of these rocks, indicating continued slight thickening towards the northeast (Fig. 5c).

Some deposition did occur to the south of the Southern Uplands fault, in a basin apparently oriented with its long axis normal to the SUF (Fig. 1). The amount of post Permo-Triassic denudation in this area is difficult to quantify.

It is not yet possible to decide whether the

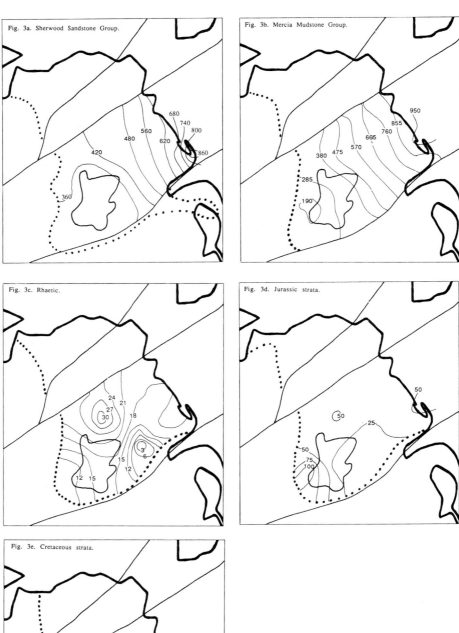

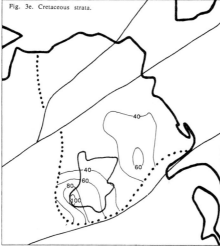

Fig. 3. (a–e) Computer-generated isopach maps for Permo-Triassic and Cenozoic strata in northeast Ireland. Borehole locations and thicknesses as on Fig. 1 and Table 2. In areas where a unit is indicated as occurring, but where there are no isopachs there is insufficient data for effective interpolation. Off-shore isopachs are tentative. (a) Sherwood Sandstone Group; (b) Mercia Mudstone Group; (c) Rhaetic; (d) Jurassic strata; (e) Cretaceous Hibernian Greensand and Ulster White Limestone Formations.

SHERWOOD SANDSTONE GROUP (hand-drawn)   MERCIA MUDSTONE GROUP (hand-drawn)

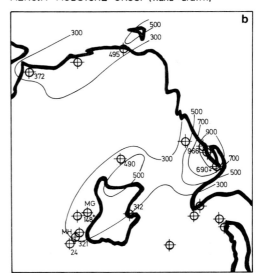

JURASSIC (hand-drawn)   CRETACEOUS ULSTER WHITE LIMESTONE (hand-drawn

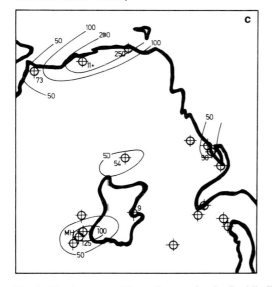

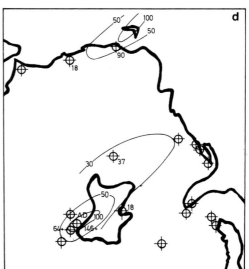

Fig. 4. Hand-contoured isopach maps for the Rathlin Trough and the Lough Neagh-Larne Basin.

Lough Neagh−Larne basin and the Rathlin Trough were separate at this period or whether they were linked around the northeast of the present Highland Border Ridge. There is little seismic and no drilling data for the area. However, the available sea bed mapping (Evans et al. 1983) would suggest a linkage.

Mercia Mudstone Group

In the Rathlin Trough, paucity of drilling makes effective interpolation difficult. However, data from seismic reflection work (Hall et al. 1984) indicates that deposition of the Mercia Mudstone Group may also extend 25−30 km off-

Table 2. *Borehole records, northeast Ireland* (borehole key in Fig. 1; ub = unbottomed)

Group/Formation	Location	KG	MG	MH	TM	LL	AD	BM	L1	L2	NM	BH	MA	CR	PM
Lough Neagh Group	Top	65		14			29								
	Thickness	144		298			30								
Antrim Lava Group	Top	209		312		9	59	0						0	1
	Thickness	223		252		780	302	769						152	76
UWL	Top	432		564		789	361	769						247	77
	Thickness	8+64		54		18	146 ub	37						18	1+90
Liassic	Top	fault?		618		807		806	38				111	265	168
	Thickness			125		9		54	50				73	11 ub	250
Rhaetic	Top	fault?		743		816		925	88				184		661
	Thickness			10		18		32	21				25		4
Mercia Mudstone Group	Top	504	14	753	10	834		957	109	17	5		209		665
	Thickness	122	148	321	24	312		490	966	951	690		372		495
Sherwood Sandstone Group	Top	626	183	1074	34	1146		1447	1075	968	695	32	581		1192
	Thickness	272	385	157 ub	288	270		421	209 ub	648	867	158	409		630

MA sill			PM sill			CR sill	
top	52		top	438		top	152
thickness	59		thickness	223		thickness	95

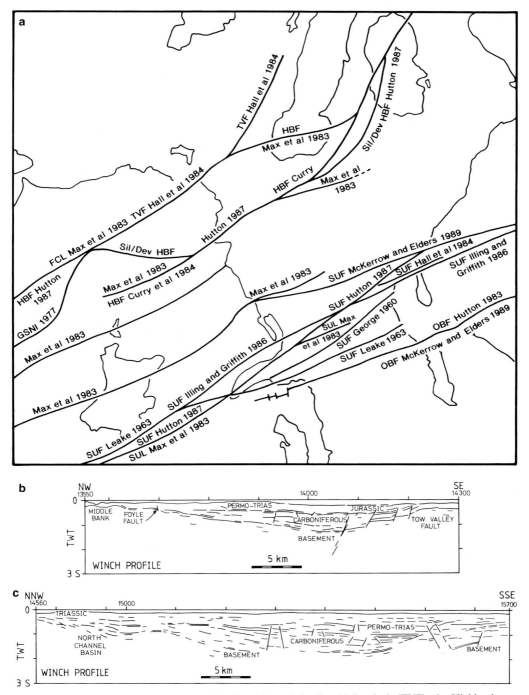

Fig. 5. (a) Map showing the recently postulated positions of the Tow Valley fault (TVF), the Highland Boundary fault, and the Southern Uplands fault. Max *et al.* (1983) also defined a Southern Uplands Linear (SUL), and a Fair Head-Clew Bay Lineament (FCL). (b) Interpretation of the WINCH seismic reflection profile for the Rathlin Trough, from Hall *et al.* (1984). (c) Interpretation of the WINCH profile for the Firth of Clyde and North Channel Basins, the off-shore equivalent of the Lough Neagh-Larne Basin.

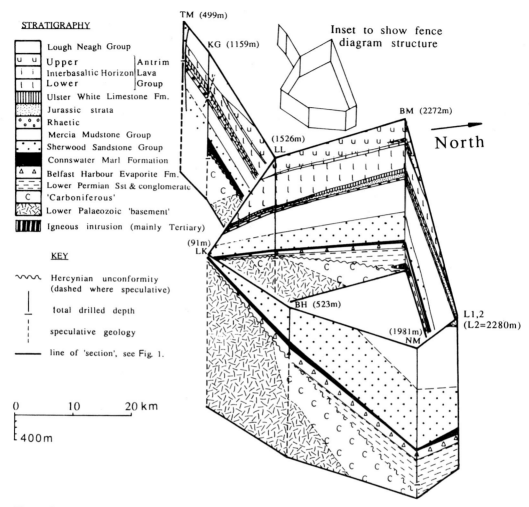

Fig. 6. Correlation ribbon diagram, located in Fig. 1. (See text for discussion). Borehole codes are as given for Fig. 1. Total depths (in metres) are given beside each borehole. Figure bottomed at 2000 m.

shore. The thickness of the Group in the Lough Neagh–Larne Basin increases to the northeast, but on the basis of gravity data a thinning between the Lough Neagh and Larne parts of the basin is suggested (Fig. 4b). The present-day absence of the Mercia Mudstone Group south of the SUF implies either non-deposition, possibly due to the existence of an upstanding topographic area during the Triassic, or subsequent erosion.

Rhaetic and Jurassic strata

Borehole records in northeast Ireland use the term Rhaetic. This obsolete term has been superseded by, but is not synonymous with, the Penarth Group. Due to the difficulty of reinterpreting old borehole records accurately, the term Rhaetic is retained in this paper.

In the Rathlin Trough, Rhaetic and Jurassic strata are known from only two boreholes, so computer interpolation is not possible. In the Lough Neagh–Larne Basin, the few data points available suggest on the computer-generated map (Fig. 3c) that the Rhaetic strata thicken north-westwards, whereas both computer and hand-drawn maps (Figs 3d & 4c) indicate irregular thickness distributions for the Jurassic strata.

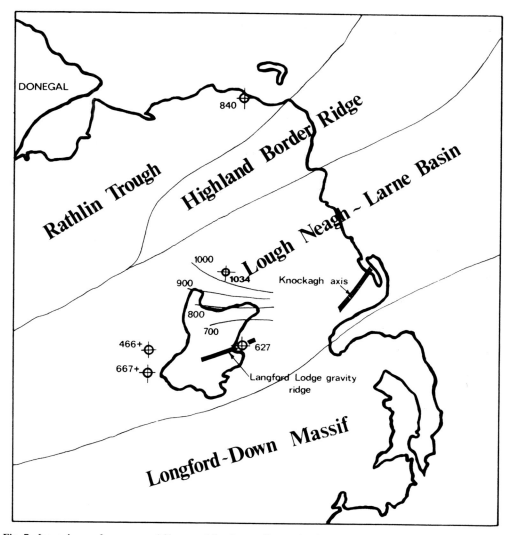

Fig. 7. Isopach map for preserved Sherwood Sandstone Group-Antrim Lava Group strata and main structural element map. See text for discussion.

Cretaceous Ulster White Limestone and Hibernian Greensand Formations

The Ulster White Limestone Formation, stratigraphically broadly equivalent to the Chalk of England (Reid 1971; Fletcher 1977), forms spectacular cliffs in both basins. Also, two outliers within 15 km southeast of the Portmore borehole rest unconformably on the Dalradian rocks of the Highland Border Ridge. Only two boreholes are available for the Rathlin Trough, suggesting thickening northeastwards while seismic data (Hall *et al*. 1984) suggests off-shore thinning towards the north. In the southern

basin seven boreholes reached Cretaceous, but only five penetrated these rocks completely. Information on the shallow holes at Upton Park and Templepatrick reported by Wilson (1983) has been used only for the computer-generated map (Fig. 3e). The Aughrimderg borehole (Fig. 4d) to the west of Lough Neagh (Hartley 1948; Fowler & Robbie 1961; McCann 1991) proved 146 m (unbottomed) of limestone. This contrasts markedly with the 18 m sequence in the Langford Lodge borehole to the east of the lough and also the area of reduced Cretaceous thickness further to the northeast (Reid 1971). This area, the Knockagh Axis (Fletcher & Wood in Griffin & Wilson 1982), may possibly be related to the northeast-trending gravity ridge upon which the Langford Lodge borehole was drilled (see Fig. 7).

Antrim Lava Group

Sub-aerial erosion and glaciation have removed unknown thicknesses of this Group and in particular the Upper Basalt Formation. Thicknesses for the Lower Basalt Formation, where protected beneath the Upper Basalt cover, are known only from the Ballymacilroy (417 m) and Langford Lodge (531 m) boreholes.

Discussion

During the Caledonian movements of the Lower Palaeozoic, the Grampian Terrane was displaced and eventually sutured to the Midland Valley Terrane along the line of the Highland Border Fault (Hutton 1987). The rocks of the Longford−Down Massif were displaced by transcurrent faulting along the SUF until their eventual suturing to the Midland Valley Terrane in the Devonian (cf. Hutton 1987; McKerrow & Elders 1989). Thus the basic structural framework of northeast Ireland has existed since at least mid-Devonian times. After this point, the bounding faults of the major structural elements (see Fig. 1) were relatively inactive (Hutton 1987).

In the Rathlin Trough, Kerr (1987) determined a Triassic ENE−WSW extensional fracture system through examination of Eocene Basalts along the north Antrim coast. E−W extension, possibly due to early Pangean instability, has been suggested as the cause for basin development in the Permo-Triassic (Shannon 1991). In the Lough Neagh−Larne Basin, deepening towards the northeast can be explained by progressive down-faulting on a series of NNW−SSE trending faults. Such a system of faults, several downthrowing to the east, is observed south of Larne (Griffith & Wilson 1982). The general absence of major faults on the limited seismic sections of the area (Illing & Griffith 1986) is because exploration lines have been shot parallel to the fault trend, thus relatively minor faults seen on sections may be oblique transform faults for larger normal faults.

The development of asymmetrical basins in northeast Ireland, during deposition of both late Triassic and lower Jurassic strata, is problematic. However, further south in the Celtic sea there was a change in the stress regime, from transtensional E−W extension in Late Triassic times to a period of regional tectonic quiescence in the Early Jurassic (Shannon 1991). One possible model for the development of a Late Triassic and early Jurassic asymmetrical Lough Neagh−Larne Basin would be movement on a NE−SW trending fault at the northwestern margin of the basin. In an otherwise tectonically quiescent period, either reactivation or continued movement of the HBF or a strand in the HBF zone could have produced normal dip-slip movement and would have created a northward-deepening hangingwall basin.

The late Jurassic−early Cretaceous ESE−WNW compressive regime deduced by Kerr (1987) for onshore northeast Ireland is represented in both the Rathlin Trough and the Lough Neagh−Larne Basin by non-deposition. The onset of regional thermal subsidence after early Cretaceous rifting, as described in the Celtic Sea region (Shannon 1991), coincides with eustatic variations in the Cretaceous (e.g. Jenkyns 1980) which also tend to produce transgressive changes. Reid (1971) and Fletcher (1977) have demonstrated that the Ulster White Limestone Formation is transgressive onto the Highland Border Ridge although the contribution of subsidence or eustatic variation to basin deepening is difficult to gauge.

The voluminous Antrim Lava Group, part of the British Tertiary Igneous Province, marks the initiation of rifting due to spreading between Greenland and Eurasia (Macintyre et al. 1975). Much of the basin development prior to Antrim Lava Group extrusion was initiated by pre-rifting stresses. Updoming of post-Permian strata indicates that some basin inversion occurred (McCann 1990), although the time of the deformation is unknown.

A final point serves to emphasise that the regional structural geology of the area has had a long-term effect on the history of basin development. Lower Palaeozoic basement was proven near outcrop in the Long Kesh water well, and also in the Langford Lodge borehole (Fig. 1). The latter hole was drilled on a weak ENE gravity ridge where the Permian to Cretaceous sequence is unusually thin and both the Carboniferous and the Oligocene Lough Neagh Group are absent (McCann 1991). The Knockagh axis of Cretaceous thinning (mentioned above) is about 35 km northeast of the Langford Lodge borehole. This axis is not, however, associated with a gravity ridge (GSNI 1984). The thinning cannot be accounted for by the Longford−Down Massif, which crops out some distance to the south (Fig. 7). One explanation for thinning strata over a ridge would be the presence, at depth, of a fault block of positive eustatic buoyancy which has led to a prolonged topographic high in the area. As is seen in Fig. 5a, there has been a suggestion that the SUF strikes close to the area (Illing & Griffith 1986). Although the presence of the SUF cannot be confirmed, the presence of a splay of the SUF responsible for fault block formation is possible.

Conclusions

The substantial thicknesses of sediments developed in the two post-Carboniferous basins of northeast Ireland (Fig. 7) represent long-term localized subsidence, during a period of basin formation along the northwestern seaboard of the British Isles. The main control upon the siting of sedimentary basins in northeast Ireland was pre-existing structure which controlled the distribution of major faulting. Regional tectonic events controlled the timing of reactivation of older faults, and eustatic variations have influenced the type of prevalent basin-wide sedimentation.

We would like to thank J. Parnell, J. Buckman, G. Hardy, M. Carvel and D. Jamison for their help, and M. Scott and E. Mulqueeny for drafting figures. Receipt of a research studentship from NERC is gratefully acknowledged by RJM, and NMcC wishes to record his appreciation for the support and encouragement of Down County Museum.

References

ANDERSON, T. B. 1964. The evidence for the Southern Uplands fault in north-east Ireland. *Geological Magazine*, 102, 383–92.

BENNETT, J. R. P. 1983. Investigations of the geothermal potential of the U.K. The Sedimentary basins of northeast Ireland. *Environmental and Deep Geology Division, Institute of Geological Sciences and Geological Survey of Northern Ireland*, 35.

CURRY, G., BLUCK, B., BURTON, C., INGHAM, J., SIVETER, D. & WILLIAMS, A. 1984. Age, evolution and tectonic history of the Highland Border Complex, Scotland. *Transactions of the Royal Society of Edinburgh: Earth Sciences*, 75, 113–133.

EVANS, D., KENOLTY, N., DOBSON, N. R. & WHITTINGTON, R. J. 1983. Malin sheet 1:250000 series, solid geology. *Institute of Geological Sciences, Geological Survey of Northern Ireland, Geological Survey of Ireland*.

FLETCHER, T. P. 1977. *Lithostratigraphy of the Chalk (Ulster White Limestone Formation) in Northern Ireland*. Institute of Geological Sciences Report 77/24.

FOWLER, A. & ROBBIE, J. A. 1961. Geology of the country around Dungannon. *Memoir of the Geological Survey of Northern Ireland*.

GEOLOGICAL SURVEY OF NORTHERN IRELAND (GSNI) 1977. *Geological map of Northern Ireland, 1:250000, solid edition*.

—— 1984. *Bouguer Gravity anomaly map of Northern Ireland 1:250000 scale*.

—— 1988. *Aeromagnetic Survey of Northern Ireland 1:250000 scale*.

GRIFFITH, A. E. & WILSON, H. E. 1982. Geology of the Country around Carrickfergus and Bangor. *Memoir of the Geological Survey of Northern Ireland*.

HALL, J., BREWER, J., MATTHEWS, D. & WARNER, M. 1984. Crustal structure across the Caledonides from the 'WINCH' seismic reflection profile: influences on the evolution of the Midland Valley of Scotland. *Transactions of the Royal Society of Edinburgh: Earth Sciences*, 75, 97–109.

HARTLEY, J. J. 1948. The post-Mesozoic succession south of Lough Neagh, Co. Antrim. *Irish Naturalists Journal*, 9, 115–121.

HUTTON, D. H. W. 1987. Strike slip terranes and a model for the evolution of the British and Irish Caledonides. *Geological Magazine*, 124, 405–425.

ILLING, L. V. & GRIFFITH, A. E. 1986. Gas prospects in the 'Midland Valley' of Northern Ireland. *In*: BROOKS, J., GOFF, J. & VAN HOORN, B. (eds), *Habitat of Palaeozoic Gas in N. W. Europe*, Geological Society, London, Special Publication, 23, 73–84.

JENKYNS, H. C. 1980. Cretaceous anoxic events: from continents to oceans. *Journal of the Geological Society, London*, 137, 171–86.

KERR, I. D. V. 1987. *Basement/cover Structural Relationships in the North Antrim Area, Ireland*. PhD thesis, The Queen's University of Belfast.

KLEMPERER, S., RYAN, P. & SNYDER, D. 1991. A deep seismic transect across the Irish Caledonides. *Journal of the Geological Society, London* 148, 149–164.

LEAKE, B. E. 1963. The location of the Southern Uplands Fault in Central Ireland. *Geological Magazine*, 100, 420–423.

MACINTYRE, R. M., MCMENAMIN, T. & PRESTON, J. 1975. K-Ar results from Western Ireland and their bearing on the timing and siting of Thulean Magmatism, *Scottish Journal of Geology*, 11, 3, 227–249.

MANNING, P. I., ROBBIE, J. A. & WILSON, H. E. 1970. *Geology of Belfast and the Lagan Valley*. Memoir of the Geological Survey of Northern Ireland.

MAX, M., RYAN, P. & INAMDAR, D. D. 1983. A magnetic deep structural geology interpretation of Ireland. *Tectonics*, 2, 432–451.

McCANN, N. 1988. An assessment of the subsurface geology between Magilligan Point and Fair Head, Northern Ireland. *Irish Journal of Earth Sciences*, 9, 71–78.

—— 1990. The Subsurface Geology between Belfast and Larne, Northern Ireland. *Irish Journal of Earth Sciences*, 10, 157–173.

—— 1991. The Subsurface Geology of the Lough Neagh-Larne Basin, Northern Ireland. *Irish Journal of Earth Sciences*, 11, 53–69.

McKERROW, W. & ELDERS, C. 1989. Movements on the Southern Uplands fault. *Journal of the Geological Society, London*, **146**, 393–395.

PAPWORTH, T. J. 1982. *South Antrim and East Tyrone seismic survey report by Geoconsulting Ltd.* Geological Survey of Northern Ireland open-file report No. 65.

RAMSAY, D. M. 1964. Deformation of pebbles in Lower Old Red Sandstone conglomerates adjacent to the Highland Boundary Ridge. *Geological Magazine*, **101**, 228–248.

REID, R. E. H. 1971. The Cretaceous rocks of north-eastern Ireland. *Irish Naturalists' Journal*, **17**, 105–29.

SANDERSON, D. J. 1970. The Highland Border Ridge of North-east Ireland. *Geological Magazine*, **107**, 531–538.

SHANNON, P. M. 1991. The development of Irish offshore sedimentary basins. *Journal of the Geological Society, London*, **148**, 181–189.

SMITH, R. A. 1986. *Permo-Triassic and Dinantian rocks of the Belfast Harbour Borehole*. Report of the British Geological Survey, 18.

TRENCH, A. & HAUGHTON, P. D. W. 1990. Palaeomagnetic and geochemical evaluation of a terrane-linking ignimbrite: evidence for the relative position of the Grampian and Midland Valley terranes in late Silurian time. *Geological Magazine*, **127**, 241–257.

WILSON, H. E. 1972. Regional Geology of Northern Ireland. *Geological Survey of Northern Ireland*,

—— 1983. Deep drilling in Northern Ireland since 1947. *Irish Naturalists' Journal*, **21**, 160–163.

——& MANNING, P. I. 1978. Geology of the Causeway Coast. *Memoir of the Geological Survey of Northern Ireland*.

WRIGHT, W. B. 1919. An analysis of the Palaeozoic Floor of north-east Ireland. *Scientific Proceedings of the Royal Dublin Society*, New Series, **15**, 629–650.

Aspects of the geology of the Malin Sea area

M. R. DOBSON & R. J. WHITTINGTON

Institute of Earth Studies, UCW, Aberystwyth, Dyfed SY23 3DB

Abstract: A complex of sediment-filled graben and half-graben, separated by acoustic basement, occupy much of the northwest shelf of the British Isles. Some were established in the Late Carboniferous, but most were formed during a post-Hercynian tensional phase that adopted Caledonoid-trending structures in the basement. A major graben complex occurs in the Malin Sea area; flanked by the Coll−Tiree−Skerryvore−Stanton Banks basement ridge to the north and by the Islay−Donegal Platform to the south. Rock samples obtained by divers from the two basement ridges confirm their Precambrian character. Limited commercial multichannel reflection seismic data together with BIRPS WIRE lines and structural information supplied by Texaco suggest that the graben complex consists of three major depocentres: the Inner Hebrides Trough, the Malin Basin and the South Donegal Basin. To the west lies the Main Donegal Basin. This basin, in concert with the South Donegal Basin, evolved during the Carboniferous as a result of dextral strike slip movement between the Stanton Banks in the north and the Islay-Donegal Platform to the south. Sea bed core and dredge material and well data recovered from the graben complex indicate that the basin sediments include Upper Carboniferous, Permo-Triassic, Lower Jurassic, Middle Jurassic, with thick Cretaceous and Lower Tertiary in the far west. Periods of uplift and erosion restricted sedimentation during the late Mesozoic, whilst uplift and erosion in the early Tertiary was accompanied by extensive igneous activity, with the development of two plutonic centres and twelve other smaller intrusive igneous bodies. Tertiary sediments are inferred for the Blackstones Basin by analogy with similar sequences elsewhere in the Hebridean area. A thick Quaternary section, dominated by glaciomarine sediments, contains three of the five glacial cycles that constitute the Pleistocene in this area.

Elucidation, to reconnaissance level, of the geology of that part of the British continental shelf that extends from west of the Shetland Islands to the north coast of Ireland has been accomplished, during the last twenty years, through a combination of marine geological and geophysical surveys, calibrated and constrained by adjacent land outcrops and direct rockhead sampling (Riddihough 1968; Binns *et al.* 1974; Binns *et al.* 1975; Evans *et al.* 1980; Brewer *et al.* 1983). Of that extensive shelf the least well understood remains the Malin Sea area; broadly the region that lies between the north coast of Ireland and latitude 56°30N. Indeed, uncertainty about even the basic geological framework was confirmed in a recent series of papers in the *Journal of the Geological Society* (Part 1, 1991) where each map presented was different.

The geological structure of the Malin Sea area, which has been known in outline since the early 1970s (Dobson & Evans 1974), consists of the Coll−Tiree−Skerryvore−Stanton Banks Outer Hebrides Platform basement blocks in the north, the southwestern part of the Inner Hebrides Trough with the Blackstones and Colonsay Basins, the Malin Basin, the Main Donegal Basin, the here-termed South Donegal

Basin in the central part of the region and the enigmatic Islay−Donegal Platform to the south (Fig. 1). Both the basins and the bounding basement blocks have been the subject of several specific studies (Dobson & Evans 1974; Evans & Whittington 1976; Gerard & Boillot 1977; Barber 1980; Durant 1980; Davies 1984), the results of which were incorporated in the BGS continental shelf map series (Evans *et al.* 1983, 1986).

In an attempt to clarify the shallow geology of this extensive area (23 000 km²) and explain more fully the geological history, we have drawn together all the available published data and re-examined data obtained from surveys supervised by us between 1971 and 1979 using Natural Environment Research Council (NERC) ships, together with University College of Wales (UCW) diving programmes conducted around the Blackstones Bank igneous centre and the Stanton Banks.

Shallow seismic reflection profiles and rockhead data obtained by us since 1979 are incorporated in the analysis, whilst the Quaternary sequences have been reinterpreted using a stratigraphy established for the West Scottish Shelf (Davies *et al.* 1984). More recently, the British Institutions Reflection Profiling Syndicate

From PARNELL, J. (ed.), 1992, *Basins on the Atlantic Seaboard: Petroleum Geology, Sedimentology and Basin Evolution.* Geological Society Special Publication No 62, pp 291−311.

291

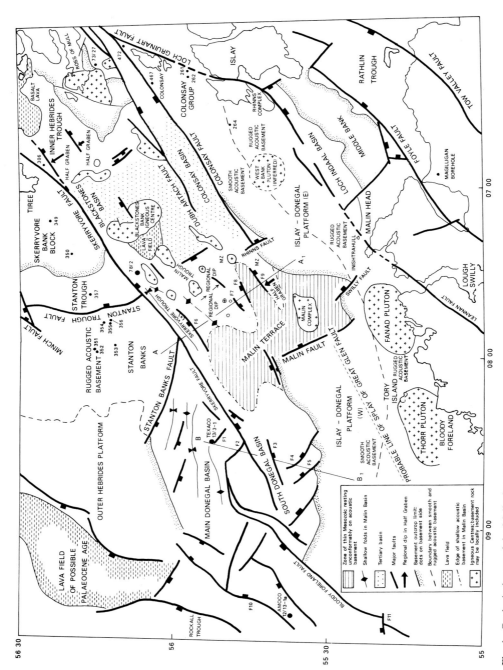

Fig. 1. Geological map of the Malin Sea area.

(BIRPS) WINCH and WIRE lines (Fig. 2) traversed part of the region (Brewer *et al.* 1983, Synder & Flack 1990), confirming the main tectonic elements and offering an opportunity for further debate on the probable course of the Great Glen Fault. Additional information was kindly supplied by Texaco, Merlin Profilers, Amoco and Western Geophysical.

As the geophysical evidence for the Malin Sea area indicates distinct seismic provinces, consisting of acoustic basement in the north, a central zone that records clear seismic reflectors and acoustic basement in the south, presentation and analysis of the geology will be given in three sections from north to south.

Coll-Tiree Block, Skerryvore and Stanton Banks Block, together with the Outer Hebrides Platform (the acoustic basement in the north)

The sharp edge of upstanding, rugged rockhead of the Coll−Tiree−Skerryvore−Stanton Banks abuts against smooth, subdued, dipping reflectors providing unequivocal evidence for the Skerryvore Fault, a major structure with normal downthrow, forming the southeastern margin to the block. The lateral continuity of this boundary is interrupted where the course of the fault is overstepped by dipping reflectors that extend into the Stanton Trough. In the west the limit of the block is determined by the northwest−southeast trending Stanton Banks Fault.

This extensive basement block, recognised in part by Binns *et al.* (1974), was re-examined and more fully described by Evans *et al.* (1980). The Coll−Tiree Block lies northeast of the Skerryvore Bank and is not included on Fig. 1.

Rock samples collected from the topographically subdued Skerryvore Bank show strong affinities with Coll and Tiree where granulite facies predominate; although modelling of a pronounced gravity low (Evans *et al.* 1980, 1986), immediately southwest of Tiree, suggests the presence of an extensive (36 km^2), granitic mass. Table 1 is a complete list, with brief descriptions, of all the samples collected to date. Rock samples collected by UCW divers from outcrop are held on file at Aberystwyth.

The Stanton Banks Block, particularly the eastern side, unlike much of the Skerryvore Block, is extremely rugged with bathymetric variation exceeding 120 m. This block is partly fault-bounded on the northwest by an extension of the Minch Fault, on the southwest by the Stanton Bank Fault, on the southeast by the

Skerryvore Fault, and on the east-north-east by the Stanton Trough Fault. A westward-thickening wedge of post-Mesozoic, presumed Quaternary sediments, beyond the outcropping part of the Bank, provides an impression that the basement block is tilted. Dive samples from the Stanton Banks confirm the presence of both granulite and amphibolite facies. Retrogression from granulite to amphibolite facies is revealed by the relict pyroxene texture whilst the appearance of microcline and biotite demonstrates a late stage potassium enrichment. Despite an apparent compositional consistency shown by these rock samples, the criterion is inadequate for confidently proposing affinities. Nevertheless, a Laxfordian interpretation is preferred (I. Cartwright & A. Barnicoat, pers. comm.); supported by a date of 1400−1600 Ma, using the Rb/Sr method, obtained from sample 351 (Evans *et al.* 1986).

The boundary between the Stanton Banks and the Outer Hebrides Platform marks the western limit of rockhead outcrop. The Platform is considered to be formed predominantly of Lewisian gneisses by extrapolation from the Stanton Banks and the Outer Hebrides to the north. Normal faults with large downthrows to the west mark the limit of the Platform. The structural relationship of the Platform with the Main Donegal Basin to the south appears to be one of onlap, although a normal fault, probably an extension of the Stanton Banks Fault, may be present at depth (James & Hitchen in press). Rugged acoustic basement is veneered in the east by Quaternary sediments. At the latitude of 08°40W, older sediments of presumed Tertiary age overstep the basement from the west. Beyond the faulted western boundary of the Platform lies an extensive lava field (Fig. 1). This field is just one small expression of a voluminous igneous outpouring that occurred along the northeastern margin of the Rockall Trough (Wood *et al.* 1988; Jones *et al.* 1986). The age of these lavas is presently unknown, although dredged rock samples from the flank of the Hebrides Terrace Seamount, which lies at the foot of the continental slope at 10°00W 56°30N and is isolated from the lavafield, have been dated as Palaeocene using the K-Ar method (Omran & Whittington 1986).

The Stanton Trough

This northwesterly orientated faulted syncline, with a major fault along its western edge, extends to the Sea of the Hebrides Basin in the north (Evans *et al.* 1986). It contains dark grey siltstones in the south with friable red

Table 1. *Stanton & Skerryvore Banks Samples*

Aberystwyth no	Tiree sheet B.G.S. NO	Lat/long	Description
4652 Dive 1	351	56.16N 07.56W	Pink microcline rich granitic pegmatite
4653 Dive 2	352	56.15.7N 07.56.2W	Amphibole bearing basic gneiss with quartzo-feldspathic bands
4653B Dive 2	352	56.15.7N 07.56.2W	Acid gneiss fragment with microcline
4653D Dive 2	352	56.15.7N 07.56.2W	Biotite and hornblende rich fragment could be a meta sediment
4564 Dive 3	353	56.12.4N 07.54.7W	Amphibolite gneiss with thin acid gneiss bands
4655 Dive 5	354	56.14.2N 07.45.8W	Amphibolite gneiss with acidic gneiss bands
4656 Dive 6	355	56.3.0N 07.45.8W	Strongly banded amphibolite facies and acid gneiss with microcline
4657 Dive 7	356	56.13.0N 07.45.1W	Banded amphibolite facies and acid gneiss
Gerard & Boillot (1976) Gravity Core & Dredge			
	SH216 (C204)	56.15N 07.56W	Microcline granite pegmatite
	SH217 (C205)	56.16N 07.55W	Microcline granite
3373 Dive	349	56.24.5N 07.10W	Siliceous marble
3374 Dive	350	56.20.5N 07.21.3W	Hornblende biotite gneiss
	183 (SH725.C227)	56.21N 07.04W	Diopside scapolite
	306 (SH727.C228)	56.25N 06.50W	Hornblende pyroxene granulite
	357 (Stanton Trough)		Red arkose

arkoses (sample 357) towards the north. BIRPS deep seismic line WINCH 2C recorded a broad faulted syncline containing reflectors that extend to 2 s TWT.

The Basins (the central zone of clear seismic reflectors)

Between the previously described basement blocks and the Islay–Donegal Platform, a narrow zone of basins have been recognized. From northeast to southwest they are the Inner Hebrides Trough, the Blackstones Basin with

the Colonsay Basin, the Malin Basin, the Main Donegal Basin and the South Donegal Basin (see Fig. 1). Table 2 lists the samples collected from this zone.

The location and geological nature of the southeastern boundary of the basins of the central zone has been uncertain since the first seismic reflection surveys in the early 1970s, due to a combination of the quality and quantity of the data, complex fault patterns, igneous intrusions and rockhead erosion.

In the east, the southeastern boundary consists largely of the Colonsay Fault, a normal

Table 2. *Basinal Zone Samples*

Aberystwyth no	Tiree/Malin sheet B.G.S. NO	Lat/long	Description
3376	482	56.09N 06.20W	Well bedded calcareous sandstones. Middle Jurassic (Bajocian)
–	(78/2) 4	56.07N 07.30W	Grey-black calcareous carbonaceous siltstone Late Lias–Mid. Jur.
Gerard & Boillot (1976) Gravity Core	–	55.55N 07.30W	Alkali basalt with olivine phenocrysts and titanaugite
	(73/27) 28	56.15N 06.14W	Greenish sandstone of Permo-Trias aspect
	493	56.28N 06.45W	Dark grey shale ?Jurassic

fault with downthrow to the north, that extends towards the southwest as far as an offset in the line of the acoustic basement. This offset is considered to be due to a fault (Gerard & Boillot 1977) and is here termed the Rhinns Fault. A short section, where thick supposed Oligocene sediment (Smythe & Kenolty 1975) oversteps the Colonsay Fault and onlaps smooth acoustic basement, occurs in the vicinity of the Rhinns Fault.

The boundary east of the Malin Complex zone (Riddihough 1968), between the Rhinns Fault and a major fault recently identified on the WIRE 4B line and here termed the Swilly Fault, was re-examined during a NERC cruise in 1983. Prior to the French work (Gerard & Boillot 1977), the basin-basement boundary had been drawn along a linear magnetic anomaly in the absence of dipping sediment reflectors (Barber 1980). From that survey a linear zone of overdeepening, which exceeds the limit of low power Sparker penetration (>300 m) and is filled with Quaternary sediments, could be traced along the flank of the Islay–Donegal Platform south from the Colonsay Basin. Although igneous intrusions, notably those close to the Rhinns Fault, further confuse the position of this margin, a few dipping reflectors were recorded terminating against steep-edged acoustic basement which allowed the Rhinns Fault (Gerard & Boillot 1977) to be confirmed. Southwest of the Rhinns Fault a short 15 km section of sharply-imaged dipping reflectors indicate onlap of sediments onto the Islay Donegal Platform and define the boundary immediately east of the Malin Complex. A sediment-filled half-graben is recorded at the south-western end of BIRPS WIRE 4B line (Fig. 2). This half-graben, here termed the

Swilly Trough, is bounded along the south-western margin by the Swilly Fault (Fig. 1). The trough may be part of a larger half-graben defined by the Malin Fault. The Swilly Fault, has a normal throw of 1.5 s, and assuming the trough has a Mesozoic or older sedimentary sequence with a velocity of 3000 m/s, this gives an infill thickness of 2250 m.

A NERC cruise conducted by us in 1976 was programmed, in part, to collect seismic profiles around the southern and western sides of the Malin Complex (Riddihough 1968). The clear, unequivocal, dipping reflectors recorded were used in the production of the BGS Solid Geology Malin map (Evans *et al.* 1983). Further analysis of the records indicated that the boundary immediately west of the Malin Complex is faulted; an interpretation based on the abrupt termination of dipping reflectors against acoustic basement. Indeed, sufficient geophysical data exists to propose a NNW/SSE trending cross fault, here termed the Malin Fault (Fig. 1).

Northwestward, beyond the Malin Fault, the basin margin is faulted along the sector shown as the Malin Terrace; thereafter, the Malin Basin is succeeded, to the southwest, by the South Donegal Basin. Here, the rugged or undulating acoustic basement of the Platform, with thin Quaternary cover (50 m), is replaced towards the northwest by thick (>200 m) superficial deposits which obscure the rockhead on single channel seismic records. The boundary is drawn either where acoustic basement dips at *c.* 20 degrees or more beneath increasing Quaternary cover or where dipping reflectors onlap the Platform. This criterion of a shallow depth to acoustic basement rockhead is used to define the boundary between the Platform and the South Donegal Basin. Further southwest, a

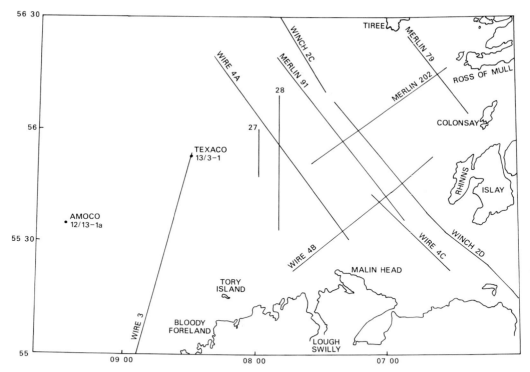

Fig. 2. Location of seismic profiles referred to in the text, including BIRPS and Merlin Profilers lines and the two shallow seismic lines shown on Fig. 6.

combination of normal faults downthrowing to the northeast and dipping acoustic basement persist to fault F4 and beyond, as far as the major NE–SW trending western bounding fault, here named the Bloody Foreland Fault (Fig. 1).

The Inner Hebrides Trough and Blackstones Basin

Only the southern part of the Inner Hebrides Trough is included on Fig. 1. In Evans *et al.* (1980) the Blackstones Basin was not separately identified, as shown on Fig. 1, but considered part of the Inner Hebrides Trough. The Skerryvore Fault forms the northwest boundary of both the Trough and Basin except that an important fault divergence is recognized off Tiree. The fracture with the larger downthrow appears to continue towards the northeast; a splay takes a more northerly route close to the Tiree–Coll coastline. Extension of the major fracture towards the northeast is limited by the masking effect of the Mull lavafield (Evans *et al.* 1986) although Kilenyi & Stanley (1985) projected it

to the Strathconan Fault on the west coast of Scotland at Loch Hourn. The Strathconan Fault, an important member of the Great Glen Fault system (Hutton & McErlean 1991), has a history of strike-slip motion.

On the southeast side of the Trough the Iona basement block acts as the boundary although this is overstepped by presumed Tertiary sediments towards the southwest. Whilst the Trough has been affected by the early Tertiary emplacement of the Blackstones igneous centre (Evans *et al.* 1986), three distinct regions are identified, the subcropping Mesozoic to the northeast, a lava field west of the Blackstones Bank, and the areally extensive Tertiary deposits (Smythe & Kenolty 1975). The first region contains two half graben; the larger along the Skerryvore Fault with a smaller structure parallel to the first but lying towards the southeast (Fig. 1). A narrow north northwest–south southeast orientated trough is also present. Northeast, beyond these depocentres, the Trough structure and sediment thickness is obscured by the Mull lavafield, although gravity modelling indicates that a 2 km depocentre occurs just to the north of 56°30N (see Fig. 1 on

BGS Tiree sheet: Evans *et al.* 1986). A core collected by the B.G.S. (493) from the Trough obtained a sample of dark grey shale of Jurassic affinity.

Presumed Tertiary deposits (Smythe & Kenolty 1975) are extensively developed in the Blackstones Basin and the western Colonsay Basin. These sediments onlap both the Blackstones igneous centre and the associated lava field. The lava field (Fig. 1), recognized on the basis of strong near-surface planar reflectors on several Merlin seismic profiles, covers a small area immediately west of the Blackstones Bank. These same profiles indicate that, southwest of the Blackstones Bank, a pronounced near-circular depocentre occurs. Assuming that the fill consists of Tertiary sediments only, and using a velocity of 2 km/s, thicknesses of 400 m are locally present, seen as two episodes of sedimentation divided by an angular unconformity. Judging from the orientation of the unconformity it could be argued that the Blackstones Bank cooled and subsided following emplacement and that this process is reflected in the sedimentary sequence.

The Malin Basin

The basin is dominated by three separate, linear, faulted synclines (Fig. 1). The Skerryvore Trough lies along the Skerryvore Fault where it varies from a 5 km wide synclinal downwarp to a graben. It extends from the Inner Hebrides Trough southwest towards the South Donegal Basin and contains 200 ms of horizontal sediments that rest on a marked erosion surface below which lies 1.6 s of sediment affected by intrabasinal faults along the southern side of the downwarp. BGS shallow borehole 78/2 penetrated Lower to Middle Jurassic sediments below 66 m of Quaternary Barra Formation (Davies *et al.* 1984), at the position shown on Fig. 1 on the northern flank of the Trough. At the nearest position to the borehole on Merlin Profilers line 91, a laterally persistent unconformity occurs at 250 ms TWT, equivalent to a Quaternary thickness of 70 m (assuming an interval velocity of 1830 m/s for the Quaternary). Using the same interval velocity, the Quaternary has a thickness of about 183 m along the axis of the Skerryvore Trough.

A broad synclinal region termed the Malin Trough (Fig. 1) is imaged both on WIRE 4A line (Fig. 3) and Merlin line 91, where it appears as a 20 km wide by more than 25 km long structure underlain along the southeastern side by a narrow graben with a sediment fill extending to 1.5 s TWT. Within the Trough, a laterally extensive unconformity occurs at 0.3 s TWT immediately below a series of horizontal reflectors; this unconformity is calculated to be the base of the Quaternary as discussed earlier.

A third depocentre, located along the southwestern extension of the Colonsay Basin (Fig. 3), consists of a small half-graben, fault-bounded to the north by fault F9 and filled with 0.5 s TWT of sediments. The structural relationship of this half-graben to the Colonsay Basin is unclear. On BIRPS WINCH 2C line (Brewer *et al.* 1983) the Colonsay Basin is confirmed as a graben, though the principal downthrow is along the southern Colonsay Fault rather than the northern Dubh Artach Fault (Fig. 1). Moreover, the Colonsay Fault, seen at Shot Point 11475 on WINCH 2C-2D line, is believed by some workers to coincide with the Great Glen Fault (Brewer *et al.* 1983). Sediment fill in this basin is about 2 km, although an irregular yet strong reflector 800 m below the seabed is thought to be Tertiary basalt that might be related either to the Blackstones Bank igneous centre or more reasonably to the Mull igneous centre, given the scale of the basalt cliffs along the north shore of the Firth of Lorne. Overlying the strong reflector at 800 m are the proposed Tertiary sediments that extend into the Blackstones Basin to the north (Smythe & Kenolty 1975; Evans *et al.* 1983).

To the west and south of these depocentres lies a broad region termed the Malin Terrace. Single channel seismic profiles record an unconformity between 70 and 120 ms TWT. The unconformity is a laterally extensive erosion surface that truncates open shallow folds. Above lies a sequence of sub-parallel reflectors that extend to the seabed. However, it would appear from the multichannel seismic profiles (Fig. 3) that this is not a true basinal region as acoustic basement occurs at about 400 ms TWT.

The southwestern limit of the Malin Basin is as a whole poorly constrained, but probably coincides with the edge of the Malin Terrace at about 08°15' west. WIRE 3 line indicates that the Skerryvore Trough persists to just beyond 08°40' west although only to a depth of 200 m below the sea bed, whilst to the south a series of troughs considered to be part of the South Donegal Basin are imaged.

In the central sector of the Malin Basin, glacial erosion has caused overdeepening; to the east, the rockhead lies at 150 m below sea bed; westward deepening of this surface is prominent, reaching 200 m total depth at 55°44'N 08°00'W. Minor, negative bedrock irregularities of about 20 m and more pronounced features with relief of 90 m have only a local

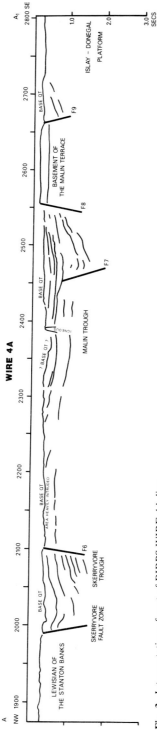

Fig. 3. Interpretation of part of BIRPS WIRE 4A line.

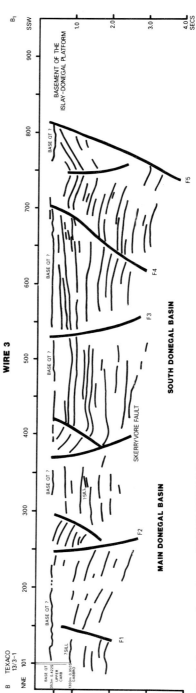

Fig. 4. Interpretation of part of BIRPS WIRE 3 line.

dimension and are considered the result of channelling. Positive irregularities are due to both concordant and discordant intrusive igneous bodies, which frequently stand 90 m above the surrounding rockhead, although without any bathymetric expression. In the southwest sector, across the Malin Terrace, rockhead lies between 50 and 100 m below the seabed and even at the seabed, over the Malin Complex (Riddihough 1968). Severe (>300 m) overdeepening occurs along the eastern margin of the Malin Terrace. In the east, the Blackstones Bank igneous centre is sharply positive, coming to within 25 metres of the sea surface.

Sediments forming the rockhead west of the Colonsay Basin have an acoustic character which allow up to 150 m penetration by low power Sparker (1 kJ). The usual seismic record consists of uniform, closely spaced, regular reflectors. Line 28 on Fig. 6 records the subdued topography of the Mesozoic rockhead, the broad open style of folding, schematically drawn on the section, and the concentration of igneous intrusions found in this part of the basin. This reflector pattern occurs throughout the eastern basin except for an area immediately north of the Malin Complex where internal reflections are poorly defined or absent. West of 08°00W dipping reflectors are rare, probably because the thick Quaternary cover absorbs most of the acoustic energy. Where reflectors are recorded they reveal regular open upright folds with consistent axial trends in a ENE/WSW direction that may be traced for distances in excess of 20 km. Apparent dips throughout are low, between 6−12°, with fold wavelengths of 4 to 5 km. Minor flexures, probably periclinal in character, are common although weaker in development as compared to those recorded by us in the Sea of Hebrides Basin where structural interference produces patterns of periclinal dome structures. Many of the major fold structures have been intruded, usually by concordant sill-like structures; elsewhere, isolated domes, the result of boss-like intrusions, are recorded. In addition, the folds have been affected by a pattern of minor faults that are orientated broadly east−west and northwest−southeast.

The three linear depocentres, the Skerryvore Trough, the Malin Trough and the half graben forming the western extension of the Colonsay Basin, record sediment thicknesses in excess of 1.6 s TWT. Significantly, the Malin Trough records two episodes of tectonic activity. The first generated a sediment-filled graben structure located between faults F7 and F8, whereas the second resulted in a wider regional downwarp

that extends from fault F6 to fault F8 (Fig. 3). An unconformity is recorded in the Malin Trough immediately above fault F7.

Direct sediment rockhead evidence is limited to three sources (Evans et al. 1983, 1986): (i) B.G.S. borehole 78/2 drilled at 56°07.65′N 07°30.35′W, in the Skerryvore Trough, recovered grey-black, calcareous, carbonaceous siltstone, with thin argillaceous limestone layers and a coaly band dated as Late Liassic to early Middle Jurassic (Evans et al. op cit.). (ii) Dredge sample 3376 at 56°09.00′N 06°20.00′W, located on the southern flank of the Colonsay Basin, recovered a large block of thinly bedded calcareous siltstone dated, using palynology, as Middle Jurassic, probably Bajocian (Barber et al. 1979). (iii) Two dive sites on the Blackstones Bank igneous centre (Nos. 337 & 339) recorded the existence of xenolithic blocks of calc-silicate hornfels, the detailed mineralogy of which suggests that they were originally, a siliceous magnesian limestone, and a calcareous siltstone. Thus, calcareous siltstone appears as a consistent lithology in the eastern Malin Basin.

The South Donegal Basin

This basin lies wholly southeast of the Skerryvore Fault and extends to the Islay-Donegal Platform. BIRPS WIRE 3 line (Fig. 4) reveals the relationship between the sediment-fill and the faults. The antithetic fault associated with the Skerryvore Fault (and another with fault F2) is not included on the main map of the region (Fig. 1) to avoid confusion. It is possible that this antithetic fault is the lateral equivalent of fault F6 on Fig. 3; in which case the Skerryvore Trough structure might persist into this basin. In the absence of further seismic data the limit of the South Donegal Basin towards the northeast is placed at the boundary with the Malin Terrace. However, it is possible, indeed likely, that Upper Palaeozoic sediments not only floor the Skerryvore Trough but also persist beneath the Malin Terrace.

The structural evidence, derived from shallow penetration seismic profiling, BIRPS data, and information provided by Texaco indicate that this basin has a thicker sediment section than the Main Donegal Basin. WIRE 3 line reveals 3 s TWT section between fault F4 and fault F5, equivalent to about 6 km of sediment. The reflective character of the sequences in this basin compare closely with those in the Main Donegal Basin, suggesting that the fill consists, at least in part, of Upper Palaeozoic sediments similar to those logged in the Texaco well.

Fig. 5. Depth from seabed to rockhead for the central Malin Basin, based on shallow seismic profiles and B.G.S. borehole 78/2 using a velocity of 1750 m/s

The Main Donegal Basin

This Basin is here defined as that region lying northwest of the Skerryvore Fault and its extension. The Basin is bounded to the northeast by the Stanton Banks Fault and to the northwest by the margin of the Outer Hebrides Platform. Clear definition of the structural limit of this depocentre to the west and southwest awaits further surveys and drilling, but for convenience, the area between the Bloody Foreland Fault and fault F10 (Fig. 1) is assumed to be part of the Main Donegal Basin. Beyond fault F10 lies a region where at least one major normal fault downthrows to the west; this region is considered part of the Rockall Trough. A cross fault F11 has been recognized as the southern limit of the basin (see Tate & Dobson 1989b, Fig. 1). Line 27 on Fig. 6 located in the extreme northeastern corner of the basin shows the relationship between the basement, the Stanton Banks Fault and the basin fill. Basin fill is indicated on the section as undifferentiated Mesozoic; this interpretation is based on seismic character alone.

Two exploration wells, Texaco 13/3−1 and Amoco 12/13−1a, provide the only evidence for the age of the sediment-fill. Texaco 13/3−1 proved 949 m of Westphalian B to Stephanian B unconformably overlain by thin marine Miocene sediments and a thick Quaternary sequence. The well bottomed in a microgabbro of unknown age. Westphalian B and C sediments consist of grey claystones, thin limestones and thick carbonaceous sandstones with coals. More than 50 coal horizons are recorded in this well. The Westphalian D to Stephanian B section consists of red and grey to green fine-grained siliciclastics, the upper 60 m of which are interbedded with volcaniclastics (Tate & Dobson 1989a).

Amoco well 12/13−1a was drilled to a total depth of 2870 m. The 27 m of red pre-Permian sandstones at the base represent undifferentiated Upper Palaeozoic. These are overlain by 665 m of Zechstein to Rhaetic sediments that pass from dolomites and anhydrite-rich siltstones at the base, to red-brown shales and claystones with evaporites characteristic of playa-plain conditions for much of the higher part of the section. Towards the top, oolitic limestones with dolomites and calcareous claystones become common. The top of the Rhaetic is marked by the appearance of dark grey claystone (Tate & Dobson 1989a). A 1893 m section of Cretaceous and Cenozoic sediments rest, with marked unconformity, on the Permo-Triassic. The Lower Cretaceous consists of glauconitic sandstones interbedded with thin white cryptocrystalline limestones and occasional coals, succeeded by light grey-green claystones with foraminifera characteristic of shallow shelf conditions. In the Albian the sediments become distinctly calcareous with marls and occasional dolomites. Significantly, Amoco report the presence of miospores of Carboniferous age in these marls. White-grey limestones with chert persist throughout the attenuated 153 m of the Upper Cretaceous. The Cretaceous−Tertiary boundary is marked by a pronounced shift on both the resistivity and sonic logs, reflecting the hardness and high chert content of the Danian sediments. Above the Danian there is a marked lithological change to claystones. Most of the Palaeogene contains claystones, siltstones and thin limestones that persist to the top of the logged sequence, which occurs in the late Middle Eocene at 853 m below the kellybushing (Tate & Dobson 1989b).

Recently, BIRPS WIRE 3 line, which was shot from the vicinity of Texaco well 13/3−1 (Figs 1 & 4) in a south−southwest direction across the basin, records a very considerable Upper Palaeozoic section. The thickness of the section, imaged on the BIRPS line, exceeds 2 s TWT which, assuming a velocity of 4 km/s, gives an overall thickness of more than 4 km. Individual throws on the faults range from 500 m to at least 1000 m.

Igneous intrusions

Acoustically opaque masses, that have a distinct magnetic signature on ship magnetometer profiles, occur throughout the basins. They are considered to be intrusive igneous rocks and include significant centres like Blackstones Bank (Durant et al. 1976), now believed to be of Palaeocene age (58 Ma, see Evans et al. 1986) and the Malin Complex (Riddihough 1968), together with lesser bodies which range in area from 1 to 6 km^2. A group of five distinct igneous masses, occur in the eastern part of the Basin (Fig. 1); two are flat lying asymmetrical bodies with stepped upper surfaces which suggest sill-like intrusions, the remainder have a plug or boss-like morphology (see Fig. 6, line 28). A sample collected from a sill-like body exposed at the sea bed (Gerard & Boillot 1977) has been described as a phenocrystic alkali basalt (see Table 2). Two igneous masses, each more than 8 km in diameter, lying immediately west of the Blackstones Bank, are seen as large bosses (Fig. 1). The scale and abundance of the igneous intrusions decline westwards. Apart from discrete bodies, prominent acoustic hyperbolae

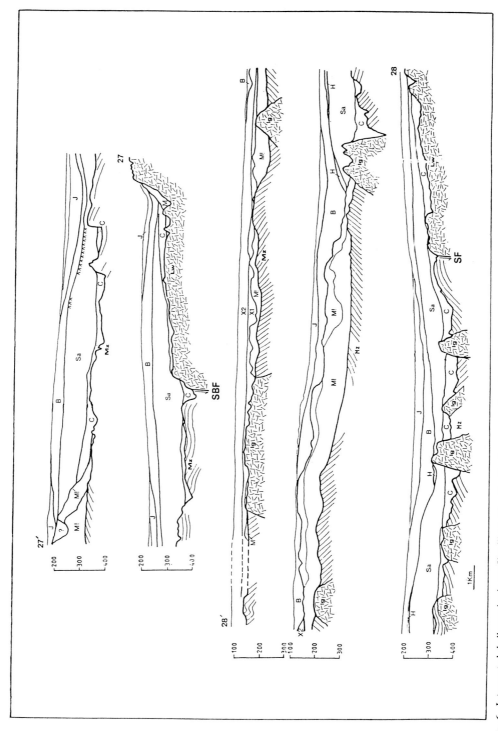

Fig. 6. Interpreted shallow seismic profiles illustrating the Quaternary stratigraphy of the central part of the Malin Basin. Abbreviations refer to formations listed in Table 4 and the following: SBF, Stanton Banks Fault; SF, Skerryvore Fault; Mz, Mesozoic; Ig, Igneous; Lw, Lewisian, X1 and X2 uncertain, but probably lateral equivalents of Stanton and Hebrides Formations respectively. Vertical scale: ms TWT.

on the single channel seismic records suggest minor, probably dyke-like, intrusions.

The Malin Complex, located in the southern part of the Malin Terrace, intrudes gently dipping sediments of Mesozoic aspect. Invariably, the structural relationship between acoustic basement, with strong magnetic signature, and the dipping reflectors that terminate against it, is sharp. Thus, the sub-Quaternary outcrop area of the complex of 125 km^2 is defined both by Sparker evidence and magnetic anomaly data. It has an outer annulus of positive anomalies with an interior of relatively low values (Riddihough 1968). An internal magnetic lineation, trending north of east in the direction of elongation of the complex, is regarded as a bisecting fault zone (Riddihough 1968). Riddihough compared the magnetic values recorded for the Malin Complex with those published for the Criffell−Dalbeattie granodiorite of southern Scotland (Phillips 1956). The Criffell−Dalbeattie central magnetic low coincides with a coarse grained granite, and the outer magnetic high with the main granodiorite. Whilst acid complexes of this type are characteristic of the Caledonian zone, the intrusive relationship with folded Mesozoic strata implies either a reactivation of an older centre or a Late Mesozoic to Tertiary age for the complex.

Riddihough (1968) emphasizes that this complex lacks the 'violent' magnetic characteristic produced by reversely magnetised Tertiary basic rocks, but may be compared with some ring complexes of Tertiary type. Additionally, there is now geophysical evidence to support an associated dyke swarm. The subcrop, although rugged or irregular, is broadly subdued, being virtually at the same erosion level as the surrounding sedimentary rocks. None of the Hebridean Tertiary centres, including the Blackstones Bank, nor even bosses referred to previously, display this level of erosion. The Malin Complex could conceivably be either a Tertiary granodioritic intrusion which did not achieve a high level of crustal emplacement or a reactivated Caledonoid centre, comparable to the Barnsmore Centre in Ireland (Riddihough 1968). However, the lack of an associated gravity anomaly (Evans et al. 1980) indicates that whether acid or basic in composition, the Complex is of no great thickness.

The Blackstones Bank igneous centre generates immense magnetic and gravity (up to +134 mGal) anomalies and has been modelled as a vertical cylinder of dense ultrabasic rock 16 km in diameter, extending to 22−30 km (McQuillin et al. 1975). During 1974, 1975 &

1980, 31 sites were sampled by scuba divers and the rocks examined petrographically and geochemically (Durant 1977; Evans et al. 1986). Radiometric dating of a dyke rock initially gave a figure of 70.4 Ma (Durant et al. 1976). Although the sample gave a minimum age due to argon loss the figure compared closely with many from the Rockall area (Roberts et al. 1974). Subsequently, an age of 57 Ma by Mitchell et al. (1976) using dredged basalt samples was published. Later, amphibole from granophyre gave an age of 134 ± 3 Ma, and three feldspars ages of 58.4, 58.6 and 58.8 Ma (all ±1.2 Ma) (Evans et al. 1986). These three ages are believed to give the best estimate of emplacement; they compare closely with dates from other adjacent Hebridean igneous centres (Curry et al. 1978).

Durant recognized that, as with the Skye igneous centre, cumulates crop out widely over the Blackstones, implying the presence of more than one layered intrusion. In addition, an intense concentric magnetic anomaly with a focal point in the south of the centre may be viewed as a ring dyke complex; inclined sheets have been recorded in the area. Although microgranite was sampled, there is a significant absence of granitic material, which makes a Walker-type (1975) emplacement mechanism difficult to envisage. With the possible exception of a lavafield located immediately west of the Bank there is a noticeable lack of associated extrusives compared with the Mull and Skye centres, suggesting that a shield volcano failed to develop. Furthermore, judging from the few samples collected and particularly the observations made by divers along the eastern side where the metamorphic rocks were recovered, the level at which the complex is exposed must be close to the top of the original emplacement, although the Tertiary sediment sequence in the Blackstones Basin indicate that some post-emplacement subsidence occurred.

Evidence for igneous intrusions in the Donegal Basins is limited to a micrograbbro located at the bottom of Texaco well 13/3−1. There is some reflector evidence on WIRE 3 line (Fig. 4) which suggests that a laterally extensive sill occurs at this depth. The age of the intrusion, which penetrates Upper Carboniferous sediments, has not been determined because of alteration, although by comparison with other igneous intrusions in the region (Tate & Dobson 1988) it is probably Lower Tertiary in age. This same WIRE line contains evidence for a further sill-like body between fault F2 and the Skerryvore Fault.

Islay—Donegal platform (the acoustic basement in the south)

The region recognised on the BGS Malin map (Evans *et al.* 1983) as the Islay—Donegal Platform (Fig. 1) is bounded to the southeast by the Loch Gruinart Fault and its extension, the Leannan Fault in Ireland. The former is considered a splay of the Great Glen Fault (Dobson *et al.* 1975) but with normal fault motion along the northwest flank of the Loch Indaal Basin (Evans *et al.* 1980).

The Platform embraces Colonsay, western Islay (Rhinns), Inishtrahull and the north coast of Ireland. Colonsay and western Islay are believed to be part of an allochthonous terrane consisting of basement termed the Rhinns Complex (Daly & Menuge 1989) and low grade sedimentary cover rocks called the Colonsay Group (Bentley 1988). The Rhinns Complex comprises an alkalic igneous association consisting of syenite, granodiorite, gabbro, ultrabasic and other rocks emplaced *c.* 1800 Ma ago. Elements of this Complex also occur on the islet of Inishtrahull off Malin Head where the rocks are predominantly deformed, coarse-grained, pink, syenite gneiss with sheets of coarse-grained gabbro. The Tor Rocks, 2 km northwest of Inishtrahull, consist of the same rock types (Roddick & Max 1983). The Colonsay Group (Fitches & Maltman 1984) cover rocks were deposited unconformably on this basement and subsequently intruded by alkaline and subalkaline igneous plugs about 600—635 Ma ago (Bentley 1986).

Although the geology of the offshore part of the Platform is poorly known, some constraint is provided by geophysical data, which have allowed delineation of several important sections, and by five dive samples (Evans *et al.* 1983). Side scan sonar surveys have assisted in the recognition of the Rhinns Complex which extends offshore towards the southwest. Evans (1974) recognized a further block of supposed Rhinns Complex located 10 km south of the West Bank Pluton, from magnetic and sonar data. Using seismic reflection signature as a rockhead discriminator in the region between the Rhinns of Islay and Malin Head and beyond to Bloody Foreland, two distinct zones are apparent. The more northwesterly acoustic basement is rounded and subdued, with a persistent Quaternary cover exceeding 70 m; to the southwest acoustic basement is strongly reflective, rugged, forming outcropping rock pinnacles and deep (>100 m), Quaternary filled rock basins (Fig. 1). Samples collected from the seabed by divers of the Irish Geological Survey (Evans

et al. 1983) confirm that Rhinns Complex lithologies extend several kilometres northeast from Inishtrahull islet and that lithologies of Moinian affinities occur immediately to the east. The structural relationship between the inferred Moinian sequences and the rocks of Inishtrahull remains unknown.

Support for a westward extension of the Colonsay Group across the Platform is derived from samples of siltstone and phyllite and fine-grained sandstone collected by UCW divers (Table 3). Virtually all these samples may be directly compared with rocks on Colonsay. Several dives, located further south on the West Bank shoal (sample No. 264, Table 3 and Fig. 1 for location), were made expressly to assess the extent of the cover rocks. Material from the West Bank dive consists of poorly sorted paraconglomerates with weak pebble alignment. Clasts range in size from >4 cm down to coarse sand (2 mm) and appear to be waterlain. The following pebble types occur: quartz feldspar pegmatite vein quartz, acid gneiss granulite facies, acid volcanic pebble with epidote rim alteration and other igneous pebbles. Many of the larger clasts are in long contact or sutured to each other and are held in a complex matrix consisting of aligned chlorite and epidote with quartz, feldspar and sericite. The fabric of the rock, notably in the matrix, is weak compared to that in the quartz feldspar clasts, many of which show very strong affinities to the Rhinns Complex. If it is regarded as a basal conglomerate, and the divers report suggests that the facies is at least 3 m thick, it could be part of the Colonsay Group, although the contact on Islay between the Rhinns Complex and the Colonsay Group has been interpreted as a slide or high strain zone (Fitches & Maltman 1984). A boundary based on acoustic character of the rockhead across the offshore part of the Platform may relate to the two rock groups (Fig. 1).

From Malin Head westwards, rockhead character is again the only distinguishing criterion. Rugged acoustic basement is confined to a zone containing the Fanad and Thorr plutons, the outlines of which were derived from gravity, magnetic and seismic data (Evans & Whittington 1976) and the geology on Tory Island. To the north the Islay—Donegal Platform (W) rockhead is noticeably smooth with an average Quaternary veneer of 70 m.

The Great Glen Fault

The age and phases of movement along this fault, including both the amount and sense, remains unknown, although the general view is

Table 3. *Islay Donegal Platform Samples*

Aberystwyth no	Malin sheet B.G.S NO	Lat/long	Description
3337	261	55.57N 06.17W	Siltstone and Phyllite alternations
3338 Appendix 4 of Barber 1980	262	55.57N 06.19W	Siltstone and Phyllite alternations with fine sandstones
3343		56.10N 06.10W	Sandstone & Dolerite
3348		55.44N 06.43W	Sandstone
4669	264	55.44N 06.43W	Lewisian pebble
4670			conglomerate with clinozoisite-epidote matrix
	(3		Banded granitic
	(4		Lewisian gneiss dated
Collected by Irish Geological Survey	close to Inishtrahull islet		at 1750 Ma
	(5		
	(6		
	(13		Orthoquartzite of the
	located in area of Fanad Pluton outcrop		Ards Quartzite Formation.
	(14–18		Hornfelsed pelite with extensive granite veining.

of a few hundred kilometres sinstral displacement at the end of the Caledonian orogeny (Smith & Watson 1983), with later Carboniferous dextral movements of a few tens of kilometres (Ziegler 1982).

Objective criteria for setting limits to the line of the Great Glen Fault were in the past restricted to mainland basement relationships. With the availability of BIRPS data overall crustal reflectivity variations have been employed. The starting point for any assessment of the course of this fracture across the west Scottish shelf must be in the Loch Linnhe area and Mull (Lee & Bailey 1925), where the Moinian and Dalradian basement are separated by a shatter zone about 1.6 km wide and where Lower Old Red Sandstone is confined to the south of the fracture. From dive sample evidence collected in the Firth of Lorne, together with shallow seismic data, the course of the fault appears to lie within a restricted zone less than 3 km wide in the east and 5 km wide in the longitude of Colonsay (Barber *et al.* 1979). This zone is wholly within the Colonsay Basin, a narrow linear graben defined by the Dubh Artach Fault and the Colonsay Fault. Neither of these normal faults have been identified west of 07°00W.

The Great Glen Fault line, beyond the Colonsay Basin, may be inferred using three deep seismic lines, WINCH 2C, WIRE 4A and 3, all of which reveal contrasts in reflective characteristics in the lower crust, the abrupt termination of which may used as an indicator of crustal fracture commensurate with a vertical and horizontal displacement (Klemperer *et al.* 1991). As there is no unequivocal evidence for the presence of the Great Glen Fault on the BIRPS records only one of the splays of Klemperer *et al.* (1991) is indicated on the geological map (Fig. 1). This caution is partly due to the fact that the BIRPS lines display poorly reflective anomalous lower crust for the region between the Islay-Donegal Platform and the Skerryvore Fault; an observation which could be used to suggest that the region contains an extensive shear zone. A magnetic lineation trending north of east, which bisects the Malin Complex, was proposed by Riddihough (1968) as a possible course for the Great Glen Fault. This evidence may provide support for the course of the splay drawn by Klemperer *et al.* (1991). In this analysis, Klemperer *et al.* (1991) has the fault passing through the Malin Complex and diverging into two splays north of the Thorr Pluton, thus having it lie wholly within the Islay Donegal Platform. Their map Fig. 2b shows the fault splay locally separating Lewisian basement from Moinian and Dalradian basement. Our shallow seismic data across the Islay–Donegal Platform (W) fails to record any high level discontinuity or evidence that might allow the juxtapositioning of different basement terranes. Thus, although this master shear zone must across this region, it does not appear to have a near surface expression and its course beyond the Colonsay Basin remains obscure. This assessment has implications for the southern extent of the Archaean crust as discussed earlier. Any tectonic analysis of this region must consider the possible role of the Great Glen Fault, for despite a lack of surface expression the shear zone must traverse the region at depth.

The nature of the Quaternary

Quaternary sediments are recorded throughout the whole of the central graben zone with only the Blackstones Bank igneous centre, and the Malin Complex together with smaller intrusive masses exposed at the seabed. Extensive areas of the Stanton and Skerryvore Banks are similarly exposed, although most of the north-western side of the Islay Donegal Platform is veneered by Quaternary sediment.

Quaternary sediment thickness data for the eastern half of the Malin area (Fig. 5) extends the published evidence 40 km south of the BGS Tiree Quaternary sheet (Evans et al. 1986). Thicknesses exceed 200 m across the Malin Basin whereas on the basement ridges the thickness rarely exceeds 100 m; frequently only a 30 m veneer of Quaternary is recorded. Earlier workers (Barber 1980; Evans et al. 1980) adopted the threefold divisions of Binns et al.

(1974). However, a detailed examination of shallow seismic reflection profiles and borehole data across the whole Hebridean area (Davies 1984; Davies et al. 1984) has resulted in a revised Quaternary stratigraphy (Table 4).

Two line drawings (Fig. 6), interpreted from shallow seismic profiles (Davies 1984), illustrate the form and relative thickness of the Quaternary sequences in the central part of the Malin Basin. Davies believes that the rockhead in the sedimentary basins of the west Scottish shelf attained its present form before the Devensian. From the stratigraphy of the infill it is thought to have originated in the Middle or even Lower Pleistocene, partly because glaciations which excavated the pre-Quaternary rockhead are thought to have been more erosive than the Late Devensian glaciation. The initial erosion of the rockhead by ice occurred, therefore, prior to the deposition of the Skerryvore Formation, whilst the apparent subsequent decrease in erosive power of ice ensured a continuing legacy of subdued landscape, aided probably by increasing aridity. It is logical to assume that basal ice paths were located along the axes of the Inner Hebrides Trough and Malin Basin, with one originating from the Firth of Lorne and moving south of the Blackstones Bank, the other down the Trough and to the north of the Blackstones Bank. Both streams would have been constricted by the Stanton Banks to the north and the Islay–Donegal Platform (W) in the south, which might account for the pronounced overdeepening in the Malin Terrace region. Further west the ice streams would have been able to spread out across both Donegal Basins.

Table 4. *Revised Quaternary stratigraphy*

Formation	Description	Age
Lorne Formation	mobile modern sediments	Recent
Jura Formation (J)	a thick, fine grained shelf deposit	Post Glacial
Barra Formation (B)	silty clays with dropstones	26 ka
Hebrides Formation (H)	till remnants	
(Main Erosion Surface)		
Stanton Formation A & B (Sa)	silt and clays with dropstones	118–50 ka
(Canna-Stanton Erosion Surface)		
Canna Formation (C)		
(Canna-Malin Erosion Surface)		
Malin Formation (M!)	diamicton, a clay with boulders	
(Skerryvore-Malin Erosion Surface)		
Skerryvore Formation	stiff micaceous clay with dropstones	

Geological history of the region

Improved understanding of the relationship between the Lewisian of the northern blocks and the Islay−Donegal Platform must await further offshore sample data. Meanwhile, both the geological composition and structural location of the Platform in relation to probable movements on the Great Glen Fault implies that it should contain the Caledonian Front. Indeed if a dominantly sinistral movement pattern is adopted for the Great Glen Fault, then the Loch Skerrols Thrust or shear zone is suitably located as the continuation of the Moine Thrust. However, according to Fitches & Maltman (1984) the Loch Skerrols Thrust is only a single, poorly defined, flat-lying shear zone and does not itself define the Caledonian Front as is commonly held. Thus, the true Front on this analysis lies west of Colonsay and Islay, but at a higher structural level than the Loch Skerrols Thrust onland. Bentley (1986) has been able to confirm from dating, that most if not all the major upright folds developed in the Colonsay Group are younger than 600 ma and are, therefore, part of the orthotectonic Caledonides; this further implies that the Caledonian Front must lie to the west of Colonsay.

The structural relationship between the Irish Dalradian and the Rhinns Complex remains unknown, although Menuge & Daly (1991) have recognized Early Proterozoic crust in north Mayo. On this evidence Daly & Menuge (1989) reasonably suggest that 1800 million years old crust underlies the Caledonian rocks of northwest Ireland. Muir (1990) believes that the Rhinns Complex underlies the Dalradian of eastern Islay. Any assessment of the regional extent of this protolith, despite being approximately coeval with Laxfordian events, is hampered by a lack of offshore samples. If the southeastern limit of the Archaean coincides with the trace of the Great Glen Fault (Fitches et al. 1990), a view that receives support from the WINCH deep seismic data (Brewer et al. 1983), then the Rhinns Complex could underlie much of the eastern (E on Fig. 1) Islay−Donegal Platform.

Klemperer et al. (1991), on their Fig. 2, have the northern margin of the Islay−Donegal Platform or the southern margin of the South Donegal Basin defined by an extension of the Colonsay Fault, although from their small-scale map it would appear to be drawn from the Dubh Artach Fault. They have the Skerryvore Fault traversing the two Donegal basins. However, on our evidence, this fracture appears to attenuate and rapidly lose its linearity. The broad plan of the two basins on their Fig. 2b invites a dextral strike-slip solution, not between the Colonsay Fault extension and the Skerryvore Fault as they propose, but rather between faults on the northern flank of the Islay−Donegal Platform and the Stanton Banks Fault. Our evidence suggests that the Islay−Donegal Platform margin of the basin is traversed obliquely by a series of localized NW−SE faults. In addition, we see no evidence for a basement block at the northern end of the WIRE 3 line as shown on Fig. 2 of Klemperer et al. (1991).

The sigmoidal configuration of the Main Donegal Basin and the South Donegal Basin when taken together, and the location of these basins between the Platform and the fault bound Stanton Banks, may reflect strike-slip displacement with a dextral sense. NNW−SSE trending faults developed across this region are in structural accord with a dextral strike-slip regime. As the oldest dated sediments in the Main Donegal Basin are Westphalian in age, a Late Carboniferous phase of strike-slip movement is inferred. This inference may relate to Asturian tectonic activity (Stephanian−Autunian), which is viewed by Ziegler (1982) as an interplay between dextral transcurrent faulting and rifting.

The question of whether Carboniferous sediments are present in the Malin and Inner Hebrides Troughs may be addressed from a structural standpoint. Two structural trends, one northeast−southwest (Caledonoid) and another north-northwest−south-southeast dominate the region. The former trend is exemplified by the Skerryvore Fault and the Colonsay Fault. Both have marked normal throw components. This trend occurs throughout the Hebridean area and has been linked, in some cases convincingly, to extension along earlier thrust planes. Faults aligned towards the north-northwest include those that define the Stanton Trough in the north of the area and the Malin-Swilly Fault system around the Malin Complex. This trend is much in evidence throughout the Irish Sea and includes the Cheshire Basin, Kish Basin (Bray Fault) and the North Channel Basin. To the west of Ireland, several basins, but especially the Porcupine Basin, contain evidence of similar, although more north−south, fault trends. This N−S aligned rift-basin system has been discussed in the context of late Palaeozoic basin development north of the Hercynian Front (Tate & Dobson 1989a). Moreover, the discussion was driven by the presence of a thick, conformable Permo-Carboniferous succession preserved along the western margin. As both Permian and Carboniferous sediments are present in the Irish Sea basins, whilst Upper Carboniferous Westphalian rocks occur in Innimore Bay, Morvern, at Macrihinish in Kintyre and in the Donegal Basin (Tate & Dobson 1989*b* and see Fig. 3), it is tempting to suggest that a similar sequence might be found filling the Swilly half graben south of the Malin Complex and in the Malin Trough between F7 and F8. Late Carboniferous sediments may also occur towards the base of the Skerryvore Trough.

As with much of northwest Europe, the west of Scotland suffered crustal extension during the Permo-Triassic and Jurassic. Morton (1987), using subsidence history curves derived largely from exposure in Skye, Mull and Morvern, suggests a three phase history of crustal stretching for the Hebrides Basin: (1) Triassic to earliest Toarcian, (2) latest Toarcian to late Bathonian, and (3) early Oxfordian to early Kimmeridgian, but emphasized that only the first phase is well developed in the Mull area. Along the northwest coast of Scotland, sedimentary basins developed in the hanging walls of reactivated Caledonoid thrusts, promoting a series of half-graben (Brewer *et al.* 1983); further south, in the Hebridean–Malin area, crustal extension may have utilized similar thrust detachment surfaces; certainly the BIRPS WINCH 2D and WIRE 4B and 4C lines record dipping reflectors within the upper mantle. Seismic records for the region confirm that the principal fractures controlling basin development are the Minch, Skerryvore, Bloody Foreland, Colonsay, Loch Gruinart and Tow Valley Faults where synsedimentary movement has allowed between 2 and 3 km of sediment to be accommodated (Evans *et al.* 1980). In the Skye area, shallow seismic (Evans *et al.* 1980) and adjacent onshore evidence indicates that the Camasunary Fault moved initially in the Upper Triassic (Steel *et al.* 1975). Although fault movement is thought to have been continuous during the Upper Triassic, sediment evidence indicates that there was a general decrease in relief with a trend from low to high sinuosity and less ephemeral stream systems (Steel & Wilson 1975) followed by a rapid transgression in the Rhaetic.

Red beds at Inch Kenneth in Western Mull imply the existence of Triassic sediments in the Inner Hebrides Trough where gravity modelling suggests a 2.5 km total thickness of sediment along the basin axis (Evans *et al.* 1986). By extrapolation, the Malin Basin may contain a similar thickness, though direct evidence is lacking. Assuming that the northern margin of the Islay–Donegal Platform represents an earlier passive margin, with marked crustal attenuation, this feature could have acted as a ramp, both during Caledonoid compressional phases and the later extensional episodes, particularly in the early Mesozoic. Extensional episodes orientated orthogonal to the margin, and indeed the Caledonoid trend, could have generated a series of graben and half graben throughout the zone between the Platform margin and the Skerryvore Fault.

In the context of the Malin Basin, early or pre-Jurassic extensional movement on the Skerryvore Fault can only be inferred. The average thickness of Liassic rocks in basins to the northwest of Britain is 250 m, with a maximum thickness in Skye of 350 m. If the Malin Basin depocentres contain 300 m of Liassic, 200 m of Middle Jurassic and 200 m of Quaternary, giving a total post-Triassic figure of 700 m, and if this figure were applied to the average sediment-fill thickness of 2400 m, then a further 1700 m of sediment must be accounted for. Restored isopach values for the Triassic in the Malin Sea give a figure of 2000 m (Ziegler 1982). It must be presumed that sediments of Permo-Triassic age account for a large proportion of the infill, particularly in the Malin Trough. B.G.S. borehole 73/27 located south of the Ross of Mull encountered sandstones of Permo-Triassic aspect. The Magilligan Point borehole (Evans *et al.* 1983) penetrated 700 m of Keuper marls and sandstones; further east on Arran the Permo-Triassic is 1300 m thick, the Larne borehole penetrated at least 1224 m of Trias (Warrington *et al.* 1980), whilst the Port More borehole, located on the Northern Ireland coast, recorded more than 1300 m of Permo-Triassic sediments. In the Main Donegal Basin, movement on the major faults like F10 allowed nearly 1 km of Permo-Triassic sediments to be preserved.

Although it is assumed that all the Hebridean and Malin basins contain Liassic sediments, direct evidence for the Malin Basin relies on just one B.G.S. borehole (78/2). However, a distinct seismic signature, and conformable sequences that pass into sampled Middle Jurassic sediments, strongly support the inference that Lower Jurassic sediments occur over a wide area of the basin. Both offshore and onshore evidence is available to confirm the existence of Liassic in the Inner Hebrides Trough (Binns *et al.* 1974) although, as with the Triassic, northeasterly thinning is evident. The age of the sediments in B.G.S. borehole 78/2 and the dredged outcrop northwest of Colonsay, together with the apparent absence in any of the samples of Upper Jurassic sediments, lends support to the notion that this region was affected by the pre-Bathonian erosion event. This event was recently documented for the North Porcupine Basin (Tate & Dobson 1989a), but recognized as an E–W axis of uplift developed at the end of the Liassic, coeval with events in the North Sea and extending from the North Porcupine area eastwards to Northern Ireland and the Irish Sea.

In the western part of the Main Donegal Basin in Amoco well 12/13–1a Lower and Upper Cretaceous rocks rest unconformably on Rhaetic rocks (Tate & Dobson 1989b). It seems reasonable to assume that both Lower Jurassic and Middle Jurassic sediments were deposited in the region, but thermally induced uplift due to the development of the Rockall Trough (Jones et al. 1986) promoted erosion. This phase of uplift was followed in the Lower Cretaceous by renewed subsidence which persisted into the Upper Cretaceous. Indeed, it can be surmised from isolated outcrops of Santonian 'chalk' in Mull (Rawson et al. 1978) that post-Cenomanian, Upper Cretaceous deposits were once common in the Hebridean area. With the exception of the Santonian to Late Eocene succession in Amoco well 12/3–1a, a gap of some 20 million years separates the deposition of the youngest Cretaceous sediments from the oldest Tertiary lavas. During this period Scotland and the western Scottish shelf were subjected to uplift and erosion.

High relief dictated by thermal influence and seen as Palaeocene and Eocene volcanic activity in the Hebridean area, ensured that the Malin area remained positive. Subsequently, in the Late Oligocene and Miocene, further fault-controlled subsidence allowed non-marine sedimentation, notably in the Blackstones and Colonsay Basins (Smythe & Kenolty 1975) and southwest of Skye (Evans et al. 1979) in the Canna Basin and at Lough Neagh in the Ulster Basin. Almost without exception, these Tertiary depocentres are located over lava fields more than 100 m thick. This observation may be partly explained as due to isostatic adjustment following introduction of the dense igneous material. Marine Neogene encroachment across the shelf is confirmed by the presence of a thin Miocene deposit in Texaco well 13/3–1. The eastern limit of the present Neogene subcrop is unknown because of difficulties in distinguishing it on shallow seismic records from Quaternary deposits. However, it is tempting to infer that deposition extended into the Malin Trough. It is clear that there was active glacial erosion of the basinal sediments which was followed by several cycles of deposition and further though weaker erosion, ensuring the preservation of a thick and complex sequence of Quaternary sediments.

Special thanks are owed to Texaco for allowing us to examine their structural map of the Main and South Donegal Basins. Their map was in part based upon Western Geophysical seismic data, who readily gave their approval. Several seismic lines located in the eastern Malin Sea area were made available to us by Merlin Geophysical for which we are most grateful. The geological staff at Murphy Oil freely gave of their views on the geological evolution of the Malin Sea area. We acknowledge the permission given to us by the BIRPS Chairman Professor D. Blundell to use the WIRE and WINCH data and to AMOCO to refer to their well 12/13–1a. The authors would particularly like to thank the reviewers whose comments greatly improved the paper. Support for this work was provided by NERC in the form of shiptime and studentships.

References

BARBER, P. L. 1980. Geological studies in the Malin Sea and Donegal Bay. PhD thesis, University of Wales, Aberystwyth.

——, DOBSON, M. R. & WHITTINGTON, R. J. 1979. The geology of the Firth of Lorne as determined by seismic and dive sampling methods. Scottish Journal of Geology, 15, 217–230.

BENTLEY, M. R. 1986. The Tectonics of Colonsay, Scotland. PhD thesis, University College of Wales, Aberystwyth.

—— 1988. The Colonsay Group. In: WINCHESTER, J. A. (ed.) Later Proterozoic Stratigraphy of the Northern Atlantic Regions. Blackie, Glasgow, 119–130.

BINNS, P. E., McQUILLIN, R. & KENOLTY, N. 1974. The Geology of the Sea of the Hebrides. Report Institute Geological Sciences. 73/14.

——, McQUILLIN, R., FANNIN, N. G. T., KENOLTY, N. & ARDUS, D. A. 1975. Structure and stratigraphy of sedimentary basins in the Sea of the Hebrides and Minches. In: WOODLAND, A. W. (ed.) Petroleum and the Continental Shelf of North West Europe. Vol. 1. Applied Science, Barking, 93–102.

BRADLEY, D. C. 1982. Subsidence in the late Palaeozoic basins in the northern Appalachians. Tectonics, 1, 107–123.

BREWER, J. A., MATTHEWS, D. H., WARNER, M. R., HALL, J., SMYTHE, D. K. & WHITTINGTON, R. J. 1983. BIRPS deep seismic reflection studies of the British Caledonides. Nature, 305, 206–210.

CURRY, D. C., ADAMS, C. G., BOULTER, M. C., DILEY, F. C., EAMES, F. E., FUNNELL, B. M. & WELLS, M. K. 1978. A Correlation of Tertiary Rocks in the British Isles. Geological Society, London, Special Report, 12.

DALY, J. S. & MENUGE, J. F. 1989. Nd isotopic

evidence for the provenance of Dalradian Supergroup sediments in Ireland. *Terra Abstracts*, **1,**,
12.

DAVIES, H. C. 1984. *Quaternary geology of the Malin
Hebridean Sea area*. PhD thesis, University of
Wales, Aberystwyth.

——, DOBSON, M. R. & WHITTINGTON, R. J. 1984. A
revised seismic stratigraphy for Quaternary deposits on the Inner Continental shelf West of
Scotland between 55 30'N and 57 30'N. *Boreas*,
13, 49–66.

DOBSON, M. R. & EVANS, D. 1974. Geological structure of the Malin Sea. *Journal of the Geological
Society, London*, **130**, 475–478.

——, EVANS, D. & WHITTINGTON, R. J. 1975. The
offshore extensions of the Loch Gruinart fault
system, Islay. *Scottish Journal of Geology*, **11**,
23–35.

DURANT, G. P. 1977. *The Blackstones igneous centre
the Islay–Jura dyke swarm and minor igneous
bodies in the eastern Malin Sea area*. PhD thesis,
University of Wales, Aberystwyth.

—— 1980. Blackstones igneous centre. *In*: Evans
et al. The Geology of the Malin Sea, Report
Institute Geological Sciences, 79/15.

——, DOBSON, M. R., KOKELAAR, B. P., MACINTYRE,
R. M. & REA, W. J. 1976. A preliminary report
on the nature and age of the Blackstones Bank
igneous centre, West Scotland. *Journal of the
Geological Society, London*, **132**, 319–327.

EVANS, D. 1974. *Geophysical studies in the Malin Sea*.
PhD thesis, University of Wales, Aberystwyth.

——, KENOLTY, N., DOBSON, M. R. & WHITTINGTON,
R. J. 1980. *The geology of the Malin Sea*. Report
Institute Geological Sciences, No. 79/15.

——, ——, —— & —— 1983. *Malin-Solid Geology
1:250000 scale (map)*. Institute of Geological
Sciences.

—— & WHITTINGTON, R. J. 1976. The submarine
extensions of the Thorr and Fanad plutons, Co.
Donegal. *Proceedings Royal Irish Academy*, **76B**,
111–120.

——, —— & DOBSON, M. R. 1985. *Tiree-Solid
Geology, 1:250000 Scale (map)*. Institute of
Geological Sciences.

——, —— & —— 1987. *Tiree-Quaternary, 1:250000
Scale (map)*. Institute of Geological Sciences.

——, WILKINSON, G. C. & CRAIG, D. L. 1979. The
Tertiary sediments of the Canna Basin, Sea of
the Hebrides. *Scottish Journal of Geology*, **15**,
329–332.

FITCHES, W. E. & MALTMAN, A. J. 1984. Tectonic
development and stratigraphy at the western
margin of the Caledonides: Islay and Colonsay,
Scotland. *Transactions Royal Society Edinburgh:
Earth Sciences*, **75**, 365–385.

——, MUIR, R. J., MALTMAN, A. J. & BENTLEY,
M. R. 1990. Is the Colonsay-West Islay block of
the SW Scotland an allochthonous terrane? Evidence from Dalradian tillite clasts. *Journal of the
Geological Society, London*, **147**, 417–420.

GERARD, J. P. & BOILLOT, C. 1977. Geology of the
north Irish continental shelf. *Marine Geology*,
23, 171–179.

HUTTON, D. H. W. & MCERLEAN, M. 1991. Silurian
and early Devonian sinistral deformation of the
Ratagain granite, Scotland: constraints on the
age of Caledonian movements on the Great Glen
Fault system. *Journal of the Geological Society,
London*, **148**, 1–4.

JAMES, J. W. C. & HITCHEN, K. in press, *Peach Solid
Geology 1:250000 scale (map)*. Institute of
Geological Sciences.

JONES, E. J. W., PERRY, R. G. & WILD, J. L. 1988.
Geology of the Hebridean margin of the Rockall
Trough. *Proceedings Royal Society of Edinburgh*,
88B, 27–51.

KILENYI, T. & STANLEY, R. 1985. Petroleum prospects
in the northwest seaboard of Scotland. *Oil & Gas
Journal*, Oct.

KLEMPERER, S. L., RYAN, P. D. & SNYDER, D. B.
1991. A deep seismic reflection transect across
the Irish Caledonides *Journal of the Geological
Society, London*, **148**, 149–164.

LEE, G. W. & BAILEY, E. B. 1925. *The pre-Tertiary
geology of Mull, Loch Aline and Oban*. Memoir
Geological Survey. U.K.

McQUILLIN, R. & BINNS, P. E. 1973. Geological
structure of the Sea of the Hebrides. *Nature*, **241**,
2–4.

——, BACON, M. & BINNS, P. E. 1975. The Blackstones Tertiary igneous complex. *Scottish Journal
of Geology*, **11**, 179–192.

MAX, M. & BARBER, P. L. 1978. The westward continuation of the Leannan Fault of Donegal and
its bearing on the Great Glen Fault system.
Geological Magazine, **115**, 3, 215–218.

MENUGE, J. F. & DALY, J. S. 1991. Proterozoic evol-
ution of the Erris Complex, N. W. Mayo, Ireland:
Neodymium isotope evidence. *In*: GOWER, C. F.,
RIVERS, T. & RYAN, B. (eds) *Mid-Proterozoic-
Laurentia-Baltica*. Geological, Association of
Canada Special Paper, 38.

MITCHELL, J. G., JONES, E. J. W. & JONES, G. T.
1976. The composition and age of basalts dredged
from the Blackstones igneous centre, Western
Scotland. *Geological Magazine*, **113**, 525–533.

MORTON, N. 1987. Jurassic subsidence history in the
Hebrides, N. W. Scotland. *Marine and Petroleum
Geology*, **4**, 226–242.

MUIR, R. J. 1990. *The Precambrian Basement and
Related Rocks of the Southern Inner Hebrides*,
Scotland. PhD thesis, University of Wales,
Aberystwyth.

OMRAN, M. A. & WHITTINGTON, R. J. 1986. Geophysical studies of the Hebrides Terrace Seamount. *Geological Society Newsletter*, **15**, 43.

PHILLIPS, W. J. 1956. The Criffell-Dalbeattie granodiorite complex. *Quarterly Journal of the
Geological Society, London*, **112**, 221–239.

RAWSON, P. F., CURRY, D., DILLEY, F. C., HANCOCK,
J. M., NEALE, J. W., WOOD, C. J. & WORSSAM,
B. C. 1978. A correlation of Cretaceous rocks in
the British Isles. Geological Society, London,
Special Report, **9**.

RIDD, M. F. 1981. Petroleum geology West of the
Shetlands. *In*: ILLING, L. V. & HOBSON, G. D.
(eds). *Petroleum Geology of the Continental Shelf*

of North-West Europe. Heyden London, 414–425.

RIDDIHOUGH, R. P. 1968. Magnetic surveys off the North Coast of Ireland. *Proceedings Royal Irish Academy*. **66**(3), 215–220.

RODDICK, J. C. & MAX, M. D. 1983. A Laxfordian age from the Inishtrahull Platform, County Donegal, Ireland. *Scottish Journal of Geology*, **19**, 97–102.

ROBERTS, D. G., FLEMING, N. C., HARRISON, R. K., BINNS, P. E. & SNELLING, N. J. 1974. Helen's Reef: a microgabbroic intrusion in the Rockall intrusive centre, Rockall Bank. *Marine Geology*, **16**, M21–30.

SMITH, D. I. & WATSON, J. V. 1983. Scale and timing of movements on the Great Glen Fault, Scotland. *Geology*. **11**, 523–526.

SMYTHE, D. K. & KENOLTY, N. 1975. Tertiary sediments in the Sea of the Hebrides. *Journal of the Geological Society, London*, **131**, 227–233.

STEEL, R. J. & WILSON, A. C. 1975. Sedimentation and tectonism (?Permo-Triassic) on the margin of the North Minch Basin, Lewis. *Journal of the Geological Society, London*, **131**, 183–202.

——, NICHOLSON, R. & KALANDER, L. 1975. Triassic sedimentation and palaeogeography in Central Skye. *Scottish Journal of Geology*, **11**, 1–13.

SNYDER, D. B. & FLACK, C. A. 1990. A Caledonian age for reflectors within the mantle lithosphere north and west of Scotland. *Tectonics*, **9**, 903–922.

TATE, M. & DOBSON, M. R. 1988. Syn- and post-rift igneous activity in the Porcupine Seabight Basin and adjacent continental margin W of Ireland. *In*: MORTON, A. C. & PARSON, L. M. (eds) *Early Tertiary Volcanism and the Opening of the N. E. Atlantic*, Geological Society, London, Special Publication **39**, 309–334.

—— & —— 1989a. Pre-Mesozoic geology of the western and northwestern Irish continental shelf. *Journal of the Geological Society, London*, **146**, 229–240.

—— & —— 1989b. Late Permian to early Mesozoic rifting and sedimentation offshore NW Ireland. *Marine and Petroleum Geology*, **6**, 49–59.

WOOD, M. V., HALL, J. & DOODY, J. J. 1988. Distribution of early Tertiary lavas in the NE Rockall Trough. *In*: MORTON, A. C. & PARSON, L. M. (eds) *Early Tertiary Volcanism and the Opening of the N. E. Atlantic*. Geological Society, Special Publication, **39**, 283–292.

WALKER, C. P. L. 1975. A new concept of the evolution of the British Tertiary intrusive centres. *Journal of the Geological. Society, London*, **131**, 121–141.

WARRINGTON, G. *et al.* 1980. *A correlation of Triassic rocks in the British Isles*. Geological Society, London, Special Report, **13**.

ZIEGLER, P. A. 1982. *Geological Atlas of western and Central Europe*. Shell International Petroleum. Maatschappij B. V. Elsevier, Amsterdam.

Offshore west and south of Ireland

Petroleum geology of the Slyne Trough and adjacent basins

STEPHEN TRUEBLOOD

*Hamilton Brothers Oil and Gas Ltd, Devonshire House, Piccadilly,
London W1X 6AQ, UK*

Abstract: The Slyne Trough lies to the west of Ireland, northeast of the Porcupine Basin and southeast of the margin of the Rockall Trough. The Slyne Trough can be demonstrated to have adequate source, reservoir and seal rocks, but the timing of hydrocarbon migration is more problematical. Structures exist on both large and small scales within the Central and Northern Slyne Troughs, with the possibility of hydrocarbon entrapment at a number of horizons. An excellent source rock has been identified in the Toarcian (Portree Shale Formation) with up to 7% TOC. A secondary source exists within the Sinemurian/Pleinsbachian (Pabba Shale Formation) with up to 4% TOC. Reservoir quality sands have been encountered in the Bathonian (Elgol Sandstone Formation) and Hettangian/Sinemurian (Broadford Beds Formation). A possibility for further reservoir development can be demonstrated in the Bajocian and Pleinsbachian. Sealing intervals have been found in the Bathonian (various levels in the Great Estuarine Group), the Toarcian/Aalenian (Portree Shale Formation/Dun Caan Shale Member) and the Sinemurian/Pleinsbachian (Pabba Shale Formation). The Liassic source rocks are marginally mature in the 27/13−1 well. In the deeper parts of the basin they are probably mature for generation and migration. The Lower and Middle Jurassic evolution of the basin can be estimated with fair accuracy from the 27/13−1 well. The Post−Middle Jurassic history can be interpreted from analogous basins in the region. The North Porcupine sub-basin section shows the complete erosion of the Liassic source horizons. The oil found within the Porcupine basin is believed to be sourced from the Upper Jurassic, which are mature here due to a post-Jurassic history different to that of the Slyne Trough. The Erris Trough is believed to have had a similar Jurassic evolution to the Slyne Trough, but with locally much greater erosion during the Lower Cretaceous. The Jurassic petroleum potential within this basin relies on preservation of the full Liassic sequence in downthrown fault blocks.

The Slyne Trough is one of a number of NNE−SSW trending basins of predominantly Mesozoic age which lie offshore Ireland and NW Scotland. Onshore exposure of these rocks is limited to the Hebrides and the northern Irish coast. The stratigraphy of the Slyne Trough has been correlated in detail to the age-equivalent sequence in the Hebridean basins (Trueblood & Morton 1991) and other West of Britain basins (Morton this volume). The structure of the Slyne Trough has been considered by Naylor & Shannon (1982), Tate & Dobson (1988, 1989) and Trueblood & Morton (1991). However, only one seismic line across the southern part of the basin has been published (Tate & Dobson 1989). An analysis of the seismic and well data from the Slyne Trough allows an estimate of its petroleum geology, and the implications from this can be extended to adjacent basins.

Structure

The structure of the basin is shown in Fig. 1, and is interpreted to consist of three sub-basins (Trueblood & Morton 1991). The three sub-basins are separated from each other and the adjacent basins by a variety of tectonic structures. The South Slyne Trough is bounded at its southern margin by a gravity and magnetic anomaly which has been interpreted as a Tertiary igneous centre (Riddihough & Max 1976) named the Brendan igneous complex (Tate & Dobson 1988), possibly similar to those seen in NW Scotland. The exact nature of the relationship between the basin and the anomaly is unknown. Seismic lines across the South Slyne Trough show the major basin-bounding fault to be to the west, with other faulting to the south and east which is possibly post-depositional. The inset in Fig. 1 shows a two-way-time map for a near top Bajocian limestone reflector in the Central and Northern Troughs. Five reflection seismic lines are marked on this map and illustrated in Fig. 2. The Slyne Trough is interpreted as an extensional basin (Trueblood & Morton 1991) similar in style to the East African Rift Valley (Rosendahl *et al.* 1986).

Seismic line 1 is the nearest to the only available well control in the basin, 27/13−1 (12 km to the south), and can be correlated to

From PARNELL, J. (ed.), 1992, *Basins on the Atlantic Seaboard: Petroleum Geology, Sedimentology and Basin Evolution.* Geological Society Special Publication No 62, pp 315−326.

315

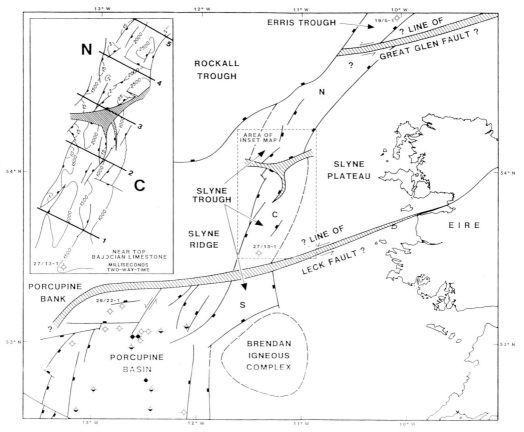

Fig. 1. Principal elements of the Slyne Trough and adjacent basins showing location of wells. Inset: Near Top Bajocian Limestone structure map for North and Central Slyne Trough (after Trueblood & Morton 1991).

the stratigraphy in the well. Three horizons in particular have been correlated: the Base Quaternary/Recent, Near Top Bajocian Limestone and Base Jurassic. The section shows the 'trapdoor' nature of the basin with the sequence above and below the Top Bajocian limestone reflector gradually thickening into the basin centre. The equivalent location on line from the 27/13−1 well is near the minor fault at the southeast end of the section. The well penetrated a Bathonian and possibly Callovian sequence between the Base Quaternary reflector and the Top Bajocian Limestone horizon. In the deep centre of the basin a more complete Middle and Upper Jurassic sequence is preserved, which is eroded at the well location. It is noticeable that the major basin-bounding fault has not been recently active in this part of the Central Slyne Trough, as no change of thickness is seen in the Recent/

Quaternary sediments. The thickness of Triassic sediments underlying the Rhaetic section penetrated in well 27/13−1 is also difficult to estimate; although reflectors can be seen extending below the Base Jurassic for some distance.

Line 2 shows the same broad structural pattern seen in line 1 and extending over the whole sub-basin. At this location the preserved Jurassic section is thinner, with greater sediment input from the northwest, the hangingwall side of the main fault. This is seen in the thickened footwall section below the Top Bajocian Limestone horizon. Possible structures for hydrocarbon entrapment have been created by the rollover into the hangingwall and the collapsed 'flower' structure seen in the middle of the line which is characteristic of extensional tectonic settings. The Quaternary section appears undisturbed, indicating quiescence

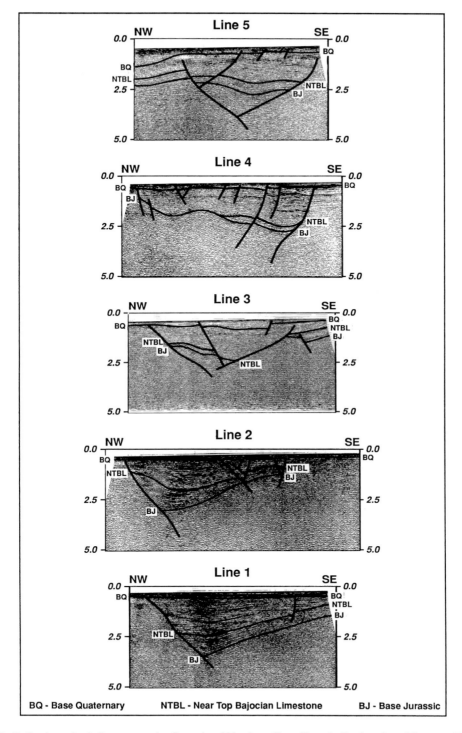

Fig. 2. Reflection seismic lines across the Central and Northern Slyne Trough. For location of lines see Fig. 1.

along the major faults in the Central Trough, a requisite for the retention of fault-trapped hydrocarbons in areas where the sealing formations are not exceptionally thick.

Line 3 is located across the main transfer fault separating the Central and Northern Slyne Troughs. At the southeastern end of the line is the northernmost area of the Central Slyne Trough, throughout which a direct correlation can be made with the stratigraphy of the 27/13−1 well. Northwest of the transfer fault, an estimate of the stratigraphy in the Northern Slyne Trough has been made on the basis of seismic character. The thickness of the pre-Bathonian Jurassic in the southern part of the Northern sub-basin is considerably thinner than that south of the transfer fault. Disruption of the Quaternary section at the northwest end of the line indicates that the faults in the Northern Trough are active at the present time. This effect becomes progressively more extensive further north in the sub-basin and is probably related to impingement of the Rockall Trough on the northern end of the sub-basin.

Line 4 shows the switch of the main basin-controlling fault from the northwestern to the southeastern margin. The pre-Bathonian Jurassic section is very thin and confined to the deepest part of the basin. A four-way dip closed structure exists over the basement high in the central part of the line. Again, minor faulting of the shallow section is evident. In this upper section a thin Tertiary sequence may be preserved further north in the sub-basin.

Line 5 is located at the northern end of the Slyne Trough. The structural pattern here is noticeably different from the remainder of the basin. The main basin-controlling fault persists on the southeastern side of the basin. However, on the northwestern side of the basin, the section falls away towards the Rockall Trough rather than showing a complete erosion of the Jurassic sequence. Overlying this section is a thicker post-Jurassic section approaching 1s TWT. The pre-Bathonian sequence is also thicker in this part of the sub-basin, approaching the thickness of the 27/13−1 area in the Central sub-basin. The structurally high area in the central part of the line is open to hydrocarbons sourced from both northwest and southeast.

Source potential

Two main source rock intervals exist in the 27/13−1 well: the Portree Shale and Pabba Shale Formations (Fig. 3). The Toarcian Portree Shale Formation (Fig. 4) is the principal source rock in the well. It is 84 m thick and two measure-ments of Total Organic Content (TOC) within the section yielded 7.15% and 3.58% with a high sapropel content. These are similar to the TOC values in the Posidoniaschiefer which is the principal oil source rock in the Dutch sector of the North Sea, and the Schistes Carton, the main source rock in the Paris Basin. However, the thickness of the Formation is unusual, as the maximum thickness in the Hebrides is only 14 m. In the 27/13−1 well this interval is only marginally mature ($R_o = 0.45\%$). However the well is located at the margin of the basin and in the central, deeper part of the basin the source rock is likely to be fully mature. Figure 5 shows a calculated burial and maturity history for the Portree Shale Formation in the deeper part of the Central Slyne Trough, equivalent to the deepest part of the section seen on line 1. Allowance has been made for the undrilled section described in the discussion on line 1. The results are necessarily general due to the absence of direct information on the Late Jurassic to Tertiary depositional and thermal history. Accepting these uncertainties the Portree Shale Formation is seen to be mature for oil generation and migration from the Mid-Cretaceous onwards.

The Sinemurian−Pliensbachian Pabba Shale Formation (Fig. 6) contains a lower percentage of organic matter than the Portree Shale Formation based on two TOC readings of 1.72% and 4.04%, but constitutes an important secondary source rock as it is over 150 m deeper and consequently more mature ($R_o = 0.70\%$ in 27/13−1). The vitrinite reflectance readings may, however, be affected by minor Tertiary intrusions in the underlying Broadford Beds Formation, such as the sill seen at 2520 m. Figure 7 shows a burial and maturity history similar to that for the Portree Shale Formation, demonstrating the higher maturity level of this source rock in the deeper parts of the basin.

Reservoir potential

Two zones of reservoir rock were encountered in 27/13−1 and two further sections show potential for reservoir development away from the well. The principal reservoir encountered in well 27/13−1 consists of nine sandstone units from 1427 m to 1698.5 m.

The upper six sandstones are represented in Fig. 8. The cumulative thickness is 66 m, of which 59 m are net reservoir sandstone (based on a minimum of 6% porosity). Porosities computed from logs vary between 17% in sandstone 4 to 23% in sandstone 6 (average 20%). Calculated water saturations vary from 74% to

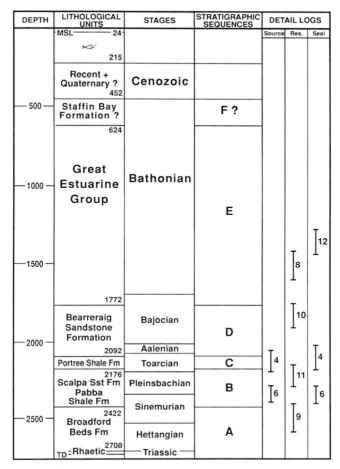

DEPTH	LITHOLOGICAL UNITS	STAGES	STRATIGRAPHIC SEQUENCES	DETAIL LOGS		
				Source	Res.	Seal
	MSL ———— 24					
	215					
	Recent + Quaternary ? 452	Cenozoic				
500	Staffin Bay Formation ? 624		F ?			
1000	Great Estuarine Group	Bathonian	E			12
1500					8	
	1772					
2000	Bearreraig Sandstone Formation 2092	Bajocian	D		10	
		Aalenian				4
	Portree Shale Fm 2176	Toarcian	C	4		
	Scalpa Sst Fm	Pleinsbachian	B		11	
	Pabba Shale Fm	Sinemurian		6		6
2500	2422 Broadford Beds Fm				9	
	2708	Hettangian	A			
	TD = Rhaetic	Triassic				

Fig. 3. Stratigraphy of the 27/13−1 well showing the principal source, reservoir and sealing intervals and marking the extent of the detailed logs (Figs 4, 6, 8−12).

100%. Hydrocarbon shows were present in the first six sandstones, consisting of direct and crush fluorescence, with the best show between 1427−1435 m in sandstone 1. Although individual sandstones are not expected to be laterally continuous throughout the basin, this package of sandstones can be correlated with the Elgol Sandstone Formation of the Hebrides, which suggests a significant overall lateral extent.

The second reservoir section in well 27/13−1 is in the Broadford Beds Fromation (Fig. 9) below 2422 m. Porosities in these sandstones vary from 7 to 12%. No hydrocarbon shows were recorded. In less deeply buried locations, especially at the basin margins, higher porosity sandstones may be preserved.

The Bearreraig Sandstone Formation

(Fig. 10) is not of reservoir quality in 27/13−1, in large part due to the high carbonate content of the sandstones. However, by analogy with the Hebridean region (Morton, this volume) it may be developed as a sandier facies in other parts of the basin or in adjacent basins. The Scalpa Sandstone Formation in 27/13−1 consists of a broadly coarsening-up sequence (Fig. 11). It does not, however, coarsen beyond sandy siltstone. Again, as in the Hebrides, a reservoir-quality sequence of this Formation may exist in other parts of the basin.

Sealing potential

The sealing horizon for the principal reservoir in 27/13−1, the Elgol Sandstone Formation, is the overlying Lealt Shale Formation (Fig. 12)

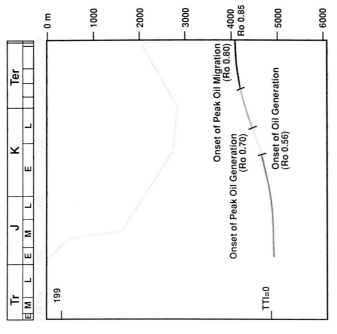

Fig. 5. Estimated burial and maturity histories for the Portree Shale Formation in the depocentre of the Central Slyne Trough. (Temperature gradient 30°C/km till end Middle Jurassic, declining to 25°C/km at present day.)

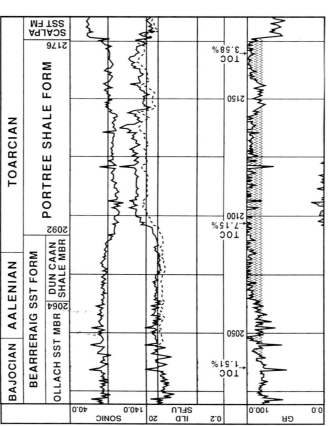

Fig. 4. Geophysical well log signature: Portree Shale Formation. Depths in metres below rig table. (GR, gamma ray: API units. DIL, Deep induction log; SFLU, shallow induction log: resistivity, log scale) (SONIC, sonic log: units in dT).

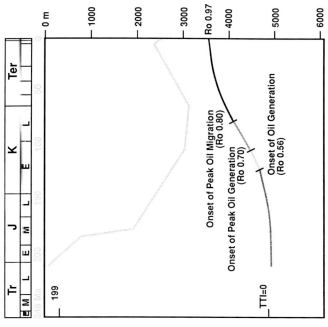

Fig. 7. Estimated burial and maturity histories for the Pabba Shale Formation in the depocentre of the Central Slyne Trough. (Temperature gradient as per Fig. 5).

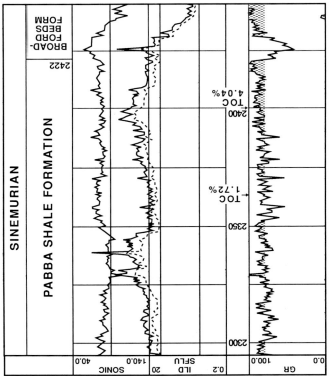

Fig. 6. Geophysical well log signature: Pabba Shale Formation.

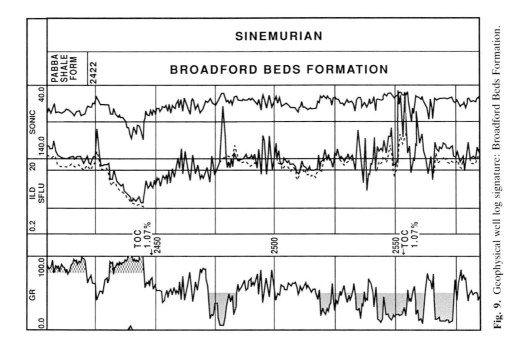

Fig. 9. Geophysical well log signature: Broadford Beds Formation.

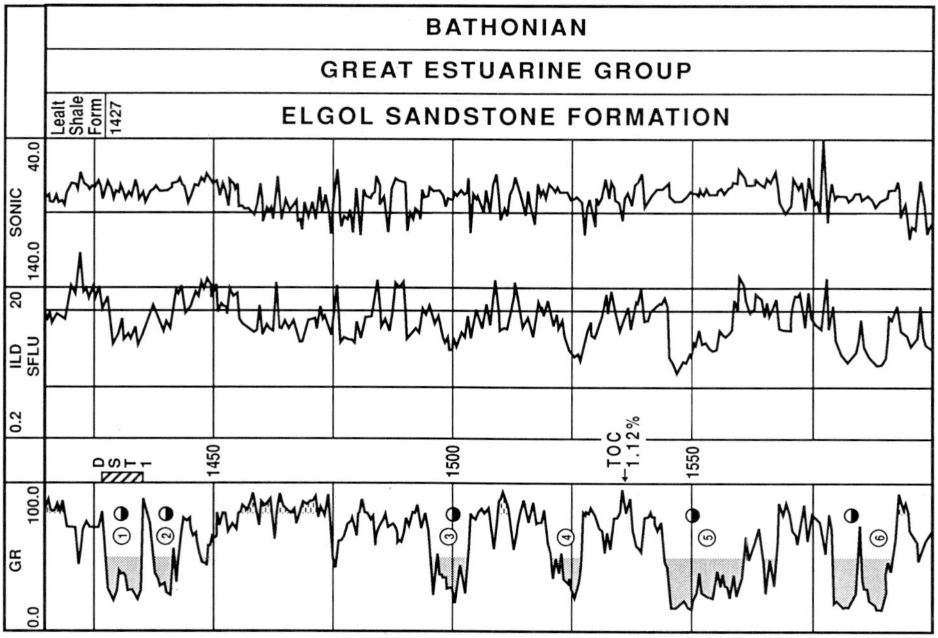

Fig. 8. Geophysical well log signature: Elgol Sandstone Formation.

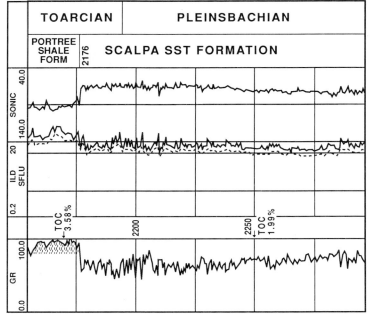

Fig. 11. Geophysical well log signature: Scalpa Sandstone Formation.

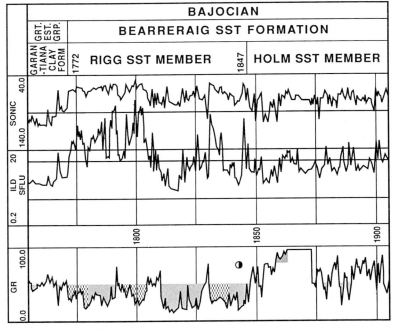

Fig. 10. Geophysical well log signature: Bearraraig Sandstone Formation.

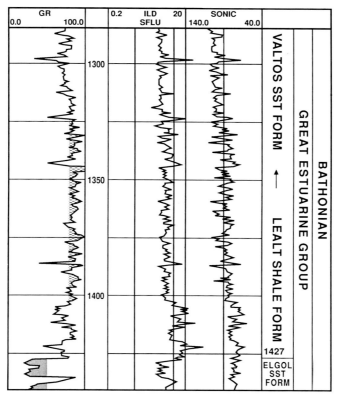

Fig. 12. Geophysical well log signature: Lealt Shale Formation.

which in the well is 100 m thick and grades upwards into the Valtos Sandstone Formation. The Broadford Beds Formation is sealed by the overlying Pabba Shale Formation (Fig. 6) which is over 150 m thick. The absence of a sandy facies of the Scalpa Sandstone Formation increases the sealing potential for this section. Should a coarse equivalent of the Scalpa Sandstone Formation be encountered then the overlying Portree Shale Formation (Fig. 4) might act as both source and seal to any reservoir section.

Timing of hydrocarbon migration

The absence of well data for the Late Jurassic to Tertiary thermal and burial history in the Slyne Trough makes an accurate estimation of the maturity, migration and emplacement of hydrocarbons impossible. Figures 5 and 7 show the burial/maturation histories for the Portree Shale and Pabba Shale Formations which are based on data from 27/13−1, seismic extrapolation into the deeper parts of the basin and

comparison with the stratigraphy of adjacent basins (Morton, this volume). These show that in the Central Slyne Trough, the large scale migration of hydrocarbons probably commenced in the Late Cretaceous for the Pabba Shale Formation and in the Early Tertiary for the Portree Shale Formation.

Estimation of the timing of the formation of the existing structures in the basin similarly suffers from many of the same constraints in the available data. The absence of activity along faults in the Central Slyne Trough may point to a lack of major structural activity in the basin during the Tertiary at the time of possible hydrocarbon emplacement. Observations in modern rifts confirm that much of the structure seen on lines 1 and 2 develops during the rifting phase (Rosendahl et al. 1986).

In the Northern Slyne Trough, faulting was active during the Tertiary and probably also the Quaternary. Long-lived fault-sealed traps are less likely in this sub-basin, although recently sourced fault-bounded traps may be prospective. In the northern sub-basin, 4-way dip closed

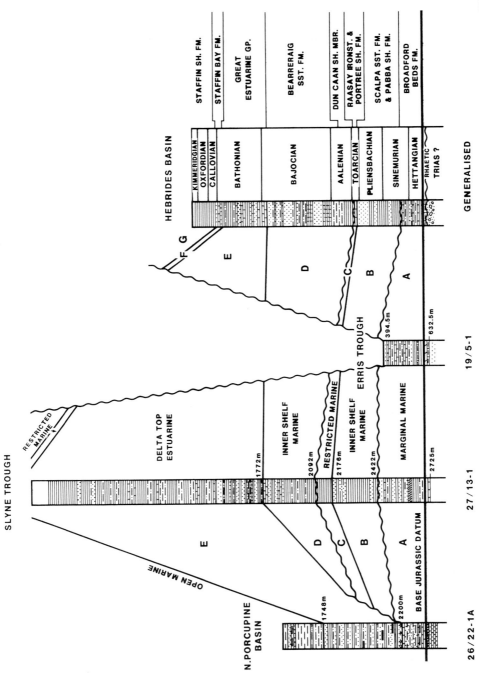

Fig. 13. Correlation of Jurassic sections west of Ireland and Scotland showing major sequence stratigraphic boundaries: (after Trueblood & Morton 1991).

prospects exist and are more likely to contain any migrated hydrocarbons than structures which rely on fault-seal. At the northwest margin of the northern sub-basin the Jurassic section is seen dipping down to the west towards the Rockall Trough (Fig. 2: line 5). This deeper burial, in a region of more recent structural development, may have facilitated the generation of fault traps and the recent/current migration of hydrocarbons.

Petroleum prospectivity of adjacent basins

Figure 13 (after Trueblood & Morton 1991) shows a correlation of the Slyne Trough sequence stratigraphy to that of the adjacent North Porcupine Basin and Erris Trough and to the Hebrides Basin. The principal Slyne Trough source rocks, the Portree Shale and Pabba Shale Formations, are eroded in both of the adjacent basins according to the evidence of wells drilled to date (Trueblood & Morton 1991).

In the North Porcupine Basin the source for the Connemara oilfield is the Upper Jurassic Kimmeridge Clay Formation. This formation is unproven in the Slyne Trough, but may be present in the deeper, as yet unpenetrated, part of the basin. It is unlikely on the evidence of 27/ 13-1 to be mature for oil generation. The major part of the Lower Jurassic is absent in the North Porcupine Basin below the erosive base of the Great Estuarine Group.

In the Erris Trough the 19/5-1 well shows the complete absence of any Jurassic section above the Broadford Beds Formation and consequently a lack of any Jurassic source rock intervals. However, in the deeper parts of the Erris Trough and on the margin of the Rockall Trough large tilted fault blocks can be seen on seismic lines similar in structure to that of the northwestern end of line 5 (Fig. 2). These offer the best opportunity for mature Jurassic source rocks in the Erris Trough.

Conclusion

The depositional history of the Slyne Trough is favourable to hydrocarbon potential in the Jurassic rocks. Structure, source, reservoirs and seal can all be demonstrated. Due to the absence of sufficient well data the timing of hydrocarbon generation and migration cannot be determined with accuracy in relation to the structural history of the basin. However, considerable potential remains within this underexplored basin.

I acknowledge Murphy Eastern Oil Company who have generously allowed me to publish the seismic lines in Fig. 2 and the well data in Figs 4-12. Much of the initial work for this paper derives from my employment with Murphy.

References

NAYLOR, D. & SHANNON, P. M. 1982. *Geology of Offshore Ireland and West Britain*. Graham & Trotman, London.

RIDDIHOUGH, R. P. & MAX, M. D. 1976. A geological framework for the continental margin to the west of Ireland. *Geological Journal*, **11**, 109-120.

ROSENDAHL, B. R., REYNOLDS, D. H., LORBER, P. M., BURGESS, C. F., McGILL, J., SCOTT, D., LAMBIASE, J. J. & DERKSEN, S. J. 1986. Structural expressions of rifting: lessons from Lake Tanganyika, Africa. *In*: FROSTICK, L. E., RENAUT, R. W., REID, I. & TIERCELIN, J. J. (eds) *Sedimentation in the African Rifts*. Geological Society, London, Special Publication, **25**, 29-43.

TATE, M. P. & DOBSON, M. R. 1988. Syn- and post-rift igneous activity in the Porcupine Seabight Basin and adjacent continental margin. *In*: MORTON, A. C. & PARSON, L. M. (eds) *Early Tertiary Volcanism and the Opening of the NE Atlantic*. Geology Society, London, Special Publication, **39**, 309-334.

—— & —— 1989. Late Permian to Early Mesozoic rifting and sedimentation, offshore N.W. Ireland. *Marine and Petroleum Geology*, **6**, 49-59.

TRUEBLOOD, S. P. & MORTON, N. 1991. Comparative sequence stratigraphy and structural styles of the Slyne Trough and Hebrides Basin. *Journal of the Geological Society, London*, **148**, 197-201.

Lithospheric stretching in the Porcupine Basin, west of Ireland

NICKY WHITE, MICHAEL TATE,[1] & JOHN-JOE CONROY[2]

BIRPS, Bullard Laboratories, Cambridge CB3 0EZ, UK

[1] Total Oil Marine PLC., 16 Palace St., London SW1E 5BQ, UK

[2] Marathon Petroleum Co. (Ireland), Centre Park House, Centre Park Rd., Blackrock, Co. Cork, Ireland

Abstract: The Porcupine Basin is a N–S trending Mesozoic extensional sedimentary basin situated on the continental shelf west of Ireland. All available datasets have been examined in order to see how well the stretching model accounts for the structure and evolution of the basin. Subsidence data indicates that there have been two phases of stretching: at the end of the Jurassic and during the Palaeogene. The earlier phase is of more significance; stretching factors varying from 1.2 at the northern end of the basin to greater than six at the southern end. Stretching factors for the later phase are generally less than 1.1. Crustal thinning information, determined principally from gravity data, is consistent with the above estimates. The timing of volcanism within the basin is broadly consistent with these stretching phases. Significantly, the location of a 150 km long and 20 km wide median igneous ridge is broadly consistent with the steady increase in stretching southwards.

A large amount of geological and geophysical information is now available for the Porcupine Basin, a N–S trending Mesozoic extensional sedimentary basin situated on the continental shelf west of Ireland (Fig. 1). Much of the detailed structure and stratigraphy relies on the considerable quantity of non-exclusive seismic reflection data which can be calibrated with well-log information at the northern end of the basin. A limited amount of seismic refraction data (Makris et al. 1988) and a single deep seismic reflection line shot to 18 s TWTT (Croker & Klemperer 1989) can be combined with gravity data to constrain crustal thickness variations. Much research has been carried out on all aspects of the basin's development (see e.g. Scrutton et al. 1971; Buckley & Bailey 1975; Roberts et al. 1981; Naylor & Shannon 1982; Masson & Miles 1986; Naylor & Anstey 1987). However, as yet no attempt has been made to apply the stretching model (McKenzie 1978; Jarvis & McKenzie 1980). This short contribution reports on a preliminary study of the stretching history of the basin and assesses whether the stretching model in its simplest form accounts for the observed subsidence, crustal thinning and normal faulting.

Water-loaded subsidence curves were calculated from well-log information using the standard backstripping technique (Steckler & Watts 1978; Sclater & Christie 1980). This procedure was undertaken in order to remove the effects of sediment loading and variable sediment supply. The most important source of uncertainty concerns water depth at the time of deposition. As in previous studies, our estimates of water depth are based on sedimentological information combined with inferences made from benthic foraminiferal assemblages (e.g. Barton & Wood 1984). Additional water-loaded subsidence curves were determined at 150 positions throughout the basin using calibrated and depth-converted seismic reflection data, since most of the basin is still undrilled.

Theoretical subsidence curves which allow for a finite period of rifting (Jarvis & McKenzie 1980) were then fitted to the data. Four of the backstripped wells are shown in Fig. 2. As has already been suggested by Masson & Miles (1986) and Naylor & Anstey (1987), the main phase of extension occurred during the Jurassic, starting at about 180 Ma and lasted 40 Ma. Although the basin clearly has had a Carboniferous and Permo-Triassic history (e.g. Robeson et al. 1988), we assume that any associated thermal anomalies would have decayed by Jurassic times. We also assume that the crust was a uniform 30 km thick prior to Jurassic extension (Whitmarsh et al. 1974).

Figure 1 shows how the Jurassic phase of stretching varies throughout the basin. At the northern end, β factors are ~1.2. Stretching increases steadily down the axis of the basin, reaching $\beta > 6$ in the Seabight. The extension across the basin can be calculated by integrating a $(1-1/\beta)$ profile across the basin. Hence at 53°N there has been ~30 km extension while at 50°N there has been ~120 km. The simplest

From PARNELL, J. (ed.), 1992, *Basins on the Atlantic Seaboard: Petroleum Geology, Sedimentology and Basin Evolution.* Geological Society Special Publication No 62, pp 327–349.

327

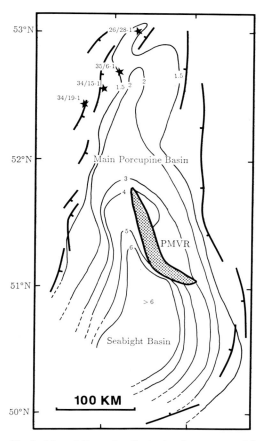

53°N

26/28-1

35/6-1

34/15-1   1.5   2   2   1.5

34/19-1

52°N   Main Porcupine Basin

3

4

5   PMVR

6

51°N   > 6

Seabight Basin

100 KM

50°N

Fig. 1. Map of Porcupine Basin showing contoured β values. Basin-bounding normal faults indicated in thick solid line with ticks on down-thrown side. PMVR, Porcupine Median Volcanic Ridge (shaded irregular shape). Stars indicate locations of four back-stripped wells shown in Fig. 1.

explain this increase as being due to variation in palaeowater depth. It cannot be explained by variation in eustatic sea level either, since allowing for the late Cretaceous highstand predicted by all of the published sea-level curves would actually amplify the increase in subsidence. At the moment, we interpret the increase in subsidence as being caused by a phase of minor stretching ($\beta \sim 1.05$). Small amounts of Tertiary normal faulting are observed in the basin, supporting this interpretation. It is interesting to note that a similar increase in subsidence rate has been observed to occur during the Palaeogene within Mesozoic basins on the conjugate Newfoundland margin (Keen *et al.* 1987).

It is difficult even when the degree of stretching is small (e.g. the East Shetland Basin in the northern North Sea) to calculate with any degree of accuracy the amount of stretching accommodated by normal faulting. The very large amounts of stretching calculated for the Porcupine Basin make this task virtually impossible: imaging of syn-rift sediments is very poor (Naylor & Anstey 1987; Tate & Dobson 1989) and in any case it is likely that several generations of normal faulting are required if $\beta > 2$ (e.g. Proffett 1977).

Estimates of β based on gravity-derived crustal thinning (Conroy & Brock 1989) combined with deep refraction and reflection profiles are sparse and are subject to large errors. Nevertheless, the values obtained are broadly consistent with those calculated from subsidence (Tate *et al.*, unpublished data). A possible exception occurs within the Seabight, where crustal thickness is about 10 km giving, within error, stretching values consistently less than those predicted by subsidence calculations.

The distribution of stretching within the Main Porcupine Basin is unusual — many extensional sedimentary basins are approximately two-dimensional: β does not vary significantly along strike. In the Porcupine Basin, β varies both across and down the axis of the basin. Recent research in igneous petrology suggests that the volume and composition of melt produced during extension is strongly controlled by three parameters: the degree of stretching, the initial mechanical boundary layer thickness, and the potential temperature of the asthenosphere (Foucher *et al.* 1982; McKenzie & Bickle 1988). Assuming that we can estimate the last two parameters, it is clear that the pattern of stretching within the Porcupine Basin has interesting implications for the magmatic history. For normal asthenospheric temperature (1280°C potential temperature) and lithospheric thick-

way of accommodating this difference is to allow the Porcupine Ridge west of the basin to have rotated through ~25° away from the Irish shelf. In contrast, Croker & Klemperer (1989) believe that extension across the basin was small and that formation of the basin by detachment and pivoting of the Porcupine Ridge away from the Irish Shelf is unrealistic. Given the considerable amounts of rotation about vertical axes which have recently been reported from areas of active extension (see Kissel & Laj 1988 for recent review), we see no difficulty in rotating the Porcupine Ridge by such a modest amount.

All of the subsidence curves which we calculated show a rapid increase in subsidence during the early Tertiary (Fig. 2). It is difficult to

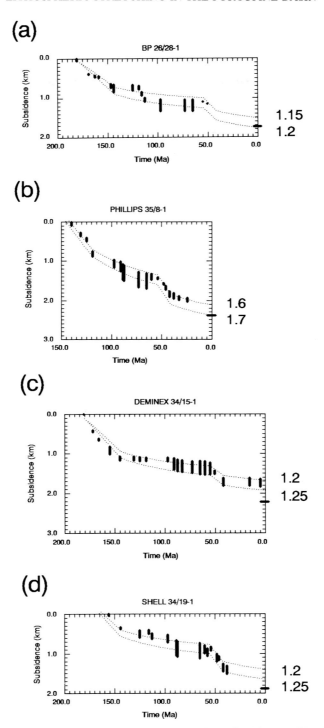

Fig. 2. Four backstripped and water-loaded subsidence curves determined from well-log information. Error bars indicate uncertainty in palaeowater depth. Dotted lines: best-fitting maximum and minimum theoretical subsidence curves assuming stretching period from 180–144 Ma. Numbers to right indicate β values. See Fig. 1 for location.

ness (a mechanical boundary layer thickness of 100 km), we would expect significant melting to commence when $\beta \sim 3$. This prediction agrees well with observation: the Porcupine Median Volcanic Ridge, which is at least Aptian/Albian in age and possibly older (Masson & Miles 1986; Tate & Dobson 1988), occurs when β reaches about 3 or 4 (Fig. 1). Unfortunately, the composition of the ridge is unknown. Significantly, Conroy & Brock (1989) argue on the basis of gravity and magnetic modelling that there are other intrusive bodies further south.

Once β reaches values of 6–10, the stretching model predicts that about 5 km of basaltic melt would be produced by adiabatic decompression of the asthenosphere. Assuming that much of this material could be underplated beneath the crust, the density of the frozen melt would be such as to make the thinned crust beneath the Seabight appear twice as thick as it really is. If this is the case, then the discrepancy between subsidence-derived β and crust-derived β can be explained.

Another important episode of igneous activity occurs at the start of the Tertiary (e.g. Tate & Dobson 1988). Although the degree of stretching calculated for this time is very small (~ 1.05), it may be sufficient to account for the observed magma compositions and volumes. If the basin were in close proximity to the Iceland hotspot at this time (less than ~ 1500 km) then the potential temperature of the asthenosphere would have been $\sim 200°C$ higher than $1280°C$. However, until further petrological work is carried out, this conclusion must remain speculative.

Finally, the calculated stretching history can be used to predict heat flux as a function of time throughout the basin. Hence the time/temperature history of buried sediment can be estimated and used to calculate vitrinite reflectance and maturation of oil- and gas-prone kerogen. These calculated values can be calibrated with the measured values at the northern end of the basin (e.g. Robeson *et al.* 1988; Tate *et al.* unpublished data) and then used as a predictive tool in the southern, undrilled, part of the basin.

M. T. and J. J. C. were supported by BIRPS short-term visiting fellowships funded by NERC. We are particularly grateful to S. G. Peacock of British Petroleum for generously allowing access to unreleased well-log information. GECO and Western Geophysical allowed us access to their extensive grids of seismic reflection data. Other well information was provided by Amerada Hess, BP, Chevron, Deminex, Elf, Esso, Gulf, Phillips, Shell and Texaco. We also thank D. Latin, R. Hobbs, S. Klemperer and K. Robinson for their help. This is Cambridge Earth Sciences Contribution No 2078.

References

BARTON, P. & WOOD, R. 1984. Tectonic evolution of the North Sea basin: Crustal stretching and subsidence. *Geophysical Journal of the Royal Astronomical Society*, **79**, 987–1022.

BUCKLEY, J. S. & BAILEY, R. J. 1975. A free-air gravity anomaly contour map of the Irish continental margin. *Marine Geophysical Research*, **2**, 185–194.

CONROY, J. J. & BROCK, A. 1989. Gravity and magnetic studies of crustal structure across the Porcupine basin west of Ireland. *Earth & Planetary Science Letters*, **93**, 371–376.

CROKER, P. F. & KLEMPERER, S. L. 1989. Structure and stratigraphy of the Porcupine Basin: Relationships to deep crustal structure and the opening of the North Atlantic. *In*: TANKARD, A. J. & BALKWILL, H. R. (eds) *Extensional tectonics and stratigraphy of the North Atlantic margins*. American Association of Petroleum Geologists Memoir, **46**, 445–457.

FOUCHER, J. P., LE PICHON, X. & SIBUET, J. C. 1982. The ocean-continent transition in the uniform lithospheric stretching model: role of partial melting in the mantle. *Philosophical Transactions of the Royal Society of London*, **A305**, 27–43.

JARVIS, G. T. & MCKENZIE. D. P. 1980. Sedimentary basin formation with finite extension rates. *Earth & Planetary Science Letters*, **48**, 42–52.

KEEN, C. E., STOCKMAL, G. S., WELSINK, H., QUINLAN, G. & MUDFORD, B. 1987. Deep crustal structure and evolution of the rifted margin northeast of Newfoundland: results from LITHOPROBE East. *Canadian Journal of Earth Sciences*, **24**, 1537–1549.

KISSEL, C. & LAJ, C. 1988. *Palaeomagnetic rotations and continental deformation*. Kluwer, Utrecht.

MAKRIS, J., EGLOFF, R., JACOB, A. W. B., MOHR, P., MURPHY, T. & RYAN, P. 1988. Continental crust under the southern Porcupine Seabight west of Ireland. *Earth & Planetary Science Letters*, **89**, 387–397.

MASSON, D. G. & MILES, P. R. 1986. Structure and development of Porcupine Seabight sedimentary basin, offshore southwest Ireland. *AAPG Bulletin*, **70**, 536–548.

MCKENZIE, D. 1978. Some remarks on the development of sedimentary basins. *Earth & Planetary Science Letters*, **40**, 25–32.

—— & BICKLE, M. J. 1988. The volume and composition of melt generated by extension of the lithosphere. *Journal of Petrology*, **29**, 625–679.

NAYLOR, D. & ANSTEY, N. A. 1987. A reflection seismic study of the Porcupine Basin, offshore west Ireland. *Irish Journal of Earth Sciences*, **8**, 187–210.

—— & SHANNON, P. M. 1982. *Geology of offshore Ireland and West Britain*. Graham & Trotman, London.

PROFFETT, J. M. JR. 1977. Cenozoic geology of the Yerington district, Nevada, and implications for the nature and origin of Basin and Range faulting. *Geological Society of America Bulletin*, **88**, 247–266.

ROBERTS, D. G., MASSON, D. G., MONTADERT, L. & DE CHARPAL, O. 1981. Continental margin from the Porcupine Seabight to the Armorican marginal basin. *In*: ILLING, L. V. & HOBSON, G. D. (eds) *Petroleum Geology of the Continental Shelf of Northwest Britain*. Institute of Petroleum, London, 455–473.

ROBESON, D., BURNETT, R. D. & CLAYTON, G. 1988. The Upper Palaeozoic geology of the Porcupine, Erris and Donegal Basins, offshore Ireland. *Irish Journal of Earth Sciences*, **9**, 153–175.

SCLATER, J. G. & CHRISTIE, P. A. F. 1980. Continental stretching: An explanation of the post-mid-Cretaceous subsidence of the Central North Sea Basin. *Journal of Geophysical Research*, **85**, 3711–3739.

SCRUTTON, R. A., STACEY, A. P. & GRAY, F. 1971. Evidence for the mode of formation of Porcupine Seabight. *Earth & Planetary Science Letters*, **11**, 140–146.

STECKLER, M. S. & WATTS, A. B. 1978. Subsidence of the Atlantic-type continental margin off New York. *Earth & Planetary Science Letters*, **41**, 1–13.

TATE, M. P. & DOBSON, M. R. 1988. Syn- and post-rift igneous activity in the Porcupine Seabight Basin and adjacent continental margin W of Ireland. *In*: MORTON, A. C. & PARSON, L. M. (eds) *Early Tertiary Volcanism and the Opening of the N.E. Atlantic*. Geological Society, London, Special Publication, **39**, 309–334.

—— & —— 1989. Late Permian to early Mesozoic rifting and sedimentation offshore NW Ireland. *Marine & Petroleum Geology*, **6**, 49–59.

WHITMARSH, R. B., LANGFORD, J. J., BUCKLEY, J. S., BAILEY, R. J. & BLUNDELL, D. J. 1974. The crustal structure beneath Porcupine Ridge determined by explosion seismology. *Earth & Planetary Science Letters*, **22**, 197–204.

A syn-rift to post-rift transition sequence in the Main Porcupine Basin, offshore western Ireland

JOHN G. MOORE

Department of Geology, University College Dublin, Belfield, Dublin 4, Ireland

(Present address: Conoco (UK) Ltd, Park House, 116 Park Street, London W1Y 4NN, UK)

Abstract: The evolution of the Main Porcupine Basin can be divided into pre-rift, syn-rift and post-rift stages. The syn-rift/post-rift transition represents a gradual change from extensive fault activity through localized faulting and passive infill to sporadic faulting during post-rift times. This Transition Sequence is present in localized areas (sub-basins). It infills the remnant syn-rift topography after which the post-rift stage begins. Sub-basins developed during the syn-rift stage have a general N−S to NE−SW orientation and range in size from approximately 30 km × 20 km to approximately 12 km × 8 km. Their shapes range from symmetrical fault-bounded depocentres to half-graben. The sub-basins have several internal unconformities which merge into a single composite erosion surface at the margins. Areas in which the Transition Sequence is developed usually have an element of fault control, especially during the early stages. Clastic fans are identified prograding from fault scarps. Later passive onlap during a rising sea-level progressively infills the sub-basins. The age of the Transition Sequence is problematical, but borehole data suggests that it spans uppermost Kimmeridgian/Tithonian to end-Berriasian times. The sub-basins appear to be broadly coincident with small Permo-Triassic basins. This may point to a deep-seated fault control on the location of the Transition Sequence sub-basins. Comparable syn- to post-rift Transition Sequences are also present in the Orphan and Jeanne d'Arc Basins, offshore Eastern Canada, and possibly in other North Atlantic rift basins also.

The Main Porcupine Basin (MPB), a Mesozoic to Cenozoic ensialic basin, lies in deep North Atlantic waters (150 metres in the north to over 1000 metres in the south) on the continental shelf off the west coast of Ireland (Naylor & Shannon 1982). It is a N−S orientated grabenal feature bounded to the north by the Slyne Ridge, to the west by the Porcupine Ridge, to the east by the Irish Mainland Shelf and it merges with the Goban Spur to the south (Fig. 1). The basin contains up to 10 km of Mesozoic and Cenozoic sediments (Naylor & Anstey 1987). Its development appears to conform to a general McKenzie (1978) simple shear extensional model, showing a typical 'steer's head' profile (Croker & Shannon 1987). Mesozoic basin development was in response to two rifting episodes. The first, in the Permo-Triassic, produced a series of small rift basins and the second, in the Middle and Late Jurassic, represents a period of major crustal extension (Shannon 1991). Cretaceous and Tertiary sediments, up to approximately 5 km thick, represent deposition during major post-rift thermal subsidence following cessation of crustal extension.

The period spanning the Middle and Late Jurassic syn-rift stage and the Cretaceous and Tertiary post-rift stage, where extensive tectonism gives way to thermal subsidence, has important implications in the complete understanding of the basin's evolution. The strata deposited during this period have hydrocarbon potential and therefore are of economic as well as academic importance. This paper describes and discusses this transition zone. Approximately 6000 km of multichannel seismic reflection data, together with information from 21 wells, were used in this study.

The principle of seismic stratigraphy, developed by EXXON in the 1970s (Vail *et al.* 1977), was used in this work. Seismic stratigraphy is basically a geological approach to the stratigraphic interpretation of seismic reflection data. Lithofacies and rock type cannot be determined directly from seismic data; some well information is also required (Vail & Mitchum 1977). The fundamental unit of this concept is a sequence, defined as a relatively conformable succession of genetically related strata bounded by unconformities and their correlative conformities (Mitchum 1977). It should be noted that the term 'sequence' in the present paper is used loosely to define tectonic episodes *sensu* Coward & Trudgill (1989) and not the EXXON group. The concepts and principles of seismic

From PARNELL, J. (ed.), 1992, *Basins on the Atlantic Seaboard: Petroleum Sedimentology and Basin Evolution.* Geological Society Special Publication No 62, pp 333−349.

333

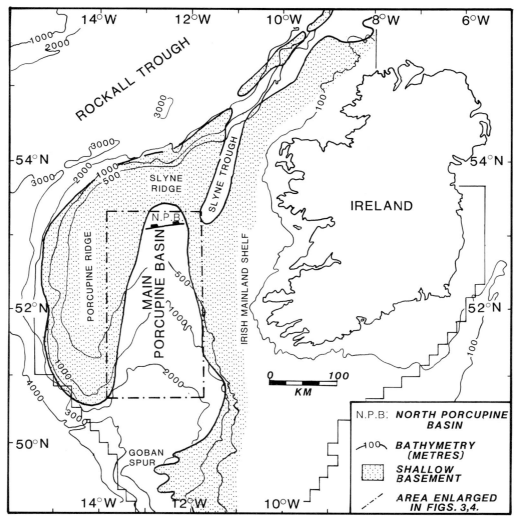

Fig. 1. Map showing the location of the Main Porcupine Basin and the location of Figs 3 & 4. Figure modified from Croker and Shannon (1987).

stratigraphy are well documented in Vail *et al.* (1977), Hubbard *et al.* (1985) and Brown & Fisher (1982).

The Transition Sequence

A Transition Sequence has been recognized between the Middle–Late Jurassic syn-rift stage and the Cretaceous and Tertiary post-rift stage in the evolution of the MPB. The sequence consists of faulted, remnant syn-rift, topographic lows (sub-basins) bounded at the base and top by unconformities. It is, therefore, a seismic megasequence in the terminology of

Hubbard *et al.* (1985). The basal and upper unconformities (together with internal unconformities within the sub-basins) merge into one composite erosion surface at the margins of the sub-basins. Internally the sub-basins consist of various unconformable downlapping, concordant, onlapping, and faulted seismic sedimentary packages. The sub-basins are recognized in five areas throughout the MPB (Figs 3 & 4) and there is an element of fault control in the formation of all of them. The Transition Sequence is recognized on seismic reflection data because of the presence of several unconformities at Base Cretaceous level within the area of the sub-

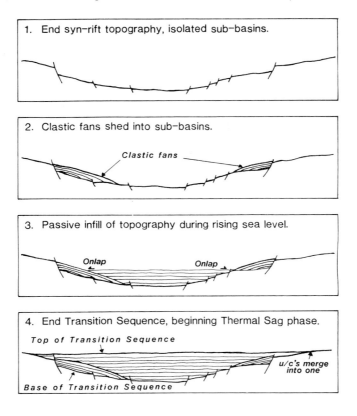

1. End syn–rift topography, isolated sub–basins.

2. Clastic fans shed into sub–basins.

Clastic fans

3. Passive infill of topography during rising sea level.

Onlap   **Onlap**

4. End Transition Sequence, beginning Thermal Sag phase.

Top of Transition Sequence

u/c's merge into one

Base of Transition Sequence

EVOLUTION OF TRANSITION SEQUENCE.

Fig. 2. Schematic diagram showing the general evolution of a Transition Sequence sub-basin.

basins (the lowermost unconformity marks the base of the sequence and the uppermost one marks the top). In addition, the sub-basins are topographically low areas situated between basement highs. Croker & Klemperer (1989) have also recognized the presence of several unconformities merging into one erosion surface at Late Jurassic/Early Cretaceous level on the western margin of the MPB.

The Transition Sequence marks a gradual change from extensive, basinwide faulting and mechanical crustal extension (syn-rift stage) through to localized faulting and later passive onlap within the Transition Sequence sub-basins. They are fault-bounded, and therefore at least a certain element of fault activity is anticipated in their formation. Areas outside of the sub-basins were topographically higher and lacked fault movement and control. Fault activity was not necessarily involved in the sedimentary fill of the sub-basins, and unequivocal evidence for active faulting cannot be seen on the present database. However, the presence of

fault bounded topographic lows (the sub-basins) proves that faulting was certainly active during their formation. Therefore, during the formation of the Transition Sequence sub-basins, fault activity was confined to these localized sub-basins rather than being basinwide as during syn-rift times. The basal unconformity of the Transition Sequence is locally disrupted by normal faulting. The boundary between the syn-rift and the Transition Sequence is taken as the basal unconformity to the Transition Sequence package. The top of the sequence is marked by the uppermost unconformity of the package and this marks the end of the Transition Sequence. The sub-basins were subsequently infilled and the sequence is overlain by the tectonically quiescent deposits of the main thermal sag phase.

Figure 2 shows the evolution of a typical sub-basin. Downlapping packages emanate from basin margin faults; well data (Shell 34/19−1) and seismic character suggest that these packages are clastic fans. The presence of these packages suggests possible syn-sedimentary movement on the faults or, alternatively, fan progradation during a sea-level lowstand. When fan progradation had ceased, passive infill of the sub-basins began during a period of rising sea-level (Haq *et al.* 1987). These sediments passively onlap the older clastic fans and the sub-basin margins (Figs 3–8).

The morphology of the sub-basins ranges from broad symmetrical depocentres to half grabenal features. Four of the sub-basins (*a*–*d*) are present in the northern half of the MPB, while the fifth (*e*) is in the southeastern part of the basin (Figs 3 & 4). All of the sub-basins are geographically separate. Each shows many similar characteristics, such as the presence of medium–high amplitude onlapping seismic reflectors, several unconformities and some degree of internal faulting. Despite these similarities each individual sub-basin has distinctive morphological features.

A seismic facies map is presented for the Transition Sequence sub-basins (Fig. 3). The procedure used in constructing the map was similar to that of Mitchum and Vail (1977). It shows the distribution and direction of onlap, downlap and concordance at the base of the mapped Transition Sequence. An overall depositional environment map of the seismic facies is shown in Fig. 4.

Jurassic-Cretaceous sub-basins of the Main Porcupine Basin

Sub-basin a (Figs 3, 4, 5)

This is the largest of the sub-basins (approximately 30 km × 20 km) and has a N–S elongate, symmetrical depocentre. Two easterly down-lapping packages (approximately 4 km × 3 km in size) thicken towards N–S orientated normal faults. The seismic reflectors within these packages are discontinuous and of medium–high amplitude, with a shallow angle of downlap. The basin margins, together with the down-lapping packages, are onlapped by later medium–high amplitude, parallel reflectors. The thicker central part (500 ms thick) shows medium–high amplitude, concordant parallel reflectors that are often laterally continuous. At the northern limit of the sub-basin some toplap is evident. Numerous normal faults cut the basal unconformity (Fig. 5). The two major unconformities within this sub-basin define the Transition Sequence top and base. They are angular unconformities at the margins, becoming conformable towards the centre of the sub-

basin. Another minor unconformity occurs in the central part of the sequence close to the eastern margin, but this also becomes conformable towards the centre. There is reasonable evidence from the seismic data that the bounding faults of sub-basin *a* extend down to at least Palaeozoic basement. The faults show evidence of reactivation and last moved in lower Cretaceous times. There is abundant normal faulting at, and below, the basal unconformity, especially in the northern part of the sub-basin. The amount of faulting decreases southwards. In the northern and western areas there are fault-bounded depocentres at about Permo-Triassic level. Some of these faults also control the margins of the Transition Sequence sub-basins.

Sub-basin b (Figs 3, 4, 6)

Sub-basin *b* (approximately 16 km × 7 km) is a NE–SW orientated linear feature, bounded to the NE and SW by normal faults. The north-western and southeastern limits are ill-defined due to the lack of good quality seismic reflection data. The main features are two NW–SE orientated normal faults that form the northeastern and southwestern boundaries of the sub-basin. A downlapping package, up to 5 km × 4 km in in size, lies basinwards of these faults. The seismic reflectors in the southern package are high amplitude and relatively continuous, with a shallow angle of downlap. The more northerly package has diffuse, low-amplitude, discontinuous reflectors with a shallow downlap angle. These packages are subsequently onlapped by later medium–low amplitude discontinuous reflectors. The basal unconformity is not faulted but the upper unconformity is offset by minor normal faulting. There is later passive onlap by the remainder of the Transition Sequence reflectors. Sub-basin *b* is bounded by two normal faults both of which extend deep into the economic basement. These basement related faults, with initial activity during the Palaeozoic (or possibly even earlier), have been reactivated with the last movement in late Aptian times. Adjacent to the SW margin of the sub-basin a deep-seated MPB bounding fault juxtaposes the pre-Mesozoic basement against the Cretaceous succession.

Sub-basin c (Figs 3, 4)

Towards the north–central part of the MPB sub-basin *c* (approximately 12 km × 8 km in size) is a broadly N–S orientated depocentre with several internal unconformities and faults.

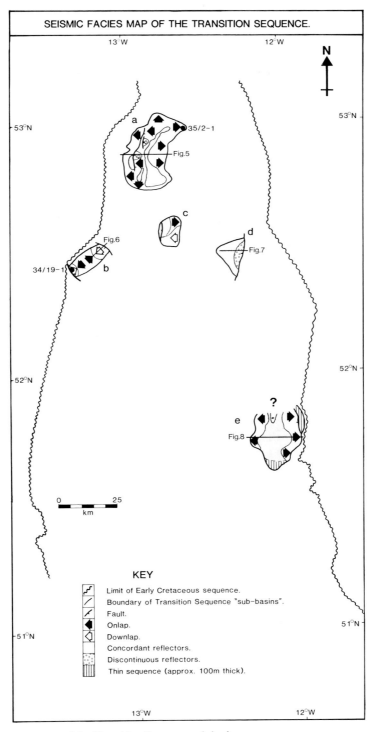

Fig. 3. Seismic facies map of the Transition Sequence sub-basins.

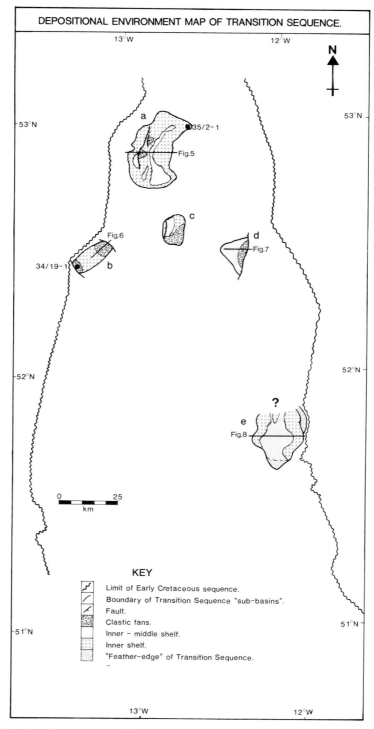

Fig. 4. Depositional environment map of the Transition Sequence sub-basins.

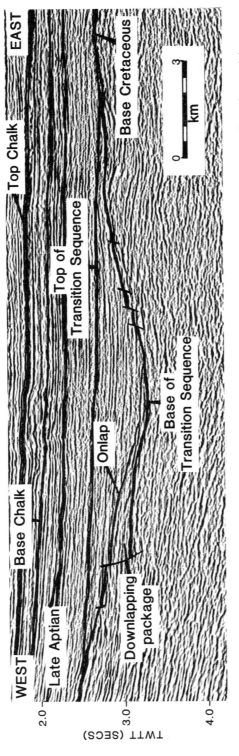

Fig. 5. Seismic section showing a downlapping package (clastic fan) emanating from a fault in sub-basin *a*. Note the later passive onlap at the package and the western margin.

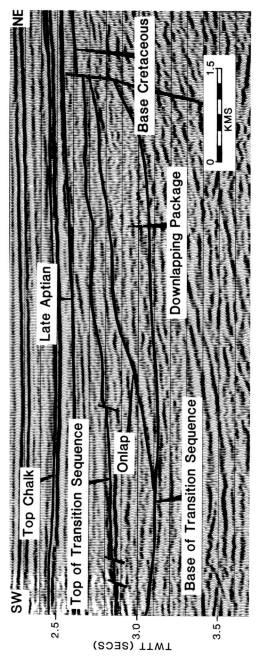

Fig. 6. Seismic section showing a downlapping package (clastic fan) from sub-basin *b*. Note the later passive onlap onto the package.

This is an asymmetrical depocentre with a large bounding fault on the western margin. The NE margin is defined by a basement high. Two discrete units are present: Unit 1, downlapping, medium–high amplitude seismic reflectors, relatively continuous prograding package coming from the eastern margin. The angle of downlap is shallow and becomes virtually horizontal towards its western end. This package is then cut by a normal fault and is subsequently onlapped by the overlying strata. Unit 2 is a discontinuous, high-amplitude package which passively infills and onlaps the remainder of the sub-basin. The northern part of the sub-basin is less complex, with low-amplitude discontinuous reflectors onlapping the margins. The basal unconformity is cut by numerous normal faults. There is abundant normal faulting associated with sub-basin c. None of the faults, except the main western bounding fault, appear to extend to any great depth. Adjacent to the NE margin of the sub-basin is a basement high which defines its limit in this area. This may be a volcanic ridge, because of the large amount of basic sills present in the section above the sub-basin. Tate & Dobson (1988) show the presence of numerous volcanic ridges within the Porcupine Basin.

Sub-basin d (Figs 3, 4, 7)

The eastern side of the MPB contains sub-basin d. This is a 14 km × 10 km (approximately) half-grabenal feature with the bounding fault on the eastern side. Proximal to the fault, the seismic reflectors are medium–high amplitude and discontinuous in nature. They gradually become very continuous and higher in amplitude away from the fault. Continuous, high amplitude reflectors overlie the discontinuous proximal reflectors in the upper part of the sequence. The entire sequence thins to the west away from the fault, as well as to the north and south. The basal unconformity is unfaulted and the upper unconformity is only affected by very minor normal faults which are antithetic to the major bounding fault. The upper unconformity is onlapped by overlying reflectors. Internally there are approximately two minor unconformities, causing truncation of reflectors. In sub-basin d the eastern margin is defined by a large, deep-seated fault which has been reactivated up to lower Miocene times. This fault also controls a Jurassic (and ?Permo-Triassic) tilted fault block below the sub-basin. The sub-basin thins to the south against a fault-controlled basement high.

Sub-basin e (Figs 3, 4, 8)

Sub-basin e (approximately 18 km × 21 km in size) is a symmetrical depocentre and broadly N–S in orientation. Its northern limit is uncertain due to a lack of good quality seismic reflection data in the area. This sub-basin is lozenge-shaped in cross section, thinning to the west against a basement high and to the east

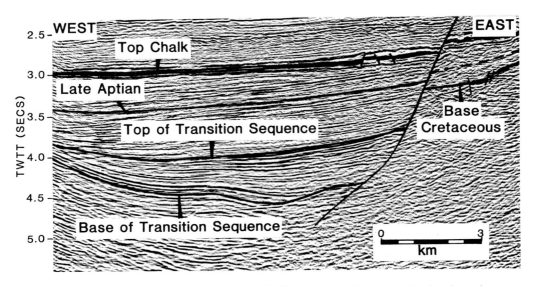

Fig. 7. East–west seismic section through sub-basin d. Discontinuous reflectors proximal to the main bounding fault and continuous reflectors distally.

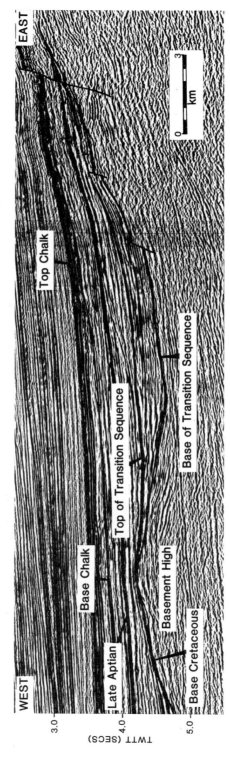

Fig. 8. East–west seismic section through sub-basin *e*. Note the high amplitude, continuous reflectors within the sub-basin.

against the shoulders of the MPB (Fig. 8). It
consists of a package of high amplitude, continuous seismic reflectors, sometimes chaotic,
with several internal unconformities. The western and eastern margins are passively onlapped
and there are thin seismic sequences along
the eastern, western and southern margins. The
succession thins towards the north but the
northern margin is not defined. In the thicker
(400 ms) central part of the sub-basin the reflectors are generally concordant but there is some
toplap and onlap. There is less internal faulting
present than in any of the other sub-basins,
although some normal faults disrupt the basal
unconformity (Fig. 8). There is also later onlap
and blanketing of the entire sub-basin by
younger sediment. Sub-basin *e* is bounded by a
major basin margin fault on its east side and a
basement high (probably fault controlled) on
the west (Fig. 8). This major fault extends deep
into the basement and has been reactivated,
with movement up to late Eocene times. Therefore, it appears that major reactivated Palaeozoic structures controlled the siting of the
sub-basin.

Discussion

Facies

The Transition Sequence is only locally preserved within the MPB as a series of isolated
sub-basins. It is suggested that each of these
were relative topographic lows, generally fault-
controlled, at the end of syn-rift times and the
intervening areas were relative topographic
highs which received very little sedimentary fill.
The early downlapping sequences emanating
from fault scarps, interpreted as clastic fan/fault
apron deposits, may reflect fault activity at the
beginning of the Transition Sequence. Alternatively the fans may represent deposits formed
by the erosion of the fault block, with no fault
activity during sedimentation. The Haq *et al.*
(1987) global sea-level curve shows a sudden
relative sea-level drop at approximately uppermost Jurassic times. Therefore, it is possible
that a Berriasian sea-level lowstand was responsible for the clastic fan deposition. Indeed, a
sea-level lowstand is seen in many basins in
the North Atlantic region at approximately
Berriasian times, for example the Lusitanian
and Cantabrian basins (Hiscott *et al.* 1990 and
their figure 6). It is difficult to resolve these
alternatives in an unequivocal manner using the
available seismic data. However, there is evidence of fault activity throughout the MPB in
late Jurassic/early Cretaceous times (Croker &

Shannon 1987). It is proposed that this faulting
was part of a basinwide uplift and erosion event
(part of the Late Cimmerian tectonic phase
sensu Ziegler 1982) which supplied the sediment
for the downlapping and prograding clastic fans
of the sub-basins. Evidence for a basinwide
uplift and erosion event comes from the lack of
Berriasian strata in all but two of the wells in
the basin, Elf 35/2−1 and Shell 34/19−1. Significantly, these are also the only wells that have
drilled through the Transition Sequence in the
sub-basins. The uplift of the topographic highs
meant that Berriasian strata was only preserved
in the Transition Sequence sub-basins. However, it was probably a combination of this
uplift and erosion event with the sea-level lowstand that facilitated clastic fan deposition.
Evidence from well data (Shell 34/19−1)
suggests that the clastic strata are alluvial fan
deposits, with the distal part deposited in a
marginal marine setting. The Shell 34/19−1
well was drilled through the proximal part of an
alluvial fan and recovered approximately 445 m
of conglomerates and breccias with intercalations of claystone, siltstone and sandstones.
The seismic character of the undrilled downlapping packages differs slightly from the drilled
package, the reflectors are medium−low amplitude (occasionally high amplitude) and generally discontinuous (Figs 5 & 6), rather than high
amplitude continuous reflectors. Despite the
fact that these features are undrilled and have a
slightly different seismic character, these downlapping packages are believed to be distal alluvial fan type deposits. This is due to their
similarity in external morphology to the drilled
downlapping package and also their close association with faults. A similar facies type but a
with different morphology (no downlapping
events are evident) is thought to be pesent in
sub-basin *d*. The medium−high amplitude discontinuous reflectors close to the main bounding
fault in sub-basin *d* (Fig. 7) are interpreted as
sand-prone fault-scree/apron type deposits,
while the more distal high amplitude continuous
reflectors are interpreted as mud-prone shallow
marine shelf deposits. These high amplitude
shallow shelf deposits also overlie the fault
scree/apron deposits. This is evidence for a
progressively rising sea level and a more marine
environment becoming established with time.
  When fault activity and alluvial fan deposition
had ceased, the passive infill of the sub-basins
began. The interbasinal areas were still topographically relatively high after the major phase
of uplift and erosion had ended. The palaeogeography envisaged at the end of the alluvial
fan depositional phase is one of a relatively flat,

topographically high interbasinal area, and six topographically low depocentres (the Transition Sequence sub-basins) with alluvial fans deposited in them.

Throughout Transition Sequence times, relative sea-levels were probably rising (Haq *et al.* 1987). It is proposed that a northerly directed transgressive episode occurred at this time. Tate *et al.* (1990) suggest that lithospheric stretching factors (during the Middle Jurassic — earliest Cretaceous rifting episode) increase progressively from north to south in the Porcupine Basin, from β 1.2 to >6. Therefore, with this deepening and widening of the basin southwards it is likely that marine conditions existed earlier in the south of the region and progressed northwards with time. This proposed transgression from the south agrees with a transgression from the southwestern quadrant at a similar time in the Fastnet and Celtic Sea Basins (Robinson *et al.* 1981; Petrie *et al.* 1989). It is thought that by the end of the clastic fan depositional phase this transgression had inundated the entire MPB. Therefore, deposition was confined to the sub-basins and these were gradually infilled by passive shallow marine shelf deposits. The Elf 35/2−1 well, drilled at the margin of sub-basin *a* through the onlapping infill succession, encountered a relatively uniform succession of claystones with occasional thin interbeds of fine calcareous sandstone and dolomitic limestone. Dipmeter data from this well shows the strata as having a shallow (6°−20°) south−southeasterly stratigraphic dip which is consistent with the onlapping nature of the sequence and the position of the well in sub-basin *a*. The section overlying the Transition Sequence is a deeper marine shelf environment. The onlapping deposits are thought to be innermost shelf while the concordant reflectors in the central part of the sub-basins are believed to be slightly deeper but are still inner shelf deposits (Fig. 6). These depositional environments are interpreted from the seismic character of the succession together with well data and the palaeogeographic setting of the sub-basins with respect to the northerly-migrating marine transgression. With time the deposits in the central part of the sub-basins became progressively deeper due to the continually rising sea level. The distal part of the alluvial fan merges with the shelf sediment. Reworking of the fan sediments by shelf processes would be expected at the boundary between the two facies but the seismic resolution is not good enough to show this. The precise depositional environment of the main fill deposits within the sub-basins is relatively difficult to ascertain. However, from well data (Shell 34/

19−1, Elf 35/2−1), seismic reflection characters, passive onlap and early Cretaceous palaeogeography it is believed, with a strong degree of certainty, that the deposits have a shallow marine shelf origin.

Little or no strata equivalent in age to that in the sub-basins are preserved in the interbasinal areas. The presence of condensed sequences, however, cannot be discounted. It is also possible that a thick sequence was deposited, and subsequently eroded, in the interbasinal areas, but there is no evidence to support this. Robeson *et al.* (1988) mentioned the possibility of Middle Jurassic- Lower Cretaceous sediment being deposited and then eroded in the NE part of the MPB, but do not provide supporting evidence. However, they also mention that vitrinite reflectance data suggests that there is a minimal amount of post-Westphalian erosion in the basin. The uppermost unconformity probably represents a time of uplift and erosion (or a widespread sea-level fall) at top Transition Sequence times. This event would have resulted in the erosion of any sediment deposited in the interbasinal areas. The thermal sag phase then began and sediment was deposited and preserved in a regular and regional fashion throughout the MPB.

Age of the Transition Sequence

The Transition Sequence is uppermost Jurassic to lowermost Cretaceous in age (Croker & Klemperer 1989). The alluvial fan deposit in Shell well 34/19−1 suggests a Tithonian age (Croker & Shannon 1987) and it is believed that this marks the beginning of the sequence. Therefore, although dating of the initiation of the Transition Sequence is rather speculative, a mid−late Tithonian age is in general agreement with the ending of the syn-rift stage (Croker & Klemperer 1989). The termination of the Transition Sequence is better constrained. Wells 35/2−1 and 34/19−1 occur within the sub-basins *a* and *b* respectively. These are also the only wells in the MPB which contain Berriasian strata, and the uppermost unconformity is coincident with (probable) late Berriasian strata in these wells. This suggests that deposition of the Transition Sequence had terminated by end-Berriasian times. All other wells within the MPB contain only Valanginian or younger deposits overlying Upper Jurassic strata.

From this time onwards a change in tectonic and sedimentary style occurred and syn-rift tectonism gave way to thermal subsidence (Croker & Klemperer 1989). The Transition Sequence sub-basins are passively onlapped and blanketed by Valanginian and younger sediment. Therefore, the regional post-rift subsidence is believed to have begun in early Valanginian times. However, very few wells have been drilled in the MPB (23 to date) and more well information is required in order to date the Transition Sequence more accurately.

As mentioned above, the small amount of internal faulting and the lack of fault-controlled downlapping clastic fans within sub-basin *e* may mean that it evolved later than the other sub-basins. The high amplitude continuous events in sub-basin *e* have a similar seismic character to the late stage passive infill succession present in the sub-basins further north. This suggests that the sequence in sub-basin *e* has a similar age to the main fill deposits of the more northern sub-basins. This correlation is further evidence for sub-basin *e* evolving later than the others and suggests a southerly younging direction within the Transition Sequence. The northerly directed marine transgression would have infilled sub-basin *e* and then later infilled the remaining sub-basins and onlapped the clastic fans within them. It is also possible that there was a variable strain regime within the MPB (P. M. Shannon, pers. comm). This would have resulted in differential stresses throughout the basin and, therefore, confine faulting to certain areas at certain times. The sub-basins could have formed within this regime.

Coincidence with older structures

The location of the Transition Sequence sub-basins appears to be coincidental with small Permo-Triassic basins that have been postulated by Shannon (1991). The poor data quality at deeper levels hinders the precise delineation of the Permo-Triassic basins. All of the sub-basins show elements of fault-control in their formation. The close relationship, demonstrated earlier between deep-seated reactivated faults, basement highs (generally fault-controlled) and the sub-basins suggests that there is an older deep-seated structural control on the location of the Transition Sequence sub-basins. Shannon (1991) proposes the development of relatively small, localized NE–SW intracontinental transtensional basins during the Permo-Triassic in the Porcupine Basin, whose location was determined by reactivated basement lineaments. The probable coincidence of the Transition Sequence sub-basins with these Permo-Triassic basins, both of which appear to be controlled by similar reactivated basement lineaments, suggests a possible explanation as to why the Transition Sequence sub-basins are located in localized areas throughout the MPB.

Correlation with other North Atlantic Rift Basins

The presence of a Transition Sequence between syn-rift and post-rift stages is not unique to the MPB. Possible comparable sequences are present in other North Atlantic rift basins, especially on the western side of the ocean.

The sedimentary basins within the North Atlantic region (Fig. 9) have broadly similar stratigraphic histories, due to the fact that they evolved in a similar plate tectonic regime (Hiscott *et al.* 1990). The MPB differs in the timing of the ending of rifting from most of the other basins. The last rifting event in the Porcupine ended in Tithonian times (Shannon 1991) whereas in other basins, such as, the Jeanne d'Arc (Tankard & Welsink 1987), Celtic Sea (Shannon 1991) and Lusitanian (Wilson *et al.* 1989), rifting ended in Aptian times. Hubbard (1988) states that rifting in some of the Grand Banks basins ended during the Cenomanian. Therefore, the boundary between syn- and post-rift events is older in the MPB than in the other basins. This also means that any Transition Sequence type successions will also be older in the MPB (Fig. 10). The offset in the timing of these events, along with other sequence boundaries (Moore & Shannon 1990), shows that the major control in the evolution of each basin is local tectonics rather than global effects.

Comparable successions to the Transition Sequence of the MPB have been recognized in some rift basins offshore eastern Canada and Newfoundland on the western side of the North Atlantic ocean (Fig. 10). Keen *et al.* (1987) recognized a 'transitional unit, perhaps representing a transition from the rift to the postrift era of mid–late Cretaceous age' on their LITHOPROBE EAST deep seismic reflection study in the Orphan Basin (Fig. 9 and their figures 3, 5, 6 & 8). The unit consists of a number of unconformities and is characterized by strong continuous reflectors. The transition unit is separated by basement highs over which the succession is absent. This is similar to the situation in the MPB described in the present paper. The seismic coverage does not appear to be sufficient to allow Keen *et al.* (1987) to fully map the extent of the transition unit. Tankard & Welsink (1987) also recognized a transition unit of Aptian–Albian age between rift and post-rift stages of basin development in the

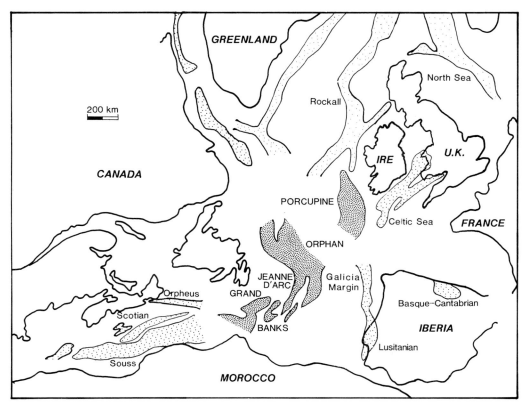

Fig. 9. Predrift (early Cretaceous) rift basins of the North Atlantic margins. Figure redrawn from Tankard & Balkwill (1989).

Jeanne d'Arc Basin (Fig. 9 and their figure 3). The sequence appears similar to that of the MPB and the 'transition from the post-rift era occurred over several million years and involved several unconformities'.

Hubbard (1988) describes the sequence stratigraphic evolution of basins in the Grand Banks area offshore Newfoundland (Fig. 9). In this area the termination of the early Cretaceous rifting event is marked by a mid-Cenomanian topographically irregular megasequence boundary (94 Ma). This marks the beginning of an 'early stage passive wedge' sequence which occurs in the early part of the post-rift stage. This is a transgressive, onlapping sequence which appears to infill the area between remnant syn-rift highs (see figure 6 in Hubbard 1988). The sequence has abundant high amplitude continuous seismic reflectors, internal unconformities and onlap onto syn-rift highs. The earliest middle Eocene megasequence boundary (52 Ma), which appears from the published data

to be relatively flat, marks the end of the early stage passive wedge succession. The presence of an irregular basal boundary and a more flat-lying upper boundary together with its seismic character and the presence of many internal unconformities makes the early stage passive wedge succession broadly similar to the Transition Sequence in sub-basin *e* of the MPB (Fig. 8). The duration of the succession in the Grand Banks (approximately 42 Ma) is longer than that of the Transition Sequence in the MPB (approximately 8 Ma). The Grand Banks passive wedge appears to be present throughout the basin and not confined to sub-basins as the Transition Sequence is in the MPB. However, the physical similarities between the two sequences may mean that they both represent the transition from syn-rift to post-rift albeit in slightly different ways and over different time durations.

In Hiscott *et al.* (1990) there may be evidence for a transition from syn-rift to post-rift being

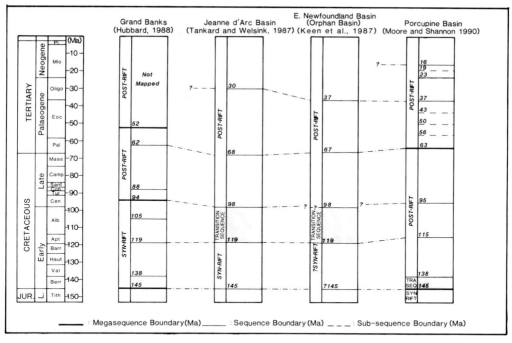

Fig. 10. Correlation of megasequence and sequence boundaries between the Porcupine Basin and basins on the western side of the North Atlantic ocean.

present in some of the other Mesozoic rift basins of the North Atlantic region. They state that there is a composite unconformity present during Aptian times (end syn-rift) in the Jeanne d'Arc and Cantabrian basins (Fig. 9). In addition, when studying rates of apparent basement subsidence their results suggest that a 'time lag may occur between the formation of the first oceanic crust and the change from differential fault-driven subsidence to broad regional subsidence due to thermal effects'. They state that such a 'transitional phase' is well displayed in the Cantabrian basin and the Parentis sub-basin of the Aquitaine basin (in France). Therefore, these sequences (the composite unconformity sequence and the 'transitional phase') may represent a type of syn-rift to post-rift transition sequence.

The possible presence of transition sequences in many of the rift basins in the North Atlantic region means that there is potential for correlation over a wide area. These sequences appear to be tectonically controlled and, therefore, the similarities in the tectonic evolution of each basin, within the regional context of the North

Atlantic plate tectonic regime, is the probable underlying control of this correlatability.

Petroleum potential

The Porcupine Basin has been the focus of intermittent petroleum exploration with the first well drilled in 1977. To date 25 wells (23 in the MPB and 2 in the North Porcupine Basin) have been drilled by a variety of companies. Four of these wells flowed quantities of hydrocarbons while most of the others reported oil and/or gas shows. A more complete study of the overall petroleum potential of the basin is given by Croker & Shannon (1987). The recognition of a Transition Sequence provides another potential hydrocarbon target in the basin. The main hydrocarbon potential within the Transition Sequence is the emanation of clastic fans from fault scarps. These fans are up to 400 m thick and may represent significant targets. Good quality reservoir rocks can be expected in the proximal-mid and mid-fan regions where sandstones should be present, as well as in the fan tops which have been reworked by shelf processes. The proximal area of the fan contains poor reservoir quality unsorted conglomerates (from Shell well 34/19−1) while the distal part should contain fine siltstone and shale. Source rocks occur adjacent to the fans and are mature for oil and gas (Croker & Shannon 1987).

The overall trap is a combination of structural and stratigraphic features, the main bounding fault acts as a seal on one side and there is stratigraphic pinchout of the fan into the distal fan area and the onlapping lower Cretaceous shales on the other sides. The hostile environmental conditions and the very deep waters (150−1000 m in the areas of the Transition Sequence) continue to make exploration very expensive. However, the Transition Sequence play along with all other play types within the basin are likely to offer reasonable exploration potential.

Conclusions

1. A Transition Sequence of latest Jurassic to earliest Cretaceous age is present between the end of the syn-rift and the beginning of the post-rift stages in the development of the Main Porcupine Basin. The sequence is identified in five areas (sub-basins) throughout the basin. All of these show elements of fault control.

2. The main facies within the sub-basins are likely to be prograding clastic fans emanating from fault scarps, together with onlapping marine shelf deposits.

3. The presence of a Transition Sequence is due to the cessation of crustal extension (end of the syn-rift stage) which left five distinct, fault-bounded topographic lows (sub-basins) throughout the MPB. During the Berriasian these sub-basins acted as sediment depocentres for alluvial fan and shallow marine shelf sedimentation. With infilling of the sub-basins and cessation of the associated faulting, quiescent thermal sag phase sedimentation occurred over the entire MPB rather than being confined to isolated sub-basins.

4. There is an apparent coincidence in location between the Transition Sequence sub-basins and localized Permo-Triassic basins. This suggests that a deep-seated structural feature may have controlled the siting of the depocentres.

5. Similar Transition Sequences are seen in the Jeanne d'Arc and Orphan Basins offshore Eastern Canada and Newfoundland, and possibly in other North Atlantic rift basins also.

The seismic sections reproduced in figures 5, 7 & 8 of this paper are part of a non-exclusive proprietary survey provided by GECO Exploration Services, a division of GECO Geophysical Company Limited. Permission to use this data is gratefully acknowledged. I am also very grateful to the Petroleum Affairs Division of the Irish Department of Energy for supplying the seismic section used in Fig. 6. I sincerely thank Dr Pat Shannon for critically reading an early draft of the manuscript and for improvements in the final draft. John Kennedy is sincerely thanked for the photography. This work is part of PhD research funded by a Research Demonstratorship at University College Dublin. The comments of two anonymous referees are also gratefully acknowledged.

References

BROWN, L. F. & FISHER, W. L. 1982. *Seismic Stratigraphic Interpretation and Petroleum Exploration*. American Association of Petroleum Geologists, Continuing Education Course Note Series 16.

COWARD, M. P. & TRUDGILL, B. D. 1989. Basin development and basin structure, West of Britain. *Bulletin of the Geological Society, France*, **8**, 483−496.

CROKER, P. F. & KLEMPERER, S. L. 1989. Structure and stratigraphy of the Porcupine Basin: Relationships to Deep Crustal Structure and the Opening of the North Atlantic Ocean. *In*: TANKARD, A. J. & BALKWILL, H. R. (eds) *Extensional Tectonics and Stratigraphy of the North Atlantic Margins*. American Association of Petroleum Geologists, Memoir **46**, 445−459.

—— & SHANNON, P. M. 1987. The evolution and hydrocarbon prospectivity of the Porcupine Basin, offshore Ireland. *In*: BROOKS, J. & GLENNIE, K. W. (eds) *Petroleum Geology of North West Europe*. Graham & Trotman, London, 633−642.

HAQ, B. U., HARDENBOL, J. & VAIL, P. R. 1987. Chronology of fluctuating sea-levels since the Triassic. *Science*, **235**, 1156−1167.

HISCOTT, R. N., WILSON, R. C. L., GRADSTEIN, F. M., PUJALTE, V., GARCIA-MONDEJAR, J., BOUDREAU, R. R. & WISHART, H. A. 1990. Comparative stratigraphy and subsidence history of Mesozoic rift basins of the North Atlantic. *AAPG Bulletin*, **74**, 60−76.

HUBBARD, R. J. 1988. Age and significance of sequence boundaries on Jurassic and early Cretaceous rifted continental margins. *AAPG Bulletin*, **72**, 49−72.

——, PAPE, J. & ROBERTS, D. G. 1985. Depositional sequence mapping to illustrate the evolution of a passive continental margin. *In*: BERG, O. R. & WOOLVERTON, D. (eds) *Seismic Stratigraphy II: an integrated approach to hydrocarbon exploration*. American Association of Petroleum Geologists, Memoir **39**, 93−115.

KEEN, C. E., STOCKMAL, G. S., WELSINK, H., QUINLAN, G. & MUDFORD, B. 1987. Deep crustal structure and evolution of the rifted margin northeast of Newfoundland: results from LITHOPROBE East. *Canadian Journal of Earth Sciences*. **24**, 1537−1549.

McKenzie, D. P. 1978. Some remarks on the development of sedimentary basins. *Earth and Planetary Science Letters*, **65**, 182–202.

Mitchum, R. M. 1977. Seismic stratigraphy and global changes in sea-level, part 11: Glossary of terms used in seismic stratigraphy. *In*: Payton, C. E. (ed.) *Seismic Stratigraphy: Applications to hydrocarbon exploration*. American Association of Petroleum Geologists, Memoir, **26**, 205–212.

—— & Vail, P. R. 1977. Seismic stratigraphy and global changes in sea-level, part 7: Seismic stratigraphic Interpretation Procedure. *In*: Payton, C. E. (ed.) *Seismic Stratigraphy: Applications to hydrocarbon exploration*. American Association of Petroleum Geologists, Memoir **26**, 135–143.

Moore, J. G. & Shannon, P. M. 1990. Cretaceous and Tertiary Seismic Stratigraphy of the Porcupine Basin, offshore Ireland. *In*: *Abstracts of the 13th International Sedimentological Congress*.

Naylor, D. & Anstey, N. A. 1987. A reflection seismic study of the Porcupine Basin, offshore Ireland. *Irish Journal of Earth Sciences*, **8**, 187–210.

—— & Shannon, P. M. 1982. *The Geology of Offshore Ireland and West Britain*. Graham & Trotman, London.

Petrie, S. H., Brown, J. R., Granger, P. J. & Lovell, J. P. B. 1989. Mesozoic History of the Celtic Sea Basins. *In*: Tankard, A. J. & Balkwill, H. R. (eds) *Extensional Tectonics and Stratigraphy of the North Atlantic Margins*. American Association of Petroleum Geologists, Memoir, **46**, 433–444.

Robeson, D., Burnett, R. D. & Clayton, G. 1988. The upper Palaeozoic Geology of the Porcupine, Erris and Donegal Basins, offshore Ireland. *Irish Journal of Earth Sciences*, **9**, 153–175.

Robinson, K. W., Shannon, P. M. & Young, D. G. G. 1981. The Fastnet basin: an integrated analysis. *In*: Illing, L. V. & Hobson, G. D. (eds) *Petroleum Geology of the Continental Shelf of Northwest Europe*: London, Heyden, 444–454.

Shannon, P. M. 1991. The development of Irish offshore sedimentary basins. *Journal of the Geological Society, London*, **148**, 181–189.

Tankard, A. J. & Balkwill, H. R. 1989. Extensional Tectonics and Stratigraphy of the North Atlantic Margins: Introduction. *In*: Tankard, A. J. & Balkwill, H. R. (eds) *Extensional Tectonics and Stratigraphy of the North Atlantic Margins*. American Association of Petroleum Geologists, Memoir, **46**, 1–6.

—— & Welsink, H. J. 1987. Extensional Tectonics and Stratigraphy of Hibernia Oil Field, Grand Banks, Newfoundland. *AAPG Bulletin*, **71**, 1210–1232.

Tate, M. P., White, N. & Conroy, J. J. 1990. Application of the Lithospheric Stretching Model to the Porcupine Seabight Basin, offshore Western Ireland. *In*: *Post-Devonian Basin Development, North Western Seaboard of the British Isles (Abstracts)*.

—— & Dobson, M. R. 1988. Syn- and post-rift igneous activity in the Porcupine Seabight Basin and adjacent continental margin West of Ireland. *In*: Morton, C. E. & Parson, L. M. (eds) *Early Tertiary Volcanism and the Opening of the NE Atlantic*. Geological Society, London, Special Publication, **39**, 309–334.

Vail, P. R. & Mitchum, R. M. 1977. Seismic stratigraphy and global changes in sea-level, part 1: Overview. *In*: Payton, C. E. (ed.) *Seismic Stratigraphy: applications to hydrocarbon exploration*. American Association of Petroleum Geologists, Memoir, **26**, 51–52.

——, Mitchum, R. M. & Thompson, S. 1977. Seismic stratigraphy and global changes in sea-level, part 4: global cycles of relative changes of sea-level. *In*: Payton, C. E. (ed.) *Seismic Stratigraphy: applications to hydrocarbon exploration*. American Association of Petroleum Geologists, Memoir, **26**, 83–97.

Wilson, R. C. L., Hiscott, R. N., Willis, M. G. & Gradstein, F. M. 1989. The Lusitanian Basin of West-Central Portugal: Mesozoic and Tertiary Tectonic, Stratigraphic and Subsidence History. *In*: Tankard, A. J. & Balkwill, H. (eds) *Extensional Tectonics and Stratigraphy of the North Atlantic Margins*. American Association of Petroleum Geologists, Memoir, **46**, 341–361.

Ziegler, P. A. 1982. *Geological Atlas of Western and Central Europe*. Shell International Petroleum Maatschappij B.V.

Early Tertiary submarine fan deposits in the Porcupine Basin, offshore Ireland

PATRICK M. SHANNON

Department of Geology, University College, Belfield, Dublin 4, Ireland

Abstract: The Porcupine Basin, offshore western Ireland, contains up to 10 km of Mesozoic and Cenozoic sediments. Seismic sequence analysis of the Palaeocene–Eocene strata on the southwestern and southeastern margins of the basin reveals a mounded and draped geometry. Four seismic sequences are defined and are coeval with a series of deltaic deposits in the northern and central parts of the basin. In the southwestern area these are interpreted as stacked submarine fan deposits. In the southeastern area the lower two sequences are interpreted as shelf-slope deposits which are overlain by two submarine fan complexes. Funnelling of the sediment was controlled by erosive channelling through interfan topographic lows. The seismic response indicates that the fans are dominated by lower fan sheet sand deposits with minor amounts of upper fan channellized sandstones. They probably developed in response to an interplay of eustatic sea level changes, tectonic uplift on the basin margins, and thermal subsidence towards the basin centre.

The Porcupine Basin, lying off the west coast of Ireland (Fig. 1), contains up to approximately 10 km of post-Palaeozoic sediments. The basin developed largely in response to the extensional stresses of the evolving North Atlantic Ocean. The sediments were deposited in a range of tectonic settings. Late Palaeozoic to Jurassic sedimentation took place in a syn-rift setting and the Cretaceous and Tertiary sediments formed during a phase of post-rift thermal subsidence. The general geology and the development of the region has been described and discussed in a number of publications including Naylor & Shannon (1982), Croker & Shannon (1987), MacDonald *et al.* (1987), Naylor & Anstey (1987), Croker & Klemperer (1989) and Shannon (1991*a*). The generalized stratigraphy of the basin is shown in Fig. 2. This is based largely on the results of most of the 25 wells which have been drilled in the basin (Fig. 1). One well has been drilled in the southwestern area of the basin but no geological information from it has been released to date.

The data presented come from a 3×7 km seismic grid shot as part of a large regional speculative survey in 1981 by Merlin Geophysical (now GECO Geophysical Company Ltd). These data are typically of high quality and reveal a wealth of seismic stratigraphic information, particularly in the post-Jurassic section. Various aspects of the seismic stratigraphy of the Porcupine Basin have been described (Naylor & Anstey 1987; Macurda & Nelson 1988; Croker & Klemperer 1990; Moore & Shannon 1991).

Seismic mapping allows the definition of a series of seismic sequences. Three important seismic reflectors are the Base Cretaceous, Top Chalk and Base Oligocene. These have been tied to well control in the northern part of basin and can be mapped with confidence throughout most of the basin.

The Base Cretaceous reflector is mapped on the basin margins as an unconformity between dipping syn-rift Jurassic strata and onlapping post-rift Lower Cretaceous sediments. It varies in amplitude throughout the basin, reflecting lithologically controlled impedence contrasts across the unconformity. This reflector is difficult to map in the basin centre, largely due to its depth beneath up to 6 km of post-Jurassic sediment.

The Top Chalk reflector is the most pronounced reflector in the basin and occurs as an event of high amplitude and high continuity (Sangree & Widmier 1977). It marks a change from carbonate to clastic deposition. In parts of the basin it coincides with the top of the Cretaceous while in other areas it lies within the Danian of earliest Tertiary age (Croker & Shannon 1987; MacDonald *et al.* 1987; Naylor & Anstey 1987) The Top Chalk forms a strong event with high amplitude and continuity, which can be mapped as a marker horizon with a high degree of confidence throughout the basin. It is clearly seen in the southwestern region. In places, it is cut by a series of Tertiary basic sills (Seeman 1984; Tate & Dobson 1988). These occur as high to very high amplitude events, making identification of the Top Chalk event

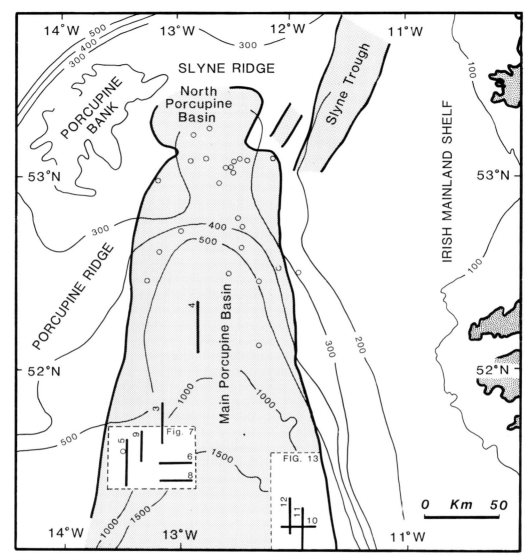

Fig. 1. Location of the Porcupine Basin, with areas of thick Mesozoic and Tertiary sediments stippled. Exploratory wells are shown by open circles. The location of seismic lines illustrated by Figs 3–6 and 8–12 is indicated (numbers refer to the figure numbers). The locations of Figs 7 and 13 are indicated on the southwestern and southeastern margins respectively. Water depth contours are in metres.

somewhat difficult. However, close examination shows that the sills sometimes transect the bedding reflectors (Fig. 3). The Top Chalk has a catenary shape across the basin, onlapping beyond the edge of the pre-Cretaceous graben-fill basin and resting upon shallow basement.

The Base Oligocene reflector is a high amplitude continuous reflector. It lies at the base of a sequence of generally shale-prone deep marine

sediments, which occur on seismic sections as continuous reflectors unconformably overlying the Eocene sandstone-prone sediments.

A series of mounded structures occur towards the southwestern and southeastern basin margins (Fig. 1). At the present day they lie in approximately 800–1800 m of water. They are coeval with a set of seismic features in the northern and central parts of the basin inter-

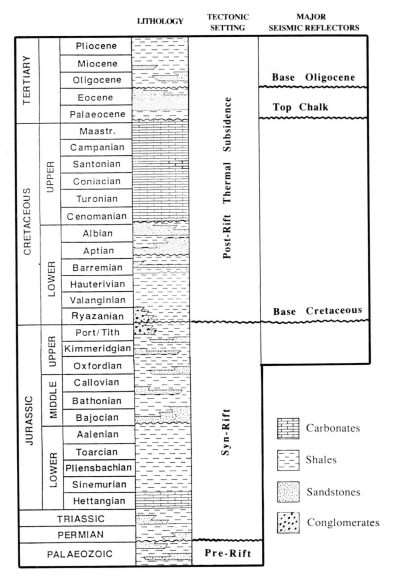

Fig. 2. Generalized stratigraphy of the Porcupine Basin. The general tectonic setting of the basin and the position of the major seismic reflectors are indicated.

preted as deltaic (Fig. 4), but their external geometry and internal reflector configuration differ from that of the deltaic sequence.

Mounded structures, seen on seismic sections as a convex-upward external configuration, may originate in a variety of ways. They may occur as a result of internal mounding, in which case there will typically be evidence of internal convex-upward structures, bidirectional down-lap and primary depositional thinning towards the edges of the mound. These are classed as Type-1 mounds. By Mitchum's (1985) criteria, this type of mound typically represents submarine fan deposits. Mounds may also occur by differential compaction of sandstones isolated within mudstones (Type-2 mounds). Where such a sequence has been deposited in a channel or topographic low, compaction of originally

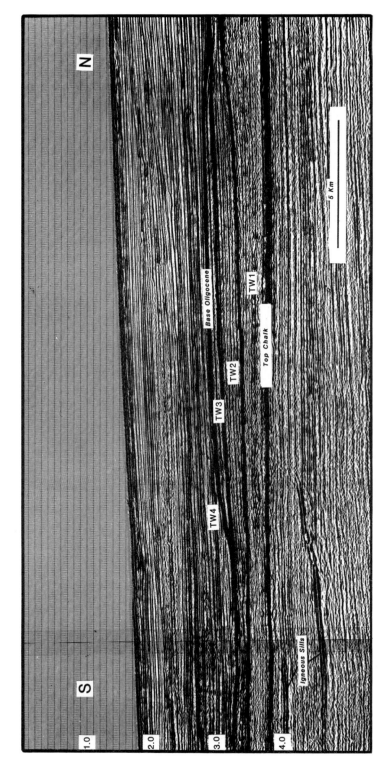

Fig. 3. North–south seismic section showing sequences TW1–4 in the southwestern region. This profile (see location on Fig. 1) shows mounding in sequences TW2 and TW3. Sequence TW4 onlaps onto the mound adjacent to a large canyon towards the south of the section. Igneous sills are seen below the Top Chalk in the south of the profile and display typical high-amplitude seismic character. The upper sill is parallel to bedding while the lower sill transects the stratigraphy towards the north. The vertical scale is in seconds (TWT).

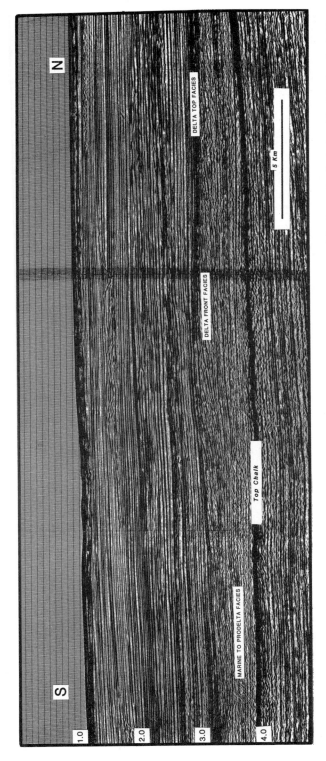

Fig. 4. Seismic section showing the deltaic facies which typify the Palaeocene and Eocene of the northern part of the Porcupine Basin (see Fig. 1 for location). The vertical scale is two-way-travel time (TWT) in seconds.

flat-lying reflectors onlapping the channel margin, and differential compaction between the sandstones and mudstones may result in apparent downlapping reflectors. However, the different lithologies are likely to produce different seismic responses (continuous low amplitude reflectors in the mudstones, discontinuous high amplitude reflectors in the sandstones), thereby allowing their identification. Such mounds are post-depositional (diagenetic) structures and on geometry alone are not diagnostic of any unique depositional setting. Thirdly, mounding may be created by erosion, in which case the convex-upward geometry will be an entirely external feature (Type-3 mounds). This type of mounding is typically created by unconformity-related erosion, but can also be created by erosive canyon-forming currents in the context of submarine fan development. Mounds of all three types occur in the areas described in the present paper. Many of them are composite mounds, with erosion modifying depositional mounds. In such instances identification of the depositional mounding is regarded as diagnostic of the submarine fan origin of the relevant sequences.

Description of seismic facies

Four seismic sequences are defined in both the southwestern and southeastern areas. Those in the southwestern area are labelled TW1 to TW4, while those in the southeastern area are TE1 to TE4. The sequences are coeval, but in some instances differences occur in external geometry between the areas and even within the areas. The part of the basin lying north of 52°N is referred to as the northern and central area and here the Palaeocene–Eocene is dominated by a series of southward-prograding sediments interpreted as deltaic (Croker & Shannon 1987; Shannon 1991b). Topset reflectors are clearly preserved and change basinwards to foreset reflectors with a high-amplitude discontinuous character. These, in turn, give way southwards to low amplitude continuous and relatively flat-lying reflectors (Fig. 4). The deltaic facies are mapped from the northern part of the basin southwards for approximately 120 km. The mounded deposits which are described in the present paper are coeval with these deltaic deposits.

Southwestern area

The oldest Tertiary sequence (TW1) in the southwestern part of the basin onlaps and downlaps the Top Chalk. It is typified by relatively low amplitude events with moderate to high continuity. The amplitude of the reflectors decreases away from the basin edge. Sequence TW1 pinches out by onlap onto the Top Chalk in a landward (westward) direction and by downlap onto the Top Chalk in a basinward (eastward) direction. North–south profiles (Fig. 5) show a number of mounded forms within the sequence. A series of variable amplitude downlapping reflectors are clearly visible within these Type-1 mounds. At least two phases of stacked mound development are seen, with the later mounds onlapping the smaller earlier knolls (Fig. 5). The mounds are approximately 5 km in width. They extend from the basin edge eastwards to the thickest part of the sequence, but are absent on lines in the eastern part of this region. The mounds are elongate and have an approximate east–west orientation.

Sequence TW1 shows some examples of low angle eastward-prograding reflectors towards its distal (eastern) end (Fig. 6). The sequence has an elongate isochrone pattern, thickening eastwards from less than 100 ms to a maximum in excess of 400 ms and then thinning eastwards to zero (Fig. 7). The overall package thickens in a northward direction away from the mounded region. The isochrone map (Fig. 7) illustrates the rapid thickness variations associated with the mounds towards the basin edge, in contrast to the relatively smooth thickness changes seen further basinwards.

Sequence TW2 consists of a package of typically high amplitude reflectors with good continuity. The boundary with Sequence TW1 is taken as the basal reflector of a package of high amplitude seismic events. This boundary is frequently apparently conformable (Fig. 4), although an erosive base to Sequence TW2 is sometimes seen which truncates the reflectors towards the top of TW1, onlapping and infilling the resultant topography (Fig. 6).

Mounding is spectacularly developed within the sequence (Fig. 5). The mounds, which are elongate in approximate east–west direction, become greater in lateral extent in an easterly direction. They vary in size from 6 km to approximately 25 km. Smaller mounds coalesce in a basinward (eastward) direction to form larger but somewhat flatter structures. The east–west elongate geometry is shown on the isochrone map (Fig. 7). In the western part of the area the internal reflectors of sequence TW2 onlap, drape and infill the underlying intermound topographic lows before taking on a mounded and downlapping aspect during their later development (Fig. 5). The lower infilling strata consist of continuous and fairly low amplitude reflectors, while the mounded

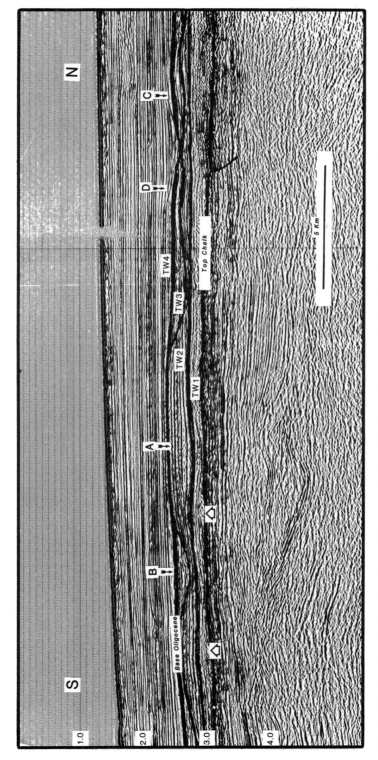

Fig. 5. Seismic section showing dramatic mounding at various levels in the southwestern region (see Fig. 1 for location). Mounding in Sequence TW1, with downlap towards the mound edges, is indicated by the large arrows. Further north the smaller TW2 mounds downlap onto the top of Sequence TW1. At A, the large mound in Sequence TW2 shows a progressive development from an early drape and infill form to a later mounded aspect. At B, Sequence TW3 consists of relatively flat-lying reflectors which onlap onto the TW2 mound and which are interpreted as canyon fill deposits. At C, Sequence TW3 is mounded and rests upon a small earlier mound. Channelling within Sequence TW4 is shown at D. The vertical scale is in seconds (TWT).

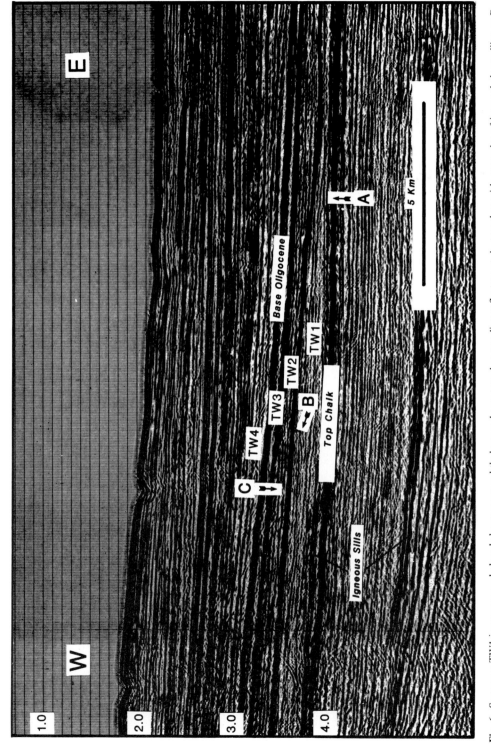

Fig. 6. Sequence TW1 is non-mounded and shows some subtle low-angle eastward prograding reflectors at A, together with examples of internal channelling at B. Sequence TW2 shows low-angle downlap onto TW1 at C, and onlap onto the TW1 topography in the eastern part of the seismic section. Igneous sills, discontinuous in nature and characterized by high-amplitude reflectors, occur at a number of levels.

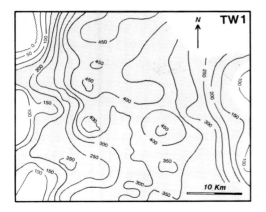

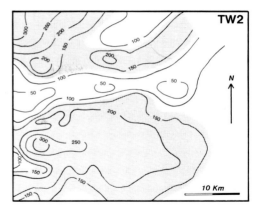

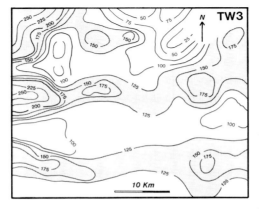

Fig. 7. Isochrone map of sequences TW1, TW2 and TW3 (see Fig. 1 for location). All sequences display substantial thickness variations in the western part of the region, reflecting the canyon and mound deposits. The areas of major mounded deposition are stippled. TW1 shows a broad band of sediments, 300–400 ms thick, running north–south through the region, with local east–west depocentres. The sequence is interpreted as a large amalgamated depositional lobe. TW2 shows two major elongate bands of thick sediment which are interpreted as depositional lobes. TW3 shows a markedly linear pattern of depocentres which is interpreted as erosion-modified elongate depositional lobes. Contours are in milliseconds two-way-travel time.

upper parts of the lobes typically consist of higher amplitude events. Evidence from progradational directions suggests a fanning of the overall mounded complex, with a general east–west progradation but with a northerly component in the north, and a southerly component in the south of the region.

Although the internal configuration of the sequence is dominated by relatively continuous high-amplitude reflectors, a number of instances of hummocky and discontinuous reflectors occur. These are interpreted as internal channel and infill structures. In addition, amplitude variations occur both within individual mounds and also from west to east across the area. In general, the reflector amplitude decreases in an eastward direction, while the continuity remains high (Fig. 8). While the mound edges were undoubtedly modified by erosion, the mounds are not simply due to channel erosion of a 'layer-cake' sequence (Type-3 mounds). Thinning of the sequence from the centre to the edges of the mounds (continuous reflectors converge towards the mound edges), the bidirectional downlap, and the internally domed geometry of the mounds (Figs 5 & 9) indicate a depositional component (Type-1 mounding) to the structures.

Sequence TW3 is characterized by lower amplitude reflectors than Sequence TW2. Its

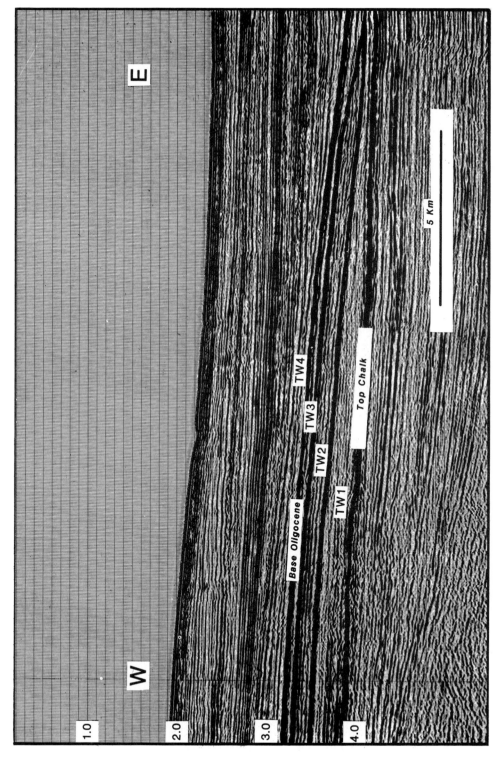

Fig. 8. Eastward thinning of TW1 which is conformably overlain by Sequence TW2. The amplitude of the reflectors within this sequence decrease from west to east. Erosion of the eastward end of TW2 results in onlap of TW3 at the east but a conformably contact further west.

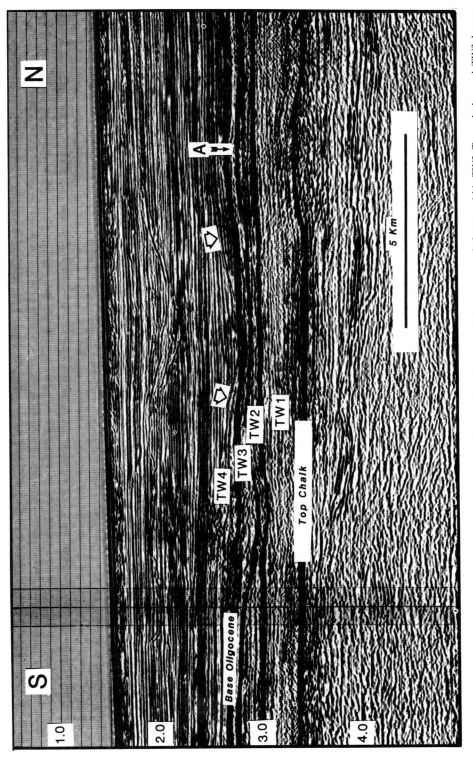

Fig. 9. Sequence TW1 is non-mounded and the seismic profile marks the transition from mounded to non-mounded strata within TW2. Towards the south TW3 drapes the edge of a large TW2 mound and infills the adjacent post-TW2 channel. Towards the north Sequence TW3 begins to take on a mounded form, downlapping onto the underlying sequence. Mounding and channelling within the lower part of Sequence TW4 are indicated by the arrows. Bidirectional downlap in sequences TW2 and TW3 are shown beneath A.

contact with the underlying sequence is variable. Towards the centre of the basin the contact is frequently apparently conformable (Fig. 6). However, local instances are seen where TW3 onlaps the eroded distal edge of TW2 (Fig. 8). In the southwestern part of the area TW3 onlaps the underlying sequence, infilling the erosion-modified intermound areas as a series of flat-lying reflectors (Fig. 5). This infill is typically variable in amplitude and has relatively discontinuous reflectors. However, further north along strike the sequence takes on a primary mounded form (Type-1 mounds) with bidirectional downlap onto the underlying TW2 topography (Figs 5 & 9). The mounding tends to occur preferentially in the palaeotopographic lows between the mounds of Sequence TW2. In general, the location of the main locus of mounding in this sequence appears to have shifted northwards from that of the underlying sequence. In the more basinward part of the area the sequence often shows a continuation of mounding onto the underlying TW2 mounds, downlapping onto these mounds towards the edges (Fig. 3). The reflectors within this sequence have a relatively discontinuous high-amplitude signature in the west of the area, with the continuity increasing in a northerly direction. Some hummocky, discontinuous and clinoform reflectors occur locally and indicate the presence of channellized deposits (Fig. 9).

The top of Sequence TW3 is marked by the Base Oligocene uncomformity, which shows a typically high amplitude, continuous and undulatory profile. This occasionally bevels the tops of the underlying depositional (Type-1) mounds (Fig. 5) and also erodes and further accentuates the topography on the intermound regions. This results in composite mound type (Type-1 modified by Type-3). A number of obvious channellized features occur at this horizon, with one prominent channel extending in an approximate east—west direction for 35 km.

Sequence TW3 is typically thinner than the underlying sequences, ranging up to 350 ms. The isochrone map (Fig. 7) illustrates the east—west elongate nature of this sequence, generally thinning in an eastward direction.

Sequence TW4 overlies the Base Oligocene unconformity. In places it onlaps Sequence TW3, infilling the erosion-modified lows and producing a flat palaeotopography (Fig. 4). However, in some areas mounding occurs in the lower part of the sequence. These mounds tend to be either Type-3 erosion-related features (Fig. 5) or, in instances where reflectors appear to downlap onto the unconformity surface

(Fig. 9), Type-2 differential compaction structures. A number of infilled channel features also occur within the lower part of TW4, truncating the underlying strata and infilled by generally flat-lying continuous reflectors (Figs 5 & 9). The internal reflector configuration within this sequence is typically of continuous and moderate to occasionally high-amplitude reflectors. The highest amplitude occurs in the mounded regions. Apart from the occasional examples of channelling and mounding (Figs 5 & 9) this sequence is dominated by reflectors which onlap the residual mounds and lows, burying the topography and creating a generally flat package of continuous reflectors.

Southeastern Area

The four seismic sequences (TE1–4) are comparable in age with those of the southwestern region. Although some similarities in internal reflector configuration are seen, there are also marked differences in terms of mound age, geometry and style.

The base of Sequence TE1 is marked by the prominent Top Chalk reflector. This dips gradually westwards into the basin and extends eastwards beyond the limit of the Jurassic fault-bounded basin. Sequence TE1 is a relatively transparent seismic package of low amplitude reflectors (Fig. 10). Its internal character resembles Sequence TW1 except that no mounds are seen. Consequently it does not display the thickness variations of TW1 (cf. Figs 6, 7) and is typically of the order of 200–300 ms thick. It is generally horizontally stratified but some low-angle westerly dipping progradational downlapping reflectors are seen, especially in the eastern part of the region (Fig. 10). Therefore, while Sequence TE1 can be correlated seismically across the basin with confidence to Sequence TW1, the external geometry differs between the areas.

Sequence TE2 rests with a slight unconformity on TE1 and locally shows a rather subtle low angle downlap onto the top of Sequence TE1 (Figs 11 & 12). It is typified by relatively continuous moderate-to-high amplitude events and in this respect it is similar to Sequence TW2. In common with the underlying sequence Sequence TE2 has a generally constant thickness, being in the range 200–300 ms. Some low-relief Type-1 mounds are developed, but these are restricted to the northeastern and eastern part of the region. Some minor internal channel structures accompany the mounding.

The base of Sequence TE3, like the underlying sequence, is slightly unconformable. In

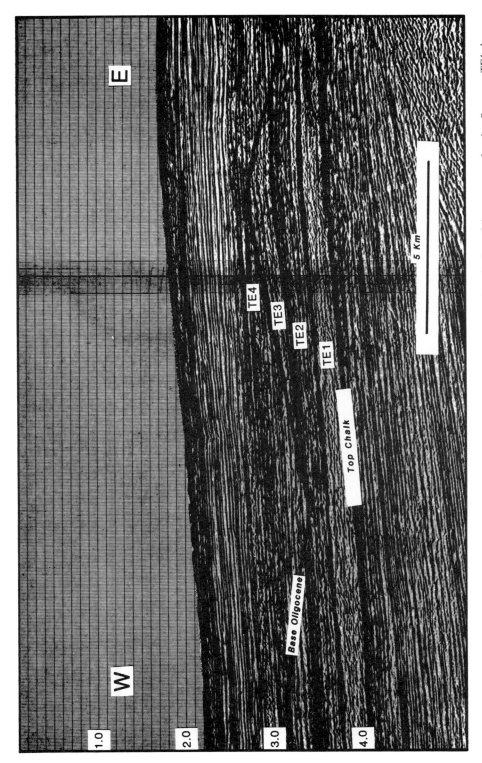

Fig. 10. Seismic profile from the southeastern region illustrating the dramatic mounds (largely Type 3) at the Base Oligocene unconformity. Sequence TE1 shows some low-angle westward-prograding reflectors. The large asymmetric mound in the eastern part of the profile shows an internal variation in the seismic character of TE3. The reflectors towards the eastern margin are discontinuous, while those on the shallow-dipping western slope of the mound are more continuous and of higher amplitude. Sequence TE4 onlaps the mound.

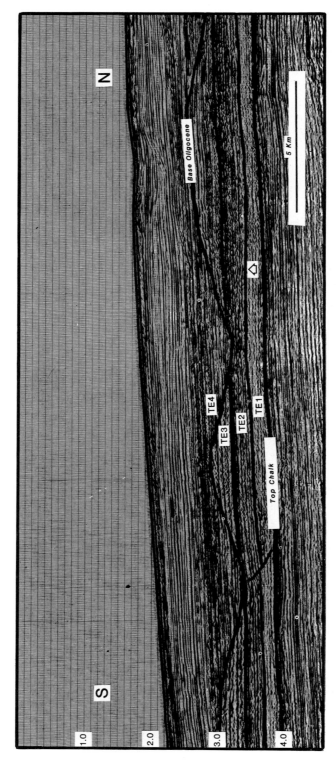

Fig. 11. Sequence TE1 consists of parallel reflectors of relatively low amplitude. TE2 is characterised by high amplitude events and shows some examples of downlap onto TE1 (marked by the arrow). Note the variation in seismic character of Sequence TE3 between the two most northerly mounds. The large mound consists of a lower package of parallel, closely spaced and continuous reflectors and an upper package of wider spaced reflectors. The small mound contains a package of variable amplitude widely spaced reflectors, distinctly different from the package at a similar level in the large mound. This suggests that the mounds represent deposits of different fan lobes, modified by erosion.

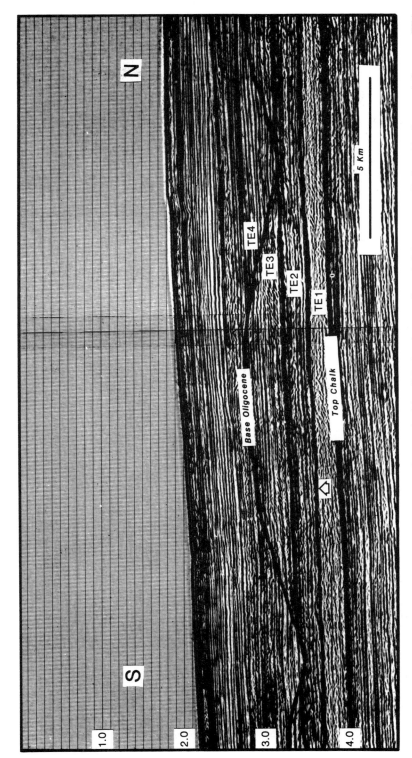

Fig. 12. The lower part of Sequence TE2 contains some low angle mounds with a slight downlap onto the underlying sequence (indicated by the arrow). Sequence TE4 onlaps the Base Oligocene unconformity. Note the slight TE4 mounds (probably Type-2 compactional mounds). This mounded package has a slightly higher amplitude than the overlying flat-lying continuous reflectors.

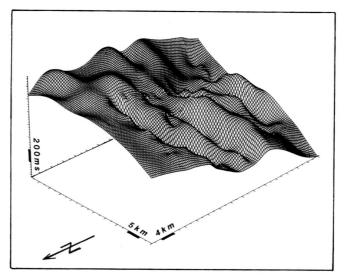

Fig. 13. Three-dimensional contour plot of the top of Sequence TE3 from the southeastern region. The scales and orientations are indicated on the diagram. The plot was produced from the database using Zycor Z-map software on a Sun Sparcstation. The diagram illustrates the pronounced canyons and mounds (largely Type-3) developed at this horizon.

places mounded structures occur, but these are significantly less pronounced than in the southwestern area. At first glance it might be argued that the topography at the top of TE3 is totally a function of erosion at the Base Oligocene unconformity (Figs 10–12), creating scoured palaeocanyons and intervening highs from an original parallel layered sequence (Type-3 mounds). However, a closer examination reveals differences in the internal reflector character of the palaeohighs (Fig. 11). This supports the supposition that the unconformity-related erosion merely strongly modified an existing Type-1 mounded palaeotopography. East–west profiles through the mounds reveal a slight asymmetry, with a steeper eastern and a shallower western margin (Fig. 10). The elongate nature of the mounds and canyons, with a strong NNE–SSW orientation, is clearly visible on the 3D contour plot (Fig. 13).

A range of reflector types occurs within the mounds. In some, closely spaced, moderately continuous reflectors occur whereas others contain fewer reflectors, of moderate-to-high amplitude and with good continuity. Some internal variability occurs, best seen on the east–west dip lines. Here, some hummocky or discontinuous clinoform reflectors occur adjacent to the steep eastern edges of the mounds, giving way to high-amplitude more continuous reflectors in a westerly direction (Fig. 10). Sequence TE4 rests above the erosive

Base Oligocene unconformity. In common with Sequence TW4 it onlaps and infills the topography produced by the TE3 mounded structures and erosion (Figs 10–12). However, an important attribute of TE4 is that the lower part of the sequence infills the palaeolows and frequently has a convex shape, downlapping onto the underlying TE3 mound edges. This results in a mounded infill within the lows immediately above the unconformity (Fig. 12). The seismic reflector amplitude of the mounded part of the sequence is typically higher than that of the overlying part of the sequence. These mounds are interpreted as Type-2 mounds. The mounding gradually dies out upwards to give way to a flat-lying succession that onlaps the higher parts of the pre-Oligocene mounds.

Interpretation of seismic facies

The oblique progradational sequence (Sangree & Widmier 1977) seen in the northern and central parts of the basin shows a range of seismic stratigraphic features that unequivocally demonstrate a southward-prograding deltaic origin. The high-amplitude continuous reflectors at the top of the deltaic package (Fig. 4) are interpreted as marshy delta top lithofacies. The high-amplitude steep southward-dipping discontinuous reflectors probably represent sand-prone delta front facies. The relatively flat to slightly inclined low-amplitude continuous reflectors are thought to represent prodelta to marine shale-prone lithofacies. The build-up and preservation of the delta top reflectors suggests that subsidence and sedimentation rates were finely balanced. Drilling results confirm a Palaeocene–Eocene age for the succession (Croker & Shannon 1987, Naylor & Anstey 1987).

The mounded sequences described from the southwestern and southeastern parts of the basin are coeval with the deltaic succession. Sequences TW1 and TE1 are laterally equivalent to the most extensive and penultimate phase of the four phases of deltaic progradation which occur in the basin (J. Moore, *pers. comm.*) However, these sequences display radically different seismic stratigraphic attributes to those of the deltaic environment in the northern and central areas.

The sequences include mounded features which thin towards palaeovalleys. While undoubtedly sculptured by erosion they are not considered to be simply erosive features (Croker & Shannon 1978), but are suggested to be turbidite deposits. The overall morphology, geometry and internal configuration of most of the seismic facies described from the margins of the basin are interpreted as representing the deposits of successive phases of submarine fan development.

While several sedimentary fan models have been described from modern and ancient deposits (e.g. Normark 1970, 1978; Nelson & Nilson 1974; Howell & Normark 1982), the majority of these involve canyon, lower fan and upper fan deposits. Each of these deposits within the fan complex contains a diagnostic set of seismic characteristics, which are summarized in an excellent review by Mitchum (1985). These diagnostic characteristics have been used in the following interpretation.

The intermound areas at various levels, in both the southwestern and southeastern regions, are typically scoured and modified by erosion. They frequently show erosional truncation of the original (Type-1) mound edges (Figs 5, 9–12) and are interpreted as canyons; the conduits for sediment funnelled from the basin edges towards the basin centre. The typical canyon-fill sediments of Sequence TW3 (Figs 5 & 9) are interpreted as sandstone-prone channellized lithofacies. This is based upon the discontinuous nature of the reflectors which onlap the adjacent mounds. In a number of instances in the southeastern region, the basal canyon-fill sediments of Sequence TE4 have a mounded convex-upwards shape (Fig. 12). This, together

with the higher amplitude and relatively continuous nature of the seismic facies in these instances, is interpreted as being due to high-energy sand-prone sheet sediments. These may be either sand-prone feeder channel or sandy upper fan deposits with marginal or levee shales. This is broadly similar to the origin suggested in the North Sea Frigg fan complex by Heritier *et al.* (1981). While compaction may have modified the overall geometry of the convex-upward canyon-fill deposits, compaction of a shale-prone package would provide a synclinal 'lickup' structure rather than the observed mounded geometry. The canyons have an elongate pattern, being most pronounced towards the basin edges and gradually becoming less obvious towards the basin centre. They typically extend across most of the fan complex areas. Those in the southwestern region run approximately perpendicular to the basin edge, although the axial directions diverge somewhat down the palaeoslope. The canyons in the southeastern region have a strong northeast–southwest orientation (Fig. 13) and are most pronounced at the top of the Eocene (Sequence TE3).

The mounds seen at all levels in the southwestern region, and at a number of levels in the southeastern region, are interpreted as lower fan deposits. In his description of the criteria for the recognition of such sediments from seismic data, Mitchum (1985) cites the overall mound shape, the convex-upward reflection pattern and the common occurrence of high amplitude reflections. The examples illustrated in that review are very similar to the reflection pattern observed from the Porcupine Basin. Particularly obvious are the downlapping reflectors of the lobe axis mounds and the onlap of the overlying strata. The high amplitude and relatively continuous reflectors are thought to represent an alternating sand–shale succession. The topographic relief on some of the mounded structures is often quite considerable, and is typically greater than that observed on modern fans. This is interpreted as being primarily due to compactional effects, with greater compaction of the shale-prone fan fringes than in the sandier lobe axes, and in part to modification by erosion.

The principal characteristic of the upper fan deposits is the presence of large channel features, sometimes flanked by levees, other times being amalgamated. However, the scale of such features are frequently below the limits of resolution of seismic data. In such instances, while a clear outline of the channels may not be obvious, hints at their existence may be provided by either hummocky or complex reflector patterns. The hummocky clinoforms, high-amplitude discontinuous reflectors and concave-upward reflectors seen on a number of profiles especially in the SW3 canyon-fill deposits (e.g. Figs 5 & 9), are thought to represent such features. These are thought to be upper fan deposits including leveed channels. Hummocky clinoform upper fan deposits also occur in the proximal parts of the TE3 mounds in the south-eastern region (Fig. 10). The TE4 canyon-fill deposits, with high-amplitude reflectors and slightly mounded onlap onto the TE3 top-ography, are interpreted as relatively un-confined deposits, which differ in their geometry from the channellized upper fan strata. The channel and fill deposits observed towards the tops of some of the lobes also probably rep-resent such features.

However, mounded structures on seismic sections may be interpreted in a variety of alter-native ways, some of which were outlined by Mitchum (1985). These alternatives are dis-regarded for the following reasons. Mounded structures can develop in deltaic and alluvial fan environments. The mounding is generated by the lobate nature of the sedimentary succession and/or by differential compaction with shale-prone strata compacting to a greater degree than the coarser clastics of the deltaic or alluvial fan lobes. However, both these settings typically generate pronounced oblique progradational clinoform reflectors, similar to those described from the northern part of the basin (Fig. 4) and also to the earlier Mesozoic and later Tertiary deltaics and clastic fan-wedges described by Croker & Shannon (1987) from further north in the Porcupine Basin. In addition, such deposits tend to show a greater diversity of lithofacies, giving different seismic reflector character, while the lateral extent and continuity of facies is likely to be significantly less than that seen in the present structures. Mounded, shale-prone chaotic-fill seismic facies may result from slumping, but internal reflector configuration in the present examples, together with the very significant lateral extent of the structures on both basin margins, argues against such an origin. Similarly, the well organized and gener-ally continuous reflectors argue against the mounding being due to sand-rich slumps (e.g. ponded lobes of Shanmugam & Moiola 1991). Mounded structures may also be created by contourite currents. Contourites are frequently internally asymmetrical, with one long gentle and another short steep slope (e.g. Markl & Bryan 1983; Mitchum 1985). They typically have an elongate geometry, hugging and parallelling the continental margin, and tend to be prefer-entially developed only on one basin margin. The elongate mounded structures in the Por-cupine Basin are clearly aligned orthogonal to both basin edges, which argues against depo-sition by contour-following currents. Finally, mounding can result from structural movement along detached normal listric faults on steep outer slopes. There is no evidence of significant faulting during the Early Tertiary in the Por-cupine Basin. Overall, therefore, the elongate lobate geometry shown on the isochrone maps (Fig. 7), together with the assemblage of seismic attributes, best fits a submarine fan model.

History of deposition

The Top Chalk and Base Oligocene reflectors in the southwest and southeast areas can be tied back to wells in the northern part of the basin. The other sequence boundaries are less con-fidently dated, largely due to lateral facies changes between the basin margins and the northern area of well control. Nevertheless, it is likely that sequences TW1 and TE1 are Palaeocene in age, TW2 and TE2 are Lower Eocene, TW3 and TE3 are Upper Eocene and TW4 and TE4 are of Lower Oligocene age.

The several phases of mounding are inter-preted as submarine fan progradational episodes. Some obvious differences in external configuration occur between the two margins. The mounds are tentatively suggested as representing depositional lobe complexes (Shanmugam & Moiola 1991). However, as pointed out by these authors, a definitive inter-pretation requires evidence of both horizontal and vertical components typical of the lobe type. In the present examples the distinctive sheet-like geometry is present but thickening-upward cyclicity cannot be unequivocally demonstrated on the basis of the present data-base. Shanmugam & Moiola (1991) highlight the fact that it is unclear why depositional lobes with sheet-like sand bodies should appear mounded on seismic profiles. It is likely that it is a combination of a primary depositional thick-ness variation (thicker sediments in the centre of the lobes) together with a degree of differ-ential compaction resulting from a gradual in-crease in the shale content away from the lobe centre. This will result in a Type-1/Type-2 combination mound.

Sequence TW1 marks the onset of submarine fan development on the western basin margin. A number of small composite depositional mounds (Fig. 5) coalesce to form a thick elongate mound that thins by downlap towards the basin centre (Figs 7 & 8). The equivalent strata on the southeastern basin margin (Sequence TE1) has a broadly uniform thickness with no mounding. The low-angle progradational reflectors seen on the dip lines in this area are suggestive of these strata being sheet-like shelf or slope sediments, devoid of submarine fan deposits. The principles of seismic stratigraphy (Vail *et al.* 1977) suggest that the low amplitude, relatively transparent seismic character of sequences TW1 and TE1 represent relatively uniform energy deposits, probably shale-prone. The differences in geometry between the coeval sequences on opposite margins of the basin may point to either a steeper slope, or a greater degree of earthquake- or fault-related tectonism on the southwestern margin of the basin. It is worth noting that some impressive Miocene slump structures occur in this region of the basin and are interpreted as having been triggered by such tectonism (Moore & Shannon 1991). Such structures are not as conspicuously developed on the eastern margin of the basin (J. Moore, *pers. comm.*).

The major period of fan progradation in the southwestern area is represented by Sequence TW2 and probably occurred during the Early Eocene. The main locus of progradation appears to have shifted northwards, and rests upon generally non-mounded strata of Sequence TW1. A number of episodes of elongate fan lobe development can be recognized within the sequence, with periods of drape, infill and finally mounding above the underlying sequence (Figs 5 & 7). The coeval sequence (TE2) on the southeastern margin only shows subdued and localized mounding. This may reflect continued development in a shelf or slope environment. Alternatively, it may represent the onset of shale-prone submarine fan progradation in this region. The predominant bedforms within the sequence are likely to be sheet-like, as evidenced by the typically continuous nature of the reflectors. Minor channelling and infill structures are interpreted as sandier upper fan facies. The small proximal fans in the southwestern region coalesce in a basinward (westward) direction to form a large lobate lower fan complex, cut by a number of canyons which die out towards the basin centre. The amplitude differences observed in a distal direction, seen especially in the southwestern region (Fig. 8), are interpreted as reflecting a basinward decrease in the sand content of the fan complex.

The location of individual depositional fan lobes in Sequence TW3 on the southwestern margin appears to have been controlled by the palaeotopography of Sequence TW2. The main

mounded parts of the fan complex are located in the intermound areas of the underlying fan. This suggests that the erosive feeder canyons exploited the original topographic lows. In addition, the main depositional axis appears to have shifted northwards with time. Horizontal canyon-fill facies of Sequence TW3 onlap and infill the intermound areas left by Sequence TW2 in the south of the area. To the north the TW3 facies are mounded and the internal reflection configuration and external mounded geometry are interpreted as sand-prone lower and upper fan deposits. The sediments of Sequence TW3 towards the basin centre are stacked upon the large distal TW2 mounds. This suggests that, while the individual conduits of sediment funnelling from the shelf appear to have shifted northwards through time, the broad pattern of the southeastern fan complex remained approximately constant through the Eocene.

Fan development and progradation on the southeastern margin were more pronounced during deposition of Sequence TE3 than during the previous sequences. A series of separate depositional lobes developed with the difference in seismic character between the lobes (Fig. 11), suggestive of the development of different lithofacies distributions. The lobes are interpreted to contain outer fan sand sheets and inner fan channellized sandstones. This sequence represents submarine fan development in succession to the shelf or slope successions of the preceding sequences.

The Base Oligocene unconformity is strikingly developed throughout the basin. Drilling results in the northern part of the basin confirm an Early Oligocene age. This unconformity enhances the topographic variations throughout the southwestern and especially the southeastern region, largely through incision of the intermound lows with the creation of a number of deep canyons. In the southwestern region the canyons are filled with TW4 deposits. While some mounding occurs, largely located on the crests of SW3 mounds, the sequence is typified by onlapping flat-lying reflectors. The internal character of these strata, with high reflector continuity and moderate amplitude, is interpreted as being more shale-prone than the underlying sequences. The pattern of sedimentation in the coeval Sequence TE4 on the southeastern margin is broadly similar, with some mounding by silt- or shale-prone strata lying on the TE3 mounds. The TE4 and TW4 facies may represent a slope front fill unit (Sangree & Widmier 1977) similar to that recorded above the Frigg fan complex in the North Sea

(McGovney & Radovich 1985). However, the mounded canyon-fill sediments seen locally in the southwestern region are likely to be sand-prone unconfined sediments.

Discussion

Submarine fans typically occur in deep water environments below wave base. The sediment deposited in the basinal fan lobes is generally sourced at the basin edge either from a delta complex or a submarine canyon. In the present examples, although the submarine fans are coeval with deltaic development, they are not genetically related. The deltaics prograded from north to south while the submarine fans were derived from the eastern and western basin margins. Clear evidence of the direction of fan progradation is provided by the orientation of the canyons and the shape of the fan lobes (Fig. 7). The fans on the southwestern margin show no evidence of derivation from previous sediment buildup on the shelf edge and the abundance of canyon features in all four sequences points towards canyon-related fan development. The head of the canyons may have intercepted sediment moving along the coastline by longshore drift. The sequences on the southeastern margin may have a somewhat different origin, with sediment for the fans of sequences TE3, TE4 and possibly TE2 provided by reworking and sediment gravity flow of detritus from the shelf or slope sediments of Sequence TE1.

A spectrum of submarine fan compositions and types has been described in the literature, ranging from sand-rich to shale-rich (Mutti 1977; Normark 1978, 1980; Nardin 1983). One end-member is the sand-rich 'poorly efficient' dispersal model type (Nardin 1983). This tends to produce significant upper fan deposits which are characterized by radial geometry, significant facies changes and large upper fan deposits. The other end-member is the shale-rich type, conforming to a 'high-efficiency' sediment dispersal model type (Mutti 1979), which forms large fans often with an elongate geometry (Stow 1985) characterized by lower to mid fan assemblages. The fans produced from the margins of the Porcupine Basin appear to lie towards the 'high-efficiency' end of the spectrum, both in terms of their overall geometry and their seismic configuration.

The Lower Tertiary deposits of the North Sea contain a significant number of submarine fan complexes of Palaeocene and Eocene age which act as prolific petroleum reservoirs. These include the Andrew, Balder, Forties, Frigg, Heimdal, Maureen, Lomond, Montrose and Odin fields (Johnson & Stewart 1985). Whilst published geological information on many of these has typically been of a general nature, seismic stratigraphic details have been published on the Frigg fan complex (Heritier et al. 1981; McGovney & Radovich 1985) which developed during the Ypresian (Early Eocene), and the Balder fan (Sarg & Skjold 1981) of Thanetian (Late Palaeocene) age. These descriptions afford the opportunity for comparison with the Porcupine Basin examples. The age and approximate size of the fans are comparable. Some seismic similarities are also immediately noted. In particular the North Sea examples consist of a series of stacked mounded structures. The mounding of sand-prone lobes was accentuated by compaction and provides large stratigraphic petroleum traps. The individual lobes are defined by a convex-upward external geometry. Internal bidirectional downlapping continuous reflectors are interpreted as outer fan sheet sands and are typically overlain by channellized inner fan sandy strata characterized by more discontinuous reflectors. A series of fan lobe progradational events occur in both areas, with lobe stacking sometimes recorded (McGovney & Radovich 1985). In these instances the topography appears to have influenced facies development in that the peripheral belt of downlapping sheet sands is thin or absent where, for example, the East Frigg lobe onlaps the central topographic high of the West Frigg lobe. However, as would be anticipated in a comparison between separate basins, there are also a number of differences between these North Sea fans and those of the Porcupine Basin. The Balder and Frigg complexes contain abundant channellized upper fan sandy facies, seen on seismic profiles as discontinuous reflectors, with subordinate lower fan facies. In the Porcupine Basin examples fewer discontinuous high amplitude packages are seen within the mounds, suggestive of a more shaly and sheet-like geometry. Consequently the North Sea fans, while they may have a higher net/gross sand value, have a large degree of lateral facies variation as a consequence of the significant channelling. Johnson & Steward (1985) state that the North Sea submarine fans typically 'display substantial variability in sand distribution, particularly on a field scale'. Furthermore, although there is evidence of reworking and erosion of lobe tops in the North Sea examples, descriptions and published seismic sections do not feature obvious canyon deposits, in contrast to the Porcupine examples. These differences suggest that, while the Porcupine examples tend to fall towards the 'high-efficiency' end of the fan spectrum, the North Sea fans are of a sandier 'low-efficiency' type. These differences are interpreted as being due largely to the nature of the sedimentary provenance, to the timing of provenance uplift and to local tectonic differences between the basins.

The age of the Porcupine Basin deposits is identical to that of a major phase of submarine fan development in the North Sea. In particular, the Balder and Frigg submarine fans developed during the Palaeocene (Balder) and Eocene (Frigg). The main deposition in these instances appears to be coincident with, and instigated by, periods of sea level fall and lowstands (Sarg & Skjold 1981; McGovney & Radovich 1985). This coincidence is also noted in submarine fans of other ages elsewhere in the world (Nardin 1983). In general; sea-level changes strongly affect the rate of sediment supply and dispersal, together with the number and position of active canyons, grain size distribution of sediment supplied to particular canyons and the depositional gradient. The fans in the Porcupine Basin are located towards the edges of the basin, where the post-Jurassic thermal subsidence deposits onlap beyond the edges of underlying syn-rift basins. Eustatic falls and lowstands of sea level are times of preferential deposition of submarine fans (see Mitchum 1985). It is therefore likely that the Porcupine Basin fans were triggered during a relative sea level lowstand. Sea-level curves for the Palaeocene and Eocene suggest a number of global eustatic sea level falls during the Palaeocene and Eocene (Haq *et al.* 1987). Throughout much of Northwest Europe, Alpine tectonic events during the Palaeogene are likely to have accentuated (or perhaps caused) a number of the observed relative sea-level falls. In the North Celtic Sea Basin offshore southern Ireland, for example, Alpine-related basin inversion occurred in the Early Tertiary (Shannon 1991c), causing the uplift and erosion of approximately 1 km of Upper Cretaceous sediments from the basin centre. A eustatic sea-level drop, combined with Alpine-related basin inversion, is therefore likely to have resulted in the exposure of a potential sediment provenance region. The relative sea-level rise suggested during deposition of the Palaeocene−Eocene deltaics in the northern and central part of the Porcupine Basin (Louis & Mermey 1978) may be explained in terms of thermal subsidence, following the cessation of the significant stretch-ing which took place during the pre-Cretaceous. Basinwards of the submarine fans the stretching factor (β) is likely to have been of the order of 3−5 (Tate *et al.* 1990). Consequently, while a number of eustatic and regional sea-level falls and lowstands exposed sedimentary provenances on the margins of the basin, the relative sea level within the central part of the basin rose due to thermal subsidence. This resulted in an increasing gradient towards the basin edge which probably facilitated sediment gravity movement and may have been influential in triggering the basinward prograding submarine fans.

The submarine fans in the southwestern region display a consistent northwards migration with time. This may be interpreted in a number of ways. The stepwise migration may simply reflect lobe switching similar to the process that occurs with deltaic lobes. However, while this could explain the lateral overlap of successive fan lobes, it would not be expected to result in a consistent sense of migration of successive lobes. Alternatively, the lobe migration may reflect the fact that the canyon route into the basin was affected by the topographic lows of the inter-mound regions. The major fans could have been forced northwards as the location of the major canyons, the conduits for the sediment, were deflected around the existing lobes. Again, however, southerly by-pass canyons and resultant fan lobes might be expected to be more commonly developed. As a third option, the northward migration of fan lobes may be due to the northward progression of erosion in the hinterland as it was worn down and gradually eroded or inundated by thermal subsidence-driven marine transgression in a northward direction. The β factor in the southern part of the basin is greater than in the north and the degree of thermal subsidence will have been commensurately greater in this area. The major feeder zone canyons will therefore have moved northwards in sympathy with the sediment source area. A fourth alternative suggests that the northward migration may have been controlled by the Coriolis force. This would be expected to have occurred preferentially along the western margin of the basin. Interestingly, there does not appear to be an equivalent northward migration of fan lobes on the eastern margin of the basin, in the area where contour-driving forces are likely to have been weakest. However, the available database and the current understanding of the development of the fans is insufficient to resolve the various alternative explanations.

Conclusions

1. A series of mounded elongate lobate seismic sequences identified on the southwestern margin of the Porcupine Basin are interpreted as submarine fans. Coeval strata on the southeastern margin of the basin also contain submarine fans but these overlie possible shelf or slope deposits. The sequences in both areas are of Palaeocene and Eocene age.

2. Seismic sequence analysis suggests that the fan sequences are the deposits of 'high-efficiency' sediment distribution systems which are dominated by lower fan sand sheets interbedded with shales, with minor upper fan channellized sands. The fans occur basinwards of well preserved feeder canyons.

3. Evidence from a number of regions indicates that submarine fans are generally instigated and preferentially develop during periods of relative sea level falls. Global sea level curves indicate that eustatic sea level falls and lowstands occurred during the Palaeocene and Eocene. It is proposed that a combination of eustatic sea level falls associated with regional early Alpine uplift and post-rift thermal subsidence within the central part of the basin provided sediment sources on the basin margins and the basinal environment for submarine fan deposition.

The seismic sections illustrated in the paper come from a non-exclusive proprietary survey provided by GECO Exploration Services, a division of GECO Geophysical Company Limited. Permission to use the data is gratefully acknowledged. The paper benefitted greatly from the constructive suggestions of Dr G. Shanmugam and an anonymous referee. Thanks are also due to Tommy McCann and John Moore for their assistance, helpful contributions and comments.

References

CROKER, P. F. & KLEMPERER, S. L. 1989. Structure and stratigraphy of the Porcupine Basin: relationships to deep crustal structure and the opening of the North Atlantic. *In*: TANKARD, A. J. & BALKWILL, H. R. (eds) *Extensional Tectonics and Stratigraphy of the North Atlantic Margin.* American Association of Petroleum Geologists Memoir, **46**, 445–460.

—, SHANNON, P. M. 1987. The evolution and hydrocarbon prospectivity of the Porcupine Basin, Offshore Ireland. *In*: BROOKS, J. & GLENNIE, K. (eds) *Petroleum Geology of North-West Europe.* Graham & Trotman, London, 633–642.

HERITIER, F. E., LOSSEL, P. & WATHNE, E. 1981. The Frigg Gas Field. *In*: ILLING, L. V. & HOBSON, G. D. (eds) *Petroleum Geology of the Continental Shelf of North West Europe.* Heyden, London, 380–391.

HAQ, B. U., HARDENBOL, J. & VAIL, P. R. 1987. Chronology of fluctuating sea levels since the Triassic. *Science*, **235**, 1156–1167.

HOWELL, D. G. & NORMARK, W. R. 1982. Sedimentology of submarine fans. *In*: SCHOLLE, P. A. & SPEARING, D. (eds) *Sandstone Depositional Environments.* American Association of Petroleum Geologists, Memoir, **31**, 365–404.

JOHNSON, H. D. & STEWART, D. J. 1985. Role of clastic sedimentology in the exploration and production of oil and gas in the North Sea. *In*: BRENCHLEY, P. J. & WILLIAMS, B. P. J. (eds) *Sedimentology: Recent Developments and Applied Aspects.* Geological Society, London, Special Publication, **18**, 249–310.

LOUIS, P. R. & MERMEY. P. 1979. An example of seismic stratigraphy. The Porcupine Basin — Western Ireland. Paper presented at *49th Annual International Meeting of the Society of Exploration Geophysicists, New Orleans.*

MACDONALD, H., ALLAN, P. M. & LOVELL, J. P. B. 1987. Geology of oil accumulation in Block 26/28, Porcupine Basin, offshore Ireland. *In*: BROOKS, J. & GLENNIE, K. W. (eds) *Petroleum Geology of North West Europe.* Graham & Trotman, London, 643–651.

MACURDA, D. B. Jr. & NELSON, H. R. Jr. 1988. Interactive interpretation of a submarine fan, offshore Ireland: a case history. *Geophysics: The Leading Edge*, 28–34.

MARKL, R. G. & BRYAN, G. M. 1983. Stratigraphic evolution of Blake Outer Ridge. *AAPG Bulletin*, **67**, 666–683.

McGOVNEY, J. E. & RADOVICH, B. J. 1985. Seismic stratigraphy and facies of the Frigg fan complex. *In*: BERG, O. R. & WOOLVERTON, D. W. (eds) *Seismic Stratigraphy II: An Integrated Approach to Hydrocarbon Exploration.* American Association of Petroleum Geologists, Memoir, **39**, 139–154.

MOORE, J. G. & SHANNON, P. M. 1991. Late Tertiary slump structures in the Porcupine Basin, offshore Ireland. *Marine and Petroleum Geology*, **8**, 184–197.

MITCHUM, R. M. Jr. 1985. Seismic stratigraphic expression of submarine fans. *In*: BERG, O. R. & WOOLVERTON. D. W. (eds) *Seismic Stratigraphy II: An Integrated Approach to Hydrocarbon Exploration.* American Association of Petroleum Geologists Memoir, **39**, 117–136.

MUTTI, E. 1977. Distinctive thin-bedded turbidite facies and related depositional environments in the Eocene Hecho Group (south-central Pyrenees, Spain). *Sedimentology*, **24**, 107–131.

—— 1979. Turbidites et cones sous-marins profonds. *In*: HOMEWOOD, D. (ed.) *Sedimentation de 'trotique. Cours zeme Cycle Romand en Aciences de la Terre*, **1**, 353–419.

NARDIN, T. R. 1983. Late Quaternary depositional systems and sea level changes — Santa Monica and San Pedro basins, California continental borderland. *AAPG Bulletin*, **67**, 1104–1124.

NAYLOR, D. & ANSTEY, N. 1987. A reflection seismic study of the Porcupine Basin, offshore western Ireland. *Irish Journal of Earth Sciences*, **8**, 187–210.

—— & SHANNON, P. M. 1982. *The Geology of Offshore Ireland and West Britain*. Graham & Trotman, London.

NELSON, C. H. & NILSON, T. H. 1974. Depositional trends of modern and ancient deep-sea fans. *In*: DOTT, Jr. R. H. & SHAVER, R. H. (eds) *Modern and Ancient Geosynclinal Sedimentation*. Society of Economic Palaeontologists and Mineralogists Special Publication, **19**, 69–91.

NORMARK, W. R. 1970. Growth patterns of deep-sea fans. *AAPG Bulletin*, **54**, 2170–2195.

—— 1978. Fan valleys, channels and depositional lobes on modern submarine fans, characters for recognition of sandy turbidite environments. *AAPG Bulletin*, **62**, 912–931.

—— 1980. Modern and ancient submarine fans: reply. *AAPG Bulletin*, **64**, 1108–1112.

SANGREE, J. B. & WIDMIER, J. M. 1977. Seismic stratigraphy and global changes of sea level, Part 9: seismic interpretation of clastic depositional facies. *In*: PAYTON, C. E. (ed.) *Seismic stratigraphy – applications to hydrocarbon exploration*. American Association of Petroleum Geologists Memoir, **26**, 165–184.

SARG, J. E. & SKJOLD, L. J. 1981. Stratigraphic traps in Paleocene Sands in the Balder area, North Sea. *In*: HALBOUTY, M. T. (ed.) *The Deliberate Search for the Subtle Trap*. American Association of Petroleum Geologists Memoir, **32**, 197–206.

SEEMANN, U. 1984. Tertiary intrusives on the Atlantic continental margin off Southwest Ireland. *Irish Journal of Earth Sciences*, **6**, 229–236.

SHANMUGAM, G. & MOIOLA, R. J. 1991. Types of submarine fan lobes: models and implications. *AAPG Bulletin*, **75**, 156–179.

SHANNON, P. M. 1991a. The development of Irish offshore sedimentary basins. *Journal of the Geological Society of London*, **148**, 181–189.

—— 1991b. Irish offshore basins: geological development and petroleum plays. *In*: SPENCER, A. M. (ed.) *Generation, accumulation and production of Europe's hydrocarbons*. Special Publication of the European Association of Petroleum Geoscientists. Oxford University Press, **1**, 99–109.

—— 1991c. Tectonic framework and petroleum potential of the Celtic Sea, Ireland. *First Break*, **9**, 107–122.

STOW, D. A. V. 1985. Deep-sea clastics: where are we and where are we going? *In*: BRENCHLEY, P. J. & WILLIAMS, B. P. J. (eds). *Sedimentology: Recent Developments and Applied Aspects*. Geological Society Special Publication, **18**, 67–93.

TATE, M. P., WHITES, N. & CONROY, J.-J. 1990. Application of the lithospheric stretching model to the Porcupine Seabight basin, offshore western Ireland. Abstracts for Conference on *Basins on the North West Seaboard: Post-Devonian basin development. North Western Seaboard of the British Isles*. Queen's University of Belfast.

—— & DOBSON, M. R. 1988. Syn- and post-rift igneous activity in the Porcupine Seabight basin and adjacent continental margin west of Ireland. *In*: MORTON, A. C. & PARSON, L. M. (eds) *Early Tertiary Volcanism and the Opening of the NE Atlantic*. Geological Society, London, Special Publication, **39**, 309–334.

VAIL, P. R., MITCHUM, Jr. R. M., TODD, R. G., WIDMIER, J. M., THOMPSON, S., SANGREE, J. B., BUBB, J. N. & HATLELID, W. G. 1977. Seismic stratigraphy and global changes of sea level. *In*: PAYTON, C. E. (ed.) *Seismic stratigraphy – applications to hydrocarbon exploration*. American Association of Petroleum Geologists Memoir, **26**, 49–212.

The Clare Lineament: a relic transform fault west of Ireland

MICHAEL P. TATE

Total Oil Marine plc, 16 Palace Street, London SW1E 5BQ, UK

Abstract: The Porcupine Seabight Basin is dissected at *c.* 51°N by a major ESE–WNW trending structure which separates the Main Porcupine Basin from the Seabight Basin. This structure was initially mapped across the southern boundary of the Rockall Trough, where it was termed the Clare Lineament and interpreted as a Mesozoic precursor to the present-day Charlie Gibbs Fracture Zone. Evidence is presented here for its extension to the eastern margin of the Porcupine Seabight Basin. There it lies to the south of the Iapetus suture zone imaged by deep seismic data west of Ireland, to which it does not appear to be related as had previously been suggested. At the onset of sea-floor spreading during the mid-Cretaceous, the Clare Lineament evolved as an incipient transform fault. It separated volcanism to the north, which produced N–S ridges above attenuated continental crust in the axes of the southern Rockall Trough and Main Porcupine Basin, from the rift–drift transition in the proto-Atlantic rift to the southwest, now occupied by oceanic crust of the Porcupine Abyssal Plain. The Clare Lineament was probably then superseded by the Charlie Gibbs Fracture Zone during the Late Cretaceous.

Mapping of continental shelf areas commonly reveals deep, vertical structures lying orthogonally to the respective passive margin (Le Pichon & Sibuet 1981). These structures invariably originate in the early development of the passive margin, from when they remain active until at least the rift–drift transition. The continental shelf west of Ireland is dissected by a network of sedimentary basins lying between Ireland and the eastern North Atlantic passive margin. Recent structural mapping of these basins, when integrated with results of recent geophysical work in the region, has enabled deeper structures to be recognized and their influence on the development of the margin to be assessed.

The Clare Lineament is an ESE–WNW aligned structure that was first identified at the southern boundary of the Rockall Trough (Dingle *et al.* 1982) where it predates the Charlie Gibbs Fracture Zone, a major North Atlantic transform fault. The Clare Lineament also forms a prominent lineation on gravity/magnetic maps that extends eastwards into the Porcupine Seabight Basin where, in the absence of more definitive structural detail, it was termed the 'Clare Trend' (Naylor & Shannon 1982; Megson 1987). This paper highlights new structural work by Tate (1990), which when integrated with previous geophysical work in the region (Dingle *et al.* 1982; Bentley & Scrutton 1987; Megson 1987), attempts to substantiate an eastward extension to the Clare Lineament across the Irish continental shelf and intervening basins. The paper also explores how the Clare Lineament may have influenced the site of

transform fault development on the evolving continental margin and assesses the validity of previously proposed genetic links between the Clare Lineament/Charlie Gibbs Fracture Zone and the Iapetus suture zone.

Data available for the structural mapping comprised *c.* 10 000 km of seismic data integrated with all available well data west of Ireland. These data were then used to prepare a series of structure–contour and isopach maps, constructed down to the base of the Cretaceous. The results of gravity and magnetic modelling over the Porcupine Seabight/southern Rockall area (Megson 1987; Bentley & Scrutton 1987; Conroy & Brock 1989; Conroy 1989) have also been examined to help identify deep basement structures.

Regional geology

The Clare Lineament divides two pairs of basinal areas: the Main Porcupine Basin from the Seabight Basin, and the southern Rockall Trough from the Porcupine Abyssal Plain (as shown in Fig. 1). It is important to describe and account for the evolution of these contrasting areas, especially the Porcupine Seabight Basin where the extension of the Clare Lineament is newly described, in order to better understand the role that the Clare Lineament may have played during their development.

Immediately to the west of the Irish mainland lies the Irish Shelf, and beyond it the Porcupine Seabight Basin. This intra-cratonic rift basin evolved through repetitive episodes of crustal stretching during the Carboniferous, probably

From Parnell, J. (ed.), 1992, *Basins on the Atlantic Seaboard: Petroleum Geology, Sedimentology and Basin Evolution*. Geological Society Special Publication No 62, pp 375–384.

375

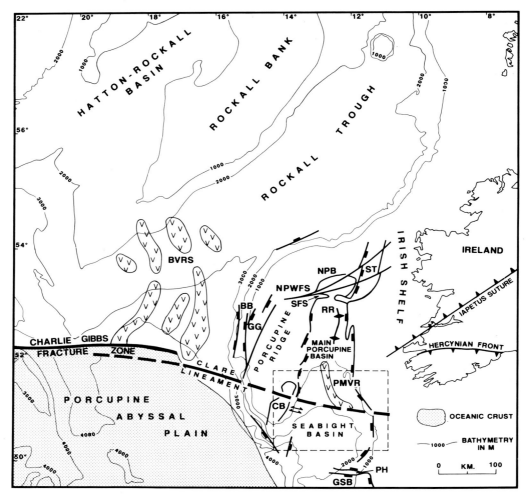

Fig. 1. Map of the Irish continental shelf and margin, outlining the main structural elements, modified from Megson (1987) and Tate (1990). Thick dashed line indicates the extension of the Clare Lineament eastwards as presented here and westwards as taken from Bentley & Scrutton (1987). Location of Figs 2a–d is shown by a thin dashed line. Abbreviations as follows: BB, Bean Basin; BVRS, Barra Volcanic Ridge System; CB, Canice Basin; GG, Galway Graben; GSB, Goban Spur Basin; NPB, North Porcupine Basin; NPWFS, North Porcupine wrench fault-system; PMVR, Porcupine Median Volcanic Ridge; PH, Portmarnock Horst; RR, Ruadan Ridge; SFS, St. Finnians Spur; ST, Slyne Trough.

the Permo-Triassic and also the Mid-Late Jurassic. Thermal subsidence during the Cretaceous and Tertiary led to the development of a 'steers head' profile to the basin. Structure–contour and isopach maps constructed from an extensive grid of seismic data have allowed the structural framework of the basin to be elucidated. The collectively termed Porcupine Seabight Basin comprises two principal basins, the N–S aligned Main Porcupine Basin, separated from the more elliptical Seabight

Basin by the proposed trajectory of the Clare Lineament (Fig. 1). In the extreme north, the North Porcupine Basin is a structurally complex area partly separated from the Main Porcupine Basin by the basement promontory of St Finnians' Spur. The neighbouring Slyne Trough is a half-graben with sinistrally offset margins. These structural complexities result from the intersection with the North Porcupine wrench fault-system (Tate & Dobson 1989a).

The Main Porcupine Basin lies in water depths

of 300–2000 m and the shallower northern part has been extensively explored for hydrocarbons. As a consequence, a reasonably clear stratigraphic picture has emerged that enables the timing of tectonic events to be determined. In plan, the basin displays an overall N–S configuration which in detail comprises a NE–SW structural grain in the north and along the western margin, with a N–S to NNW–SSE trend in the southeast and along the eastern margin. Rejuvenation of these basement anisotropies in an E–W extensional regime produced the N–S basin. In profile, there is a general deepening and broadening of the basin southwards, with clear E–W symmetry. Marginal sub-basins are locally developed along the western and eastern margins adjacent to major basin-boundary faults and contain up to 3.5 km of syn-rift sediments. The thermal subsidence infill comprises up to c. 5 km of Cretaceous and up to c. 4 km of Cenozoic sediments in the deepest parts of the basin axis. A zone of complex N–S faulting lies in the northeastern quadrant of the Main Porcupine Basin. This area forms a topographic high on the base Cretaceous unconformity map and comprises a series of N–S curvilinear ridges. The most prominent of these is the Ruadan Ridge which was drilled by the Phillips 35/8–2 well, encountering an Upper Jurassic succession. Fault geometries in this area are inconsistent with simple normal faulting, but rather allude to the existence of a N–S wrench fault system (Tate 1990). It is proposed that transpressional movement on such faults during the latest Jurassic produced inversion prior to being onlapped by early Lower Cretaceous basinal shales. The Porcupine Median Volcanic Ridge is a striking feature obliquely aligned along the southern basin axis with a NNW–SSE trend (Tate & Dobson 1988). This ridge principally evolved as an Early Cretaceous (possibly originating during the mid-late Jurassic) fissure volcano, 150 km long, c. 20 km wide and up to 3 km high and forms an abrupt skewed southern termination.

The Seabight Basin, in contrast, lies in water depths of 2–4 km and has a more elliptical outline with NE–SW trending isopachytes. On its southern margin the Portmarnock Horst divides it from the contiguous Goban Spur Basin (Cook 1987) and its western extremity is delimited by the continental–oceanic crustal boundary. The basin is known to be underlain by highly attenuated continental crust intruded by basaltic magma (Conroy & Brock 1989). It contains up to 6 km (2.85 s TWT) of Cretaceous sediments, but since the early Tertiary it has remained relatively starved of sediment, ac-counting for its development as a modern-day bathymetric embayment.

The Porcupine Ridge is a cratonic massif that separates the Porcupine Seabight Basin from the Rockall Trough. This feature has long been a positive topographic feature, certainly since the beginning of the Mesozoic and probably also during the Permo-Carboniferous (Tate & Dobson 1989b). Parts of the Ridge are cut by several shallow basins, notably in the south by the previously unmapped 'Canice Basin' (Figs 2 & 3). This basin has an irregular outline with abrupt faulted margins and contains up to 800 m of sediment.

Further west still, the Rockall Trough is a NE–SW aligned, tongue-shaped area of deep water some 1000 km in length, extending from offshore north-western Scotland southwards to the northeastern corner of the Porcupine Abyssal Plain. The exact nature of the underlying crust has been a contentious issue but is currently reputed to be composed of highly attenuated continental crust. This is believed to be heavily intruded by basaltic magma, resulting from crustal extension with β stretching estimates of 6–10 (Joppen & White 1990). Sediments in the basin are estimated to date back to the Early Cretaceous–(?)Late Jurassic and may possibly have formed part of a late Palaeozoic proto-Atlantic rift-system (Tate & Dobson 1989b). The southern part of the Rockall Trough has been mapped using single channel seismic data. This work enabled the Charlie Gibbs Fracture Zone as well as the Clare Lineament to be recognized and a provisional seismic stratigraphy (in the absence of nearby well data) to be established (Dingle et al. 1982; Bentley & Scrutton 1987; Megson 1987; Masson & Kidd 1986). In addition, the axis of the southernmost part of the Trough is occupied by a series of curvilinear ridges which form the Barra Volcanic Ridge System (Scrutton & Bentley 1988).

The Porcupine Abyssal Plain forms the northeastern corner of the Atlantic oceanic crust. Its boundary with the Rockall Trough is underlain by the Charlie Gibbs Fracture Zone–Clare Lineament and produces an abrupt bathymetric break. The Porcupine Abyssal Plain resulted from early Cretaceous rifting which led to the onset of sea-floor spreading during the Albian between the Goban Spur and Grand Banks continental margins (Masson et al. 1984; Peddy et al. 1989). However, prior to the Cretaceous it may have formed the southern part of a more continuous rift-system extending into the Rockall Trough.

The Clare Lineament

Background

The Clare Lineament was first recognized from the results of single channel seismic profiling on the western side of the Porcupine Ridge (Dingle *et al.* 1982). It was reported to comprise a zone of *en echelon* basement highs with a WNW−ESE trend that appeared to converge north-westwards with the E−W aligned Charlie Gibbs Fracture Zone (CGFZ). More recent work demonstrates that the CGFZ between 17°W and 20°W comprises a pair of parallel basement ridges separated by an intervening trough (Bentley & Scrutton 1987, their Figs 2, 7 & 8). The mapped orientation of the more southerly of these two ridges, east of 18°N, was noted to change to ESE and may continue into the Clare Lineament, mapped only as far west as 16°40′W. Whilst the CGFZ is known to extend eastwards to *c.* 17°W, unlike the Clare Lineament, there is no evidence for its extension onto the continental shelf. Moving across the CGFZ−Clare Lineament there is an abrupt northward increase in the thickness and age of the sediment column. This provides up to 2 s TWT of topographic relief and a shallowing of the isobaths at the junction of the Porcupine Abyssal Plain and southern Rockall Trough (Bentley & Scrutton 1987; Megson 1987).

Evidence for an extension of the Clare Lineament into the Porcupine Seabight Basin

The continuation of the Clare Lineament across the Porcupine Seabight Basin can be discerned from magnetic and gravity maps, as well as from a series of structure-contour/isopach maps constructed from seismic data. A total magnetic intensity anomaly contour map (Conroy 1989), together with a free-air gravity anomaly map (Masson *et al.* 1985) (Figs 2a & 2b respectively) across the Porcupine Seabight area, both show N−S trends over the Main Porcupine Basin and NE−SW trends over the Seabight Basin. In both cases these trends are separated by an ESE−WNW break in the anomaly pattern.

The base Cretaceous unconformity is the deepest horizon that can be mapped throughout the basin (Fig. 2c). It lies close to the top of the faulted syn-rift succession. Across the eastern part of the Porcupine Seabight Basin, where sufficient seismic line spacing exists, there is a deflection in the structure-contours (in TWT) that is areally coincident with the observed break in the magnetic and gravity anomaly contour pattern. It is probably not fortuitous that this lineament also crosses the skewed southern termination of the Porcupine Median Volcanic Ridge and coincides with an observed widening of the basin on its eastern margin. On the western half of the basin, gaps in the data-base and the wider seismic line spacing do not enable a break in the contour pattern to be discerned. However, close to the western basin margin, two approximately E−W faults that extend up to the base of the Tertiary as vertical zones dividing areas of contrasting dip, can be discerned and are inferred to be strike-slip in origin. At base Cretaceous level, an angular discordance is indicated close to these two faults in the southwestern corner of the Main Porcupine Basin and in the vicinity of the Ruadan Ridge, implying some degree of contemporaneous tectonic activity.

An isopach map of the Cretaceous interval (up to and including the Danian) provides another indication of the palaeo-bathymetry and subsidence patterns that prevailed over this part of the basin (Fig. 2d). Cretaceous iso-pachytes also have a N−S (to NNW−SSE) trend in the north, compared with NE−SW trends to the south where they delimit a greater thickness of sediment and are consistent with a southward increase in calculated crustal extension (White *et al.*, this volume). A similar gentle deflection of the isopachytes over the eastern half of the basin is also evident.

Altogether, these various disturbances and lineaments lie on an ESE−WNW trend that lies precisely along strike from the mapped position of the Clare Lineament west of the Porcupine Ridge. In between, on the eastern part of the Porcupine Ridge, the previously described Canice Basin (Fig. 3) lies exactly above the path of the trend, and is likely to be in some way

Fig. 2. Series of four inset maps (see Fig. 1 for location) from which the eastward extension of the Clare Lineament has been interpreted, crossing the centre of each map with an ESE−WNW trend. See text for details: (a) total magnetic intensity anomaly contour map (nT) (taken from Conroy 1989); (b) free-air gravity anomaly map (mGal) (taken from Masson *et al.* 1985); (c) structure-contour map (TWT secs) of the base Cretaceous unconformity; (d) isopach map (TWT secs) of the Cretaceous interval including Danian chalk (c and d both taken from Tate 1990). Abbreviations same as for Fig. 1, otherwise: MPB, Main Porcupine Basin; PR, Porcupine Ridge; SB, Seabight Basin.

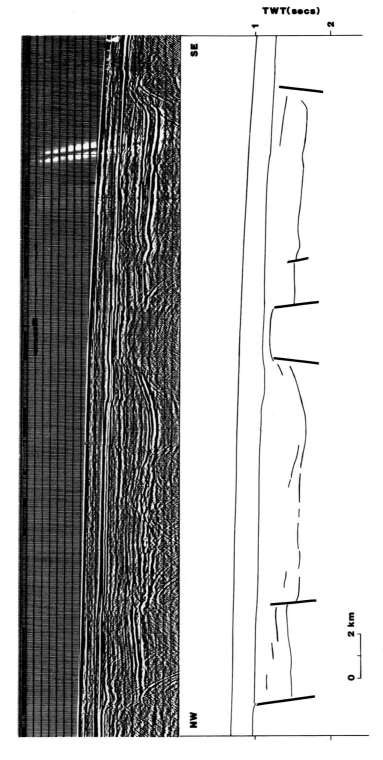

Fig. 3. Seismic reflection profile (unmigrated) and interpreted line drawing across the previously unmapped Canice Basin that lies above site where the Clare Lineament intersects the Porcupine ridge. Depth from the seabed to the high amplitude reflector at 1.6–1.7 s (TWT) indicates a sedimentary thickness of c. 800 m. Courtesy of Western Geophysical.

related. To the south of its intersection with the western basin margin, two wrench faults may represent associated fault splays.

Interpretation of the Clare Lineament and its relationship to the Atlantic margin

The Clare Lineament appears to dissect the Porcupine Seabight Basin and provides an important structural discontinuity in the basin. Its passage across the southern boundary of the Rockall Trough forms a hinge-line, providing not only a bathymetric break but has also influenced palaeo-bathymetry and subsidence rates (see Figs 2c & d). Whilst its extension across the Porcupine Seabight Basin is more subtle, it has still influenced the location of submarine canyon and fan development as recently as the mid-Tertiary, most notably on the eastern margin (Tate 1990). Prior to the Early to mid Cretaceous, it probably behaved as a wrench fault, as implicated from data west of the Porcupine Ridge and some evidence within the basin. The recognition of this structure as a clear lineation on both structure–contour and gravity/magnetic maps, allied to its apparent behaviour as a wrench fault, indicates that it has a vertically inclined sub-surface profile. In the Main Porcupine Basin, there still remains a structural problem in accounting for the dramatic inversion (up to 2 km) of the Ruadan Ridge and parallel ridges. It may have been that at the climax of Late Jurassic extension, the Clare Lineament may have moved as a wrench fault, creating the rhomb-shaped Canice Basin, angular discordance across parts of the basin, and induced a sufficent couple (perhaps in combination with the North Porcupine wrench fault system further to the north) to invert the Ruadan Ridge, which is itself believed to be underlain by a wrench fault-zone (Tate 1990). However, with the exception of its intersection with the western basin margin, there is an absence of evidence for significant post-Early Cretaceous movement, indicating that it has remained relatively quiescent.

The early history of the Clare Lineament is better constrained on the western side of the Porcupine Ridge, where together with the CGFZ, it forms the southern boundary of the Rockall Trough (Dingle et al. 1982; Bentley & Scrutton 1987; Megson 1987). The CGFZ is the largest transform fault in the North Atlantic and in the eastern part of the area it divides the highly attenuated continental crust of the southern Rockall Trough from oceanic crust of the Porcupine Abyssal Plain, and probably originated during the Santonian (Upper Cretaceous) or slightly after (Bentley & Scrutton 1987; Megson 1987). The onset of sea-floor spreading on the nearby Goban Spur continental margin is dated as middle Albian following Early Cretaceous rifting (Masson et al. 1984). Therefore it seems that during the Mesozoic, the Clare Lineament evolved as a precursor to the CGFZ (Bentley & Scrutton 1987; Megson 1987).

Previous work on passive continental margins has shown that transform faults are situated along predisposed crustal weaknesses that existed prior to the onset of oceanic spreading and are aligned approximately orthogonal to the axis of extension (Le Pichon & Sibuet 1981). Such 'palaeo-continental shear zones' are thought to be responsible for delimiting punctiform oceanic spreading in embryonic oceans such as the Red Sea (Crane & Bonatti 1987). In an analogous way during the mid-Cretaceous, the Clare Lineament appears to have been a major fault dividing the southern Rockall Trough from the proto-Atlantic rift (that is now occupied by oceanic crust of the Porcupine Abyssal Plain), such that when spreading commenced and prior to the inception of the CGFZ, the Clare Lineament behaved as a transform fault dividing newly emplaced oceanic crust to the south (west of 17°W) from attenuated continental crust to the north. Perhaps as spreading progressed and became more organized, the younger CGFZ was initiated at a slightly different angle to the Clare Lineament in adjustment to a modified spreading direction. Spreading later commenced on the north side in the northern North Atlantic during the 60–85 Ma interval.

Magmatism

While the Clare Lineament appears to have behaved as an incipient transform fault, it also formed the southern boundary to voluminous igneous activity in contiguous basins. The Barra Volcanic Ridge System (BVRS) comprises a series of c. N–S curvilinear volcanic ridges in the southern Rockall Trough (Scrutton & Bentley 1988; Megson 1987) (Fig. 1). These are analogous to the Porcupine Median Volcanic Ridge (PMVR) in their location, morphology, and possibly age and relationship with the Clare Lineament. High amplitude magnetic anomalies along the Clare Lineament over the Porcupine Ridge, and at its intersection with the eastern basin margin of the Porcupine Seabight Basin, may also be igneous in origin (Tate & Dobson 1988). The PMVR, like the BVRS, also displays a skewed southern termination at the point where it abuts the Clare Lineament (and CGFZ). As described, strike-slip movement may have occurred on the Clare Lineament during the latest Jurassic episode of structural readjustment. The onset of magmatism at that time, or shortly after during the earliest Lower Cretaceous, may have imposed a dextral Reidel shear, resulting in extrusion of magma along the direction of least compressive stress in the strain ellipsoid, producing an obliquity to the volcanic ridge comparable to the intersection of the Atlantic mid-oceanic ridge with the CGFZ (Lonsdale & Shor 1979).

The magmatism in the axis of the Porcupine Seabight Basin appears to have had a complex history. It probably commenced as syn-rift magmatism during the Mid–Late Jurassic over an area of maximum crustal attenuation (White et al., this volume). However, within the Cretaceous interval, evidence from ash bands and seismic-stratigraphy (Tate & Dobson 1988) indicates that activity resumed initially during the early Lower Cretaceous, with further evidence for activity during the Aptian–Albian, whereupon the Porcupine Median Volcanic Ridge acquired its present-day morphology. This latest activity would appear to be post-rift and unusually does not extend south across the Clare Lineament, where greater estimates for β stretching have been calculated with increased likelihood of magmatism. Moreover, this Cretaceous episode of magmatism above attenuated continental crust and on the north side of an incipient transform fault, may be related to advanced extension and the rift-drift transition in the proto-Atlantic rift. By analogy with the Red Sea (Crane & Bonatti 1987), this may be envisaged to have occurred through the northward propagation of the rift, during punctiform oceanic spreading, until its intersection with a transform fault, whereupon magmatism occurred. The BVRS and PMVR, abutting the north side of the transform above attenuated crust in the basin axis, may have resulted as a peripheral effect above a 'leaky transform' or an abortive attempt to localize renewed spreading across the transform boundary/crustal discontinuity at an established centre. Contemporaneous volcanism on the western North Atlantic continental margin is similarly believed to be related to reactivated fracture zones, or possibly to the formation of new fracture zones generated in response to changing stress fields during times of plate re-organization (Jansa & Pe-Piper 1988).

Both the BVRS and the PMVR became temporarily reactivated yet again 50–60 Ma later, as indicated by the existence of sills radiating from their apex and intruding mid to Upper Cretaceous sediments (Scrutton & Bentley 1987; Tate & Dobson 1988). This final episode may have been contemporaneous with the British Tertiary Igneous Province and the onset of sea-floor spreading on the north side of the CGFZ.

Is the Clare Lineament an extension of the Iapetus Suture?

Deep seismic data (BIRPS WIRELINE 2) recorded along the west coast of Ireland has imaged reflectors dipping southwards at 25°, believed to represent the frontal thrust sheets associated with part of the Iapetus suture zone (Fig. 1), where it occurs along strike from its mapped extent onshore to the east (Klemperer et al. 1991). In addition, to the south on the same deep seismic line, some northward dipping reflectors have been associated with the Hercynian front (Klemperer et al. 1991). The recognition of the Clare Lineament to the west in the southern Rockall Trough aroused speculation as to whether it constituted an offshore extension of an important crustal suture (Megson 1987).

Prior to structural mapping in the Porcupine Seabight Basin, and also the delineation of the probable Iapetus suture zone west of the Dingle peninsula, the eastward continuation of the Clare Lineament along the gravity/magnetically defined 'Clare Trend' was considered to extend into the Iapetus suture zone (Megson 1987), then mapped only as far west as onshore western Ireland. It seemed appropriate that a major oceanic transform fault should become located at a major crustal boundary, especially since on the eastern Canadian margin it had already been proposed that the CGFZ recognized from aeromagnetic data extends into the Dover fault (Haworth 1977; Srivastava et al. 1988a). The Dover fault dissects Newfoundland along a NE–SW trend, dividing the Gander and Avalon crustal terranes. It was speculated to be equivalent to the Iapetus suture zone in the western Atlantic (Haworth & Lefort 1979; Haworth et al. 1988; Srivastava et al. 1988b), as opposed to the Hercynian front, as was originally proposed by Cherkis et al. (1973, 1975). By analogy, on the Irish margin, the supposition that the Clare Lineament may be an offshore extension of the Iapetus suture zone has remained largely conceptual until the eastward extent of the Clare Lineament and the westward extent of the Iapetus suture had been determined more accurately. Recent structural mapping presented here and independent gravity/magnetic modelling by Conroy (1989) have confidently extended the Clare Lineament to 51°N/11°W (Fig. 1). Since the Iapetus suture has been confidently extended to c. 52°N/11°W, the location of the Clare Lineament with a contrasting trend, located 1° of latitude south of the Iapetus suture, would indicate that the two structures are unrelated. Irrespective of this, the vertical profile inferred for the Clare Lineament contrasts with the more gently inclined frontal thrusts of the Iapetus suture. This alone would appear to make the Clare Lineament a more likely candidate for the site of detachment of a potential transform fault. Only further deep seismic profiling can reveal the true identity of the Clare Lineament and the westward extension of the Iapetus suture zone.

Financial support was provided by a NERC studentship whilst resident at the Institute of Earth Studies, University College of Wales, Aberystwyth. I am especially grateful to Geco and Western Geophysical for provision of an extensive grid of seismic data; the Department of Energy, Dublin, and all the oil companies that have drilled in the basin, for access to well data. Total Oil Marine plc are acknowledged for drafting assistance. Thanks are also due to M. R. Dobson, J. J. Conroy and three referees for critically reviewing an earlier manuscript.

References

BENTLEY, P. A. D. & SCRUTTON, R. A. 1987. Seismic investigations into the structure of southern Rockall Trough. *In:* BROOKS, J. & GLENNIE, K. W. (eds) *Petroleum Geology of North West Europe.* Graham & Trotman, London, 667–75.

CHERKIS, N. Z., FLEMING, H. S. & MASSINGILL, J. V. 1973. Is the Gibbs Fracture Zone a westward projection of the Hercynian Front into North America? *Nature Physical Science*, **245**, 113–115.

——, ——, —— & —— 1975. Evidence for the emergence of the Hercynian front on the North American continent, *Canadian Journal of Earth Sciences*, **12**, 1474–1479.

CONROY, J. J. 1989. *Marine Geophysical Investigations on the Continental Margin, west of Ireland.* PhD thesis, University College Galway.

—— & BROCK, A. 1989. Gravity and magnetic studies of crustal structure across the Porcupine basin west of Ireland, *Earth and Planetary Science Letters*, **93**, 371–376.

COOK, D. 1987. The Goban Spur: Exploration in a deep water frontier basin. *In:* BROOKS, J. & GLENNIE, K. W. (eds) *Petroleum Geology of North West Europe.* Graham & Trotman, London, 623–632.

CRANE, K. & BONATTI, E. 1987. The role of fracture zones during early Red Sea rifting: structural analysis using Space Shuttle radar and LANDSAT imagery. *Journal of the Geological Society, London*, **144**, 407–420.

DINGLE, R. V., MEGSON, J. B. & SCRUTTON, R. 1982. Acoustic stratigraphy of the sedimentary succession west of Porcupine Bank, NE Atlantic Ocean: a preliminary account, *Marine Geology*, **47**, 17–35.

HAWORTH, R. T. 1977. The continental crust northeast of Newfoundland and its ancestral relationship to the Charlie Fracture zone, *Nature*, **266**, 246–249.

—— & LEFORT, J. P. 1979. Geophysical evidence for the extent of the Avalon Zone in Alantic Canada. *Canadian Journal of Earth Sciences*, **16**, 552–567.

——, HIPKIN, R., JACOBI, R. D., KANE, M., LEFORT, J. P., MAX, M. D., MILLER, H. G. & WOLFF, F. 1988. Geophysical framework and the Appalachian–Caledonide connection. *In:* HARRIS, A. L. & FETTES, D. J. (eds) *The Caledonian–Appalachian Orogen,* Geological Society, London Special Publication, **38**, 3–20.

JANSA, L. F. & PE-PIPER, G. 1988. Middle Jurassic to early Cretaceous Igneous Rocks Along Eastern North American Continental Margin, *AAPG Bulletin Petroleum Geologists*, **72**, 347–66.

JOPPEN, M. & WHITE, R. S. 1990. The structure and subsidence of Rockall Trough from two-ship seismic experiments, *Journal of Geophysical Research*, **95**, 19821–37.

KLEMPERER, S. L., RYAN, P. D. & SNYDER, D. B. 1991. A deep seismic reflection transect across the Irish Caledonides. *Journal of the Geological Society, London*, **148**, 149–164.

LE PICHON, X. & SIBUET, J-C, 1981. Passive margins: a model of formation. *Journal of Geophysical Research*, **86**, 3708–3720.

LONSDALE, P. & SHOR, A. 1979. The oblique intersection of the Mid-Atlantic Ridge with Charlie-Gibbs transform fault. *Tectonophysics*, **54**, 195–209.

MASSON, D. G. & KIDD, R. B. 1986. Revised Tertiary seismic stratigraphy of the Southern Rockall Trough. *In:* RUDDIMAN, W. F., KIDD, R. B., THOMAS, E., *et al.* (eds) *Initial Reports of the Deep Sea Drilling Project.* (US Government Printing Office), Washington, Leg 48, 1117–1126.

——, MILES, P. R., MAX, M. D., SCRUTTON, R. A. & INAMDAR, D. D. 1985. A free-air gravity anomaly map of the Irish continental margin and a new gravity model across the southern Porcupine Seabight. *Geological Survey of Ireland*, Report Series, RS B85/4.

——, MONTADERT, L. & SCRUTTON, R. A. 1984. Regional geology of the Goban Spur continental margin. *In:* DEGRACIANSKY, P. C., POAG, C. W. *et al.* (eds). *Initial Reports of the Deep Sea Drilling Project.* US Government Printing Office, Washington, **80**, 1115–39.

MEGSON, J. B. 1987. The evolution of the Rockall Trough and implications for the Faeroe-Shetland Trough. *In:* BROOKS, J. & GLENNIE, K. W. (eds)

Petroleum Geology of NW Europe. Graham & Trotman, London, 653–665.

NAYLOR, D. & SHANNON, P. M. 1982. *The Geology of Offshore Ireland and West Britain.* Graham & Trotman, London.

PEDDY, C., PINET, B., MASSON, D., SCRUTTON, R., SIBUET, J. C., WARNER, M. R., LEFORT, J. P. & SHROEDER 1989. Crustal structure of the Goban Spur continental margin, Northeast Atlantic, from deep seismic reflection profiling. *Journal of the Geological Society, London,* **146**, 427–437.

SCRUTTON, R. A. & BENTLEY, P. A. D. 1988. Major Cretaceous volcanic province in southern Rockall Trough. *Earth and Planetary Science Letters,* **91**, 198–204.

SRIVASTAVA, S. P., VERHOEF, J. & MACNAB, R. 1988a. Results from a detailed aeromagnetic survey across northeast Newfoundland margin, Part I: Spreading anomalies and relationship between the magnetic anomalies and the ocean-continent boundary. *Marine and Petroleum Geology,* **5**, 306–323.

——, —— & —— 1988b. Results from a detailed aeromagnetic survey across northeast Newfoundland margin, Part II: Early opening of the North Atlantic between the British Isles and Newfoundland. *Marine and Petroleum Geology,* **5**, 324–337.

TATE, M. P. 1990. *Structural framework and tectonostratigraphic evolution of the Porcupine Seabight Basin, offshore western Ireland.* PhD thesis, University of Wales, Aberystwyth.

—— & DOBSON, M. R. 1988. Syn- and post-rift igneous activity in the Porcupine Seabight Basin and adjacent continental margin. *In:* MORTON, A. C. & PARSON, L. M. (eds) *Early Tertiary Volcanism and the Opening of the NE Atlantic.* Geological Society, London, Special Publication, **39**, 309–334.

—— & —— 1989a. Late Permian to early Mesozoic rifting and sedimentation offshore NW Ireland. *Marine and Petroleum Geology,* **6**, 49–59.

—— & —— 1989b. Pre-Mesozoic geology of the western and northwestern Irish Shelf. *Journal of the Geological Society, London,* **146**, 229–240.

Basement tectonics and their relationship to Mesozoic megasequences in the Celtic Seas and Bristol Channel area

A. H. RUFFELL[1] & M. P. COWARD

Department of Geology, Imperial College, Prince Consort Road, London SW7 2BP, UK
[1] *Present address: Department of Geology, Queen's University, Belfast BT7 1NN, UK*

Abstract: A synthesis of new and pre-existing data on the deep geological structure of the Celtic Sea and Bristol Channel basins shows similarities to published models of deep structure from the onshore Wessex Basin to the east. A series of Variscan thrust planes, reactivated in the Mesozoic as normal faults, underlie the study area. Beneath the Bristol Channel, one such southward-dipping thrust may be equated with the 'Variscan Front'. This structure is offset by NW−SE orientated transcurrent faults, structures thought to be active from the late Palaeozoic to the present-day. Mesozoic stratigraphic successions from the North Celtic Sea Basin and South Celtic Sea; Bristol Channel, and northern Wessex Basins suggest uplift and erosion of the latter areas in the late Jurassic. This is contrasted with increased subsidence at the same time in the North Celtic Sea. This uplift may have been facilitated by reactivation of the 'Variscan Front' thrust as a thrust in the east of the area, and by similar thrusts beneath the Pembrokeshire Ridge to the west. This reactivation and uplift during North Atlantic opening is suggested to have controlled the preservation of Upper Jurassic−Lower Cretaceous sedimentary megasequences.

Studies of the Palaeozoic−Mesozoic structure and influence of Variscan thrusts have been made in southern Ireland (Gardiner & Sheridan 1981), the Celtic Seas (BIRPS & ECORS 1986), Bristol Channel (Brooks *et al.* 1988), Southwestern Approaches (Day & Edwards 1983) and western Wessex Basin (Chadwick *et al.* 1983). These areas have been studied with respect to the line of the 'Variscan Front' (the northernmost limit of late Palaeozoic major thrusting) from outcrop, seismic and gravity data. The reactivation of Variscan thrusts as low-angle normal faults during Mesozoic times is thought to have facilitated crustal extension in the major sedimentary basins of the area (Fig. 1). This has been well demonstrated by Chadwick *et al.* (1983) for the western parts of the Wessex Basin, as well as by Brooks *et al.* (1988) for the Bristol Channel Basin. In both cases Variscan thrusts can be linked to specific normal faults in the overlying Mesozoic sediments, seen from both deep and commercial seismic lines. Such thrusting is well known in outcrop sections of the Palaeozoic, rocks surrounding Mesozoic basins, for instance in southern Ireland, South Wales (Gardiner & Sheridan 1981); and east and south of the Bristol Channel (Chadwick *et al.* 1983; Donato 1988).

The secondary reactivation of Variscan thrusts during basin inversion was conjectured by Coward & Trudgill (1989) for the Celtic Seas area: thus, while studies previous to this explained Mesozoic basin formation through crustal extension, accommodated along Variscan thrust planes, Coward & Trudgill (1989) suggested that re-thrusting along such planes might occur in order to explain the uplift (specifically) of the South Celtic Sea Basin in late Jurassic times. Using the information on deep geological structure reviewed above for the whole study area (Fig. 1), we might test whether a similar scenario might be developed for adjacent Mesozoic sedimentary basins.

The study of the possible interaction between basement tectonics and cover sedimentary sequences relies upon geological information about the basement to sedimentary basins, constrained by deep seismic data linked to outcrop structures on the basin margins, as well as gravity models. The northern limits of this study can be summarized therefore as the probable northern limit of Variscan thrusting. To the west, basement reflections are clearly defined on the deep seismic profile SWAT 4 (Fig. 1), but not on SWAT 5 further to the southwest (BIRPS & ECORS, 1986; p 45). There thus seems little point in discussing the role of basement structures in areas where they are not evident. Similarly to the east, the structure of the Bristol Channel Basin, and margins of the Wessex Basin are well constrained (Brooks *et al.* 1988; Chadwick *et al.* 1983, respectively), becoming less-so toward the centre of the Wessex Basin in southern England.

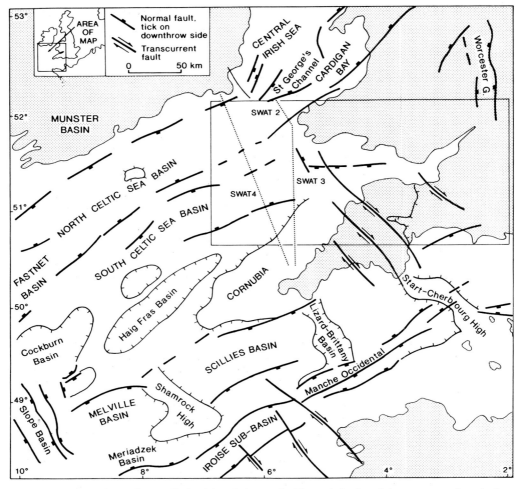

Fig. 1. Location of the study area (in box) in relation to the Mesozoic basins of the western seaboard of England and Wales and offshore southern Ireland.

Deep geology & structure

Deep and shallow (i.e. commercial) seismic data across the study area (Fig. 1) indicate that these basins are underlain by low-angle crustal detachments, evident as shallow-dipping seismic reflections in the Variscan basement. Such reflections are thought to represent Variscan thrusts, the most northern of which corresponds to the 'Variscan Front'. These thrusts may also have been reactivated as normal (dip-slip) faults during Mesozoic crustal extension (BIRPS & ECORS 1986; Shannon 1991).

In the eastern margin of the onshore Wessex Basin (at the limits of the present study),

Chadwick et al. (1983) observed a planar suite of high-amplitude reflections, below Mesozoic cover, dipping at around 27° to the south and southeast. These reflections were thought to be a thrust or series of thrusts of Variscan 'affinity' (Chadwick et al. 1983, p 899), and depths to these reflections were given by depth-converting the deep seismic profiles by reference to nearby boreholes: these data are included on Fig. 2. Chadwick et al. (1983) linked these Variscan thrusts, at depth, to the major outcropping faults of the Mesozoic of the Wessex Basin (i.e. the Vale of Pewsey & Mere Faults: Fig. 2), along which Mesozoic crustal extension was facilitated.

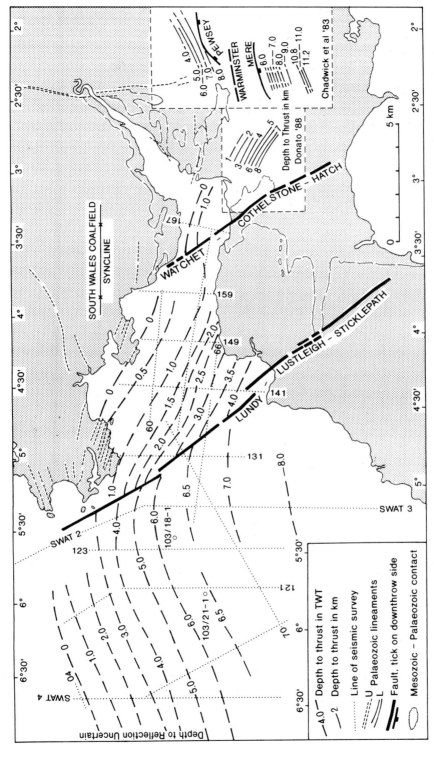

Fig. 2. Synthesis of depth data on the main Variscan thrust below the South Celtic Sea, Bristol Channel and northwestern Wessex Basin. Original seismic two-way time structures and published depth-converted contours are used for comparison to original data (e.g. Figs 3 & 4). Numerous small normal faults are omitted.

In the southwestern margin of the Wessex Basin, Donato (1988) also observed similar seismic reflections, linked to possible Variscan thrusting. These were mapped in a similar manner to that employed by Chadwick *et al.* (1983), and thus can be directly compared (on Fig. 2 of this study). These features were linked to gravity anomalies of the area to explain the juxtaposition, in north Somerset, of deformed Variscan rocks typical of the southern Culm basin, with undeformed Upper Palaeozoic rocks found north of the Variscan Front.

The Mesozoic succession of the Bristol Channel area is structurally linked (laterally) to both the onshore Wessex Basin to the east (Kammerling 1979) and to the South Celtic Sea Basin to the southwest (Petrie *et al.* 1989). This area then forms the geographic focus of the study (Figs 1 & 2), as well defined Variscan crustal reflections become less apparent to the east and west of this area. Seismic reflections representative of Variscan thrusts, and possibly of the Variscan Front itself are known from beneath the Bristol Channel (Brooks *et al.* 1988; see Fig. 3). Here, reactivation of the thrust in Mesozoic times has been linked not only to the regional crustal extension of the area, but specifically to the development of the Central Bristol Channel Fault Zone (see Brooks *et al.* 1988 figure 6 for specific details). An analogous deep crustal reflection is observed at the western limit of the Bristol Channel, on deep seismic data (BIRPS & ECORS 1986; see Fig. 4), as well as beneath the Celtic Sea Basins on SWAT 4 (see Figs 1 & 2 for location). As mentioned above, no similar or clearly defined structure is thought to have been imaged by SWAT 5, some 150 km to the southwest of SWAT 4, even though this line still crosses both Celtic Sea basins (BIRPS & ECORS 1986). Conversely, Coward & Trudgill (1989) demonstrated that a number of low-angle seismic reflections occur below the Mesozoic cover of the Celtic Seas, and that these may represent reactivated Variscan thrusts. Apparently, over the whole Celtic Sea area, Mesozoic crustal extension did not only occur along a single major thrust, as in the Bristol Channel, but along several reactivated thrust planes. Thus while the northernmost thrust is thought to represent the 'Variscan Front' of Gardiner & Sheridan (1981), and which crosses southern Ireland (BIRPS & ECORS 1986), a second reactivated thrust occurs beneath the Pembrokeshire (or St. David's) Ridge (Coward & Trudgill 1989, and see Fig. 1).

While the outcrop tectonic lineaments suggested to represent the 'Variscan Front' of Gardiner & Sheridan (1981) match closely the reflections seen in basement rocks on seismic data beneath the Bristol Channel (Brooks *et al.* 1988), such good correlation is not applicable offshore in the Celtic Sea basins. Here a number of postulated Variscan thrusts occur below Mesozoic sedimentary successions, all of which may have been reactivated as normal faults (Petrie *et al.* 1989). The northernmost basement thrust of the North Celtic Sea Basin is taken to represent the 'Variscan Front' (Gardiner & Sheridan 1981; BIRPS & ECORS 1986), although the number of similar structures to the south, and indeed their apparently reactivated behaviour in the Mesozoic, may make the Celtic Sea area similar to the broader 'front' of Variscan deformation described by Matthews (1974). Coward & Trudgill (1989) suggest that it is the thrusts beneath the Pembrokeshire Ridge, passing into the onshore Variscan Front in South Wales, that facilitated uplift of the South Celtic Seas in late Jurassic times.

All previous, and areally restricted, studies of basement structure and its effect on Mesozoic basins (summarized above) focused on the reactivation of Variscan thrusts in crustal extension. The relationship of these various studies may aid in our understanding of how the Variscan thrusts of each area relate to, and how they might control the development of Mesozoic sedimentary sequences. Figure 2 is an attempt to demonstrate how the main Variscan thrust(s) of the area relate, by combining data from the west of the study area (SWAT Profiles 3 & 4), with the Merlin seismic profiles utilized by Brooks *et al.* (1988). This structure is shown in two-way travel time to the main Variscan 'thrust' of the area in order to allow direct comparison to the original seismic data (shown in: BIRPS & ECORS 1986; Brooks *et al.* 1988; Fig. 4). This data can be compared to the depth-converted contours from the studies of the Wessex Basin to the east (Chadwick *et al.* 1983; Donato 1988), again left in Fig. 2 so as to allow comparison with original data. This synthesis (Fig. 2) suggests that the northern depositional basin margin of the Bristol Channel (Kammerling 1979) and Wessex Basin (Whittaker 1985) roughly corresponds to the northern outcrop/subcrop of this major Variscan thrust; possibly the Variscan Front. Interestingly, both areas possess a similar stratigraphic succession, comprising Permian−Triassic deposits resting unconformably on faulted Variscan basement, passing into Lower−Middle Jurassic successions, unconformably overlain by mid-Cretaceous strata, with isolated pockets of Upper Jurassic pre-

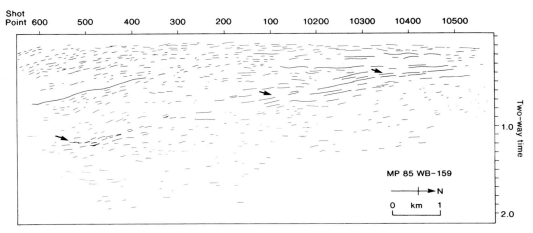

Fig. 3. Line drawing of Merlin Geophysical Ltd Seismic Line MP 85 WB-159 (location on Fig. 2). Open arrows indicate the reflection thought by Brooks *et al.* (1988) to represent a Variscan thrust.

served below this unconformity (Kammerling 1979). This is the initial observation which might suggest that the Coward & Trudgill (1989) model of latest Jurassic uplift along Variscan

thrusts, developed for the South Celtic Sea Basin, might find application elsewhere.

Figure 2 demonstrates the similarity in orientation and dip between the Variscan thrusts

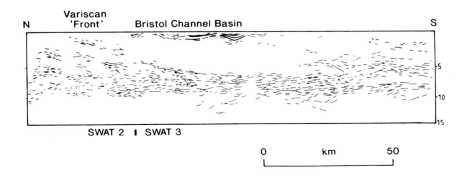

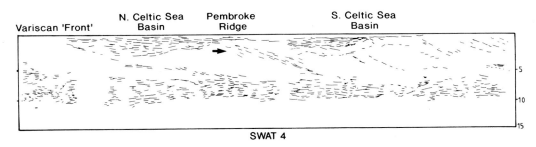

Fig. 4. Line drawings of SWAT lines 3 (with part of line 2) and 4. Location on Figure 1. Depth in seconds, two-way time. Arrow indicates the Variscan thrust thought to be reactivated in late Jurassic uplift (Coward & Trudgill 1989).

identified in the east of the study area by Chadwick *et al.* (1983), Donato (1988) and Brooks *et al.* (1988) in the west of the study area. It should be noted that such structural contours are drawn on the upper surface of the most prominent seismic reflections of the area: such reflections are likely to represent a number of closely spaced thrust planes forming an impedence contrast, and in no way imply that a simple, single thrust plane is represented. It is also quite probable that other thrusts occur beneath the Bristol Channel that are not clearly imaged on seismic data. Two interpretations of the direct effect of deep Variscan thrusts on Mesozoic faults can be offered: one is the view of Brooks *et al.* (1988), who depict normal faults emanating from the thrust; the other is that Mesozoic normal faults also cut the thrust planes, some of which continue to surface and are expressed as outcrop thrust planes in South Wales.

NW−SE orientated transform faults of the area

Offsets in the depths recorded on seismic data to the main Variscan thrust in the study area are frequently orientated NW−SE (Brooks *et al.* 1988), and some undoubtedly are the continuation (or relate to) the known major transcurrent faults of the area (Fig. 2: Lundy−Lustleigh−Sticklepath; Quantock or Watchet−Cothelstone−Hatch Faults). Such offsets are best constrained in the Bristol Channel area by a dense network of seismic lines. Onshore, the variable orientation of the structure contours to the Variscan thrust given by Donato (1988), as opposed to Chadwick *et al.* (1983), may be due to the presence of more than one thrust beneath the Wessex Basin (as occurs in the Celtic Seas). However, such a change in orientation may also be produced through more complex offsets where the NW−SE transcurrent faults of the area intersect with the dominantly E−W reactivated Variscan−Mesozoic structures of the Wessex Basin to the south and Worcester Graben to the north (Whittaker 1985).

NW−SE orientated transcurrent faults that affect Devonian through to Tertiary (and possibly recent) strata are well documented throughout the study area (Zeigler 1982). Webby (1966) demonstrated how the Quantock Fault (Watchet−Cothelstone−Hatch: see Fig. 2) affected Devonian strata. Similarly Whittaker (1972) and Holloway & Chadwick (1986) showed how this structure, as well as the Lustleigh−Sticklepath Fault (respectively) to the southwest, affects the distribution of

Mesozoic and Cenozoic sediments. Shearman (1967) modelled such faults and demonstrated how movement along the Quantock Fault could facilitate E−W extension. From these studies it would appear that the NW−SE faults of the area are inherently basement structures, kept active from Palaeozoic times until the present-day (Smithurst 1990). They are evident as transcurrent faults in the basement, and thus it is interesting to note the offset to the major Variscan thrust of the area. This suggests that later extension and possibly re-thrusting during Mesozoic−Cenozoic compression may have been compartmentalized and accommodated along these faults.

Study of such transcurrent offsets of the main Variscan thrust of the Bristol Channel area (Fig. 2) suggests that the dominant feature of the area is the Lundy−Sticklepath−Lustleigh Fault, a feature described in detail by Holloway & Chadwick (1986). This fault offsets the main Variscan thrust of the area by over 3 km (laterally in basement rocks) whereas the Quantock (Watchet−Cothelstone−Hatch) Fault to the east only offsets the 'thrust' (here it is a series of thrust planes) by a maximum of 1 km. It is notable that the association of Cenozoic granites (of the North Atlantic Province) and strike-slip pull-apart basins (i.e. Bovey−Petrockstow−Lundy) occur along the Sticklepath Fault, yet these are not developed along other NW−SE orientated transcurrent faults of the area. This near vertical fault is most obviously highlighted by such offsets: on seismic data (e.g. Line 131 of Fig. 2) this feature is evident as a zone of vertical faults and chaotic reflections.

NW−SE orientated faults were affecting sedimentation, either in an active or passive manner, in the early Triassic in the western part of the study area, but are less evident in late Triassic to later Mesozoic successions (where an E−W orientation is dominant; Ruffell 1990). Later evidence for NW−SE orientated control is most evident in the late Jurassic−mid-Cretaceous (Drummond 1970; Ruffell & Wignall 1990) and in the Cenozoic (Holloway & Chadwick 1986). It is thus of note that the well documented episode of basin inversion in the late Cretaceous−mid Cenozoic was directed along E−W trends in the centre of the Wessex Basin (Whittaker 1985), passing west into NW−SE orientated faults. Similarly therefore, the late Jurassic−early Cretaceous phase of uplift, less obvious as compression or inversion (see Coward & Trudgill 1989; Ruffell & Wignall 1990 as examples), but equally well known as the 'late Cimmerian' (Chadwick 1986) and/or 'Austrian' (Zeigler 1982; Karner *et al.* 1987) phase of tectonics, was also characterized by E−W deformation in the basin centre, passing into a NW−SE trend in the basin margins. The late Jurassic−early Cretaceous re-thrusting model of basin inversion described by Coward & Trudgill (1989) for the Celtic Sea area, may find further applicability to surrounding basins, and to the east may be further refined as possible re-thrusting accommodated along NW−SE transfer faults. The effect on sedimentary megasequences of all the areas would be similar if such a model is applied, and it is by a comparison of the stratigraphy that the model may be further tested.

Effects of basement tectonics on Mesozoic sequences

Mesozoic basin development in the study area is discussed by Chadwick (1986), Karner et al. (1987) and Petrie et al. (1989). An early Permian−Triassic syn-rift phase, followed by late Triassic−early Jurassic thermal relaxation and later Jurassic−early Cretaceous uplift is evident in all the basins of the area. The exception is the North Celtic Sea Basin, which underwent renewed subsidence in the late Jurassic. The early Cretaceous movements in southern England and in the Celtic Seas have been suggested to represent a second syn-rift phase (Karner et al. 1987; Petrie et al. 1989), again followed by Cretaceous thermal relaxation (during deposition of the Chalk), and later basin inversion due to Alpine compression (see above) in the Cenozoic.

Similarities in the Mesozoic stratigraphy immediately south of the main Variscan thrust (Fig. 2) suggests that here there may be a genetic link between basement tectonics and the major late Jurassic−early Cretaceous unconformity developed in the South Celtic Sea, Bristol Channel and Northern margins of the Wessex Basin. It is also notable that it is not the traditional line of the 'Variscan Front' (Gardiner & Sheridan 1981) that forms the structural boundary between areas of differing Mesozoic stratigraphies: instead it is the Pembrokeshire Ridge, a positive structure throughout the Mesozoic history of the area, and thought to be underlain by Variscan thrusts (Coward & Trudgill 1989; Petrie et al. 1989). Why then did a thick late Jurassic succession develop in the North Celtic Sea Basin north of the Pembrokeshire Ridge, when erosion was occurring in adjacent basins, as well as many of the basins along the margins of the North Atlantic? Coward & Trudgill (1989) suggested that

Variscan thrusts beneath the Pembrokeshire Ridge were reactivated as thrusts at this time, causing uplift of the South Celtic Sea Basin, and the redeposition of eroded material in the North Celtic Sea Basin. It is possible therefore that the Bristol Channel Basin, and northern Wessex Basin, both underlain by Variscan 'Front' thrusts, had a similar history, being inverted in late Jurassic times, the inversion being accommodated by renewed (i.e. Mesozoic) thrusting on pre-existing Variscan thrust planes. Whilst in the South Celtic Sea Basin eroded material may have been redeposited in the North Celtic Sea Basin, in the Bristol Channel and Wessex Basin similar material may have been redeposited to the south in the Wessex−Channel Basins. In both areas the uplift resulted in the source-area for the non-marine clastic 'Wealden' facies.

The occurrence of similar Wealden facies as well as a widespread Jurassic−Cretaceous unconformity south of the study area (Paris Basin; Lusitanian Basin) suggests that similar uplift occurred here too. A major late Jurassic−early Cretaceous unconformity also occurs north of the study area, beyond the influence of postulated reactivated Variscan thrusts (e.g. in the Hebridean basins: see Morton, this volume). Such regional uplift is not at variance with a reactivated thrust model: uplift of the North Atlantic margins and continental break-up to the south probably occurred at the same time as some compression and crustal shortening to the west, facilitated by Variscan thrusts, and probably accommodated along NW−SE transcurrent faults. These now compartmentalize basins such as the Wessex Basin (Karner et al. 1987; also Fig. 2). It is the close proximity of thickened Jurassic−Cretaceous successions to basins with a major unconformity (separated by areas underlain by Variscan thrusts) that requires a more dynamic tectonic explanation than simple regional uplift, when crustal shortening over a wide area could also have occurred. This model may thus find application to many similar basins along the margins of the North Atlantic and NW seaboard of the United Kingdom, especially where thick sedimentary successions (of any age, but most specifically, late Jurassic−early Cretaceous) of one basin occur close to another basin with a major unconformity of similar age. Figure 6 shows the development of similar successions to the Celtic Sea−Bristol Channel example over the North Atlantic region. Such a comparison of stratigraphic megasequences predicts that plate movement, rotation during North Atlantic rifting, and episodes of inversion in many areas,

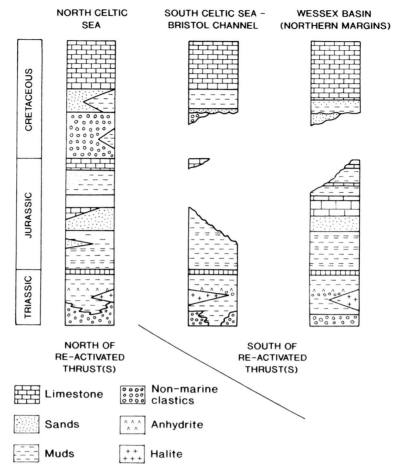

Fig. 5. Mesozoic stratigraphic successions from the four main basins of the study area (from Whittaker, 1985; Petrie *et al.* 1989). Basement (e.g. the Welsh-Anglo-Brabant Massif) may also occur north of a reactivated Variscan thrust as foreland.

was similar to that in the study area. Similar structural controls in basement rocks may also be predicted.

Discussion

Whether the late Jurassic inversion along the Variscan thrusts, or in surrounding uplifted basins, was rapid or gradual is difficult to assess. The number of late Jurassic—early Cretaceous unconformities and other depositional breaks in the North Celtic Sea sedimentary succession (Colin *et al.* 1981: figure 11.3; Petrie *et al.* 1989) would, taken in isolation, be one indication of spasmodic uplift and erosion. The existence of similar, stratigraphically closely spaced and

major unconformities in southern England (Hesselbo & Allen 1991; Wignall 1991), the North Sea area (Rawson & Riley 1982), other North Atlantic continental margin basins (e.g. the Lusitanian, Parentis, Jeanne d'Arc basins of Wilson *et al.* 1989 and Fig. 6), and not least on the Exxon Global Cycle Chart (Haq *et al.* 1988), must be counted as evidence for a wider, regional, control, either through eustacy (*sensu* Haq *et al.* 1988) or through intra-plate stress mechanisms (*sensu* Cloetingh 1986). This applies directly to the Upper Jurassic—Lower Cretaceous of the North Celtic Sea Basin, while basement tectonics and the crustal deformation associated with the opening of the Atlantic area are thought to account for the Mesozoic mega-

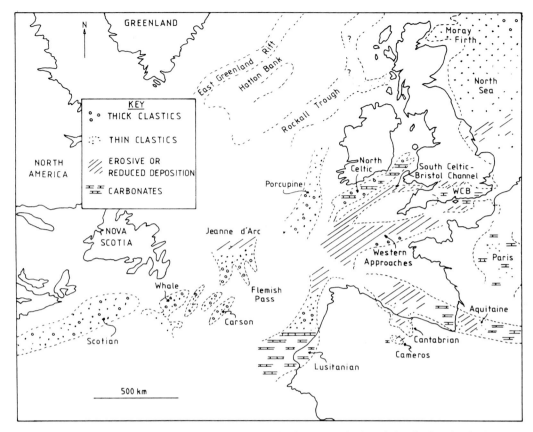

Fig. 6. Sedimentary successions of the late Jurassic–early Cretaceous basins of the North Atlantic. Data sources: Wilson *et al.* (1989); Shannon (1991).

sequences (Petrie *et al.* 1989) and most specifically, the widespread Jurassic–Cretaceous unconformity of the surrounding basins.

Conclusion

Subsidence and crustal extension during the opening of the North Atlantic was accommodated by dip-slip movement on basement thrusts in the Celtic Sea, Bristol Channel and Wessex Basins. Phases of compression and uplift due to plate rotation during extension and the effects of the 'late Cimmerian' (late Jurassic–early Cretaceous) movements to the south were facilitated by similar reactivation of thrusts as compressive structures. The late Jurassic–early Cretaceous megasequence of the North Celtic Sea Basin is in effect preserved in the foreland of reactivated thrusts beneath the Pembrokeshire Ridge and Bristol Channel. Basement thrusts, along with overlying Mesozoic–

Cenozoic sediments, are cross-cut by NW–SE transcurrent faults that were also active at various times in the Mesozoic–Cenozoic.

This study forms part of a BP International-funded project, in which the help of Chris Banks is acknowledged. AR would also like to thank John Donato (Goal Petroleum plc) and Marios Miliorizos for their help, and Pat Shannon for his encouragement. Seismic line MP 85 WB-159 is reproduced with permission from Merlin Geophysical Ltd, in which the help of Tom Kileyni is acknowledged.

References

BIRPS & ECORS 1986. Deep seismic profiling between England, France and Ireland. *Journal of the Geological Society, London*, **143**, 45–52.

BROOKS, M., TRAYNER, P. M. & TRIMBLE, T. J. 1988. Mesozoic reactivation of Variscan thrusting in the Bristol Channel area, UK. *Journal of the Geological Society, London*, **145**, 439–444.

CHADWICK, R. A. 1986. Extension tectonics in the Wessex Basin, southern England. *Journal of the Geological Society, London*, **143**, 465−488.

CHADWICK, R. A., KENOLTY, N. & WHITTAKER, A. 1983. Crustal structure beneath southern England from deep seismic reflection profiles. *Journal of the Geological Society, London*, **140**, 893−911.

COLIN, J. P., LEHMANN, R. A. & MORGAN, B. E., 1981. Cretaceous and Late Jurassic Biostratigraphy of the North Celtic Sea Basin, Offshore Southern Ireland. *In*: NEALE, J. W. & BRASIER, M. D. (eds) *Microfossils from Recent and Fossil Shelf Seas*. Ellis Horwood, Chichester, 122−155.

COWARD, M. P. & TRUDGILL, B. 1989. Basin development and basement structure of the Celtic Sea basins (SW Britain). *Bulletin Societie geologique Francais*, **3**, 423−436.

CLOETINGH, S. 1986. Intraplate stresses: a new tectonic mechanism for fluctuations of relative sea level. *Geology*, **14**, 617−620.

DAY, G. A. & EDWARDS, J. W. F. 1983. Variscan thrusting in the basement of the English Channel and SW Approaches. *Proceedings of the Ussher Society*, **5**, 432−436.

DONATO, J. A. 1988. Possible thrusting beneath the Somerton Anticline, Somerset. *Journal of the Geological Society, London*, **145**, 431−438.

DRUMMOND, P. V. O. 1970. The mid-Dorset swell. Evidence of Albian−Cenomanian movements in Wessex. *Proceedings of the Geologists Association*, **81**, 679−714.

GARDINER, P. R. R. & SHERIDAN, D. J. R. 1981. Tectonic framework of the Celtic Sea and adjacent areas with special reference to the Variscan Front. *Journal of Structural Geology*, **3**, 317−331.

HAQ, B. U., HARDENBOL, J. & VAIL, P. R. 1988. Mesozoic and Cenozoic chronostratigraphy and cycles of sea level change. *In*: WILGUS, C. K., HASTINGS, B. S., KENDALL, G. ST. C., POSAMENTIER, H. W., ROSS, C. A. & VAN WAGONER, J. C. (eds) *Sea-level changes: an integrated approach*. Special Publication of the Society of Economic Paleontologists and Mineralogists, **42**, 71−108.

HESSELBO, S. P. & ALLEN, P. A. 1991. Major erosion surfaces in basal Wealden Beds, Lower Cretaceous, south Dorset: a sequence stratigraphic interpretation. *Journal of the Geological Society, London*, **148**, 105−113.

HOLLOWAY, S. & CHADWICK, R. A. 1986. The Sticklepath−Lustleigh fault zone: Tertiary reactivation of a Variscan dextral strike-slip fault. *Journal of the Geological Society, London*, **142**, 447−452.

KAMMERLING, P. 1979. The geology and hydrocarbon habitat of the Bristol Channel Basin. *Journal of Petroleum Geology*, **2**, 75−93.

KARNER, G. D., LAKE, S. D. & DEWEY, J. F. 1987. The thermo-mechanical development of the Wessex Basin, southern England. *In*: HANCOCK,

P. L., DEWEY, J. F. & COWARD, M. P. (eds) *Continental Extensional Tectonics*. Geological Society, London, Special Publication, **28**, 517−536.

MATTHEWS, S. C. 1974. Exmoor Thrust? Variscan Front? *Proceedings of the Ussher Society*, **3**, 82−94.

PETRIE, S. H., BROWN, J. R., GRANGER, P. J. & LOVELL, J. P. B. 1989. Mesozoic history of the Celtic Sea Basins. *In*: TANKARD, A. J. & BALKWILL, H. (eds) *Extensional Tectonics and Stratigraphy of the North Atlantic Margins*. American Association of Petroleum Geologists, Memoir **46**, 433−444.

RAWSON, P. F. & RILEY, L. A. 1982. Latest Jurassic− Early Cretaceous events and the 'late Cimmerian' unconformity in North Sea area. *AAPG Bulletin*, **66**, 2628−2648.

RUFFELL, A. 1990. Stratigraphy and structure of the Mercia Mudstone Group (Triassic) in the western part of the Wessex Basin. *Proceedings of the Ussher Society*, **7**, 263−267.

—— & WIGNALL, P. B. 1990. Depositional trends in the Upper Jurassic−Lower Cretaceous of the northern margin of the Wessex Basin. *Proceedings of the Geologists' Association*, **101**, 279−288.

SHANNON, P. M. 1991. The development of Irish offshore sedimentary basins. *Journal of Geological Society, London*, **148**, 181−189.

SHEARMAN, D. J. 1967. On Tertiary fault movements in north Devonshire. *Proceedings of the Geologists' Association*, **78**, 555−566.

SMITHURST, L. J. M. 1990. Structural remote sensing of south-west England. *Proceedings of the Ussher Society*, **7**, 236−241.

WEBBY, B. D. 1966. The stratigraphy and structure of the Devonian rocks in the Quantock Hills, west Somerset. *Proceedings of the Geologists' Association*, **76**, 321−343.

WHITTAKER, A. 1972. The Watchet Fault − a post-Liassic transcurrent reverse fault. *Bulletin of the Geological Survey*, **41**, 75−80.

—— 1985. (ed.) *Atlas of Onshore Sedimentary Basins in England and Wales*. Blackie, Glasgow & London.

WIGNALL, P. B. 1991. Test of the concepts of sequence stratigraphy in the Kimmeridgian (Late Jurassic) of England and northern France. *Marine & Petroleum Geology*, **8**, 430−441.

WILSON, R. C. L., HISCOTT, R. N., WILLIS, M. G. & GRADSTEIN, F. M. 1989. The Lusitanian Basin of west central Portugal: Mesozoic and Tertiary tectonic, stratigraphic and subsidence history. *In*: TANKARD, A. J. & BALKWILL, H. (eds) *Extensional Tectonics and Stratigraphy of the North Atlantic Margins*, American Association of Petroleum Geologists, Memoir **46**, 341−361.

ZIEGLER, P. A. 1982. *Geological Atlas of Western and Central Europe*. Shell International Petroleum Mij BV, The Hague.

The Atlantic Seaboard beyond the British Isles

Evolution of Mesozoic sedimentary basins around the North Central Atlantic: a preliminary plate kinematic solution

S. P. SRIVASTAVA & J. VERHOEF

Geological Survey of Canada, Atlantic Geoscience Centre, Bedford Institute of Oceanography, P.O. Box 1006, Dartmouth, NS, B2Y 4A2, Canada

Abstract: There is significant correlation between the tectono-stratigraphic record in the sedimentary basins round the Central North Atlantic and the seafloor spreading history of the North Atlantic. This has been taken as an indication that the formation of these basins can be related to the relative motion between lithospheric plates. Based on many criteria, plate kinematics of the North Atlantic have been derived for the rifting periods of these basins. Reconstructions of the North Atlantic based on these plate kinematic solutions show a progressive overlap between the reconstituted plate boundaries. These overlaps exist because the margins of the original plates stretched during rifting: present-day plate boundaries are therefore extended beyond their pre-rift locations. From the overlaps, it is possible to calculate the amount of extension during rifting and to restore the plates and their enclosed basins to their pre-stretched configurations. The paper discusses techniques for the de-stretching of plate margins and describes a set of reconstructions showing the configuration of these basins as they evolved. For the first time, the reconstructions give a pictorial presentation of the formation of these basins.

The accumulation of a vast amount of information on sedimentary basins on both sides of the North Central Atlantic (Fig. 1) has enabled a number of authors to compare evolution histories (e.g. Masson & Miles 1986; Manspeizer 1988; Tankard & Balkwill 1989; Verhoef & Srivastava 1989). In a recent paper, Hiscott *et al.* (1990) compared the stratigraphy and subsidence history of these basins and showed that most of them share features like unconformities of similar age and subsidence rates. They suggested that the basins shared a common origin controlled by intercontinental rifting and the subsequent separation of Europe from North America. If these basins were contiguous prior to seafloor spreading, then we should expect to see a direct relationship between tectonic events in these basins and those observed in the evolution of the North Atlantic.

The opening of the North Atlantic was not an instantaneous process. The episodic northward propagation of the separation of North America from Africa, Iberia and Europe has been summarized by Srivastava & Tapscott (1986) and Klitgord & Schouten (1986). Prior to their separation, rifting took place between the plates and their final separation occurred gradually, as suggested by Vink (1982) and Courtillot (1982). Thus when portions of plates separated in one region, other portions were still undergoing stretching. These events should then be recorded in the evolution of the basins. This is illustrated in Table 1, adapted from a compilation of the tectono-stratigraphy of the sedimentary basins around the North Atlantic (Fig. 1) by Tankard & Balkwill (1989). For example, event L relates to the separation of Africa from North America (175 Ma, Klitgord & Schouten 1986) even though the sedimentary basins onshore and offshore North America suggest that rifting between these plates started as early as Late Triassic to Early Jurassic (Manspeizer 1988). This episode also affected the basins to the north, like the Jeanne d'Arc and Lusitanian basins (Table 1). Event J relates to the separation of Galicia Bank (northwestern part of Iberia) from Flemish Cap, and to the concurrent formation of a volcanic ridge between North America and Iberia (118 Ma, Boillot *et al.* 1989, Srivastava *et al.* 1988). Event G relates to the complete separation of Eurasia south of Greenland from North America (Srivastava *et al.* 1988) and appears as an unconformity in several of the basins surrounding the North Central Atlantic. The timing of the separation of Iberia from North America is less certain, but the suggestion that its southern part began to separate from North America as early as Kimmeridgian (chron M25, 156 Ma, Srivastava *et al.* 1990*a*, *b*; Malod & Mauffret 1990) is well reflected in many of the basins (event K, Table 1). The presence of a large number of major unconformities in many of the basins between events L and J and their absence afterwards attests to the hypothesis that they originated during the gradual separation of

From PARNELL, J. (ed.), 1992, *Basins on the Atlantic Seaboard: Petroleum Geology, Sedimentology and Basin Evolution.* Geological Society Special Publication No 62, pp 397–420.

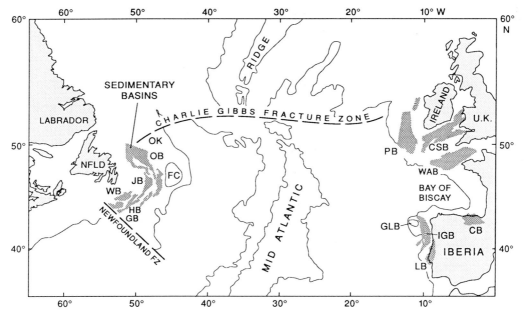

Fig. 1. Simplified bathymetry of the North Central Atlantic showing the location of the sedimentary basins. OK, Orphan Knoll; OB, Orphan Basin; FC, Flemish Cap; JB, Jeanne d'Arc Basin; WB, Whale Basin; HB, Horseshoe Basin; GB, Grand Banks; PB, Porcupine Basin; CSB, Celtic Sea Basin; WAB, Western Approaches Basin; GLB, Galicia Bank; IGB, Inner Galicia Basin; LB, Lusitanian Basin; CB, Cantabrian Basin.

Iberia from North America (Srivastava *et al.* 1990*a*).

By comparing the timing of major seafloor spreading events with stratigraphic records of sedimentary basins, we can relate the processes involved in the development of these basins to associated events. The existence of a direct linkage between the evolution of sedimentary basins and seafloor spreading was shown by Welsink *et al.* (1989) and Verhoef & Srivastava (1989) who correlated the tectonic fabric of these basins with the direction of the initial plate motion in the North Atlantic. What needs

to be resolved now is how a plate kinematic solution of the ocean basins can be used to explain the development of sedimentary basins during rifting.

The problem is to determine the configuration of the plates and their boundaries during the formation of the sedimentary basins. In other words, we need to relate the timing and the amount of basinal extension to the magnitude and direction of rifting that occurred between the plates at various times. It is difficult to obtain these parameters for the periods when the plates were being pulled apart, on account

Table 1. Tectono-stratigraphy of the sedimentary basins around the Central North Atlantic (Fig. 1) and seafloor spreading events (A to L) in the North Atlantic. A, Iberia moving with Eurasia (Srivastava *et al.* 1990*a*); B, seafloor spreading in the Labrador Sea ceases and Greenland starts to move with North America (Roest & Srivastava 1989); C, Iberia moving as an independent plate (Roest & Srivastava 1991); D, separation of Greenland from Eurasia and volcanism in North America (Srivastava and Tapscott 1986); E, change in direction of motion between Eurasia and North America (Srivastava *et al.* 1988); F, active seafloor spreading starting in the Labrador Sea (Roest and Srivastava 1989); G, complete separation of Eurasia from North America (Srivastava *et al.* 1988); H, separation of Goban Spur from Flemish Cap (De Graciansky *et al.* 1985); I, separation of Galicia Bank from Flemish Cap (Boillot *et al.* 1988); J, formation of volcanic ridges (known as "J" anomaly ridge) between Iberia, North America and Africa and excessive volcanism along the Newfoundland Fracture Zone; K, possible separation of southern part of Iberia from North America (Mauffret *et al.* 1989; Srivastava *et al.* 1990*a*); L, separation of Africa from North America (Klitgord & Schouten 1986)

of a lack of reliable information that can be used as constraints: when plates have been pulled apart over a long period of time and in varying directions, it is not easy to differentiate the time-dependent evidence for this deformation. However, if the separation between the plates has been progressive in nature, as in the region of Fig. 1 (Table 1, Srivastava *et al.* 1988,

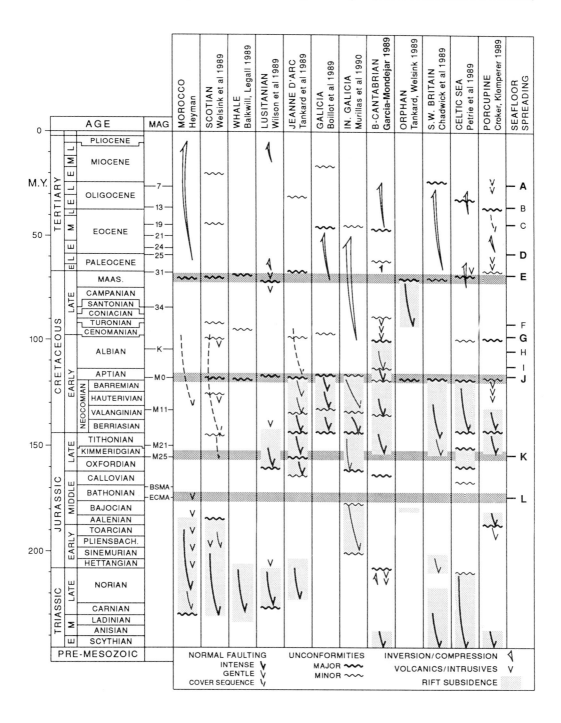

De Graciansky *et al.* 1985, Boillot *et al.* 1989 and Montadert *et al.* 1979), then it should be possible to determine how much each plate was stretched at different times. This is achieved by systematically bringing together the plate boundaries along which the plates had progressively separated. In doing so, one finds that when older regions of the plate boundaries are matched, regions that separated later overlap in the reconstruction. The amount of overlap can be related to the stretching of the plates.

As an example, Fig. 2 shows the configuration of the North American, Eurasian and Iberian plates and their basins, at chron M0 (Aptian, 118 Ma), when Iberia had completely separated from North America. The parallelism between the direction of plate motion at M0 and the geophysical trends over these basins suggests that part of the extension of these basins took place along that direction of motion. North of

Flemish Cap, there are overlaps between the boundaries of the Rockall, Eurasian and North American plates. These are boundaries along which the plates are supposed to have separated (i.e. the ocean–continent boundaries); the overlaps imply that the regions were still undergoing rifting while separation had already occurred to the south. A similar overlap between the plate boundaries south of Flemish Cap results when the plates are restored to earlier times (Srivastava *et al.* 1990*a*). The amount of overlap of plate boundaries at a given time essentially tells us how much these plates were extended.

If we know the magnitude of overlap and the direction of plate motion at a given time, we should be able to restore plates to their pre-extensional state at that time. This provides us with a technique for determining the configurations of sedimentary basins as they evolved.

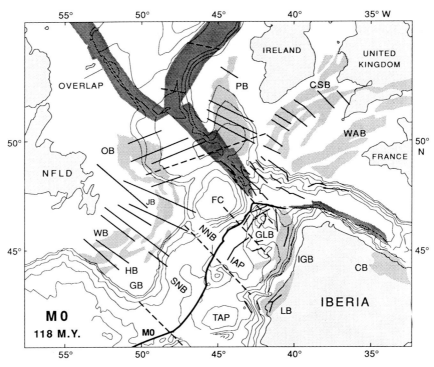

Fig. 2. Reconstruction of the North Central Atlantic at chron M0 showing a simplified bathymetry on each plate, outlines of the sedimentary basins (shaded regions) and their tectonic features (continuous lines, after Verhoef & Srivastava 1989). Also shown are the direction of plate motion (dashed lines) and the resulting overlap between plate boundaries (dark stippled regions). JB, Jeanne d'Arc Basin; WB, Whale Basin; HB, Horseshoe Basin; OB, Orphan Basin; FC, Flemish Cap; CSB, Celtic Sea Basin; WAB, Western Approaches Basin; PB, Porcupine Basin; GLB, Galicia Bank; IGB, Inner Galicia Basin; LB, Lusitanian Basin; CB, Cantabrian Basin; NNB, North Newfoundland Basin; SNB, South Newfoundland Basin; IAP, Iberia Abyssal Plain; TAP, Tagus Abyssal Plain.

In this paper, we have restored some North Atlantic plate margins to their pre-extensional configuration at various times. For this we used the plate kinematics of the North Atlantic described by Srivastava *et al.* (1988, 1989, 1990*a*) and Roest & Srivastava (1989, 1991). The present study describes a technique for deriving the positions of plates and sedimentary basins at various times in their evolution, and discusses some implications of these reconstructions.

Poles for pre-drift plate reconstructions

To obtain the amount of overlap between plate boundaries we need to know the positions of the plates at pre-drift periods. Figure 2 illustrates one such reconstruction at Aptian time (chron M0): at this time active seafloor spreading had already started south of Flemish Cap while regions to the north were undergoing stretching. A number of initial-opening reconstructions of the North Atlantic exist in the literature (Bullard *et al.* 1965; Le Pichon *et al.* 1977; Savostin *et al.* 1986; Srivastava & Tapscott 1986; Klitgord & Schouten 1986; Rowley & Lottes 1988). Most models assume an instantaneous separation between the plates, contrary to what geological (Table 1) and recent geophysical evidence (Srivastava *et al.* 1990*a*, *b*) suggest.

Recently, Van der Voo (1990) showed that the Bullard *et al.* (1965) reconstruction, based on a least square fitting of 500 fathoms contours across the North Atlantic, results in a best fit between Ordovician to Early Jurassic palaeomagnetic poles of North America and Europe (Fig. 3). As the Late Triassic to Early Jurassic is the oldest episode which can be recognized in the sedimentary basins around the North Atlantic, this reconstruction may be considered a fair approximation of the pre-drift configuration of the North Atlantic. A similar conclusion was reached by Chadwick *et al.* (1989), from a comparison of crustal extension factors between the Grand Banks and the British Isles obtained from two models: a simple shear model of extension from Permian to mid-Cretaceous gave a factor of 1.19 while Bullard's reconstruction gave 1.16.

However, the Bullard *et al.* (1965) reconstruction is not compatible with the evolution of the Arctic (Rowley & Lottes 1988): if we assume that no deformation has taken place within the Eurasian plate since the Early Triassic, the reconstruction implies a large compression within the Arctic oceanic regions at later times (Fig. 3). Similarly, it produces a large overlap between France and Iberia, perhaps caused by

major extension within the North Sea during Triassic and Jurassic (Ziegler & van Hoorn 1989). It is difficult, therefore, to use the Bullard *et al.* (1965) reconstruction as a definitive model for calculations of the pre-drift configurations of the basins round the North Atlantic. However, it can be applied as a guide for determining the pole positions for other pre-drift stages between Eurasia and North America.

Chron M25 (Kimmeridgian, 156 Ma) pole

Poles of rotation between Eurasia, Greenland, Rockall and North America for chron M25 (Kimmeridgian) are listed in Table 2. This is the oldest episode recognized from seafloor spreading data in this region (Srivastava *et al.* 1990*a*; Malod & Mauffret 1990). It has been inferred that at this time the southern part of Iberia separated from North America. The pole between Eurasia and North America gives rise to an overlap between their boundaries that is some what less than that obtained from the Bullard *et al.* (1965) pole. However, the listed pole results in a strike-slip motion between the Eurasian and North American plates in the Arctic (Fig. 3). At the same time, the rotation of the palaeomagnetic poles for Eurasia of this age (shown as No. 4 in Fig. 3) using our pole, brings them within the 95% confidence circle for the pole of North America (Van der Voo 1990).

Figure 4 shows a bathymetric reconstruction of the North Atlantic at chron M25 using the poles of Table 2. This was used to determine the configuration of the basins at that time. To obtain the amount of stretching implied by this reconstruction, we followed a scheme similar to that of Chadwick *et al.* (1989). For this we used the plate configuration of Srivastava *et al.* (1988) at the onset of seafloor spreading between Europe and North America and the one at the pre-drift period, given in Fig. 5 where the plates have been de-stretched to take into account the overlap shown in Fig. 4. To calculate the amount of extension of the plates between these two configurations, we took a quadrangle ABCD (Fig. 5) enclosing the region where most of the stretching may have taken place. The ratio of the area enclosed by these quadrangles in both configurations (ABCD and AB'C'D) gives a stretching factor of 1.23. A similar calculation carried out using the Bullard *et al.* (1965) pole gave a value of 1.37.

As obtained above, the estimate for the stretching is highly dependent on the size of the quadrangle. A larger area would have resulted in a smaller stretching factor. Our selection of

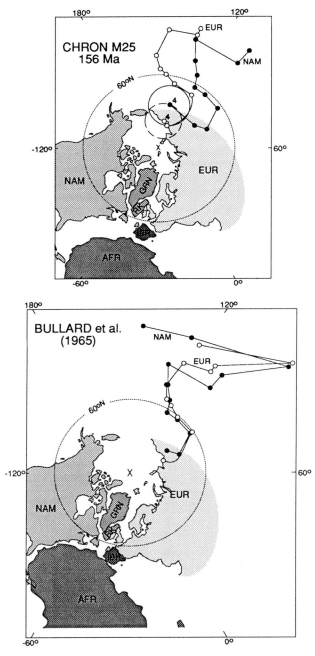

Fig. 3. Fit between the palaeomagnetic poles of Eurasia (EUR) relative to those for North America (NAM) at various times. Circles of 95% confidence limits are shown for the considered periods. The reconstructions were obtained by rotating Eurasia, Greenland, Rockall, Iberia and Africa to the west using the poles of rotations from Table 2 while keeping the North America fixed. In Bullard's reconstruction Eurasia has been moved using Bullard's pole (Table 2) for Eurasia while rest of the plates have been rotated using the poles from Table 2.

Table 2. *Reconstruction poles for Africa, Iberia, Rockall, Greenland and Eurasia relative to North America*

Anomaly (age) Plate	MO (118 Ma)			M25 (156.5 Ma)			CL (? 175 Ma)		
	Lat +°N	Long +°E	Angle +°E	Lat +°N	Long +°E	Angle +°E	Lat +°N	Long +°E	Angle +°E
Africa	66.30	−19.90	−54.25[1]	67.15	−16.00	−64.70[1]	65.97	−12.76	−76.44[3]
Iberia	68.88	−15.00	−50.62[2]	66.90	−12.93	−60.45[2]	65.72	−12.82	−66.32[3]
Eurasia	69.67	154.26	−23.17[2]	70.53	154.95	−24.88[3]	88.50	27.70	−38.00[4]
Greenland	67.50	−118.48	−13.78[5]	67.23	−120.29	−14.45[3]	67.23	−120.29	−14.45[3]
Rockall	75.32	159.59	−23.47[5]	75.29	162.20	−24.11[3]	75.29	162.29	−24.11[3]

1, Klitgord & Schouten (1986)
2, Srivastava *et al.* (1990*a*)
3, Calculated
4, Bullard *et al.* (1965)
5, Srivastava and Roest (1989)

the area was governed by the landward limit of the hinge line on either side of the North Atlantic (the hinge line is defined as the region where little or no horizontal or vertical motion took place during the formation of the basins). On the Grand Banks the hinge line lies roughly along the Bonavista Platform (Enachescu 1987), while on the European side it is assumed to lie along the east coast of British Isles, which is the eastern limit of the basins. By using these hinge lines as limits, we imply that most of the stretching took place within the basins lying west of the British Isles and not in the North Sea where stretching is presumed to have taken place mainly during Triassic and Early Jurassic (Ziegler & van Hoorn 1989). The stretching factor derived in this study is similar to those obtained in other investigations (Keen *et al.* 1987*a*; Masson *et al.* 1984) for this part of the North Atlantic. A stretching factor for the

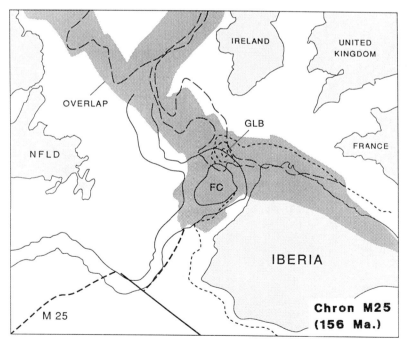

Fig. 4. Reconstruction of the North Central Atlantic at chron M25 using simplified bathymetry of each plate showing the amount of overlap between plate boundaries. FC, Flemish Cap; GLB, Galicia Bank.

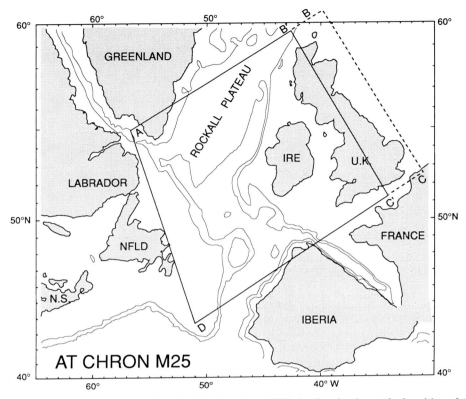

Fig. 5. Reconstruction of the North Central Atlantic at chron M25 showing the destretched position of the plates and their simplified bathymetry. Also shown is the position of the quadrangle ABCD at the time of initial separation between Eurasia and North America and its de-stretched position at chron M25 (AB'C'D).

Grand Banks region could not be determined because its separation from Iberia was not synchronous throughout its length.

Closure pole

Other than palaeomagnetic poles, there are too few constraints to determine the configuration of the Central North Atlantic plates accurately for times earlier than chron M25. The tectono-stratigraphic information of the sedimentary basins (Table 1) suggests formation as early as Late Triassic to Early Jurassic. However, a pole of rotation between Eurasia and North America obtained using these palaeomagnetic poles for a pre-chron M25 time (Fig. 3) would have resulted in a large compression in the Arctic and a large overlap between Iberia and France. Therefore, in determining the closure pole for the present study, we made the assumption that most of the motion during this period occurred between Iberia and North

America, and not much motion occurred between Porcupine Bank and Orphan Basin. During this time, some strike-slip motion must have occurred in the Western Approaches Basin (also known as Western Approaches Trough) while basins in the North Sea were undergoing rifting. However, considering the uncertainties in the determination of the pole position between Eurasia and North America for this period, we felt justified in excluding such motions between Eurasia and North America for the time being. We assumed that during this period Iberia was moving in the same direction as Africa, although the former was being pulled away from North America at a much slower rate than the latter. This is evident in the depth to basement map compiled by Oakey *et al.* (1989) from existing maps of the Grand Banks region (Grant & McAlpine 1990) and shown in the reconstruction of the basins at Aptian time (Fig. 9).

The depth to basement under the Grand

Banks shows two isolated highs, one forming the Flemish Cap to the north and another forming part of the southern Grand Banks. Several deep sedimentary basins (Whale, Horseshoe and Jeanne d'Arc Basins) lie between these two highs. The overall basement pattern formed by these basins may be interpreted as the result of the two highs pulled away not only from each other, but also from the western part of the Grand Banks. The stratigraphy of these basins (Balkwill & Legall 1989; Tankard & Welsink 1989) and the evolution of the North Atlantic suggest that this started when Africa was moving away from North America in Bajocian time (Table 1). The motion of Africa at this time was along the Newfoundland Fracture Zone (Klitgord & Schouten 1986). It appears that Africa was not completely separated from the Grand Banks but remained partly attached to the southern Grand Banks. As a result, the southern high may have been pulled away from the western Grand Banks as the African plate moved along the Newfoundland Fracture Zone. Such a dragging motion could arise from the flow pattern under the lithosphere as proposed by Reid (1989), based on seismic refraction results. This motion may have continued until chron M25, when the high was finally detached from Africa. This was also the time when the southern part of Iberia separated from the Grand Banks (Srivastava et al. 1990a; Mauffret et al. 1989; Malod & Mauffret 1990). While the southern high was moving in this fashion with Africa, the Flemish Cap was perhaps also being pulled away with Galicia Bank.

The pole position for Iberia for this period was determined by assuming that its motion was parallel to that of Africa, giving rise to an overlap between chron M25 plate boundaries for North America and Iberia that accounts for the formation of most of the Whale, Horseshoe and Lusitanian basins. Eurasia was kept at its chron M25 position in the closure reconstruction.

De-stretched reconstructions

Method

Figure 6 illustrates the method of determining the unstretched position of the plates. When the plates are restored from their present configuration to their pre-opening positions, there is an overlap between the ocean-continent boundaries (OCB) along which separation originally occurred. The problem is to compress the two plates along the direction of their motion

until their OCBs coincide along the dotted line. This results in the de-stretched configuration. For this we assume a line of zero stretching (the hinge line) and distribute the overlap between plates. This was done equally, unless there was evidence for doing otherwise.

Input data

The input data used in this paper come from several recent compilations. The depth to basement in the western North Atlantic was compiled by Oakey et al. (1989), in the eastern north Atlantic by de Chassy et al. (in press), and in the northeastern Atlantic by Tucholke (1988). For bathymetry we used ETOPO5 (1986); magnetic data were obtained from Verhoef et al. (1986) and Srivastava et al. (1988, 1990a).

Reconstruction at chron M0 (118 Ma, Aptian)

The method described above was applied to determine the de-stretched configuration of the plates at chron M0. Details of the procedure are given in the Appendix. Figure 7 shows the results for the bathymetry reconstruction (cf. Fig. 2 for the stretched configuration). The overlaps between the North American, Greenland, Rockall and Eurasian plates have been removed by uniformly destretching these plates along directions obtained from the rotation poles (Table 2). This was mainly due to a lack of destretching information between these plates for different times. However, the model did not allow deformation for continental fragments such as Flemish Cap, Orphan Knoll and Galicia Bank, nor for portions of the continents that are devoid of sedimentary basins of the appropriate age. It is important to remember that Fig. 7 does not represent the Aptian bathymetry, as we have not allowed any vertical movement of present day topographies in the reconstructed framework.

Three observations can be made from this reconstruction: (1) Orphan Knoll and Porcupine Bank form a continuous feature; (2) Rockall and Porcupine Troughs have decreased in width (Rockall Trough by about 20%); (3) Ireland has rotated anticlockwise from its present position because of the de-stretching of the Celtic Sea Basins. Rockall and Porcupine Troughs and Orphan Basin form a continuous deep bathymetric low at this time.

In our model, we assumed that little or no stretching took place on either side of

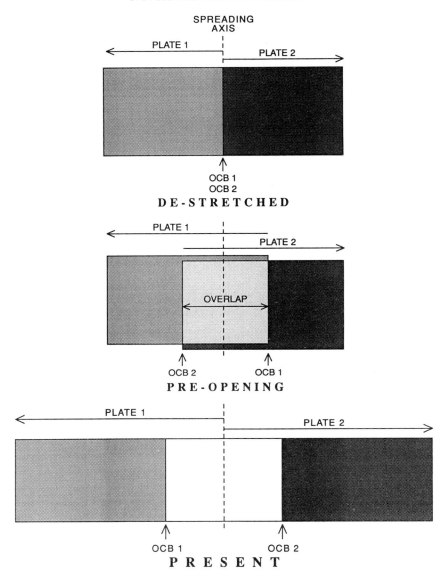

Fig. 6. Sequential positions and sizes of plates at present, at the time of their separation, and when they have been restored to their destretched shapes. OCB, Ocean Continent Boundary.

Greenland, and that all the stretching occurred seaward of Labrador and the east Rockall Banks. The reconstruction shows that the Labrador Sea is completely closed. No destretching was applied south of Flemish Cap and Galicia Bank, as active seafloor spreading already took place there at that time.

Similar reconstructions using the magnetic and depth to basement data were carried out, and are shown in Figs 8 & 9 respectively. The

magnetic reconstruction shows the continuation of a large magnetic high at 55°N between Labrador and Greenland. A similar continuation of a large magnetic high can also be seen between south Rockall Bank and the Labrador shelf at 52°N/50°W. A more dramatic change is observed in the depth to basement reconstruction (Fig. 9), where Galicia Bank and Goban Spur appear to form part of a continuous basement high in a north–south direction. Orphan

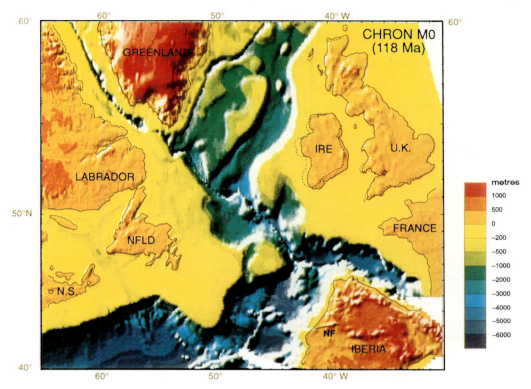

Fig. 7. Shaded relief bathymetry map showing positions of the destretched plates at chron M0, illuminated from the northwest. OK, Orphan Knoll; FC, Flemish Cap; GLB, Galicia Bank; NF, Nazare Fault. The dotted outlines of continents refer to their positions relative to North America if the basins around them were left in their stretched positions.

Basin appears to lie along the southwestward extension of the Celtic Sea Basin. The Orphan and Porcupine Basins are reduced by 15% of their present sizes while the Celtic Sea basins are reduced by 13% in the south and about 9% in the north. The Western Approaches Basin is reduced only by 5%. The reconstruction also shows that the basement under the basins on the Grand Banks is deeper than the basement under the basins off the British Isles.

Reconstruction at chron M25 (Kimmeridgian, 156.5 Ma)

A second set of reconstructions were carried out for chron M25 using the plate configuration as shown in Fig. 4. The large overlaps in this reconstruction were used to destretch each plate along its direction of motion relative to neighbouring plates. De-stretched configurations were derived by assuming that both the North American and Eurasian plates were stretched equally from chron M0 to M25 time. We further made the assumption that most of the stretching on the Eurasian plate took place west of the 3°E meridian, even though geological information from the North Sea suggests some rifting there during this time (Badley et al. 1984). Since we have no estimates for the distribution of motion on either side of the British Isles during this time, we assumed that all stretching took place west of 3°E. As in our M0 reconstructions (Figs 7–9), no deformation was allowed across the British Isles and continental fragments like Flemish Cap, Galicia Bank and the southern Grand Banks High. Figure 10 shows the plate configuration for the present bathymetry.

Several interesting features stand out from this reconstruction: (1) Rockall Trough has been reduced to about 45% of its present size, and joins Orphan Basin to form a deep trough. (2) Galicia Bank lies east of Flemish Cap. Flemish Cap has moved in a northwest direction relative to the Grand Banks, closing most of Flemish

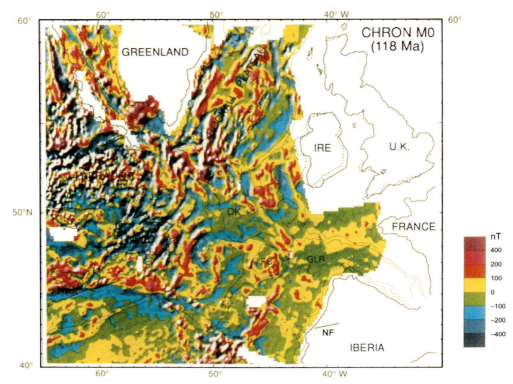

Fig. 8. Shaded relief map, of reduced to the pole magnetic anomalies, showing positions of the destretched plates at chron M0, illuminated from the northwest. Also shown are 1000 and 2000 m isobaths. OK, Orphan Knoll; FC, Flemish Cap; GLB, Galicia Bank; NF, Nazare Fault. The dotted outlines of continents refer to their positions relative to North America if the basins around them were left in their stretched positions.

Pass. Similarly, Galicia Bank has moved to the north from its M0 position relative to Flemish Cap. A portion of the Inner Galicia Basin is reduced in size. (3) The eastern edge of the Grand Banks along 48°W has a much less arcuate shape. (4) Similarly the size of Porcupine Basin is decreased. Porcupine Bank lies closer to Goban Spur and Flemish Cap. (5) Porcupine Bank together with Flemish Cap, Goban Spur and Galicia Bank form a major basement high. This configuration of the basement high may have had important implications for deep water circulation throughout the region during this period. (6) Ireland has rotated further anticlockwise relative to the United Kingdom, closing more of the Celtic Sea Basins. Part of the Western Approaches Basin is also closed.

A similar reconstruction carried out using the depth to basement data (Fig. 11) shows several additional features: (1) Several basins on the Grand Banks and on the Iberian and European

shelves have been reduced in size. The Jeanne d'Arc Basin is reduced to about half its size. On the Iberian shelf, the Inner Galicia basin is reduced by about 34% since M0 time. Similarly the Lusitanian and Cantabrian basins are also reduced by 25% and 22% respectively. On the European shelf, the north Biscay margin is heavily compressed and the basin east of Goban Spur is partly closed. The southern end of the Western Approaches Basin is reduced to half its size since M0 (Aptian) time. Similarly the Celtic Sea basin is reduced by a further 14% since M0 time. (2) The Lusitanian Basin on the southern Iberian shelf lies adjacent to the south Salar basin off the Grand Banks (Tucholke *et al.* 1989). (3) The Western Approaches Basin and Inner Galicia Basin form a continuous feature. (4) Further motion between the plates is required if we wish to close the remainder of these basins to their initial configuration. This is especially true for the Whale and Horseshoe Basins on the southern Grand Banks. The for-

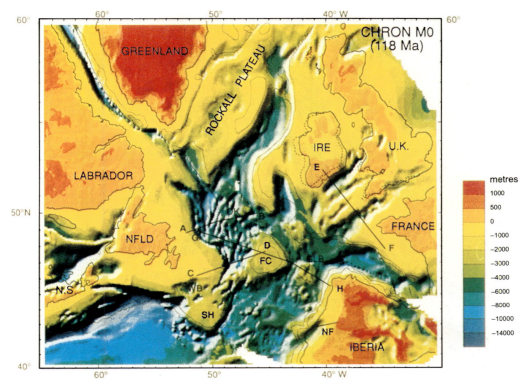

Fig. 9. Shaded relief depth to basement map showing positions of the destretched plates at chron M0, illuminated from the northwest. Also shown are the locations of cross sections AB, CD, EF and GH shown in Figs 15–18 and the 1000 and 2000 m isobaths. OK, Orphan Knoll; FC, Flemish Cap; GLB, Galicia Bank; NF, Nazare Fault. The dotted outlines of continents refer to their positions relative to North America if the basins around them were left in their stretched positions.

mation of these basins was perhaps caused by the motion of Africa and the southern basement high in this region, as mentioned earlier and discussed in the next section.

Reconstruction at closure time (Early–Middle Triassic to Middle Jurassic, 180–230 Ma)

A set of reconstructions were carried out at closure time, i.e. at the time of onset of rift between the North American, Eurasian and Iberian plates. No definite date can be assigned to this event but, as pointed out earlier, the sedimentary records from the basins suggest that it extended from Early–Mid-Triassic to Mid-Jurassic when separation between Africa and North America took place (Table 1). The reconstructions (Figs 12–14) were obtained by rotating Iberia further to the west using the

closure pole (Table 2) while keeping Eurasia at its M25 position.

The bathymetric reconstruction (Fig. 12) shows that Flemish Cap has moved to line up completely with the southern end of the Grand Banks. As a result it closes off most of Flemish Pass. The Orphan basin is further closed by 30% (Fig. 13) and Flemish Cap lies much closer to Orphan Knoll than at chron M0 time (Aptian). On the European side the Porcupine basin and Porcupine Bank have been reduced further by 20% because of the northwest movement of Iberia. Similarly off Iberia, Galicia Bank has moved closer to the mainland closing off most of the Inner Galicia basin. The Lusitanian basin has closed by 30%. Most noticeably, the Whale and Horseshoe basins on the Grand Banks appear to be completely closed (Fig. 13). The small gap between the Bonavista Platform and the Southern High (SH) on the Grand Banks lines up with the line of separation

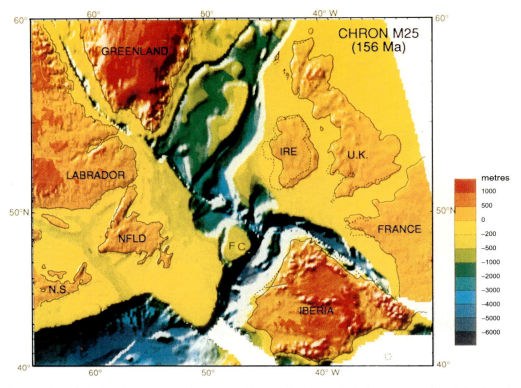

Fig. 10. Shaded relief bathymetry map showing positions of the destretched plates at chron M25, illuminated from the northwest. OK, Orphan Knoll; FC, Flemish Cap; GLB, Galicia Bank; NF, Nazare Fault. The dotted outlines of continents refer to their positions relative to North America if the basins around them were left in their stretched positions.

between Africa and North America. This confirms our observations from the depth to basement map, as well as the Balkwill and Legall (1989) interpretation that these basins were created due to cratonic extension by the movement of the southern high from the Bonavista platform before and during the opening of the western North Atlantic Ocean.

In the magnetic reconstruction (Fig. 14), the east−west high north of Flemish Cap in M0 reconstruction, Fig. 8, (Cumberland High, Enachescu, 1987) is very much reduced in size. A north−south oriented anomaly which joins this east−west anomaly at its western end in M0 reconstruction (Fig. 8) is dislocated towards the northwest (Fig. 14), reflecting the northwest motion of Flemish Cap along the northeastern edge of the Bonavista platform from chron M25 to closure (Fig. 13). Anomaly dislocations appear to continue even farther northwest on the platform itself, indicating that the northeastern edge of Bonavista platform was acting as the main extensional fault during the development

of several basins in this region. In the depth to basement reconstruction, the Nazare fault on Iberia appears co-linear with this edge of the Bonavista platform (Fig. 13).

Discussion

The restoration of plates to their pre-drift positions can provide some very useful information on the evolution of their sedimentary basins. The procedure requires accurate gravity, magnetic and depth to basement data in digital form. The success of the method depends on several factors: knowledge of the plate kinematics for the periods in question; the selection of initial boundaries along which plates separated; and the location of the zero stretching boundary during the various rifting stages.

The accuracy of the pole determinations for the pre-drift periods depends on the constraints that can be used. In this paper we used the Bullard *et al.* (1965) reconstruction combined with Arctic geological constraints as a guide for

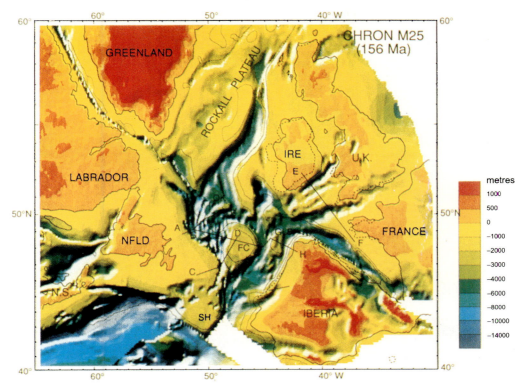

Fig. 11. Shaded relief depth to basement map showing positions of the destretched plates at chron M25, illuminated from the northwest. Also shown are the location of cross sections AB, CD, EF and GH shown in Figs 15–18 and the 1000 and 2000 m isobaths. OK, Orphan Knoll; FC, Flemish Cap; GLB, Galicia Bank; NF, Nazare Fault. The dotted outlines of continents refer to their positions relative to North America if the basins around them were left in their stretched positions.

determining the Eurasia to North America pole. The determination of the pole for Iberia is uncertain, due to the disputed nature of the crust in the Newfoundland Basin (cf. Srivastava *et al.* 1990a) and the lack of a definitive indication about the direction of Iberia's motion relative to North America. For chron M25, we used the pole of Srivastava *et al.* (1990a), which was determined under the assumption that most of the Newfoundland Basin is underlain by oceanic crust, and that the ocean-continent boundary (OCB) follows the line described by Keen & de Voogd (1988). The age for this pole is based on Mauffret *et al.*'s (1989) interpretation of the age of the OCB in the Tagus Abyssal Plain, estimated to be about chron M21–M25. Other pole positions for Iberia exist (e.g. Malod & Mauffret 1990) but they result in significant overlap between Iberia and Africa at this time.

An even greater uncertainty exists for the pole position at the start of the rifting stage (Mid-Triassic to Mid-Jurassic). Our pole deter-

mination is based on the assumption that the motion of Iberia was parallel to that of Africa and that there was little or no motion between Orphan Knoll and Porcupine Bank during this period.

The location of the zero stretching line is perhaps the most critical factor in influencing the shapes of the basins. We chose it to lie along the Bonavista Platform on the Grand Banks, along the eastern side of the UK (along the 3°E meridian as the model permitted no destretching in the North Sea), and along the eastern end of the Lusitanian basin on Iberia. These locations were kept fixed for the whole period, although it seems likely that the position of this line may have varied at different times depending on where the maximum extension took place.

Lastly, we divided the overlap equally between plates to calculate the amount of stretching between them. We also used uniform stretching in all our computations. These were

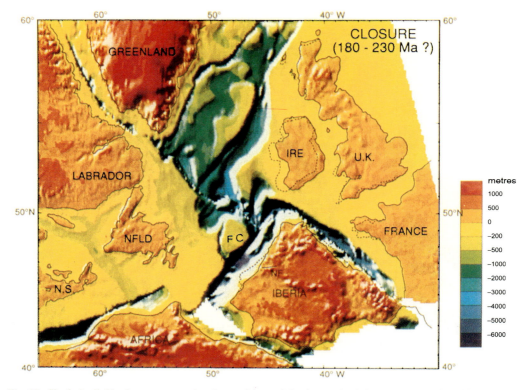

Fig. 12. Shaded relief bathymetry map showing positions of the destretched plates at closure time, illuminated from the northwest. OK, Orphan Knoll; FC, Flemish Cap; GLB, Galicia Bank; NF, Nazare Fault. The dotted outlines of continents refer to their positions relative to North America if the basins around them were left in their stretched positions.

done because of the lack of information about them for these regions. Little or no information exists as to the amount of extension which the sedimentary basins on each sides of the Atlantic have been subjected to at different times.

As a result of these uncertainties, we caution that our present model for the evolution of the basins is only preliminary. In the absence of additional constraints to justify the use of more complicated models, we have adopted the simplest model possible. The question to address now is how well the present model represents the development of some of the sedimentary basins in this region.

To illustrate the effects of the de-stretching, we constructed four cross sections: two on the North American side along deep seismic reflection lines (Figs 15, 16), one on the European side (Fig. 17) and one across the North American and Iberian rift (Fig. 18).

Section AB (Fig. 15) lies along seismic line 84−3 (Keen *et al*. 1987*a*) and crosses the Orphan Basin. We have labelled features for easy com-

parison between profiles. For example, features A on both the seismic line and on the depth to basement profile can be compared. Overall, there is good agreement between the seismic line section and the cross section obtained from the digital depth to basement compilation (labelled present). Comparison with the same section in the chron M0 framework, after de-stretching, shows that Orphan Basin has narrowed. By chron M25 the basin has been reduced to about 64% of its present size. In the de-stretching, we have compressed some of the smaller basins to the extent of elimination, which is exactly what one would expect. These smaller basins were formed subsequently and their elimination is not surprising. Profile AB also shows that the basins are not further compressed at closure time.

Section CD (Fig. 16) is along seismic line 85−3 (Keen *et al*. 1987*a*), located on the northern flank of Flemish Cap (Fig. 9) and crossing the Jeanne d'Arc basin at its western end. Again a fair match is obtained between the

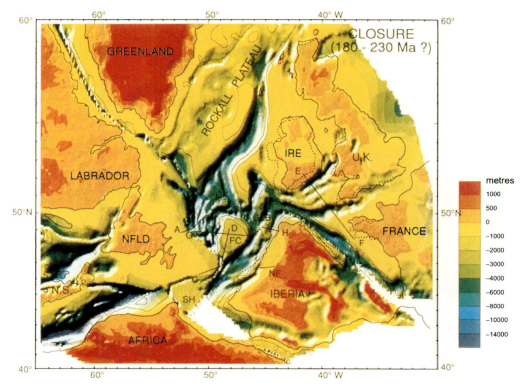

Fig. 13. Shaded relief depth to basement map showing positions of the destretched plates at closure time, illuminated from the northwest. Also shown are the locations of cross sections AB, CD, EF and GH shown in Figs 15–18 and the 1000 and 2000 m isobaths. OK, Orphan Knoll; FC, Flemish Cap; GLB, Galicia Bank; NF, Nazare Fault. The dotted outlines of continents refer to their positions relative to North America if the basins around them were left in their stretched positions.

depth to basement data and the seismic section. As the Flemish Cap had separated from Galicia Bank just after chron M0 time (Boillot *et al.* 1988), the cross section for chron M0 differs only marginally from the one labelled present. Note also that some smaller basins east of the Jeanne d'Arc basin are reduced in size. At chron M25 time (Kimmeridgian), the cross section shows that the Jeanne d'Arc basin is reduced to 70% of its present size; it remains at the same size at closure time.

The third cross section, EF (Fig. 17), crosses the Celtic Sea and the Western Approaches basins. The overall sizes of the two basins have been reduced to about 87% of their present sizes at chron M0 time, and to about 74% at chron M25 time.

The fourth cross section GH (Fig. 18) was taken across the plate boundary between the North American and Iberian plates (cf. Figs 9, 11, and 13). The cross sections at different times have been stacked with the plate boundary as common point: they clearly show the effects

of the stretching on the basins on both sides. For example, the Orphan Basin is stretched by 25% from its initial position to that at chron M25, and by 102% that at chron M0. On the Iberian side the inner Galicia basin is stretched by 47% by chron M25, and 76% by chron M0.

The above examples clearly show the effectiveness of our method in destretching the basins. They have destretched to about 50% to 70% of their present sizes; the question which arises is how realistic are these figures, and how do they compare with previous estimates of the stretching factors for these basins.

Not much is known about stretching factors for various basins in this area. For the Orphan Basin lithosphere, Keen *et al.* (1987*a*) calculated a stretching factor of about 2 to 2.7 from modelling of the subsidence history of this region and from study of deep seismic reflection data. Assuming a linear relationship between the thinning of the lithosphere and the size of the resulting basin, these values are consistent with our estimate that Orphan basin increased by a

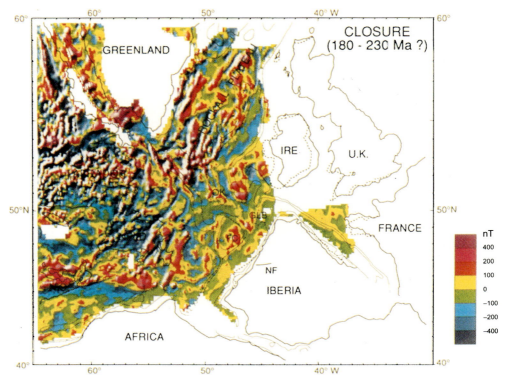

Fig. 14. Shaded relief map, of the reduced to the pole magnetic anomalies, showing positions of the destretched plates at closure time, illuminated from the northwest. Also shown are the 1000 and 2000 m isobaths. OK, Orphan Knoll; FC, Flemish Cap; GLB, Galicia Bank; NF, Nazare Fault. The dotted outlines of continents refer to their positions relative to North America if the basins around them were left in their stretched positions.

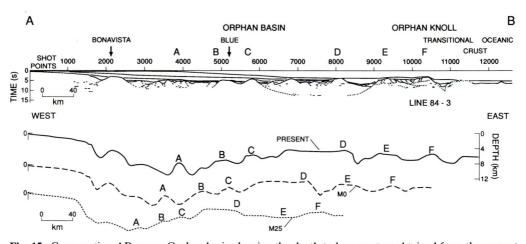

Fig. 15. Cross section AB across Orphan basin showing the depth to basement as obtained from the present depth to basement map, and those from the reconstruction maps (Figs 9, 11 & 13) at chron M0, M25 and closure. Also shown is a line drawing of the deep seismic reflection line 84−3 along this cross section (Keen *et al.* 1987*a*). The location of this cross section at different times is shown in Figs 9, 11 & 13. Labels A,B,C,D,E and F refer to locations of features at different times.

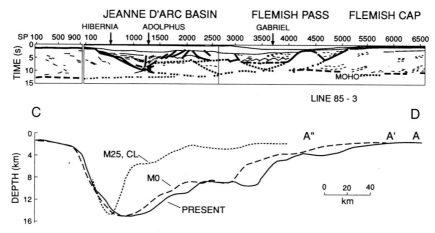

Fig. 16. Cross section CD across Jeanne d'Arc basin showing the depth to basement as obtained from the present depth to basement, and those from the reconstructions maps (Figs 9, 11 & 13) at chron M0, M25 and closure (CL). Also shown is the line drawing of deep seismic reflection line 85−3 along this cross section (Keen *et al.* 1987*a*). The location of this cross section at different times is shown in Figs 9, 11 & 13. Labels A, A' and A" refer to locations of the same feature at different times.

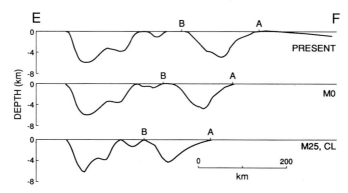

Fig. 17. Cross section EF across Celtic Sea basins and the Western Approaches basin showing the depth to basement as obtained from the present depth to basement, and those from the reconstructions maps (Figs 9, 11 & 13) at chron M0, M25 and closure (CL). The location of this cross section at different times is shown in Figs 9, 11 & 13. Labels A and B refer to the same features at different times.

factor of 2. Other estimates exist for the Goban Spur margin where Masson *et al.* (1985) found stretching factors ranging between 1.13 and 2.2 using deep seismic profiles. Our estimates for the Porcupine basin give an extension by a factor of more than 2.

Kusznir & Egan (1989) modelled the formation of the Jeanne d'Arc basin by extension of the upper crust by simple shear mechanism and of the lower crust by pure shear. They estimated that a maximum of 15 km of extension of the basin took place in this process. This equals an extension of only about 15%, considering that the extension took place over 100 km of lithosphere. We find that the minimum extension of the Jeanne d'Arc basin in the north is about 30%. In the south, the extension is considerably greater.

One has to bear in mind that the basin sizes determined in this study depend solely on the amount of overlap produced in the reconstructions and how it is distributed over the plate at various times. These overlaps are then removed by uniformly de-stretching the basins. The reduction of the basin, therefore, depends on the size of the area the overlap is distributed over.

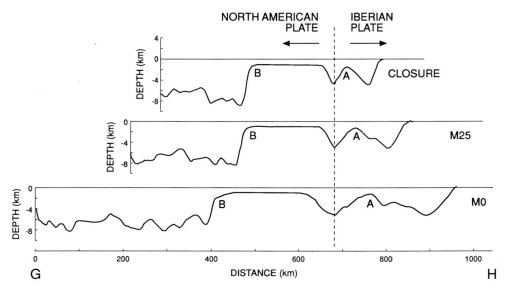

Fig. 18. Cross section GH across Galicia Bank and northern part of Flemish Cap including Orphan basin. The cross sections have been aligned along the boundary between the North American and Iberian plates. The depth to basement along these cross sections are obtained from the reconstruction maps (Figs 9, 11 & 13) at chrons M0, M25 and closure. The location of this cross section at different times is shown in Figs 9, 11 & 13. Labels A and B refer to features on the cross sections at different times.

It is possible to de-stretch the basins along the basin bounding faults to obtain a more realistic picture of their original size. This requires detailed structural information for the entire area, which does not exist.

Also the above method does not take into account the mechanism of creation of the sedimentary basins and changes in their depth with age. These can be incorporated into the method but needs detailed stratigraphic information for the entire region which do not exist.

The basin formation scenarios presented by this procedure raise some interesting questions which need to be considered for further studies: If the Orphan basin has doubled in size, what crustal processes were involved? What crustal parameters can be studied to substantiate these results? A possible independent approach is to consider the variation in crustal thickness obtained from gravity, which would indicate an amount of stretching that can subsequently be used to de-stretch the plates prior to the reconstruction.

Conclusions

The following conclusions can be drawn from this study:

1. The de-stretching method provides a new quantitative technique for plate kinematic studies of sedimentary basin evolution and it provides a way to relate the development of sedimentary basins to seafloor spreading in adjacent ocean basins.

2. Correlation of Palaeozoic and other old basement trends across the North Atlantic has been problematic (Lefort 1989) because of deformation and modification of these trends by younger events. Mismatches between these trends are therefore often observed when plates are restored to their position of initial separation. The present method provides a technique of restoring these plates and their internal trends to pre-drift stages.

3. Understanding paleocirculation in the ocean basins, requires knowledge of the deep water passages that existed at various times. Until now this information has only been available for the time following initial plate separation. The method described here offers the potential for new insights related to circulation paths in earlier times.

4. The reliability of the present model of sedimentary basin evolution is highly dependent on the accuracy achieved in determining predrift plate positions. Until we can determine positions of various plates in the North Atlantic more accurately than at present, the present reconstructions can only be viewed as preliminary.

The assistance rendered by Gordon Oakey and Allen Stark in compiling depth to basement data used in this paper is gratefully acknowledged. Antoine de Chassy compiled several of our initial data sets. Karl Usow of Blue Vajra Computing assisted in the development of the computer code. Drafting of the illustrations, done by the Drafting and Illustration Section of the Bedford Institute of Oceanography is acknowledged. Sonya Dehler and Ron Macnab read critically an earlier version of the paper and offered many suggestions for improvement.

This is Geological Survey of Canada contribution No 25991.

Appendix. De-stretching procedure

The procedure followed in the de-stretching of the plates is illustrated in Fig. A1. At first we remove the seaward portion of the plate along the boundary labelled OCB. In essence, this means eliminating the part of the plate that was created during seafloor spreading, leaving only the 'continental' portion of the plate. Part of this remaining plate may be stretched: in that

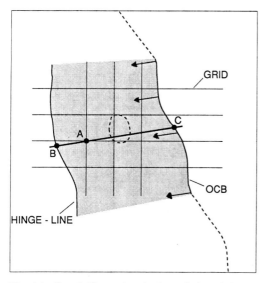

Fig. A1. Sketch illustrating the boundaries of the plate. OCB denotes the boundary with maximum stretching (arrows denote the direction and amount of stretching) and the hinge line, the boundary with no stretching. Therefore, the stretching is confined to the shaded region. The dotted region denotes a part of the plate that has moved with the plate but was not deformed. For each grid point we obtain the amount of stretching by linear interpolation between the stretching at point C and at point B (see text).

case, when restored to its original position, it would overlap onto its conjugate plate. Let us assume that we have found the amount of stretching for each point of the OCB (illustrated in Fig. A1 by the size of the arrows). In this paper we used the overlap as an indication of the amount of stretching, but there are other ways of finding it, e.g. from the crustal thickness.

We also need the direction of the stretching for each point of the boundary OCB (illustrated in Fig. A1 by the direction of the arrows). We can obtain the direction for each point from the differential pole of rotation of the plate during the period we want to calculate the destretching. From the amount and direction of the motion of each point of the present OCB, we can calculate the location of the boundary in its initial position. However, for all points landward of the OCB we have to decide how they have moved. If all these points move the same distance and direction as the corresponding points on the boundary, then we would have a translation of the plate, not a deformation. Therefore, we have to define a hinge-line, or line of zero stretching, landward of the boundary OCB, assuming that all points landward of the hinge-line have not been deformed by the stretching process (see Fig. A1). The stretching of the plate is now confined to the region between the OCB and the hinge-line (see shaded area in Fig. A1) and may be distributed over this region. In this paper, we took the simplest approach and assumed that the deformation was distributed linearly over those parts of the region that were allowed to deform; more complicated non-linear distributions are possible.

The procedure to obtain the destretched gridded data is as follows. Figure A1 illustrates the grid over the deformed region. For each grid point in the deformed region (A in Fig. A1), we have to define the direction of motion, in our case from a differential rotation pole. We then calculate the intersection points of the line through point A with the boundary OCB (point C) and with the hinge-line (point B). From the distances to these two boundaries, measured along the direction of motion, we obtain the amount of stretching for grid point A, in this case from a linear interpolation between the stretching at point C and the zero stretching at point B. Note that we allow for the following complication: There may be parts of the region that have moved with the deformed plate, but have not been deformed, i.e. like the movement of steel balls in mud. In this case we have to find the portion of the line through grid point A that has not been deformed (in this example the portion that intersects the dotted outline in

Fig. A1) and distribute the deformation over the remainder of the line. This procedure was applied to handle continental fragments like Flemish Cap, Orphan Knoll and Galicia Bank.

This procedure now gives us the destretched position for each grid point in the deformed region. However, since the deformation is not uniform, the resulting grid is irregular. Therefore, we calculate a surface through the deformed grid points and then sample this surface at a regular grid interval. We used the procedure of splines under tension (Smith & Wessel 1990) to obtain the surface through the deformed points.

The destretched grid now replaces the original grid in the deformed region (the shaded region in Fig. A1). We follow this procedure for all the plates involved; in the region discussed in this paper, this involved five plates. After this, we rotate the deformed plate to their configuration in the reconstructed frame work using a procedure described by Verhoef et al. (1990), and obtain the images of Figures 7–14.

References

BADLEY, M. E., EGEBERG, T. & NIPEN, O. 1984. Development of rift basins illustrated by the structural evolution of the Oseberg feature, Block 30/6, offshore Norway. *Journal of the Geological Society, London*, **141**, 639–650.

BALKWILL, H. R. & LEGALL, F. D. 1989. Whale basin, offshore Newfoundland: Extension and salt diapirism. *In*: TANKARD, A. J. & BALKWILL, H. R. (eds) *Extensional Tectonics and Stratigraphy of the North Atlantic Margins*. American Association of Petroleum Geologists Memoir, **46**, 233–246.

BOILLOT, G., MOUGENOT, D., GIRARDEAU, J. & WINTERER, E. L. 1989. Rifting processes on west Galicia margin, Spain. *In*: TANKARD, A. J., BALKWILL, H. R. (eds) *Extensional Tectonics and Stratigraphy of the North Atlantic Margins*. American Association of Petroleum Geologists Memoir, **46**, 363–378.

——, WINTERER, E. L. & MEYER, A. W. 1988. *Proceedings of the Ocean Drilling Program, Scientific Results*. Ocean Drilling Program, College Station, TX, **103**, 858.

BRIGGS, I. C. 1974. Machine contouring using minimum curvature. *Geophysics*, **39**, 39–48.

BULLARD, E., EVERETT, J. E. & SMITH, A. G. 1965. The fit of the continents around the Atlantic. *Philosophical Transactions of the Royal Society of London, Series A.*, **258**, 41–75.

CHADWICK, R. A., LIVERMORE, R. A. & PENN, I. A. 1989. Continental extension in southern Britain and surrounding areas and its relationship to the opening of the North Atlantic. *In*: TANKARD, A. J. & BALKWILL, H. R. (eds) *Extensional Tectonics and Stratigraphy of the North Atlantic Margins*. American Association of Petroleum Geologists Memoir, **46**, 411–424.

COURTILLOT, V. 1982. Propagating rifts and continental breakup. *Tectonics*, **1**, 239–250.

CROKER, P. F. & KLEMPERER, S. L. 1989. Structure and stratigraphy of the Porcupine Basin: relationships to deep crustal structure and the opening of the North Atlantic. *In*: TANKARD, A. J. & BALKWILL, H. R. (eds) *Extensional Tectonics and Stratigraphy of the North Atlantic Margins*. American Association of Petroleum Geologists Memoir, **46**, 445–460.

DE CHASSY, A., PINET, B., VERHOEF, J., EDWARDS, A. E. *Conjugate Margin Atlas*. GSC Special Paper, In Press.

DE GRACIANSKY, P. C. et al. 1985. The Goban Spur transect: Geologic evolution of a sediment-starved passive continental margin. *Geological Society of America Bulletin*, **96**, 58–76.

ENACHESCU, M. E. 1987. Tectonic and Structural Framework of the Northeast Newfoundland Continental Margin. *In*: BEAUMONT, C. & TANKARD, A. J. (eds) *Sedimentary Basins and Basin-Forming Mechanisms*. Canadian Society of Petroleum Geologists, Memoir **12**, 117–146.

ETOPO5. 1986. Relief map of the earth's surface. *EOS*, **67**, 121.

GARCIA-MONDEJAR, J. 1989. Strike-slip subsidence of the Basque-Cantabrian Basin of northern Spain and its relationship to Aptian-Albian opening of Bay of Biscay. *In*: TANKARD, A. J. & BALKWILL, H. R. (eds) *Extensional Tectonics and Stratigraphy of the North Atlantic Margins*. American Association of Petroleum Geologists Memoir, **46**, 395–410.

GRANT, A. C. & McALPINE, K. D. 1990. The continental margin around Newfoundland. *In*: KEEN, M. J. & WILLIAMS, G. L. (eds) *Geology of the Continental Margin of Eastern Canada*. Geological Society of North America. **I**, 239–292.

HEYMAN, M. A. W. 1989. Tectonic and depositional history of the Moroccan continental margin. *In*: TANKARD, A. J. & BALKWILL, H. R. (eds) *Extensional Tectonics and Stratigraphy of the North Atlantic Margins*. American Association of Petroleum Geologists Memoir, **46**, 323–340.

HISCOTT, R. N., WILSON, R. C. L., GRADSTEIN, F. M., PUJALTE, V., GARCIA-MONDEJAR, J., BOUDREAU, R. R. & WISHART, H. A. 1990. Comparative Stratigraphy and Subsidence History of Mesozoic Rift Basins of North Atlantic. *AAPG Bulletin*, **74**, 60–76.

KEEN, C. E., BOUTILIER, R., DE VOOGD, B., MUDFORD, B. & ENACHESCU, M. E. 1987a. Crustal Geometry and Extension Models for the Grand Banks, Eastern Canada: Constraints From Deep Seismic Reflection Data. *In*: BEAUMONT, C. & TANKARD, A. J. (eds) *Sedimentary Basins and Basin-Forming Mechanisms*. Canadian Society of Petroleum Geologists, Memoir **12**, 101–115.

—— & DE VOOGD, B. 1988. The Continent-Ocean Boundary at the Rifted Margin off Eastern Canada: New Results From Deep Seismic

Reflection Studies. *Tectonics*, **7**, 107–124.

——, STOCKMAL, G. S., WELSINK, H., QUINLAN, G. & MUDFORD, B. 1987*b*. Deep crustal structure and evolution of the rifted margin northeast of Newfoundland: results from LITHOPROBE East. *Canadian Journal of Earth Sciences*, **24**, 1537–1549.

KLITGORD, K. D. & SCHOUTEN, H. 1986. Plate kinematics of the central Atlantic: The Geology of North America *In*: VOGT, P. R. & TUCHOLKE, B. E. (eds) *Vol.M., The Western North Atlantic Region*, Geological Society of America, 3351–3378.

KUSZNIR, N. J. & EGAN, S. S. 1989. Simple shear and pure shear models of extensional sedimentary basin formation: Application to the Jeanne d'Arc Basin, Grand Banks of Newfoundland. *In*: TANKARD, A. J. & BALKWILL, H. R. (eds) *Extensional Tectonics and Stratigraphy of the North Atlantic Margins*, American Association of Petroleum Geologists Memoir, **46**, 305–322.

LEFORT, J. P. 1989. *Basement Correlation Across the North Atlantic*. Springer, Berlin.

LEPICHON, X., SIBUET, J. C. & FRANCHETEAU, J. 1977. The fit of the continents around the North Atlantic Ocean. *Tectonophysics*, **38**, 169–209.

MALOD, J. A. & MAUFFRET, A. 1990. Iberian plate motions during the Mesozoic. *Tectonophysics*, **184**, 261–278.

MANSPEIZER, W. 1988. Triassic–Jurassic rifting and opening of the North Atlantic: An overview. *In*: MANSPEIZER, W. (ed) *Triassic-Jusassic Rifting, Continent Breakup and Origin of the Atlantic Ocean and Passive Margins, Part A. Development in Geotectonics*, **22**, Elsevier, 41–80.

MASSON, D. G. & MILES, P. R. 1986. Development and Hydrocarbon Potential of Mesozoic Sedimentary Basins Around Margins of North America. *APPG Bulletin*, **70**, 721–729.

——, MONTADERT, L. & SCRUTTON, R. A. 1984. Regional Geology of the Goban Spur Continental Margin. *In*: DE GRACIANSKY, P. C., POAG, C. W. (eds) *Initial Reports of the Deep Sea Drilling Project*, U.S. Government Printing Office, Washington, **LXXX**, 1115–1139.

MAUFFRET, A., MOUGENOT, D., MILES, P. R. & MALOD, J. A. 1989. Results from Multichannel Reflection Profiling on the Tagus Plain (Portugal)-Comparison with the Canadian Margin. *In*: TANKARD, A. J., BALKWILL, H. R. (eds) *Extensional tectonics and Stratigraphy of the North Atlantic Margins*, American Association of Petroleum Geologists Memoir, **46**, 379–393.

MONTADERT, L., DE CHARPAL, O., ROBERTS, D., GUENNOC, P. & SIBUET, J. C. 1979. Northeast Atlantic Passive Continental Margins: Rifting and Subsidence Processes. *In*: TALWANI, M., HAY, W. & RYAN, W. B. F. (eds) *Deep Drilling Results in the Atlantic Ocean: Continental Margin and Paleoenvironment*, Maurice Ewing Series, **3**, 154–186.

MURILLAS, J., MOUGENOT, D., BOILLOT, G., COMAS, M. C., BANDA, E. & MAUFFRET, A. 1990. Structure and evolution of the Galicia interior basin (Atlantic western Iberian continental margin). *Tectonophysics*, **184**, 297–319.

OAKEY, G. N., CURRIE, C. & DURLING, P. 1989. A digital compilation of depth to basement of the east coast of Canada and adjacent areas. *Geological Survey of Canada Open File #1964*.

PETRIE, S. H., BROWN, J. R., GRANGER, R. J. & LOVELL, J. P. B. 1989. Mesozoic history of the Celtic Sea basins. *In*: TANKARD, A. J. & BALKWILL, H. R. (eds) *Extensional Tectonics and Stratigraphy of the North Atlantic Margins*. American Association of Petroleum Geologists Memoir, **46**, 433–444.

REID, I. 1989. Effects of lithospheric flow on the formation and evolution of a transform margin. *Earth and Planetary Science Letters*, **95**, 38–52.

ROEST, W. R. & SRIVASTAVA, S. P. 1989. Seafloor spreading in the Labrador Sea: A new reconstruction. *Geology*, **17**, 1000–1004.

—— & —— 1991. Kinematics of the plate boundaries between Eurasia, Iberia and Africa in the North Atlantic from the Late Cretaceous to Present. *Geology*, **19**, 613–616.

ROWLEY, D. B. & LOTTES, A. L. 1988. Plate-kinematic reconstructions of the North Atlantic and Arctic: Late Jurassic to Present. *Tectonophysics*, **155**, 73–120.

SAVOSTIN, L. A., SIBUET, J. C., ZONENSHAIN, L. P., LE PICHON XAVIER, & ROULET, M. J. 1986. Kinematic Evolution of the Tethys Belt from the Atlantic Ocean to the Pamirs since the Triassic. *Tectonophysics*, **123**, 1–35.

SMITH, W. H. F. & WESSEL, P. 1990. Gridding with continuous curvature splines in tension, *Geophysics*, **55**, 293–305.

SRIVASTAVA, S. P. & ROEST, W. R. 1989. Seafloor spreading history II–VI. *In*: BELL, J. S. (ed.) *East Coast Basin Atlas Series: Labrador Sea. Atlantic Geoscience Centre, Geological Survey of Canada, Map sheets*, L17-2-L17-6.

—— & —— 1991. King's Trough: reactivated pseudo fault of a propagating rift. *Geophysical Journal*. (In Press).

——, ——, KOVACS, L. C., LEVESQUE, S., VERHOEF, J. & MACNAB, R. 1990*a*. Motion of Iberia since the late Jurassic: Results from detailed aeromagnetic measurements in the Newfoundland Basin. *Tectonophysics*, **184**, 229–260.

——, SCHOUTEN, H., ROEST, W. R., KLITGORD, K. D., KOVACS, L. C., VERHOEF, J. & MACNAB, R. 1990*b*. Iberian plate kinematics: a jumping plate boundary between Eurasia and Africa. *Nature*, **344** (6268), 756–759.

—— & TAPSCOTT, C. R. 1986. Plate kinematics of the North Atlantic: The Geology of North America, Vol. M. *In*: VOGT, P. R., TUCHOLKE, B. E. (eds) *The Western North Atlantic Region*, The Geological Society of America, 379–404.

——, VERHOEF, J. & MACNAB, R. 1988. Results from a detailed aeromagnetic survey across the northeast Newfoundland margin, Part II: Early opening of the North Atlantic between the British Isles and Newfoundland. *Marine and Petroleum*

Geology, **5**, 324–337.

TANKARD, A. J. & BALKWILL, H. R. 1989. Extensional tectonics and stratigraphy of the North Atlantic margins. *In*: TANKARD, A. J. & BALKWILL, H. R. (eds) *Extensional Tectonics and Stratigraphy of the North Atlantic Margins*, American Association of Petroleum Geologists Memoir **46**, 1–6.

—— & WELSINK, H. J. 1989. Mesozoic extension and styles of basin formation in Atlantic Canada. *In*: TANKARD, A. J. & BALKWILL, H. R. (eds) *Extensional Tectonics and Stratigraphy of the North Atlantic Margins*, American Association of Petroleum Geologists Memoir, **46**, 175–195.

—— & —— 1987. Extensional Tectonics and Stratigraphy of Hibernia Oil Field, Grand Banks, Newfoundland. *AAPG Bulletin*, **71**, 1210–1232.

——, —— & JENKINS, W. A. M. 1989. Structure styles and stratigraphy of the Jeanne d'Arc basin, Grand Banks of Newfoundland. *In*: TANKARD, A. J. & BALKWILL, H. R. (eds) *Extensional Tectonics and Stratigraphy of the North Atlantic Margins*. American Association of Petroleum Geologists Memoir, **46**, 265–282.

TUCHOLKE, B. E. 1988. Sediment distribution. *In*: SRIVASTAVA, S. P., VOPPEL, D. & TUCHOLKE, B. E. (eds) *Geophysical Atlas of the North Atlantic between 50° to 72°N and 0° to 65°W*. Deutsches Hydrographisches Institut, Hamburg, No. 2302.

——, AUSTIN, JR. J. A. & UCHUPI, E. 1989. Crustal Structure and Rift-Drift Evolution of the Newfoundland Basin. *In*: TANKARD, A. J. & BALKWILL, H. R. (eds) *Extensional Tectonics and Stratigraphy of the North Atlantic Margins*. American Association of Petroleum Geologists Memoir, **46**, 247–263.

VAN DER VOO, R. 1990. Phanerozoic paleomagnetic poles from Europe and North America and comparisons with continental reconstructions. *Reviews of Geophysics*, **28**, 167–206.

VERHOEF, J., COLLETTE, B. J., MILES, P. R., SEARLE, R. C., SIBUET, J. C. & WILLIAMS, C. A. 1986. Magnetic anomalies in the northest Atlantic Ocean (35°–50°). *Marine Geophysical Researches*, **8**, 1–25.

—— & SRIVASTAVA, S. P. 1989. Correlation of sedimentary basins across the North Atlantic as obtained from gravity and magnetic data, and its relation to the early evolution of the North

Atlantic. *In*: TANKARD, A. J. & BALKWILL, H. R. (eds) *Extensional Tectonics and Stratigraphy of the North Atlantic Margins*, American Association of Petroleum Geologists Memoir, **46**, 131–147.

——, USOW, K. H. & ROEST, W. R. 1990. A new method for plate reconstructions: the use of gridded data, *Computers and Geoscience*, **16**, 51–74.

VINK, G. E. 1982. Continental rifting and the implications for plate tectonic reconstructions. *Journal of Geophysical Research*, **87**, 10677–10688.

WELSINK, H. J., DWYER, J. D. & KNIGHT, R. J. 1989. Tectono-stratigraphy of passive margin off Nova Scotia. *In*: TANKARD, A. J. & BALKWILL, H. R. (eds) *Extensional Tectonics and Stratigraphy of the North Atlantic Margins*. American Association of Petroleum Geologists Memoir, **46**, 215–232.

——, SRIVASTAVA, S. P. & TANKARD, A. J. 1989. Basin architecture of the Newfoundland continental margin and its relationship to ocean crust fabric during extension. *In*: TANKARD, A. J. & BALKWILL, H. R. (eds) *Extensional Tectonics and Stratigraphy of the North Atlantic Margins*. American Association of Petroleum Geologists Memoir, **46**, 197–214.

WILSON, R. C. L., HISCOTT, R. N., WILLIS, M. G. & GRADSTEIN, F. M. 1989. The Lusitanian basin of west-central Portugal: Mesozoic and Tertiary tectonic stratigraphy and subsidence history. *In*: TANKARD, A. J. & BALKWILL, H. R. (eds) *Extensional Tectonics and Stratigraphy of the North Atlantic Margins*. American Association of Petroleum Geologists Memoir, **46**, 341–362.

ZIEGLER, P. A. 1989. Evolution of the North Atlantic-An overview. *In*: TANKARD, A. J. & BALKWILL, H. R. (eds) *Extensional Tectonics and Stratigraphy of the North Atlantic Margins*. American Association of Petroleum Geologists Memoir, **46**, 111–130.

—— & VAN HOORN, B. 1989. Evolution of the North Sea rift system. *In*: TANKARD, A. J. & BALKWILL, H. R. (eds) *Extensional Tectonics and Stratigraphy of the North Atlantic Margins*. American Association of Petroleum Geologists Memoir, **46**, 471–500.

Synoptic palaeogeography of the Northeast Atlantic Seaway: late Permian to Cretaceous

A. G. DORÉ

Conoco Norway Inc., Post Box 488, 4001 Stavanger, Norway

Abstract: The NE Atlantic rift system was a key element in marine connectivity between the northern (Boreal) and southern (Tethyan) marine realms. Palaeogeographic summary maps in this account emphasize the exploitation of pre-existing basement grain on a regional scale, particularly that of the Caledonian Orogen, in the development of the Mesozoic linked rift systems. Also emphasized are the importance of extension across the rift system during successive tectonic episodes and, as implied by restoration of the stretching, the narrowness of the proto-North Atlantic seaway in the Late Permian — Early Mesozoic.

The palaeogeographic maps document a sequence of tectonic events leading to the break-up of Pangea. Block-faulting in the mid-Permian enabled marine conditions to penetrate southwards from the Boreal Sea to the Zechstein and Bakevillia Seas of NW Europe, although no link with the Tethyan realm can be documented. The Triassic was characterized by intense differential movement and sediment accumulation. Sporadic marine ingressions took place into the NE Atlantic and North Sea basins. However, no throughgoing connection between marine tracts in the Barents Sea and Tethys was established until the Early Jurassic, when a series of transgressions brought widespread marine conditions and faunal unification between north and south. In the Middle Jurassic, regional uplift in the central North Sea, and probably in the NE Atlantic rift system, ran counter to an overall transgressive regime, suggested by regional sea-level curves and by overstepping of the East Greenland and Mid-Norwegian basin margins. These restrictions re-established acute provinciality between the Boreal and Tethyan realms. Marine connections were restored by intense rifting and transgression in the Late Jurassic, but the evolution of a complex seaway with major land barriers in the earliest Cretaceous saw a return of marine provinciality. Transgressions associated with probable ocean floor development to the southwest (Rockall Trough, Hatton—Rockall Basin) and northwest (Canada Basin) of the study area in the Albian and Late Cretaceous finally established an open seaway through the NE Atlantic rift. Massive subsidence in the Faeroes Trough and Mid-Norwegian basins, and dextral shear along the Barents Sea margin, were precursors to final crustal separation in the Early Tertiary.

This account provides an outline palaeogeography of the NE Atlantic rift system (defined herein as the basins lying between East Greenland and the northwestern coast of Norway) and its borderlands, described principally through a sequence of sedimentary—tectonic reconstruction maps. Earlier syntheses for the area have been provided by Gage & Doré (1986), Doré & Gage (1987), Larsen (1987), Ziegler (1988) and Doré (1991). Ideas are, however, constantly being revised. The pace of change is, in particular, driven by the continuing search for hydrocarbons in NW European waters and by a rapidly improving understanding of the mode of extensional basin formation. The present reconstructions are best-fit models incorporating the most recent data. It is expected that these models will be substantially modified as more knowledge becomes available.

The reconstructions utilize plate-tectonic base maps that draw upon the compilations of Scotese (1987) and on the University of Chicago PALEOATLAS program. The work of Rowley & Lottes (1988), probably the most kinematically sophisticated plate reconstruction available for the Arctic region, was also extensively consulted.

The base maps include an attempt to convey the importance of continental extension in palaeogeographic reconstruction. In the absence of definitive data, the maps invoke an average stretching factor of two across the NE Atlantic rift system in the Mesozoic, as indicated by the PALEOATLAS program. Most of this extension is assigned to the Late Jurassic. However, the potential significance of less well understood rifting episodes, such as those of the Permo-Triassic and Early Tertiary, should not be underestimated. These factors emphasize the probable narrowness of the NE Atlantic portal in Early Mesozoic times, a concept that is strongly reinforced by some striking similarities

From PARNELL, J. (ed.), 1992, *Basins on the Atlantic Seaboard: Petroleum Geology, Sedimentology and Basin Evolution*. Geological Society Special Publication No 62, pp 421–446.

between facies assemblages on the East Greenland and mid-Norway flanks of the rift. Farther southwest, the region of the Rockall Trough presents a perennial problem of reconstruction. Although it is generally agreed that lithosphere in this area is highly extended, the timing and nature of the stretching is extremely controversial (Roberts *et al.* 1988; Smythe 1989 and later sections of this paper). The palaeogeographic reconstructions of this region should therefore be regarded as particularly speculative.

No attempt has been made here to allow for the much more difficult problem of continental shortening. It is fortunate that this effect is only significant at the northern margin of the area studied, where crust was attenuated during the Tertiary West Spitsbergen and Eurekan orogenies. The amount of shortening during the West Spitsbergen episode was probably small, while the effect of the Eurekan episode of Arctic Canada may have been considerably more significant (Jackson 1985; de Paor *et al.* 1989).

Fundamental to the palaeogeographic reconstructions shown in this sudy is the importance attached to basement anisotropy in influencing the development of the Mesozoic basin systems. This interpretation is readily apparent from Fig. 1 (Caledonian−Variscan/Uralian tectonic setting) and Fig. 2 (Mesozoic structural elements). This relationship has been explored in detail in a separate paper (Doré 1991), and for the present account a very brief summary of the essential conclusions will suffice.

The Caledonian orogen is considered to be the single most important influence on subsequent basin development. The Iapetus Suture, marking the junction between plates accreted during the culmination of the orogeny, approximately 400 Ma, has been delineated in the Irish Sea, UK mainland and western North Sea using palaeontological evidence and deep reflection profiles (Beamish & Smythe 1986; Freeman *et al.* 1988; McKerrow & Soper 1989) (Fig. 1). Recent work on the feature in the North Sea (Klemperer & Hurich 1990; J. Hospers, pers. comm.) suggests that a branch of the suture probably bends eastwards into the North German−Polish arm of the Caledonides, bounded to the north by a deeply-buried deformation front extending ENE−WSW through the southern part of Denmark (EUGENO-S Working Group 1988). This front merges to the southeast with the Tornquist Alignment, a deeply-rooted and frequently reactivated zone of disturbance traversing the southernmost Baltic Shield (e.g. Pegrum 1984). It is likely that a further branch of the Iapetus suture

extends northwards through the northern North Sea, and thence into the proto-Atlantic rift system between the Caledonian fronts of West Norway and East Greenland. Here, the suture system may have been extensively sheared during oblique closure of the Baltic and Laurentian plates. Further north at the margin of the Barents Sea the Inuitian fold belt, extending through Spitsbergen, North Greenland and Arctic Canada, records a series of movements broadly contemporaneous with those of the Caledonian (e.g. Ohta *et al.* 1989). It probably represents closure of an arm of Iapetus running normal to the main NE−SW Caledonian orogen. There is ample evidence, however, that a 'main' Iapetus suture continues northeastwards beneath the Barents Shelf (Fig. 1). This evidence is described in detail in Doré (1991) and incorporates deep reflection profiling, the strong northeasterly basement grain observed directly off the Finnmark coast and indirectly through the trend of the offshore Mesozoic basins and highs, and numerous references to Caledonian events in the Franz Joseph's Land, Novaya Zemlya and Severnaya Zemlya archipelagos in the Russian literature.

Exploitation of the Caledonian basement grain during subsequent stretching episodes is evident in numerous Caledonoid-trending molasse half-grabens, for example alongside the Great Glen Fault, west of Shetlands, along the SE margin of the Møre Basin (offshore mid-Norway) and onshore East Greenland. These trends were subsequently reinvoked and substantially modified during the later Mesozoic. This concept is particularly well exemplified in the mid-Norway/East Greenland area, where the Mesozoic basin-high system, and the subsequent Early Tertiary crustal separation, can be regarded as a direct exploitation of the Caledonian suture zone (e.g. Surlyk 1977 and many subsequent publications). By implication, the northeasterly basins and highs traversing the Barents Shelf are a continuation of this trend. Caledonian fracture zones regarded as particularly important to later palaeogeographic development include the Senja-Hornsund Alignment (also known in the literature as the De Geer Line), a major belt of fractures extending northward along the Barents Shelf and cross-cutting the main Caledonian trend (Fig. 1); and the Hitra Fault Alignment, a shorthand term given here for the intensely clustered faults that define the section of Norwegian coast between 62° and 64°N (Møre−Trøndelag Fault Zone) and their projection, with about 100 km of offset due to extension of the Viking Graben, into the West Shetland margin (Fig. 2). Both of

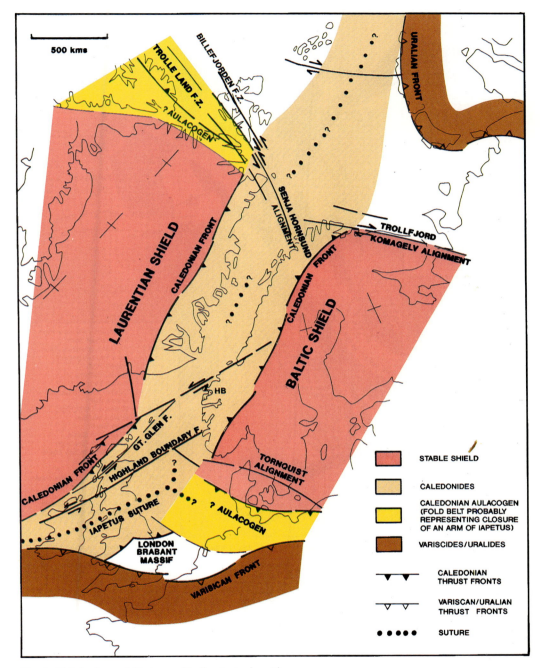

Fig. 1. Caledonian and Variscan−Uralian tectonic setting.

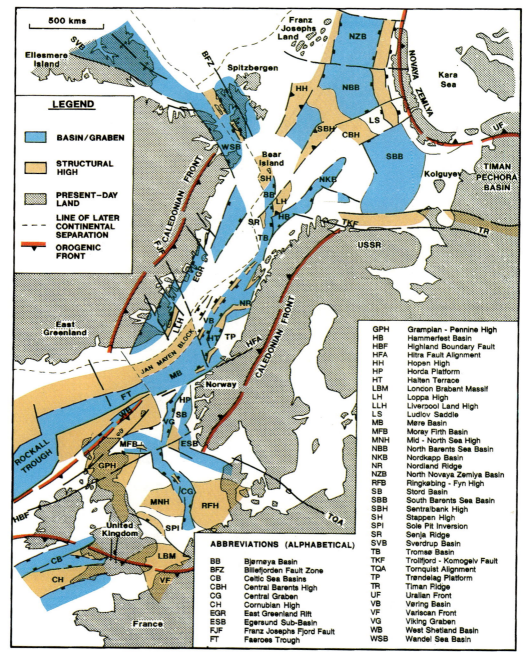

Fig. 2. Principal Mesozoic structural elements of Northwest Europe, Northeast Atlantic and Barents Shelf, assembled on Cretaceous plate reconstruction.

these fault zones were active in the closing stages of the Caledonian orogeny as lines of strike-slip and foci for molasse deposition; both exercised important palaeogeographic control in the late Palaeozoic and Mesozoic; and both influenced the morphology of the developing North Atlantic Ocean in Late Cretaceous–Tertiary times. Evidence for the significance of these deep-seated fracture zones has been reviewed in detail by Doré (1991).

In the North Sea the relationship between Caledonian basement structure and Mesozoic extensional basin development is more difficult to unravel, possibly because (as stated above) a 'triple junction' in the suture system may underlie the region. The extension of lines such as the Highland Boundary Fault across the North Sea, postulated by the author to be a Late Palaeozoic–Early Mesozoic palaeogeographic control, has been contested from deep profiling evidence (Klemperer & Hurich 1990). It appears that, by the late Mesozoic at least, this line may have become inactive. It has also been argued that both the Highland Boundary Fault and Hitra Fault Alignment (Møre–Trøndelag–West Shetlands fault zone) cannot extend across the North Sea, since to do so they would have to intersect basement complexes originally situated on opposite sides of the Iapetus Ocean (Roberts et al. 1990; Klemperer & Hurich 1990). If, however, the fault zones propagated as lines of shear during the terminal phases of the orogeny, as a result of crustal accommodation to oblique closure of Iapetus, then such arguments need not apply.

The Caledonian basement framework was modified in the south by the Variscan Orogeny (culminating in the Late Carboniferous about 280 Ma) and in the northeast by the Uralian Orogeny, a complex closure event culminating approximately 240 Ma in the earliest Triassic. The Variscan collision of Laurasia with Gondwanaland created highlands in the south of the study area, and imposed an E–W and N–S structural overprint that was, in all probability, exploited in the development of such features as the Mid North Sea/Ringkøbing–Fyn High, Oslo Graben, and precursor versions of the Viking and Central Graben. The Uralian collision was accompanied by the development of massive foredeep basins (South Barents Sea Basin, North Barents Sea Basin and North Novaya Zemlya Basin) along the western margin of Novaya Zemlya (Fig. 2). These basins were the dominant structural units of the eastern Barents Shelf throughout Mesozoic time.

Late Permian (Figs 3 & 4)

Of key significance in the Late Permian was the development of marine basins in the previously continental North Sea and Atlantic Rift domains; for example in Britain (Smith 1980), the North Sea (Taylor 1981) and East Greenland (Surlyk et al. 1986). On the western Barents Shelf, this transgression was marked by a change from restricted evaporitic and sabkha facies to a more open marine depositional style (e.g. Worsley & Aga 1986). The overall transgressive regime may be attributable to eustatic sea-level rise, but was undoubtedly also facilitated by widespread extensional tectonic activity. Surlyk et al. (1984) record major mid-Permian block-faulting in East Greenland, while contemporaneous tectonic episodes are recorded on the Mid-Norwegian Shelf and in the Oslo Graben. The mid-Permian rifting penetrated through the Senja–Hornsund fault system, which had previously confined marine sedimentation to the Barents Sea domain (Doré & Gage 1987) and provided the avenue for a marine connection from the Boreal Ocean to Northern England, the North Sea and mainland Europe.

On the Barents Shelf, deposition in eastern areas (adjacent to Novaya Zemlya and in the Timan–Pechora Basin) was dominated by thick terriginous sediment sourced from the developing Uralian fold belt. From here there was a diachronous transition westwards into a carbonate shelf. Locally developed bioherms within the carbonate unit form distinctive features on industry seismic lines across the eastern Norwegian Barents Sea (Bruce & Toomey, in press). Fine siliceous clastics (Kap Starostin facies) were laid down in deeper and more distal areas. Uplift of marginal source areas, probably associated with the Uralian orogenesis, resulted in the development of a marine coarse clastic fringe round the Baltic and Laurentian margins, and north of Spitsbergen ('Lomonosov Land').

The eastwards shedding of coarse clastics from the Hornsund-Sørkapp High (south Spitsbergen; Worsley & Aga 1986), a mid-Permian unconformity on Bear Island (Worsley & Edwards 1976) and on the western margin of the Loppa High (Riis et al. 1985) all provide evidence of activity on the north–south Senja–Hornsund trend along the western margin of the Barents Shelf. Penetration of the Late Permian transgression across this barrier into the Atlantic Rift domain brought marine sedimentation to East Greenland, where sediments of the Foldvik Creek Group accumulated in a restricted basin setting. Facies types include

LEGEND FOR SEDIMENTARY/TECTONIC RECONSTRUCTIONS

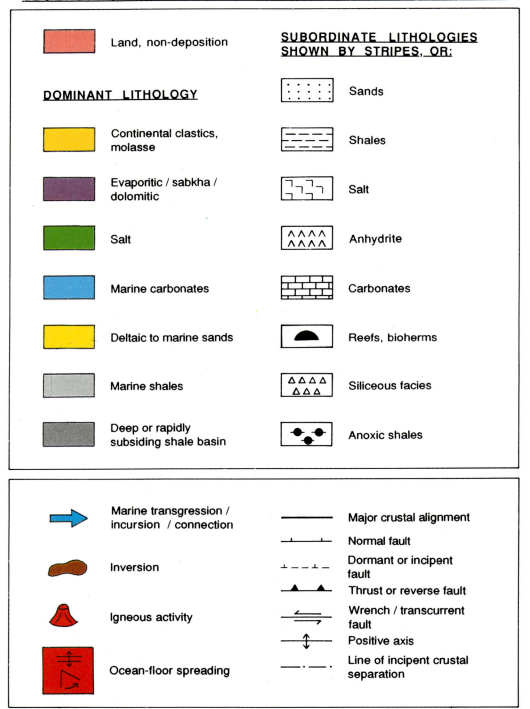

Fig. 3. Legend for sedimentary/tectonic reconstructions.

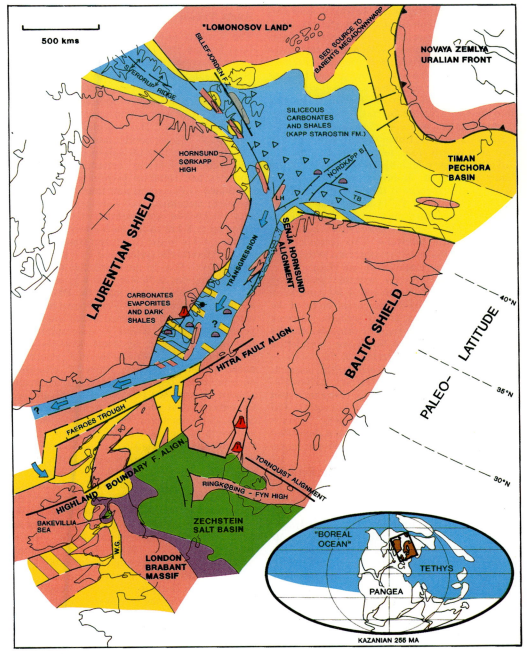

Fig. 4. Late Permian sedimentary/tectonic reconstruction. Abbreviations: LH, Loppa High; WG, Worcester Graben.

coarse clastics, evaporites, bryozoan reef carbonates and organic-rich shales (Surlyk *et al.* 1986). The association of organic shales (Ravnefjeld Formation) with porous reef facies (Wegener Halvø Formation) may also exist on the Mid-Norwegian side of the rift, and is thus of interest to the oil industry.

The transgression of the Late Permian Sea into the North Sea Basins has been described as a catastrophic, or at least geologically rapid, event (Glennie & Buller 1983). It is possible that southwards transgression through the NE Atlantic rift was initially blocked at the Hitra Fault Alignment. In-house seismic mapping along the SE margin of the Møre Basin (J. K. Best, pers. comm. 1991) shows that Permo-Triassic deposition in this area was dominated by NE–SW half-grabens with basement exposed in the footwalls. This tectonic configuration is similar to that observed in the West Shetlands Basin (Duindam & van Hoorn 1987). The dominant NE–SW tectonic grain may eventually have been breached by continuing transgression and by the precursor faults of the northern North Sea graben system, allowing marine conditions to penetrate through a narrow portal into the southern North Sea. Inundation of the low-lying desert terrain of the southern North Sea Basins was followed by the accumulation of the Zechstein Group carbonate-evaporite cycles, in a subsiding, restricted basin bounded northwards by the Tornquist and Highland Boundary Fault trends. Thinner anhydrites and shelf dolomites were deposited in marginal areas and on intra-basinal highs (Taylor 1981).

Smith (1980) identifies a Late Permian (Kazanian) marine ingression in NW Britain (the 'Bakevillia Sea'), separate from the Zechstein Basin of NE Britain and the North Sea. Transgression from the Arctic may therefore have reached the Bakevillia Sea via an alternative route, perhaps through a precursor of the Faeroes Trough or another southwesterly propagating rift system. There is no recorded evidence, however, of this marine connection in the West Shetlands area, where the limited evidence suggests that red-bed deposition persisted through the Late Permian interval (Duindam & van Hoorn 1987).

Faunal evidence confirms the link between the Zechstein and Late Permian sequences of the Boreal Realm, but indicates no connection with the Tethyan region (Smith 1980) which was presumably separated from the study area at the time by the recently formed Variscan uplands.

Early Triassic (Fig. 5)

The Uralian suturing in the earliest Triassic (e.g. Scotese 1987) marked an important stage in the assembly of the Pangean supercontinent. Nance *et al.* (1988) have shown that heat accumulation under a region of low-conductivity continental crust, on supercontinent scale, should lead to widespread updoming and subsequent break-up. This postulate may explain the typical Triassic configuration over much of the study area; that of widespread emergence and withdrawal of the Zechstein seas to the northern and southern extremity of the area, combined with extensional faulting and rapid sediment accumulation. Substantial sedimentary thicknesses are recorded throughout the area; up to 8 km in the basins west of Novaya Zemlya, 6 km in the Nordkapp Basin, 2–3 km in the Atlantic rift system and 4–6 km in parts of the North Sea. In the North Sea and proto-Atlantic regions sedimentation was in an arid, fluvial-lacustrine setting, while the Barents Sea at higher palaeolatitudes was characterized by marine-deltaic cycles formed under more temperate conditions. Rapid Triassic subsidence has been described by some workers (e.g. Gabrielsen *et al.* 1990) as a thermal subsidence phase to Permian rifting. However, extensive documentation of major normal faulting in the eastern Barents Sea (Gramberg 1988), in East Greenland, west of Shetlands, and the North Sea (Clemmensen *et al.* 1980; Lervik *et al.* 1989) and south of the study area (Manspeizer 1988) indicates that the Triassic marked an important stretching phase in its own right. In the North Sea, extension was followed by a thermal subsidence phase lasting from mid-Triassic to mid-Jurassic (Badley *et al.* 1988). Further south, on the eastern seaboard of America and in northwest Africa, Triassic rifting was a precursor to central Atlantic spreading in Middle Jurassic times (Manspeizer 1988). Triassic faulting largely followed the tectonic grain of the fused orogenic belts of the Pangean supercontinent. In the eastern Barents Sea the foredeep basins bordering the Uralian front were the dominant factor, while in the western Barents Sea, Atlantic rift domain, and west of Shetlands, Caledonoid trends predominated. Variscan influences became more important southwards through the North Sea, and south of the study area Triassic rifting broadly followed the lines of the Variscan–Alleghanian orogen (Manspeizer 1988).

In the far northeast of the study area Early Triassic deposition consisted of continental red-beds shed from the uplifted Arctic Urals. From

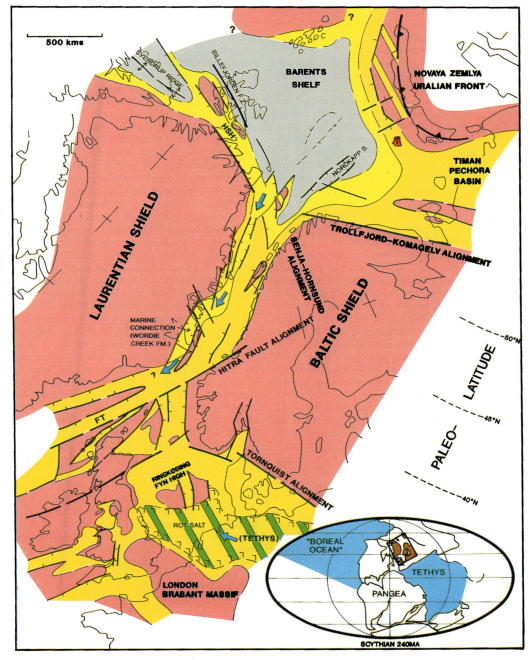

Fig. 5. Early Triassic sedimentary/tectonic reconstruction. Abbreviations: FT, Faeroes Trough; HSH, Hornsund Sørkapp High.

here, there was a transition westwards into a marginal marine to deltaic environment in the Norwegian Barents Sea. Much of the substantial sediment thickness may again have been sourced from the Uralides, although the large transport distances required suggest that southerly sources such as the northern Baltic margin may also have been important. Marginal marine environments also prevailed in both Svalbard (Steel & Worsley 1984) and the Sverdrup Basin (Embry 1989). Sands emanating from the Laurentian margin gave way eastwards and northwards to areas dominated by fine clastic sedimentation. This depositional area probably connected northwards to the Boreal Ocean. Transgressive-regressive cycles within the sequence can be correlated, with some certainty, between the Sverdrup Basin, Spitsbergen and Barents Shelf (Mørk et al. 1989).

Rejuvenation of the Hornsund-Sørkapp High on Spitsbergen (e.g. Worsley & Aga 1986) and onlap on to the eastern margin of the Loppa High (in-house data) provide evidence that elements of the Senja-Hornsund trend remained high in the Early Triassic. These features probably formed barriers between the predominantly marine Barents Shelf and the Atlantic Rift domain, where marine influences were more transient. A transgression in the early Scythian deposited marine sand/shale with a Boreal fauna (Wordie Creek Formation) in East Greenland (Clemmensen 1980) but this was replaced in the late Scythian by the continental coarse clastics of the Pingo Dal Formation. There is no evidence of marine incursions on the eastern (Mid-Norway) side of the Atlantic Rift, although Scythian well penetrations are limited.

Further south, the North Sea domains were almost entirely dominated by continental red-bed deposition, with coarse clastic units (Skagerrak Formation and equivalents) accumulating proximal to rapidly-eroding highs (Vollset & Doré 1984; Lervik et al. 1989). The Røt Halite, deposited at the end of the Scythian, marks the first of a series of brief Triassic marine ingressions into the southern North Sea domain from the Tethyan realm in the southeast.

Middle to Late Triassic (Fig. 6)

The general tectono-sedimentary pattern of the Early Triassic continued in the Middle to Late Triassic, with the development of further marine ingressions from the Boreal Realm into the Atlantic Rift domain, and from the Tethyan Realm into the southern North Sea domain.

Continental deposits continued to accumulate in the foredeep to the Uralian uplift. West of

Novaya Zemlya a Late Triassic transgression terminated this regime and brought fully marine conditions to the area (in-house data). Shallow marine-deltaic deposition prevailed over the remainder of the Barents Shelf, although there is evidence for the emergence of new land-areas in Carnian times. Such a positive area is postulated in Fig. 6, to explain delta-front deposits identified on Edgeøya, eastern Svalbard (Worsley and Aga 1986) and coastal sediments in Franz Joseph's land. The area of the Sentralbank High probably also became emergent during the Carnian (in-house data).

In Svalbard, deposition occurred in a series of north-south facies belts with their axis in the Billefjorden Trough (e.g. Steel & Worsley 1984). Deltas prograded into this depocentre from the east and west. Mudstones deposited in axial parts of the basin included the organic-rich Botneheia Member, which formed during a Middle Triassic (Anisian-Ladinian) sea-level high-stand (Mørk et al. 1982). Roughly contemporaneous bituminous developments are also identified in the Sverdrup Basin (Murray Harbour Formation; Embry 1989) and in structural lows of the Barents Shelf (Kobbe and Klapmyss Formations; in-house data).

Evidence of activity on fault blocks along the N−S Senja−Hornsund trend at the western Barents Sea margin is indicated by uplift of the Hornsund−Sørkapp High, and by the probable existence of an analogous sediment source west of the Hammerfest Basin in the Late Triassic (Rønnevik et al. 1982). Additional evidence is provided by a major Middle Triassic disconformity on the Bear Island (Mørk et al. 1989) and by uplift of the Loppa High, which was finally inundated in the Late Triassic (Riis et al. 1985). Southwest of this barrier, the East Greenland area was dominated by lacustrine, anhydritic sedimentation (Gipsdalen Formation) and continental coarse clastics (Fleming Fjord Formation). A brief but widespread marine transgression brought sandy calcarenites and limestones with a Boreal fauna (Gråklint Beds) to the area in the Middle Triassic (Clemmensen 1980). On the Mid-Norway side, in Haltenbanken, two halite units represent short-lived marine incursions from the Boreal Realm into an otherwise continental sequence. Seismic evidence suggests that the units are widespread over Haltenbanken. They have been dated as Latest Ladinian − Early Carnian and Late Carnian respectively. The lower salt interval has been tentatively correlated with the Gråklint Beds of East Greenland by Jacobsen and van Veen (1984).

Interior continental deposition in the North

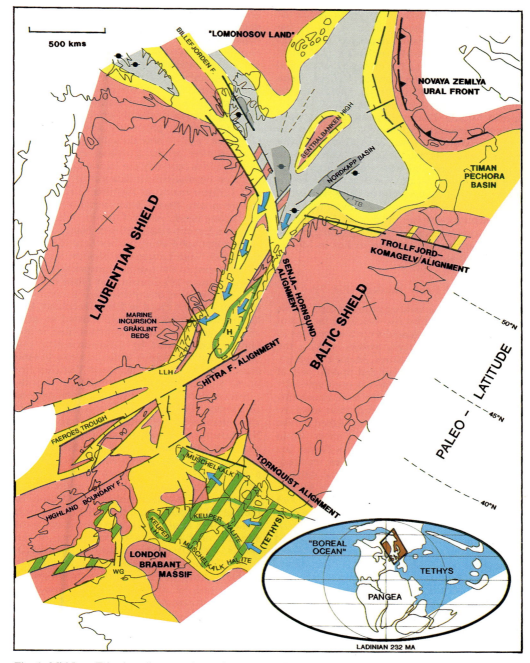

Fig. 6. Mid-Late Triassic sedimentary/tectonic reconstruction. Abbreviations: LLH, Liverpool Land High; H, Haltenbanken; WG, Worcester Graben.

Sea area was also interrupted by periodic marine ingressions from the Tethyan realm in the southeast. These events deposited the halites and carbonates of the Muschelkalk in the Middle Triassic (Anisian–Ladinian) and halites and anhydrites in the Late Triassic (Keuper Halite and other units) (Rhys 1974). These deposits represent the northermost outpost of a widespread Middle Triassic–Sinemurian evaporite regime characteristic of basins on the western margin of Tethys (Holser et al. 1988). Tethyan marine incursions into the North Sea have been tentatively correlated with Boreal ingressions into the Atlantic rift domain in terms of worldwide sea level changes (Jacobsen & van Veen 1984). It should be stressed, however, that both the palaeogeographic and faunal evidence argues strongly against any throughgoing marine connection between the two realms in Middle to Late Triassic times.

Rhaetian and Early Jurassic (Fig. 7)

The latest Triassic and beginning of the Jurassic saw a general sea level rise which, by the end of the Early Jurassic, created a continuous seaway through the Atlantic rift system, linking the Boreal and Tethyan Realms. Major transgressive pulses in the Rhaetian and middle part of the Early Jurassic deposited a predominantly marine suite in the south of the area, inundating the Triassic basins and flooding their margins. The earlier (Rhaetian) pulse established paralic conditions in the Norwegian-Danish Basin (Gassum Formation) and northern North Sea (Statfjord Formation). This general environment extended along the flanks of the Atlantic rift domain, depositing the coaly Kap Stewart Formation in East Greenland (Surlyk 1990a) and the very similar Åre Formation on the mid-Norwegian side (Fig. 8).

The succeeding Sinemurian-Pliensbachian transgression established marine shale deposition in the North Sea (e.g. Dunlin Formation), although sandy deposits continued to accumulate close to the basin margins (Cook and Johansen Formations). The same transgression brought fully marine conditions and the deposition of tide-dominated sands to the NE Atlantic rift system. There is again a close equivalence between the East Greenland (Neill Klinter Formation) and mid-Norwegian (Tilje Formation) facies (Fig. 8). The marine pulse extended across the Senja–Hornsund trend into the southern Barents Shelf, where the earlier shallow marine-deltaic environment persisted with the deposition of the Tubåen and Nordmela Formations (Dalland et al. 1988). This trans-

gression culminated in the Toarcian with the deposition of anoxic shales in the southern North Sea and Paris Basin regions, a phenomenon attributed by Jenkyns (1988) to deepening water and impingement of a Tethyan oxygen-minimum water layer on to marginal shelf areas. Dark marine shales of the Ror Formation, on the mid-Norwegian Shelf, date from this phase (Fig. 8). The poorly dated Sortehat Member of East Greenland, previously assigned a later (Bajocian) age, is now thought to be a further manifestation of the Toarcian event (Surlyk 1990a) and is probably the lateral equivalent of the Ror Formation. Unification of the Boreal and Tethyan realms at this time is reflected in the ammonite faunas from western Svalbard, East Greenland, Arctic Canada, Alaska and Western Europe (Bäckström & Nagy 1982).

Regional uplift along the northern margins of the Baltic and Laurentian Shields formed a counterpoint to the overall transgressive trend. In the Atlantic rift domain, this phase included the establishment of a palaeohigh to the north of Kong Oscar's Fjord in East Greenland. Uplifted blocks must also have existed in axial areas of the rift system, demonstrated in the Halten Terrace area by sedimentological evidence, from exploration wells, of westerly sand sources in the Plienbachian and Toarcian (in-house studies; see also Doré 1991). This interpretation runs counter to the reconstructions of Ziegler (1988), which show a transition to shale-dominated deposition in the axis of the NE Atlantic rift system between Haltenbanken and East Greenland. In the Barents Sea and marginal areas, the same event may account for a major hiatus in the Timan–Pechora Basin (Kelly 1988), periodic emergence in the central Barents Sea (in-house studies), condensing of the Early Jurassic west of the Billefjorden Fault Zone (Mørk et al. 1982), and for the apparent absence of Early Jurassic sediments in the Wandel Sea Basin (Håkansson & Stemmerik 1984). Continuation of the Triassic high to the west of Spitsbergen may explain the westward progradation of the Wilhelmøya Formation deltaic sands across the islands in the Rhaetian–Early Jurassic, and a similar clastic fringe in Franz Joseph's Land. An alternative (or additional) sediment source may have existed in the region of the Sentralbank High, as postulated by Johannessen & Embry (1989).

Middle Jurassic (Fig. 9)

An overall transgressive trend continued in the Middle Jurassic, although this regime was interrupted locally by very significant tectonic events.

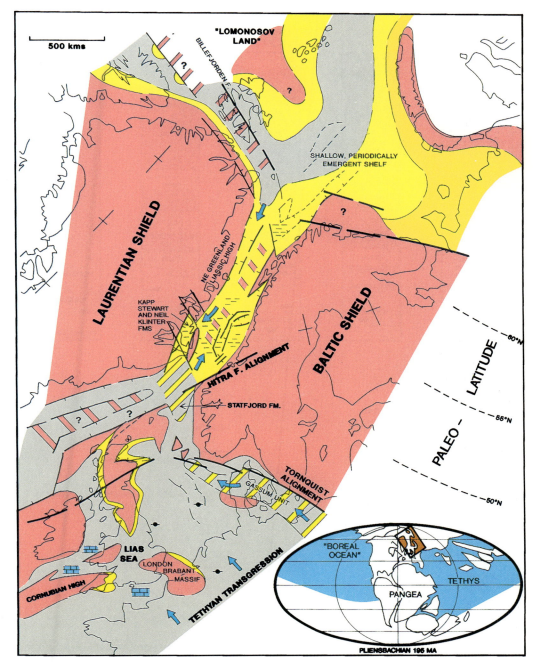

Fig. 7. Rhaetian to Early Jurassic sedimentary/tectonic reconstruction.

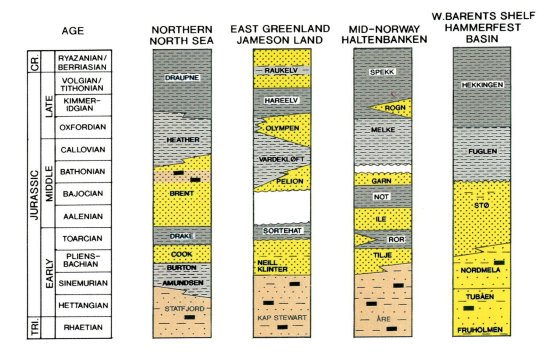

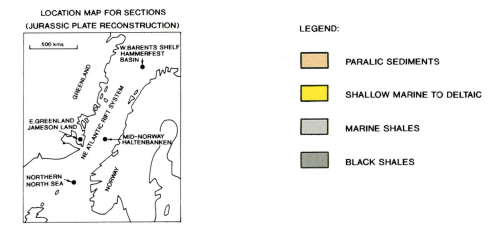

Fig. 8. Comparison of Jurassic clastic sequences in and adjacent to the NE Atlantic Rift domain. Simplified after Dalland *et al.* (1988), Surlyk *et al.* (1981) and Vollset & Doré (1984).

In the Atlantic rift domain a series of transgressions took place over the basin margins. In East Greenland, a hiatus in the Aalenian–Early Bajocian was followed in the later Bajocian by transgression and deposition of marine sand-stone (Pelion Member). The marine advance progressively inundated portions of the East Greenland Rift throughout the remainder of the Middle Jurassic (Surlyk 1990*b*). The Aalenian–Lower Bajocian hiatus does not

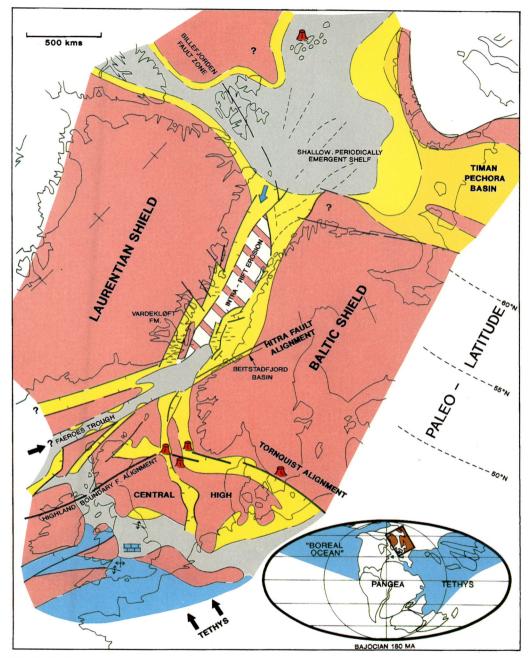

Fig. 9. Middle Jurassic sedimentary/tectonic reconstruction. Stripes show *maximum* area of intra-basinal uplift (see text). Deposition in parts of this area is also possible.

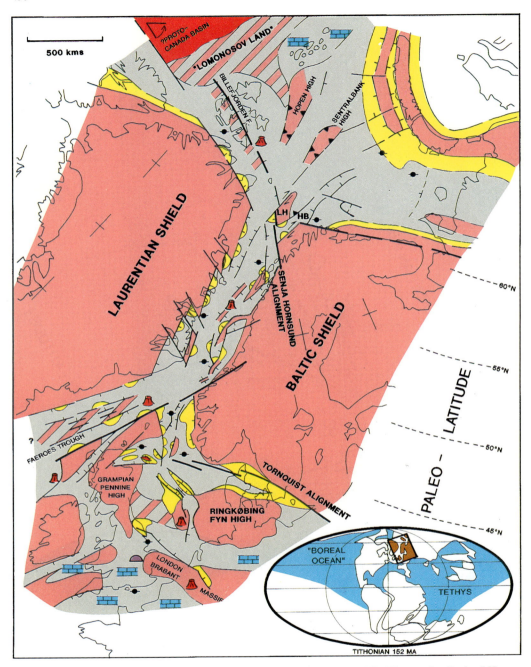

Fig. 10. Late Jurassic sedimentary/tectonic reconstruction. Abbreviations: HB, Hammerfest Basin; LH, Loppa High.

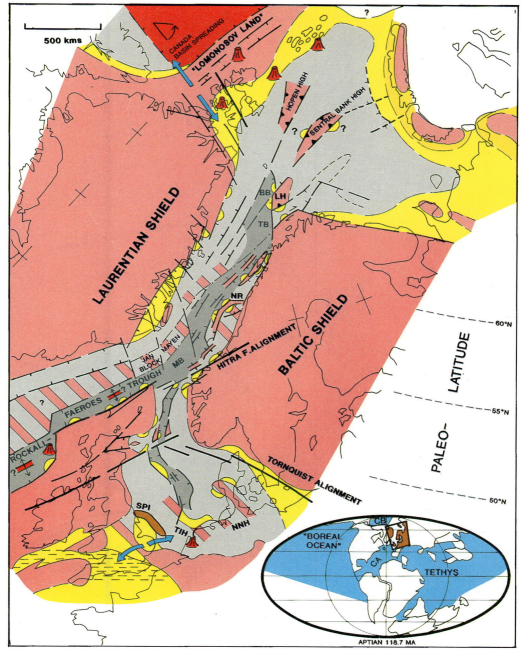

Fig. 11. Early Cretaceous sedimentary/tectonic reconstruction. Abbreciations: BB, Bjørnøya Basin; CA, Central Atlantic; CB, Canada Basin; LH, Loppa High; MB, Møre Basin; NNH, North Netherlands High; NR, Nordland Ridge; SPI, Sole Pit Inversion; TB, Tromsø Basin; TIH, Texel-Ischelmeer High.

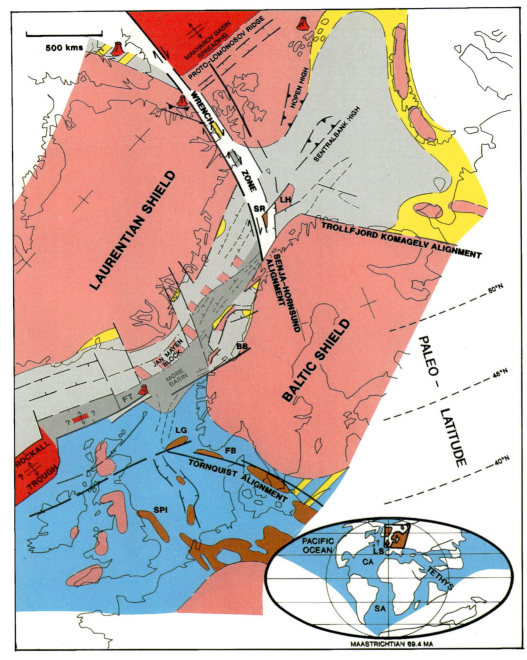

Fig. 12. Late Cretaceous sedimentary/tectonic reconstruction. Abbreviations: BB, Beitstadfjord Basin; CA, Central Atlantic; FB, Farsund Basin; LG, Ling Graben; LH, Loppa High; LS, Labrador Sea; SA, South Atlantic; SPI, Sole Pit Inversion; SR, Senja Ridge.

appear to be present on the Mid-Norway side, where marine sand-shale deposition prevailed and a significant Bajocian transgression deposited dark mudstones (Not Formation; Fig. 8). The Middle Jurassic transgression overstepped the basin flanks in Mid-Norway and brought marginal marine deposition to the Frohavet Basin, just offshore, and paralic deposition to fault-preserved outliers in the Norwegian fjords along the Møre–Trøndelag Fault Zone (Bøe 1990).

Shallow marine sedimentation continued on the southern Barents Shelf, where coastal sands of the Stø Formation show evidence of several transgressive pulses (Dalland et al. 1988). Further north on Spitsbergen, however, uplift and condensing of sequences, a regime established in the Early Jurassic, continued through the Aalenian and Bajocian. This local regressive tendency was also prevalent in the Timan–Pechora Basin (e.g. Kelly 1988) and Arctic Canada (Embry 1989). On Spitsbergen, open marine conditions were once again established in the Bathonian and Callovian with deposition of the Janusfjellet Formation shales (Worsley & Aga 1986).

Important tectonic uplifts in the study area ran counter to the overall picture of Middle Jurassic transgression suggested by sea-level curves from East Greenland (Surlyk 1990b) and by the overstepping of the East Greenland and Mid-Norway basin margins. Most significant amongst these was uplift and restriction in the central North Sea area, a phenomenon probably genetically associated with the well-known basic igneous activity occurring at, and predating, the trilete junction between the Central, Viking and Witch Ground Graben systems (e.g. Ritchie et al. 1988). The uplift was the focal point for the establishment of delta systems in the northern North Sea (Sleipner Formation/Brent Group) along the Fennoscandian Border Zone (Bryne/Haldager Formations) and in the southern North Sea (Yorkshire Deltaic sequence).

The magnitude of the Middle Jurassic uplift is a subject of some controversy (see Leeder, 1983). Nevertheless, in palaeogeographic terms it is hard to ignore. The uplift was undoubtedly a major contributing factor to the acute faunal provinciality (Callomon 1984) established between the Boreal (Arctic–NE Atlantic seaway) and Tethyan (southern Britain–central Europe) realms from the Late Bajocian onwards. The palaeogeographic barrier was probably breached by transgression and extensional faulting in the Callovian, when north–south faunal connections were re-established. The

transgression brought marine shale deposition (Heather Formation) to the northern North Sea, although marginal sands of the Fensfjord and Krossfjord Formations continued to accumulate adjacent to the Fennoscandian margin (Vollset & Doré 1984).

A notable body of evidence also points to the continued existence of substantial emergent areas in axial parts of the NE Atlantic rift system in Middle Jurassic times (see Fig. 9). In-house sedimentological studies of exploration wells in the Haltenbanken region indicate coarse clastic contributions from northerly and westerly sources during deposition of the Ile Formation (Aalenian–Bajocian) and Garn Formation (Bajocian–Bathonian). This concept is supported by onshore outcrop data in the Lofoten Islands, which indicate a westerly provenance (Dalland 1979) and by westwards thickening of contemporaneous sand units in the Hammerfest Basin, possibly towards uplifted palaeo-highs along the Senja–Hornsund trend. Larsen (1987) has used this evidence to propose the existence of a land bridge between north-east Greenland and north Norway in the Middle Jurassic. Such an extreme interpretation is, however, contradicted by the faunal evidence (Callomon 1984), which demonstrates continuing marine connections between East Greenland and Arctic Canada in Late Bajocian–Callovian times.

The side-by-side existence of an overall transgressive regime with local deep erosion and coarse clastic sourcing in the Middle Jurassic presents an intriguing puzzle. Attempts have been made to explain this phenomenon using crustal stretching models such as non-uniform extension, which predicts thermal uplift of the rift flanks (Leeder 1983). Other heterogenous stretching hypotheses, such as the simple shear and depth-dependent extension models (Wernicke 1985; Badley et al. 1988) also predict a degree of uplift, its geographical location varying according to the model used. In any of these scenarios, significant crustal thinning could eventually result in magmatism and thermal updoming in the basin centre, as is presumed to have occurred in the central North Sea (see Latin et al. 1990, for a very thorough discussion of alternative models). A key problem, however, is that the Middle Jurassic sand sequences that were sourced from the thermally uplifted hinterlands show only minor signs of syndepositional fault activity. Although rifting probably began in the latest Middle Jurassic, the peak activity was in the Late Jurassic–Early Cretaceous. Therefore, it is necessary to explain the significant delay between crustal stretching to a point where extensive volcanism and thermal uplift is possible, and its manifestation as brittle failure in the upper crust. Failing this, a more active thermal drive for pre-rift up-doming, for example, the currently unfashionable hypothesis of mantle pluming (Torske 1975; Ziegler 1982), should be sought to explain the widespread uplift and restriction in the Middle Jurassic.

Late Jurassic (Fig. 10)

The Late Jurassic saw a continuing strongly transgressive regime, occurring against a background of continent-wide extensional tectonic activity, usually referred to as the Cimmerian diastrophic cycle. Badley *et al.* (1988) have, with some justification, pointed out that use of the term 'Cimmerian' in the literature to imply a single tectonic pulse belies the true situation; that of a complex sequence of tectonic events that varied in timing from area to area. The present author believes that use of the term is acceptable if it is taken to represent the whole spectrum of tectonic effects associated with the same, roughly synchronous, continent-wide controls. These include the break-up of northern Pangea associated with crustal separation and spreading in the Central Atlantic (see inset to Fig. 10), concomitant clockwise rotation of the Laurentian plate relative to the Baltic plate (Rowley & Lottes 1988) and important closure events on the north-western margin of Tethys in the Crimea–Caucasus region (Sengör 1979).

The widespread rifting and fault block rotation was most intense in the latest Middle Jurassic – earliest Cretaceous interval. The movements were accompanied by extrusive igneous activity in the Atlantic rift domain, evidenced by tuff deposits on the islands of Skye and Andøya (Dalland & Thusu 1977), and by dolerite sill injection in the Svalbard region (Worsley & Aga 1986). Recent, unpublished clay mineral data on the Callovian–Kimmeridgian shales of East Greenland (F. Surlyk, pers. comm.) also show a very strong volcanic component. In the Central Graben, Viking Graben and Witch Ground Graben systems of the North Sea, major rifting probably commenced in latest Middle Jurassic times (see previous section). A similar timing is recorded in the Atlantic rift system, although in East Greenland particularly intense normal faulting occurred in the Volgian/Tithonian (Surlyk 1978). On the mid-Norwegian side of the rift, the faulting was accompanied by thin-skinned tectonics involving soling-out of faults onto Triassic salt layers. In the Barents Sea domain,

tectonic events more or less synchronous with the mid-Norway activity initiated or re-invoked the bounding faults of the Hammerfest Basin (Rønnevik *et al.* 1982), and re-activated elements of the ancient Senja-Hornsund fault zone, creating a N–S sequence of basins and highs. These include the Bjørnøya Basin, Loppa High and Tromsø Basin. Extensional tectonism is documented as far east as the Mesozoic basins adjacent to Novaya Zemlya (in-house studies).

In northern parts of the linked rift system, on the mid-Norway and Barents shelves, a wrench component to the 'Cimmerian' movements becomes more apparent. These movements are consistent with the Late Jurassic clockwise (sinistral) rotation of the Laurentian plate postulated by Rowley & Lottes (1988). Stresses associated with incipient rotational opening of the Canada Basin, a process which culminated in the Early Cretaceous (Rowley & Lottes 1988) could also have emphasized the strike-slip component.

Flexural uptilting of the rift margins and footwall uplift of individual fault blocks locally overcame the effects of the pervasive transgression and created emergent sand source areas within the study area. These developments include coarse clastic submarine fans deposited on the hangingwall blocks of major faults; for example in the northern North Sea at the Brae, Magnus and Miller Fields, at Brora in the Moray Firth, and in East Greenland. An excellent synopsis of this depositional mode, characteristic of the Late Jurassic, is given by Surlyk (1989). Other depositional styles include shallow marine transgressive–regressive sheet sands such as the Sognefjord Formation of the northern North Sea (e.g. Vollset & Doré 1984) and barrier-bar complexes deposited on the dip-slope of major intra-basinal fault blocks; for example, the Rogn Formation of Mid-Norway (Dalland *et al.* 1988). All of these sands were local in extent (Fig. 10). Away from the emergent highs, the predominant transgressive mode was reflected in the deposition of dark marine shales. Anoxic, organic-rich shales developed within this interval constitute the well-known 'supersource' for the North Sea fields. Similar, roughly contemporaneous facies developments can be shown to extend northwards through the NE Atlantic rift system to the Barents Sea, and in the Arctic region are developed as far afield as Alaska and West Siberia (Doré 1991; Table 2). The continent-wide distribution of a facies type frequently described as 'restricted' is a situation that has long intrigued geologists. Its pervasive nature is probably not attributable to a single cause, but to a coincidence of several.

Principal among these was the creation of a complex seaway (with limited and narrow connections to Tethys in the south and the Boreal Ocean to the north), within which the strongly transgressive regime created a stagnant bottom layer. The globally warm climate of the Jurassic, without major temperature differentials between the equator and poles (Hallam 1967), probably enhanced a tendency to stagnation and salinity stratification within the complex network of rift systems. This convergence of causes was terminated in post-Berriasian time with the creation of new open marine systems north (Canada Basin) and south (Rockall Trough, Hatton−Rockall Basin) of the study area.

The marine seaway between northwest Europe and the Arctic, re-established in the Callovian, continued to exist through the early part of the Late Jurassic. This is demonstrated by ammonite faunas described in East Greenland and the northern North Sea, which indicate links between southern Britain and the Russian Platform in the Oxfordian (Callomon 1975) and Kimmeridgian (Callomon & Birkelund 1982). However, the intense tectonic activity of the Late Jurassic added increasing complexity to the evolving seaway. This effect, combined with a widely recorded sea level fall in the Mid-Volgian/Tithonian (e.g. Rawson & Riley 1982), resulted in the re-establishment of faunal provinciality. While most of the study area was within the 'Boreal Realm' in terms of ammonite palaeobiogeography, the Boreal Realm itself contained numerous sub-provinces (e.g. Casey 1971). Significant faunal differences between Britain and East Greenland in Mid-Volgian/Tithonian times (Callomon & Birkelund 1982) can readily be visualized in terms of fault-induced re-activation of the central North Sea highs.

Early Cretaceous (Fig. 11)

The continuing evolution of structural highs as a result of Late Jurassic−Early Cretaceous tectonics created land barriers in the earliest Cretaceous that are reflected in the faunal provinciality of the interval. Ammonite provincialism was at its most pronounced during the Berriasian. Boreal and Tethyan communities were completely cut off from each other during much of this interval, with the area north of the London−Brabant Massif lying within the Boreal realm. However, a late Berriasian transgression (Rawson & Riley 1982) paved the way for subsequent 'spreads' of ammonite genera between the two realms through the complex Early Cretaceous seaway.

Widespread emergence resulted in deltaic developments in England, East Greenland and Svalbard. In southern England the paralic Wealden deposits accumulated south of the London−Brabant Massif in Berriasian−Barremian times, while in East Greenland probable deltaic rocks of Valanginian-Hauterivian age are identified on Milne Land (Birkelund et al. 1984). Major deltaic developments in the Svalbard region (Helvetiafjellet Formation) prograded away from emergent areas in the north and west in Barremian times. Uplift of source areas in this region was probably associated with rotational opening of the Canada Basin to the north, dated as Hauterivian−Barremian (131−110 Ma) by Rowley & Lottes (1988). Basaltic lava flows interbedded with the deltaic sediments in Kong Karl's Land (east Svalbard) and Franz Joseph's Land (Kelly 1988) add weight to this interpretation. Farther east in the USSR Barents Sea, marine clastics continued to accumulate in the subsiding troughs west of Novaya Zemlya.

Away from the developing deltas, marine shale deposition predominated in the North Sea (Speeton Clay Formation, Valhall Formation), mid-Norway (Lange Formation) and Barents Shelf (Knurr and Kolje Formations) in Berriasian−Barremian times. Footwall uplift on rift margins and other Cimmerian faults continued to be active to a varying extent across the area, depositing clastic wedges against the fault scarps. Such developments include the Devil's Hole Formation of the Central Graben (Hesjedal & Hamar 1983), the Lyr and intra-Lange sands in Mid-Norway, and Berriasian to (?) earliest Hauterivian sands within the Wollaston Foreland Group in northern East Greenland (Surlyk 1978). Farther north, faulting continued to control clastic accumulations on Andøya (Dalland 1979), in offshore basins west of Lofoten where seismic records show major Early Cretaceous half-graben development (J. H. Snow, pers. comm. 1991), and in the southwestern Barents Sea where Early Cretaceous sands are currently an exploration target. In the latter area, this tectonic activity again carried a wrench component, manifested as dextral strike-slip motion and associated reverse faulting (Riis et al. 1985).

Regionally significant oceanic and transgressive events in the Aptian−Albian interval overturned the tectono-sedimentary regime of the earliest Cretaceous. The North Sea began a transition towards a more stable regime of epicontinental subsidence, while the Atlantic rift continued the sequence of events that was to culminate in crustal separation. The history of ocean-floor spreading in the Rockall Trough is controversial, largely due to the absence of linear magnetic anomalies to date this event. A small body of opinion (e.g. Haszeldine & Russell 1987) believes that the ocean floor was emplaced as early as the Carboniferous. On the other hand, some recent studies suggest that the Rockall Trough and Hatton−Rockall Basin, although highly extended, may never have proceeded to full oceanic status and are underlain by highly thinned continental lithosphere (see summary by Smythe 1989). Figure 11 in this account shows the more usual model, in which a long history of rifting within the Rockall Trough culminated with spreading in the Albian (100 Ma) during the Middle Cretaceous magnetically 'Quiet Zone' (e.g. Rowley & Lottes 1988). Indirect support for the idea of significant Cretaceous extension across the Rockall area comes from the NE−SW belt of rapid subsidence and sedimentary infill that was initiated seaward of the ancient Møre-Trøndelag/West Shetlands trend (Hitra Fault Alignment on Fig. 11). Sills and/or lava flows within this sequence (Bukovics and Ziegler 1985) suggest upwelling of magmas into a region of thinned crust already stretched threadbare by preceding episodes of extension. Rapid downwarping of the Møre and Vøring Basins, which accelerated in the Late Cretaceous, presumably represents a thermal subsidence phase of this activity. The line of subsiding basins continued northwards to the Barents Shelf, where the Tromsø and Bjørnøya Basins contain an expanded Early Cretaceous sequence. These depocentres were disengaged from the eastern Barents Shelf by the Ringvassøy−Loppa Fault Zone (Gabrielsen 1984), an element of the northerly Senja−Hornsund trend.

A major Aptian−Albian transgression, probably associated with the northwards propagation of Atlantic spreading described above, deposited uniform reddish calcareous claystones of the Rødby Formation over most of the North Sea (Hesjedal & Hamar 1982). This major transgression submerged most of the upstanding areas created by Late Jurassic−Early Cretaceous movements, and overstepped the margins of the Atlantic rift. It established an open seaway from southern England, through the North Sea and Atlantic rift, to the Barents Shelf in Albian times and resulted in faunal connections between Spitsbergen and the Mediterranean by the mid-Albian (Casey & Rawson 1973).

Late Cretaceous (Fig. 12)

The Late Cretaceous saw the most significant of the Mesozoic transgressions. This event flooded much of the remnant Early Cretaceous topography south of the Barents Sea, and gave rise to fine-grained deposition over much of the area. In the North Sea region, the Late Cretaceous seas transgressed over the remnant highs, and probably parts of the western Baltic margin. High-level peneplains in western Norway may represent erosion surfaces formed before or during the Late Cretaceous transgression, and subsequently exhumed and elevated during the Tertiary uplift of Fennoscandia (Doré in press). The pelagic carbonate (chalk) deposition that predominated in the south gave way through the northern North Sea to fine clastic deposition, perhaps as a function of increased clastic input from the Atlantic rift flanks (Hancock & Scholle 1975) or northwards climatic change. The transgression overstepped the reduced rift margins in the mid-Norway region, depositing shales with some local sands (Lysing Formation) around persistent highs such as the Nordland Ridge. Evidence of Late Cretaceous sedimentation is more sparse on the East Greenland side of the rift, but where present suggests a milder continuation of the tectono-sedimentary style established in the late Jurassic and Early Cretaceous; block faulting, with locally-developed proximal coarse clastic wedges and dark mudstones predominating away from the fault scarps (Surlyk et al. 1981).

Significant tectonic events of the Late Cretaceous included continued spreading (or continental extension; see previous section) in the Rockall Trough, which ceased in the Santonian (84 Ma) with the development of a spreading centre in the Labrador Sea. The orthogonal spreading of the Makharov Basin, north of Svalbard and the Sverdrup Basin, probably also dates from this phase and continued until Campanian time (Rowley & Lottes 1988). This Late Cretaceous plate reorganization may have induced contemporaneous North Sea inversion structures, such as those observed along the Tornquist Alignment in the Danish Basin, the Farsund basin (Fig. 12) and Central Graben (e.g. Roberts et al. 1990). However, a connection with compressional events on the northwestern Tethyan margin is also likely.

The line of basins extending northeastwards from the Rockall Trough continued to be the site of intensive downwarping. Up to 2 km of monotonous grey shales are recorded in the West Shetland Basin (Mudge & Rashid 1987), thickening to 5 km or more in the Faeroes

Trough, where the sequence contains sills and lava flows. Similarly impressive thicknesses of Late Cretaceous sediments are observed in the Møre and Vøring Basins. The rapid downwarping of the mid-Norwegian basins in the Late Cretaceous is a phenomenon that is still not satisfactorily explained using thermal subsidence models (e.g. Brekke & Riis 1987). Similarly unexplained is the provenance for the vast quantities of fine clastics filling these basins, deposited during a time of transgression when sediment starvation might have been expected. Resolution of these problems requires more detailed work on the Late Cretaceous sequence, which is not a hydrocarbon target and is thus largely unstudied. A potential line of investigation is suggested by in-house studies of high resolution reflection seismic lines across the western Vøring Basin. These data indicate thinning of the Cretaceous sequences towards the western margin of the basin (J. H. Snow & S. Vassmyr, pers. comm. 1991). A palaeohigh in this region (as suggested in Figs 11 & 12) could, therefore, have contributed to the Cretaceous basin-fill. Even more speculatively, such a feature could have been a precursor to the well documented thermal uplift and subaerial exposure of the Vøring Plateau region in the earliest Tertiary (Skogseid 1990).

The zone of Cretaceous downwarping extended northwards to the Senja–Hornsund fault system, along which it became decoupled from the Barents Sea domain in a broad zone of dextral transcurrent activity. In the Wandel Sea Basin this motion was expressed along the Trolle Land master fault and other parallel faults, producing a series of isolated pull-apart basins containing disparate sedimentary types ranging from marine to continental (Håkansson & Pedersen 1982). The same motion probably gave rise to inversion structures in the southwestern Barents Sea (in-house reports) and, at the southern termination of the Senja–Hornsund Alignment against the Baltic Craton, to NNE faulting in Andøya (Dalland 1979). The Late Cretaceous dextral stress field along the Senja–Hornsund Alignment was a precursor to the more extensive transcurrent motion that occurred in the Early Tertiary, when the line acted as a relay zone between spreading centres in the Nansen Basin and North Atlantic (e.g. Myhre et al. 1982).

In the Barents Sea east of the Senja–Hornsund trend, the tectono-sedimentary regime differed markedly from that of the Atlantic rift domain. Svalbard was uplifted and eroded, with result that Palaeocene sediments rest unconformably on rocks of Aptian–Albian age (Steel & Worsley 1984). Farther south, on the southern Barents Shelf, the mid-Cenomanian to Maastrichtian interval is condensed or eroded east of the Tromsø Basin depocentre. Late Cretaceous sediments are absent from wide areas of the central Barents Sea due to Cenozoic erosion. However, the existence of known marine depocentres west of Novaya Zemlya, and the presence of thin Cenomanian marine clastics in Franz Joseph's Land (in-house reports) suggest a continuation eastwards of the marine depositional area in the Late Cretaceous.

I extend thanks to the explorationists of Conoco Norway Inc., whose reports, ideas and observations I have freely used; to Ann-Kristin Larsen for drafting the text-figures; to Linda Moen for typing the manuscript; and to my wife, Barbara, for tolerating yet another diversion from family life.

References

BÄCKSTRÖM, S. A. & NAGY, J. 1985. Depositional History and Fauna of a Jurassic Phosphorite Conglomerate (the Brentskardhaugen Bed) in Spitsbergen. *Norsk Polarinstitutt Skrifter*, **183**, 1–61.

BADLEY, M. E., PRICE, J. D., DAHL, C. & AGDESTEIN, T. 1988. The Structural Evolution of the Northern Viking Graben and its Bearing on Extensional Modes on Basin Formation. *Journal of the Geological Society, London*, **145**, 455–472.

BEAMISH, D. & SMYTHE, D. K. 1986. Geophysical Images of the Deep Crust: The Iapetus Suture. *Journal of the Geological Society, London*, **143**, 489–497.

BIRKELUND, T., CALLOMON, J. H. & FÜRSICH, F. T. 1984. The Stratigraphy of the Upper Jurassic and Lower Cretaceous Sediments of Milnes Land, Central East Greenland. *Grønlands Geologiske Undersøgelse, Bulletin*, **147**.

BREKKE, H. & RIIS, F. 1987. Tectonics and basin evolution of the Norwegian shelf between 62°N and 72°N. *Norsk Geologisk Tidsskrift*, **67**, 295–322.

BRUCE, J. R. & TOOMEY, D. F. 1992. *Late Palaeozoic Bioherm Occurrences of the Finnmark Shelf, Norwegian North Sea: Analogues and Regional Significance*. Norwegian Petroleum Society, Elsevier.

BUKOVICS, C. & ZIEGLER, P. A. 1985. Tectonic Development of the Mid-Norway Continental Margin. *Marine and Petroleum Geology*, **2**, 2–22.

BØE, R. 1990. Structural Development of the Mesozoic Rocks in Frohavet, Beitstadfjorden and Edøyfjorden, Central Norway. *Geonytt*, **17**, 37.

CALLOMON, J. H. 1975. Jurassic Ammonites from the Northern North Sea. *Norsk Geologisk Tidsskrift*, **55**, 373–386.

—— 1984. A Review of the Biostratigraphy of

the Post-Lower Bajocian Jurassic Ammonites of Western and Northern North America. *In*: WESTERMANN, G. E. G. (ed) *Jurassic-Cretaceous Biochronology and Paleogeography of North America*. Geological Association of Canada Special Paper 27, 143–174.

—— & BIRKELUND, T. 1982. The Ammonite Zones of the Boreal Volgian (Upper Jurassic) in East Greenland. *In*: EMBRY, A. F. & BALKWILL, H. R. (eds), *Arctic Geology and Geophysics*. Canadian Society of Petroleum Geologists, Memoir **8**, 349–369.

CASEY, R. 1971. Facies, Faunas and Tectonics in the Late Jurassic–Early Cretaceous Britain. *In*: MIDDLEMISS, F. A., RAWSON, P. F. & NEWELL, G. (eds) *Faunal Provinces in Space and Time*. Seel House Press, Liverpool, 153–168.

—— & RAWSON, P. F. 1973. A Review of the Boreal Lower Cretaceous. *In*: CASEY, R. & RAWSON, P. F. (eds) *The Boreal Lower Cretaceous*. Geological Journal Special Issue, **5**, 415–430.

CLEMMENSEN, L. B. 1980. Triassic Lithostratigraphy of East Greenland between Scoresby Sund and Kejser Franz Joseph's Fjord. *Grønlands Geologiske Undersøgelse, Bulletin* **139**.

——, STEELE, R. J. & JACOBSEN, V. W. 1980. Some Aspects of Triassic Sedimentation and Basin Development: East Greenland, North Scotland and North Sea. *In*: *The Sedimentation of North Sea Reservoir Rocks*, Norwegian Petroleum Society, Geilo. Article **17**.

DALLAND, A. 1979. The Sedimentary Sequence of Andøya, Northern Norway. *In*: *Norwegian Sea Symposium*, Norwegian Petroleum Society, Trømso, 1979, Article **26**.

—— & THUSU, B. 1977. Kimmeridgian Volcanic Ash in Andøya, Northern Norway. *In*: Mesozoic Northern North Sea Symposium, Norwegian Petroleum Society, Oslo, 1977, Article **9**.

——, WORSLEY, D. & OFSTAD, K. 1988. A Lithostratigraphic Scheme for the Mesozoic and Cenozoic Succession Offshore Mid- and Northern Norway. NPD Bulletin **4**.

DE PAOR, D. G., BRADLEY, D. C., EISENSTADT, G. & PHILLIPS, S. M. 1989. The Arctic Eurekan Orogen: A Most Unusual Fold-and-Thrust Belt. *Geological Society of America Bulletin*, **101**, 952–967.

DORÉ, A. G. 1991. The structural Foundation and Evolution of Mesozoic Seaways between Europe and the Arctic. In: CHANNEL, J., JANSA, L. F. & WINTERER, E. L. (eds) *Palaeogeography, Palaeoclimatology, Palaeoecology*, special issue.

—— 1992. The Base Tertiary Surface of Southern Norway and the Northern North Sea. *In*: JENSEN, L. N. & RIIS, F. (eds) Post-Cretaceous Uplift and Sedimentation along the Western Fennoscandian Shield. *Norsk Geologisk Tidsskrift*, special issue.

—— & GAGE, M. S. 1987. Crustal Alignments and Sedimentary Domains in the Evolution of the North Sea, Northeast Atlantic Margin and Barents Shelf. *In*: BROOKS, J. & GLENNIE, K. W. (eds) *Petroleum Geology of North West Europe*.

Graham & Trotman, London, 1131–1148.

DUINDAM, P. & VAN HOORN, B. 1987. Structural Evolution of the West Shetland Continental Margin. *In*: BROOKS, J. & GLENNIE, K. W. (eds), *Petroleum Geology of NW Europe*. Graham & Trotman, London.

Eugeno-S Working Group. 1988. Crustal structure and tectonic evolution of the transition between the Baltic Shield and the North German Caledonides (the EUGENO-S Project). *In*: FREEMAN, R., BERTHELSEN, A. & MUELLER, ST. (eds) *The European Geotraverse, Part 4*. *Tectonophysics*, **150**, 253–348.

EMBRY, A. F. 1989. Correlation of Upper Palaeozoic and Mesozoic Sequence between Svalbard, Canadian Arctic Archipelago and Northern Alaska. *In*: COLLINSON, J. D. (ed.) *Correlation in Hydrocarbon Exploration*. Norwegian Petroleum Society. Graham & Trotman, London, 89–98.

FREEMAN, B., KLEMPERER, S. L. & HOBBS, R. W. 1988. The Deep Structure of Northern England and the Iapetus Suture Zone from BIRPS Deep Seismic Reflection Profiles. *Journal of the Geological Society, London*, **145**, 727–740.

GABRIELSEN, R. H. 1984. Long-lived Fault Zones and Their Influence on the Tectonic Development of the Southwestern Barents Sea. *Journal of the Geological Society, London*, **141**, 651–662.

——, FAERSETH, R. B., STEEL, R. J., IDIL, S. & KLØVJAN, O. S. 1990. Architectural styles of basin fill in the northern Viking graben. *In*: BLUNDELL, D. G. & GIBBS, A. D. *Tectonic Evolution of the North Sea Rifts*. Oxford Science Publications, 158–179.

GAGE, M. S. & DORÉ, A. G. 1986. A Regional Geological Perspective of the Norwegian Exploration Provinces. *In*: SPENCER, A. M. *et al.* (eds), *Habitat of Hydrocarbons on the Norwegian Shelf*. Norwegian Petroleum Society. Graham & Trotman, London, 21–38.

GLENNIE, K. W. & BULLER, T. A. 1983. The Permian Weissliegend of North West Europe: The Partial Deformation of Aeolian Dune Sands caused by the Zechstein Transgression. *Sedimentary Geology*, **35**, 43–81.

GRAMBERG, I. S. (ed.) 1988. The Barents Shelf Plate. Trudy PGO 'Sevmorgeologiya', L., Nedra, 196, 263 (in Russian).

HALLAM, A. 1967. The Depth Significance of Shales with Bituminous Laminae. *Marine Geology*, **5**, 481–493.

HANCOCK, J. M. & SCHOLLE, P. A. 1975. Chalk of the North Sea. In: WOODLAND, A. W. (eds) *Petroleum and the Continental Shelf of North West Europe*. Vol. 1. Geology. Barking, England, 413–427.

HASZELDINE, R. S. & RUSSELL, M. J. 1987. The late Carboniferous North Atlantic Ocean; implications for hydrocarbon exploration from Britain to the Arctic. *In*: BROOKS, J. & GLENNIE, K. W. (eds) *Petroleum Geology of North West Europe*. Graham & Trotman, London, 1163–1175.

HESJEDAL, A. & HAMAR, G. P. 1983. Lower Cretaceous Stratigraphy and Tectonics of the South-Southeastern Norwegian Offshore. *In*: KAASSCHIETER, J. P. H. & REIJERS, T. J. A. (eds), *Petroleum Geology of the Southeastern North Sea and the Adjacent Onshore Areas* (The Hague, 1982). *Geologie en Mijnbouw*, **62**, 135–144.

HOLSER, W. T., CLEMENT, G. P., JANSA, L. F. & WADE, J. A. 1988. Evaporite Deposits of the North Atlantic Rift. *In*: MANSPEIZER, W. (ed.) *Triassic-Jurassic Rifting*. Elsevier, Amsterdam, 525–553.

HÅKANSSON, E. & PEDERSEN, S. A. S. 1982. Late Paleozoic to Tertiary Tectonic Evolution of the Continental Margin in North Greenland. *In*: EMBRY, A. F. & BALKWILL, H. R. (eds) *Arctic Geology and Geophysics*, Canadian Society Petroleum Geologists Memoir **8**, 331–348.

—— & STEMMERIK, L. 1984. Wandel Sea Basin — The North Greenland Equivalent to Svalbard and the Barents Shelf. *In*: SPENCER, A. M. *et al.* (eds) *Petroleum Geology of the North European Margin*. Norwegian Petroleum Society. Graham & Trotman, London, 97–108.

JACKSON, H. R. 1985. Nares Straight — A Suture Zone: Geophysical and Geomagnetic Implications. *Tectonophysics*, **114**, 11–28.

JACOBSEN, V. W. & VAN VEEN, P. 1984. The Triassic Offshore Norway North of 62°N. In SPENCER, A. M. *et al.* (eds), *Petroleum Geology of the North European Margin*. Norwegian Petroleum Society. Graham & Trotman, London, 317–328.

JENKYNS, H. C. 1988. The Early Toarcian (Jurassic) Anoxic Event: Stratigraphic, Sedimentary and Geochemical Evidence. *American Journal of Science*, **288**, 101–151.

JOHANNESSEN, E. P. & EMBRY, A. F. 1989. Sequence Correlation: Upper Triassic to Lower Jurassic Succession, Canadian and Norwegian Arctic. *In*: COLLINSON, J. D. (ed.) *Correlation in Hydrocarbon Exploration*. Norwegian Petroleum Society. Graham & Trotman, London, 155–170.

KELLY, S. R. A. 1988. Jurassic through Cretaceous Stratigraphy of the Barents Shelf. *In*: HARLAND, W. B. & DOWDESWELL, E. K. (eds), *Geological Evolution of the Barents Shelf Region*. Graham & Trotman, London, 109–129.

KLEMPERER, S. L. & HURICH, C. A. 1990. Lithospheric Structure of the North Sea from Deep Seismic Reflection Profiling. *In*: BLUNDELL, D. G. & GIBBS, A. D. *The Tectonic Evolution of the North Sea Rifts*. Clarendon, Oxford.

LARSEN, V. B. 1987. A Synthesis of Tectonically Related Stratigraphy in the North Atlantic-Arctic Region from Aalenian to Cenomanian Time. *Norsk Geologisk Tidsskrift*, **67**, 281–293.

LATIN, D. M., DIXON, J. E., FITTON, J. G. & WHITE, N. 1990. Mesozoic magmatic activity in the North Sea Basin: implications for stretching history. *In*: HARDMAN, R. F. P. & BROOKS, J. (eds) *Tectonic Events Responsible for Britain's Oil and Gas Reserves*. Geological Society, London, Special Publication, **55**, 207–227.

LEEDER, M. R. 1983. Lithospheric Stretching and North Sea Jurassic Clastic Sourcelands. *Nature*, **305**, 510–514.

LERVIK, K. S., SPENCER, A. M. & WARRINGTON, G. 1989. Outline of Triassic Stratigraphy and Structure in the Central and Northern North Sea. *In*: COLLINSON, J. D. (ed.), *Correlation in Hydrocarbon Exploration*. Norwegian Petroleum Society. Graham & Trotman, London, 173–190.

MANSPEIZER, W. 1988. Triassic-Jurassic Rifting and Opening of the Atlantic: An Overview. *In*: MANSPEIZER, W. (ed.), *Triassic-Jurassic Rifting*. Elsevier, Amsterdam, 41–79.

McKERROW, W. S. & SOPER, N. J. 1989. The Iapetus Suture in the British Isles. *Geological Magazine*, **126**, 1–8.

MUDGE, D. C. & RASHID, B. 1987. The Geology of the Faeroe Basin Area. *In*: BROOKS, J. & GLENNIE, K. W. (eds), *Petroleum Geology of North West Europe*. Graham & Trotman, London, 751–764.

MYHRE, A., ELDHOLM, O. & SUNDVOR, E. 1982. The Margin between Senja and Spitsbergen Fracture Zones: Implications from Plate Tectonics. *Tectonophysics*, **89**, 33–50.

MØRK, A., KNARUD, R. & WORSLEY, D. 1982. Depositional and Diagenetic Environments of the Triassic and Lower Jurassic Succession of Svalbard. *In*: EMBRY, A. F. & BALKWILL, H. R. (eds) *Arctic Geology and Geophysics*. Canadian Society Petroleum Geologists, Memoir **8**, 371–398.

——, EMBRY, A. F. & WEITSCHAT, W. 1989. Triassic Transgressive-Regressive Cycles in the Sverdrup Basin, Svalbard and the Barents Shelf. *In*: COLLINSON, J. D. (ed.), *Correlation in Hydrocarbon Exploration*. Norwegian Petroleum Society. Graham & Trotman, London, 113–130.

NANCE, R. D., WORSLEY, T. R. & MOODY, J. B. 1988. The Supercontinent Cycle. *Scientific American*, July Issue, 44–51.

OHTA, Y., DALLMEYER, R. D. & PEUCAT, J. J. 1989. Caledonian Terranes in Svalbard. *Geological Society of America Special Paper* **230**.

PEGRUM, R. M. 1984. Structural development of the southwestern margin of the Russian-Fennoscandian Platform. *In*: SPENCER, A. M. *et al.* (eds), *Petroleum Geology of the North European Margin*. Norwegian Petroleum Society, Graham and Trotman, London, 359–369.

RAWSON, P. F. & RILEY, L. A. 1982. Latest Jurassic-Early Cretaceous Events and the 'Late Cimmerian Unconformity' in the North Sea Area. *AAPG Bulletin*, **66**, 2628–2648.

RHYS, G. H. (compiler). 1974. *A Proposed Standard Lithostratigraphic Nomenclature for the Southern North Sea and an Outline Structural Nomenclature for the Whole of the (UK) North Sea*. Report of the Institute of Geological Sciences, 74/8.

RIIS, F., VOLLSET, J. & SAND, M. 1985. Tectonic Development of the Western Margin of the Barents Sea and Adjacent Areas. Norwegian Petroleum Directorate Contribution **22**.

RITCHIE, J. D., SWALLOW, T. J., MITCHELL, J. G. & MORTON, A. C. 1988. Jurassic Ages from Intrusives and Extrusives within the Forties Igneous Province. *Scottish Journal of Geology*, **24**, 81–88.

ROBERTS, A. M., PRICE, J. D. & OLSEN, T. S. 1990. Late Jurassic Half-Graben Control on the Siting and Structure of Hydrocarbon Accumulations: UK/Norwegian Central Graben. *In*: HARDMAN, R. F. P. & BROOKS, J. (eds) *Tectonic Events Controlling Britain's Oil and Gas Reserves*. Geological Society, London, Special Publication, **55**, 229–257.

ROBERTS, D. G., GINZBERG, A., NUNN, K. & McQUILLIN, R. 1988. The structure of the Rockall Trough from seismic refraction and wide-angle reflection measurements. *Nature*, **332**, 632–635.

ROWLEY, D. B. & LOTTES, A. K. 1988. Plate-Kinematic Reconstructions of the North Atlantic and Arctic: Late Jurassic to Present. *Tectonophysics*, **155**, 73–120.

RØNNEVIK, H., BESKOW, B. & JACOBSEN, H. P. 1982. Structural and Stratigraphic Evolution of the Barents Sea. *In*: *Offshore Northern Seas Conference, The Geological Framework and Hydrocarbon Potential of Basins in Northern Seas*, Article E/3.

SCOTESE, C. R. 1987. *Phanerozoic Plate Tectonic Reconstructions*. Paleoceanographic Mapping Project. Institute for Geophysics, University of Texas Technical Report 90.

SKOGSEID, J. 1990. *Vøring Continental Margin: Magmatic-tectonic Evolution, Sedimentation and Basin Subsidence*. Doctor Scient. Thesis, University of Oslo, Norway.

SENGÖR, A. M. C. 1979. Mid-Mesozoic Closure of Permo-Triassic Tethys and Its Implications. *Nature*, **279**, 590–593.

SMITH, D. B. 1980. The United Kingdom: Permian. *In*: *Geology of the European Countries*. Graham & Trotman, London, 399–402.

SMYTHE, D. K. 1989. Rockall Trough — Cretaceous or Late Palaeozoic? *Scottish Journal of Geology*, **25**, 5–43.

STEEL, R. & WORSLEY, D. 1984. Svalbard's Post-Caledonian Strata: An Atlas of Sedimentational Patterns and Palaeogeographic Evolution. *In*: SPENCER, A. M. *et al.* (eds) *Petroleum Geology of the North European Margin*. Norwegian Petroleum Society, Graham & Trotman, London, 109–136.

SURLYK, F. 1977. Mesozoic Faulting in East Greenland. In FROST, R. T. C. & DIKKERS, A. J. (eds). Fault tectonics in N.W. Europe. *Geologie en Mijnbouw*, **56**, 311–327.

—— 1978. Jurassic Basin Evolution of East Greenland, *Nature*, **274**, 130–133.

—— 1989. Mid-Mesozoic Syn-Rift Turbidite Systems: Controls and Predictions. In COLLINSON, J. D.

(ed), *Correlation in Hydrocarbon Exploration*. Norwegian Petroleum Society. Graham and Trotman, London, 231–242.

—— 1990*a*. Timing, style and sedimentary evolution of Late Palaeozoic — Mesozoic extensional basins of East Greenland. *In*: HARDMAN, R. F. P. & BROOKS, J. (eds) *Tectonic Events Responsible for Britain's Oil and Gas Reserves*. Geological Society Special Publication, **55**, 107–125.

—— 1990*b*. A Jurassic sea-level curve for East Greenland. *Palaeogeography, Palaeoclimatology, Palaeoecology*, **78**, 71–85.

——, CLEMMENSEN, L. B. & LARSEN, H. C. 1981. Post-Paleozoic Evolution of the East Greenland Continental Margin. *In*: KERR, J. W. & FERGUSON, A. J. (eds), *Geology of the North Atlantic Borderland*. Canadian Society of Petroleum Geologists, Memoir, **7**, 611–645.

SURLYK, F., HURST, J. M., PIASECKI, S., ROLLE, F., SCHOLLE, P. A., STEMMERIK, L. & THOMPSEN, E. 1986. The Permian of the Western Margin of the Greenland Sea — A Future Exploration Target. *In*: HALBOUTY, M. T. (eds.), *Future Petroleum Provinces of the World*. American Association of Petroleum Geologists, Memoir, **40**, 630–659.

——, PIASECKI, S., ROLLE, F., STEMMERIK, L., THOMSEN, E. & WRANG, P. 1984. The Permian Basin of East Greenland. In SPENCER, A. M. *et al.* (eds), *Petroleum Geology of the North European Margin*. Norwegian Petroleum Society. Graham & Trotman, London, 303–315.

TAYLOR, J. C. M. 1981. Zechstein Facies and Petroleum Prospects in the Central and Northern North Sea. *In*: ILLING, L. V. & HOBSON, G. D. (eds), *Petroleum Geology of the Continental Shelf of NW Europe*. Institute of Petroleum, Heyden, London, 176–185.

TORSKE, T. 1975. Possible Mesozoic Mantle Plume Activity beneath the Continental Margin of Norway. *Norges Geologiske Undersøkelse*, **322**, 73–90.

VOLLSET, J. & DORÉ, A. G. (eds). 1984. *A Revised Triassic and Jurassic Lithostratigraphic Nomenclature for the Norwegian North Sea*. Norwegian Petroleum Directorate Bulletin 3.

WERNICKE, B. 1985. Uniform-Sense Normal Simple Shear of the Continental Lithosphere. *Canadian Journal of Earth Sciences*, **22**, 108–125.

WORSLEY, D. & AGA, O. J. 1986. The Geological History of Svalbard. Statoil, Stavanger, Norway.

—— & EDWARDS, M. B. 1976. The Upper Palaeozoic Succession of Bjørnøya, *Norsk Polarinstitutt Årbok 1974*, 17–34.

ZIEGLER, P. A. 1982. *Geological Atlas of Western and Central Europe*, SIPM, Elsevier, Amsterdam.

—— 1988. *Evolution of the Arctic-North Atlantic and the Western Tethys*. American Association of Petroleum Geologists, Memoir **43**.

Excursion Guide

Excursion Guide: Basins and petroleum geology in the north of Ireland

JOHN PARNELL, BRYAN MONSON & JIM BUCKMAN

Department of Geology, Queen's University of Belfast, Belfast BT7 1NN, UK

Introduction to basins in the north of Ireland

The pre-Devonian terranes of the north of Ireland consist, from northwest to southeast, of Dalradian and Moinian rocks forming the upland regions of Cos. Donegal, Londonderry and Tyrone, an Ordovician volcanic terrane which crops out in Co. Tyrone, and the Ordovician–Silurian Longford–Down Massif. The volcanic terrane is related to an ophiolite complex (Hutton *et al.* 1985), equivalent to the Highland Border Group in Scotland, while the Longford–Down outcrop is a continuation of the Southern Uplands of Scotland. Also, as in Scotland there are small outcrops of Ordovician and Silurian strata between these terranes which are relatively unmetamorphosed (Pomeroy and Lisbel-law inliers). These occur in the 'Midland Valley', unconformably overlain by Devonian (Old Red Sandstone) sediments which constitute the Fintona Block in Co. Tyrone.

The outcrop of Carboniferous rocks (Fig. 1) includes the North West Basin, which is contiguous with the Omagh and Slieve Beagh Basins, and thick sequences in East Tyrone and North Antrim. Permo-Triassic rocks accumulated in two major basins, the Magee or Larne–Lough Neagh Basin and the Rathlin Trough, separated by the 'Highland Border Ridge', a partly fault-bound high of Dalradian rocks. Triassic continental rocks are succeeded by Rhaetic–Lower Jurassic and subsequently Upper Cretaceous marine sediments which transgressed across the entire region. The northeast of Ireland was flooded by Palaeocene basalt lavas, while the Mourne plutonic complex intruded the crust of Co. Down. The youngest sedimentary basin is the Oligocene Lough Neagh Basin, a fault-bounded complex which developed on the basalt surface.

Reservoir prospects are in the Carboniferous and Permo-Triassic basins (Fig. 2). Potential source rocks are in the Carboniferous, which includes coals and several Dinantian shales (Fig. 3), and possibly the 'Midland Valley' Lower Palaeozoic outcrops.

Itinerary

1. *Scrabo*

Scrabo Hill is formed by a Tertiary sill complex intruded into Permo-Triassic sandstones. The sandstones were formerly quarried for building stone, particularly on the east face of the hill where it is possible to examine quite fresh faces in Triassic sandstone. The quarries can be reached by a footpath north of a car park at J 475724. The sandstones exhibit low to medium angle cross-stratification, with ripple marks, pebble lags, mudflakes, desiccation cracks and (?) rain pits. These rocks have in the past been interpreted as aeolian, but there is no supporting evidence for this. Rather they are the deposits of dune bedforms in river channels (Fig. 4A). Rounded grains in the Triassic sandstones are probably reworked from underlying Permian sandstones (Permian sandstones in the Enler borehole 4 km to the west consist of very well rounded grains) or from a desert hinterland beyond the main basinal region. The Triassic sandstones at Scrabo Hill have been partly baked by the sill, and have also been affected by hydrothermal activity associated with the intrusion. An unusual feature is a widespread cementation by the amphibole actinolite, first recorded by Preston (1962) and subsequently observed by electron microscopy as a network of pore-bridging fibres. The sandstone is also patchily cemented by calcite.

The Scrabo Hill outcrop occurs in a deep trough of Carboniferous to Triassic sediments developed within the Lower Palaeozoic Longford–Down Massif, the equivalent of the Southern Uplands of Scotland which similarly supports extensional basins of Carboniferous to Permian age.

2. *Larne*

The coastal section at Waterloo (Fig. 5), north of Larne is best approached from the swimming pool at D 412031, where vehicles can be parked. The coastal promenade passes a shore and cliff

From PARNELL, J. (ed.), 1992, *Basins on the Atlantic Seaboard: Petroleum Geology, Sedimentology and Basin Evolution*. Geological Society Special Publication No 62, pp 449–464.

449

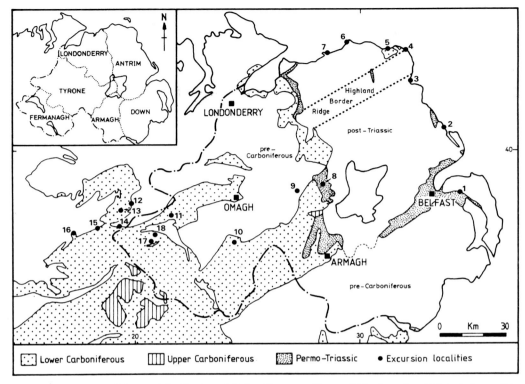

Fig. 1. Excursion localities, and distribution of Carboniferous and Permo-Triassic rocks which include possible hydrocarbon reservoirs.

section of upper Triassic (Mercia Mudstone Group, Rhaetic) and lower Jurassic (Liassic). The section is slightly complicated by faulting. The Larne No. 1 borehole, less than 2 km distant, penetrated 51.5 m Liassic beneath the drift, 20.5 m Rhaetic, 10.8 m Collin Glen Formation and 29.0 m Port More Formation, the latter two being subdivisions of the Mercia Mudstone Group (Manning & Wilson 1975). The thicknesses at Waterloo are of similar magnitude: the Rhaetic is 14.3 m thick on the shore, possibly with some loss due to faulting (Ivimey-Cook 1975).

The Port More Formation consists predominantly of brick red siltstones, with some horizons containing dark accretionary nodules within reduction spots. The nodules contain vanadium minerals here, and uranium and copper minerals elsewhere in Co. Antrim (Parnell 1988). Similar phenomena elsewhere are formed by an interaction of migrating hydrocarbons and metalliferous red bed groundwaters, and this explanation has also been suggested for the Larne nodules (Parnell & Eakin 1987).

It is not possible accurately to delimit the Port More Formation from the overlying Collin Glen Formation, but there is a transition upwards into grey-green mudrocks. In places these beds contain abundant pseudopisoliths; millimetre-scale concretionary structures which are clearly diagenetic and not mechanically deposited. Their origin has been attributed to volcanic emissions from the Larne Lough Fault offshore (Ivimey-Cook 1975), or to precipitation from saline fluids migrating from halite units lower in the Mercia Mudstone Group (Reid 1983). The grey mudstones contain no more than 0.5% total organic carbon (TOC).

The Rhaetic (Rhaetian) and Lower Liassic rocks are grey-black mudrocks with thin (<15 cm) limestone beds. The Rhaetic includes beds of compacted bivalve shells, particularly *Protocardia*. The boundary with the Lias is in the vicinity of an outfall pipe. The Lias contains numerous ammonite fragments, particularly *Psiloceras planorbis*, and represents the Hettangian and lower Sinemurian stages. Over 100 m of Liassic is present at Larne, and

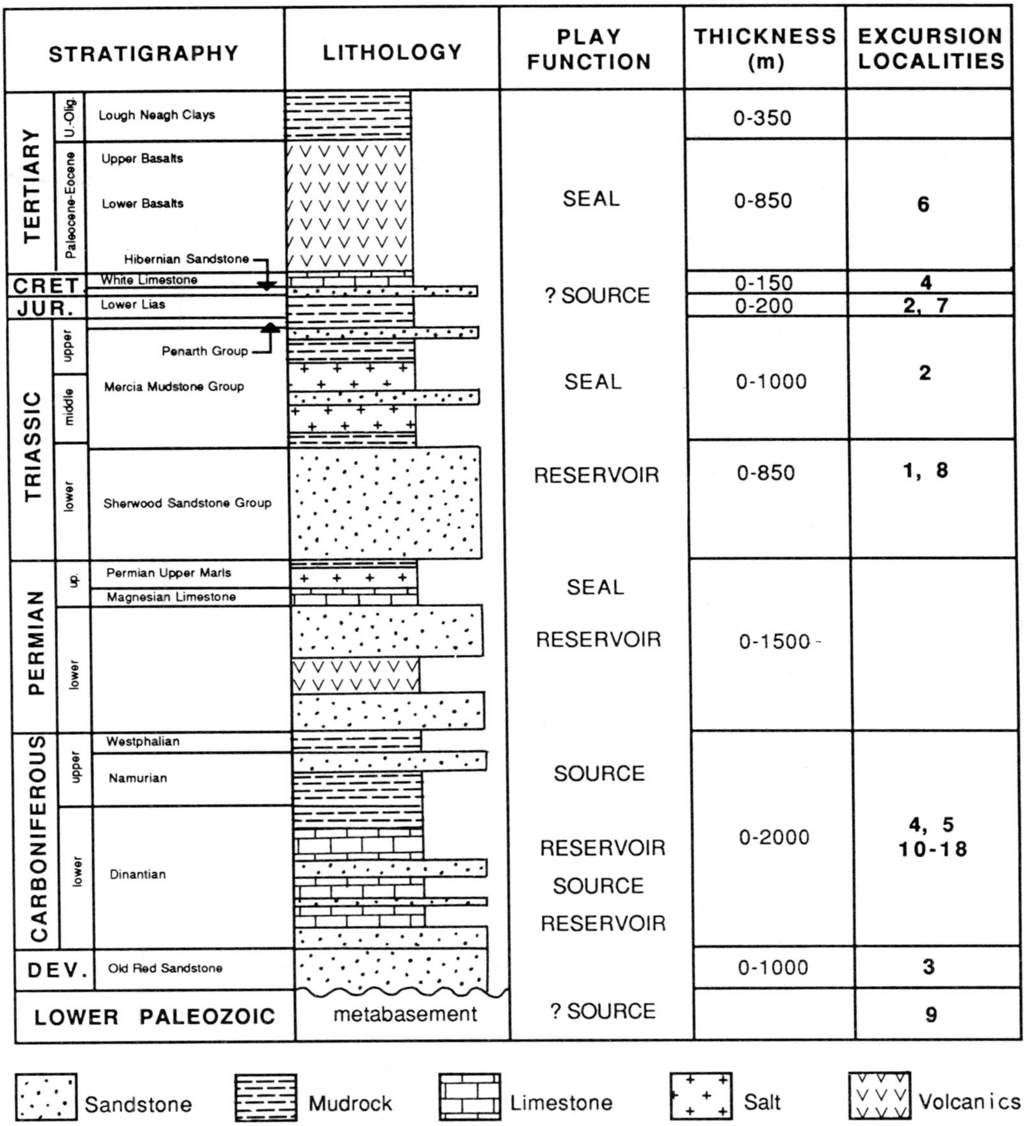

STRATIGRAPHY			LITHOLOGY	PLAY FUNCTION	THICKNESS (m)	EXCURSION LOCALITIES
TERTIARY	Paleocene-Eocene	U.-Olig.	Lough Neagh Clays			0-350	
			Upper Basalts		SEAL	0-850	6
			Lower Basalts				
			Hibernian Sandstone				
CRET.			White Limestone		? SOURCE	0-150	4
JUR.			Lower Lias			0-200	2, 7
TRIASSIC	upper		Penarth Group		SEAL	0-1000	2
	middle		Mercia Mudstone Group				
	lower		Sherwood Sandstone Group		RESERVOIR	0-850	1, 8
PERMIAN	up.		Permian Upper Marls		SEAL	0-1500-	
			Magnesian Limestone				
	lower				RESERVOIR		
CARBONIFEROUS	upper		Westphalian		SOURCE	0-2000	4, 5 10-18
			Namurian				
	lower		Dinantian		RESERVOIR SOURCE RESERVOIR		
DEV.			Old Red Sandstone			0-1000	3
LOWER PALEOZOIC			metabasement		? SOURCE		9

Sandstone   Mudrock   Limestone   Salt   Volcanics

Fig. 2. Outline composite stratigraphy for Northern Ireland, indicating possible hydrocarbon play functions.

on the north Antrim coast the Liassic is almost 250 m thick in the Port More borehole, extending up to the Lower Pleinsbachian. Loose blocks suggest that even younger beds, of Middle Liassic age (Hartley 1933), were deposited in the region. The black mudstones have yielded up to 4% TOC.

3. *Cushendall*

Immediately adjacent to a jetty at the lifeboat station, Red Bay, Cushendall, are exposures of red conglomerate probably attributable to the Upper Old Red Sandstone. They form the base of an upward fining sequence about 400 m

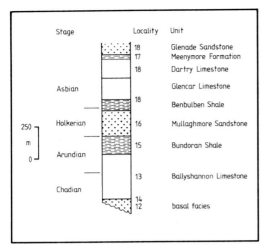

Stage	Locality	Unit
	18	Glenade Sandstone
	17	Meenymore Formation
	18	Dartry Limestone
Asbian		Glencar Limestone
	18	Benbulben Shale
Holkerian	16	Mullaghmore Sandstone
	15	Bundoran Shale
Arundian		
	13	Ballyshannon Limestone
Chadian		
	14 / 12	basal facies

Fig. 3. Carboniferous stratigraphy for north west Ireland, highlighting shale and sandstone units.

thick. Conglomerate beds 0.5 to 1.5 m thick are interbedded with cross-stratified and parallel-laminated beds of pebbly sandstone. The conglomerates have erosive bases, weakly developed internal bedding, exhibit poor sorting and are clast-supported. The clasts are cemented with calcite and/or dolomite, and the most dolomitic rocks exhibit some vuggy porosity, as also seen in dolomitic basal beds of the Carboniferous on the west coast (see Assaroe Lake locality below). The remainder of the succession, exposed southwards along the coast to the Red Arch, has a generally fining-up trend and the sandstones become progressively more mature. The succession has been termed the Red Arch Formation by Simon (1984), who interprets it as an alluvial fan system. A major lineament which at present bounds the Dalradian 3 km to the northwest may have been an active fault boundary during fan sedimentation. Palaeocurrent data confirms the derivation of clasts from this

Fig. 4. Cross-bedded units of the Sherwood Sandstone Group, which has reservoir potential in some districts. A, dune bedforms, Scrabo Hill (locality 1); B, cross-bedded oolitic sandstone-limestone body and interbedded sandstones and mudrocks, Drapersfield (locality 8).

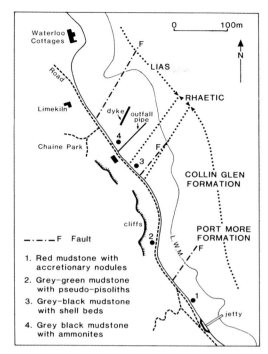

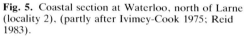

Fig. 5. Coastal section at Waterloo, north of Larne (locality 2), (partly after Ivimey-Cook 1975; Reid 1983).

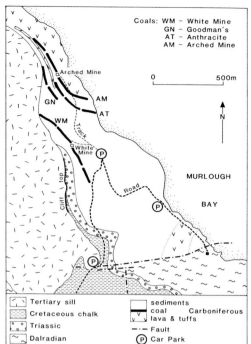

Fig. 6. Geology of Murlough Bay district (locality 4).

direction (Simon 1984). Along this major lineament Devonian sandstones are potential reservoirs where they occur updip from the Carboniferous which may include source rocks. They are sealed by Tertiary basalts inland to the west.

4. *Murlough Bay*

The cliff sections west of Murlough Bay expose a wide range of rocks, from Dalradian metamorphic basement, through Carboniferous, Triassic and Cretaceous sediments, to Tertiary intrusions (Fig. 6). The cliffs are capped by the Tertiary Fair Head Sill, which has a very distinctive profile when viewed from the west (locality 5, Fig. 7, and see Figure 184 of Holmes 1965). The dolerite sill transgresses upwards to the southeast in several stages, penetrating Carboniferous rocks in the north and Cretaceous chalk in the south. The region between the cliff and the shoreline includes several major landslips, in which successions of dolerite and Cretaceous to Carboniferous sediment appear undisturbed despite falling up to 100 m from their original positions.

At Murlough Cottage, Dalradian mica schists are seen at the shore in faulted contact with Carboniferous sandstones. On the cliff above, Triassic rocks lie directly upon the Dalradian to the south of the fault. There has clearly been movement on the fault between Carboniferous and Triassic sedimentation although it also cuts the chalk and must have a multi-phase history. Further south along the Antrim coast near Larne, evidence for the earlier phase of tectonic activity is available from a seismic section which shows the Permo-Triassic truncating older reflectors (Illing & Griffith 1986). The Carboniferous sandstones near Murlough Cottage are overlain by about 12 m of porphyritic basalt lavas, best seen at the shoreline. These Carboniferous volcanics can be correlated with similar rocks in the Midland Valley of Scotland, but do not occur elsewhere in the north of Ireland beyond northeast Antrim. Above the lavas are tuffaceous sediments followed by an extensive succession of sandstone, shales and coal seams, which have been mined at several points. The traces of the coal seams are indicated on Fig. 7.

A track from the car park half-way up the

Fig. 7. Aerial view of Murlough Bay, dominated by the Fair Head Sill. Traces of coal seams and adits (encircled) marked, as on Figure 6. (Photograph courtesy of the Geological Survey of Northern Ireland).

coastal slope leads to the Arched Mine, which exploited the lowest coal (Dinantian) in the Ballycastle district. Immediately inside the right hand portal of the mine, black mudstone and canneloid coal are exposed in the walls of the workings. However, entering the workings is not advised; samples can be obtained from the spoil heap outside. Above and slightly south of the Arched Mine, other adits and spoil heaps can be found on workings into an 'Anthracite' horizon and Goodman's coal. A lower leaf of the Tertiary sill is prominent here, transgressing the 'Anthracite' horizon. Above these coal levels are about 100 m of red sandstones within beds of mudrock. Some Carboniferous sandstones to the west of Fair Head are similarly red. The red colouration is a late diagenetic pigment, probably due to deep weathering during the Permian. Sandstones are well exposed along the side track to the White Mine, which entered the highest coal seam on this side of Fair Head. The sandstones are mineralogically very mature and very porous.

The most accessible exposures of Triassic rock are at the base of the cliff to the south of the upper car park. Eight metres of red sandy mudrock lie upon 10 m of red sandstone which is pebbly towards the base and underlain by a further 10 m of breccia derived from the

Dalradian. This Triassic succession is very thin in comparison with most in Northern Ireland, reflecting deposition on the northern edge of the 'Highland Border Ridge'. In the Port More borehole, just 12 km to the west but within the onshore part of the Rathlin Trough, over 1354 m (unbottomed) red beds were penetrated which may include beds of Permian age. The sandstone at Murlough Bay is tightly cemented with poikilotopic calcite despite the exposed position: waters draining downwards from the overlying chalk would be bicarbonate-saturated and incapable of leaching out the cement from the Triassic beds. By contrast some sandstones in the Port More borehole are porous.

Above the red Triassic rocks, the cliffs are composed of the distinctive white chalk. A basal facies includes glauconitic sandstone, with Dalradian, Triassic and Liassic pebbles, although the Liassic is not exposed in this district. Regional correlations of chalk stratigraphy show that the Highland Border Ridge was progressively drowned by the Cretaceous chalk sea and the marginal clastic facies localized about the ridge gave way to normal micritic chalk deposition (Reid 1971). The chalk (the Ulster White Limestone) does not exhibit the high intergranular porosity of equivalent rocks in England and the North Sea, possibly due to metamorphism/hydrothermal activity associated with Tertiary vulcanism. However it does exhibit fracture porosity and functions as an aquifer in this way.

5. *Colliery Bay, Ballycastle*

The shore/cliff section to the east of Ballycastle was once the scene of extensive coal mining operations, exploiting coal seams in both the Lower and Upper Carboniferous. Several adits are still visible and the track east of the cottage/car park at D 150419 is floored with much debris from the mines. Representative sediments can be examined by following the track to the old harbour at Murray's Port, and veering right and upwards towards a cliff section where black shale is visible (Fig. 8). The base of the section consists of a massive sandstone with an upper 10 cm bioturbated phase passing upwards into coaly black shale. The shale has prominent weathering blooms of sulphur (yellow) and gypsum (white). The shale is overlain by about 6 m of sandstone, generally massive but beds of quartz pebbles display some low angle cross-stratification. The underside is flaggy towards the top where it is interlaminated with siltstone, bioturbated and includes *in situ* plant rootlets. Above is a second shale unit, less coaly than the first and including a bed of siderite nodules. The shale is overlain by a further unit of coarse sandstone, which is red-pink and porous. The section as a whole can be traced for 50 m along strike, and viewed from below the sandstone units exhibit channel forms. The very high porosities in these sandstones are also found in boreholes in the region, and are secondary after carbonate dissolution.

The section is immediately below the position of the Main Coal (mostly worked out) at the Dinantian–Namurian boundary (details in Wilson & Robbie 1966). Although most of the sequence represents fluvio-deltaic environments, marine bands allow stratigraphic dating and show the sequence to be comparable with those in western Scotland rather than elsewhere in Northern Ireland.

The black shales and coals are barely mature at outcrop, but have a good hydrocarbon yield upon pyrolysis and could prove a viable gas source if they occur at depth further south in Co. Antrim, where the Carboniferous rocks may be buried beneath a thick Mesozoic basin.

6. *Giant's Causeway*

The Tertiary basalt lavas of Co. Antrim are generally divisible into Lower and Upper Basalts, whose deposition was separated by an Interbasaltic Period. In the vicinity of the Giant's Causeway the Interbasaltic Period includes the distinctive group of Tholeiitic Basalts (Fig. 9). These rocks are very fine grained, rarely contain megascopic crystals, and occur as lava flows typically 20 m thick. Following slow cooling, they exhibit a pronounced jointing, which is

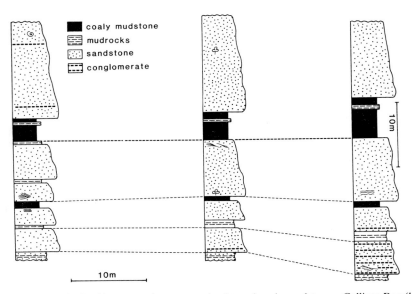

coaly mudstone
mudrocks
sandstone
conglomerate

10m

10m

Fig. 8. Cliff section of Carboniferous sandstones, mudrocks and coaly mudstones, Colliery Bay (locality 5), showing limited lensing of channel sandstones (logs courtesy of W. Wang).

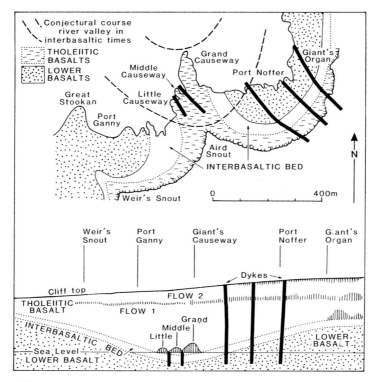

Fig. 9. Geology of Giant's Causeway district (locality 6; after Department of the Environment for Northern Ireland 1987).

divisible into a lower columnar portion (colonnade structure) and an upper more rubbly portion (entablature structure). At the Causeway itself a deep hollow, possibly a river valley, in the Lower Basalts was filled by the first flow of the tholeiitic lavas. Subaerial weathering of these basalts produced a red-purple lithomarge which consists largely of kaolinite and iron minerals, and which can be readily traced along the coastline. The weathered beds are sufficiently extensive to have formerly supported numerous small mines for bauxite and iron ore. Thin sediment layers also accumulated between flows, and lignitic beds can be seen on the cliff side of the Shepherd's path, east of the Causeway.

A number of texts record the occurrence of hydrocarbons in basalt at the Giant's Causeway. The ultimate source of this record is an account by Knox (1823) who distilled hydrocarbons from a number of igneous rocks. It is conceivable that hydrocarbons could have been generated from the lignitic beds as has been observed in Tertiary basalts above lignite in Iceland (Jakobsson & Fridleifsson 1990).

7. Portrush

Rocks of historical importance are exposed adjacent to an exhibition centre on the eastern side of the headland at Portrush (C 856413). Jurassic (Liassic: upper Sinemurian) mudstones are intruded by a Tertiary sill of olivine gabbro. At the contact, the mudstones are metamorphosed to a hornfels and the top of the sill is chilled to basalt. The margin between hornfels and basalt can be distinguished but they are sufficiently similar to cause some confusion and, 200 years ago, considerable debate. At that time, the origin of igneous rocks was fiercely contested by Plutonists who advocated a magmatic origin, and Neptunists who envisaged a subaqueous origin. The occurrence of numerous ammonites in the hornfelsed Liassic, which was mistaken for an igneous rock, was seen as evidence for the Neptunist theory and attracted visitors from far afield. The Liassic mudstones are particularly susceptible to intrusion: in the Port More borehole to the east 496 m of Rhaetic–Liassic section includes 223 m of Tertiary intrusion (Wilson & Manning 1978).

8. *Drapersfield*

A riverside quarry at Drapersfield (H 842767), reached through the grounds of a private nursing home, exposes over 10 m of the Sherwood Sandstone Group. Drapersfield is near the western limit of a 2 km deep Permo-Triassic basin which extends westwards from Larne across the Lough Neagh region. The bright red cross-bedded rocks (Fig. 4B) are typical of exposures in the valleys of East Tyrone. However, on closer examination much of this section is found to consist of cross-bedded oolitic limestone (either pure limestone or mixed siliciclastic–oolitic rock), whereas at many other localities the rocks are normal sandstones. The oolitic facies has been identified in boreholes in East Tyrone and South Antrim and extends to the east coast on Belfast Lough.

The section at Drapersfield also includes non-oolitic sandstones and mudrocks (Fig. 10). The beds exhibit broad channel structures, and planar cross-bedding representing dune forms in the river channels. Smaller scale cross-bedded sandstones, with some low-angle cross-lamination, were deposited under low flow regimes, and the mudrocks represent overbank deposits. The whole section is probably of fluviatile origin. The oolitic beds are the equivalent of the 'Rogenstein' recorded in the lower half of the Sherwood Sandstone Group in the southern North Sea and in continental Europe. They have not been recorded onshore elsewhere in the UK. Much of the oolitic rock is tightly cemented with calcite, i.e. it is non-porous. However some high porosity values are recorded in both oolitic and non-oolitic sandstones (Fig. 10). Borehole data show that the porosity is not simply a surficial feature. The porosity is secondary after dissolution of calcite, and in the porous oolitic rocks there is inter-layer porosity leached within individual ooliths. Porosity is more extensive in non-oolitic sections elsewhere, where bicarbonate activity in the local groundwaters would be lower. The distribution of the oolitic facies broadly coincides with the occurrence of Lower Carboniferous limestones beneath the Triassic.

Beneath the Permo-Triassic in East Tyrone is a thick Carboniferous sequence which includes shales and coals including canneloid shales which are likely to have a mixed potential for oil and gas (Parnell 1991).

9. *Pomeroy*

The Lower Palaeozoic rocks of the Pomeroy and Lisbellaw inliers are at the mature limit of the oil window and possibly have gas potential (Illing & Griffith 1986; Parnell 1989). The Pomeroy inlier contains graptolitic shales of Ordovician and Silurian age. A roadside cutting at H 702709 exposing the Ashgill Desertcreat Group and a riverbank adjacent to the road at H 711732 exposing the Llandovery Little River Group both yield samples with TOC contents up to 1%.

10. *Cole Bridge*

Clastic Lower Carboniferous sediments are extensively distributed between Lough Erne and Lough Neagh, but poorly exposed. One of the few informative localities is a roadside stream section north of Cole Bridge, near Fivemiletown, palynologically dated as Tournaisian (Sheridan *et al.* 1967). The section shows a fining upward transition from basal Carboniferous rudaceous sediments (Ballyness Formation) to sandstones and interbedded mudrocks and limestones of the Clogher Valley Formation (Fig. 11). Conglomerates occur in the stream at the northeast end of the section (H 443525) and sandstones with quartz cement can be examined beneath a small bridge over the stream. Some of these basal sediments are red, reflecting a transition from the underlying Old Red Sandstone. The Clogher Valley Formation includes tabular cross-bedded sandstones near a rubbish dump, overlain by alternating mudrocks and thin limestones. The mudrocks include grey to black shales, which are presently in the oil window. The limestones include beds with evaporite dissolution cavities and finely laminated beds which are probably algal deposits. These beds are accessible at a ford across the stream (H 443523).

11. *Clonelly*

In the Clonelly district and on Boa Island there are several small exposures of the Holkerian Clonelly Sandstone (= Mullaghmore Sandstone, locality 16). The Holkerian sandstones are generally regarded as fluviodeltaic, but the Clonelly Sandstone additionally contains bioclasts and ooliths which indicate a marine component. Over much of Northwest Ireland, the Holkerian sandstones contain sub-millimetre-sized bitumen nodules which contain thorite inclusions and represent an interaction between migrating hydrocarbons and thorium-rich groundwaters draining off the Caledonian granites of Co. Donegal (Parnell & Monson 1990). The nodules occur scarcely in the Clonelly Sandstone. A convenient roadside sampling stop is

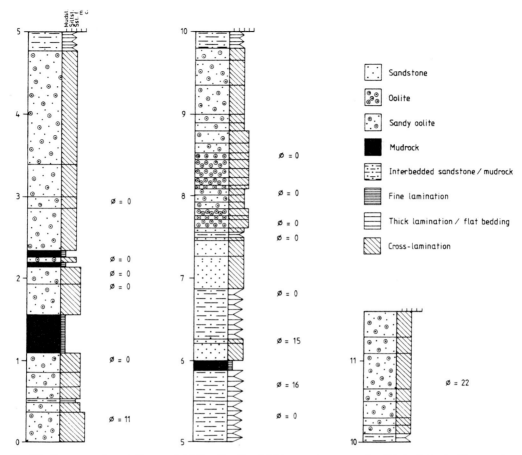

Fig. 10. Quarry section at Drapersfield (locality 8) exhibiting sandstones and oolitic beds in the Sherwood Sandstone Group. Porosity values (%) determined from point counts.

on the Kesh-Pettigo road (H 147663) where the sandstone occurs in the bank along the northern side.

12. *Shinnan Hill*

Between Clonelly and Shinnan Hill, which are in the distinct sub-basins of the Omagh Syncline and Donegal Syncline respectively, the route crosses boggy uplands formed by Moinian rocks. The Carboniferous rocks between the Moinian uplands and the coast of Donegal Bay are predominantly the Ballyshannon Limestone, a marine succession of interbedded limestones and calcareous mudrocks. However at the very margin with the Moinian basement is a thin fringe of coarse siliciclastic sediment, which represents a beach facies passing laterally into the Ballyshannon Limestone. At Shinnan Hill

this facies is more quartzose than most sandstones in North West Ireland, and is also relatively porous. Exposures in a roadside ditch and the adjacent hillside north of a farmhouse at G 960705 show sandstones impregnated with solid bitumen (Fig. 12). To the south of the farmhouse the unconformity with the Moinian basement can be determined upon close inspection (N.B. The Moinian is quartzose and granular here and may initially be confused with Carboniferous sandstone).

13. *Bridgetown*

There are several working quarries in the Ballyshannon Limestone near the main road between Laghy and Ballyshannon, which can be visited with permission. In most of them traces of bitumen can be found in calcite/dolomite veins

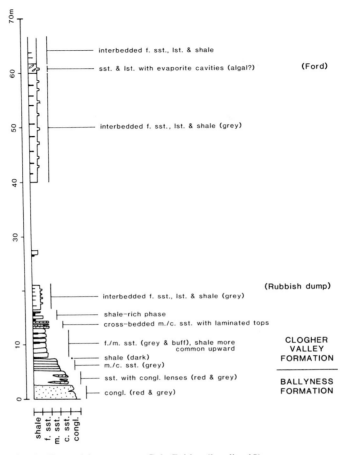

Fig. 11. Stream section in Tournaisian strata at Cole Bridge (locality 10).

cutting the limestone. The bitumen is almost certainly derived from within the Ballyshannon Limestone, which is bituminous particularly in the lower half. The rocks can also be examined at a convenient roadside exposure in Bridgetown, where interbedded limestones and dark shales form an anticlinal structure. A bituminous odour can be detected from freshly fractured surfaces of the limestone. Reflectance values from the kerogen in these rocks show that they are either at the extreme limit of the oil window ($R_o = 1.3\%$) or have passed through it. Vein-hosted bitumens yield higher reflectance values and may have experienced higher temperatures due to hydrothermal activity; the veins also contain traces of sphalerite, galena and fluorite with fluid inclusion homogenization temperatures up to 140°C (Parnell & Monson 1990).

14. *Assaroe Lake*

Along the roadside on the north side of Assaroe Lake are several exposures of the unconformity between Carboniferous and Moinian. The unconformity is most clearly seen in a field behind the road, where there is a clear angular discordance between the two groups. The basal Carboniferous is a cement-supported pebbly sandstone, best seen opposite a small island. The coral *Syringopora* is locally conspicuous. The cement is dolomite, which has partially replaced the sandstone grains and exhibits vuggy cavities. The same phenomenon is seen in the basal Carboniferous sediments on the other side of the border on the north shore of Keenaghan Lough, Co. Fermanagh (G 975600). At Keenaghan the dolomitization also affects the overlying Ballyshannon Limestone and ap-

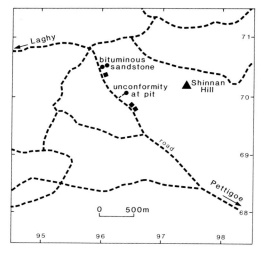

Fig. 12. Location of basal Carboniferous bituminous sandstones and unconformity in Shinnan Hill district (locality 12).

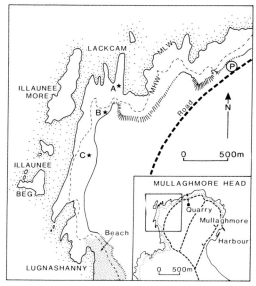

Fig. 13. Map of Mullaghmore Head showing location of quarry and shore sections (locality 16).

pears to be related to hydrothermal mineralization. Traces of copper mineralization are evident at the roadside (G 981597) and the locality was formerly mined. (N.B. The direct cross-border road along the north side of Assaroe Lake is closed).

15. *Bundoran*

In the centre of Bundoran, a car park between the main street and the shore is sited immediately above a good exposure of the Bundoran Shales. The Bundoran Shales are thinly interbedded marine limestones and shales, with conspicuous large crinoid stems orientated by currents. The shales have TOC values of up to 6%.

16. *Mullaghmore Head*

There are several good exposures of the Holkerian Mullaghmore Sandstone on Mullaghmore Head (Fig. 13). The sandstones represent shallow marine/deltaic sedimentation. The excursion incorporates a quarry section (Fig. 14) exhibiting bitumen-bearing sandstones, and a shore section (Fig. 15) in which the ichnofauna is important in reconstructing the environment.

At the south end of the quarry (furthest from the road), an 8 m section shows stacked channel sandstones, which near the top of the section are bituminous. The bitumen, which can be identified in the field, is intergranular and

probably occupies secondary porosity after the dissolution of carbonate cement.

From a car park a kilometre west of the quarry, access to the shore can be gained by a five minute walk westwards along the cliff top, descending to the beach on the west side of the bay to the south east of Lackcam. Walking westwards to Illaunee Beg one ascends through the succession of approximately 25 m shown in Figure 15. The lower half of the succession is repeated south of Illaunee Beg, but access to this is only possible from the Lugnashanny side.

Sedimentologically, three broad facies units can be distinguished, these being shales/siltstones with varying amounts of interbedded sandstone, bedded sandstones with minor shales/siltstones, and major thick channel sandstones (with southward dipping cross sets). The first two facies also commonly contain channels, these typically being of a much smaller scale than those of the channel sandstones. Low angle and trough cross bedding are the major bedforms seen within the thinner sandstone units, lenses and streaks of sand often being seen in the more shale/siltstone dominated facies. 'Mega' and large-scale rippled surfaces are also seen, as are soft sediment deformation structures (often truncated), mudcracks, sandstone dykes, shelly lags, and large woody logs. Carbonaceous material is relatively abundant, particularly within the laminated sandstone on the northwest corner of the headland.

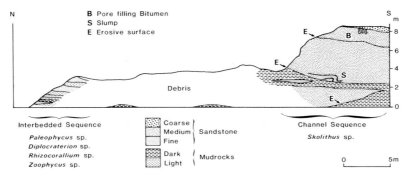

Fig. 14. Quarry section at Mullaghmore Head, exhibiting bituminous sandstones.

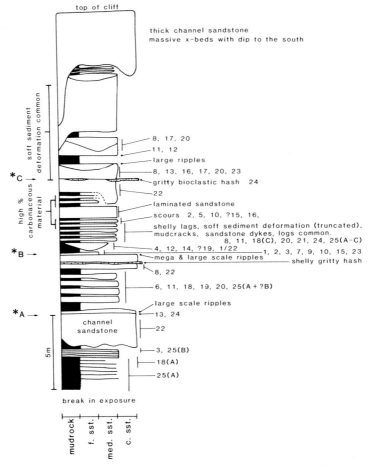

Fig. 15. Log of shore section, Mullaghmore Head, exhibiting diverse trace fossils: 1, *Arenicolites*; 2, *Asteriacites*; 3, *Aulichnites*; 4, Anemone resting marks; 5, bilobed hyporeliefs; 6, *Chondrites*; 7, *?Curvolithus*; 8, *Diplocraterion*; 9, furrow trace; 10, groove trace; 11, branched hyporeliefs; 12, *Lockeia*; 13, mounds cf. *Chomatichnus*; 14, *Neonereites*; 15, *Olivellites*; 16, *Archaeonassa*; 17, *Palaeophycus*; 18, *Phycodes*; 19, *Planolites*; 20, *Rhizocorallium*; 21, *Scalarituba*; 22, *Skolithos*; 23, *Taenidium*; 24, *Teichichnus*; 25, walled burrows (3 types).

Ichnologically the sequence is diverse and varied, with at least 25 common ichnogenera being represented. These are generally well displayed, but both ends of the section need to be visited to appreciate the full diversity and laterally somewhat sporadic occurrence of the ichnofauna. The predominant trace fossils seen within this section are the walled burrows (*Palaeophycus*, *Schaubcylindrichnus* and *Arenicolites*), *Skolithos*, *Diplocraterion*, *Teichichnus* and *Rhizocorallium*. Also more exotic traces such as *Asteriacites* (star fish resting marks), anemone resting/dwelling marks and *Archaeonassa* are found in varying abundance and state of preservation.

The Mullaghmore Sandstone is thought to represent shallow marine/deltaic conditions. At this locality the shale/siltstone-dominated facies represents lagoonal or intertidal environments, as indicated by the occurrence of both anemone resting marks and *Archaeonassa*, with intermittent subaerial exposure producing mudcracks. The bedded sandstones represent (?) storm deposits, and the thick channel sandstones represent deltaic migrating channel deposits, possibly fluviatile in part.

17. *Glennasheevar*

Vehicles may be parked at the entrance to a disused quarry on the north side of the road (H 035532) (Fig. 16). The quarry exposes the Meenymore Formation. The low hill to the north of the quarry is formed by an outcrop of the Tertiary Garrison Sill. The effects of contact metamorphism on the Meenymore Formation may be seen at the base of the sill, and are also very well exposed at a quarry at Slisgarrow (H 015516) where abundant garnetiferous clots have developed (Jones & Galwey 1966). The Meenymore Formation consists predominantly of mudrock and thin limestones, but the quarry at Glennasheevar exposes sandstones (the Quarry Sandstone Member) as well as some shale. The sandstone is well cemented with calcite and dolomite (orange-weathering), contains horizons of rolled marine fossils, and exhibits low-angle cross-stratification. Clasts also include drifted plant debris and fragments of a dolomitic limestone with worm borings (Mason 1980). This limestone is exposed *in situ* with other micritic limestones and mudrocks in a stream section on the opposite side of the road, accessible about 30 m east of the quarry entrance.

The section has also yielded fossil fish (Gardiner & Mason 1974) and it is important *not to hammer* the fossiliferous beds in this section.

The sandstone in the quarry is loaded down into the underlying mudrock in a small exposure which is modified by faulting. Nearby fractures through the sandstone are coated with brittle bitumen which may have been generated from the mudrocks. Analyses of the Meenymore Formation give good pyrolysis yields with potential for a mixture of oil and gas (Parnell 1991). Generation of the bitumen may possibly be related to the intrusion of the sill.

The Meenymore Formation is generally thought to represent a sabkha-type environment (there is evidence for evaporites in a stream section to the west at Meenacloyabane, and fluid bitumen in evaporite dissolution porosity), in which shallow marine micrites and mudrocks are interbedded with fluviodeltaic sandstones (Brandon 1977). The rolled marine fossils in the sandstones were probably eroded from underlying units.

18. *Lough Navar Forest*

A forest drive through the Blackslee part of Lough Navar Forest can be entered from the public road at Correl Glen (H 073546). At the first viewpoint, Aghameelan (Fig. 16), is the first of several exposures of a composite Tertiary dolerite dyke, which is intruded into a fault through the shales of the Meenymore Formation. The dolerite contains abundant xenoliths of sandstone which may be from the Carboniferous, Dalradian or Moinian. The dyke may belong to a swarm exposed extensively in Cos. Antrim and Down (Wilson 1964).

Further along the drive, at a left-hand bend shortly after a track junction to the right, there is a large quarry in the Dartry Limestone. The limestone is cherty and interbedded with dark shales which yield brachiopods.

The forest drive leads to a viewpoint above the Magho escarpment which gives excellent views across Lower Lough Erne to the basement rock uplands of Co. Donegal. The escarpment itself consists of steep cliffs of Glencar and Dartry Limestones above gentler slopes of Benbulben Shale. Landslides (rotational slumps and debris slides) occur on the slope due to failure on or within the shale (Prior & Graham 1974). To the south are further escarpments of the Glenade Sandstone. As the drive returns to the public road the sandstones are most accessible at Lough Achork. (N.B. The forest drive is a one-way system, and must be driven from east to west).

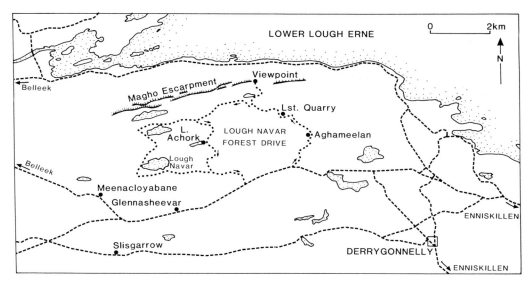

Fig. 16. Map of Lough Navar Forest region showing location of Glennasheevar Quarry (locality 17) and stops along forest drive (locality 18).

References

BRANDON, A. 1977. *The Meenymore Formation — an extensive intertidal evaporitic formation in the Upper Visean (B₂) of north-west Ireland.* Report of the Institute of Geological Sciences, No. 77/23.

DEPARTMENT OF THE ENVIRONMENT FOR NORTHERN IRELAND 1987. *Giant's Causeway,* The Universities Press Ltd, Belfast.

GARDINER, B. G. & MASON, T. R. 1974. On the occurrence of the Palaeoniscid fish *Elonichthys serratus* in the Visean of County Femanagh. *Proceedings of the Royal Irish Academy,* **74,** 31–36.

HARTLEY, J. J. 1933. Notes of fossils recently obtained from the 'chloritic' conglomerate of Murlough Bay, Co. Antrim. *Irish Naturalists' Journal,* **4,** 238–240.

HOLMES, A. 1965. *Principles of Physical Geology.* Thomas Nelson, London.

HUTTON, D. H. W., AFTALION, M. & HALLIDAY, A. N. 1985. An Ordovician ophiolite in County Tyrone, Ireland. *Nature,* **315,** 210–212.

ILLING, L. V. & GRIFFITH, A. E. 1986. Gas prospects in the 'Midland Valley' of Northern Ireland. In: BROOKS, J., GOFF, J. C. & VAN HOORN, B. (eds), *Habitat of Palaeozoic Gas in N.W. Europe,* Geological Society, London, Special Publication, **23,** 73–84.

IVIMEY-COOK, H. C. 1975. The stratigraphy of the Rhaetic and Lower Jurassic in East Antrim. *Bulletin of the Geological Survey of Great Britain,* **50,** 51–69.

JAKOBBSSON, S. P. & FRIDLEIFSSON, G. O. 1990. Asphaltic petroleum in amygdales in Skyndida-lur, Lon, SE Iceland. *Natturufraedingurinn,* **59,** 169–188.

JONES, K. A. & GALWEY, A. K. 1966. Size distribution, composition, and growth kinetics of garnet crystals in some metamorphic rocks from the west of Ireland. *Quarterly Journal of the Geological Society, London,* **122,** 29–44.

KNOX, G. 1823. On bitumen in stones. *Philosophical Transactions,* 517–528.

MANNING, P. I. & WILSON, H. E. 1975. The stratigraphy of the Larne borehole, Co. Antrim. *Bulletin of the Geological Survey of Great Britain,* **50,** 1–50.

MASON, T. R. 1980. Formation and diagenesis of Visean trace fossils from Ireland. *Lethaia,* **13,** 229–237.

OSWALD, D. K. 1955. The Carboniferous rocks between the Ox Mountains and Donegal Bay. *Quarterly Journal of the Geological Society, London,* **111,** 167–186.

PARNELL, J. 1988. The mineralogy of red bed uranium-vanadium mineralization in the Permo-Triassic of Belfast. *Irish Journal of Earth Sciences,* **9,** 119–124.

—— 1989. Hydrocarbon potential of Lower Palaeozoic of the British Isles. *Oil and Gas Journal,* August, 82–86.

—— 1991. Hydrocarbon potential of Northern Ireland: 1. Burial histories and source rock potential. *Journal of Petroleum Geology,* **14,** 65–78.

—— & EAKIN, P. 1987. The replacement of sandstones by uraniferous hydrocarbons: significance for petroleum migration. *Mineralogical Magazine,* **51,** 501–515.

—— & Monson, B. 1990. Sandstone-hosted thorium-bitumen mineralization in the North-West Irish Basin. *Sedimentology*, **37**, 1011–1022.

Preston, J. 1962. Explosive volcanic activity in the Triassic sandstone of Scrabo Hill, Co. Down. *Irish Naturalists' Journal*, **14**, 45–51.

Prior, D. B. & Graham, J. 1974. Landslides in the Magho district of Fermanagh, Northern Ireland. *Engineering Geology*, **8**, 341–359.

Reid, M. B. 1983. *The sediments, stratigraphy and geochemistry of the late Triassic rocks of Larne, County Antrim.* MSc thesis The Queen's University of Belfast.

Reid, R. E. H. 1971. The Cretaceous rocks of north-eastern Ireland. *Irish Naturalists' Journal*, **17**, 105–129.

Sheridan, D. J. R., Hubbard, W. F. & Oldroyd, R. W. 1967. A note on Tournaisian strata in Northern Ireland. *Scientific Proceedings, Royal Dublin Society, Series A*, **3**, 33–37.

Simon, J. B. 1984. Sedimentation of a small complex alluvial fan of possible Upper Old Red Sandstone age, northeast County Antrim. *Irish Journal of Earth Sciences*, **6**, 109–119.

Wilson, H. E. & Manning, P. I. 1978. The geology of the Causeway Coast. *Memoir of the Geological Survey of Northern Ireland*, Her Majesty's Stationery Office, Belfast.

—— & Robbie, J. A. 1966. The geology of the country around Ballycastle. *Memoir of the Geological Survey of Northern Ireland*, Her Majesty's Stationery Office, Belfast.

Wilson, R. L. 1964. The Tertiary dykes of Magho Mountain, Co. Fermanagh. *Irish Naturalists' Journal*, **14**, 254–257.

Index